The Papers of
George Washington

Philander D. Chase, *Editor*

Frank E. Grizzard, Jr., and

Beverly H. Runge, *Associate Editors*

Robert F. Haggard, David R. Hoth, Edward G. Lengel,
and Christine S. Patrick, *Assistant Editors*

Presidential Series
11

August 1792–January 1793

Christine Sternberg Patrick, *Edit*

UNIVERSITY OF V

CHARLOTTESVILLE AND LONDON

This edition has been prepared by the staff of
The Papers of George Washington
sponsored by
The Mount Vernon Ladies' Association of the Union
and the University of Virginia
with the support of
the National Endowment for the Humanities and
the National Historical Publications and Records Commission.
The publication of this volume has been supported by a grant from
the National Historical Publications and Records Commission.

UNIVERSITY OF VIRGINIA PRESS
© 2002 by the Rector and Visitors
of the University of Virginia

First published in 2002

Library of Congress Cataloging-in-Publication Data
Washington, George, 1732–1799.
    The papers of George Washington, Philander D. Chase, ed.

    Presidential series vol. 11 edited by Christine Sternberg
Patrick.
    Includes indexes.
    Contents: 1. September 1788–March 1789—[etc.]—11.
August 1792–January 1793
    1. United States—Politics and government—1789–1797.
2. Washington, George, 1732–1799—Correspondence.
3. Presidents—United States—Correspondence.   I. Chase,
Philander.   II. Patrick, Christine Sternberg. Presidential
series.
E312.72   1987b   973.4′1′092   87–410017
ISBN 0-8139-1103-6 (v. 1)
ISBN 0-8139-2123-6 (v. 11)

Contents

NOTE: Volume numbers refer to the *Presidential Series.*

Contents   xiii

Contents

Illustrations

Maps

Editorial Apparatus

Transcription of the documents in the volumes of *The Papers of George Washington* has remained as close to a literal reproduction of the manuscript as possible. Punctuation, capitalization, and spelling of all words are retained as they appear in the original document; only for documents printed in annotations has paragraphing been modified. Dashes used as punctuation have been retained except when a dash and another mark of punctuation appear together. The appropriate marks of punctuation have always been added at the end of a paragraph. When a tilde (~) is used in the manuscript to indicate a double letter, the letter has been doubled. Washington and some of his correspondents occasionally used a tilde above an incorrectly spelled word to indicate an error in orthography. When this device is used the editors have silently corrected the word. In cases where a tilde has been inserted above an abbreviation or contraction, usually in letter-book copies, the word has been expanded. Otherwise, contractions and abbreviations have been retained as written except that a period has been inserted after an abbreviation when needed. If the meaning of an abbreviation or contraction is not obvious, it has been expanded in square brackets: "H[is] M[ajest]y." Editorial insertions or corrections in the text also appear in square brackets. Angle brackets 〈 〉 are used to indicate illegible or mutilated material. A space left blank in a manuscript by the writer is indicated by a square-bracketed gap in the text [   ]. Deletion of material by the author of a manuscript is ignored unless it contains substantive material, and then it appears in a footnote. If the intended location of marginal notations is clear from the text, they are inserted without comment; otherwise they are recorded in the notes. The ampersand has been retained, and the thorn transcribed as "th." The symbol for per (℔) is used when it appears in the manuscript. The dateline has been placed at the head of a document regardless of where it occurs in the manuscript. All of the documents printed in this volume, as well as omitted routine Washington documents and various ancillary material cited in the notes, may be found in the CD-ROM edition of Washington's Papers (CD-ROM:GW). The reports of Washington's farm managers at Mount Vernon, some of which have been printed in previous volumes of the *Presidential Series,* from now on will appear only in CD-ROM:GW.

During both of Washington's administrations, but particularly in the period shortly before and after his first inauguration, he was besieged with applications for public office. Many of the applicants continued to seek appointment or promotion. The editors have usually printed only one of these letters in full and cited other letters both from the applicant and in support of his application in notes to the initial letter. When Washington replied to these requests at all, the replies were generally pro forma reiterations of his policy of noncommitment until the appointment to a post was made. In such cases his replies have been included only in the notes to the original application and do not appear in their chronological sequence. These and other letters to or from Washington that, in whole or in part, are printed out of their chronological sequence are listed in the table of contents with an indication of where they may be found in the volumes.

Since Washington read no language other than English, incoming letters written to him in foreign languages were generally translated for his information. Where this contemporary translation has survived, it has been used as the text of the document, and the original version has been included in CD-ROM:GW. If there is no contemporary translation, the document in its original language has been used as the text.

During the early years of the new government, the executive sent out a large number of circular letters, under either Washington's name or that of one of his secretaries. Circular letters covered copies of laws passed by Congress and sent to the governors of the states. They also covered commissions and announcements of appointment for public offices sent to individuals after their nominations had been approved by the Senate. In both instances, the circulars requested recipients to acknowledge receipt of the documents. The circulars and the routine acknowledgments of these circulars, usually addressed to Washington but sometimes to one of his secretaries, have been omitted unless they contain material of other interest or significance. In such cases the letters are either calendared or printed in full. The entire text of the documents is available in the CD-ROM edition.

Individuals mentioned in the text in each series are usually identified only at their first substantive mention in the series. The index to each volume indicates where an identification appears in an earlier volume of the *Presidential Series*.

During Washington's first administration, he depended upon the services of several secretaries: both Tobias Lear and David Humphreys, who had been in his service at Mount Vernon, went with him to New York. Two of Washington's nephews also joined his secretarial staff: Robert Lewis of Fredericksburg joined the staff in May 1789, and Bartholomew Dandridge sometime in the spring of 1791. Thomas Nelson and William Jackson assumed secretarial duties in 1789; the former left Washington's service in November 1790, and the latter resigned in December 1791. Relatively few drafts in Washington's hand of letters from early 1791 have survived, and the sequence in which outgoing letters and documents were drafted and copied is often difficult to determine. In Record Group 59, State Department Miscellaneous Letters, in the National Archives, are numerous documents that appear to be the original retained copies of letters written by Washington shortly before he became president and in the first years of his first administration. Much of this correspondence is in the hand of Lear or Humphreys. In early 1791 letterpress copies of documents drafted by Lear in Philadelphia also began to appear. Occasionally the frequency with which the secretary's emendations and insertions appear suggests that the document was a draft prepared by him for Washington. More rarely Washington himself made changes and corrections to a document. On other occasions the documents appear to be simply retained copies either of his original draft or of the receiver's copy. For most of the letters found in Miscellaneous Letters, there are also letter-book copies in the Washington Papers at the Library of Congress. Some of the letters for this period probably were copied into the letter books close to the time they were written, but others obviously were entered much later. Occasionally Thomas Nelson's writing appears in the letter-book copies for the summer of 1789, as does Bartholomew Dandridge's, although Nelson did not join the staff until October and Dandridge was not employed until 1791. Finally, a few letter-book copies are in the handwriting of Howell Lewis, Washington's nephew, who did not assume his duties until the spring of 1792. When the receiver's copy of a letter has not been found, the editors have generally assumed that the copy in Miscellaneous Letters was made from the receiver's copy or the draft and have used it as the text, rather than the letter-book copy, and have described the document either as a copy or a draft, depending on the appearance of the manuscript.

Symbols Designating Documents

AD	Autograph Document
ADS	Autograph Document Signed
ADf	Autograph Draft
ADfS	Autograph Draft Signed
AL	Autograph Letter
ALS	Autograph Letter Signed
D	Document
DS	Document Signed
Df	Draft
DfS	Draft Signed

L	Letter
LS	Letter Signed
LB	Letter-Book Copy
[S]	Used with other symbols to indicate that the signature on the document has been cropped or clipped.

Repository Symbols and Abbreviations

Arch. Aff. Etr.	Archives du Ministère des Affaires Etrangères, Paris (photocopies at Library of Congress)
CD-ROM:GW	*See* "Editorial Apparatus"
CSmH	Henry E. Huntington Library, San Marino, Calif.
CtHi	Connecticut Historical Society, Hartford
DLC	Library of Congress
DLC:GW	George Washington Papers, Library of Congress
DNA	National Archives
DNA:PCC	Papers of the Continental Congress, National Archives
DSI	Smithsonian Institution, Washington, D.C.
MB	Boston Public Library
MdAA	Maryland Hall of Records, Archives, Annapolis
MHi	Massachusetts Historical Society, Boston
MiU-C	William L. Clements Library, University of Michigan, Ann Arbor
Nc-Ar	North Carolina State Department of Archives and History, Raleigh
NHi	New-York Historical Society, New York
NIC	Cornell University, Ithaca, N.Y.
NjMoNP	Washington Headquarters Library, Morristown, N.J.
NjP	Princeton University, Princeton, N.J.
NN	New York Public Library, New York
NNGL	Gilder-Lehrman Collection at The Pierpont Morgan Library, New York
NNMM	Metropolitan Museum of Art, New York
NNPM	Pierpont Morgan Library, New York
OMC	Marietta College, Marietta, Ohio
OHi	Ohio State Historical Society, Columbus
PBbCald	Caldwell Consistory, A.A.S. Rite of Freemasonry, Bloomsburg, Pa.
PHi	Historical Society of Pennsylvania, Philadelphia
PPL	Library Company of Philadelphia
PPRF	Rosenbach Foundation, Philadelphia

PWCD	David Library of the American Revolution, Washington Crossing, Pa.
RG	Record Group (designating the location of documents in the National Archives)
Vi	Library of Virginia, Richmond
ViFaCt	Fairfax County Courthouse, Fairfax, Va.
ViLxW	Washington and Lee University, Lexington
ViMtV	Mount Vernon Ladies' Association of the Union
ViU	University of Virginia, Charlottesville

Short Title List

Alvord, *Illinois Country.* Clarence Walworth Alvord. *The Illinois Country, 1673–1818.* Chicago, 1922.

Alvord, *Kaskaskia Records.* Clarence Walworth Alvord, ed. *Kaskaskia Records, 1778–1790.* Springfield, Ill., 1909.

Annals of Congress. Joseph Gales, Sr., comp. *The Debates and Proceedings in the Congress of the United States; with an Appendix, Containing Important State Papers and Public Documents, and All the Laws of a Public Nature.* 42 vols. Washington, D.C., 1834–56.

Arbuckle, *Pennsylvania Speculator and Patriot.* Robert D. Arbuckle. *Pennsylvania Speculator and Patriot: The Entrepreneurial John Nicholson, 1757–1800.* University Park, Pa., 1975.

Archives parlementaires. M. J. Mavidal, ed. *Archives parlementaires de 1787 à 1860.* Paris, 1877.

Arnebeck, *Through a Fiery Trial.* Bob Arnebeck. *Through a Fiery Trial: Building Washington, 1790–1800.* Lanham, Md., and London, 1991.

ASP. Walter Lowrie et al., eds. *American State Papers: Documents, Legislative and Executive, of the Congress of the United States.* 38 vols. Washington, D.C., 1832–61.

Aupaumut, "Narrative." Hendrick Aupaumut. "A Narrative of an Embassy to the Western Indians, from the Original Manuscript. . . ." *Memoirs of the Historical Society of Pennsylvania* 2 (1827): 61–131.

Bayley, *National Loans.* Rafael A. Bayley. *The National Loans of the United States, from July 4, 1776, to June 30, 1880.* 1881. Reprint. New York, 1970.

Bond, *Correspondence of Symmes.* Beverley W. Bond, Jr., ed. *The Correspondence of John Cleves Symmes, Founder of the Miami Purchase.* New York, 1926.

Brown, *Old Frontiers.* John P. Brown. *Old Frontiers: The Story of the Cherokee Indians from Earliest Times to the Date of Their Removal to the West, 1838.* Reprint. Kingsport, Tenn., 1938.

Buell, *Putnam Memoirs.*   Rowena Buell, ed. *The Memoirs of Rufus Putnam and Certain Official Papers and Correspondence.* Boston and New York, 1903.

Burton, "General Wayne's Orderly Book."   C. M. Burton, ed. "General Wayne's Orderly Book." Michigan Pioneer and Historical Society. *Historical Collections* 34 (1904): 341–733.

Calendar of Virginia State Papers.   William P. Palmer et al., eds. *Calendar of Virginia State Papers and Other Manuscripts.* 11 vols. Richmond, 1875–93.

Campbell, *Lives of the Lord Chancellors.*   John Campbell. *Lives of the Lord Chancellors and Keepers of the Great Seal of England, from the Earliest Times till the Reign of Queen Victoria.* 10 vols. New York, 1875.

"Canadian Archives. Colonial Office Records: Michigan."   "Canadian Archives. Colonial Office Records: Michigan." Michigan Pioneer and Historical Society. *Historical Collections* 24. Lansing, Mich., 1895.

Carter, *Little Turtle.*   Harvey Lewis Carter. *The Life and Times of Little Turtle: First Sagamore of the Wabash.* Urbana, Ill., and Chicago, 1987.

Carter, *Territorial Papers.*   Clarence E. Carter et al., eds. *The Territorial Papers of the United States.* 27 vols. Washington, D.C., 1934–69.

Cash Memorandum Book H.   Manuscript Cash Memorandum Book in Beineke Rare Books and Manuscript Library, Yale University.

Caughey, *McGillivray of the Creeks.*   John Walton Caughey. *McGillivray of the Creeks.* Norman, Okla., 1938.

Chase, *History of Dartmouth.*   Frederick Chase. *A History of Dartmouth College and the Town of Hanover, New Hampshire.* 2 vols. Cambridge, Mass., 1891–1913.

Collins, *History of Kentucky.*   Lewis Collins. *Collins' Historical Sketches of Kentucky. History of Kentucky: by the Late Lewis Collins. . . .* 2 vols. Covington, Ky., 1878.

Columbia Historical Society Records.   *Records of the Columbia Historical Society.* Washington, D.C., 1895—.

Copeland and MacMaster, *The Five George Masons.*   Pamela C. Copeland and Richard K. MacMaster. *The Five George Masons, Patriots and Planters of Virginia and Maryland.* Charlottesville, Va., 1975.

Cruikshank, *Simcoe Papers.*   E. A. Cruikshank, ed. *The Correspondence of Lieut. Governor John Graves Simcoe, with Allied Documents Relating to His Administration of the Government of Upper Canada.* 5 vols. Toronto, 1923–31.

Darlington, *Fort Pitt.*   Mary C. Darlington, ed. *Fort Pitt and Letters from the Frontier.* Pittsburgh, 1892.

Decatur, *Private Affairs of George Washington.*   Stephen Decatur, Jr. *Private Affairs of George Washington, from the Records and Accounts of Tobias Lear, Esquire, His Secretary.* Boston, 1933.

Delaware Archives.   *Delaware Archives.* 5 vols. 1911–19. Reprint. New York, 1974.

DenBoer, "The House of Delegates."   Gordon Roy DenBoer. "The House of Delegates and the Evolution of Political Parties in Virginia, 1782–1792." Ph.D. dissertation, University of Wisconsin, Madison, 1972.

"Denny Journal."   "Military Journal of Major Ebenezer Denny, an Officer in the Revolutionary and Indian Wars. With an Introductory Memoir. By William H. Denny." *Memoirs of the Historical Society of Pennsylvania* 7 (1860): 204–498.

Detweiler, *George Washington's Chinaware.*   Susan Gray Detweiler. *George Washington's Chinaware.* New York, 1982.

DHFC.   Linda G. De Pauw et al., eds. *Documentary History of the First Federal Congress of the United States of America.* 14 vols. to date. Baltimore, 1972—.

Diaries.   Donald Jackson and Dorothy Twohig, eds. *The Diaries of George Washington.* 6 vols. Charlottesville, Va., 1976–79.

Douglas, "Boundaries, Areas, Geographic Centers."   Edward M. Douglas. "Boundaries, Areas, Geographic Centers and Altitudes of the United States and the Several States, with a Brief Record of Important Changes in Their Territory." *United States Geological Survey. Bulletin 689.* 1923.

Downes, *Council Fires.*   Randolph C. Downes. *Council Fires on the Upper Ohio.* Pittsburgh, 1940.

"Early Proceedings."   "Early Proceedings of the American Philosophical Society . . . from the Manuscript Minutes of Its Meetings from 1744 to 1838." *Proceedings of the American Philosophical Society* 22 (1884–85).

Executive Journal.   *Journal of the Executive Proceedings of the Senate of the United States of America.* Vol. 1. Washington, D.C., 1828.

Fairfax Index.   Edith Moore Sprouse, ed. *A Surname and Subject Index of the Minute and Order Books of the County Court, Fairfax County, Virginia, 1749–1800.* Fairfax County History Commission. Fairfax, Va., 1976. Microcard.

Farrand, *Records of the Federal Convention.*   Max Farrand, ed. *The Records of the Federal Convention of 1787.* 4 vols. rev. ed. New Haven, 1966.

Felder, *Fielding Lewis.*   Paula S. Felder. *Fielding Lewis and the Washington Family.* n.p., 1998.

Ford, *Spurious Letters.*   Worthington Chauncey Ford. *The Spurious Letters Attributed to George Washington.* Brooklyn, 1889.

Green, *The Spanish Conspiracy.*   Thomas Marshall Green. *The Spanish Conspiracy.* Cincinnati, 1891.

Greene Papers.   Richard K. Showman et al., eds. *The Papers of General Nathanael Greene.* 11 vols. to date. Chapel Hill, N.C., 1976—.

Griffin, *Boston Athenæum Washington Collection.*   Appleton P. C. Griffin, comp. *A Catalogue of the Washington Collection in the Boston Athenæum.* Cambridge, Mass., 1897.

Guthman, *March to Massacre.*   William H. Guthman. *March to Massacre: A History of the First Seven Years of the United States Army, 1784–1791.* New York, 1975.

Gwathmey, *Historical Register.*   John H. Gwathmey. *Historical Register of Virginians in the Revolution.* Richmond, 1938.

Harris, *William Thornton.*   C. M. Harris, ed. *The Papers of William Thornton.* Vol. 1. Charlottesville, Va., 1995.

Hayden, *Va. Genealogies.*   Horace Edwin Hayden. *Virginia Genealogies: A Genealogy of the Glassell Family of Scotland and Virginia, . . .* 1891. Reprint. Baltimore, 1973.

Heads of Families (Maryland).   *Heads of Families at the First Census of the United States Taken in the Year 1790* (Maryland). 1907. Reprint. Baltimore, 1965.

Heard, *Handbook of the American Frontier.*   J. Norman Heard. *Handbook of the American Frontier: Four Centuries of Indian-White Relationships.* 5 vols. Metuchen, N.J., and London, 1987.

Hening.   William Waller Hening, ed. *The Statutes at Large; Being a Collection of All the Laws of Virginia from the First Session of the Legislature, in the Year 1619.* 13 vols. 1819–23. Reprint. Charlottesville, Va., 1969.

Hirschfeld, *Washington and Slavery.*   Fritz Hirschfeld. *George Washington and Slavery: A Documentary Portrayal.* Columbia, Mo., 1997.

Hoig, *Cherokee Chiefs.*   Stanley W. Hoig. *The Cherokees and Their Chiefs: In the Wake of Empire.* Fayetteville, Ark., 1998.

JCC.   Worthington C. Ford et al., eds. *Journals of the Continental Congress.* 34 vols. Washington, D.C., 1904–37.

Jefferson Papers.   Julian P. Boyd et al., eds. *The Papers of Thomas Jefferson.* 29 vols. to date. Princeton, N.J., 1950—.

Journal of the House.   Martin P. Claussen, ed. *The Journal of the House of Representatives: George Washington Administration 1789–1797.* 9 vols. Wilmington, Del., 1977.

Journal of the Senate.   *The Journal of the Senate Including the Journal of the Executive Proceedings of the Senate: George Washington Administration, 1789–1797.* Ed. Martin P. Claussen. 9 vols. Wilmington, Del., 1977.

JPP.   Dorothy Twohig, ed. *Journal of the Proceedings of the President, 1793–1797.* Charlottesville, Va., 1981.

Kappler, *Indian Treaties.*   Charles Joseph Kappler, ed. *Indian Affairs: Laws and Treaties.* 5 vols. Washington, D.C., 1903–41.

Kelly, "Cedar Park."   J. Reaney Kelly. "Cedar Park, Its People and Its History." *Maryland Historical Magazine* 58 (1963): 30–53.

Kinney, *Church and State.*   Charles B. Kinney, Jr. *Church and State: The Struggle for Separation in New Hampshire, 1630–1900.* New York, 1955.

Knopf, *Wayne.*   Richard C. Knopf, ed. *Anthony Wayne, a Name in Arms: Soldier, Diplomat, Defender of Expansion Westward of a Nation: The Wayne-Knox-Pickering-McHenry Correspondence.* Pittsburgh, 1960.

Laws of Maryland, . . . 1790.   Laws of Maryland, Made and Passed at a Session of Assembly, Begun and Held at the City of Annapolis on Monday the First of November, in the Year of Our Lord One Thousand Seven Hundred and Ninety. Annapolis, 1791.

Laws of Maryland, . . . 1792.   Laws of Maryland, Made and Passed at a Session of Assembly, Begun and Held at the City of Annapolis on Monday the Fifth of November, in the Year of Our Lord One Thousand Seven Hundred and Ninety-Two. Annapolis, 1793.

Ledger B.   Manuscript ledger in George Washington Papers, Library of Congress.

Ledger C.   Manuscript ledger in Morristown National Historical Park, Morristown, N.J.

Linn and Egle, *Whiskey Insurrection Papers.*   John B. Linn and William H. Egle, eds. *Papers Relating to What Is Known as the Whiskey Insurrection in Western Pennsylvania.* Vol. 4 of *Pennsylvania Archives,* 2d ser. Harrisburg, Pa., 1890.

Lists and Returns of Conn. Men.   Lists and Returns of Connecticut Men in the Revolution, 1775–1783. Connecticut Historical Society. *Collections* 12. Hartford, 1909.

Madison Papers.   William T. Hutchinson et al., eds. *The Papers of James Madison* [1st series]. 17 vols. Chicago and Charlottesville, Va., 1962–91.

Madison Papers, Secretary of State Series.   Robert J. Brugger et al., eds. *The Papers of James Madison: Secretary of State Series.* 5 vols. to date. Charlottesville, Va., 1986—.

Marcus and Perry, *Documentary History of the Supreme Court.*   Maeva Marcus, James R. Perry, et al., eds. *The Documentary History of the Supreme Court of the United States, 1789–1800.* 6 vols. to date. New York, 1985—.

Mathews, *Andrew Ellicott.*   Catharine Van Cortlandt Mathews. *Andrew Ellicott: His Life and Letters.* New York, 1908.

Miller, *Artisans and Merchants of Alexandria.*   T. Michael Miller, comp. *Artisans and Merchants of Alexandria, 1780–1820.* 2 vols. Bowie, Md., 1991–92.

Miller, *Treaties.*   Hunter Miller, ed. *Treaties and Other International Acts of the United States of America.* Vol. 2. Washington, D.C., 1931.

Morris, *Diary of the French Revolution.*   Beatrix Cary Davenport, ed. *A Diary of the French Revolution by Gouverneur Morris.* 2 vols. Boston, 1939.

Morris, *Diary and Letters of Gouverneur Morris.* Anne Cary Morris, ed. *The Diary and Letters of Gouverneur Morris.* 2 vols. New York, 1888.

Murray, *The Story of Some French Refugees.* Louise Welles Murray. *The Story of Some French Refugees and Their "Azilum," 1793–1800.* Elmira, N.Y., 1917.

Pa. 1820 Census Index. Ronald Vern Jackson et al., eds. *Pennsylvania 1820 Census Index.* Bountiful, Utah, 1977.

Philadelphia Directory, 1793. James Hardie. *The Philadelphia Directory and Register.* Philadelphia, 1793.

Presidential Household Accounts. Presidential Household Accounts, 4 March 1793–25 March 1797. Manuscript ledger on deposit at PHi.

Prussing, *Estate of George Washington.* Eugene E. Prussing. *The Estate of George Washington, Deceased.* Boston, 1927.

Randall, "Washington's Ohio Lands." E. O. Randall. "Washington's Ohio Lands." *Ohio Archæological and Historical Society Publications* 19 (1910), 303–18.

Reps, *Monumental Washington.* John W. Reps. *Monumental Washington: The Planning and Development of the Capital Center.* Princeton, N.J., 1967.

Slaughter, *Whiskey Rebellion.* Thomas P. Slaughter. *The Whiskey Rebellion: Frontier Epilogue to the American Revolution.* New York, 1986.

Smith, "James Seagrove and the Mission to Tuckaubatchee." Daniel M. Smith. "James Seagrove and the Mission to Tuckaubatchee, 1793." *Georgia Historical Quarterly* 44 (1960): 41–55.

Sorley, *Lewis of Warner Hall.* Merrow Egerton Sorley. *Lewis of Warner Hall: The History of a Family.* 1935. Reprint. Baltimore, 1979.

Spangler, "Memoir of Major John Clark." E. W. Spangler. "Memoir of Major John Clark, of York County, Pennsylvania." *Pennsylvania Magazine of History and Biography* 20 (1896): 77–86.

Sparks, *Writings.* Jared Sparks, ed. *The Writings of George Washington.* 12 vols. Boston, 1855.

1 *Stat.* Richard Peters, ed. *The Public Statutes at Large of the United States of America.* Vol. 1. Boston, 1845.

6 *Stat.* Richard Peters, ed. *The Public Statutes at Large of the United States of America.* Vol. 6. Boston, 1848.

9 *Stat.* George Minot, ed. *The Statutes at Large and Treaties of the United States of America.* Vol. 9. Boston, 1851.

Syrett, *Hamilton Papers.* Harold C. Syrett et al., eds. *The Papers of Alexander Hamilton.* 27 vols. New York, 1961–87.

Tanner, "The Glaize in 1792." Helen Hornbeck Tanner. "The Glaize in 1792: A Composite Indian Community." *Ethnohistory* 25 (1978): 15–39.

Teetor, *Life and Times of Col. Israel Ludlow.*   Henry Benton Teetor. *Sketch of the Life and Times of Col. Israel Ludlow, One of the Original Proprietors of Cincinnati.* Cincinnati, 1885.

Weelen, *Rochambeau.*   Jean-Edmond Weelen. *Rochambeau, Father and Son: A Life of the Maréchal de Rochambeau.* New York, 1936.

White, *Genealogical Abstracts.*   Virgil D. White. *Genealogical Abstracts of Revolutionary War Pension Files.* 4 vols. Waynesboro, Tenn., 1990–92.

Williams, "Memoir."   Jonathan Williams. "Memoir of Jonathan Williams, on the Use of the Thermometer in Discovering Banks, Soundings, etc." *Transactions of the American Philosophical Society Held at Philadelphia for Promoting Useful Knowledge* 3 (1793): 82–100.

The Papers of George Washington
Presidential Series
Volume 11
August 1792–January 1793

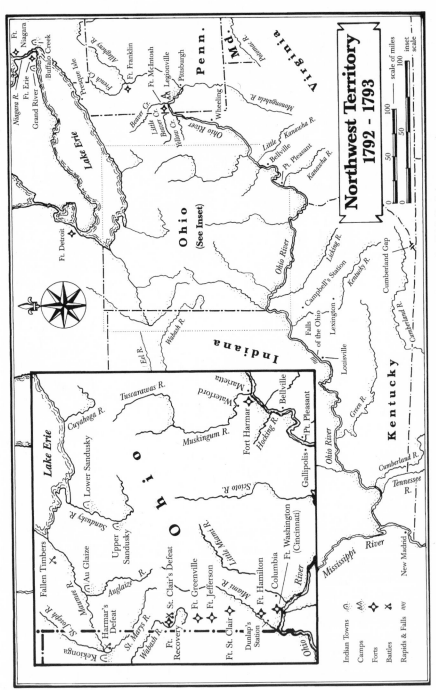

Map 1. *Northwest Territory, 1792–1793.* (Illustrated by Rick Britton. Copyright Rick Britton 2002.)

From Henry Knox

Sir   War department August 16th 1792

I have the honor to submit a copy of a Letter from Brigadier General Putnam of the 14th Ultimo, & another of the same date from Brigadier General Wilkinson containing enclosures.[1] and I shall transmit copies of the several papers which have been received, to Major General Wayne, as I conceive it highly proper for him to be informed of every thing relative to the objects of his command.[2]

I confess I think the accuracy of the information of the prisoners to be questioned—their sphere of observation must have been very small indeed—I think however there cannot be a doubt about Trueman.[3]

We may expect to hear of the reception of Captain Hendricks daily, as he probably arrived at the Miami River of Lake Erie about the latter end of June.[4]

That the Shawanese and some others are inveterate, I have no doubt, but I think if they have fairly explained to them the ample message sent by Trueman, that the mass of the hostile Indians will probably accede to a Treaty—But in any event the Executive of the United States will be considered by all impartial and moderate men as having taken every rational expedient to bring matters to an amicable termination.

I intimated to General Wayne some time since that the lateness of the Season would probably render it inexpedient to employ any Chickesaws or Choctaws this year.[5]

I have the honor to transmit a copy of my letter to Governor Blount of the 15th instant.[6]

The affairs in the South Western quarter are in a very ill position if Colonel Arthur Campbells letter is to be entirely credited—I have the honor to enclose a copy of his Letter to Lieut. Governor Wood who transmitted it to me.[7]

The Governor of Virginia set out on the 25th Ultimo for the South Western frontier.[8]

Since writing the above I have the honor to acknowledge the receipt of your favour of the 13th instant—the letter of General Putnam relative to the post on the Muskingum and the Fish

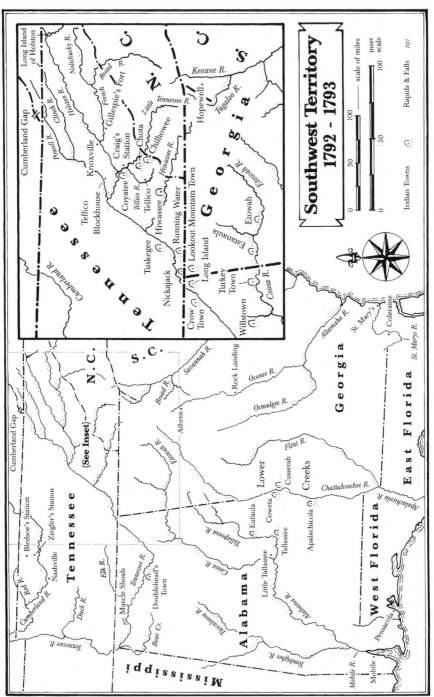

Map 2. *Southwest Territory, 1792–1793.* (Illustrated by Rick Britton. Copyright Rick Britton 2002.)

Carriers Speech are now enclosed.[9] I have the honor to be with the greatest respect Your most obedt servt

H. Knox

LS, DLC:GW; LB, DLC:GW.

1. On 14 July, Rufus Putnam wrote to Knox from Fort Washington in the Northwest Territory: "Captain Armstrong, the Commanding officer of Fort Hamilton, in his letter to General Wilkinson of yesterday writes thus 'one man of the first Regiment taken prisoner on the 19th of October 1791 when under my command, and one of the 4th of November after our late defeat, have reached this post, they made their escape from an Indian Village on the St Joseph 50 Miles above the Miami, passed that place, and early next day reached Jefferson, they came through the place where our Army was defeated and can no doubt give much information. Three different Flags from us have been received at the glaze River, when the messengers were tomahawked and throun in the water, The last was a great Captain (I suppose poor Trueman).'

"From this account it seems that nothing but War is to be expected from the Indians collected at the grand Council on the Oma, or Tawa River—That our only prospect of effecting any thing by way of Treaty is with the more Western tribes; my opinion with respect to them I have expressed in my letters of the 5th 8th and 11th instant.

"The Interpreter [William Wells] who (I informed you in my letter of the 5th instant) was sent for to Kentucke, arrived last evening" and "is of opinion that the Weya and Eel river Indians are disposed for peace they say its their Wish, but they are great liars, and he cannot answer for their intention, he has also heard some of the other tribes towards lake Michigan say they were for peace and others that they had never been at War with the Americans—Mr Wells also informs that when he left the Eel river Town the great chief was gone to see the Shawanoes and Delawares, and to know their intentions concerning the War.

"He also tells me that he expects a number of the Wabash Chiefs will arive here in two or three Weeks, which should it happen it is probable that through their influence a great number of Indians may be drawn together at Vincennes agreeably to the plan I have in my former letter recommended in which case it will be necessary that a quantity of provisions be furnished at that place, for the purpose, which circumstance cannot be too early attended to, if the Contractors are not already instructed on the Subject.

"The Prisoners who have lately made their escape from the Indians, and now at Fort Hamilton will be here in a few days, after the examination of whom I hope a more certain opinion of the intentions of the Indians, in the North, may be formed than at present" (DLC:GW). For an account of Putnam's September meeting at Vincennes with the Eel River Indians and other friendly tribes, see Buell, *Putnam Memoirs,* 335–62.

Like Putnam, James Wilkinson wrote Knox from Fort Washington on 14 July about the arrival of the escaped prisoners at Fort Hamilton. Wilkinson also reported: "In my letter by Mr Hodgdon I enclosed a copy of my correspondence with the Contractors on the subject of throwing an additional quantity of salted meat into Fort St Clair—which it would appear requires the immediate attention of Government—Escorts, Scouts and detached posts have greatly diminished our stock in that article—at this post and at Fort Hamilton the quantity on hand is very inconsiderable—at Fort St Clair about twenty days allowance for the Garrison and at Fort Jefferson about Seventy—But at the last post we have more than eight hundred small Casks of Flour and at St Clair five Months full allowance.

"I will not hazard another convoy of Pack Horses to Fort Jefferson before I have the Country well reconnoitred, but shall necessarily send up a quantity of live Beef after having delayed a sufficient time to disconcert the immediate plans and expectations of the Enemy; and I have it in contemplation so soon as the first Crop of Hay is secured at Fort Hamilton to move on to Fort Jefferson with the mounted Riflemen, mounted Infantry and Captain Peters's company and in spite of the Enemy to secure a magazine of forage at that post; however this will depend on Contingencies, and I shall take my measures with cautious deliberation" (DLC:GW).

2. Knox wrote Anthony Wayne on 17 Aug. enclosing "The Invoices of all the Stores forwarded since the 17th. of July to this day" and copies of James Wilkinson's letter to Knox of 14 July, Rufus Putnam's letter to Knox of 14 July, and John Belli's letter to Knox of 12 July (Knopf, *Wayne*, 69–71). For Wilkinson's and Putnam's letters, see note 1, and for Belli's letter, see GW to Knox, 22 Aug. 1792, n.5.

3. For the background to Maj. Alexander Trueman's peace mission to the northwest Indians, see Thomas Jefferson's Memorandum of a Meeting of the Heads of the Executive Departments, 9 Mar. 1792, and Knox to GW, 1 April 1792, and note 2. Wayne sent Knox more detailed information about Trueman's death in a letter of 6 Aug. from Pittsburgh. The letter, which was docketed by John Stagg, Jr., chief clerk of the War Department, as "Recd: Augt: 18th; since the departure of the Secy of War for New York," reads: "I have this moment examined two men just from *Detroit,* by the way of Niagara, who were taken prisoners by the Indians, one of them near Fort Jefferson, on the 27th of October and the other a Mr John Cleghorn near the falls of Ohio. in April last, who was carried to Michilimackinac, and from thence to Detroit, where he arrived the 24 June and says, that, whilst he was at Michilimackinac, accounts were received that a Captain Hardin, and one or two others, were killed by the Indians, and the papers that were found upon them, were sent, or given to Captain McKee, he was also informed at detroit (where the report was common) that a Captain Trueman and another man, were killed near the Miami towns by two Indians, who were in company with them, in the evening, that, the Indians affected to be very uneasy, upon which Captain Trueman, told them they might *tie* the other man, so that the numbers should be equal, which was accordingly done. that they then shot Captain Trueman, & *tomahawked,* the man, that was tied—that the Interpreter made his escape into a Swamp or wood—that the Indians called to him and promised not to hurt him, upon which he came to them, and they carried him to the Council as a Prisoner, and reprobated the foolish conduct of *Trueman* (as they termed it) for suffering the

man to be *tied;* that their papers were also, given up to McKee, and said this was a *fifth* flag, they had killed, nor had they any intention, or wish, to make peace with us, as the Americans had already deceived them, both last summer and before.

"He further says—that a certain *Simon Girty* with four hundred Indians, had left Detroit, some days before he arrived—say about the 15th June, and swore that he would make an immediate Stroke at the Americans, and kill or be killed, in the attempt.

"Query—may not this be the person in *red* or *Scarlet* who was seen with the Indians, in the attack upon the Serjeants party, near Fort Jefferson on the 25th June, as mentioned in General Wilkinsons letter of the 6th Ultimo, and do not all the accounts, from the different quarters, and Channels strongly corroborate, so as to amount, almost, to positive proofs, of the *Murder* of our *Flags* and the inveterate, *hostile* intentions of the Indians" (DLC:GW; the date on which this copy was sent to GW has not been identified).

4. Knox is referring to the Maumee River, which flows northeast from Indiana through Ohio and empties into the southwestern end of Lake Erie at present-day Toledo, Ohio.

Hendrick Aupaumut's first peace mission to the western Indians had failed in the summer of 1791 (see Knox to GW, 18 April 1792, n.2) as did a second attempt in February 1792, when he failed to pass the Iroquois settlement of Grand River in Canada. He made a third effort in the summer of 1792, leaving Buffalo Creek, in western New York, on 18 June and arriving among the western Indians in early July. Aupaumut delivered the American peace message on numerous occasions, both formally and informally; the last occasion was during the grand council that convened at Au Glaize between 30 Sept. and 9 October. He and other U.S. envoys failed to persuade the hostile Indians to accept the American terms of peace (see Aupaumut, "Narrative," 61–131). For Knox's report on the failure of Aupaumut and of the peace mission in general, see Knox to GW, 6 Dec. 1792.

5. Knox wrote Wayne from Philadelphia on 27 July 1792: "The Season is so far advanced that it is not probable any very serious offensive operations can be undertaken before the cold weather sets in.

"If this should be the case it will not be proper to endeavour to obtain a body of the Chickasaws to join our army—Should they be brought to Fort Washington with the expectation of seeing there a large army ready for offensive operations and find it otherwise, disgust would ensue.

"But perhaps they would like to make a stroke by themselves. *In this however they cannot be indulged* unless the negociations should be at an end and it shall be discovered that the War must progress" (Knopf, *Wayne,* 52).

6. In his letter to William Blount of 15 Aug., Knox wrote: "it is to be hoped this may find you at Holstein after having made satisfactory arrangements with all the ⟨*illegible*⟩.

"By letters from Colonel Arthur Campbell of Washington to the Governor of Virginia and myself, it would seem that all the conferences at Coyatte and Estanula amounted to nothing, and that parties of the lower towns had set off not only to attack the Boats under the charge of Mr Allison with the Goods, and also to attack you and General Pickens. These ideas are said to have arisen from the information of a friendly Chief of the upper towns.

"I am very much inclined to believe and sincerely hope from your Letter of the 4th of July, that these fears will prove groundless—and I am the more encouraged in this as I have been informed verbally that Mr Chisholm had brought in some prisoners who had lately been taken near the Cumberland settlements at a place called Bledsoes station. If my information, given by Mr Vigo of post Vincennes lately from Kentuckey, be true, the above mentioned station was attacked by a banditti formed of Shawanese, Cherokees and Creeks, partly of the very men who attacked Major Doughty in 1790. . . . The five companies of Infantry and one of horse you have ordered into service if the companies are nearly full would amount to a pretty formidable force. If sufficiently alert and active it would seem to be a reasonable expectation, that they would intercept and chastise some of the banditti that lately have given your government so much trouble, and the south western frontiers of Virginia such serious alarms. . . . Every thing indeed depends upon your exertions to avert the event of a war, that will be reluctantly entered into, and at best but illy supported.

"Every just pretence of grievances on the part of the Indians, if any such exist must be removed, and if a war must inevitably ensue, it ought to be made appear to all the world that the government and Citizens of the United States have not been the cause of bringing it on.

"Understanding as you do the wishes of the President of the United States, a full persuasion must be entertained that you will leave no reasonable expedient unattempted, to effect a general tranquility. Indeed your efforts to preserve peace must, and I flatter myself will be rendered conspicuous.

"General Wayne seems at a loss what steps to take relative to any of the Chickasaws or Choctaws joining the army this Campaign. I have written him intimating that the bad season would be so far advanced before the result of our pacific overtures should be known, as to preclude any important offensive operations—That therefore it would be best not to engage any Indians for the present year—this point will be left to his judgment, his orders are to be obeyed.

"But it would appear that it would be the preferable arrangement to calling any Indians this year to an ineffectual Campaign, to make an agreement with them that they should hold themselves in readiness at an early period of the next year to obey our call if necessary."

Regarding allegations that deputy Indian agent Leonard Shaw was "deficient in prudence and sobriety," Knox advised Blount "to enquire into these charges, and if you find them well founded it is the orders of the President of the United States that he be dismissed from all employment in the Indian Department" (DLC:GW).

7. In his letter to James Wood, written from Washington County, Va., on 19 July 1792, Arthur Campbell reported that since the departure of Governor Blount "from Knoxville for Cumberland, the place appointed to hold a treaty with the Chickasaws and Choctaws. We have the alarming intelligence, that all the lower towns of the Cherokees have seceded from their late engagements to the United States, that a large party of warriors had set out to intercept the

Boats carrying the Goods for the treaty, and as the river has been remarkably low, it is to be feared they have succeeded in their design.

"There are also serious apprehensions that Governor Blount and General Pickens have been attacked on their way out as their guard was but weak. One party of the enemy set out to attack the settlements in Virginia on Clinch and Powell's river. This intelligence was brought a few days ago to Knoxville by a friendly Chief of the Upper Towns. . . . From Fort Washington I learn, that the Indians have lately been uncommonly furious, often killing people within view of the Garrisons—in a late attack of a guard of Twenty men, eighteen were killed on the spot" (DLC:GW).

8. Gov. Henry Lee left Richmond around 20 July for an extended tour of the militia outposts in southwest Virginia. For Lee's observations on the militia, see Knox to GW, 15 Sept. 1792, n.7.

9. Putnam's letter may be the one he wrote to Knox on 9 July (see GW to Knox, 22 Aug. 1792, n.2).

The "Speech of the *Fish Carrier* the Head Chief of the Cyuga Nation of indians to Israel Chapin Esqr: D. Superintendant of the Five Nations," delivered at Buffalo Creek on 3 July 1792, reads: "Brother Canadasago. Open your ears and hear me speak a few words.

"You have told me all—you have hid nothing. I heard our brothers before you came—My heart was then bad—My ears were shut—Your talk entered a little way—I began to listen, and my ears were opened. I have received your words, and the words of my brothers—I have pondered them well—My heart is glad for the Union ratifyed by our brothers who went to Philadelphia, and the great council of your nation at the council fire lighted at that place; and which your talk has made me take hold of.

"Brother. As I now think your minds are good towards us, my path looks straight. I will now with a glad heart join my brothers in carrying the talk of peace to the southward. In confidence of justice, I will do all—I will risque all for my brothers of Congress—I look and expect the assistance of the Great Spirit to do good—He can conquer the stubborn hearts of proud warriors, and make peace.

"Brother—You tell me Gen: Washington is a father to your people—You tell me too he is a father to indians—Will he not see justice done me and my people—I will then return if it pleases the *Great Spirit,* and visit my father at Philadelphia.

"Brother Canadasago. Will you present this my talk to our common father" (DLC:GW).

From James McHenry

Sir.   Fayetteville [Md.] 16 Augt 1792.
I had the honor to recieve your letter of the 13th yesterday.[1]

The business of the maritime court as you remark requires that the district attorney should be a resident of Baltimore. With respect to Mr Tilghman and Hammond both stand extremely fair in politics, and would either settle here would be acceptable. The former will sooner yield to transient circumstances than the latter who as far as I have known him seems to possess a fixedness of thinking in the discharge of public trusts that renders him in my eyes a valuable man.[2] I have more than once endeavoured to persuade Mr Craike to settle in Baltimore where I beleive he would soon acquire practice. I have promised him such interest as I can exert.[3] If he would remove thither I think him qualified, tho' not in a higher degree than either Mr Smith or Mr Hollingsworth.[4] As to these gentlemen the public opinion would be in favor of Mr Smith. He is more steady, cautious, industrious and painstaking than Mr Hollingsworth, and has obtained a character of perhaps greater probity in his profession. Mr Hollingsworth is more of a wit and not less of a lawyer. Marriage has corrected some of his levities and study must make him a much superior lawyer to Mr Smith, whose medeocrity of talents will for ever preclude from eminence at the bar.[5] But all things considered (if a resident of Baltimore is preferr'd) political opinions character, connexions and *present qualifications* Mr Smith seems to me the most eligible. This being the case and you wishing to know whether if appointed he would accept I fell in with him yesterday evening. I mentioned to him what was true, that I had been told Mr Hollingsworth was desirous of having the appointment, and might call on me for a recommendation; that I therefore wished to know whether he would accept if appointed in which case I should sign nothing that could stand in his way. He told me he would accept and confirmed it this morning.[6]

It is to be lamented that the best qualified man in the State is the last person who merits this appointment. I mean Mr Luther Martin. Very few of his description have so far altered their principles as to be safely trusted with power.[7]

Mr Paca told me the other day that Col. Lloyd and he intended to pay you a visit about the 1st Septr Col. Lloyd you know is a good man of some influence and vast property.[8] If he makes the visit it will afford you the occasion to speak of the necessity of gentlemen like him using their opportunities to remove any misrepresentations respecting the laws which may be made to the people to answer electioneering or other purposes. I think you can produce it by a happy effect upon him while it may serve as an admonition to Mr Paca not to interfere in Mr Mercers election, who is if possible more desperately mischievous than when the open decided and declared enemy of the constitution, and for whom Mr Paca may perhaps retain some regard.[9]

May god bless you and long preserve you in your present station. I am my ever Dear Sir most sincerely and truely your affectionate

James McHenry

Perhaps it would be proper to destroy this communication?[10]

ALS, DLC:GW; ADf (three pages), MdAA: James McHenry Collection; ADf (one page), MdAA: James McHenry Collection. The docket on the longer draft reads: "To Gen. Washington. with a note from Revr. Smith." The author of this note, which has not been identified, may have been Robert Smith (1732–1801), a South Carolina clergyman who had been the chaplain general of the southern department of the Continental army during the Revolutionary War and who became the Protestant Episcopal bishop of South Carolina in 1795. Related by marriage to the prominent Tilghman family of Maryland and Pennsylvania, Smith visited GW at Mount Vernon with British diplomat George Hammond from 24 to 26 Sept. 1792 (see Knox to GW, 18 Sept., GW to Knox, 24 Sept., and to Andrew Ellicott, 26 Sept. 1792).

1. Neither draft includes this opening sentence.

2. In place of this sentence, the shorter draft reads: "The former is more yielding than the latter, and may be less inflexible in politics. Both are valuable men."

After Richard Potts notified GW on 12 June of his resignation as federal district attorney for Maryland, GW solicited McHenry's opinion on the candidacies of prominent Maryland lawyers William Tilghman, Nicholas Hammond, Robert Smith, and Zebulon Hollingsworth. He later instructed McHenry to make informal inquiries about Tilghman's and Hammond's interest in the position (see GW to McHenry, 13, 31 Aug. 1792).

3. William Craik (1761–1814), the eldest son of Dr. James Craik, GW's close friend, practiced law at Port Tobacco and Leonardtown, Maryland. He later moved to Baltimore and was elected to Congress, serving from 1796 to 1801, when he became chief justice of the fifth judicial district of Maryland. The section regarding William Craik does not appear in the shorter draft.

4. At this place in the text, the longer draft reads: "It may be a consideration too should the appointment fall on one out of B. that he be thought by the public to be better qualified than any in it, as it is introducing a new practitioner who will change the practice of those who now enjoy it."

5. The shorter draft does not include the phrase about Robert Smith's "medeocrity of talents."

6. Baltimore attorney Robert Smith (1757–1842) declined the position when GW offered it to him in a letter dated 31 August. He later became secretary of the navy under Thomas Jefferson and secretary of state under James Madison. Hammond and Tilghman had withdrawn their names from consideration before Smith was offered the position (see McHenry to GW, 4 Oct. 1792, and note 1).

7. Luther Martin (c.1748–1826), attorney general of Maryland from 1788

to 1805 and from 1818 to 1822, had been a Maryland delegate to the Federal Convention in 1787. Opposing the establishment of a strong central government, he and fellow Maryland delegate John Francis Mercer left the convention before its conclusion and afterwards actively campaigned against ratification of the U.S. Constitution. This paragraph on Martin is not included in the shorter draft.

8. Edward Lloyd III (1744–1796) of Talbot County, Md., actively supported the American Revolution and voted for ratification of the federal Constitution as a delegate to the 1788 Maryland ratifying convention. In 1792 he was serving his third term in the state senate as a representative for the Eastern Shore. Lloyd shared with William Paca a joint investment in over 5,000 acres in Allegany County, Md., as well as an interest in thoroughbred racing, both having been stewards of the Annapolis Jockey Club. The rest of this paragraph is not included in the shorter draft.

9. John Francis Mercer, who had been selected to fill the vacancy in Maryland's second congressional district created by the resignation of William Pinkney in November 1791, took his seat in the U.S. House of Representatives on 6 Feb. 1792 and was reelected in the 1792 fall election.

10. This sentence is not in either draft.

From Henry Knox

Sir,   War department August 17th 1792

I have received a letter from General Wayne of the 10th instant of which the enclosed is a copy.[1]

Every thing he has requested has been forwarded excepting a full supply of blankets & shoes for the old regiments and clothing for about one company of the old troops, which number is deficient as not standing the rigid inspection which has been made.[2]

The powder he requests is a fine grained powder, which, in his opinion, will prime the musket from within, on the cartridge being rammed down and the touch hole being enlarged.

I have complied with his request, reluctantly, so far as to order forty quarter barrells—The Powder sent him has been brought from West Point and is as good as ever was made, or used—I have had every barrell proved. The grain of the Rifle Powder is sufficiently fine, but not quite so fine as General Wayne requires.

I shall set off for New York in the Morning to be absent a few days. I have the honor to be with perfect respect Your most obedt Servant

                                        H. Knox secy of war

LS, DLC:GW; LB, DLC:GW.

1. In his letter to Knox of 10 Aug. from Pittsburgh, Wayne wrote: "I have the

honor to inclose a copy of a Letter from Major George McCully of the 7th Inst., nothing further has yet been received respecting those parties of Indians, I therefore conclude that McCully is following upon their trail, and probably may come up with them, one of the *Spies* has made oath, that the party he discovered amounted to two hundred Indians.

"I am informed that part of the Militia of Westmoreland have voluntiered it with Major McCully.

"Desertions have become frequent & alarming, two nights since, upon report, that a large body of Indians were close in our front, I ordered the troops to form for action, and rode along the line to inspire them with confidence, and gave orders to those in the redoubts, which I had recently thrown up in our front, and right flank, to maintain those posts, at every expence of blood, until I would gain the enemies rear with the dragoons, but such was the defect of the human heart, that from excess of Cowardice, one *third* part of the *sentries* deserted from their stations, so as to leave the most accessable places unguarded. however I do not conceive myself weakened by this kind of defection, as it was only the effect of pusillanimity, in a few individuals; but as it may become infectious, unless suddenly checked, I am determined to make a severe example, of part of those who deserted their posts in the hour of danger.

"I expect the most of them are secured by a detachment of dragoons under Cornet [James] Taylor, who I sent in pursuit of them, he had found their trail, and was not far in their rear yesterday Noon, his orders are, if they attempt resistance, to put them to instantaneous death.

"By the enclosed papers you will see the measures I have adopted to prevent desertion in future, two deserters were brought in yesterday, by two Country men; for which they received ten dollars ℔ head—the written descriptive list of deserters, are those who deserted from their posts at the alarm, and who I expect to see in the course of the day, it however may be possible, Notwithstanding the near approach of the Dragoons, that they may escape, it will therefore not be amiss, to have the whole inserted, and republished in the Philadelphia Papers.

"I have in contemplation a brand, with the word *Coward* to stamp in the forehead of one or two of the greatest *Caitiffs* and to divest them of every Military ensignia, and cause them to be constantly employed, in the most menial services about Camp. You'l please to observe that there has scarcely been any desertions from this place, except those occasioned by the *alarm*, they have generally taken place on the march from the respective rendezvouses, Apropós, would it not be adviseable, to furnish the Officers marching Detachments, with printed blank descriptions by way of Advertisement.

"Eight Howitzers, have arrived, but without Wheels or Carriages, no account of clothing! permit me again to reitterate my request for a quantity of fine grained powder, of equal fineness and quality with the sample sent you Pr post.

"I cause the whole of the Guards to load, when they take post, and discharge at *Marks* when relieved, under the inspection of their respective Officers, I give one gill of Whisky as a reward for the *best,* and half a gill for the *second* best, shot each day which will cause an emulation: the troops and Dragoons, improve rapidly in Maneouvre, but our *Coats* begin to be out at the elbows, and under the Arms. I have therefore to request, that you will order on a quantity of remnants of blue Cloth with needles and thread, by which means we can furbish up, and keep our clothing decent and Comfortable, which will tend to inspire the troops with pride, and pride, in a soldier I esteem as a substitute for almost every other virtue, make him ashamed of committing a mean Act, and it answers every purpose of Virtue, dress will greatly facilitate this desirable end.

"I have sent off a large quantity of grain to Fort Washington under an escort, together with two, three pounders—and six tons of three and six pound shot, I have also ordered the purchase of One hundred and fifty *Tons* of the best Clover and timothy hay at Whelen, to be delivered on board the boats, at six dollars ℔ Ton, which with the addition of the price of the boats, will not amount to more than eight dollars ℔ tun, delivered at Fort Washington so that our Cavalry can be supported there as cheap, and as well, as in any part of the United States. if we can amuse the savages for this Campaign—(for from present appearances, peace is out of the question) I think I could venture to insure success, against three times our numbers the next season, nor shall We ever have a permanent peace with those Indians, until they experience our superiority in the field.

"6. oClock. P.M. the post has this moment arrived and I am honored with yours of the 3d Inst. containing a number of Inclosures—to which due attention shall be paid.

"Before this reaches you, you will probably have received my letters of the 3d & 6th Instant which will remove every doubt respecting the fate of Colonel Hardin & Major Trueman.

"Cornet Taylor has returned without success. but the *Cowards* cant escape" (DLC:GW). For GW's reaction to this letter, see GW to Knox, 26 Aug. 1792.

2. Knox added the phrase "& shoes" in his own hand.

From Alexander Hamilton

Sir   Philadelphia Aug. 18. 1792

I am happy to be able, at length, to send you, answers to the objections, which were communicated in your letter of the 29th of July.[1]

They have unavoidably been drawn in haste, too much so, to do perfect justice to the subject, and have been copied just as they flowed from my heart and pen, without revision or correction. You will observe, that here and there some severity[2] appears—I have not fortitude enough always to hear with calmness, calumnies, which necessarily include me, as a principal Agent in the measures censured, of the falsehood of which, I have the most unqualified consciousness. I trust that I shall always be able to[3] bear, as I ought, imputations of errors of Judgment; but I acknowledge that I cannot be entirely patient under charges, which impeach the[4] integrity of my public motives or conduct. I feel, that I merit them *in no degree:* and expressions of indignation sometimes escape me, in spite of every effort to suppress them⟨.⟩ I rely on your goodness for the proper allowance. With high respect and the most affectionate attachment, I have the honor to be Sir Your most Obedient & humble servant

Alexander Hamilton

ALS, DLC: GW; ADf, DLC: Hamilton Papers; copy, DLC: Hamilton Papers. GW docketed the ALS "Private."

1. For background on the objections to the financial policies of the Washington administration that were contained in GW's letter to Hamilton of 29 July, see Jefferson to GW, 23 May 1792 (second letter), and notes. For Hamilton's enclosure, which has been found only in draft form in DLC: Hamilton Papers, see Syrett, *Hamilton Papers,* 12:229–58.

2. At this place on the draft manuscript, Hamilton wrote and then struck out the phrase "has been deserved indulged."

3. At this place on the draft manuscript, Hamilton wrote and then struck out the words "submit properly to."

4. At this place on the draft manuscript, Hamilton wrote and then struck out the word "purity."

From Thomas Jefferson

Sir   Monticello Aug. 19. 1792.

I was yesterday honored with your's of the 13th inst. covering the Governor of Vermont's of July 16. I presume it cannot now be long before I shall receive his answer to the two letters I wrote him from Philadelphia on the same subject.[1] I now inclose letters received by yesterday's post from mister Hammond, mister William Knox, and mister Paleske, with answers to the two latter.[2] should these meet your approbation, you will be so good as to seal and let them go on under the cover to mister Taylor, who will have them co⟨nvey⟩ed according to their address. should you wish an alteration of them, it shall be made on their being returned.[3] the Prussian treaty is, I believe, within four years of it's expiration. I suspect that personal motives alone induce mister Paleske to press for a convention which could hardly be formed & ratified before it would expire; and that his court cannot lay much stress on it.[4] mister Hammond's former explanations of his notification of the 12th of April, having been laid before Congress, may perhaps make it proper to communicate to them also his sovereign's approbation of them.[5] I have the honor to be with sentiments of the most perfect respect & attachment, Sir, your most obedt & most humble servt

Th: Jefferson

ALS, DNA: RG 59, Miscellaneous Letters; ALS (letterpress copy), DLC: Jefferson Papers; LB, DNA: RG 59, Domestic Letters; LB, DNA: RG 59, George Washington's Correspondence with His Secretaries of State; LB (photocopy), DLC:GW.

1. Conflicting jurisdictional claims by Vermont and Canada over the town of Alburg, Vt., were the focus of this correspondence with Gov. Thomas Chittenden. For background on this dispute, see Chittenden to GW, 16 June, 16 July, GW to Jefferson, 23 July, and Jefferson to GW, 30 July 1792. Jefferson's letters to Chittenden of 9 and 12 July are in *Jefferson Papers*, 24:200, 218–19.

2. In his letter to Jefferson of 3 Aug. from New York, George Hammond, minister from Great Britain, wrote: "I have received a dispatch from my Court, communicating to me his Majesty's entire approbation of my conduct, relative to my conversations and explanatory correspondence with you, on the subject of the circular notification which I transmitted to you on the 12th of April.

"Having obtained this sanction to the sentiments, which I expressed to you upon those occasions, it is necessary for me at present only to add that that notification was then, and is now, intended to apply solely to Merchant-vessels *strictly foreign;* under which denomination ships belonging to Citizens of the United States cannot be generally comprehended, so long as the Kings proclamations, regulating the commercial intercourse between Great Britain and this country, shall continue in force, and assign to the ships of the latter those *distinctions,* which they now possess" (DNA: RG 59, Notes from Foreign Legations, Great Britain; see also Hammond to Jefferson, 12 April 1792, *Jefferson Papers*, 23:418).

William Knox, consul at Dublin, reported in a letter to Jefferson of 28 May that despite recent concessions from Parliament, the Irish Catholics "think any thing less than a participation in the elective franchise, will not relieve them from the numerous inequalities under which they labour." He noted that twenty-eight American ships carrying over 12,000 hogsheads of flaxseed had arrived in Dublin since 1 Jan. and that this cargo sold "at more than the ordinary price" due to increased linen manufacture in Ireland. Knox warned Jefferson that American ships carrying tobacco were subject to seizure if they attempted to enter any Irish port or even if they appeared off the coast, and he asked Jefferson "to request the President of the United States to excuse my returning to America, at least for a few months" (DNA: RG 59, Despatches from Consular Offices: Dublin). On 19 Aug., Jefferson wrote Knox that his letter had been communicated to GW and that "as the Consulships of the U.S. have no salaries or perquisites for the support of those who hold them . . . the government does not expect that the office should so far tie the holder to a constant presence at his residence as would be inconsistent with that business by which he is supported." Knox was therefore free to return home for a short time (*Jefferson Papers,* 24:308). He left Ireland on 22 July and arrived in Philadelphia on 15 Sept. (William Knox to Jefferson, 18 Sept. 1792, ibid., 389). Knox never resumed his consular post, and Jefferson recorded Knox's resignation in a "Memorandum on Consuls and Consular Appointments," 15 Feb. 1793 (ibid., 25:202–4).

Charles Gottfried Paleske of Philadelphia, who had been commissioned the Prussian consul general in the United States on 14 Aug. 1791 and served until 1801, announced his appointment to Jefferson in a letter dated 2 Jan. 1792 and sent a certified copy of his commission two days later (DNA: RG 59, Notes from Foreign Consuls in the United States). Paleske wrote Jefferson on 9 Aug. that the king of Prussia had instructed him to request "that agreable to the existing treaty of comerce, His consul-general be acknowledged, as belonging to a most favoured nation, with which the United States have formed a treaty of comerce, and that the privileges and immunities, due to a consul general of the most favoured nation be also granted to the consul general of His Prussian Majesty, as due conformable to treaty." Paleske asked "that comissioners be appointed by the United States, as speedily as possible, to regulate by particular convention, the functions of the consuls and vice consuls of the respective nations" (DNA: RG 59, Notes from Foreign Consuls in the United States). For previous suggestions from Paleske concerning commercial and diplomatic relations between the United States and Prussia, see Paleske to Jefferson, 19 June 1792, in *Jefferson Papers,* 24:99–101.

Jefferson replied to Paleske on 19 Aug.: "Treaties of the U.S. duly made & ratified, as is that with his Prussian Majesty, constitute a part of the law of the land, and need only promulgation to oblige all persons to obey them, and to entitle all to those privileges which such treaties confer. that promulgation having taken place, no other act is necessary, or proper, on the part of our government, according to our rules of proceeding, to give effect to the treaty. this treaty however has not specified the privileges or functions of consuls; it has only provided that these 'shall be regulated by particular agreement.' to the proposition to proceed as speedily as possible to regulate these functions by a convention, my absence from the seat of government does not allow me to give a definitive answer. I know in general that it would be agreeable to our government, on account of the recent changes in it's form, to suspend for a while the contracting specific engagements with foreign nations, until something more shall be seen of the direction it will take, and of it's mode of operation, in order that our engagements may be so moulded to that as to ensure the exact performance of them which we are desirous ever to observe. should this be the sentiment of our government on the pre⟨sen⟩t occasion, the friendship of his Prussian majesty is a sufficient reliance to us for that delay which our affairs might require for the present: and the rather as his vessels are not yet in the habit of seeking our ports, and for the few cases which may occur for some time, our own laws, copied mostly in this respect from those of a very commercial nation, have made the most material of those provisions, which could be admitted into a special convention, for the protection of vessels, their crews, and cargoes coming hither. we shall on this however, and every other occasion, do every thing we can to manifest our friendship to his Prussian majesty, & our desire to promote commercial intercourse with his subjects" (DLC: Jefferson Papers).

3. GW returned the enclosed letters from Hammond, Knox, and Paleske to Jefferson on 3 Sept., and although GW said in his cover letter to Jefferson that he did not "perfectly comprehend an expression in the one to Mr Palaske," he forwarded Jefferson's answers to Knox and Paleske to George Taylor, Jr., chief clerk in the State Department (ALS, DLC: Jefferson Papers; ADfS, DNA: RG 59, Miscellaneous Letters; LB, DNA: RG 59, George Washington's Correspondence with His Secretaries of State; LB [photocopy], DLC:GW).

4. The Prussian Treaty of Amity and Commerce of 10 Sept. 1785 was due to expire on 8 Aug. 1796, ten years after the exchange of ratifications (see Miller, *Treaties*, 2:162–84).

5. See GW to the U.S. Senate and House of Representatives, Jefferson to GW, both 13 April 1792.

To Henry Knox

Sir   Mount Vernon Augt 19th 1792

In my letter of the 15th I promised you my sentiments on Mr Seagroves communications; and though I am not enabled to do it so fully as I could wish, I shall nevertheless give them as fully as I can.

His letters, and the enclosures there in contained, with the evidence in support, go to points, which may be classed under six heads.[1]

1st—Spanish interference, to prevent the treaty between the United States & the Creek Nation from being carried into effect—To accomplish which, these Indians, together with the Cherokees, chicasaws & Chactaws, are envited to a grand Council at Pensacola; where, if they will attend, it is intimated to them, they shall be furnished with Arms, Ammunition, & goods of all sorts. An Agent of Spain, (a Captn Oliver) who is established at little Tallassee in the Creek Nation, & supposed to be acting in concert with McGillivray, has *forbid* their running the line that was established by treaty with these people; promising them the support of Spain against any measures which may be pursued by the U. States, in case of their refusal—and in a word, aided by McGillivray & Panton, is stimulating *all* the Southern Indians to acts of hostilities against the United States; to facilitate which he is distributing goods, & holding talks with the chiefs. Three things, it is said, will be attempted at the proposed meeting in Pensacola—1st to established Posts in the Indian Country—2d To fix three Agents amongst them, of whom McGillivray is to be the principal; & 3d to exclude the Citizens of the United States from having any trade with these Indians—To carry the whole of this plan into effect, it is further said that five Regimts of about 600 men each & a large quantity of Ordnance & Stores are actually arrived from old Spain, & the like number of Troops are expected from the Havanna; and suspns are alive, that the Capture of Bowles, was a preconcerted scheme between the Spanh Govt & himself.

2d—The turbulant disposition of the settlers on the Western frontier of Georgia—and their endeavors (as appear by the declaration of Colo. Alexander—and others which could be adduced)—to oppose the measures of the General Government; and to bring on a War between the United States and the Creek Nation, with the nefarious means practiced by them to accomplish this project and the effect it has had upon the latter; who are affraid, though generally well disposed towards the U. States and in all their public talks have given strong assurances of their intention to execute the treaty, to meet at the Rock landing on the Oconee in the vicinity of these characters.

3d—His conditional engagement to meet the lower Creeks on the head of St Marys River in November next—His opinion that with more extensive powers, and a larger field to display in, he should be able, not only to counteract the unprovoked interference of the Spaniards by keeping the Indians in our Interest, but could even engage them to Act for us, if circumstances should make it desirable—but to do this he must be furnished with goods, and be authorised to distribute them as occasions should require. That but for his endeavors to support the authority of McGillivray, & to reinstate him in the good opinion of his Nation who began to see into his views, and nine tenths of it to dispise him, this might have been in a more progressive state, than it is at present.

4th—The necessity of restricting the licenses of Traders— and passes to people of other descriptions; who, under various pretences (but oftentimes with bad intentions) go into the Indian Villages—And of the expediency, & the advantages which would result, from having proper forms for both, with checks, to prevent counterfeits and impositions on the Indians.

5th—The probable consequence of a severe drought, to the Indians—and the policy of relieving them from impending famine.

6th—The intemperence of Major Call—His improper conduct in raising three troops of horse with promise of paymt from the Genl Government—leaving a party on the So. Western frontier of Georgia without an Officer, or even a Sergeant—And the Agents opinion of the necessity of a respectable force on the So. Western frontier of that State & the little use of them in their present Stations.

These heads, as well as I can recollect, contain the substance of Mr Seagroves communication, on which I give the following sentiments & observations.

1st—The conduct of Spain in this business is so unprovoked (by any event that has come to my knowledge)—so misterious—and so hostile in appearance, that although the evidence is strong, and corroborated by a variety of information through a variety of channels, and even confirmed by McGillivray himself, yet the mind can scarcely realise a proceedure so base & inhuman as the encouraging (not only without the exhibition of complaint, but under professions of good neighbourhood & friendship towards us) a war which must expose helpless women & children to the relentless fury of Savages, & to the cruelties of the Tomahawk & Scalping knife. But the evidence of their intreigues to set aside the treaty, & to exclude the U. States from having trade or intercourse with the Southern Indians, will scarcely admit of a doubt; and there is but too much reason to suspect that McGillivray has an agency in promoting these measures.

My opinion therefore is, that the Commissioners of Spain, in Philadelphia, shd be informed, delicately, & perhaps informally (until matters can be more fully investigated, or developed) that though we are ready to acquit the Spanish *government* of measures so unfriendly to the U. States, yet that the evidence of these proceedings in some of its Officers, is too strong to admit of a doubt, & of too important a nature to pass over in silence. That it creates serious alarm in the minds of our Citizens in the Southern quarter, and gives much trouble to the Government of the

U. States; which has no views incompatible with good faith towards Spain, and with justice and honor towards the Indns.

Something to this effect was written, or spoken to these Gentlemen by the Secretary of State on the first representation of this matter from the Southern Agent for Indian Affairs, but what notice was taken of it by them, or whether any, I do not recollect to have been informed. Enquiry, however, should be made —but whether the documents respecting it are to be found in his Office, or are deposited among the private transactions in his own keeping, is uncertain: in the latter case no information can be obtained in time.[2]

2d—My opinion on this head is, that Governor Tellfair should be written to, and informed in delicate, but in firm & unequivocal terms—That the United States from a concatination of causes, are so delicately circumstanced as to render Peace in the Southern quarter indispensably necessary, if it be possible to preserve it upon just, & honorable terms. That Government has received information unequivocal in its nature, of designs in some of the frontier Inhabitants of Georgia, not only to *impede,* but absolutely to *oppose* running the line which was agreed upon as a boundary between that State & the Creeks; and, of conduct in some of them, tending to provoke war, rather than to promote peace with these Indians—That it was (and subsequent events have proved it) with great difficulty that the boundary then agreed on could be obtained—That now it has become a law of the Land; and if the Indians can be prevailed on to carry it into execution it must be enforced—And lastly, to exhort him, by every motive to peace & good order, that he would use his influence & address to repress[3] all turbulent & illegal proceedings in this behalf, as the consequences cannot fail to be distressing from a contrary conduct.[4]

3d—Although the opinions, and propositions of the Southern Agent ought, in this case, to be received with a due degree of caution, inasmuch as he is removing the theatre of action from the Rock landing to his own (or brothers store) at the head of St Marys—covering thereby that frontier, where his interest is more immediately affected—building his own consequence upon the ruins of another as occasion & circumstances may require—Acquiring a power to distribute goods (which, tho' limited, & issued under certn restrictions, may nevertheless be abused)—Investing him with more ample power to act from the circumstances of the moment—I say, notwithstanding the liability of abuse in some, or all of these cases; I am of opinion from the circumstances which exist, & press, and from the delay which would result from references at the distance He is from the Seat of the Government, that he ought, as far as I have power to give them, to be instructed To—hold a meeting with the Indian *Chiefs* at the time & place mentiond in his letter of the 27th ulto—and—That he should—under defined restrictions—have authority given him—to distribute goods as circumstances, & his own judgment shall dictate. That he ought to counteract the nefarious schemes of Spain by all the influence & address he is master of. That if, upon further, & more unequivocal proof, McGillivrays duplicity & treachery should appear more evident; that he is, in that case, to destroy, as far as it is in his power, the consequence of that man in the Creek nation; and, as the most effectual step towards it, & serving the U: States, to take, if he can, his place in the Nation.[5]

4th—The propriety of this restrictive proposition is apparent —but to draw the line is difficult. To vest it *solely* (which I believe wd be the least evil) with the Indian Agents, wd encrease their consequence amazingly, & would, in a man[ne]r, give them, if they are indirectly engaged in Trade, a monopoly thereof; and all other intercourse with the Indians: and in the instance before us, would create much Jealousy & disgust in the Executive of the State of Georgia. Under this impression of my sentiments, decide as shall appear best, upon a full view of the case.

The idea of an engraving with the proposed check, to prevent counterfeit passes & impositions, is a good thought, and merits adoption.[6]

5th—If the Indians should be reduced to the deplorable State which is apprehended, by an Act of Providence which human foresight is unable to avert; It is my opinion that we ought, if they exhibit signs of good dispositions towards us, as well from motives of policy as those of humanity, to afford them relief. But the power of the Executive to do this—the state of the treasury— the extent of the evil—& the consequences of giving to one Nation & not to all, if it should be asked—are matters to be considered before any explicit assurance is given, that Supplies will be granted.[7]

6th—There can be no doubt of the propriety of bringing Ma-

jor Call before a Genl Court Martial for his intemperate conduct—for authorising the raising of three troops of Horse at the
expence of the Union (unless as commanding officer he was
instructed, or empowered to do it; of which I have no recollection)—and for leaving a party of Soldiers on the So. Westn frontier without an Officer, or even a sergeant to comd & provide
for them.[8]

As to the necessity of having a respectable force on the South
western frontier of Georgia, and of the little use of those on the
more western part of the State no reasons are assigned for either,
by which a judgment can be formed; & havg no accurate map of
that Country with me, I am unable to give any other sentimt on
either of these points, than that (for the reason which has been
given under another hd) this measure should be decided on with
caut[ion].

I do not give these opinions, or any one of them as decisive, or
as directions to be implicitly followed; because that would render
deliberation, & the request contained in my letter of the 15th,
nugatory. They are given as crude & indigested first thoughts,
only; to be closely examined, & compared & combined with
other information which may be found in the public Offices, and
the letters & Instructions, draughted accordingly.

Let these (except the communication if any to the Comrs of
Spain) pass through my hands unsealed—I am persuaded there
will be no delay on acct of disapprobation, & consequent alterations. The Express not expecting (as he says) to have proceeded
further than Mount Vernon, will want a supply of money to take
him back—to be accounted for with the Indian Agent. He has
already received two guineas from me.

I presume Mr Seagrove would wish to be placed upon some
more permanent establishment with respect to his pay; but if
there be any doubt of my power to fix this, & to render his Office
more stable, matters (with assurances that his Services will neither pass unnoticed, or unrewarded) must remain as they are
until the meeting of Congress: And as he appears to have acted
with zeal and intelligence, he ought to be informed of the satisfaction his conduct has given; & to be requested in a particular,
& pointed manner, to have someone or more persons in whom
entire confidence can be placed (as well in their abilities, as fidelity) to attend the meeting at Pensacola—to watch the motions
of Oliver—and to be informed precisely—and accurately—of

the Spanish movements in both East and West Florida. Money (reasonably bestowed) must not be spared to accomplish these objects.

What is become of the Surveyor—Ellicot—& what is proper to be done with him? he ought not to be retained in that Country at a *certain* expence, awaiting a very *uncertain* event.[9]

I did not think of it when I was writing my letter of the 15th but now request that the Attorney General may be called on to aid with his sentiments in the several matters which are referred for your consideration and decision.

Not having thought of any character more eligable for Adjutant General than Majr Fish, I request that he may be sounded, or even directly applied to.[10] Should he be indisposed to the Office, some other must be appointed without delay. With esteem & regard I am Affectly Yours

Go: Washington

ADfS, DLC:GW; LB, DLC:GW.

1. For background on the six points outlined and analyzed by GW in this letter, see the letters that James Seagrove, Indian agent of the southern department, wrote to GW on 5 and 27 July 1792.

2. Jefferson had written the Spanish consuls José Ignacio de Viar and José de Jaudenes on 17 May 1792 to express U.S. concerns about Spanish intrigues with the southern Indians (see *Jefferson Papers*, 23:523). While Jefferson was away at Monticello, Knox attempted to solicit further information from the Spanish consuls by inviting Viar and Jaudenes to "a family dinner" on 6 Sept. at his home in Philadelphia. During the course of the evening, Knox questioned the consuls about reports of Spanish intrigue among the Creek Indians, and in the minutes that he later recorded, he wrote: "the conversation was naturally introduced by themselves about Bowles, who they said he was in jail at Cadiz, and would not easily be liberated. I inquired whether they would find cause of putting him to death—they said they did not know but they beleived not—I mentioned Mr Hammonds having disclaimd on the behalf of the british court any support or authority to save Bowles—They said they had so understood, but that this did not preclude the idea of support being given to Bowles by Individuals as McGaliavray and perhaps by the Governor.

"I mentioned to them, that one Wellbanks seemed to retain part of Bowles authority Among the Indians. They said they had understood one Connelly was a sort of successir to Bowles but Knew nothing about Wellbanks.

"I mentioned to them that a new Character had sprung up among the Creeks by the name of Olivar, a frenchman by birth who styled himself a spanish agent, and a Capt. of the regimt of new Orleans, and that he wore a Spanish ⟨milirty⟩ Uniform. That however he talked in such a manner, as to excuse in our minds all aspects of havg any authority on the part of the spanish governt—⟨For⟩ he exhorted the Indians not to run the line agreably to the treaty made with the Creeks at New York and assured them of the support [of] the Spaniards and he also invited them ⟨to apear in⟩ New Orleans." In reponse to Knox's request for more information about Pedro Olivier, the consuls replied that they "had never heard of him until Mr Jefferson had written to them a letter on the subject."

According to Knox, the consuls also said: "That they did not conceive the said Olivar could have any authority from the spanish governt for if their court had any exceptions to the treaty of New York—they conceived it would be made Known in the ordinary channells of Communication.

"That the spanish government had some exception to a treaty made by the US with the Choctaws in the year 1786, wherein ⟨to⟩ the 31st degree of latitude is mentioned and the district of the natchez is included as confined to the Indians. That the district of the Natchez is a seperate ⟨governt⟩, and that the ⟨functions thereof⟩ are at present exercised by [   ].

"That if Capt. Olivar was in the spanish ser[vice] where to them was unknown, it must be in a regimt of two battalions, which the spanish government had lately authorized Governor Condorelet of New Orleans, to raise under the title of the regimt of the Mississippi—that a Capt. While of the 112th brigade in the spanish service—who was in New York about the year 1789, was a Colonel of one of the battalions, he being a leut. col. or in the line of the Spanish army—That Capt. Woorster son of the late Genl Woorster was also a Capt. in the second regiment.

"I read to them Mr Seagroves letter to Governor Quesadas of East Florida, and the Govrs Answer, thereto They observed that We Might rest assured that the ⟨casual⟩ answer of the said governor breathed the true spirit of the Spanish governt towards the US" (Minutes of a Conversation with Viar and Jaudenes, 6 Sept., NNGL: Knox Papers). For the official response of Viar and Jaudenes to American concerns, see Jefferson to GW, 29 Oct. 1792 (second letter), n.1.

3. The word "redress" is used in the letterbook copy.

4. For Knox's letter to Edward Telfair of 31 Aug., see Knox to GW, 31 Aug. (second letter), n.1.

5. Seagrove had informed Knox on 5 July that he had given the Creeks a "conditional promise, that, if agreeable to the President of the United States, I will meet them at the head of the St. Mary's, on the first day of November next, at which time and place they think every thing can be settled to our wish" (*ASP, Indian Affairs*, 1:303). For Knox's letter to Seagrove of 31 Aug., see Knox to GW, 31 Aug. (second letter), n.2. Seagrove and his brother Robert, along with James Armstrong and Noble Hardee, owned a trading post in the town of Coleraine, approximately sixty miles up St. Marys River, which served both local white settlers and nearby Creek Indians. See Smith, "James Seagrove and the Mission to Tuckaubatchee," 42.

While GW, Seagrove, and Knox suspected Alexander McGillivray of treachery against the United States, the Spanish government was trying to discredit McGillivray for his supposed loyalty to the Americans. By late 1792 ill health contributed to McGillivray's declining influence, and his death on 17 Feb. 1793 left the Creeks without one of their most skillful diplomats (see Caughey, *McGillivray of the Creeks*, 45–53).

6. The Trade and Intercourse Act, which Congress passed in 1790, stipulated that "no person shall be permitted to carry on any trade or intercourse with the Indian tribes, without a license for that purpose under the hand and seal of the superintendent of the department, or of such other person as the President of the United States shall appoint for that purpose." The act was to remain in effect for "the term of two years, and from thence to the end of the next session of Congress, and no longer" (1 *Stat.* 137–38). Since this act did not end frontier unrest, GW outlined a basic Indian policy in his annual address to Congress on 25 Oct. 1791, but no legislation resulted. In 1792, with the act of 1790 about to expire, GW pointed out the need for new legislation in his annual message to Congress on 6 Nov., and a new, stronger act was approved on 1 Mar. 1793 (ibid., 329–32).

7. James Seagrove wrote Knox on 17 Oct. that the "situation for bread is very bad indeed; the Cussetah town, which contains three thousand souls, did not actually make fifty bushels of corn this year; many other towns are equally destitute," despite the arrival eight days earlier at St. Mary's of the sloop *Polly* and the schooner *Oak* "with corn and goods on public account" (*ASP, Indian Affairs,* 1:311). Knox had notified Seagrove on 31 Aug. that "Goods, corn, and money," totaling $13,314.61, would be shipped to St. Mary's "in due season," and he instructed Seagrove to "make such distribution of the goods and corn to the Lower towns as your judgment shall direct. . . . If the real necessities of the Lower Creeks require a larger quantity than the five thousand bushels intended to be transported to St. Mary's, you may intimate to them that the President of the United States, actuated by his humanity and regard for them, will order a further quantity, provided they exhibit, on their parts, similar dispositions of kindness and attachment to the United States" (ibid., 260, printed under the incorrect date of 31 October). Knox, in his letter to Seagrove of 24 Sept., enclosed an invoice totaling $7,336.81 for the supplies being sent on the *Polly* and the *Oak* and wrote that about 450 more bushels of corn would follow on another vessel (ibid.).

8. Maj. Richard Call died on 28 Sept. 1792 before he could be court-martialed (see GW to the U.S. Senate, 22 Feb. 1793).

9. For background on Joseph Ellicott's appointment to survey the boundary line negotiated between the Creeks and the United States in the 1790 Treaty of New York, see Tobias Lear to Knox, 1 Sept. 1791, and note 2.

10. Knox wrote Nicholas Fish on 29 Aug. to offer him the office of adjutant general (NNGL: Knox Papers).

To Alexander Hamilton

Sir,   Mount Vernon 22d Augt 1792.

This will merely inform you that your letter of the 10th with it's enclosure—and that of the 11th Inst: have been duly received; and that if the Regulations of your Department, mentioned in the former, are carried strictly into execution, the most happy consequences, it is to be hoped, will result from them. I am sir &c.

G. Washington

LB, DLC:GW.

To Henry Knox

Dear Sir, Mount Vernon Augt 22 1792

In my letter of the 15th I acknowledged the receipt of yours of the 11th;[1] since which your dispatches of the 16th are come to hand, and convey but a gloomy prospect of peace with the Indians, in either hemisphere; but shew the necessity of preparing more vigorously if possible for the dernier resort. That the Western Indians are stimulated to acts of hostility on one side, and every mean which can be devised to set aside the treaties wch exist between the Southern Indians and the U. States, & to encourage the former to break with us on the other admits of no doubt in my mind; and that it may be a concerted plan between certn Powers to check the growth of this rising Country, is far from improbable—diabolical as it may seem.

The enclosure of Genl Putnams letter of 9th of July, enables me (which I could not do before) to form some idea of his proposition to establish a Post on the Muskingham;[2] and 'though I shall give no decided opinion on *this* particular case, my sentiments, generally, with respect to Posts, are not changed—and are shortly these. that except for the preservation of Stores, and the security of convoys upon a communi[catio]n they are of no use but to protect the people within them—for unless the Garrison is of such strength, & can detach in such force, as to bid defiance to the enemy it is always cooped up. Except for the purposes I have mentioned, of what advantage are Forts Hamilton, St Clair & Jefferson? The strength of Stationary parties are soon discovered by the Indians and when discovered, are liable to be cut off, unless they confine themselves *solely* to the defence of the Post—& of what avail would this be on the Muskingham or elsewhere? Posts can be insulted, or avoided at the option of the enemy in a covered Country—but the best vigilence of the most cautious Ene[my] cannot prevent scouting parties falling on their trail. Besides, we shall never be respectable at any point if

the Troops are divided, & subdivided for the quietude of particular settlements or neighbourhoods: nor will they ever be disci-
plined, and under due subordination whilst they are scattered
over the Country in small parties under Subaltern Officers; except when they are employed in ranging, which is an essential
part of their Military educatn in the Service for which they are
designed.

If all the measures which have been pursued by Governmt to
convince the hostile Indians of the just & honorable intentions
of the U. States towards them should prove ineffectual we may
certainly calculate upon a powerful opposition from their Combind force; in which case, we shall not only be unprepared to
penetrate their Country, this Year, but there appears to me to be
very little prospect of doing it early in the next; unless there can
be some stimulus to the recruiting Service; and the Officers *absolutely* restrained from enlisting improper men—for I am told,
notwithstanding the pointed instructions which have been issued to them on this head, that *boys* in *many instances,* and the
worst miscreants in others are received: to the last of which may be
attributed the number of desertions that are reported to the War
Office.[3] Under this view of the matter, your intimation to Genl
Wayne respecting the Chicasaws and Choctaws was prudent &
proper; but I conceive, nevertheless, if a few of each Southern
Nation say a Six or 8 respectable characters was to visit & remain
with the Army as long as should be agreeable to themselves—Be
well fed & cloathed—& in all respects treated with attention &
kindness, it would be an effectual inducement to the coming of
the number that might be required next year?[4]

I perceive by Mr Belli's letter that the difference between supplying the Troops with their Rations by Contract, and by a purchasing Commy must be very great indeed, although he has not
given the Wages, & other charges of the latter gentry. I am of
opinion that the difference in favor of the latter will be found
from the nature of things much greater on the exterior than it
would be in the interior Country—and as the public pay for all
lost provisions (by the enemy) is at the expence of Stores Guards
&ca it is a matter worthy of serious investigation & consequent
decision—Consult therefore with the Secretary of the treasury,
& act as the result shall appear best.[5]

The *hair* must have *stood* on Major S——— *head,* & a *stake* full in his view, when his letter of the 8th of July was writing to Genl Wilkinson, or the style of it would certainly have been varied.[6] With esteem & regard I am Dr Sir Yrs &ca

G. W——n

ADfS, DLC:GW; LB, DLC:GW.

1. The letter of 11 Aug. from Knox has not been found.

2. In his letter from Fort Washington of 9 July, Putnam wrote Knox: "Whether the plan of making an Establishment on Lake Erie at Cayahoga as proposed in my letter of yesterday be adopted or not, I beg leave to suggest the propriety of fixing a post some where on the Muskingum River to be occupied by about three companies two of which should be riflemen, they should be employed in scouting up the Muskingum and towards the Hockhocking—they would be a great protection to Ohio County and Washington in Pennsylvania, as well as to the settlements on the Muskingum and the Inhabitants on both sides of the Ohio as far down as Belleville (from whence there is no settlement until we come to the great Kenhawa) until offensive operations are determined on, these troops should be posted at the Waterford Station which is twenty three miles by Water up the Muskingum (and fourteen by land) but as soon as the business of treating is over they should be posted farther up the river; and provided supplies can be furnished they ought to be fixed as far up as the Mouth of Licking Creek—to this place loaded Boats may pass at almost any season—the only difficulty lies in the danger in passing up the River.

"The greatest part of these troops on the advance of the Militia towards San Dusky should join them on the march and after alarming San Dusky if thought necessary may fall away North East and join the Army" (DLC:GW).

3. The problem of desertion was addressed in the general orders issued at Pittsburgh on 9 Aug. 1792 by Henry De Butts, aide-de-camp to Wayne: "Desertion having become very prevalent among the Troops at this place particularly upon the least appearance or rather apprehension of Danger that some man (for they are unworthy of the name of Soldiers) have so lost in every sence of honor and duty as to desert their posts, as Sentries by w[h]ich treacherous, base and cowardly conduct, the lives and Safety of their brave Companions, and worthy citizens, where committed to Savage fury.

"The Commander in Chief therefore determined to put a stop to such a banefull practice, by the most exemplary punishment, as well as by liberal rewards, and hereby promises to every citizen, or *Soldier,* the Sum of *ten* dollars, for each and every deserter, that may be apprehended and brought to this place with reasonable costs.

"The Commander in Chief also promises a reward of ten *dollars,* to any *Soldier,* who will discover any intention of desertion in any other Soldier or Soldiers—to the end that such Soldier or Soldiers, may be secured and punished agreeably to the rules and Articles of War" (Burton, "General Wayne's Orderly Book," 358; printed in the *Federal Gazette and Philadelphia Daily Advertiser* on 17 Aug. 1792).

4. For Knox's statement in a 27 July letter to General Wayne that it was too late in the year to launch a military campaign using Chickasaw and Choctaw

Indians against the hostile Indians in the Northwest Territory, see Knox to GW,
16 Aug. 1792, and note 5.

5. Deputy quartermaster general John Belli wrote Knox on 12 July from
Lexington, Ky., that he had "purchased 230. cavalry horses" and "19 Yoke working oxen," that forage was impossible to obtain at that time, and that he anticipated a plentiful corn crop in October. He expected the cost of the horses
to average $70 each and oxen $35.25 each, the oxen to weigh from 1,200 to
1,800 lbs. per yoke. He noted that prices for supplies were lower when bought
with cash rather than merchandise. Belli informed Knox that "should the mode
of supplying the army (with provisions) by a purchasing commissary be preferred to the present plan," he was interested in such an appointment (DLC:
GW). He also enclosed a "Short Sketch of the Cost of a Ration at Fort Washington" in which he analyzed the cost of buying and transporting beef, flour,
and whiskey to that fort. Belli concluded that after allowing 10 percent for lost
cattle, damaged flour, and "lost whiskey by leakage," the daily ration per soldier would not cost "above 3½ pence virginia currency" (DLC:GW).

For the regulations that Hamilton had already developed for purchasing
supplies for the U.S. Army, see Hamilton to GW, 10 Aug. 1792. For "proposals
for the supply of rations for the Western Posts" and for a list of the daily rations
allowed each recruit, see Hamilton to Otho H. Williams, 11 Aug. 1792, n.1, in
Syrett, *Hamilton Papers*, 12:195–96.

6. The letter to Gen. James Wilkinson has not been identified.

To Thomas Jefferson

(Private)

My dear Sir,   Mount Vernon Augt 23d 1792.

Your letters of the 12th & 13th came duly to hand—as did
that enclosing Mr Blodgets plan of a Capitol. The latter I forwarded to the Commissioners, and the enclosures of the two first
are now returned to you.[1]

I believe we are never to hear *from* Mr Carmichael; nor *of him*
but through the medium of a third person. His —— I realy do
not know with what epithet to fill the blank, is, to me, amongst
the most unaccountable of all the unaccountable things! I wish
much to hear of the arrival of Mr Short at Madrid, and the result of their joint negotiations at that Court, as we have fresh,
and much stronger Representations from Mr Seagrove of the
extraordinary interference of the Spaniards in West Florida, to
prevent running the boundary line which had been established
by treaty between the United States & the Creeks—of their
promising them support in case of their refusal—and of their
endeavouring to disaffect the four Southern tribes of Indians to-

wards this Country. In the execution of these projects Seagrove is convinced McGillivray & his partner Panton are embarked, & have become principal Agents and there are suspicions entertained, he adds, that the Capture of Bowles was a preconcerted measure between the said Bowles & the Spaniard⟨s⟩—That the former is gone to Spain (& to Madrid I think) is certain. That McGillivray has removed from little Tellassee to a place he has within, or bordering on the Spanish line. That a Captn Oliver, [(]a Frenchman, but) an Officer in a Spanish Regiment at New Orleans has taken his place at Tellassee and is holding talks with the Chiefs of the several Towns in the Nation. And that every exertion is making by the Governor of West Florida to obtain a full & general meeting of the Southern Tribes at Pensicola, are facts that admit of *no doubt.* It is also affirmed that five Regiments of about 600 men each, and a large quantity of Ordnance & Stores arrived lately at New Orleans, and that the like number of Regiments (but this can only be from report) was expected at the same place from the Havanna. Recent accts from Arthur Campbell (I hope without *much* foundation) speak of very hostile dispositions in the lower Cherokees, and of great apprehension for the safety of Govr Blount & Genl Pickens who had set out for the proposed meeting with the Chicasaws & Choctaws at Nashville— & for the Goods which were going down the Tenessee by Water, for that Meeting.[2]

Our accounts from the Western Indns are not more favourable than those just mentioned. No doubt remains of their having put to death Majr Trueman & Colo. Hardin; & the Harbingers of their mission.[3] The report from their grand Council is, that War was, or soon would be, decided on; and that they will admit no Flags. The meeting was numerous & not yet dissolved that we have been informed of. What influence our Indn Agents may have at it, remains to be known. Hendricks left Buffaloe Creek between the 18th & 20th of June, accompanied by two or three of the Six Nations; some of the Chiefs of those Nations were to follow in a few days—only waiting, it was said, for the Caughnawaga Indians from Canada. And Captn Brandt would not be long after them. If these attempts to disclose the just & pacific disposition of the United States to these people, should also fail, there remains no alternative but the Sword, to decide the difference; & recruiting goes on heavily.[4]

If Spain is really intrieguing with the Southern Indians as represented by Mr Seagrove, I shall entertain strong suspicions that there is a very clear understanding in all this business between the Courts of London and Madrid; & that it is calculated to check, as far as they can, the rapid encrease, extension & consequence of this Country; for there cannot be a doubt of the wishes of the former (if we may judge from the conduct of its Officers) to impede any eclaircissment of ours with the Western Indians, and to embarrass our negotiations with them, any more than there is of their Traders & some others who are subject to their Government, aiding and abetting them in acts of hostilities.

How unfortunate, and how much is it to be regretted then, that whilst we are encompassed on all sides with avowed enemies & insidious friends, that internal dissentions should be harrowing & tearing our vitals. The last, to me, is the most serious—the most alarming—and the most afflicting of the two. And without more charity for the opinions & acts of one another in Governmental matters—or some more infalible criterion by which the truth of speculative opinions, before they have undergone the test of experience, are to be forejudged than has yet fallen to the lot of fallibility, I believe it will be difficult, if not impracticable, to manage the Reins of Government or to keep the parts of it together: for if, instead of laying our shoulders to the machine after measures are decided on, one pulls this way & another that, before the utility of the thing is fairly tried, it must, inevitably, be torn asunder—And, in my opinion the fairest prospect of happiness & prosperity that ever was presented to man, will be lost—perhaps for ever!

My earnest wish, and my fondest hope therefore is, that instead of wounding suspicions, & irritable charges, there may be liberal allowances—mutual forbearances—and temporising yieldings on *all sides*. Under the exercise of these, matters will go on smoothly, and, if possible, more prosperously. Without them every thing must rub—the Wheels of Government will clog—our enemies will triumph—& by threwing their weight into the disaffected Scale, may accomplish the ruin of the goodly fabric we have been erecting.

I do not mean to apply these observations, or this advice to any particular person, or character—I have given them in the same general terms to other Officers of the Government—because the disagreements which have arisen from difference of opinions—and the Attacks wch have been made upon almost all the measures of government, & most of its Executive Officers, have, for a long time past, filled me with painful sensations; and cannot fail I think, of producing unhappy consequences at home & abroad.[5]

The nature of Mr Seagroves communications was such, and the evidence in support of them so strongly corroborative, that I gave it as my sentiment to Genl Knox that the Commissioners of Spain ought to have the matter brought before them again in the manner it was before, but in stronger (though not in committing) language; as the Government was embarrassed, and its Citizens in the Southern States made uneasy by such proceedings, however unauthorised they might be by their Court.[6]

I pray you to note down, or rather to frame into paragraphs or sections such matters as may occur to you as fit & proper for general communication at the opening of the next Session of Congress—not only in the department of State, but on any other subject applicable to the occasion, that I may, in due time, have every thing before me.[7] With sincere esteem & friendship I am, always, Your Affectionate

Go: Washington

ALS, DLC: Jefferson Papers; copy, DNA: RG 59, Miscellaneous Letters; LB, DNA: RG 59, George Washington's Correspondence with His Secretaries of State; LB (photocopy), DLC:GW.

1. Along with his letter of 12 Aug., Jefferson sent GW, under a cover letter addressed to the D.C. commissioners that was left open for GW's examination, the plan which Samuel Blodget, Jr., had enclosed in his letter to Jefferson of 10 July (see *Jefferson Papers*, 24:205–6). The plan has not been identified. Jefferson's letter to the D.C. commissioners has not been found, although its receipt was recorded on 27 Aug. (see DNA: RG 42, Records of the Commissioners for the District of Columbia, Proceedings, 1791–1802). The commissioners informed Blodget, in a letter written from the Federal City on 29 Aug., that his plan was "under Consideration" (DNA: RG 42, Records of the Commissioners for the District of Columbia, Letters Sent, 1791–1802). For descriptions of the returned enclosures, see the notes for Jefferson to GW, 12 and 13 Aug. 1792.

2. The Senate on 24 Jan. 1792 approved the appointment of William Carmichael and William Short as joint commissioners plenipotentiary to negotiate with Spain for the U.S. right of free navigation on the Mississippi River (see GW to the U.S. Senate, 11 Jan. 1792; *Executive Journal*, 1:99). Jefferson sent Carmichael and Short their commissions on 18 Mar. along with "Observations on these several subjects reported to the President and approved by him, which will therefore serve as instructions for you" (*Jefferson Papers*, 23:292–

93). Under these "Observations" Jefferson added the settlement of the disputed boundary between Georgia and Florida and the attainment of a commercial treaty with Spain as two additional subjects for negotiation (ibid., 296–317). Carmichael was already in Madrid serving as the U.S. chargé d'affaires. Short did not arrive there until February 1793.

For background on U.S. difficulties with Spanish intrigues among the southern Indians, see Seagrove to GW, 5 and 27 July, and GW to Knox, 19 Aug. 1792. For the account from Arthur Campbell, see Knox to GW, 16 Aug. 1792, n.7.

3. For a report on the deaths of Trueman and Hardin, see Knox to GW, 16 Aug., and note 3.

4. Au Glaize, the place where the Auglaize River flows into the Maumee at present-day Defiance, Ohio, was the central meeting site for the Indian confederacy that opposed the growing American presence in the Northwest Territory (see Tanner, "The Glaize in 1792," 15–36). For background on the peace mission of Hendrick Aupaumut, see Knox to GW, 16 Aug., n.4. For the Mohawk leader Joseph Brant's failure to reach Au Glaize before the Indian council adjourned on 9 Oct., see Knox to GW, 6 Dec. 1792. Knox and GW hoped that diplomatic intervention by Brant and other Iroquois chiefs, as well as by Stockbridge chief Aupaumut, would produce a peaceful settlement of U.S. differences with the western Indians.

5. For evidence of the internal dissension within the Washington administration, see Hamilton to GW, 18 Aug., GW to Hamilton, 26 Aug., Jefferson to GW, 9 Sept., and Jefferson's Conversations with GW, 10 July and 1 Oct. 1792.

6. For Knox's discussion with Spanish consuls José Ignacio de Viar and José de Jaudenes on 6 Sept., see GW to Knox, 19 Aug., and note 2.

7. Jefferson sent GW two paragraphs, written on 15 Oct., for inclusion in the president's message to Congress (see GW's Address to the U.S. Senate and House of Representatives, 6 Nov., and note 10). GW made a similar request to each of his other cabinet officers (see GW to Alexander Hamilton, 26 Aug., to Henry Knox, 3 Sept. [second letter], and Edmund Randolph to GW, 28 October).

From Henry Knox

Sir   New-York 23d August 1792

The express, with your letter of the 15th instant and Mr Seagroves and Major Calls dispatches, arrived at the War office about the hour of twelve on the 21st instant, and I received the letters by express yesterday in this City.[1]

I shall return to Philadelphia either to day or tomorrow, and will immediately take up the subjects of Mr Seagroves communications, in conjunction with the secretary of the treasury, and submit the result sir to you.[2]

Major Gaither has probably arrived and will soon be on the

frontiers of Georgia. The Mr Rosecrantz of whom you are pleased to inquire appears to have been an agent of Gen. Waynes, employed through Capt. Cass at Fort Franklin, to obtain information of the movements of the Senekas.[3]

The dangerous situation of Major Washington is greatly to be regretted, I sincerely pray he may recover and again comfort his friends, by his virtues and amiable qualities.[4] I have the honor to be sir with the highest respect Your obedient Servant

H. Knox

ALS, DLC:GW; LB, DLC:GW.

1. Knox left Philadelphia for a visit to New York City on the morning of 18 Aug. (see Knox to GW, 17 August). James Seagrove's dispatches included his letters to GW of 5 and 27 July and his letters to Knox of the same dates. Those from Maj. Richard Call have not been identified.

2. For the result of Knox's meeting with Hamilton, see Knox to GW, 28 and 31 Aug. (second letter).

3. Knox wrote to Anthony Wayne on 13 July 1792: "The President of the United States has directed Major [Henry] Gaither to repair to Georgia, to take the command of the troops there—Major Call will be ordered to join you" (Knopf, *Wayne*, 32). Call's reputed intemperance was the reason for this change in command (see Seagrove to GW, 5 July, and GW to Knox, 19 Aug. 1792).

In a letter of 27 July from Pittsburgh, Wayne had informed Knox that he expected Nicholas Rosecrantz to "accompany the *Legation* of the Five Nations to the Grand Council of the Hostile Indians, he speaks the Seneka, Delaware, & Shawanese Language's" (Knopf, *Wayne*, 47–48).

Capt. Jonathan Cass (1753–1830), a native of New Hampshire and a veteran of the Revolutionary War, was appointed a captain in the U.S. Army on 4 Mar. 1791 and promoted to major on 21 Feb. 1793. He resigned from active duty on 15 Feb. 1801. Fort Franklin was located at the mouth of French Creek, in present-day Franklin, Pennsylvania.

4. GW's nephew George Augustine Washington, who was ill with tuberculosis, died on 5 Feb. 1793.

From William Deakins, Jr.

Sir   Bath [Va.] August 24th 1792

Your much Esteem'd favor of the 13th Instant (Covering a Letter for my Brother & Mr Jones) came safe to hand yesterday.[1] My Brother is now here. I have Enquired of him, respecting Mr Benja. Jones, he thinks him an honest reasonable Man, & will Act with him to Value Mr Mercers Land agreeable to your request.

Doctr James Stewart who holds one third of the same Tract with Mr Mercer, is now here, he has (I believe,[)] received letters from Mr Mercer, he leaves this tomorrow, & will call in his way home, to see the Land, and give Orders for a Division to take place.[2]

I hope whenever I can be usefull to your Excellency, you will freely command me, Assuring Yourself it gives me the Utmost pleasure to execute any of your commands. With every Sentiment of Respect & Esteem—I am Your Excellency's Most Obt Servt

Will. Deakins Junr

ALS, DLC:GW. In addition to the address to GW at Mount Vernon, Deakins wrote "George Town 31st Augt" and indicated "Free" postage on the cover.

1. For the covered letter, see GW to Francis Deakins and Benjamin Jones, 8 Aug. 1792.

2. For GW's earlier attempts to collect a long-standing debt from the estate of John Mercer (d. 1768), father of James and John Francis Mercer, see GW to James Mercer, 18 Mar. 1789, and note 1, and 4 April 1789, and GW to John Francis Mercer, 5 April 1789, 30 June and 23 July 1792. In April 1793 GW accepted a 519-acre tract in Montgomery County, Md., as a final payment for the debt (see Ledger C, 4). This land was one-half of Woodstock Manor, which John Francis Mercer's wife, Sophia Sprigg Mercer, had inherited (see GW to Francis Deakins and Benjamin Jones, 8 Aug. 1792). Dr. James Steuart was married to Rebecca Sprigg Steuart, a sister of Sophia Mercer.

From the Citizens of Marseilles

Marseilles, 24th August 1792,
Sir,   the 4th Year of Liberty

Free Nations are always in alliance, and are alike interested in affording mutual aid and assistance to each other.

A common interest has already united the inhabitants of the American States to the interests of regenerated France. Their three-coloured flags are unfurled upon every sea, proclaiming that the free Americans and French are brethren. The name of Washington is as much revered here as at Philadelphia. It is to Washington that we address ourselves in order to convey the Sentiments of our fellow citizens to a nation for whom he has done and suffered so much.

Commerce is one of the first ties in the fraternity of mankind, and engaged as we are in the destructive trade of war, which unfortunately has become necessary in order to establish the cause of Liberty, free citizens ought nevertheless to leave no possible means untried to extend their commercial intercourse, and ensure the means of subsistence.

The time will arrive, and doubtless it is not far off, when the genius of liberty, having crossed the ocean, and hovered over France will kindle over the whole earth that sacred fire which now animates our breasts. The demons of discord will then be chained up forever, the sword will be rendered useless, and the great bond of nations will be confidence and brotherly affection.

We have therefore to propose to our American brethren to form more extensive commercial connexions with us than heretofore. Above all, we present to their view an object of speculation, which while it supplies our wants, offers emoluments to the adventurer by no means contemptible. The article of provisions, for which we have contracted, cannot be supplied during the present year, on account of the indifferent crops, which are disproportionate to the quantities that Marseilles annually lays up either for the use of her own citizens, for the southern districts of France, or for a part of Spain and Italy.

Such being our situation, we have petitioned the National Assem⟨bly⟩ to grant a premium of fifty Sous per quintal/mark weight of grain that shall be imported from abroad into the southern Districts of France: and we have every reason to believe that our patriotic legislators will comply with our request.[1]

But this is not the only Step we will take in favour of our American brethren. We will petition the executive council that the American flag be protected by the French cruising vessels of w⟨ar⟩ and we have every reason to believe that our solicitations on this subject will not be fruitless.

Exert your influence then, Sir, to engage our American brethren to export to us the superfluity of their crops. Be pleased to inform them that in exchange for their produce they will be supplied in our port with oils and wines, besides other articles and commodities which may suit their market. Inform them, Sir, that the citizens of Marseilles will do every thing in their power to encourage the American trade, and that in this instance in particular they will consider a compliance with their wishes as a proof of the fraternal friendship that exists between the two nations.

It is worthy of your character, Sir, to cherish such sentiments, the dissemination of which will constitute the happiness of your nation. You have toiled for the liberty of your country, and by meriting the universal esteem of all nations, you have gained that, in particular, of the mayor, municipal officers, and public attorney for the community of Marseilles.

Mourraille, mayor[2]

here follow also the signature of the other officers of the municipality of Marseilles.[3]

Translation, DNA: RG 59, Despatches from Consular Offices: Marseilles; DS, in French, DNA: RG 59, Despatches from Consular Offices: Marseilles; DS, in French (marked "Duplicate"), DNA: RG 59, Despatches from Consular Offices: Marseilles; DS, in French, DNA: RG 59, Miscellaneous Letters. The French version appears in CD-ROM: GW.

Stephen Cathalan, Jr., vice-consul at Marseilles, prepared the English translation. For background on this document, see Cathalan's letter to Thomas Jefferson of 24 Aug. from Marseilles, in which this document was enclosed, and its notes in *Jefferson Papers*, 24:319–21. Jefferson replied to the citizens of Marseilles in a letter dated 6 Nov. 1792 (ibid., 589).

1. Jefferson corrected Cathalan's translation in this sentence by replacing "ninety" with "fifty," and an unidentified third hand inserted the word "weight" above an illegible deletion.

2. Mathematician and astronomer Jean-Raymond-Pierre Mourraille (1720–1808) was mayor of Marseilles from 1791 to 1793.

3. This sentence was added by Jefferson to replace the struck-out text: "(A Number of other Signatures: See original)." Jefferson made his corrections to this letter in preparation for its publication in the *National Gazette* (Philadelphia) on 10 Nov. 1792.

From William Moultrie

Charleston, S.C., 24 Aug. 1792. Recommends for work in the Federal City "Mr Gevan a Stone Cutter," who had "done the Cornice & other stone work on the State house in Charleston in a masterly manner" and who "is an industrious sober man."[1]

ALS, DNA: RG 42, General Records, Letters Received, 1791–1867.

1. Although Charleston resident Robert Given (died c.1801) apparently was not hired to work on the federal buildings in the Federal City, he was employed in 1795 to work in Philadelphia on the First United States Bank (*City Gazette & Daily Advertiser* [Charleston], 13 April 1795).

At GW's request Tobias Lear forwarded Moultrie's letter to the D.C. commissioners on 5 Nov. 1792 (DNA: RG 59, Miscellaneous Letters).

From the National Assembly of France

du 26. aout 1792.

l'assemblée Nationale considérant que les hommes qui par leurs Ecrits et par leur Courage ont Servi la Cause de la liberté et preparé l'affranchissement des peuples ne peuvent Etre Regardés Comme Etrangers par une Nation que Ses lumiéres et Son Courage ont Rendue libre,

Considerant que Si cinq ans de domicile en France Suffisent pour obtenir à un Etranger le titre de Citoyen français ce titre est bien plus Justement dû à Ceux qui, quelque soit le Sol qu'ils habitent, ont consacré leurs Bras et leurs Veilles à Deffendre la Cause des peuples contre le Despotisme des Rois, à Bannir les préjugés de la terre, et à Reculer les Bornes des connaissances humaines,

Considérant que S'il n'est pas permis D'Espérer que les hommes ne forment un jour devant la loi comme devant la Nature qu'une Seule famille, une Seule association, les amis de la liberté de la fraternité universelles n'en doivent pas etre moins chers à une Nation qui a proclamé Sa Renonciation a toutes conquetes et Son desir de fraterniser avec tous les peuples,

Considerant Enfin qu'au moment ou une Convention Nationale Va fixer les Destinees de la France, et preparer peut-Etre Celles du genre humain, il appartient a un peuple généreux et libre D'appeller toutes les lumiéres et de Déférer le droit de concourir à ce grand acte de Raison à des hommes qui par leurs Sentimens, leurs Ecrits et leur Courage S'en Sont Montrés Si Eminement Dignes.

Déclare Déférer le titre de Citoyen français au Docteur Joseph Prietsley, à Thomas payne, a Jérémie Bentham à William Wilberforce, à Thomas Clarkson, à Jacques Makinstosh, à David Williams, à N Gorani, à Anacharsis Cloots, à Corneille Paw. à Joachim-henry Campe, à N pestalozzi, à George Washington à Jean hamilton, à N Maddison, à H Klopstack, et à Thadée Kociusko.

Guadet Rapporteur[1]

DS, Archives Nationales, Paris.

In this document the French National Assembly grants French citizenship to persons who it believes have promoted the cause of liberty. In addition to GW, Alexander Hamilton, and James Madison, the list includes: English scientist Joseph Priestley (1733–1804), revolutionary pamphleteer Thomas Paine, English jurist and essayist Jeremy Bentham (1748–1832), English abolitionists William Wilberforce (1759–1833) and Thomas Clarkson (1760–1846), Scottish philosopher and historian Sir James Mackintosh (1765–1832), Welsh dissenting minister and essayist David Williams (1738–1816), Milan native and political writer Giuseppe Gorani (c.1740–1819), Prussian participant in the French Revolution Anacharsis Cloots (Jean-Baptiste, baron du Val-de-Grâce; 1755–1794), Dutch author Cornelius de Pauw (1739–1799), German pedagogue Joachim Heinrich Campe (1746–1818), Swiss educational reformer Johann Heinrich Pestalozzi (1746–1827), German poet Friedrich Gottlieb Klopstock (1724–1803), and Polish engineer and cavalry officer Tadeusz Kościuszko (1746–1817).

1. Marguerite-Élie Guadet (1758–1794), an administrator in the Gironde department, was elected to the Legislative Assembly in 1791 and became its president on 22 Jan. 1792. He subsequently fell out of favor and was executed on 17 June 1794.

To Alexander Hamilton

(Private)

My dear Sir,   Mount Vernon Augt 26th 1792

Your letter of the 18th, enclosing answers to certain objections communicated to you in my letter of the 29th Ulto came duly to hand; and although I have not, as yet, from a variety of causes, been able to give them the attentive reading I mean to bestow, I feel myself much obliged by the trouble you have taken to answer them; as I persuade myself, from the full manner in which you appear to have taken the matter up, that I shall receive both satisfaction and profit from the perusal.

Differences in political opinions are as unavoidable as, to a certain point, they may perhaps be necessary; but it is to be regretted, exceedingly, that subjects cannot be discussed with temper on the one hand, or decisions submitted to without having the motives which led to them, improperly implicated on the other: and this regret borders on chagrin when we find that Men of abilities—zealous patriots—having the same *general* objects in view, and the same upright intentions to prosecute them, will not exercise more charity in deciding on the opinions, & actions of one another. When matters get to such lengths, the natural inference is, that both sides have strained the Cords beyond their bearing—and that a middle course would be found the best, until experience shall have pointed out the right mode—or, which is not to be expected, because it is denied to mortals—there shall be some *infallible* rule by which we could *fore* judge events.

Having premised these things, I would fain hope that liberal allowances will be made for the political opinions of one another; and instead of those wounding suspicions, and irritating charges with which some of our Gazettes are so strongly impregnated, & cannot fail if persevered in, of pushing matters to extremity, & thereby tare the Machine asunder, that there might be mutual forbearances and temporising yieldings *on all sides.* Without these I do not see how the Reins of Government are to be managed, or how the Union of the States can be much longer preserved.

How unfortunate would it be, if a fabric so goodly—erected under so many Providential circumstances—and in its first stages, having acquired such respectibility, should, from diversity of Sentiments, or internal obstructions to some of the acts of Government (for I cannot prevail on myself to believe that these measures are, as yet, the deliberate Acts of a determined party) should be harrowing our vitals in such a manner as to have brought us to the verge of dissolution—Melancholy thought! But one, at the sametime that it shows the consequences of diversified opinions, when pushed with too much tenacity; exhibits evidence also of the necessity of accomodation; and of the propriety of adopting such healing measures as will restore harmony to the discordant members of the Union, & the governing powers of it.

I do not mean to apply this advice to measures which are passed, or to any character in particular. I have given it in the same *general* terms to other Officers of the Government.[1] My earnest wish is, that balsam may be poured into *all* the wounds which have been given, to prevent them from gangrening; & from those fatal consequences which the community may sustain if it is withheld. The friends of the Union must wish this—those who are not, but wish to see it rended, will be disappointed—and all things I hope will go well.

We have learnt through the medium of Mr Harrison to Doctr Craik, that you have it in contemplation to take a trip this way.[2] I felt pleasure at hearing it, and hope it is unnecessary to add that it would be considerably encreased by seeing you under this roof, for you may be assured of the sincere and Affectionate regard of Yours

                                                Go: Washington

P.S. I pray you to note down whatever may occur to you, not only in your own department but other matters also of general import that may be fit subjects for the Speech at the opening of the ensuing Session.[3]

G.W.

ALS, CtHi: Oliver Wolcott, Jr., Papers; ADfS, DLC:GW; LB, DLC:GW.

1. GW expressed similar concerns about the dissension within his administration and the criticism of his administration's policies by the press in his letter to Jefferson of 23 Aug. and his letter to Edmund Randolph of 26 August.

2. Richard Harrison, the auditor of the U.S. Treasury Department, was the son-in-law of GW's friend James Craik, having married Craik's daughter Nancy in 1791. Hamilton did not visit GW at Mount Vernon at this time (see Hamilton to GW, 9 Sept. 1792).

3. For the draft message, dated 15–31 Oct., that Hamilton prepared for GW to present at the opening of the next session of Congress, see Syrett, *Hamilton Papers*, 12:558–66. For GW's final version, see his Address to the U.S. Senate and House of Representatives, 6 Nov. 1792. GW made a similar request to his other cabinet officers (see GW to Thomas Jefferson, 23 Aug., to Henry Knox, 3 Sept. [second letter], and Edmund Randolph to GW, 28 Oct. 1792).

To Henry Knox

Sir,   Mot Vernon 26. Augt 1792

I have recd your Letter of the 17th inst; with it's enclosure from Genl Wayne.

Whatever Genl Wayne may require towards the equipmt of his troops for the service for wch they are designed, provided a compliance therewith be authorised by Law, I think had better be granted. powder in particular, precisely such as he desires, I would furnish him with in order that there may be no room for complaint here after on that score; At the same time I must confess that I am no friend to his proposal with respect to enlarging the touch holes—for part of the force of the powder must be expended that way, & when the musket gets a little foul, may not communicate with the pan—it would certainly be better to employ a little more time in loading, where every shot ought to be well & deliberately aimed.[1]

Orders or Advertisements which are intended to be put in the public Gazettes, ought to be well weighed & digested before they are inserted, as they will not only appear in all parts of Europe, but may be handed to the enemy. To publish beyond the limits of the army, or the vicinity of it, the dastardly behaviour of one's own troops, is not a very pleasant thing.

Concerning his idea of having a Brand, I have great doubts both as to the legality & policy of the measure; the bad impression it may make in the country, may considerably outweigh the good effects it may produce in the army.

Printed blank Descriptions is, to me, an *Irishism;* for the true meaning of wch I am at a loss, & which requires an explanation.[2] I am Sir Yr mo: hble Servt

G.W.

Df, DLC:GW; LB, DLC:GW.

1. In the summer of 1792 Wayne was anxious to acquire fine-grain powder of the kind he enclosed in a letter to Knox on 13 July 1792 (see Knopf, *Wayne,* 27–29). In the same letter Wayne outlined experiments he had conducted "respecting the improvement of the Musket, by an alteration in the touch hole." Wayne repeated his request for the fine-grain powder in his letter to Knox of 10 Aug. (see Knox to GW, 17 Aug., n.1).

2. In his letter to Knox of 10 Aug., Wayne expressed concern about the number of deserters from the army, and he suggested several ways of dealing with the problem, including branding the word *coward* on the foreheads of the guilty men. Wayne's aide-de-camp Henry De Butts issued general orders on 9 Aug. that offered a $10 reward for the apprehension of deserters; these orders were published in the *Federal Gazette and Philadelphia Daily Advertiser* on 17 Aug. 1792 (see GW to Knox, 22 Aug. 1792, n.3).

From Henry Knox

Sir   Philadelphia 26th August 1792

I had the honor in New York, on the 23d, to acknowledge the receipt of your letter of the 15th instant with the dispatches from Georgia. Having returned to this city the last evening I found your favor of the 19th, which was received here on the 23d instant.

Tomorrow I will lay before the secretary of the treasury, and the attorney Genl, the Georgia papers and your ideas thereon; and the result shall be submitted to you as early as possible.[1]

I have now the honor to submit Copies of General Waynes letter of the 17th,[2] Capt. Jo. Cass's of the 6 instant,[3] and Genl Putnams of the 22d July.[4]

The conduct of the Waggoners mentioned by Genl Wayne, in leaving the stores upon the road shall be inquired into and remedied immediately, and proper prosecutions take place.

The conduct of Genl Putnam appears to have been judicious, and an anticipation of his instructions lately transmitted.[5]

By the next post I shall have the honor of making further communication of such circumstances as may be necessary to be submitted to your view.[6] I have the honor sir to be with perfect respect Your Obedient Servant

H. Knox

ALS, DLC:GW; LB, DLC:GW.

1. For the results of Knox's meeting with Hamilton and Randolph, see Knox to GW, 28 and 31 Aug. (second letter) 1792.

2. The copy of Wayne's letter to Knox of 17 Aug. from Pittsburgh reads in part: "By the many corroborating accounts from every quarter I believe there can be little room to doubt the fate of our three *flags* and that both Col. Harding, and Major Trueman have been victims to savage ferocity—It's also probable that the first *embassy*, if not the *second* from the *five Nations* to the hostile Indians (mentioned in the inclosed copy of a letter from Capt. Cass) have experienced the fate of our *flags*—the first had been absent for *two moons* the other *One,* when *Cornplanter* was at Fort Franklin i.e. the 23d Ultimo; had any material intelligence been received at the mouth of Buffaloe as late as the 7th instant I should have been made acquainted with it by this time.

"The alarm of two large parties of Indians being in the vicinity of this post turned out to be a party of *Six* only, who finding themselves discovered, went off without doing any damage, they were followed about Sixty Miles—Another small party made their appearance near *Whelen* about fifty Miles below this place on the Ohio the beginning of this week and fired upon three of our people who returned it, by which fire one Indian fell, and one of our people was shot thro the shoulder.

"I have in some measure anticipated the Presidents orders in firing at marks —by permitting the riflemen to practice two shot ℞ man every fair day, and by directing the Guards relieved from duty, to discharge at marks *waistband* high as mentioned in my letter of the 10th instant.

"On Wednesday [15 Aug.] we had a *sham* engagement—the rifle Corps (by reiterated attacks and highly painted) acted well the part of savages—which required all the skill and fortitude of our little legion to sustain, until by a combined maneuvre of the reserve, composed of Cavalry and Infantry—they were out flanked and charged in front and rear at the same instant (by actual surprize) part of the Cavalry having passed and repassed the Allegheny River for that purpose during the Action."

After disagreeing with Gen. Rufus Putnam's recently suggested plan of operation and promising to submit his own ideas by the next post, Wayne continued: "The Indians who were attached to Capt. [John] Jeffers's corps have been dismissed and sent home ever since early in July—except two or three who don't show a disposition to leave this place, in fact, *Jeffers's* whole corps of rangers has been dissolved near two Months, as I found the Soldiers were much averse to that kind of service, which had caused many desertions. . . . It is indispensibly necessary that some effectual mode of transportation of Stores should be adopted—probably if the Owners of Waggons were obligated to deliver the Stores committed to their charge within twenty five days at Pittsburgh it might have a good effect—Captain [Moses] Porter of the Artillery who arrived yesterday says that he seen considerable quantities of public Stores left at several taverns along the road in open sheds from the sign of the ship 34 Miles from Philada to Shippensburg" (DLC:GW).

3. The copy of Capt. Jonathan Cass's 6 Aug. letter to Wayne from Fort Franklin reads: "Inclosed are the returns of this Garrison for the Month of July— Previous to your arrival in this Country, the Secretary of War gave orders for this garrison to be constantly supplied with six Months provisions for 120 Men, beside which there was to be 5000 rations for indian issues, which order I could never prevail on the Contractors to comply with—If it is your intention that quantity should be kept in store, nothing but your authority will accomplish it. the inclosed return of provision will show the quantity now on hand, which will serve this Garrison for the troops and indian issues, about one month. the hurry in which I dispatched my last express occasioned me to neglect mentioning that the Bears-Oil Chief a Massasuaga Indian, called on me in April at this Garrison professed much friendship and on his leaving me promised to do all he could to make his Nation so; from the late Council at Buffaloe Creek where he and they generally attend he sent me a *speak* together with a string of Wampum, by the Cornplanter and new arrow declaring he had strictly attended to his promise made to me last spring that he had taken much pains among his nation that they had generally become friendly and desired I would make it known to our great Men. The Chiefs of that Nation also agreed in Council to send me a *speak* and did so, the purport of which was that they had agreed in Council with the Seneka Nations and had agreed to be friendly to them and the 13 fires, that they would do all in their power to persuade the hostile Indians to peace, this the Cornplanter and New Arrow both confirmed, and added that the Massasuaga Nation had agreed in Council to be governed by the policy of the six Nations with respect to their friendship to the 13 fires or words to that amount, that I have every reason to believe that the Senekas the Mohawks, the Massasaugas those living in Canada and many Indians who are gone from this quarter and live on the other side of Lake Erie are zealously engaged in persuading the hostile Indians to peace, and if the United States offer generous terms, I have no doubt they will obtain it, of this however your judgment and information are much better than mine, neither shall my own occasion any military relaxation on my part have received no account from [Nicholas] Rosencrantz since I wrote you—the Cornplanter informed me it is now two moons since two of their men were dispatched to the hostile Indians to discover their intentions and see if they would listen to terms of peace, those

men are hourly expected: that one moon since they had dispatched two more men to the same place and on the same business, that he promised me when those Indians returned I should be informed of their report which I will as immediately make known to General Wayne" (DLC:GW).

4. The copy of Putnam's letter to Knox of 22 July from Fort Washington reads in part: "Jean Krouch the principal chief who arrived here the 3d instant, with Mr Vego [Francis Vigo], died on the 16th.

"I mentioned in my letter of the 14th instant, two prisoners having escaped from the Indians, and being then at Fort Hamilton; these have since arrived here; and by the information they give, I think there is the highest reason to beleive, that [Isaac] Freeman. Truman, & Harden. are murdered, with all the people who went with them. except one, who they considered as servant, as a person of no consequence: and if the Squaw (who gave the information to the prisoners) told the truth, it appears that Truman must be murdered, by order of the Council, as a Confirmation of their resolution, not to make peace.

"When, add to this information, the circumstance, that I hear nothing of Captain Henderick [Aupaumut], I conclude that the Indians met on the Omee or Tawa River, have rejected the overtures made them, by the United States, in the several Speeches sent them, and that the prospect of my speaking with them, through the Channel first proposed, is at an end.

"By the information received from the Wabash, mentioned in my former letters, together with the information received by Mr Wells, the interperter, and the Indians who are now here on a visit to their families, I conceive there is very little reason to expect any more of the Chiefs from that quarter, or if they should, they will be of inferior grades, and a treaty with them will be of no Consequence.

"From all these circumstances I conclude, that my tarrying at this place much longer can be of no service whatever, except to receive your further orders, which I certainly should do or return up the river; but for the following reasons, viz., It appearing highly probable, that the principal Chiefs, from nearly all the western Tribes, with a great number of Warriors may be collected at Port Vincent, if the business is seasonably attended to, and by a proper management, there is the highest prospect they may be detached from, and return to, or be kept in, a State of peace."

Putnam informed Knox that he had resolved to go "to Port Vincent, for the purpose of holding a treaty with the Western tribes about the Twentieth of September, and shall take measures to have them invited to meet there about that time. . . . I propose to leave this, with the Indian goods, the prisoners &c. &c., about the 15th of August" (DLC:GW).

5. Knox had written Putnam from Philadelphia on 7 Aug.: "You will cultivate and make peace with the Wabash tribes to the utmost of your power, and you will judge how far your going to Post Vincennes, or any other place will facilitate the object—Extend your treaties with one tribe after another as far as possible, always subjecting them to the ratification of the President and Senate of the United States" (Buell, *Putnam Memoirs*, 313).

6. Knox next wrote GW on 28 Aug. 1792.

To Edmund Randolph

(Private)

My dear Sir, Mount Vernon Augt 26th 1792

The purpose of this letter is merely to acknowledge the receipt of your favors of the 5th & 13th instt, and to thank you for the information contained in both without entering into the details of either.[1]

With respect, however, to the interesting subject treated on in that of the 5th, I can express but one sentiment at this time, and that is a wish—a devout one—that whatever my ultimate determination shall be, it may be for the best. The subject never recurs to my mind but with additional poignancy; and from the declining State in the health of my Nephew, to whom my concerns of a domestic & private nature are entrusted it comes with aggrivated force[2]—But as the allwise disposer of events has hitherto watched over my steps, I trust that in the important one I may soon be called upon to take, he will mark the course so plainly, as that I cannot mistake the way. In full hope of this, I will take no measure, yet awhile, that will not leave me at liberty to decide from circumstances, & the best lights, I can obtain on the subject.

I should be happy in the mean time to see a cessation of the abuses of public Officers—and of those attacks upon almost every measure of government with which some of the Gazettes are so strongly impregnated; & which cannot fail, if persevered in with the malignancy they now team, of rending the Union asunder. The Seeds of discontent—distrust & irritations which are so plentifully sown—can scarcely fail to produce this effect and to Mar that prospect of happiness which perhaps never beamed with more effulgence upon any people under the Sun—and this too at a time when all Europe are gazing with admiration at the brightness of our prospects. and for what is all this? Among other things, to afford Nuts for our transatlantic—what shall I call them? Foes!

In a word if the Government and the Officers of it are to be the constant theme for News-paper abuse, and this too without condescending to investigate the motives or the facts, it will be impossible, I conceive, for any man living to manage the helm, or to keep the machine together—But I am running from my text, and therefore will only add assurances of the Affecte esteem & regard with which I am always—Yours.

ADf, PHi: Gratz Collection; LB, DLC:GW.

1. In his second letter to GW of 5 Aug., Randolph urged GW to continue as president for another term. Randolph's letter to GW of 13 Aug. 1792 has not been found.

2. GW's nephew George Augustine Washington, the manager of Mount Vernon, was ill with tuberculosis, and he died on 5 Feb. 1793.

From Edmund Randolph

Dear Sir   Philadelphia August 26. 1792.

Mr Bordley, who wrote the inclosed pamphlet, thought it too unimportant to present it to you with form. He therefore requested me, if an opportunity offered, to send it to Mount Vernon.[1]

Since I had the honor of writing to you last, nothing has occurred, worthy of a special mention.[2] The arrivals from Europe have brought nothing; and no incidents in the political line attract any notice, except those, which relate to the supposed temper of Virginia, & the measures, projected at the next session. Of these you must have heard; and therefore I omit them.[3]

The mail, which was due yesterday, has not yet arrived. (12 o'-clock)

Mr Fraunces informs me, that every thing is well; and indeed I should judge it to be the case from appearances.[4] I am dear sir with affte attachment yr obliged hbl. serv.

                                                Edm: Randolph

ALS, DLC:GW.

1. Randolph enclosed a copy of John Beale Bordley's *Sketches on Rotation of Crops*, published in Philadelphia in 1792. GW subsequently also acquired the enlarged version of this pamphlet that was printed in Philadelphia in 1797 (see GW to Randolph, 3 Sept. 1792, and Griffin, *Boston Athenæum Washington Collection*, 27–28).

2. Randolph apparently is referring to his letter to GW of 13 Aug., which has not been found (see GW to Randolph, 26 Aug. 1792).

3. For the matters discussed in the fall session of the Virginia legislature, see Randolph to GW, 10 Sept. 1792.

4. Samuel Fraunces was GW's household steward at Philadelphia.

From Alexander Hamilton

Sir, Treasury Departmt Augt 27. 1792.

By the Act of the last Session entitled "An Act supplementary to the Act making provision for the Debt of the United States," authority is given to discharge the debts due to foreign Officers out of the monies which the President is authorised to borrow by the Act making provision for the Debt of the United States.[1]

The sum authorised to be borrowed by the last mentioned Act is 12.000.000. of Dollars. The whole amount of the foreign debt, exclusive of that due to foreign Officers, was 11.710.378 Dollars & 62 cents. The difference is 289.621. Dollars & 38 cents, which is greater than the sum due to foreign Officers being about 230.000 Dollars. This debt being payable in Paris and bearing an interest of six per Cent, it is for the advantage of the United States to discharge it as soon as possible. The last loan will be a convenient fund for the purpose, and if approved by the President a part of it will be so applied.[2]

Should it appear to the President adviseable to direct this payment—a second question arises, namely whether it shall be made in Assignats, or in a mode which shall exempt the parties from the loss which would attend the depreciation of those securities—without however occasioning loss to the United States. The last appears best to accord with the justice & reputation of the Government.[3] With the highest respect and the truest attachment I have the honor to be &c.

A: Hamilton

P.S. Your Letter of the 13. instant & the Contract concerning the N. Hampshire Lighthouse were duly received.[4]

LB, DLC:GW.

1. The supplementary act was approved on 8 May 1792 during the first session of the Second Congress (see 1 *Stat.* 281–83). "An Act making provision for the (payment of the) Debt of the United States," approved on 4 Aug. 1790, authorized the president to borrow "a sum or sums, not exceeding in the whole twelve million of dollars," for payment of the foreign debt (ibid., 138–44).

2. When the Revolutionary War ended in 1783, the Continental Congress could not pay the salaries of the foreign officers who had served in the Continental army. A partial cash payment was made to them in 1782, and they received the rest of their arrears in certificates of indebtedness at 6 percent interest. Those certificates, which depreciated quickly, were exchanged for new

ones issued on 5 April 1784, again bearing 6 percent interest but with no definite redemption date. GW approved Hamilton's redemption plan in a letter to him of 31 Aug. 1792 and issued the ratification statement on 5 Nov. 1792. Monies for this redemption came from the Dutch loan contracted on 9 Aug. 1792 (see Contract, contemporary translation from the Dutch, DNA: RG 59, State Department Letters, Accounts, and Contracts Relating to European Loans). Although most of the certificates were redeemed by 1803, it was not until 1828 that all were exchanged (see Bayley, *National Loans,* 22–23, 28).

3. For GW's opinion on repayment of the debt due foreign officers, see GW to Hamilton, 31 Aug. 1792.

4. In his letter to GW of 3 Aug., Hamilton enclosed the provisional contract for the supply of the lighthouse on New Castle Island at the mouth of the Piscataqua River in Portsmouth, N.H., which GW approved in his reply of 13 Aug. 1792.

From Thomas Jefferson

Monticello [Va.] Aug. 27. 1792.

Th: Jefferson, with his dutiful respects to the President of the United States, has the honor to inclose him under an open cover to mister Taylor two letters to M. de Ternant, the one containing an Exequatur for his signature (the commission whereon it is grounded being under the same open cover to mister Taylor) the other an answer to a formal notification of the declaration of war by France against the king of Hungary, which if the President approves he will be so good as to let go on under the cover to mister Taylor, sticking a wafer in it as well as in the cover, but leaving still open the letter containing the Exequatur that mister Taylor may put the great seal to it before he seals the letter.[1] he hopes the President and mistress Washington are in perfect health.

AL, DNA: RG 59, Miscellaneous Letters; AL (letterpress copy), DLC: Jefferson Papers; LB, DNA: RG 59, George Washington's Correspondence with His Secretaries of State; LB (photocopy), DLC: GW.

1. On 27 Aug., Jefferson sent George Taylor, Jr., chief clerk in the State Department, two letters for Jean-Baptiste Ternant, French minister to the United States (see *Jefferson Papers,* 24:328). The first contained an exequatur (official recognition) for Michel-Ange-Bernard de Mangourit to act as the French consul for North Carolina, South Carolina, and Georgia. The second letter, also dated 27 Aug., concerned France's declaration of war on 20 April 1792 against Francis II, the Holy Roman Emperor and king of Bohemia and Hungary. Jefferson expressed "the sincere concern we feel on learning that the French nation, to whose friendship and interests we have the strongest attachments, are now to encounter the evils of war." He assured the French minister that the

United States "shall continue in the same friendly dispositions, and render all those good offices which shall be consistent with the duties of a neutral nation" (ibid., 328–29).

From Henry Knox

Sir   War department August 28. 1792

I have the honor to acknowledge the receipt of your favor of the 22d instant after the departure of the post on Monday Morning the 27th.

The Secretary of the Treasury, the Attorney General and myself have had two separate meetings, yesterday and to day upon the subject of the Georgia dispatches. We have, in substance, adopted the ideas, you were pleased to communicate in your favor of the 19th instant—The details will be prepared and submitted to your consideration as soon as possible.[1]

Colonel Fish is upon a tour of reviewing the Militia, which will require a considerable time to finish—I will immediately in your name offer him the appointment of the office of Adjutant General; and in order to secure an answer it shall be forwarded from New York by Express.[2]

A Lieutenant Schuylers resignation, of the Artillery, has been received. He was accused of a long course of intoxication and was ordered either to take his trial or resign—The vacancy has long been expected and was eagerly desired by Colonel Burr for a Mr Peter Van Allen a young Gentleman of the State of New York of liberal education, bred to the Law and of good Character —Mr Burr has pledged himself for his fitness for the Office—his name was brought forward, on the augmentation of the troops, as a Captain—but the local arrangements rendered that grade unattainable—If it should meet your approbation, I request leave to notify Mr Van Allen of the vacancy and offer it to him.[3] I have the honor to be with the highest respect Your obedient servant.

                                                    H. Knox

LS, DLC:GW; LB, DLC:GW.

1. For Knox's receipt of the dispatches that GW forwarded from James Seagrove and Maj. Richard Call, see Knox to GW, 23 August. For the recommendations of Alexander Hamilton, Edmund Randolph, and Knox concerning U.S. relations with Spain and the southern Indians, see Knox to GW, 31 Aug. 1792.

2. Knox wrote Nicholas Fish on 29 Aug. offering him the office of adjutant general (NNGL: Knox Papers).

3. Dirck Schuyler (1761–1811) of New York, who had served in the Continental army from 1782 to 1783, was appointed a lieutenant in the artillery in 1786 and continued in that rank throughout the various reorganizations of the U.S. Army that followed until 1792 when he resigned from the army on 20 June following his arrest earlier that year on charges of drunkenness (see GW to the U.S. Senate, 12 Mar., n.5). On Senator Aaron Burr's recommendation, Peter L. Van Alen of New York (d. 1802) was appointed a lieutenant in the artillery on 19 Nov. 1792, with rank effective from 6 Sept. (GW to the U.S. Senate, 19 Nov. 1792 [second letter]).

From Henry, Count de Nassau

Sir!   London August 28th 1792

I never am unmindful of those I think so well of as Yourself; their Number is not So great as to Confound ones Memory.

Inclosed printed Extracts from the Public Advertiser.[1] Shews Your Excellency a little what I have suffered for the brave Americans Since the Battle of Bunkershill. I was since that time persecuted and have suffered much, and more as You Could think but my good Conscience and Providence have never left me Comfortless. at last my Book *Memoires Campaigns and Travels* in 4 Volumes large Octavo will be printed after so manny strugles. the First Volume will be published about Easter next Year and every 6 months another Volume. I shall have the Honour through the american ambassador send one for Your Excellency[2] Since these few days I was very Ill a severe Coald has troubled me much that I can scarcely write a few Lines. I was 18 Years in the late King of Prussias Service, I left him 1767. made a Tour through Saxony, Bohemia, Austria Hungaria and was 4 days at Belgrad: 1768. I came home again but had the misfortune to be shipwrecked in Yoarmouth Roads where I lost all my Monney Equipage &c. this was a Very hard Trial for me but God had never forsaken me The late King of Prussia Frederick the Great holds me about 40,000£. Sterling 5 months past I wrote a Letter to the present King of Prussia and Demanded my money the Answer was I myself must Come to Berlin to wait upon the King himself I Should have the money due to me but I must not mention any things about this in my Book. Kings like their secrets not to be published.

Now I prepare me to go to Holland Brunswick Potsdam and Berlin to receive the monney due to me, and to see my Old good

Friends and whenn my Book is finished in about 2 Years time. I hope to have the Honour to give Your Excellency a Visit in America. my Book Contains manny Excillent Anecdotes Concerning the late War in America.

In the Public advertiser August the 4th this month I have published *an Essay on Duelling* as a Warning to my Brother Officers in the Navy and Army.

The late accounts from France are very melancholic. I have heard Preach that famous Dr [Joseph] Priestley 3 times he is a man of Sense, a true Philosopher and I believe an honest man, but Veritas odium parit.[3] *his appeal* is excellent Soon after Easter next year I hope to retourn from Berlin. I wish Your Excellency good Health and all Happiness here below. and so all the Inhabitans of America, Success to Trade and Commerce. Peace Unity and Concord. I wish to see America again before I Die. my Head ach permits me no more to Write. I have the Honour with the greatest Esteem to be Your Excellencys most humble servant

Henry, Count de Nassau
the Old Neglected Captain in the Royal Navy

N.B. it is to day exactly 10 years when the Royal George of 100. Guns was overset at Portsmouth. brave Admiral Kampenfeld and So many 100. about 920 Souls were lost.[4] And N.B. I saved my Life so wunderfull all is minutly explained in my Memoires &c:

ALS, DLC:GW. The cover indicates this letter's passage on the ship "Pigou Loxley."

1. The enclosed broadside contains three extracts from *The Public Advertiser* (London). The first extract, dated 15 Nov. 1784, reports the arrest on 12 Nov. of "Henry Count de Nassau, a Post Captain in the Royal Navy" and his release the next day when the authorities decided that the unspecified charges were false. "It seems this persecution had arose from the Count's constant adherence to the Protestant interest in Holland, and England," and from his recent expressions of support for Lord George Gordon, a prominent anti-Catholic activist. "The Count de Nassau is the same Nobleman who was persecuted in Lord North's Administration for refusing to fight against the Protestant Colonies in America, and their brave Dutch allies."

The second extract, from the 5 Mar. 1787 issue, announces the anticipated publication of the "memoirs, campaigns, and travels, in four volumes," by Nassau, "a Captain in the Royal Navy, who was formerly a Lieutenant Colonel, Knight of the Military Order of Merit, and Privy Counsellor to the late king Frederick the Great, of Prussia." In this extract Nassau says that he was born in 1728 at York, England, and that "In 1755, when I was a Lieutenant in the king of Prussia's service, the king trusted me with dispatches of the greatest consequence, and sent me to London to king George the Second, . . . who received me very graciously, and made me a Lieutenant in the Royal Navy, to the man of war, the Royal George. . . . I had the honour to travel with king George the Second, from London to Hanover, and from thence to Potsdam, with the king's answer to my Royal Master Frederick the Great."

In the third extract, dated 10 Mar. 1792, Nassau says that the publication of his memoirs has been delayed due to "a falling out with my Bookseller. . . . The Engravers made a mistake in the plan of the battle of Ros[s]bach, and the unfortunate battle of Collin [Kolin], where I lost my dearly beloved eldest son who was killed by a canon ball at my side."

2. Nassau's memoirs have not been identified, and no publication by Nassau was in GW's library at the time of his death.

3. This Latin phrase, which can be translated as "truth breeds hatred," was used by the Roman comic dramatist Terence (Publius Terentius Afer; c.190–159 B.C.) in his play *Andria*.

4. The *Royal George* sank on 29 Aug. 1782 while docked at Portsmouth, England, for repairs. At the time of the disaster not only the crew but also family, friends, and tradesmen were on board. Estimates of the number killed vary, but all accounts agree that hundreds died that day, including Adm. Richard Kempenfelt (1718–1782).

From John Augustine Spotswood

Dear Sir   Philadelphia August the 28. 1792

I arrived in this City the 16th of this month, and Delivered your favor to Mr Morris; Who Informed me it would be Some time before the arrival of Capt. Truxton. I have until then Engaged to Sail in Mr Crammond's Employ, Which will Commence in the Course of Next month, At the Arrival of his Ships.[1] There is no doubt but you think I have Slited your friendship, in not Writing you before this; but as I felt myself Much Indisposed at my Arrival here, I hope You will pardon me. My Love to Mrss Washington and the family; I am Dear Sir with Every Sense of Gratitude, yours

John A. Spotswood

ALS, DLC:GW.

1. GW's letter to Robert Morris of 23 July 1792, which Spotswood delivered to Morris, concerned Spotswood's desire for a maritime position with Capt. Thomas Truxtun in the China and East Indies trade or, in the event of Truxtun's long absence, a temporary position on one of Morris's ships in the West Indies trade. Spotswood achieved neither position but instead apparently found employment with either James or William Crammond (Cramond), two Philadelphia brothers who engaged in trade with Great Britain (see Alexander Spotswood to GW, 27 Aug. 1793). For a history of John A. Spotswood's search

for maritime employment, see Alexander Spotswood to GW, 4 Dec. 1791, n.1, and GW to Alexander Spotswood, 7 Feb. 1792, n.2, and 6 May 1792.

From Margaret Hay

Fort George, N.Y., 30 Aug. 1792. Writes GW in hopes of a "vindacation of my injured Charecter." She says that an earlier letter to GW asking for "pecuniary assistance" elicited no reply, even though GW had received the letter and initially was inclined to assist her,[1] "but after that you wrote a Gentelman in Albany who give me such a Charecter that you thought me unworthy of even pity. . . . I am sorry to think that . . . worthy Citizens will let an innocent woman suffer all that art and malice can invent and beleive evry falshood that a subtle unnatureal enemy [her husband] has spared no expence or truble to get circulated rether then Give them selves the truble to bring the truth to light." Her husband's "next step," she says, "is to sue for a devorce in vermount[2] I am now very ill in consequence of his treatment when he was last hear he offered me a paper relative to his intended devorce as I did not know that my accepetence of it would be proper I refused it . . . and when I a second time refused it he draged me into a dark room how he treated me I can not tell for my fright had deprived me of Reson . . . but he left convincing proofs of his brutaliaty for my side remained black for several weeks where he had trampt or kicked me the pain of it now is allmost intolorable had he put an end to my Life that would have been an act of mercy—he has got leave to go on so long with impunity I have no doubt he will close the guilty scene in that way if he is not prevented by the interposition of devine providence."

ALS, DLC:GW.

1. No other correspondence between Margaret Hay and GW has been found.

2. Margaret Hay may be the estranged wife of Udny Hay (d. 1806), assistant deputy quartermaster general for the Continental army during the Revolutionary War. After the war Hay became a land agent in Vermont and lived at Underhill, Vermont.

To Alexander Hamilton

Sir.   Mount Vernon 31st Augt 1792.

The enclosed Letter was written agreeably to the date, but by an accident, was omitted when my other letters were sent to the post office on Monday last;[1] since wch 'till yesterday afternoon, I have been absent from home.

On my return, amongst other Letters I found the enclosed from the Inspector of the 5th survey in the State of North Carolina. The picture drawn by him of the temper of the people in the District entrusted to his Inspection, is a very unpleasant & disagreeable one. It is forwarded for your consideration, & opinion of the measures necessary to be taken in the premises; particularly whether the Governor of that State ought to be written to on the subject; and in that case, to desire that you would draft a letter proper for the occasion.[2]

Your Letter of the 27. instant is also before me; and my opinion on the points therein submitted is, that part of the Loan lately obtained in Holland, should be applied in discharge of the Debt due to the foreign Officers agreeably to the Authority given by the Act alluded to in your letter, & because the interest of the United States requires it to be done; and that it ought to be paid in a mode which shall exempt the parties from the loss which would attend the depreciation of Assignats, without, however, occasioning loss to the United States. The first is an act of justice due to the officers—and the latter an act of prudence becoming the Government. I am Sir &c.

                                        G: Washington

LB, DLC:GW.

1. For the enclosed letter, see GW to Hamilton, 26 Aug. 1792. The previous Monday was 27 August.

2. The letter from Joseph McDowell, Jr., the inspector of the fifth survey, has not been identified. For McDowell's appointment to that office and the concurrent confusion over which Joseph McDowell was nominated, see Hamilton to GW, 18 Feb. 1792, n.1. Because of difficulties encountered in collecting the whiskey tax, McDowell resigned from his position in late 1792 (see GW to the U.S. Senate, 28 Jan. 1793). Hamilton responded to McDowell's letter, and to opposition in Pennsylvania, by suggesting that GW issue a proclamation urging compliance with the federal excise tax on distilled spirits (see Hamilton to GW, 8 Sept. and 9 Sept. [second letter] 1792). For GW's letter to North Carolina governor Alexander Martin, see Circular to the Governors of North Carolina, Pennsylvania, and South Carolina, 29 Sept., which enclosed the proclamation that GW issued on 15 Sept. 1792.

From Henry Knox

Sir   War department August 31st 1792

I have the honor to submit herein enclosed a letter to the Governor of Georgia and one to Mr Seagrove—the former drafted by the Attorney General and both approved by the s⟨am⟩e and the Secretary of the Treasury.

The principles you were pleased to suggest have been the basis of these papers—The manner of treating the Spaniards and McGillivray was unanimously considered as the most proper to be adopted in the present conjuncture.[1]

One of the Spanish commissioners is at present in Virginia and the other in the Country, but will return either to day or to morrow. I shall see him and conformably to the advice of the Gentlemen mention the affair verbally and informally—the result of which I will have the honor to transmit to you.[2]

Letters have just been received from Major General Wayne—all quiet—He has transmitted his ideas of the further progress of the war, in case the negociations should fail, which shall be transmitted by the next post.[3]

I have directed that the express be furnished with one hundred dollars out of which he will return the money you were pleased to advance him. I have the honor to be with the highest respect Sir Your most obed. servant

H. Knox secy of war

LS, DLC:GW; LB, DLC:GW.

1. Earlier in the month, Knox had met at least twice with Edmund Randolph and Alexander Hamilton to discuss U.S. relations with the southern Indians and with the Spanish (see Knox to GW, 28 Aug. 1792). As instructed by GW in his letter of 19 Aug., Knox wrote Edward Telfair on 31 Aug. urging the Georgia governor to control frontier settlers who opposed any attempt to survey the boundary line between Georgia and the Creeks that was established in the 1790 Treaty of New York and whose actions against the Indians could provoke a war. Knox said that it was Telfair's responsibility as "a public officer" to cooperate in halting these unlawful activities. He emphasized that an Indian war would be "so adverse to strict economy" and "would tend to protract the extinguishment of the public debt." As a new nation, the United States had not "acquired a solid and profitable confidence with the Indians," as had other countries with whom the United States had to compete for the affections of the Indians, and thus it could not "afford cause of complaint by acting unjustly. These sentiments call for the attention of no State more forcibly than of Georgia; upon which the foreign power in her vicinity might, by gaining an ascendency over the Southern tribes, let them loose with all the horrors of their warfare." Knox reminded Telfair that the Treaty of New York was negotiated in good faith and its articles must be observed by the United States. "Under these circumstances, your Excellency will easily discover what is the duty of the federal and your own Government. The constitution has been freely adopted; the regulation of our Indian connexion is submitted to Congress; and the treaties are parts of the supreme law of the land. It would be a criminal negligence in

the federal administration to pass over the gross infraction of public tranquility, and the insult to the public honor, which are said to be in contemplation. I am authorized to declare to you, sir, in order to testify the determination to uphold you in the most vigorous exertions under the laws of your State, that those of the United States will be strictly enforced and executed upon the offenders, without distinction." Knox insisted Telfair "suppress those violent and unwarrantable proceedings, of which you have been apprised" (*ASP, Indian Affairs*, 1:258–59).

Knox's letter to James Seagrove of 31 Aug., in answer to Seagrove's letters to GW of 5 and 27 July, and to Knox of the same dates and 4 Aug., incorporated the "principles" suggested by GW in his letter to Knox of 19 August. Knox instructed Seagrove to "watch closely the further movements and designs of the said Captain Olivar, and to have them attested by undeniable evidence, on oath. . . . But, in the pursuit of this business . . . you will observe an entire delicacy as it shall relate to the Spanish Government, rather holding up the idea that Captain Olivar may be acting without due authority from the said Government." Knox also cautioned Seagrove not to underestimate the power and influence of Alexander McGillivray. Until "he shall throw off the mask entirely, we ought apparently to treat him as our firm friend; but at the same time, to keep an eagle's eye upon all his conduct."

Knox stressed the importance of U.S. agents residing "within the most populous parts" of the Creek nation in order to gather reliable information and to establish a firmer friendship with the Indians. "From the abilities you have exhibited upon the subject of Indian affairs, and the favorable opinion entertained and expressed thereof, by the President of the United States, I am authorized to say, that he considers you as the suitable character to direct the affairs of the Creeks, having under you one or two subordinate agents; but at the same time, to say, that he considers an actual residence within the heart of the nation, as indispensably necessary for the affairs of the United States; and, as it is necessary to be explicit on this head, I request your immediate information, whether such residence would be agreeable to you, and where you would fix your residence. . . . If you know suitable characters, who would willingly reside among the Creeks . . . you will please to recommend them to the President."

Knox informed Seagrove that the meeting "which you propose on the first of November next, with the Lower Creeks, has been approved by the President . . . on the expectation that it will, as far as possible, be restricted to the chiefs only, agreeably to your proposal; as you have conditionally agreed to this meeting, it might have ill effects, were it not complied with. The Indians will but imperfectly conceive the distinction between a conditional and an actual promise, and therefore it must take place. But, in future . . . there [will] be no great assembling of the Creeks, but in consequence of a previous statement of the causes thereof, and the express approbation of the President of the United States is obtained."

"Goods, corn, and money," Knox wrote, will be sent for distribution to the Lower Creeks, and Seagrove should assess the loss of Indian corn and estimate the amount "which would be an effectual relief to the parts oppressed. If the real necessities of the Lower Creeks require a larger quantity than the five thousand bushels intended to be transported to St. Mary's, you may intimate to them that the President of the United States, actuated by his humanity and regard for them, will order a further quantity, provided they exhibit, on their parts, similar dispositions of kindness and attachment to the United States."

Knox concluded his letter by reminding Seagrove that the administration's policies restricted issuing passports and trading licenses and establishing trading houses within Indian territory. Knox's letter to Seagrove is printed in full in *ASP, Indian Affairs,* 1:259–60, where it is erroneously dated 31 Oct. 1792.

2. For GW's suggestion that Knox meet informally with José de Jaudenes and José Ignacio de Viar, the Spanish ministers to the United States, and for Knox's Minutes of a Conversation with Viar and Jaudenes, on 6 Sept. 1792, see GW to Knox, 19 Aug., and note 2.

3. Copies of the two letters that Wayne wrote to Knox on 24 Aug. were enclosed in Knox to GW, 1 Sept. 1792.

To James McHenry

(Private)

Dear Sir,   Mount Vernon Augt 31st 1792

The characters given of Messrs Smith & Hollingsworth by you, comports very much with those I have received from others, and therefore of the two, the preference is given to the former.[1] But as neither stand upon such high grounds as Mr Tilghman or Mr Hammond, and as it is my duty as well as inclination to fill Offices with the most suitable characters I pray you to make all the indirect enquiry you can whether either of the last named Gentlemen would accept; and, as the nature of the case seems to require, would make Baltimore the place of Residence.[2]

If the result is unfavourable, be so good as to cause the enclosed to be delivered.[3] This case requires a little delicasy in the management and I am persuaded it will receive it from you. I am with sincere esteem and regard—Your Obedt & Affecte

Go: Washington

ALS, CSmH; copy, DLC: James McHenry Papers; ADfS, DNA: RG 59, Miscellaneous Letters; LB, DLC:GW.

1. No letters to GW recommending Robert Smith for appointment as the district attorney for Maryland, other than McHenry's letter of 16 Aug., have been found. GW received several letters recommending Baltimore lawyer Zebulon Hollingsworth for this position. For William Vans Murray's recommendation of 1 Aug., see GW to McHenry, 13 Aug., n.2. John Henry wrote GW on 1 Sept. that Hollingsworth's "Integrity and professional Talents are known & acknowledged. He is a man of letters, possessing philanthropy, and indeed in

every view of his character highly deserving" (DLC:GW). Michael Jenifer Stone said in his letter to GW of 1 Sept. that Hollingsworth is "an Able and attentive Lawyer; a Gentleman of Fair reputation—Entangled with no Party or Faction—A Fast Friend to the Government he wishes to Serve. . . . I am told he has done great part of the United States Business as Locum Tenens for Mr Potts" (DLC: GW). William Paca wrote GW on 18 Sept.: "The legal knowledge and professional Talents of this Gentleman, his Attachment & Zeal for the General Government, the Extent & Influence of his Connections and the Amiableness of his Temper Disposition & Manners give him a Consequence and Respectability of Character equal to any in this State" (DLC:GW). In his letter to GW of 21 Sept., Joshua Seney said: "Mr Hollinsworth is an Attorney of some of the Courts in which I preside, and appears to possess both Industry and professional Talents" (DLC:GW).

2. For McHenry's earlier assessment of Maryland lawyers Robert Smith, Zebulon Hollingsworth, William Tilghman, and Nicholas Hammond, see McHenry to GW, 16 Aug. 1792. For Tilghman and Hammond's disinterest in the position, see McHenry to GW, 4 Oct. 1792, and note 1.

3. GW enclosed his letter to Robert Smith of 31 Aug. offering him the position of district attorney: "If you are disposed to accept the appointment, this shall be your Warrant to Act in it, until a Commission shall issue; which cannot be until the Secretary of State returns to Philadelphia" (ADfS, DNA: RG 59, Miscellaneous Letters; LB, DLC:GW). McHenry forwarded GW's letter to Smith on 5 Oct. (see McHenry to GW, 4 October). When Smith declined the position, Hollingsworth was offered the appointment, and he accepted, writing GW from Baltimore on 30 Oct. 1792 to "express my respectful acknowledgements for the Confidence you have honoured me with in appointing me attorney for this district" (DNA: RG 59, Miscellaneous Letters).

From the Commissioners for the District of Columbia

Sir   George-town 1st Septr 1792

Esteeming it necessary to have your written order for Sales in the City we have enclosed a Draft, a Copy of that given last year, to be Signed against the approaching public Sales—An Idea has been pretty generally entertained, that it would be prudent to Sink a part of the price on condition of Speedy Improvement, and we have presumed to enclose the Draft of an Order calculated for that End, which we only wish to be Signed on its meeting your fullest approbation[1]—We are Sir, with the greatest Respect &c.

Th. Johnson
Dd Stuart
Danl Carroll

Copy, DNA: RG 42, Records of the Commissioners for the District of Columbia, Letters Sent, 1791–1802.

1. The enclosed drafts have not been found. The official records of the commissioners for 1 Sept. 1792 indicate that two orders were sent for GW to sign, "one for Sale of Lots on the eighth of October next, the other for private Sales" (DNA: RG 42, Records of the Commissioners for the District of Columbia, Proceedings, 1791–1802). For the previous year's sale order, see Proclamation, 17 Oct. 1791. For the 1792 orders for public and private sales, see GW to D.C. Commissioners, 29 Sept. 1792, n.1. For the various regulations concerning the "Materials and Manner of the Buildings and Improvements" on these lots, see Broadside: Sale of Lots in the Federal City, 8 October.

From Alexander Hamilton

Sir,   Treasury Departmt 1st Septr 1792.

I have the honor to inclose sundry papers which have been handed to me by the Commissioner of the Revenue, respecting the state of the Excise Law in the western survey of the District of Pennsylvania.[1]

Such persevering and violent opposition to the Law gives the business a still more serious aspect than it has hitherto worn, and seems to call for vigorous & decisive measures on the part of the Government.[2]

I have directed that the Supervisor of the District shall repair forthwith to the Survey in question, to ascertain in person the true state of the Survey; to collect evidence respecting the violences that have been committed in order to a prosecution of the Offenders; to ascertain particulars as to the Meeting which appears to have been holden at Pittsburgh; to encourage the perseverance of the officers; giving expectations as far as it can be done with propriety, of indemnification from the Government, for any losses which they may sustain in consequence of their Offices; to endeavour to prevail upon the Inhabitants of the County of Alleghany, who appear at present the least refractory, to come into an acquiescence with the Law; representing to discreet persons the impossibility of the Governments remaining longer a passive spectator of the contempt of it's Laws.[3]

I shall also immediately submit to the Attorney General for his opinion, whether an indictable offence has not been committed by the persons who were assembled at Pittsburgh, and of what nature, the paper which contains their proceedings; with a view, if judged expedient by you, that it may be brought under the notice of the Circuit Court, which I understand is to be holden in October at York Town.[4]

My present clear conviction is, that it is indispensable, if competent evidence can be obtained, to exert the full force of the Law against the Offenders, with every circumstance that can manifest the determination of the Government to enforce it's execution; & if the processes of the Courts are resisted, as is rather to be expected, to employ those means, which in the last resort are put in the power of the Executive. If this is not done, the spirit of disobedience will naturally extend and the authority of the Government will be prostrate. Moderation enough has been shewn: 'tis time to assume a different tone. The well disposed part of the community will begin to think the Executive wanting in decision and vigour. I submit these impressions to your consideration previous to any step which will involve the necessity of ulterior proceedings; and shall hope as speedily as possible to receive your instructions.[5]

The Secretary at War will be requested to direct Captain Faulkner's attendance at this place.[6] With the highest respect and truest attachment I have the honor to be &c.

Alexander Hamilton

LB, DLC:GW.

Hamilton had proposed an excise tax on domestically produced whiskey in his "Report Relative to a Provision for the Support of Public Credit," which he completed on 9 Jan. 1790 and submitted to Congress on 14 Jan. (Syrett, *Hamilton Papers*, 6:51–168). "An Act repealing, after the last day of June next, the duties heretofore laid upon Distilled Spirits imported from abroad, and laying others in their stead; and also upon Spirits distilled within the United States, and for appropriating the same" was approved on 3 Mar. 1791 (1 *Stat.* 199–214). Congress modified the original statute with "An Act concerning the Duties on Spirits distilled within the United States," approved on 8 May 1792 (ibid., 267–71). Opposition to this tax was particularly strong in the frontier regions of all the states south of New York, and in western Pennsylvania it was often violent. As of August 1792, the federal government had failed to collect any taxes from that area (see Slaughter, *Whiskey Rebellion*, 105–18).

1. Tench Coxe, commissioner of the revenue, recently had forwarded to Hamilton papers that Coxe had received from George Clymer, supervisor of the Pennsylvania district, who had received them from John Neville, inspector of Pennsylvania's fourth survey, comprising Allegheny, Bedford, Washington, and Westmoreland counties (see Hamilton to Coxe, 1 Sept. 1792, in Syrett, *Hamilton Papers*, 12:305–10). Former congressman Clymer had been appointed supervisor of the revenue for the District of Pennsylvania in 1791 (see GW to the U.S. Senate, 4 Mar. 1791). Neville, who was a veteran of the

1755 Braddock expedition and the Continental army, served after the Revolutionary War on the Pennsylvania supreme executive council, in the state's federal ratifying convention, and in the Pennsylvania constitutional convention of 1789–90 before being appointed an inspector of the fourth survey in 1792 (see GW to the U.S. Senate, 6 Mar. 1792).

2. The enclosed papers included a letter from Neville to Clymer of 23 Aug., in which Neville recounted the recent attack on Capt. William Faulkner's home, where Neville had established his tax office. Faulkner, a resident of Washington County, was captain of the rifle company of the 3d Sub-Legion in Gen. Anthony Wayne's army currently stationed at Pittsburgh. Neither Neville nor Faulkner was home at the time of the attack, but Faulkner was in the area searching for deserters when he encountered angry citizens "who reproached him for letting his House for such purposes. They drew a knife on him, threatened to scalp him, tar & feather him, and finally to reduce his House and property to ashes if he did not solemnly promise them to prevent the office of Inspection from being there." Faulkner agreed to their demand and evicted Neville. "I do not think," Neville wrote, "it will be possible to get another House in Washington County for the purpose, of course I shall be obliged to desist from further attempts to fulfill the law. The office at Pittsburg is open but no person makes an entry, many say they would willingly comply with the Law but for the severe denunciations of fire &c. with which they are threatened in case they do" (Syrett, *Hamilton Papers*, 12:305–6, nn.2–3).

Neville's letter also contains an account of an extralegal convention held at Pittsburgh on 21–22 Aug. by opponents of the tax. "In the course of their debates," Neville wrote, "they agree'd that if I would resign no other person would '*accept* the appointment:' & that it would give a '*mortal Stab to the Business.*'" He enclosed a copy of the minutes of the meeting and concluded, "however willing I may be, I do not see at present any chance of doing my duty in the office" (ibid., 307–10, nn.5–6).

3. Supervisor of the Revenue George Clymer left for the western counties in mid-September. His ludicrous attempts at secrecy, first posing as Henry Knox and then as a servant named Smith, failed to disguise his real mission, and his personal fear of violence kept him confined primarily to Pittsburgh where Wayne's troops offered protection. Knox wrote to the commanding officer at Fort Bedford, Pa., on 11 Sept. asking him to protect Clymer "from all lawless violence, while on his journey to Pittsburg, if he should require the same. This being a matter of great delicacy, ought to be kept secret; and of course it can only be necessary to act on the defensive. Great caution and circumspection will be expected" (DLC:GW). Knox also wrote Wayne on that date asking him to protect Clymer "from all lawless violence" on his return from western Pennsylvania to Philadelphia, being sure to stay "within the limits of the law" and to act "with all due caution and circumspection" (DLC:GW). Unable to obtain any firsthand information, and becoming an object of ridicule on account of his disguises and fear, Clymer failed in his mission (see Slaughter, *Whiskey Rebellion*, 125–27).

4. The minutes of the extralegal convention held on 21–22 Aug. were published as a broadside (see Syrett, *Hamilton Papers*, 12:307–9, n.5). Edmund Randolph gave Hamilton his opinion in a lengthy letter dated 8 Sept. (see ibid., 336–40).

5. GW replied to Hamilton on 7 September.

6. Knox wrote Wayne on 21 Sept.: "The Secretary of the Treasury has requested, that in case the Supervisor George Clymer should judge it necessary, that you will peremptorily order Captain Faulkner to repair to York Town in this State in order to give his evidence before the Circuit Court of the United States which will commence its session at that place on the 11th of October ensuing" (DLC:GW).

From Henry Knox

Sir,   War department September 1st 1792

I have the honor to submit you a copy of Major General Waynes letter of the 24th Ultimo, containing his ideas of the war, in case of the failure of the pacific overtures.[1]

I have written him this day, of which the enclosed is a copy.[2]

The propriety of the expedition to the St Joseph's river at present, may be justly questioned—After we shall be well established at the Miami village, with proper posts of communication with the head and down the Wabash, and down the Miami of Lake Erie,[3] the hostile Indians on St Josephs will either submit, or remove to a greater distance.

We shall soon know with certainty, whether any Indians will remain on the Miami of Lake Erie the ensuing winter—If they should not, the establishments may be effected as far as the field of action of the 4. of November[4] and perhaps at the Miami village during the Winter or early in the spring, [(]before the Indians can assemble) either without loss or opposition—if so, our great points would be gained.

The Magazines therefore of forage, and provisions at the advanced posts will be proper and important.

The morning report made to Genl Wayne of the 24th of August I have the honor to enclose—I believe some of his detachments which had arrived are not inserted.[5]

I have the honor also to transmit enclosed the returns of recruits to this day—It is painful to reflect upon its small encrease and difficult to conjecture a remedy, excepting by increasing the pay which cannot be effected without the orders of Congress.[6] I have the honor to be with the highest respect Your most obed. Servant

H. Knox secy of war

LS, DLC:GW; LB, DLC:GW.

1. In his first letter to Knox written from Pittsburgh on 24 Aug., Wayne offered "a few general observations why I think the war must progress.

"The savages have become confident, haughty and insolent, from reiterated success, which they have recently evinced, by the wanton and deliberate massacre of our *flags.*" Wayne believed that the British from their "Possession of our posts on the *Lakes* . . . do *indirectly,* stimulate the savages to continue the War," and he cited Lord Dorchester's speech to the Indians in August 1791 "which to me is very conclusive evidence, that they don't actually encourage the Indians to continue the War—*they promise to protect them.*"

Wayne said that he "can't agree in opinion with General Putnam, that we ought to carry on part of our operation by the way of Lake Erie, Because I believe that the British would with avidity, avail themselves of that pretext to assist the savages openly—at all events they would prevent us from navigating on that Water, as long as they hold possession of our posts; . . . I will take the liberty to offer some reasons against a fall Campaign, especially that immediately ensuing.

"Because, we shall be pressed for time, and deficient in point of numbers, discipline and Manoeuvre. and Because, *we ought not to risk an other defeat with raw troops;* . . . This business—with every exertion and care, will require all this fall and winter to effect. . . . I consider the Indian—an Enemy formidable only, when he has a choice of time & Ground—in the *fall* of the year he's strong ferocious, and full of spirits, corn is in plenty, and Venison and other game, every where to be met with, in the spring he is half starved weak and dispirited. . . . Permit me to choose the season for operation—give me time to Manoeuvre and discipline the troops . . . let the component parts of the Legion be perfected. . . . Authorise me to direct ample and proper Magazines of forage stores & provisions to be thrown into the advanced posts—at the most convenient periods, from Fort Washington to fort Jefferson, I would also establish a suitable magazine of Forage and provisions at Big Beaver, from this place, and Fort Washington, I would propose two strong desultory parties, composed of Mounted Volunteers . . . the one against *Sandusky* (which has not been abandoned as mentioned by Captain Brandt) the other against the Indians, who have removed from the Miami Villages, to St Josephs river, where by several accounts, there are several New towns of Hostile Indians—these expeditions to take place as soon as the grass in the *Prairies* would answer for Pasture, and not until every thing was in readiness for a forward move, *Of the Legion,* from Fort Jefferson, at which point, the operating Army should previously assemble.

"These movements . . . should they have no other effect, they wou'd distract the Savage Councils—and create a Jealousy for the safety of their Women and Children, whilst the Legion was advancing and employed in erecting small intermediate Forts, at proper and convenient distances, between Fort Jefferson and the point intended for establishing a strong and permanent Post."

After making a favorable assessment of the availability of forage and the ability of the army to purchase and transport additional forage and provisions to Forts Jefferson and Washington, Wayne wrote: "Clothe me with Authority to make the necessary arrangements for an active War (which must from the nature of things take place) and I will establish a strong and permanent post, in any part of the Indian Country, that you may please to direct." Wayne then summarized his previous "ideas of Offensive and effectual Operation" and concluded: "I would not have it understood, that I mean to be totally on the defensive, for this *Season* on the contrary, I have in Contemplation, *One* if not two, Desultory Expeditions, with mounted Volunteers and riflemen, in order to draw the attention of the Savages, to another Quarter, whilst we make the greatest efforts, to throw Magazines of Forage, provisions and other stores into Fort Jefferson, and perhaps to establish a Post, twenty Miles in front of it, or eventually, *upon General St Clairs field of Action* which I presume may be effected, without risking too much; with the Aid of a Desultory Expedition against *Sandusky* Upon the whole I am decidedly of opinion, that the War must progress, and that We have no time to lose, in preparing for that event" (DLC:GW).

2. In this letter Knox wrote: "I have directed a person to be sent to examine the road from hence to Pittsburg to see whether there any stores lingering upon the road, and if so, to accelerate them and report the delinquents—But Major [Isaac] Craig writes on the 24th that several waggon loads of Stores have just arrived. . . . I have not yet had time to consider of your propositions for carrying on the war, in case the pacific overtures should fail—in general they upon first sight appear judicious and to have been well weighed by you, and an explicit answer shall be transmitted thereon upon the receipt of the Presidents opinion.

"I wish you had been pleased to transmit the information which gives you the belief that Sandusky is not mostly abandoned by the Women and Children—The Indians may be raising some Corn there but I believe no more—I am apprehensive that any expedition against that place without further information would be pushing against a Cloud.

"No doubt however can be entertained of the propriety of accumulating the magazines of forage and provisions you propose at Fort Washington and the posts advanced thereof—and you will please explicitly to understand, that if you had not the authority before—that it is hereby sufficiently vested in you."

Knox also wrote that it was "the season for laying up Salt provisions" and that "forty small casks" of fine-grain powder, along with clothing, had been forwarded to Wayne. Several new companies of recruits were en route to Wayne's headquarters at Pittsburgh, but Knox reported that the "recruiting service has been almost at a stand—I know not how it can be stimulated unless by an additional Sum to their pay for which no authority exists—perhaps in the autumn and winter we may complete the numbers authorized." Knox informed Wayne that he was waiting for an opportunity "to send on money to complete the pay to the first of August and also ten thousand dollars for the Quarter Master which his agent has drawn from the treasury" (DLC:GW).

3. Knox is referring to the Maumee River.

4. Gen. Arthur St. Clair and his troops were defeated by a confederation of hostile Indians on 4 Nov. 1791 while encamped at the present-day site of Fort Recovery, Ohio (see William Darke to GW, 9–10 Nov. 1791, and source note; "Denny Journal"; Guthman, *March to Massacre*).

5. According to this morning report, there were 662 present fit for duty, 45 sick present, 56 sick in the hospital, 18 sick absent, 49 on command, 6 absent

with leave, 16 on extra duty, 14 in confinement, and 9 recently joined, for a total of 875 men at Pittsburgh's Fort Fayette where Wayne maintained his head-quarters (DLC:GW).

Knox also enclosed a copy of Wayne's second, briefer letter of 24 Aug. in which Wayne wrote: "I find that the southern Indians are rather hostilly in-clined, by Colonel A. Campbells letter—If the legion was complete—and *Aug-mented* by four troops more of dragoons—I woud feel a Confidence in meet-ing the whole combined force of the savages—by the months of June or July next—Their numbers would only tend to confuse them—and they would be-come an easy prey to our cavalry (after being roused by the *bayonet*) their bare heads would invite the fall of the Sword.

"In my opinion we have more to apprehend from a temporizing peace than from the most active Indian war" (DLC:GW).

6. The enclosed "Returns of the Recruits at the respective rendezvous and who have marched" is dated erroneously 1 Sept. 1790. The recruits returned as of 28 July numbered 1,827, and by 1 Aug. there were an additional 237 re-cruits. Knox allowed for an estimated 100 deserters to reach a total of 1,954 (DLC:GW).

To Henry Knox

Sir,   Mount Vernon Sepr 3d 1792

Since my last to you—dated the 26th of Augt—I have received your dispatches of the 23d; 26th; & 28th; of the same month; and it is probable, the Messenger who will carry this & other let-ters to the Post Office, will bring me the result of your delibera-tions on the communications from Georgia.[1]

I am exceedingly glad to find by the copy of Genl Putnams let-ter to you, that he had resolved to proceed from Fort Washing-ton to Post Vincennes, even if no other good should result from it, than to shew that nothing in the compass of the Executive has been unessayed to convince the hostile Indians of the pacific and equitable measures & intentions of the Government of the Union towards them. I shd have been unwilling (as I mentioned to you in my letter of the [13] of Augt)[2] to have entrusted so important a negotiation to Majr Hamtrackt although the business might have been transacted with zeal & ability by that Officer.[3]

I hope the party of Seneca Indians when their services were dispensed with by Lieutt Jeffers were rewarded, & went off well satisfied. This, as far as it can be accomplished by reasonable at-tentions & proper compensation, ought *always* to be the case.[4]

The conduct of the Waggoners, in dropping the public stores with the transportation of which they are charged, along the

Road to Pittsburgh, ought to undergo the strictest scrutiny; & in cases of culpability, to meet with severe punishment by way of example to others.[5]

I have no objection to Peter Van Allans filling the Vacancy which has been occasioned by the resignation of Lieutt Schuyler and shd be glad to know the determination of Major Fish as soon as he has formed and you are made acquainted with it.[6] With esteem and regard I am—Yours &ca

Go: Washington

ADfS, DLC:GW; LB, DLC:GW.

1. For Knox's deliberations, see Knox to GW, 31 August.

2. At this place on the draft manuscript, GW left a blank; the date is supplied from the letter-book copy.

3. For Putnam's letter of 22 July, see Knox to GW, 26 Aug., n.4. On 22 May 1792 Knox had instructed Putnam to present American peace offers to the Miami, Shawnee, Delaware, and other Indians who would gather for a grand council scheduled that fall at Au Glaize on the Maumee River (see Buell, *Putnam Memoirs,* 257–67; see also *ASP, Indian Affairs,* 1:234–36). Putnam arrived at Fort Washington on 2 July to prepare for this mission. An attack on Fort Washington shortly before his arrival and news of the murder of peace envoys Alexander Trueman and John Hardin induced Putnam to redirect his efforts to negotiating a peace treaty at Vincennes with the Wabash tribes, who were less hostile to the United States primarily because of their strong anti-British feelings (see Putnam to Knox, 5 July, in Buell, *Putnam Memoirs,* 273–78; Putnam to Knox, 8 July, printed at Knox to GW, 5 Aug., n.2, and 14 July, printed at Knox to GW, 16 Aug., n.1). Maj. John Hamtramck, the American commander at Vincennes, already had persuaded the Eel and Wea Indian chiefs to sign a preliminary peace agreement with the United States in March and had convinced other Indians who were hostile to the British to join further peace negotiations, over which Putnam now assumed control (see "Articles of Agreement with the Wabash Indians," 14 Mar. 1792, Hamtramck to Knox, 31 Mar. 1792, in Carter, *Territorial Papers,* 2:374–75, 380–83; Knox to GW, 26 Aug., nn.4–5, and 22 Sept., n.3). For an account of Putnam's negotiations at Vincennes during September, see Buell, *Putnam Memoirs,* 335–62.

4. Knox had written Gen. Anthony Wayne on 7 Aug. from Philadelphia suggesting that the Seneca Indians serving with Capt. John Jeffers's company of rangers "ought not to be pressed to stay in service—their continuance may have bad effects" (see Knox to GW, 7 Aug., n.3). Wayne replied to Knox from Pittsburgh on 17 Aug.: "The Indians who were attached to Capt. Jeffers's corps have been dismissed and sent home ever since early July—except two or three who don't show a disposition to leave this place, in fact, *Jeffers's* whole corps of rangers has been dissolved near two Months, as I found the Soldiers were much averse to that kind of service, which had caused many desertions" (see Knox to GW, 26 Aug., n.2).

5. Wayne's letter to Knox of 17 Aug. reported difficulties in having supplies shipped to Wayne's headquarters at Pittsburgh (see Knox to GW, 26 Aug., n.2).

6. For Dirck Schuyler's resignation and Peter Van Alen's appointment, see Knox to GW, 28 Aug., and note 3. Knox wrote Nicholas Fish from Philadelphia on 29 Aug. offering him the position of adjutant general (NNGL: Knox Papers). Knox informed GW in his letter of 15 Sept. that Fish had declined the appointment.

To Henry Knox

(Private)
My dear Sir,   Mount Vernon Sep. 3d 1792.

I thank you sincerely for the medicine you were so obliging as to send for my Nephew, and for the sympathetic feeling you express for his situation. Poor fellow! neither, I believe will be of any avail. Present appearances indicate a speedy dissolution. He has not been able to leave his bed except for a few moments to set in an Arm Chair since the 14th or 15th of last Month. The paroxysm of the disorder seems to be upon him and death or a favourable turn to it must soon follow.[1]

I pray you to turn your thoughts to the communications which may be necessary for me to refer to from the War Department at the *opening* of the next Session; that such documents as shall be adjudged proper for the occasion may be prepared by *that time* for both houses of Congress; and if any thing else of a *general* nature should occur to you I would thank you for noting it for consideration that nothing proper may escape communication.[2]

I learn through the medium of a letter from the Auditor to his father in law, Doctr Craik, that Colo. Hamilton has it in contemplation to visit this part of the Country in the course of this, or the beginning of next month. Should this event take place and you could make it convenient to be of the party it will be unnecessary I hope for me to say that I should be very glad to see you under this roof. It is fair, however, to add, that this part of the Country has experienced more sickness *this* summer than is recollected to have happened for many years—first with the flux, and then with intermittant & remittant fevers. happily few deaths have been the consequence of either. The former is now over— but the latter is still prevalent. Both the French and British Ministers talked of coming this way. Should they still continue in the same mind I should be glad if by indirect enquiries you could ascertain & let me know the time, or times (if they come seperately) they may be expected.[3] My present intention, if the peculiar situation into which my affairs are thrown by the illness of my Nephew will not necessarily delay it, is to take the Sale of Lots in the Federal City in my way to Philadelphia—and this Sale is appointed to be on the 8th of October.[4] I am &ca

G. W——n

ADfS, DLC:GW; LB, DLC:GW.

1. On 31 Aug., Knox sent GW "two more bottles" of "the medicine called Antipertussis" from Philadelphia for GW's nephew George Augustine Washington, who died on 5 Feb. 1793 from tuberculosis (NNGL: Knox Papers).

2. GW made a similar request to the other members of his cabinet for material to include in the address that he delivered to the U.S. Senate and House of Representatives on 6 Nov. 1792 (see GW to Jefferson, 23 Aug., to Hamilton, 26 Aug., and Randolph to GW, 28 Oct. 1792). For Knox's response, see his letter to GW of 14 Oct., and note 1.

3. For GW's positive response to the suggestion by Richard Harrison, auditor of the Treasury Department, that Hamilton might visit Mount Vernon, see GW to Hamilton, 26 August. Hamilton and Knox did not visit Mount Vernon (see Knox to GW, 8 Sept. [first letter], and Hamilton to GW, 9 Sept. [first letter]).

In a letter marked "Private," Knox wrote GW from Philadelphia on 16 Sept.: "Agreably to your request I have sounded Mr Hammond, and Mr Ternant upon their intentions of vissiting Mount Vernon[.] The former who returned from the eastward a few days past, will set out for your house on Wednesday the 19th, and he expects to reach it in four day and an half.

"Mr Ternant who is in delicate health says he shall be unable to form any decision until the latter of the Week, but it is rather improbable that he will undertake the journey" (DLC:GW).

On 18 Sept. in another "Private" letter from Philadelphia, Knox wrote GW that "Mr Hammond in order to accommodate Mr [Robert] Smith of south Carolina, who is to accompany him to Mount Vernon will not set out until the 20th instant" (DLC:GW). Hammond arrived at Mount Vernon on 24 Sept. (see GW to Knox, 24 Sept. [second letter]).

4. GW left Mount Vernon on 8 Oct. and arrived in Philadelphia on 13 Oct. to prepare for the opening of the second session of the Second Congress (see GW to Betty Washington Lewis, 7 Oct., to Anthony Whitting, 14 October).

From John J. Pringle

Charleston, S.C., 3 Sept. 1792. Resigns as U.S. attorney for the District of South Carolina because his "business and avocations" do not permit him enough time to perform properly the duties of this office.[1]

ALS, DNA: RG 59, Miscellaneous Letters.

1. John Julius Pringle (1753–1843), a Charleston lawyer, was appointed the U.S. district attorney for South Carolina in September 1789 (see GW to the U.S. Senate, 24 Sept. 1789). He became the state attorney general in December 1792 and served in that position until 1808.

To Edmund Randolph

(Private)

Dear Sir,   Mount Vernon Sep. 3d 1792.

Since my last to you dated the 26th of Augt—I have been favoured with your letter bearing the same date, covering Mr Bordley's "Sketches on rotations of Crops[.]" Permit me, through you to offer him my sincere thank for this instance (among many others) of his politeness. The subject is interesting and important, and as soon as I have leizure, for at present I am fully occupied I will give it an attentive perusal.

You add "no incidents in the political line attract any notice, except those, which relate to the supposed temper of Virginia, & the measures projected at the next Session. Of these you must have heard; and therefore I omit them."

The truth is, I go out no where; and those who call upon me, observe a silence which leaves me in ignorance in all these matters. You wd oblige me therefore by an explanation of the above paragraph.[1] Colo. Bassett is here—he came up this day week to see my poor Nephew, who I suppose is near his end; but was siezed hand & foot, with the Gout on the Road, & has not been out of his bed since; nor in a condition to communicate what he knows if he was disposed to do it.[2] I am with sincere and affecte regard—always Yours

                                    Go: Washington

ADfS, DNA: RG 59, Miscellaneous Letters; LB, DLC:GW.

1. Randolph responded to GW's inquiries about Virginia politics in his letter of 10 September.

2. Col. Burwell Bassett, husband of Martha Washington's sister Anna Maria Dandridge Bassett (1739–1777), was the father of Frances (Fanny) Bassett Washington and thus the father-in-law of GW's nephew George Augustine Washington. Bassett died on 4 Jan. 1793 after a fall from his horse (see Henry Lee to GW, 6 Jan. 1793).

From George Gale

Sir   Baltimore September 4th 1792

I am extremely sorry that I have not been sooner able to obey your Instructions in regard to enquiring of Mr Porters fitness for the command of the cutter.[1] As he is by Birth a New England Man I first sought among the Gentlemen from that Country for his character and found them unfavourab⟨l⟩y impressed; two circumstances were alledged to his prejudice such as his having been in a manner expatriated for keeping a Public house of Ill fame in Boston and again his having lost a ship in such a way as to induce suspicions of his integrity.

On more minute enquiry the better opin[ion] seems to be that the latter charge is ground less; and Capt. Porters general deportment as a good citizen since his residence in Balta. eight or nine years is a favourable evidence of his reform and does in a degree atone for his former manner of living.

It is objected to him as an Officer that whilst in the pay of the Government he engaged in the service of a merchant of this Town for whom he made a Voyage without resigning his commission.

Having heard these reports I thought it my Duty to communicate them at the same time I must observe that it appears to me the appointment of Capt. Porter would be agreeable to many of the respectable merchants of Balta.; they think him sober & industrious though an unfortunate man and pity a numerous family of small children whose Subsistence perhaps depends on his provision from the Government.[2] I have the Honor to be with the greatest respect and permit me to add sincerest esteem Sir your most Obedt Hbe servt

Geo. Gale

ALS, DNA: RG 59, Miscellaneous Letters.

1. For GW's request that Gale, the current supervisor of revenue for the Maryland district, send him information about David Porter, see GW to Hamilton, 5 Aug. 1792.

2. Gale's mixed letter of recommendation arrived after GW had decided to appoint Porter as the master commandant of the Maryland cutter *Active* (see Hamilton to Otho H. Williams, 13 Aug. 1792, in Syrett, *Hamilton Papers*, 12:199). The appointment was effective 5 Aug. 1792 (see Tobias Lear to Jefferson, 26 Oct. 1792).

To James Seagrove

Sir,   Mount Vernon Sep. 4th 1792.

It was necessary for the Express that brought your dispatches to me to proceed to the War Office with my sentimt thereupon —Enclosed you have the result.[1] To these I have nothing to add but my entire approbation of the zeal and intelligence with which you have conducted matters with the Creek Indians—My good wishes for the perfect restoration of your health—and my hope that it may comport with your Inclination and views to superintended that business, agreeably to the Plan suggested by the Secretary of War.

As I do not perceive that any mention is made of it in the letter from the Secretary of War to you, it may not be amiss to inform you that One hundred Dollars has been advanced to Mr Jas Jordon to defray the expences of his journey; for which he must acct to you. With esteem I am Sir Yr Obedt Hble Servt

Go: Washington

ADfS, DNA: RG 59, Miscellaneous Letters; LB, DLC:GW.

1. Seagrove's dispatches, which included his letters to GW of 5 and 27 July, arrived at Mount Vernon on 15 Aug., and GW forwarded them to Knox later that same date (see GW to Knox, 15 Aug. 1792). Knox received them on 22 Aug. (see Knox to GW, 23 August). On 19 Aug., GW wrote Knox at length about Spanish interference in U.S. Indian relations in the South, the subject of the Seagrove dispatches, and he instructed Knox to confer on the matter with Alexander Hamilton and Edmund Randolph. Knox's letters to Seagrove and Georgia governor Edward Telfair of 31 Aug., copies of which he enclosed in his second letter to GW of that date, reflect both the principles proposed by GW and the result of Knox's discussions with Hamilton and Randolph. Knox's letter to Seagrove and this letter from GW were delivered to Seagrove at St. Mary's, Ga., by James Jordan on 1 Oct. (see Seagrove to Knox, 17 Oct. 1792, in *ASP, Indian Affairs,* 1:311).

From John Churchman

Baltimore September 5th 1792.

Having waited with patience for several Years, in hopes the National Legislature would do something towards fitting out one or two vessels on a Voyage of experiment, yet notwithstanding the report of the Committee of Congress was adopted last Session, & a Bill brought in and read the second time, it did not pass into a Law.[1]

Now agreeable with the advice of some of my Friends, I have proposed to go to Europe in the Ship *Friendship* Captain Smith who is to leave this port for *London* the 10th day of the present month.[2] Before my departure I had a desire of coming to *Mount Vernon,* but was afraid of interfereing with a croud of other Visitors, and it was with difficulty I could prevail upon myself to be the Occasion of so much trouble as the present *Farewell* Letter, but as I go to prove the principles of the *Magnetic Atlas,* from the favourable reception this little work has met with, I humbly hope to be pardoned. In order to bring these principles to the test, I have been engaged in making an extensive set of Tables, to reduce them to practice, without the trouble of measuring angles, or making calculations by the marriner. on this account I wish to make a number of observations, on the western coast of Europe, this business I percieve must be very expensive.[3]

As the different Governments of Europe have thought subjects of this kind worthy of their encouragement, it may be useful for me to keep up a correspondence at some of the Courts abroad, for this reason it might be highly useful for me to get into the good graces of the American Ministers residing at London and Paris. I shall therefore be happy to be the bearer of a line to each or either of them, as by these means my well meant endeavours may be promoted in part without any additional expence to the public. & if any good should arise from the present scheme, with Justice will it be said that it came by & through the President of the United States, but I dare not solicit any letter to the Marquis de la Fayette the Washington of France.[4]

Should I be favoured with any commands at this time, they will come safe to the care of James Clark Merchant in this Town, in whose Ship I am to sail.

Indeed the Secretary of the Treasury has kindly written to both of the said American Ministers at London & Paris on my behalf. yet if some thing further is now added this kindness will ever be remembered by me with gratitude. Its true I have also many other Letters to & from certain Scientific Characters. among which is one from the good Bishop White to his Friend in London. Judge Johnson has obligingly written to his Brother the Consul General in the same City in my favour. &c.[5]

I take the Liberty to mention that I have furnished myself with a number of copies of a Map & description of the Federal City of Washington, which was engraved for the Magazine, all of which I hope to put in such hands on the other side of the Ocean, as to place that new City in a favourable light, & as a larger Map of the same is expected soon to be finished & published I expect also to procure some of that impression for the same purpose.[6] With the greatest sentiments of respect, I hope to be permitted to make an humble offering of my service & esteem

John Churchman

ALS, DNA: RG 59, Miscellaneous Letters; the cover is stamped "BALT SEPT 6."

1. For background on the scientific controversy stirred up by John Churchman, Maryland surveyor and cartographer, see Thomas Ruston to GW, 20 Mar. 1789, n.1, and Rodolph Vall-travers to GW, 20 Mar. 1791, n.1. Although Congress had rejected Churchman's earlier petitions for financial support, he submitted another petition to Congress in December 1791 asking the federal government to fund a voyage to Baffin Bay "for the purpose of making discoveries to confirm his new theory of the variation of the magnetic needle." A bill to finance Churchman's research was read in Congress, but it failed to generate sufficient support for a final vote on the House floor (see *Journal of the House*, 4:67, 75, 119, 127).

2. William B. Smith was the captain of the *Friendship* (see *Maryland Journal and Baltimore Advertiser*, 4 Sept. 1792). This ship left Baltimore for London on 13 Sept. (see *Dunlap's American Daily Advertiser* [Philadelphia], 20 Sept. 1792).

3. Churchman's third pamphlet on this subject, *The Magnetic Atlas, or Variation Charts of the Whole Terraqueous Globe; Comprising a System of the Variation and Dip of the Needle, by Which the Observations Being Truly Made, the Longitude May Be Ascertained*, was published in London in 1794.

4. GW replied to Churchman on 10 Sept. from Mount Vernon and enclosed "two short letters of introduction" (ADfS, DNA: RG 59, Miscellaneous Letters; LB, DLC:GW). In identical letters dated 10 Sept., which GW labeled "un-Official," to Gouverneur Morris, minister to France, and Thomas Pinckney, minister to Great Britain, GW explained that Churchman wanted an "opportunity of explaining to you the object of his Voyage" and that he planned to make "a number of observations on the Western coast of Europe" (GW to Morris, ALS, PPL. Pinckney's receiver's copy has not been found; the letter-book copy in DLC:GW is addressed to both Morris and Pinckney).

On 15 Oct., in Philadelphia, Tobias Lear sent a brief cover letter to William Barton enclosing the "letters and papers" intended for Churchman that Vall-travers had enclosed in his letter to GW of 20 Mar. 1791, "as it appears that in case of Mr Churchman's absence from home they are to be left" with Barton (DNA: RG 59 Miscellaneous Letters).

5. Hamilton's letters of introduction have not been identified. William White (1748–1836), who helped organize the Protestant Episcopal Church from the Anglican Church of colonial America, was the first Protestant Episcopal bishop of the diocese of Pennsylvania. A 1765 graduate of the College of Philadelphia, White, unlike his brother-in-law Robert Morris, was a Loyalist during the Revolutionary War.

Thomas Johnson was the chief justice of the Maryland general court, 1790–91. GW appointed him to the board of commissioners for the federal district in January 1791 (see Commission, 22 Jan. 1791) and to the U.S. Supreme Court on 5 Aug. 1791. Failing health forced him to resign from the Supreme Court in 1793 (see Thomas Johnson to GW, 16 Jan. 1793) and from the commission in 1794. GW asked him to be his secretary of state in 1795, but poor health forced him to decline this offer. Joshua Johnson had been appointed consul to London in 1790 (see GW to the U.S. Senate, 2 Aug. 1790).

6. Churchman is referring to the "Description of the city of Washington" and the accompanying map that appeared in the March 1792 issue of the *Universal Asylum, and Columbian Magazine* (Philadelphia). It apparently was at GW's direction that his secretary Tobias Lear wrote the magazine's publisher William Young on 23 Feb. 1792: "As soon as the plan of the federal City is ultimately determined upon and approved of, you will be furnished with a sight of it, in order to have a plate prepared for the Universal Assylum & Columbian Magazine. . . . It will be a desireable thing that a *perfect & correct* plan of the city should be published in the Columbian Magazine as well as in other useful publications of a similar kind. But should an *incorre[c]t* one be brought before the public in that way, it would only serve to mislead the public mind with respect to the City, and could reflect no credit on the work in which it may be published. For this reason the friends of the proposed establishment are as desireous as you can be that you should be furnished with a *correct* plan" (MHi: Photostats). The "larger Map" was produced by Philadelphia engravers James Thackara and John Vallance in the fall of 1792 (see D.C. Commissioners to GW, 5 Oct. 1792, n.2).

Memorandum on a Statement by James Craik

[Mount Vernon, 7 September 1792][1]

Agreeably to your request, I shewed Mr Campbells letter, to you, to the P. of the U:S: who appeared to be exceedingly surprised at the contents, and at the liberty which had been taken in making declarations for him which he had never made for himself. He added, that to the best of his recollection, he never exchanged a word with Bushrod Washington on the subject of Colo. Mercers Election, much less to have given a decided opinion of his fitness or unfitness to represent the district for which he is a Candidate. That such a measure would have been inconsistent with the rule he has prescribed to himself, and which he has invariably observed of not interfering directly, nor indirectly with the suffrages of the people in the choice of their Representatives. And said he wished that Bushrod Washington might be called upon to certify what, or whether any conversation of the kind ever passed between them on this subject as it was his desire that every thing might stand upon it's proper foundation.[2]

The above, is what Doctr Craik was authorised to say, or write to Mr Fendal, on the subject of a letter from Mr Campbell to him signifying that Colo. Mercer or some of his friends were reporting that I had to B[ushrod]. W[ashington]: declard that he was the best Representative in Congress & that it was my earnest wish that he should be re-chosen by the State of Maryland.[3]

AD, DNA: RG 59, Miscellaneous Letters; LB, DLC:GW.

1. GW wrote this date on the docket of his retained copy, and the same date appears on the letter-book copy.

2. This paragraph is enclosed in quotation marks in the letter-book copy. John Francis Mercer was a successful candidate in 1792 for election from Maryland to the U.S. House of Representatives. For Mercer's denial that he inappropriately used GW's name in his election campaign, see his letter to GW of 15 Sept. 1792. For GW's chastisement of Mercer, see GW to Mercer, 26 Sept. 1792.

3. Philip Richard Fendall, a resident and merchant of Alexandria, Va., was a frequent visitor to Mount Vernon before GW's election to the presidency (see Harriot Washington to GW, 2 April 1790, source note, and GW to Philip Richard Fendall, 22 Oct. 1788, source note). William Campbell of Maryland served in John Fulford's matross company of Anne Arundel County, Md., during the Revolutionary War, and he was promoted to captain on 31 May 1777. His letter to Fendall has not been identified, but GW quotes from it in his letter to John F. Mercer of 26 September.

To Alexander Hamilton

Sir, Mount Vernon 7th Septr 1792.
The last Post brought me your letter of the first instant, with the enclosures respecting the disorderly conduct of the Inhabitants of the Western Survey of the District of Pennsylvania, in opposing the execution of what is called the Excise Law; & of the insults which have been offered by some of them to the Officers who have been appointed to collect the duties on distilled spirits agreeably thereto.

Such conduct in *any* of the Citizens of the United States, under *any* circumstances that can well be conceived, would be exceedingly reprehensible; but when it comes from a part of the community for whose protection the money arising from the Tax was principally designed, it is truly unaccountable, and the spirit of it much to be regretted.

The preliminary steps taken by you in ordering the Supervisor of the District to repair to the Survey where these disorders prevail, with a view to ascertain in person, "the true state of the Survey; to collect evidence respecting the violences that have been committed, in order to a prosecution of the Offenders; to ascertain the particulars as to the Meeting which appears to have been held at Pittsburg; to encourage the perseverance of the officers in their duty, & the well disposed inhabitants in discountenancing such violent proceedings &c. &c."—are prudent & proper, and I earnestly wish they may have the desired effect.[1] But if, notwithstanding, opposition is still given to the due execution of the Law, I have no hesitation in declaring, if the evidence of it is clear & unequivocal, that I shall, however reluctantly I exercise them, exert all the legal powers with which the Executive is invested, to check so daring & unwarrantable a spirit. It is my duty to see the Laws executed: to permit them to be trampled upon with impunity would be repugnant to it; nor can the Government longer remain a passive spectator of the contempt with which they are treated. Forbearance, under a hope that the Inhabitants of that Survey would recover from the delirium & folly into which they were plunged, seems to have had no other effect than to encrease the disorder.

If it shall be the Attorney General's opinion, under a full consideration of the case (adverting, as I presume he will as well to the Laws & Constitution of Pennsylvania, as to those of the United States) that the Meeting which appears to have been held at Pittsburg was illegal, and the members of it indictable; and it shall further appear to you from such information as you may be able to obtain, from a comparative view of all circumstances that it would be proper to bring the matter before the Circuit Court to be holden at York town in October next, you have all the sanction and authority I can give to do it.[2] I am Sir, &c.

G: Washington

LB, DLC:GW.

1. GW is quoting from Hamilton's letter of 1 September. For background on the issues and events mentioned by GW, see Hamilton to GW, 1 Sept. 1792, and notes.

2. Attorney General Randolph answered Hamilton's query on 8 Sept.: "Thus, Sir, you discover my opinion to be against an attempt to a prosecution *at this moment,* when the malignant spirit has not developed itself in acts so specific, and so manifestly infringing the peace, as obviously to expose the culpable persons to the censures of the Law. . . . I thought of a proclamation, as an eventual substitute, if the law should be found inadequate. It struck me that a proclamation was objectionable, because it seemed that the Executive ought to consign to the course of the law any violations of it, and not to animadvert upon acts to which no Law had prescribed a penalty, and because an improper interference of the President might excite an idea of usurpation and inlist

against him even those who execrate the spirit of the Pittsburg proceedings. But after the anticipation of a part only of the consequences, which the silence of Government would produce, after recollecting that these obnoxious things have been transacted in the very state which is the temporary residence of the Administration, that they will carry with them a kind of eclat, as being done at a spot where the United States are certainly not unpopular, that the western Settlers in other States, from a Sympathy of situation, and the want of intelligence may imitate the conduct of the pennsylvania counties, unless they will be restrained by a timely admonition, that few of the serious oppositions to Government have existed, which were not capable of being blasted, if encountered before men committed themselves too deeply, and that acquiescence of the President may be imputed to a suspicion of the inconstitunality or at least gross inexpediency of the Excise Laws, I yeild to the necessity of a Proclamation. I derive the Presidents right to issue it, from the duty of seeing the laws executed, and the fitness of preventing the growth of a crime by salutary advice rather then waiting to press the infliction of punishment." Randolph then suggested several alterations to a draft proclamation relative to the current opposition to the whiskey tax that Hamilton had sent him (Syrett, *Hamilton Papers* 12:336–40). GW issued a proclamation on 15 Sept. 1792 urging compliance with the excise tax. For GW's instructions to Randolph to attend the U.S. circuit court session held on 11 Oct. in York, Pa., and the results of that session, see GW to Randolph, 1 Oct., and note 1.

To Henry Knox

Sir,   Mount Vernon Sepr 7th 1792.

Your letters of the 31st of Augt and first of the present month, have been duly received. The enclosures in the first for Govr Tellfair and Mr Seagrove have been approved, and forwarded. Those of the Second I have read, but will give them a second & a more attentive consideration before I express any decisive opinion upon General Waynes Plan for carrying on the War.[1]

My first impression of it, however, is, that it differs immaterially, if in any thing from the basis—or principal features of the one that has been, and now is pursuing; except in the establishment of a Post on Big Beaver Creek, and in the two desultory strokes to be aimed at Sandusky & St Joseph. The latter will be *right,* or *wrong,* according to the actual State of things at *those places* at the time it is proposed to make them—(to be ascertained from indubitable information) and by a comparison of the hazard wch must be run of failure with the advantages to be gained in case of Success. In all other respects, I see little more than Incidents and detail of the Original Plan—for if *all* the

pacific overtures are rejected by the hostile Indians, and the
Troops are neither in for⟨ce⟩ nor discipline to make a forward
movemt the ensuing fall, it follows of course that it must be delayed until the Spring; and every exertion used in the establishment of Posts magazines &ca for as early an exped[it]ion at that
period as high Waters & the state of the forage will permit—If
Genl Wayne had any doubt of this & his power to arrange, & effectuate these, you have, I perceive by the copy of your letter to
him, very properly removed it; and it is my wish & desire that his
exertion to accomplish the objects he has contemplated, may be
commensurate to the importance of them.

With respect to the proposition for establishing a Magazine on
Big beavr—there is but one objection to it in my mind admitting
that it does not look forward to the event which is contemplated
by Genl Wayne (provided the position is judiciously chosen) and
that is, the multiplication of Posts; for it has, for a great length
of time, been my opinion that a strong Post at that place would
cover much more effectually the Western frontier of Pennsylvania and the Northern parts of Virginia, than a Post at Pittsburgh;
but habit, and the deep root the latter has taken, to which may
be added its being a convenient deposit, and a place of more
safety with a *small* garrison (on Acct of its Inhabitants) than any
other, has restrained my mentioning of it before. But in case of
a movement towards Sandusky, one there does, in that design,
become important.

If, upon more mature consideration of the ideas submitted by
Genl Wayne, I should find cause to change the sentiments herein
expressed the alterations shall be communicated in my next—if
not, you will consider what I have here said as the *substance* of my
opinion thereupon.[2]

Before the (grain) forage is purchased *above* for the Posts *below,*
it ought to be ascertained from whence (including the transportation to Fort Washington) it can be had cheapest. I have understood, as well from others (who are just from that Country)
as from the letter of Mr Belli, that the Crops of Grain in Kentucky are astonishingly great. It would have an odd appearance
therefore, & I dare say would give much dissatisfaction to the
people of that State, to have the forage carried down the River
from the Neighbd of Pittsburgh unless it is obtained on *better*
terms than they will supply it.[3]

A caution both to Genl Wayne (& through him to Genl Wilkinson) ought to be given, to guard *effectually*, the Hay at the Outposts. Unless this is done, the Indians will, most assuredly, set fire to it before the Spring. & to do it without having the stacks in the range of their defences, or as a cover to the approaches of the enemy, is no easy matter. I am Sir Yr Very Hble Servt

Go: W——n

If the enclosed represents a fact the case merits attention.[4]

ADfS, DLC:GW; LB, DLC:GW; copy, PHi: Wayne Papers. The mutilated text in angle brackets is provided from the letter-book copy.

1. For Anthony Wayne's plan and Knox's critique of it, see Wayne to Knox, 24 Aug., and Knox to Wayne, 1 Sept., both enclosed in Knox to GW, 1 Sept. 1792.

2. GW did not comment further on Wayne's ideas in his next letter to Knox on 16 Sept. 1792.

3. Deputy quartermaster general John Belli reported on 12 July 1792 to Knox the various problems in providing forage and other supplies to the army in the Northwest Territory (see GW to Knox, 22 Aug., n.5).

4. The enclosure has not been identified.

From Thomas Marshall

Sir   Septr 7th 1792

I take the liberty of writing by Capt. Obannon and in a few words mean to give you the names and rank of the Gentlemen who are most likely to Influence government & give a tone to the politics of this State.[1] Isaac Shelby Esqr. Governor. Harry Innes Esqr. (present Judge of the federal Court) first Judge of the high Court of appeals. John Brown Esqr. Senator to Congress. James Brown Esqr. Secretary. George Nicholas Esqr. Attorney General for that and almost every post of power or proffit in the state fill'd by their friends and adherants. From this you may judge of my situation who have formerly offended some of them & can never make concessions without violating my own conscience. It is true I want nothing which they have to bestow; yet they can by missrepresentation vex me, by rendering me obnoxious to the people.

Colo. Muter, who can never be forgiven for suffering the publication of Mr Browns letter, has pretty severely felt the rod of power. He has been by the choice of the Assembly of Virginia, for seven years past first judge of the supreme Court of the District of Kentucky, with a Salary of £300 pr Annum & is without any fault alleged against him turned down to the Court of Oyer & terminer where the Salary it is thought will be very trifling—for the Salary of the judges are not yet fixed.[2]

I have recieved a letter from Colo. Richard C. Anderson requesting my recommendation of him to fill the office of Commissioner of loans if such an office should be necessary in this State. To recommend a Gentleman to fill any office is a liberty I have never yet taken, nor do I think my self by any means authorised to do so, but as I have had a long acquantance with Colo. Anderson both in the Army & since it was discharged, & have the highest opinion of his merit as an officer & a Gentleman, I hope you will pardon me for being the means of his wishes having come to your knowledge.[3] I have the honor to be with the most cordial wishes for a long continuance of your health & prosperity Sir Your most obedient humble Servant

T. Marshall

ALS, DLC:GW.

Thomas Marshall, father of the future Supreme Court chief justice John Marshall, moved from Fauquier County, Va., to Kentucky in 1783. In March 1792 GW appointed him inspector of the seventh survey in Virginia, which comprised the Kentucky district (see GW to the U.S. Senate, 6 Mar. 1792). Marshall continued in this position after Kentucky became the fifteenth state on 1 June 1792.

1. Capt. John Obannon (O'Bannon; d. 1813) was deputy surveyor for Virginia's bounty lands located northwest of the Ohio River under the supervision of Richard Clough Anderson (see note 3). During the winter and spring of 1788, Obannon surveyed land purchased in the region by GW. A resident and militia officer of Fauquier County, Va., during the Revolutionary War, Obannon had moved to Kentucky about 1784, eventually settling in Woodford County (see Randall, "Washington's Ohio Lands," 305–6; Collins, *History of Kentucky*, 2:766).

2. Isaac Shelby (1750–1826) surveyed lands in Kentucky for the Transylvania Company and the military during the Revolutionary War, and he settled there after the war. In January 1791 Congress appointed Shelby to the Board of War for the District of Kentucky, which was responsible for the defense of the frontier and the management of punitive expeditions against hostile Indians. An active proponent of Kentucky's independence from Virginia, he was elected the state's first governor in May 1792. Under Shelby's leadership Kentucky supported General Wayne's military activities in the Northwest Territory.

Harry Innes, John Brown, George Nicholas, and George Muter were all Virginia natives, and all except Innes were Revolutionary War veterans. All four men moved to the Kentucky district shortly after the war. Early advocates of Kentucky's independence, they became prominent political leaders in the district and then in the new state. GW appointed Innes the U.S. district judge for

Kentucky in 1789, and Innes served in that office until his death. Brown represented the Kentucky district of Virginia in the U.S. House of Representatives in 1789, and, when Kentucky became a state in 1792, he was elected a U.S. senator, continuing in that office until 1805. Nicholas helped draft Kentucky's first constitution, and he became the state's first attorney general. Muter was appointed a district judge for Kentucky in 1785 and then to the Kentucky appellate court in 1792, serving until 1806. For background on Thomas Marshall's dispute with these men, see his letter to GW of 11 Sept. 1790, and notes.

3. Richard Clough Anderson, Sr. (1750–1826), a Virginia native and Revolutionary War veteran, was appointed the principal surveyor for Virginia's bounty lands in July 1784. He and his deputies were responsible for surveying the lands that Virginia set aside for its Continental army veterans between the Green and Cumberland rivers in Kentucky and between the Scioto and Little Miami rivers in Ohio. Settling near Louisville, Ky., Anderson opened his surveying office on 20 July 1784, and he served in the Kentucky legislature for several years. He did not receive the desired federal appointment (see Collins, *History of Kentucky*, 2:370, 375–76).

From John V. Weylie

Honoured Sir,   Alex[andri]a [Va.] Sept. 7th 1792
    Notwithstanding the inestimable Favour you have conferred upon me in paying for my Education, yet I have made bold (though with great reluctance) to beg another particular Kindness.[1]

Through your unexampled Bounty, I have made a considerable Progress in the Latin Tongue, and at the Return of the Revd Mr McWhir from Georgia, I am to begin Greek.[2] My Father bought several Latin Authors for me, and others I borrowed. But being at present unable to purchase me what Greek Books I shall want, and they being more scarse than the Latin, my only Resource is in your well known Generosity. Without your kind Interposition and Assistance, I am afraid my Education will be rendered altogether imperfect. Had I continued to learn English, I might by this time, have made myself perfect Master of my Mother Tongue. But having exchanged that for the Study of the Classics, and being, very much charmed with it, I am very loath to forsake so very agreeable a Study; as a thirsty Traveller having found a cool, refreshing Brook in his way, is very unwilling to leave it till he perfectly allayst his Thirst. Whether the Greek Language may please me as much as the Latin, is a matter I am as yet uncertain of; however I am very desirous to try. I entreat you Sir, as your unparalled Liberality has conducted me thus far, not to forsake me at the very moment I am upon the point of obtaining my Desires. I might here enlarge upon my manifold Obligations to you, but as merit is alway disgusted at its own Praises, I choose to be silent. But depend upon (illustrious Benefactor) you have my most ardent and sincere wishes for your temporal and eternal Welfare.

The principal Books necessary for learning the Greek Language are the five following, Moor's Greek Grammar, Testament, Lucian's Dialogues, Homer's Iliad and a Lexicon. Though they are but few, yet my Father's Circumstances incapacitate him to procure them for me. I therefore, hope, noble Sir, you will assist me, and thus complete the Benefits already heaped upon Your Excellency's most devoted Humble Srt[3]

John V. Weylie

ALS, DLC:GW.

1. For information about GW's previous financial support of Weylie, see Weylie to GW, 11 Mar. 1789, and source note.

2. William McWhir (1759–1851), a Presbyterian minister who had emigrated from Ireland in 1783, was headmaster of the Alexandria Academy and a reputed scholar of Greek and Latin. He moved to Sunbury, Ga., in 1793 to accept the principalship of the Sunbury Academy.

3. Because GW responded positively to his request for financial aid, Weylie sent an enthusiastic letter of thanks on 8 Sept.: "It is with great pleasure that I reflect on the many advantages, which all America recieves from you. To Your valour and prudence she owes her liberty and the peaceful enjoyment of her civil and religious rites. And if she is so infinitely indebted to you for these blessings, how much rather are those who not only enjoy them, but also are educated by Your extraordinary Bounty. But I am lost in admiration of you Liberality to myself. After giving me a considerable knowledge of the English Language, you went so far as to have me instructed in Latin. And then to crown all your Favours, and give me a complete Education, you have even offered to purchase me Books to learn the Greek language. It is utterly impossible for me to repay or enumerate my obligations to you" (DLC:GW).

From Alexander Hamilton

Sir,   Treasury Departmt 8th Septr 1792.

I have to acknowledge the honor of your Letter of the 31st of August.

Letters from the Supervisor of North Carolina confirm the

representation contained in the letter from the Inspector of the 5th Survey to you.[1] My letter which accompanies this suggests the measure which, on mature reflection, has appeared most proper to be taken upon the whole subject of the opposition to the Law.[2] If the idea is approved by you, I believe it will be adviseable to transmit a copy of the Proclamation to the Governor of each of the States of South Carolina North Carolina & Pennsylvania, calling their attention in a proper manner to the state of affairs within their respective Governments.[3]

I am taking arrangements to cary into execution the payment of the Debt due to foreign officers, agreeably to the authorisation in the close of your Letter. With the highest respect and the truest attachment, I have the honor to be &c.

Alex. Hamilton

LB, DLC:GW.

1. The letters from supervisor William Polk to Hamilton have not been identified. William Polk (1758–1834), a North Carolina native and Revolutionary War veteran, served several terms in the North Carolina house of commons after the war. GW appointed him the supervisor of the North Carolina district in March 1791 (see GW to the U.S. Senate, 4 Mar. 1791), and Polk remained in that office until 1808. For background about opposition to the excise tax on whiskey, see "Report on the Difficulties in the Execution of the Act Laying Duties on Distilled Spirits," presented by Hamilton to Congress on 6 Mar. 1791, in Syrett, *Hamilton Papers*, 11:77–106. For background on the problems that Joseph McDowell, Jr., encountered as inspector of the fifth survey in North Carolina, see GW to Hamilton, 31 Aug. 1792, and note 2.

2. For the accompanying letter, see Hamilton to GW, 9 Sept. 1792 (second letter).

3. On 15 Sept. 1792 GW issued a proclamation in which he urged compliance with the federal excise tax on distilled spirits. GW enclosed a copy of this proclamation in his circular letter of 29 Sept. to the governors of North Carolina, Pennsylvania, and South Carolina.

From Henry Knox

My dear sir   Philadelphia Septr 8 1792

I have the pleasure to acknowledge Your favor of the 3d instant. It really gives me great pain to learn the deplorable situation of your amiable Nephew. Although the tax of death be inevitable, so premature a demand, while it afflicts, perplexes and confounds us as to the arrangement upon this subject by the great author of our natures.

Poor Mrs Smith, paid this debt, to the inexpressible anguish of her friends. She died last night.

I will have prepared, such Communications as shall occur to me relatively to the war department and also upon other general subjects.[1]

Colonel Hamilton will not have the leisure he promised himself in order to visit Mount Vernon. and it would also be inconvenient for me to be absent, as I experien[c]ed in my jaunt to New York. which however I shall be constrained again to revisit in the course of this month, for three days. But I shall endevor to do it without prejudice to my public duty.

I have called twice upon the french Minister in order to sound him indirectly on his intention of paying you his respects at Mount Vernon, but he was not at home. I will as early as possible ascertain it and communicate the result—Mr Hammond has not yet returned from his eastern excursion, nor can I learn that he is soon expected.[2] With sincere respects to Mrs Washington I am my dear Sir with the highest attachment Your most Obedient Servant

H. Knox

P.S. poor france seems destined to drink deeply of the Cup of Misery. The King, and M. Fayette seem to play the parts of heroes—and probably the blood of both of them will seal their principles.[3]

ALS, DLC:GW. GW wrote "Private" on the docket.

1. See Knox's second letter to GW of this date for Knox's official communications.

2. Knox had left Philadelphia on 18 Aug. to visit New York City and returned on 25 Aug. (see Knox to GW, 17 and 26 August). For background on the proposed visits to Mount Vernon by Hamilton and Knox, see GW's letter to Hamilton, 26 Aug., and to Knox, 3 Sept. (second letter). Although French minister Jean-Baptiste Ternant did not visit Mount Vernon at this time, the English minister George Hammond arrived for a short visit on 24 Sept. (see GW to Knox, 3 Sept. 1792 [second letter], and note 3).

3. For a summary of recent events in France, including the misfortunes of Louis XVI and Lafayette, see Gouverneur Morris to GW, 23 Oct. 1792, source note and notes 1 and 3.

From Henry Knox

Sir,   War department September 8th 1792
I have the honor respectfully to acknowledge the receipt of your favor of the 3rd instant.

Upon examination it appears that no stores have been unreasonably detained by the Waggoners upon the road, as the receipts for all at Pittsburg which could have arrived have been received by Mr Hodgdon.[1]

I have the honor to submit enclosed the copy of General Wayne's letter of the 31st of August[2] and my answer thereto.[3]

I also enclose the copy of Captain Brant's letter of the 26th of July and of the Chiefs of the Six Nations dated at Buffaloe Creek the first of August.[4]

These two letters pretty amply confirm the idea of a new boundary line being desired by the English. The opinions of Brant and the Chiefs may be regarded as the opinion of the British—and not as the opinion of the Wyandots and Delawares.

The time which Brant intimates as necessary, is of great importance to us in order to complete the Legion—But it is my serious apprehension that the Indians will be influenced to demand a boundary which we cannot honorably grant, and probably the idea of it's being guaranteed by the British will be brought forward.[5]

I also submit to your consideration a letter of Governor Mifflin to the County Lieutenant of Allegany. and in order that you may have the subject fully before you, I transmit the correspondence between the Governor and me to which he alludes.

I shall lay these papers before the Attorney General and request his opinion whether the Conduct of the Governor in calling out the Militia without any previous communication thereof to the Executive of the United States be consistent with the Constitution? and I shall submit to you the result[6]—I have the honor to be with the highest respect Your most obedt servant
                                    H. Knox secy of war

P.S. Since writing the above I have received a letter from Brigadier General Wilkinson dated 6. Ultimo, a copy of which I have the honor to inclose.[7]

LS, DLC:GW; LB: DLC:GW.

1. For Anthony Wayne's earlier complaint about delays in the shipment of military supplies to Pittsburgh, see Knox to GW, 26 Aug. 1792, n.2.

2. On 31 Aug., Wayne wrote Knox from Pittsburgh: "I have the honor to enclose a copy of Captain Haskells letter to me of the 21st instant, in addition to which Captain William Mills (brother to our Captain John Mills) by whom the letter came, says that in conversation with Mr Hewill (who is a Militia Officer) he mentioned—'that whilst he was with the Indians, they expressed an anxiety for a *hostile* interview, and that nothing prevented them from committing depredations, but a full conviction of our advance into their Country. that they effect to hold us in the utmost contempt, for offering to treat of peace with a people, who neither *want* or *wish* for it.' be that as it may, I am decidedly of opinion that we ought immediately to establish our Magazines of Forage and provision, and have therefore, *privately,* directed the Quarter Master General, to contract for *Fifty thousand* bushels of Grain chiefly Indian Corn, and *five hundred tons* of hay.

"At present nothing can be done by Water—the Ohio has never been so low in the memory of the oldest inhabitants. the copy of a letter from Captain Haskell to the Quarter Master General will give you some idea of it—at the time the boats went from this place, there was a small fresh in the Monongahela, but it was evaporated before it reached Marietta.

"The Clothing for the first Regiment has generally arrived, as well as that for the rifle Corps, except shoes, and blankets, and part for the second; not a single moment shall be lost in forwarding it, when the state of the water will admit, in order to stop the mouths of *Haskell* & others.

"I enclose you a Copy of Governor Mifflins letter to the Lieutenant of Alleghany County. I shall forbear to comment upon it. I however informed Colonel [John] Nevill[e] that at present I did not think myself justifiable in calling out any Militia, or in assenting to the measure. that when there was a necessity I would do it with a full reliance upon their turning out with alacrity.

"We are in want of many Articles in the Hospital department, of which the enclosed letter and invoice from Dr [John Francis] Carmichael will inform you. the quantum is left to your Judgment.

"By this mornings report you will see the Number and Condition of our force at this post—the men in Confinement have all been tried by a General Court Martial, some are condemned to Death, some to Corporal punishment, others are acquitted or ordered to do the drudgery of the Camp, for a given time.

"The whole of the sentences will take place tomorrow and next day—I trust it will break the neck of desertion—You'l please to observe the principal part of those Criminals were lately brought here by the several detachments as prisoners.

"Be pleased to present my best compliments to Major Stagg, and inform him, that I have been honored with his letter of the 25th instant, with Invoices of Clothing &c. forwarded between the 20th and 23d of this month, And a duplicate of yours of the 17th instant" (DLC:GW).

In the enclosed letter to Wayne of 21 Aug., Jonathan Haskell, who currently commanded a small garrison protecting the residents of Marietta, Ohio, recounted the testimony of Moses Hewill, who had just arrived at Marietta after escaping from a band of Shawnee Indians who had captured him on 10 July near the mouth of the Little Kanawha River (DLC:GW). Haskell also wrote Quartermaster General James O'Hara on 21 August. In that letter, according to O'Hara's subsequent letter to Wayne on 30 Aug., Haskell complained about "the disagreeable situation the Troops at that Post and Gallipolis are in for 'want of clothing' and other necessaries" (see Darlington, *Fort Pitt,* 251). For Gov. Thomas Mifflin's letter to Presley Neville, the lieutenant of Allegheny County, Pa., and the son of John Neville, see note 6.

3. Knox replied to Wayne from Philadelphia on 7 Sept.: "I have the honor to acknowledge the receipt of your letter, with its enclosures of the 31st Ultimo.

"Whatever may be the result of the pacific overtures, or however individuals of the frontiers, or among the Indians may regard the said overtures, still the Government of the United States were constrained to make them by a respect to the opinion of probably the great majority of the Citizens of the United States—The offers being made, we must wait for the issue.

"The tranquillity of the frontiers, which will probably continue throughout the autumn, may be fairly estimated as a consequence of the Indians knowing our desires for peace.

"By the enclosed letters from Captain Brant of the 26th of July, and the Chiefs of the six Nations of the first of August; which I received yesterday, you will observe the strong impressions relatively to a new boundary—It is questionable with me, whether the Indians received this idea from the hostile Indians or from another quarter.

"The Wyandots and Delawares, who are the tribes particularly affected by the boundaries established by the treaties of Fort McIntosh in 1786 and Fort Harmar in 1789, have never complained of the said treaties, although there were three years difference between the first and second treaty. Brant was opposed to the latter treaty being unwilling to repair to Fort Harmar, and requiring it to be held at the Forks of the Muskingum—Governor St Clair refused this request, as the forks of the Muskingum had been first fixed upon, and he sent a party there with provisions and to erect the necessary buildings—As this party was fired upon and obliged to quit the spot, the Governor declined kindling the fire again at that place—Brant is therefore personally interested to get the line altered.

"I confess, in confidence, my apprehensions that the Indians will require more than we can grant consistently with any sort of dignity, and that therefore we ought to strain every nerve in making all sorts of preparation—of recruits—of discipline—and of supplies to establish such posts as shall effectually accomplish our objects of bridling and punishing the refractory tribes.

"Our Recruits may now be estimated at two thousand, exclusive of deserters—If that number with the addition of two, three or at most five hundred more arrive at Pittsburg in the course of the autumn, it will be all which may be expected—But in the above I mean to include those companies ordered to the mouth of the Kenhawa and which have not yet, nor will they arrive there much before the 15th or 20th of the present Month.

"Whether Congress will order an additional pay as an inducement to enlist, will depend upon circumstances, which cannot be estimated at this moment— On this point perhaps much reliance ought not to be placed.

"The discipline of the troops *for the nature of the service* will depend on you— I persuade myself entire confidence may be entertained, that this object will be perfectly accomplished.

"All the supplies to be transported from this place have been forwarded— and you will please to observe by the enclosed statement that *all* have arrived that could reasonably be expected—Some mistakes have been committed by Major [Isaac] Craig in reporting the articles deficient.

"The magazine of Medicines and instruments required by Doctor Carmichael shall be prepared and forwarded immediately—You will observe, on this head, that the supplies at Fort Washington are abundant, as will be perceived by your having recourse to the lists you have in your possession.

"Your providing ample magazines of forage and provisions were approved in my last of the first instant, a copy of which is herein enclosed.

"The quantity you mention of Fifty thousand bushels of Corn would appear sufficient—there will be no difficulty in obtaining that quantity after the harvest in Kentucky—but this is to include the original quantity of twenty thousand bushels.

"I flatter myself you will in all cases enjoin a proper œconomy, and particularly not suffer a greater number of horses in the Quarter Masters department, than the real demands of the service shall require; and also that you will not suffer any Officers of the Legion to keep horses, who shall not be allowed by law, forage.

"Your Cavalry at best will be expensive, and in order to be perfectly efficient at all times, a due œconomy of forage should be observed.

"Colonel [Samuel] Griffin has given me the enclosed papers relative to Thomas Gathright who has enlisted in Captain Ballard Smiths company—This young Gentleman is extremely well connected, and has a great passion for the army—His friends request he may be a serjeant in the first instance, and afterwards promoted, if he shall deserve the same—I state the circumstances and send the documents, requesting you to state his conduct if he should really merit promotion.

"The letter of Governor Mifflin to the Allegany County Lieutenant is received and the subject will be hereafter duly noticed to you—the date of the said letter is not mentioned pray inform me of it.

"Your information to Colonel Nevil was certainly just, for it would be a waste of the Money of the United States to call out Militia for the defence of the frontiers, while the public have such a solid force there—But then some of your troops ought to assume the stations proper for the protection of the exposed Counties.

"I find it will be in vain to depend upon any of the detachments for the seasonable protection of the money for the payment of the troops up to the first of August—I shall therefore send it from here under the best security which can be devised and I request you would detach a prudent Officer and twenty dragoons so as to meet it at Bedford on or about the twentieth instant.

"This intimation ought to be a profound secret otherwise bad minded people might attempt to intercept so large a sum.

"I hope you have ordered Mr [Caleb] Swan up to Head Quarters—the payments ought to be regularly made in order to prevent confusion—in case of his non arrival, the person who shall have charge of the Money will be appointed to make the payments" (DLC:GW).

For the enclosed letters from Joseph Brant and the chiefs of the Six Nations, see note 4.

4. Knox and GW hoped that diplomatic intervention by the Mohawk leader Joseph Brant and other Iroquois chiefs, as well as by Stockbridge chief Hendrick Aupaumut, would produce a peaceful settlement of differences between the United States and the Indians in the Northwest Territory. Brant wrote Knox from Niagara, N.Y., on 26 July 1792: "Since my arrival here I am sorry to have to say that intelligence respecting Major Truemans being killed (by an Indian boy who met with him a hunting) has arrived. this will induce you to recollect what passed between us, relative to messages being sent. the rout by Presque Isle I again recommend as the most eligible, from thence keeping along the lake to the Miamis at which place the Chiefs are aptest to be met with, and when once there they are safe, sending such numbers of messages rather makes the Indians suspicious of your intentions, and by any other rout they are much more liable to meet with hunters—There are now great numbers of Indians collected, and from all their Councils seem determined upon a new boundary line—in short they are sensible that what has hitherto been done (which I fully explained to you) was unfair, and I am of opinion peace will not easily be established without your relinquishing part of your Claim. the purchases were all made from Men who had no right to sell, and who are now to be thanked for the present difficulties. The Senecas and seven nations of Canada are now waiting at Ft Erie for a passage for Detroit on their way to the Miamis. I shall be able to go up by the next trip of the Vessel, my intention and wish is still for the accomplishing of Peace, tis a business will require time, things too rashly or hastily agreed upon seldom have the effect of those seriously and cooly reflected on, knowing the foundation to be just, and the benefits that will arise therefrom affords a greater space for forwarding the business" (DLC:GW).

Knox also enclosed a copy of a letter written "In behalf of the Six Nations and the Seven Nations of Canada" by Farmer's Brother, Fish Carrier, Old Smoke, and Clear Sky to Indian superintendent Israel Chapin, Sr., on 1 Aug. 1792: "Since we have returned home we are informed for a Certainty that the disturbance to the Westward between our Brethren and your people is entirely owing to your Detaining the Lands as we said in Philadelphia, which you made a purchase of and this prevents any accomodation. . . . We are now according to our promise on the eve of our departure to meet our Western Brethren in Council where we will expect an answer which we hope will be so favorable as to enable us to bring about that peace which so desirable to all parties" (DLC:GW).

5. On 21 Jan. 1785 representatives from the Wyandot, Delaware, Ottawa, and Chippewa nations concluded the Fort McIntosh treaty with the United States, and on 9 Jan. 1789 at Fort Harmar, the United States signed two additional treaties: one with the Wyandot, Delaware, Ottawa, Chippewa, Potawatomi, and Sac nations and the other with the Six Nations (see Kappler, *Indian Treaties*, 2:6–8, 18–25). Many Indian leaders opposed the extensive land cessions contained in these treaties and sought to reestablish the Ohio River as the boundary with the United States (see Downes, *Council Fires*, 283–311).

6. General Wayne, in his letter to Knox of 31 Aug. (see note 2), enclosed an undated copy of Pennsylvania governor Thomas Mifflin's letter from Philadelphia, written in late July or August 1792, to Presley Neville, the lieutenant of Allegheny County. Mifflin, who was concerned about the possibility of Indian attacks on the state's western borders, wrote, "Though I think that there is a favorable prospect of Peace, and that the measures proposed by the Federal Government are calculated to protect the Frontiers, yet I am not disposed to omit any precautions," and he issued instructions to Neville "and to the other Lieutenants of Westmoreland, Washington and Fayette, for making a draft from the Militia of your respective counties." Mifflin also sent Neville copies of his correspondence with Knox on the subject of federal protection for the Pennsylvania frontiers (DLC:GW).

Knox wrote Mifflin on 11 July from Philadelphia "that the Troops of the United States will soon arrive on the frontiers of this State in considerable numbers, and that a sufficient proportion thereof will remain there until the effect of certain pacific overtures to the Indians shall be known.

"In this state of things, and as the time for which the state troops were raised, is drawing to a close, I beg leave to know whether it would be compatible with the views and arrangements of your Excellency to permit the Continental Officers recruiting in this State to endeavour to enlist such noncommissioned and privates of the said Companies as shall be inclined thereto" (DLC:GW).

Mifflin replied from Philadelphia on 13 July: "From the present situation of our frontiers, and being unacquainted with the Plans of the Federal Government for their defence, I regret, that, . . . I cannot, consistently with the ideas, which I entertain of the trust reposed in me, acquiesce in the proposition to permit the Continental Officers to endeavour, at this period, to enlist the noncommissioned Officers and privates of the three Companies raised by Pennsylvania" (DLC:GW).

Mifflin wrote Knox again from Philadelphia on 18 July: "As the period for which the three Pennsylvania Companies were raised, will expire on the 1st of September next, and as it will be incumbent on me to pursue such farther measures for the protection and defence of the Citizens on our frontiers, as their situation shall at that time require, I am desirous of being informed, whether any and what, arrangements are made by the Federal government, that may eventually supersede the necessity of the interference of the State, In the absence of the President therefore, I address myself to you; and request such satisfaction as you may be able to give in the following points:

"1st. Whether any, and what force, will be permanently stationed on the frontiers of Pennsylvania.

"2d. Whether it is consistent with the powers and plans of the Executive of the Federal government, to include the three Pennsylvania companies in the military establishment of the Union, at the expiration of their engagement with the State, and to continue them at their present Stations" (DLC:GW).

Knox replied to Mifflin that same day from Philadelphia: "in answer to the first query therein contained I take the occasion to state.

"That the general government have sent certain messages of a pacific nature to the hostile Indians, the event of which is not yet known.

"That the enlisting of the troops authorized by Law, together with the length of time required to know the determination of the indians or the propositions made to them will probably prevent any decisive offensive operations for the present season.

"That therefore the troops not necessary for the Garrisons will for the present be assembled in two encampments of discipline, the one on the upper parts of the Ohio in Pennsylvania, and the other at or in the vicinity of Fort Washington.

"That besides the encampment at the upper parts of the Ohio, which it is presumed will be an ample protection to those parts during its continuance—there will be an adequate Garrison at Fort Franklin which will have the effect to cover Westmoreland County, and there will also be a proper garrison at Pittsburg.

"To the second Question, I answer, That the Executive of the United States having made the appointments for the military establishment, has not any authority to add thereto, by including the temporary Companies of Pennsylvania, as Companies, on the expiration of their engagements.

"If any further explanations in my power either Written or Verbal should be necessary to enable you to take your ultimate measures relatively to the three Companies, they shall be imparted by me" (DLC:GW).

7. James Wilkinson's brief letter to Knox of 6 Aug. from Fort Hamilton reported that "the enemy are quiet probably collecting for their Green Corn dance" (DLC:GW).

From Alexander Hamilton

Sir   Philadelphia September 9 1792.
  I have the pleasure of your private letter of the 26th of August.
  The feelings and views which are manifested in that letter are such as I expected would exist. And I most sincerely regret the cause of the uneasy sensations you experience. It is my most anxious wish, as far as may depend upon me, to smooth the path of your administration, and to render it prosperous and happy. And if any prospect shall open of healing or terminating the differences which exist, I shall most chearfully embrace it; though I consider myself as the deeply injured party. The recommendation of such a spirit is worthy of the moderation and wisdom

which dictated it; and if your endeavours should prove unsuccessful, I do not hesitate to say that in my opinion the period is
not remote when the public good will require *substitutes* for the
differing members of your administration. The continuance of a division there must destroy the energy of Government, which will
be little enough with the strictest Union—On my part there will
be a most chearful acquiescence in such a result.[1]

I trust, Sir, that the greatest frankness has always marked and
will always mark every step of my conduct towards you. In this
disposition, I cannot conceal from you that I have had some in-
strumentality of late in the retaliations which have fallen upon
certain public characters and that I find myself placed in a situation not to be able to recede *for the present.*[2]

I considered myself as compelled to this conduct by reasons
public as well as personal of the most cogent nature—I *know* that
I have been an object of uniform opposition from Mr Jefferson,
from the first moment of his coming to the City of New York to
enter upon his present office—I *know,* from the most authentic
sources, that I have been the present subject of the most unkind
whispers and insinuation, from the same quarter—I have long
seen a formed party in the Legislature, under his auspices, bent
upon my subversion—I cannot doubt, from the evidence I possess, that the National Gazette was instituted by him for political
purposes and that one leading object of it has been to render me
and all the measures connected with my department as odious
as possible.

Nevertheless I can truly say, that, except explanations to confidential friends, I never directly or indirectly retaliated or countenanced retaliation till very lately—I can even assure you, that
I was instrumental in preventing a very severe and systematic attack upon Mr Jefferson, by an association of two or three individuals, in consequence of the persecution, which he brought
upon the Vice President, by his indiscreet and light letter to the
Printer, transmitting *Paine's* pamphlet.[3]

As long as I saw no danger to the Government, from the
machinations which were going on, I resolved to be a silent sufferer of the injuries which were done me—I determined to
avoid giving occasion to any thing which could manifest to the
world dissentions among the principal characters of the government; a thing which can never happen without weakening its
hands, and in some degree throwing a stigma upon it.

But when I no longer doubted, that there was a formed party deliberately bent upon the subversion of measures, which in its consequences would subvert the Government—when I saw, that the undoing of the funding system in particular (which, whatever may be the original merits of that system, would prostrate the credit and the honor of the Nation, and bring the Government into contempt with that description of Men, who are in every society the only firm supporters of government)—was an avowed object of the party; and that all possible pains were taking to produce that effect by rendering it odious to the body of the people—I considered it as a duty, to endeavour to resist the torrent, and as an essential mean to this end, to draw aside the veil from the principal Actors. To thi⟨s⟩ strong impulse, to this decided conviction, I have yielded—And I think events will prove that I have judged rightly.

Nevertheless I pledge my honor to you Sir, that if you shall hereafter form a plan to reunite the members of your administration, upon some steady principle of cooperation, I will faithfully concur in executing it during my continuance in office. And I will not directly or indirectly say or do a thing, that shall endanger a feud.

I have had it very much at heart to make an excursion to Mount Vernon, by way of the Fœderal City in the course of this Month—and have been more than once on the point of asking your permission for it. But I now despair of being able to effect it. I am nevertheless equally obliged by your kind invitation.[4]

The subject mentioned in the Postcript of your letter shall with great pleasure be carefully attended to[5]—With the most faithful and affectionate attachment I have the honor to remain Sir Your most Obed. & humble servant

A. Hamilton

P.S. I had written you two letters on public business, one of which will go with this; but the other will be witheld, in consequence of a slight indisposition of the Attorney General, to be sent by express—sometime in the course of tomorrow.[6]

ALS, DLC: GW.

1. Despite the growing animosity and political differences among members of GW's cabinet, particularly between Hamilton and Thomas Jefferson, no one resigned from the cabinet until GW's second administration. Jefferson, the first to leave, sent his letter of resignation to GW on 31 Dec. 1793. Hamilton did not submit his resignation until 31 Jan. 1795.

2. In 1792 the *Gazette of the United States* (Philadelphia) published several articles by Hamilton in which he criticized the partisanship of the *National Gazette* (Philadelphia), its editor Philip Freneau, and Freneau's sponsor Thomas Jefferson. Hamilton's writings appeared on 25, 28 July and 11 Aug. under the pseudonym of "T.L." and on 4, 11, and 18 Aug. under "An American." Despite GW's concerns, Hamilton's political diatribes continued, appearing on 11 Sept. under "Amicus," on 15, 19, 29 Sept., 17 Oct., 24 Nov., and 22 Dec. under "Catullus," and on 24 Oct. under "Metellus" (see Syrett, *Hamilton Papers*, 12:107, 123–25, 157–64, 188–94, 224, 354–56, 379–85, 393–401, 498–506, 578–87, 613–17, 13:229–31, 348–57). For Jefferson's defense of his behavior and for information about the newspaper war conducted by his supporters, see Jefferson to GW, 17 Oct., and notes.

3. For background on the dispute between Jefferson and John Adams, which started after publication of an endorsement Jefferson wrote in 1791 for the American publication of Thomas Paine's *Rights of Man*, see Jefferson to GW, 8 May 1791, and notes 1 and 2.

4. For the invitation to visit Mount Vernon, see GW to Hamilton, 26 Aug. 1792.

5. For Hamilton's draft of 15–31 Oct. of an address to be presented by GW at the opening of the next session of Congress, see Syrett, *Hamilton Papers*, 12:558–66. For the final version, see GW's Address to the U.S. Senate and the House of Representatives, 6 Nov. 1792.

6. The enclosure was Hamilton's letter to GW of 8 Sept. 1792. Hamilton's other letter, also dated 9 Sept., was sent with his letter to GW of 11 Sept. 1792. Hamilton was waiting for Edmund Randolph's opinion on Hamilton's draft of a proclamation concerning recent opposition to the whiskey excise tax (see Randolph to Hamilton, 8 Sept. 1792, in Syrett, *Hamilton Papers*, 12:336–40; for the final decree, see GW's Proclamation, 15 Sept. 1792).

From Alexander Hamilton

Sir,   Treasury Departmt Septr 9th 1792.

I had the honor of writing to you by the post of Monday last, and then transmitted Sundry papers respecting a Meeting at Pittsburg on the 21st of August, and other proceedings of a disorderly nature, in opposition to the Laws laying a duty on distilled spirits; and I added my opinion, that it was adviseable for the Government to take measures for suppressing these disorders, & enforcing the laws with vigour & decision.[1]

The result of further & mature deliberation is, that it will be expedient for the President to issue a Proclamation, adverting in general terms to the irregular proceedings, which have taken place, warning all persons to desist from similar proceedings & manifesting an intention to put the Laws in force against Offenders.

The inducements to this measure are;

1st. That it is a usual course in like cases; and seems, all circumstances considered, requisite to the justification of the Executive Department. It is now more than fourteen months since the duty in question began to operate. In the four Western Counties of Pennsylvania and in a great part of North Carolina it has never been in any degree submitted to. And the late Meeting at Pittsburg is in substance a repetition of what happened last year in the same scene. The disorders in that quarter acquire additional consequence from their being acted in the State which is the immediate Seat of the Government. Hence the occasion appears to be sufficiently serious & of sufficient importance to call for such a proceedure.

II. An accommodating and temporising conduct having been hitherto pursued, a Proclamation seems to be the natural prelude to a different course of conduct.

III. There is considerable danger, that before measures can be matured for making a public impression by the prosecution of offenders, the spirit of opposition may extend & break out in other quarters; and by it's extension become much more difficult to be over come. There is reason to hope that a Proclamation will arrest it, and give time for more effectual measures.

IV. It may even prevent the necessity of ulterior coertion. The character of the President will naturally induce a conclusion that he means to treat the matter seriously. This idea will be impressive on the most refractory—it will restrain the timid & wavering, and it will encourage the well disposed. The appearance of the President in the business will awaken the attention of a great number of persons of the last description to the evil tendency of the conduct reprehended, who have not yet viewed it with due seriousness. And from the cooperation of these circumstances, good may reasonably be expected.

In either view therefore, of the propriety of conduct, or the effects to be hoped for, the measure seems to be an adviseable one. I beg leave to add that, in my judgment, it is not only adviseable, but necessary.[2]

Besides the state of things in the Western parts of North Carolina which is known to you, a letter has just been received from the Supervisor of South Carolina, mentioning that a spirit of discontent and opposition had been revived in two of the Counties of that State bordering on North Carolina, in which it had been before apparently suppressed. This shews the necessity of some immediate step of a general aspect; while things are preparing, if unhappily it should become necessary, to act with decision in the Western Counties of Pennsylvania, where the Government, from several obvious considerations will be left in condition to do it. Decision successfully exerted in one place will, it is presumeable, be efficacious every where.[3]

The Secretary at War and the Attorney General agree with me in opinion on the expediency of a Proclamation. The draft of one now submitted has been framed in concert with the latter; except as to one or two particulars which are noted in the margin of the *rough* draft in my hand writing, herewith also transmitted. In respect to these, the objections of that Gentleman did not appear to me founded, and would, I think, unnecessarily diminish the force of the instrument.[4] With the highest respect and the truest attachment, I have the honor to be &c.

Alexr Hamilton

LB, DLC: GW. This letter was sent with Hamilton's letter to GW of 11 Sept. (see Hamilton to GW, 9 Sept. [first letter], and note 6).

1. Hamilton is referring to his letter to GW of Saturday, 1 Sept. 1792, in which he recounted recent opposition, both peaceful and violent, by some western Pennsylvania citizens to attempts to collect the federal excise tax on whiskey.

2. GW agreed with Hamilton's suggestion, and on 15 Sept. he issued a proclamation urging compliance with the federal law.

3. The enclosed letter from Daniel Stevens, supervisor of South Carolina, has not been identified. For an earlier mention of problems with collecting the whiskey excise tax in North Carolina, see Hamilton to GW, 8 Sept., and note 1.

4. For the attorney general's opinion, see Edmund Randolph to Hamilton, 8 Sept., in Syrett, *Hamilton Papers,* 12:336–40. Neither draft proclamation sent with this letter has been found.

From Thomas Jefferson

Dear Sir   Monticello [Va.] Sep. 9. 1792.

I received on the 2d inst. the letter of Aug. 23. which you did me the honor to write me; but the immediate return of our post, contrary to his custom, prevented my answer by that occasion. the proceedings of Spain mentioned in your letter are really of a complexion to excite uneasiness, & a suspicion that their friendly overtures about the Missisipi have been merely to lull us while they should be strengthening their holds on that river. mister Carmichael's silence has been long my astonishment: and however it might have justified something very different from a new appointment, yet the public interest certainly called for his junction with mister Short as it is impossible but that his knolege of the ground of negotiation, of persons & characters must be useful & even necessary to the success of the mission. that Spain & Gr. Britain may understand one another on our frontiers is very possible; for however opposite their interests or dispositions may be in the affairs of Europe, yet while these do not call them into opposite action, they may concur as against us. I consider their keeping an agent in the Indian country as a circumstance which requires serious interference on our part: and I submit to your decision whether it does not furnish a proper occasion to us to send an additional instruction to messrs Carmichael & Short to insist on a mutual & formal stipulation to forbear employing agents or pensioning any persons within each others limits: and if this be refused, to propose the contrary stipulation, to wit, that each party may freely keep agents within the Indian territories of the other, in which case we might soon sicken them of the license.[1]

I now take the liberty of proceeding to that part of your letter wherein you notice the internal dissentions which have taken place within our government, & their disagreeable effect on it's movements. that such dissentions have taken place is certain, & even among those who are nearest to you in the administration. to no one have they given deeper concern than myself; to no one equal mortification at being myself a part of them. tho' I take to myself no more than my share of the general observations of your letter, yet I am so desirous ever that you should know the whole truth, & believe no more than the truth. that I am glad to seize every occasion of developing to you whatever I do or think relative to the government; & shall therefore ask permission to be more lengthy now than the occasion particularly calls for, or would otherwise perhaps justify.

When I embarked in the government, it was with a determination to intermeddle not at all with the legislature, & as little as possible with my co-departments. the first and only instance of variance from the former part of my resolution, I was duped into by the Secretary of the treasury and made a tool for forwarding his schemes, not then sufficiently understood by me; and of all the errors of my political life this has occasioned me the deepest regret.[2] it has ever been my purpose to explain this to you, when, from being actors on the scene, we shall have become uninterested spectators only. the second part of my resolution has been religiously observed with the war department; & as to that of the Treasury, has never been farther swerved from than by the mere enunciation of my sentiments in conversation, and chiefly among those who, expressing the same sentiments, drew mine from me. if it has been supposed that I ever intrigued among the members of the legislature to defeat the plans of the Secretary of the Treasury, it is contrary to all truth, as I never had the desire to influence the members, so neither had I any other means than my friendships, which I valued too highly to risk by usurpations on their freedom of judgment, & the conscientious pursuit of their own sense of duty. that I have utterly, in my private conversations, disapproved of the system of the Secretary of the treasury, I acknolege & avow: and this was not merely a speculative difference. his system flowed from principles adverse to liberty, & was calculated to undermine and demolish the republic, by creating an influence of his department over the members of the legislature. I saw this influence actually produced, & it's first fruits to be the establishment of the great outlines of his project by the votes of the very persons who, having swallowed his bait were laying themselves out to profit by his plans: & that had these persons withdrawn, as those interested in a question ever should, the vote of the disinterested majority was clearly the reverse of what they made it. these were no longer the votes then of the representatives of the people, but of deserters from the rights & interests of the people: & it was impossible to consider their decisions, which had nothing in view but to enrich themselves, as the measures of the fair majority which ought always to be respected. if what was actually doing begat uneasiness in those who wished for virtuous government, what was further proposed was not less threatening to the friends of the constitution. for, in a Report on the subject of manufactures, (still to be acted on) it was expressly assumed that the general government has a right to exercise all powers which may be for the *general welfare,* that is to say, all the legitimate powers of government:[3] since no government has a legitimate right to do what is not for the welfare of the governed. there was indeed a sham-limitation of the universality of this power *to cases where money is to be employed.* but about what is it that money cannot be employed? thus the object of these plans taken together is to draw all the powers of government into the hands of the general legislature, to establish means for corrupting a sufficient corps in that legislature to divide the honest votes & preponderate, by their own, the scale which suit⟨ed⟩, & to have that corps under the command of the Secretary of the Treasury for the purpose of subverting step by step the principles of the constitution, which he has so often declared to be a thing of nothing which must be changed. such views might have justified something more than mere expressions of dissent, beyond which, nevertheless, I never went. has abstinence from the department committed to me been equally observed by him? to say nothing of other interferences equally known, in the case of the two nations with which we have the most intimate connections, France & England, my system was to give some satisfactory distinctions to the former, of little cost to us, in return for the solid advantages yeilded us by them; & to have met the English with some restrictions which might induce them to abate their severities against our commerce. I have always supposed this coincided with your sentiments. yet the Secretary of the treasury, by his cabals with members of the legislature, & by hightoned declamation on other occasions, has forced down his own system, which was exactly the reverse. he undertook, of his own authority, the conferences with the ministers of these two nations, & was, on every consultation, provided with some report of a conversation with the one or the other of them, adapted to his views. these views thus made to prevail, their execution fell of course to me; & I can safely appeal to you, who have seen all my letters & proceedings, whether I have not carried them into execution as sincerely as if they had been my own, tho' I ever considered them as inconsistent with the honor & interest of our country. that they have been inconsistent with our interest is but too fatally proved by the stab to our navigation given by the French. so that if the question be By whose fault is it that Colo. Hamilton & myself have not drawn together? the answer will depend on that to two other questions; Whose Principles of administration best justify, by their purity, conscientious adherence? and Which of us has, notwithstanding, stepped farthest into the controul of the department of the other?

To this justification of opinions, expressed in the way of conversation, against the views of Colo. Hamilton, I beg leave to add some notice of his late charges against me in Fenno's gazette: for neither the stile, matter, nor venom of the pieces alluded to can leave a doubt of their author. spelling my name & character at full length to the public, while he conceals his own under the signature of 'an American' he charges me 1. with having written letters from Europe to my friends to oppose the present constitution while depending. 2. with a desire of not paying the public debt. 3. with setting up a paper to decry & slander the government.[4] 1. the first charge is most false. no man in the U.S., I suppose, approved of every tittle in the constitution: no one, I believe approved more of it than I did: and more of it was certainly disapproved by my accuser than by me, and of it's parts most vitally republican. of this the few letters I wrote on the subject (not half a dozen I believe) will be a proof: & for my own satisfaction & justification, I must tax you with the reading of them when I return to where they are.[5] you will there see that my objection to the constitution was that it wanted a bill of rights securing freedom of religion, freedom of the press, freedom from standing armies trial by jury, & a constant Habeas corpus act. Colo. Hamilton's was that it wanted a king and house of lords. the sense of America has approved my objection & added the bill of rights, not the king and lords. I also thought a longer term of service, insusceptible of renewal, would have made a President more independant. my country has thought otherwise, & I have acquiesced implicitly. he wished the general government should have power to make laws binding the states in all cases whatsoever. our country has thought otherwise: has he acquiesced? notwithstanding my wish for a bill of rights, my letters strongly urged the adoption of the constitution, by nine states at least, to secure the good it contained. I at first thought that the best method of securing the bill of rights would be for four states to hold off till such a bill should be agreed to. but the moment I saw mister Hancock's proposition to pass the constitution as it stood, and give perpetual instructions to the representatives of every state to insist on a bill of rights, I acknoleged the superiority of his plan, & advocated universal adoption. 2. the second charge is equally untrue. my whole correspondence while in France, & every word, letter, & act on the subject since my return, prove that no man is more ardently intent to see the public debt soon & sacredly paid off than I am. this exactly marks the difference between Colo. Hamilton's views & mine, that I would wish the debt paid tomorrow; he wishes it never to be paid, but always to be a thing wherewith to corrupt & manage the legislature. 3. I have never enquired what number of sons, relations & friends of Senators, representatives, printers or other useful partisans Colo. Hamilton has provided for among the hundred clerks of his department, the thousand excisemen, customhouse officers, loan officers &c. &c. &c. appointed by him, or at his nod, and spread over the Union, nor could ever have imagined that the man who has the shuffling of millions backwards & forwards from paper into money & money into paper, from Europe to America, & America to Europe, the dealing out of Treasury secrets among his friends in what time & measure he pleases, and who never slips an occasion of making friends with his means, that such an one I say would have brought forward a charge against me for having appointed the poet Freneau translating clerk to my office, with a salary of 250. dollars a year.[6] that fact stands thus. while the government was at New York I was applied to on behalf of Freneau to know if there was any place within my department to which he could be appointed. I answered there were but four clerkships, all of which I found full, and continued without any change. when we removed to Philadelphia, mister Pintard the translating clerk, did not chuse to remove with us.[7] his office then became vacant. I was again applied to there for Freneau, & had no hesitation to promise the clerkship for him. I cannot recollect whether it was at the same time, or afterwards, that I was told he had a thought of setting up a newspaper there. but whether then or afterwards, I considered it as a circumstance of some value, as it might enable me to do, what I had long wished to have done, that is, to have the material parts of the Leyden gazette brought under your eye & that of the public, in order to possess yourself & them of a juster view of the affairs of Europe than could be obtained from any other public source. this I had ineffectually attempted through the press of mister

Fenno while in New York, selecting & translating passages myself
at first, then having it done by mister Pintard the translating
clerk. but they found their way too slowly into mister Fenno's
papers. mister Bache essayed it for me in Philadelphia; but his
being a dayly paper, did not circulate sufficiently in the other
states. he even tried at my request the plan of a weekly paper of
recapitulation from his daily paper, in hopes that that might go
into the other states, but in this too we failed. Freneau, as translating clerk, & the printer of a periodical paper likely to circulate
thro' the states (uniting in one person the parts of Pintard &
Fenno) revived my hopes that the thing could at length be affected. on the establishment of his paper therefore, I furnished
him with the Leyden gazettes, with an expression of my wish that
he would always translate & publish the material intelligence
they contained; & have continued to furnish them from time to
time, as regularly as I recieved them.[8] but as to any other direction or indication of my wish how his press should be conducted,
what sort of intelligence he should give, what essays encourage,
I can protest in the presence of heaven, that I never did by myself, or any other, directly or indirectly, say a syllable, nor attempt
any kind of influence. I can further protest, in the same awful
presence, that I never did by myself or any other, directly or indirectly, write, dictate or procure any one sentence or sentiment
to be inserted *in his, or any other gazette,* to which my name was not
affixed, or that of my office. I surely need not except here a thing
so foreign to the present subject as a little paragraph about our
Algerine captives, which I put once into Fenno's paper.[9] Freneau's proposition to publish a paper, having been about the
time that the writings of Publicola, & the discourses on Davila
had a good deal excited the public attention,[10] I took for granted
from Freneau's character, which had been marked as that of a
good whig, that he would give free place to pieces written against
the aristocratical & monarchical principles these papers had in-
culcated. this having been in my mind, it is likely enough I may
have expressed it in conversation with others; tho' I do not recollect that I did. to Freneau I think I could not, because I had still
seen him but once, & that was at a public table, at breakfast, at
mistress Elsworth's, as I passed thro' New York the last year.[11] and
I can safely declare that my expectations looked only to the chastisement of the aristocratical & monarchical writers, & not to any

criticisms on the proceedings of the government. Colo. Hamilton can see no motive for any appointment but that of making a convenient partisan. but you Sir, who have recieved from me recommendations of a Rittenhouse, Barlow, Paine, will believe that talents & science are sufficient motives with me in appointments to which they are fitted: & that Freneau, as a man of genius, might find a preference in my eye to be a translating clerk, & make good title moreover to the little aids I could give him as the editor of a gazette, by procuring subscriptions to his paper, as I did, some, before it appeared, & as I have with pleasure done for the labours of other men of genius. I hold it to be one of the distinguishing excellencies of elective over hereditary successions, that the talents, which nature has provided in sufficient proportion, should be selected by the society for the government of their affairs, rather than that this should be transmitted through the loins of knaves & fools passing from the debauches of the table to those of the bed. Colo. Hamilton, alias 'Plain facts' says that Freneau's salary began before he resided in Philadelphia.[12] I do not know what quibble he may have in reserve on the word 'residence'. he may mean to include under that idea the removal of his family; for I believe he removed, himself, before his family did, to Philadelphia but no act of mine gave commencement to his salary before he so far took up his abode in Philadelphia as to be sufficiently in readiness for the duties of the office. As to the merits or demerits of his paper, they certainly concern me not. he & Fenno are rivals for the public favor. the one courts them by flattery, the other by censure: & I believe it will be admitted that the one has been as servile, as the other severe. but is not the dignity, & even decency of government committed, when one of it's principal ministers enlists himself as an anonymous writer or paragraphist[13] for either the one or the other of them? no government ought to be without censors: & where the press is free, no one ever will. if virtuous, it need not fear the fair operation of attack & defence: nature has given to man no other means of sifting out the truth either in religion, law, or politics. I think it as honorable to the government neither to know nor notice it's sycophants or censors, as it would be undignified & criminal to pamper the former & persecute the latter. So much for the past. a word now of the future.

When I came into this office, it was with a resolution to retire

from it as soon as I could with decency. it pretty early appeared
to me that the proper moment would be the first of those epochs
at which the constitution seems to have contemplated a periodical change or renewal of the public servants. in this I was
confirmed by your resolution respecting the same period; from
which however I am happy in hoping you have departed. I look
to that period with the longing of a wave-worn mariner, who has
at length the land in view, & shall count the days & hours which
still lie between me & it.[14] in the mean while my main object will
be to wind up the business of my office avoiding as much as possible all new enterprize. with the affairs of the legislature, as I
never did intermeddle, so I certainly shall not now begin. I am
more desirous to predispose every thing for the repose to which
I am withdrawing, than expose it to be disturbed by newspaper
contests. if these however cannot be avoided altogether, yet a regard for your quiet will be a sufficient motive for deferring it till
I become merely a private citizen, when the propriety or impropriety of what I may say or do may fall on myself alone. I may
then too avoid the charge of misapplying that time which now
belonging to those who employ me, should be wholly devoted to
their service. if my own justification, or the interests of the republic shall require it, I reserve to myself the right of then ap-
pealing to my country, subscribing my name to whatever I write,
& using with freedom & truth the facts & names necessary to
place the cause in it's just form before that tribunal. to a thorough disregard of the honors & emoluments of office, I join as
great a value for the esteem of my countrymen; & conscious of
having merited it by an integrity which cannot be reproached, &
by an enthusiastic devotion to their rights & liberty, I will not suffer my retirement to be clouded by the slanders of a man whose
history, from the moment at which history can stoop to notice
him, is a tissue of machinations against the liberty of the country
which has not only recieved and given him bread, but heaped it's
honors on his head.[15] still however I repeat the hope that it will
not be necessary to make such an appeal. though little known to
the people of America, I believe that, as far as I am known, it is
not as an enemy to the Republic, nor an intriguer against it; nor
a waster of it's revenue, nor prostitutor of it to the purposes of
corruption, as the American represents me: and I confide that
yourself are satisfied that, as to dissensions in the newspapers, not

a syllable of them has ever proceeded from me; & that no cabals or intrigues of mine have produced those in the legislature, & I hope I may promise, both to you & myself, that none will recieve aliment from me during the short space I have to remain in office, which will find ample employment in closing the present business of the department.

Observing that letters written at Mount Vernon on the Monday, & arriving at Richmond on the Wednesday, reach me on Saturday, I have now the honor to mention that the 22d instant will be the last of our post-days that I shall be here, & consequently that no letter from you after the 17th will find me here. soon after that I shall have the honor of receiving at Mount Vernon your orders for Philadelphia, & of there also delivering you the little matter which occurs to me as proper for the opening of Congress, exclusive of what has been recommended in former speeches & not yet acted on.[16] in the mean time & ever I am with great and sincere affection & respect, dear Sir, your most obedient and most humble servant

Th: Jefferson

ALS, DLC:GW; ALS (letterpress copy), DLC: Jefferson Papers.

1. GW apparently agreed with Jefferson's suggestion about sending additional instructions to U.S. envoys William Carmichael and William Short since Jefferson so instructed them in his letter of 14 Oct. 1792 (*Jefferson Papers* 24: 479–81).

2. Jefferson is referring to his role in the political compromise achieved in 1790 that encouraged congressional approval of Hamilton's assumption plan and secured the location of the federal capital on the Potomac River. See Jefferson's "Account of the Bargain on the Assumption and Residence Bills," [1792?], in *Jefferson Papers*, 17:205–8.

3. Hamilton's "Report on the Subject of Manufactures" was first presented to the House of Representatives on 5 Dec. 1791, but it was never approved by Congress (see Syrett, *Hamilton Papers*, 10:230–340).

4. Hamilton wrote three essays under the pseudonym "An American" that appeared in John Fenno's *Gazette of the United States* (Philadelphia) on 4, 11, and 18 Aug. 1792.

5. For Jefferson's proof of his support for the Constitution and for the payment of the U.S. debt, see the enclosures in the letter he wrote to GW from Philadelphia on 17 Oct. 1792.

6. For a discussion of Jefferson's relationship with Philip Freneau, the editor of the *National Gazette* (Philadelphia), see *Jefferson Papers*, 20:718–53.

7. John Pintard (1759–1844), a College of New Jersey graduate in 1776, was a New York City merchant, civil servant, and banker. Fluent in French, he was appointed a translator in the department of foreign affairs under the Con-

federation Congress, and his appointment continued when the foreign affairs office became the Department of State after the adoption of the Constitution. He resigned that position when the national capital moved to Philadelphia in 1790. Pintard helped found the New-York Historical Society in 1804 and devoted much of his later life to philanthropic activities in New York City.

8. The *Gazette de Leyde* was a favorite source of European news for Jefferson. For Jefferson's efforts to encourage publication of news items from the Leiden newspaper to counter American dependence on British sources, see the editorial note in *Jefferson Papers,* 16:237–47. Benjamin Franklin Bache established the *General Advertiser* in Philadelphia in 1790, and in 1794 he added the word "Aurora" to the beginning of the title.

9. The item about the Algerian captives, titled "Extract of a letter from James Stimpson, Esq. Russian Consul, at Gibraltar, August 30, 1790," appeared in the 3 Nov. 1790 issue of the *Gazette of the United States* (Philadelphia).

10. Jefferson is referring to John Adams's *Discourses on Davila,* essays critical of the French Revolution that were serialized in the *Gazette of the United States* in 1790, and to letters published under the pseudonym "Publicola" in the *Columbian Centinel* (Boston) in the summer of 1791 that defended the ideas in *Davila* and pointed out fallacies in Thomas Paine's recently published *Rights of Man.* Jefferson erroneously attributed these letters to John Adams, but they were the work of the vice-president's son John Quincy Adams.

11. Vandine and Dorothy Elsworth ran a boardinghouse at 19 Maiden Lane in New York City.

12. This is an allusion to a letter by "Fair Play," published in the *Gazette of the United States* on 18 Aug. 1792, which criticized Jefferson's relationship with Freneau and which Jefferson attributed to Hamilton.

13. At this place on the manuscript, Jefferson first wrote "scribbler of slander." He then struck out those words and wrote "writer or paragraphist."

14. Jefferson sent his letter of resignation to GW on 31 Dec. 1793.

15. Hamilton was born on the island of Nevis, a British colony in the West Indies, and moved to New York in 1772 at the age of 15.

16. For Jefferson's suggestions, see GW's Address to the U.S. Senate and House of Representatives, 6 Nov., nn. 9–10. Jefferson stopped at Mount Vernon on 1 Oct. (see Jefferson's Conversation with Washington, 1 October).

From Edmund Randolph

Dear Sir   Philadelphia Sepr 10. 1792.

When I had the honor of receiving your favor of the third instant, I was too much indisposed by a fever to answer it by the return of the mail.

The movements, said to be meditated at the next session of the Virginia assembly, are the disfranchisement of the excise-officers, by taking from them the right of suffrage, and also the establishment of a state-bank, in opposition to the Branch Bank. Since I wrote to you last, Mr Andrews, the delegate for Williamsburg has been here; and contradicted most of the hostile reports, which had come from the mouth of Mr Corbin.[1] Still, however, it seems probable, that the legislature will so far oppose the Branch-bank, as to refuse to permit a higher interest than five per cent: to be received, or to repeal the act, which prohibits the circulation of bank notes. It surprizes me, I confess, that these should be considered as obstacles; since no-body means to dispute, according to my information, the validity of the law itself, now that it is passed, and is in operation.[2] At a late court in Chester County, in this state several persons were indicted for an assault on an excise officer. Notwithstanding a strong defence, they were convicted and fined; the jury having said to the attorney-general, that it was not a question with them, whether the law was good, or bad; but that they would never countenance an opposition to laws in such a form.[3] This event, which I shall endeavour to have published with all its circumstances, will increase the abhorrence, which several of the very party, who are associated with Gallatin and Smilie, feel themselves compelled to express, in order to avoid the imputation of a love of anarchy. The probability is, that the proceedings at Pittsburg will contribute to defeat the ticket, which has been proposed by that party.[4] I have the honor, dear sir, to be with the most affectionate attachment yr obliged & obedient serv.

Edm: Randolph

ALS, DLC:GW. This letter is identified as "Private" on the cover sheet.

1. Robert Andrews represented Williamsburg in the Virginia house of delegates from 1790 to 1799. Francis Corbin represented Middlesex County in the Virginia house of delegates from 1784 to 1794.

2. Debate over ratification of the U.S. Constitution helped to solidify previous political differences within Virginia into Federalist and Antifederalist factions, a division which became even clearer during the post-ratification debates over which amendments should be added to the Constitution. The first ten amendments that were eventually adopted did not protect states' rights sufficiently for Virginia's Antifederalists who examined every decision by the Washington administration for signs of monarchical tendencies and who found the various components of Hamilton's financial plan particularly alarming (see DenBoer, "The House of Delegates," 277–84).

For Virginia governor Henry Lee's plan to create a state bank in opposition to the Bank of the United States, see Lee to Madison, 10 Sept. 1792, in *Madison Papers*, 14:363. The Virginia general assembly passed acts establishing state banks at Alexandria and Richmond on 23 Nov. and 23 Dec. 1792, respectively (see Hening, 13:592–607). For a later report on the political climate in Virginia's general assembly, see Randolph's Memorandum to GW, 30 Jan. 1793.

3. On 26 Sept. 1792 the *Gazette of the United States* (Philadelphia) printed the following notice: "At the last Court of Quarter Sessions for the county of Chester, in this State, Joseph Evans and Robert Fletcher, with several others, were indicted for a riot, assault and battery on Jacob Humphreys, who was in the execution of his office under what is commonly called the 'Excise Law' of the United States. The other defendants had not, at the time of the trial, been taken. The Jury convicted both the defendants, and Fletcher was fined 50l."

Jared Ingersoll (1749–1822), a prominent Philadelphia lawyer, served as the attorney general of Pennsylvania from 1790 to 1799 and from 1811 to 1817. He was born in New Haven, Conn., and graduated from Yale in 1766. Ingersoll represented Pennsylvania in the Continental Congress in 1780 and in the Constitutional Convention in 1787.

4. Albert Gallatin and John Smilie, residents of Fayette County, Pa., and members of the Pennsylvania legislature, attended the extralegal convention held by opponents of the excise tax on whiskey in Pittsburgh on 21–22 Aug. 1792. Gallatin was elected clerk of the meeting (see Linn and Egle, *Whiskey Insurrection Papers,* 25–26). For background on the opposition to the excise tax on whiskey, see Hamilton to GW, 1 Sept. 1792, and notes. For a contemporary report on efforts to defeat Federalist candidates in the upcoming national elections, see John Beckley to James Madison, 1 Aug. 1792, in *Madison Papers,* 14:345–47.

From Alexander Hamilton

Sir   Philadelphia Sepr 11. 1792

Herewith is an official letter submitting the draft of a Proclamation. I reserve some observations as most proper for a private letter.[1]

In the case of a former proclamation I observe it was under the seal of the U. States and countersigned by the Secretary of State. If the precedent was now to be formed I should express a doubt whether it was such an instrument as ought to be under the seal of the U. States; and I believe usage as well in this Country under the state Government as in Great Britain would be found against it; but the practice having been begun there are many reasons which in this instance recommend an adherence to it—and the form of the attestation is adapted to this idea.[2]

But still if the Secretary of State should be at so great a distance or if an uncertainty of his being in the way should involve the probability of considerable delay it will be well to consider if the precedent ought not to be departed from. In this case the Attestation would require to be varied so as to omit from the words "In testimony" to the words "my hand" inclusively—and to substitute the word "*Given*" to "*Done*" and it may be adviseable to direct the Atty General to countersign it.[3]

Every day's delay will render the Act less impressive & defeat a part of its object.

The propriety of issuing the proclamation depends of course upon a resolution to act in conformity to it and put in force all the *powers* and *means* with which the Executive is possessed as occasion shall require—My own mind is made up fully to this issue and on this my suggestion of the measure is founded—Your letter by the last Post, confirming former intimations, assures me that you view the matter in the same light.[4]

The words in the Proclamation "dictated by weighty reasons of public exigency and policy" are not essential to the general scope of it—They amount to an *additional commitment* of the President on the question of the merits of the law and will require to be well considered.[5]

That the Proclamation both as to *manner* and *matter* will be criticised cannot be matter of surprise if it should happen, to any one who is aware of the lengths to which a certain party is prepared to go—It ought to be anticipated as probable.

In a step so delicate & so full of responsibility, I thought it my duty to make these observations; though I was sure they would of themselves occur.

It is satisfactory to know that a Jury in Chester County in this state convicted a person who was guilty of assaulting an Officer of Inspection. On being interrogated they answered that they had found him guilty upon the Count in the Indictment which charged him with assaulting the Officer in the execution of his duty—that the law was a constitutional act of Government and was not to be resisted by violence—I have directed Mr Coxe to collect & publish the particulars.[6] The symptom is a good one. With the most faithful & affectionate attachment I have the honor to remain Sir Yr obedt & hum. Srvt

A. Hamilton

ALS, DLC:GW; copy, DLC: Hamilton Papers.

1. The enclosed draft has not been found. For background on the events leading to the writing of this proclamation in response to opposition to the excise tax on whiskey, see Hamilton to GW, 1 Sept., and notes. Hamilton ex-

pressed his private views on this matter in a second letter to GW of 9 September. GW issued the final version of the proclamation on 15 Sept. 1792.

2. Hamilton probably is referring to the Proclamation on the Treaty of Holston which GW issued on 11 Nov. 1791.

3. The proclamation that GW issued on 15 Sept. continued the precedent established earlier by including Jefferson's countersignature.

4. Hamilton is referring to GW's letter to him of 7 Sept. 1792.

5. GW did not include these words in the final version of the proclamation.

6. For the Chester County, Pa., court case, see Edmund Randolph to GW, 10 Sept., n.3.

From David Stuart

Dear Sir,   Hope Park [Va.] 11th Sept. 92

I have recieved so much pleasure and instruction from the inclosed observations, that I could wish the author would in some shape fan on the Public with them.[1] I am satisfyed more than ever, that fiew even of those who presume most on their talents, and are most clamorous and illiberal against the funding System, have a true understanding of it. But allowing that they have, and are activated in their opposition to it, by improper motives, so plain a development of its principles, and superiority to the Systems which have been opposed to it, would deprive them of the reason of misleading those who are well intentioned—The high opinion entertained of Mr Maddison's abilities, and Jefferson's, have induced most of us I suspect to nourish the prejudices we have against it—As talents for finance, are of a particular nature, and not often combined with considerable abilities in other respects, it is a question with me whether even they understand it well—It is clear, at least to me at present, that their Systems would have been equally mischievous, indeed more so, in fostering speculation, while it would have been defective as to it's object[2]—It is essential at thi⟨s⟩ m⟨o⟩ment th⟨at⟩ the people s⟨hould⟩ be well informed; but such is the chain of misrepresentations about the funding System, and bank, that fiew who wish well to the government, are able to detect them fully particularly when resting on great State authorities. I am Dr Sir, with great respect Your Affecte Servt

Dd Stuart.

ALS, DLC:GW. The text in angle brackets is mutilated.

1. The enclosure has not been identified.

2. For an introduction to James Madison's views on the funding system de-

vised by Alexander Hamilton, see "Public Debt," 31 Mar. 1792, in *Madison Papers*, 14:275–77. For an introduction to Jefferson's ideas on funding the national debt and his conflict with Hamilton on this subject, see the editorial notes in *Jefferson Papers*, 14:190–96, 20:175–97.

From Jacob Wray

The Hermitage Ashton Manour
Elizabeth City County [Va.]
Honorable Sir   Sepr 13th 1792
   My Brother George Wrays friends (Colo. Cary Mr Miles King & others) has put him in mind of asking for the care of the light house business on Cape Henry[.] my Brother is a very sober man Active in spirits & they think he would make a good superintendt to the business, & command a good watch, & Such an amusement would pleas him to see he was of Use as long as he continues in this life[.] he has no family, & always been fond of serving the publick more then himself—therefore he would be glad to live better then he does to his own will, & pleasure (as he lives with our Family in Hampton) He has bin in no business since our revolution began, but a Deligate at Times—& continues in the County business—he has no rents nor in comes—I, believe not less then a round thousand behind hand in England but he thinks the British put him out, of ever paying that debt, therefore that does not dwell on his spirits, a Home altogether in his own way, & to be of such Use to the publick, woul[d] make him thankful & Dutiful, no doubt[1]—I am in al duty bound to the Father of this New Empire—Honorable Sir your most obedt
                                                        Jacob Wray

I am a Theocratic under the Auspicious Saviour of the World that Quickening Spirit that is to influence the whole World all in good time.
                                                                    J.W.

ALS, DLC:GW.
   Merchant Jacob Wray served as the collector of customs at Hampton, Va., from 1789 until he resigned in March 1790. His son George Wray, Jr., succeeded him in this position (see Jacob Wray to GW, 24 Mar. 1790, and note 1, and GW to the U.S. Senate, 28 April 1790, and note 1).
   1. George Wray, Sr., who represented Elizabeth City County in the Virginia house of delegates 1781–85 and 1794, did not receive the appointment of lighthouse keeper at Cape Henry in spite of his recommendations from promi-

nent Virginians. Col. Richard Cary, Jr. (c.1760–1800), a member of an influential Warwick County family, attended the College of William and Mary, served in the dragoons during the Revolutionary War, and was elected to the Virginia general assembly after the war. Miles King (1747–1814) of Elizabeth City County, who had been a surgeon's mate in the 1st Virginia Regiment 1775–78, was also a member of the Virginia general assembly. He served as mayor of Norfolk from 1804 to 1805 and again in 1810. For the other candidates considered for appointment as lighthouse keeper at Cape Henry, see Hamilton to GW, 22 Sept., and note 6, and Thomas Newton, Jr., to GW, 28 Sept. 1792.

From Ferdinand Bayard

Sir   Baltimore September 15 92.

to the desire of being useful, both to America & France, this intrusion of mine is to be accounted for, & your tryed love to the rights of Man, Keeps alive the hope, that the generous & honorable project of forming a corps of American volunteers, to join the french, will be approved & supported by you.

as it has been publickly circulated, I doubt not but you are acquainted with that wish of many of your countrymen; & as their attachement to you is adequate to the services you paid your country, an expression of your desire, to see it realized, would bring to existence what may be now, but an effusion of gratitude & virtue.

the benefits the two people would gather from it, are reciprocal & obvious, & lest I should be thought wanting confidence in the generosity of the american, I will pass those to their share unnoticed.

few men added to the numbers of the French may be considered as of litle or no service to their Cause, with them who would appreciate the gift, with arithmetical rules—but with men who rely on the moral strenght, it will appear that those few will add energy, their good discipline have a salutary influence & that it may be an inducement to the friends of liberty scatered through Europe, to do the same. and as it is not so much the number of men, as their character, which determines their value, I may say without flattery, that the american corps should be worth reckoning.

the cause is a glorious one—the old world is interested in the strugle; for universal freedom or slavery must be the consequence.

the American corps of Volunteers, may be raised by individuals, to save government some inconveniences which may result from its interfering & that way would be the most expedite as well as the most brotherly.

your exertions, Sir, have exalted you above the reach of the most extravagant ⟨de⟩sires of pride & selfishness; but virtue you are indebted for it, like its parent, Knows no limits—why George Washington should not be as active for the liberty of Europe, as he has been for that of America? & while I think, that it was not so much the enjoyings of political & civil blessings which endared it to you, as the consciousness of its being the only mode, wherein, man can reach again his state of native dignity, I rest assured of your good will & support.[1] may heaven bless the old world with your exertions, as ⟨it⟩ did the new, is the daily prayer, Sir of your admirer

Ferdinand Bayard

ALS, DNA: RG 59, Miscellaneous Letters.

Ferdinand-Marie Bayard de La Vingtrie (1763–c.1818) had pursued a military career in his native France, rising to the rank of lieutenant before leaving the army in 1788. He lived in the United States from 1788 to 1794, and after returning to France, he published *Voyage dans l'intérieur des États-Unis: à Bath, Winchester, dans la vallée de Shenandoah, etc., etc., pendant l'été de 1791* in 1797. A second, expanded edition in 1798 included several spurious letters attributed to GW. For background on these fictitious letters, their first publication during the Revolutionary War, and their publication again during GW's presidency, see GW to Jeremiah Wadsworth, 6 Mar. 1797, and note 3; see also Ford, *Spurious Letters*.

1. No reply from GW to Bayard has been found. It is unlikely that GW would have encouraged Bayard's ambition to raise an American corps to fight in behalf of the new French republic. When Henry Lee wrote GW on 29 April 1793 that he contemplated resigning as Virginia's governor in order to accept a commission in the French army, GW discouraged Lee from taking such a step, and he referred Lee to the recently announced Neutrality Proclamation of 22 April, noting that it was designed not only to declare the "disposition of this Country" but also to restrain U.S. "citizens from taking part in the contest" (see GW to Henry Lee, 6 May 1793).

To Thomas Jefferson

Dear Sir,　　　　　　　　　　　Mount Vernon Septr 15th 1792

This letter goes Express, to obtain the signature of the Secretary of State to the enclosed Proclamation. The reasons for sending it in this manner, are, to avoid the circuitous rout by Richmond, and the delay it might meet with by the Post; not having reached my hands until this morning, too late for the Mail of this day—nor in time for any other before Tuesday next—and because it is unknown to me, when one will set out from Richmond for Charlottesville.[1]

If good is to result from the Proclamation, no time is to be lost in issueing of it; as the opposition, to what is called the Excise Law, in the Western Survey of the District of Pennsylvania, is become too open, violent & serious to be longer winked at by Government, without prostrating it's authority, and involving the Executive in censurable inattention to the outrages which are threatened.[2]

I have no doubt but that the measure I am about to take, will be severely criticised; but I shall disregard any animadversions upon my conduct when I am called upon by the nature of my office, to discharge what I conceive to be a duty—and none, in my opinion, is more important, than to carry the Laws of the United States into effect.

The Secretary of the Treasury; the Secretary of War and the Attorney General, concur in the expediency of the Proclamation; as forbearance seems to have produced no other effect than to spread the evil.[3]

I have *scored* a few words, which possibly may as well be omitted; and if, upon an attentive perusal of the draught, others should appear which you think might as well be expunged or altered; mark them in *like* manner with a pencil, and I will give due consideration thereto.[4]

Your note of the 27th ulto with the enclosures to Mr Tayler, were forwarded in the manner you desired, by the first Post after they came to my hands. With sincere & affectionate regard, I am Dear Sir, Your very hble Servt

Go: Washington

LS, DLC: Jefferson Papers; ADf[S] (mutilated), DNA: RG 59, Miscellaneous Letters; LB, DNA: RG 59, George Washington's Correspondence with His Secretaries of State; LB (photocopy), DLC: GW. Jefferson docketed the LS as being received on 18 September. The draft is missing the last paragraph, which has been cut off with the closing signature.

1. Earlier this morning GW had received Hamilton's letter of 11 Sept., enclosing a draft of a proclamation urging compliance with the federal excise tax on whiskey. Anxious to issue the proclamation, GW sent his tenant William Gray to deliver this letter to Jefferson. In a memorandum also written on 15 Sept.,

GW instructed Gray to "bring an Answer from the Secretary of State—Mr Jefferson—you will enquire for his Seat of Monticello. Delay no time you can avoid, in bringing back his answer—and in order to obtain it, you must if he is not at Home, go to him. . . . be here, if possible by, or before friday Noon [21 Sept.], ensuing the date of this" (ALS [photocopy], NHi: George and Martha Washington Papers).

2. For background on the events leading to the writing of the proclamation, see Alexander Hamilton to GW, 1 Sept. 1792, and notes, and Edmund Randolph to GW, 10 Sept., and notes 3 and 4.

3. For Randolph's opinion on issuing a proclamation, see his letter to Hamilton of 8 Sept. in Syrett, *Hamilton Papers*, 12:336–40.

4. Upon receiving this letter on 18 Sept., Jefferson immediately returned the enclosed proclamation with his signature and a suggested change (see Jefferson to GW, 18 September). For the final version, see Proclamation, 15 Sept. 1792.

From Henry Knox

Sir   War department September 15th 1792

I have had the honor to receive yours of the 7th instant and I have transmitted a copy of it to Major General Wayne.[1]

I have the honor to enclose you a copy of his last letter of the 7th instant. No. 1. and my answer thereto No. 2. From every account, I learn that he is indefatigable in disciplining his troops.[2]

Money to the amount of Forty five thousand six hundred and thirty seven dollars and thirty three Cents to complete the pay to the first of August left this town yesterday under the charge of two careful men—I had previously desired General Wayne to have an escort at Bedford by the 20th for the purpose of escorting the money from that place to Pittsburg—and at the request of the Secretary of the Treasury I wrote to the Officer the enclosed Note No. 3 and to General Wayne No. 4. both of which I hope will meet your approbation.[3]

As soon as the Waters of the Ohio will permit, General Wayne will forward a respectable detachment from Pittsburgh including those rifle Companies raised on the South Western frontiers of Virginia, to Fort Washington.[4]

All our pacific overtures to the Indians have been marked with misfortune excepting Captain Hendricks they have all miscarried whether conducted by Whites or Indians[5]—The enclosed letter which I have this moment received from General Chapin

No. 5. gives the account of the death of Good Peter and the sickness of Captain Brant, besides the death of others of our friends.[6]

The enclosed letter No. 6 from Governor Lee however will show that affairs are more tranquil on the South western frontier than they were expected to be by him.[7]

The Messieurs Dunn and Jones who are recommended by General Wayne were early applicants for commissions, but upon the failure of their applications they both joined as Sergeants in the dragoons on the hope of promotion conditioned on their good behaviour—there will be vacancies to be filled and they may upon further trial be promoted—Joseph Richardson mentioned by Mr Spriggs in his letter to you will be in the same predicament.[8]

I am inclined to the opinion that the orders to General Wayne for the ulterior disposition of his troops for winter may be delayed sometime without any injury—perhaps until your arrival here—but the preparations may be making of the materials for barracks.[9]

It was not until yesterday that all evidences in behalf of General St Clair against Ensign Morgan were delivered to this office —Until the evidences were forwarded, I conceived it unnecessary to order him on to the Army to undergo his trial—But as the case is now circumstanced I think no further delay should be permitted. It is probable however he will attempt to evade or disobey the order unless it is given explicitly in your name—This opinion is founded on a conversation which took place between his father and Major Stagg a few days ago. The father said his Son intended to present a memorial to you requesting that he might have his trial in this City, saying it was a matter of great importance in the minds of the people at large, and that he should prefer its being held during the session of Congress.

If after receiving your ultimate orders he should disobey them, he will place himself in a new and more critical situation—and in this event it will become a consideration what steps shall be taken upon the subject.

Whether to add this new charge to those made by General St Clair and use force to convey him to Pittsburg or whether to dismiss him the service without further process—Although in the event contemplated, no doubt could be entertained of the abstract propriety of compelling Ensign Morgan to take his trial according to law, yet considering the clamour that such a strong measure might excite, together with the probable severity of his punishment, it may be perhaps be politically expedient to adopt the second alternative.[10]

Colonel Fish has declined the office of Adjutant General as by his letter will appear No. 7. Colonel Sproat has signified his desire of that office. Colonel Posey has also been mentioned[.] It seems necessary that it should be filled immediately.[11] I have the honor sir to be with the highest respect Your obedient Servant

H. Knox

LS, DLC:GW; LB, DLC:GW. The closing and signature of the LS are in Knox's hand.

1. Knox enclosed this copy in his letter to Wayne of 14 Sept. (see note 2).

2. Wayne enclosed in his letter to Knox of 7 Sept. "an extract from General Orders, containing the arrangement of the Officers of the four *Sub Legions,* and the principles upon which rank is to be determined, . . . also for the mustering and making out the necessary Muster and pay rolls." Wayne suggested the creation of "Sub Legionary and Battalion Paymasters. . . . I am of opinion that they are really necessary; Pay however is much wanted. do have the goodness to give immediate and necessary Orders for that purpose—let us pay—and *feed* well—we then have a right to expect due subordination." Wayne complained about the poor quality and tardiness of provisions from the contracting firm of Robert Elliott and Eli Williams, and he reported that neither dragoons nor clothing intended for Fort Washington could be sent from his headquarters at Pittsburgh because "no boat can possibly pass at present down the Ohio. . . . The Paymaster General [Caleb Swan] has not been ordered to this place because there was no means of doing it by water and I am of opinion that it would be very improper for him to attempt it by land—the Ohio has never been known so low, nor is there any prospect of its rising before the Equinox and perhaps not then as it will depend upon a very heavy fall of Water—but Lieut. [Daniel] Britt is on the spot who I have directed to instruct the Officers as to the form and correctness of the Muster and pay Rolls— Query might it not be expedient to appoint him Deputy Pay Master pro tem?" Wayne mentioned that the offices of brigade major, sublegionary and battalion adjutants, and adjutant general also needed to be filled. "In fact," he wrote, "I never experienced so great a want of *Officers.*" He suggested promoting sergeants George H. Dunn and Abraham Jones. Wayne also enclosed "extracts from General orders approving the sentences of a general Court Martial held at this place by which four Soldiers were condemned to death and one to be shaved, branded and whipt. John Elias alias Ebbert alias Eli, has been pardoned—the other three were shot to death on Sunday last—these exemplary punishments, I trust will have the desired effect." Wayne concluded with a report on the frequency of

target practice and the subsequent improvement in the skills of the soldiers and with a report that the Indians were in "pretty great force at *Sandusky*" (DLC:GW; see also Knopf, *Wayne,* 87–89). For details on the court-martial and for the general orders enclosed in Wayne's letter, see Burton, "General Wayne's Orderly Book," 370–78.

In his reply to Wayne from Philadelphia on 14 Sept., Knox agreed with Wayne's request for sublegionary paymasters and quartermasters, but not battalion paymasters. He promised to submit both ideas to the president for his consideration. He enclosed a copy of his 11 Sept. letter to Wayne and reported that money for the army's pay left Philadelphia on 14 September. Concerning the future assignment of the U.S. Army in the Northwest Territory, Knox wrote: "I will write immediately to the President of the United States and request his orders on certain conditional statements relatively to the proportion of troops which may probably be necessary to retain on the upper parts of the Ohio." In the meantime "the Quarter Master should be making arrangements for scantling boards, Bricks &c. for the covering of the troops at the places which shall be decided upon for their stations."

Enclosing a copy of GW's letter to Knox of 7 Sept., in which GW reviewed Wayne's proposed plan of war, Knox wrote: "I am persuaded that the President who is highly anxious on the subject will be well pleased with your exertions to discipline the troops. Every thing depends on that pivot. The public interest, the national character and your personal reputation—Aware of the consequences, no doubt can be entertained that you will continue unremittingly to pursue in every proper way, the accomplishment of so indispensible a qualification of your troops.

"The sentences of the Courts Martial you have confirmed, seemed absolutely necessary—Hereafter it is to be hoped there may be less call for the punishment of death. The Branding however is a punishment upon which some doubts may be entertained as to its legality. Uncommon punishments not sanctioned by Law should be admitted with caution although less severe than those authorized by the articles of War."

Knox enclosed copies of letters written him on 5 and 6 Aug. by Gen. James Wilkinson and on 10 Aug. by deputy quartermaster John Belli. He reported that additional troops were on their way to Pittsburgh under Capt. William Eaton, Capt. John Peirce, and Lt. Ebenezer Massey (DLC:GW; see also Knopf, *Wayne,* 95–97). A copy of Wilkinson's letter of 6 Aug. is in DLC:GW, as is a copy of Knox's first letter to Wayne of 11 Sept. (see also ibid., 90–91).

3. For Knox's previous instructions regarding this money, see his letter to Wayne of 7 Sept., enclosed in Knox to GW, 8 Sept. 1792 (second letter). Enclosure 3 is a copy of Knox's letter to the commanding officer of Fort Bedford, Pa., of 11 Sept., directing him to protect "the persons having charge of the money, for the payment of the army." Knox also ordered that officer to arrange protection for George Clymer, supervisor of the revenue for Pennsylvania, as he traveled to Pittsburgh (DLC:GW). Enclosure 4 is a copy of Knox's second letter to Wayne of 11 Sept. instructing him to help protect Clymer when he reached western Pennsylvania (DLC:GW; see also Knopf, *Wayne,* 92). For background on Clymer's mission, see Hamilton to GW, 1 Sept., and note 3.

4. These rifle companies were commanded by captains Alexander Gibson, Howell Lewis, Thomas Lewis, and William Preston (see Knox to Wayne, 15 June, 20 July 1792, in Knopf, *Wayne*, 18, 40–41).

5. For information on the failure of peace envoys Alexander Trueman and John Hardin and the peace mission of Stockbridge chief Hendrick Aupaumut, see Knox to GW, 16 Aug., nn.3–4. For Knox's report on the failure of American efforts in 1792 to achieve a peaceful settlement with the Indians of the Northwest Territory, see Knox to GW, 6 Dec. 1792.

6. On 25 Aug. 1792 Indian superintendent Israel Chapin, Sr., wrote Knox from Canandaigua, N.Y., about the current mood of the Iroquois Indians: "An Opportunity presenting . . . I do myself the honor to write you altho' I have not received any answers to my two last letters—since which nothing material has occurred in this quarter, the Indians appear perfectly friendly and have a sincere wish for peace.

"Captain Scanando [Skenandon] one of the Oneida Chiefs returned yesterday from Buffaloe Creek not being able to proceed on to the Westward on account of his sickness—he informs me of the death of good Peter. for which I am extremely sorry as I think he was capable of doing much good among the Indians—he also informs me that twenty four Indians have died at Buffaloe Creek within the course of a few days, that Capt. Brant lay at the point of death, and it was thought there was scarce a possibility of his recovery; that a vessel and every necessary preparation was made to convey the Indians of the six Nations to attend the Council at the Westward, and it was probable they had taken their departure before this time.

"I have not as yet been able to obtain the particulars of the Murder of the Indian at the Oswego Falls, when I do will immediately inform you" (DLC:GW).

7. Enclosure 6 was a copy of a letter that Virginia governor Henry Lee wrote Knox on 7 Sept. from Richmond: "I have perused your letter to the Lieutenant Governor received during my absence, and have the pleasure to inform you that my intelligence while on the frontier confirms the opinions you therein express. Governor Blount and General Pickens had reached Nashville and I understood the Goods were safely arrived. A very numerous assemblage of Indians from the Chickasaw nation had taken place, but only a few from the Choctaws. I found the troops employed on our southern frontier inadequate to the defence of that quarter, and therefore augmented the same by the addition of fifty militia. Excepting the killing of two Men and the capturing of a Woman and six Children (all of whom were afterwards retaken) and the loss of some horses, our people in that part of the frontier have been uninjured" (DLC:GW). For Knox's letter to Virginia's lieutenant governor, James Wood, of 13 Aug., see *Calendar of Virginia State Papers*, 6:38. For information on William Blount and Andrew Pickens's journey to Nashville and their subsequent meeting with the Chickasaw and Choctaw Indians, see Blount to Knox, 4 July, and "Journal of the Grand Cherokee National Council," 26 June–1 July 1792, in *ASP, Indian Affairs*, 1:270–73.

8. For Wayne's recommendations of promotions for cavalry sergeants George H. Dunn (d. 1793) and Abraham Jones (d. 1831), see Wayne to Knox, 7 Sept., in note 2. Their promotions to cornet were effective on 18 Sept. and

7 Oct. 1792, respectively (see GW to the U.S. Senate, 22 Feb. 1793). Both men later advanced to lieutenant. Mr. Sprigg's letter to GW has not been found, but Knox enclosed a copy of it in his letter to Wayne of 28 Sept. (see Knopf, *Wayne*, 110). Neither Sprigg nor Richardson has been identified.

9. GW arrived in Philadelphia on 13 Oct. (see GW to Anthony Whitting, 14 Oct. 1792). He did not wait until his return from Mount Vernon to offer directives concerning winter quarters for the troops but included them in his first letter to Knox written on 24 September. Knox relayed these suggestions to Wayne in a letter from Philadelphia of 28 Sept. (see ibid., 110–11).

10. For background on John Morgan and his impending court-martial, see Knox to GW, 28 July 1792, and note 8. Morgan was the eldest son of Col. George Morgan, a Philadelphia merchant, fur trader, and western land speculator. After efforts to have influential family friends and associates intervene on his behalf, Ensign Morgan attempted to have his trial moved to Philadelphia, hoping this change of venue would be in his favor (see Morgan to Knox and Knox to Morgan, 19 Sept., enclosed in Knox to GW, 22 Sept., and Morgan to Knox, 20 Sept., enclosed in Knox to GW, 29 Sept. 1792). GW rejected that request (see GW to Knox, 24 Sept. 1792), and Morgan's court-martial was held at General Wayne's headquarters south of Pittsburgh in August 1793 (see Burton, "General Wayne's Orderly Book," 462). Morgan was found guilty, and after unsuccessful appeals for redress, he was cashiered from the army on 31 Dec. 1793 (see Knox to GW, 22 Nov. 1793, Edmund Randolph to GW, 24 Nov. 1793).

11. Knox wrote Nicholas Fish on 29 Aug. offering him the position of adjutant general (NNGL: Knox Papers). Fish declined the offer in a reply from Schoharie, N.Y., on 7 Sept., in which he wrote: "At present my views are so detached from military pursuits, that an appointment in that line, would not be in any degree desireable" (DLC:GW). Neither Ebenezer Sproat nor Thomas Posey received the appointment of adjutant general. For more information about Sproat's efforts to acquire a federal position, either military or civil, see Sproat to GW, 9 July 1789, and source note, and Knox to GW, 29 Sept. 1792 (second letter), n.4. For Colonel Posey's efforts to acquire a military appointment, see Posey to GW, 20 Nov. 1791, source note and notes 1 and 2.

From John Francis Mercer

Sir   West River [Md.] Sepr 15. 1792.

In proceeding to execute my part of the engagement respecting the Land in Montgomery County information has been given me that I judge proper to mention to you—The Tract will not divide to advantage into three parts, but will to very great benefit into two valuable Estates—It woud be perhaps, therefor greatly for the interest of all parties for you to take between five & six hundred Acres, & the other legatees will look to me, for their proportion of the Money. If on enquiry you find this representation just & approve of the arrangement, you will please to give me early information that I may conform accordingly.[1]

Amidst the variety of Reports which an approaching Election has given rise to—there is one that I am obliged to mention to you—It is currently said that you have written or verbally expressed great dissaprobation at some liberty that had been taken with your name by me—As this coud only have arisen from previous information to you, which I expect will prove equally false, with information of the same nature that the same dirty & desperate faction have given to these other Characters, which I have already detected & exposed, I now beg leave to state to you that it was told me at dinner in Company—that you had expressed opinions to your Nephew favorable to me or my Election—I immediately observed that I wished it might be true as it woud be the most eligible means of rejecting those infamous tales that had been so long and industriously propagated in this part of the Country, that you considered me as personally inimical—I mentioned soon afterwards what I had heard in the presence of three or four persons with this additional observation & caution that I had written to Marlbough whence the report was said to have originated to enquire into its truth—my sole object in this had I receivd a confirmation woud have been to have exposed the malignity, falsity & impudence of those who had ever made use of your name against me—for the truth of these impressions so long & so generally made here an enquiry of your Neighbour Mr Rozier, Mr Osborn Sprigg or Mr Thos Clarke or any other Gentlemen of reputation I beleive in Prince Georges County, (shoud you choose to satisfy yourself) woud convince you that these People have for five years past made very free with your name to create unfavorable impressions of me in this District.[2]

I shoud at an earlier period have mention⟨*mutilated*⟩ this, but conscious that in private life you had laid me under personal obligations that your public Character had every claim to my entire confidence & regard, & that my Enemies had never accused me of ingratitude, I did think that if ever such Reports (industriously circulated as they were) shoud reach your Ears, they might become the foundation of some explanation on your part either to me or others—& I anxiously waited for some opportunity when unsuspected of adulation I might openly express my real sentiments & the pain which reports so injurious to my feelings & so contrary to truth had given me, I write this now Sir, only to assure you that every report you may have receivd of improper use made of your name by me, is wholly without foundation & that if improper impressions with respect to me have been made on your mind, they shall not remain, from any neglect to remove them on my part, for as to any other object, the party formed here against me are so contemptible & are already become so odious to the people, that they require popular names to protect them from the general resentment their conduct has inspired—With every sentiment of real respect I am, yr mo: Obt hb. Set

John F. Mercer

ALS, DLC:GW.

1. For background on GW's attempts to collect a long-standing debt from the estate of John Mercer, father of James and John Francis Mercer, see William Deakins, Jr., to GW, 24 Aug. 1792, and note 2.

2. For further information about GW's dispute with Mercer over his alleged use of GW's name in his 1792 congressional election campaign, see GW's Memorandum of a Statement to James Craik, 7 Sept., and GW to John F. Mercer, 26 Sept. 1792. Henry Rozer (Rozier; born c.1725) lived at Notley Hall in Prince Georges County, Md., on the Potomac River about eight miles from the mouth of Piscataway Creek and nearly opposite Alexandria, Virginia. Osborn Sprigg, Jr. (c.1741–1815), a Maryland planter who lived at his estate Northampton in Prince Georges County, served as justice of the peace in 1779–86 and 1793–98, as tax commissioner in 1792 and 1798, and as a member of Maryland's ratifying convention in 1788. He was a distant cousin of Mercer's wife, Sophia Sprigg Mercer. Thomas Clark (Clarke; c.1760–1796), a stepson of Osborn Sprigg, Jr., also resided in Prince Georges County. A merchant, he served in the lower house of the Maryland legislature 1789–92 and 1794 and was a justice of the peace in 1791–92. By 1794 he had moved to Georgetown in the federal district, where he remained until his death.

Proclamation

[15 September 1792]
By the Presdent of the United States. A Proclamation.[1]

Whereas certain violent and unwarrantable proceedings have lately taken place, tending to obstruct the operation of the laws of the United States for raising a revenue upon Spirits distilled within the same, enacted pursuant to express authority delegated in the Constitution of the United States; which proceedings are subversive of good order, contrary to the duty that every Citizen owes to his Country and to the laws, and of a nature dangerous to the very being of Government: And whereas such proceedings are the more unwarrantable, by reason of the moderation which has been heretofore shewn on the part of the Government, and of the disposition which has been manifested by the Legislature (who alone have authority to suspend the operation of laws) to obviate causes of objection, and to render the laws as acceptable as possible. and whereas it is the particular duty of the Executive "to take care that the laws be faithfully executed," and not only that duty, but the permanent interests and happiness of the people require, that every legal and necessary step should be pursued as well to prevent such violent and unwarrantable proceedings, as to bring to justice the infractors of the laws and secure obedience thereto.

Now therefore I George Washington, President of the United States, do by these presents most earnestly admonish and exhort all persons whom it may concern, to refrain and desist from all unlawful combinations and proceedings whatsoever, having for object or tending to obstruct the operation of the laws aforesaid; inasmuch as all lawful ways and means will be strictly put in execution, for bringing to justice the infractors thereof and securing obedience thereto.

And I do moreover charge and require all Courts, Magistrates and Officers whom it may concern, according to the duties of their several Offices, to exert the powers in them respectively vested by law for the purposes aforesaid, hereby also enjoining and requiring all persons whomsoever, as they tender the welfare of their Country, the just and due authority of Government and the preservation of the public peace, to be aiding and assisting therein, according to law.

In Testimony whereof I have caused the seal of the United States to be affixed to these presents, and signed the same with my hand. Done this fifteenth day of September in the year of our Lord one thousand seven hundred and ninety two, and of the independence of the United States the seventeenth.

Geo. Washington

By the President
Th. Jefferson.

Copy, Nc-Ar: Governor's Papers, Alexander Martin; copy (extract), PHi: Wallace Papers. The extract omits the last paragraph.

1. For background on GW's decision to issue this proclamation, see Hamilton to GW, 1 Sept., and notes, 9 Sept. (second letter), and notes, 11 Sept. 1792, and notes, and GW to Hamilton, 7 Sept., and note 2.

To Henry Knox

Sir,   Mt Vernon Sepr 16th 1792

Your letter of the 8th, with its enclosures, came duly to hand; & requires but little in reply to it, as your answer to Genl Waynes communications contain every direction which is necessary for his governmt at this time.[1]

Whatever may be the Attorney General's opinion with respect to the *legality* of calling out Militia by the Governor of Pennsylvania—for supplying the place of the Rangers—it is not an easy matter, under the circumstances which now do and have existed during the summer, to discover any necessaty for the measure; especially if the order was subsequent to *your* solution of *his* queries.[2]

Captn Brants letter, and the Speech of the Chiefs of the Six Nations to Genl Chapin, is no more than a continuation of the Evidence, which, long since, has established a fact, & left no doubt in my mind, of the causes to which all our difficulties with the Western Indians are to be ascribed; and I am equally clear that the period is not very distant when this business will assume a less disguised appearance.[3]

Have you received any answer yet from Major Fish respecting the offer that was made him of the Office of Adjutant General?[4] This matter has been too long suspended—With esteem & regd I am Sir, Yr Hble Servt

G. W——n

ADfS, DLC:GW; LB, DLC:GW.

1. GW is referring to the enclosures in Knox's second, and official, letter of 8 Sept. (see notes 2 and 3 for the Wayne-Knox correspondence).

2. For previous correspondence between Knox and Pennsylvania governor Thomas Mifflin about the legality of calling out the Pennsylvania militia to protect inhabitants on the frontier from Indian attacks, see Knox to GW, 8 Sept. (second letter), and note 6.

3. For Joseph Brant's letter of 26 July 1792 and the 1 Aug. speech from the chiefs of the Six Nations, see Knox to GW, 8 Sept. (second letter), n.4.

4. Nicholas Fish declined the position of adjutant general in a letter to Knox of 7 Sept. (see Knox to GW, 15 Sept., n.11).

To Alexander Hamilton

Sir,   Mount Vernon Septr 17th 1792.

Your Letters of the 8 and 9. inst: are received. The latter came to me on Saturday morning by Express, from the Post Office in Alexandria. I gave the Proclamation my signature and forwarded it in the afternoon of the same day, by a special messenger, to the Secretary of State for his countersign. If no unforeseen delay happens, the return of it may be in time for *Friday's* Post, so as to be with you the Tuesday following.[1]

It is much to be regretted that occurrences of a nature so repugnant to order and good Government, should not only afford the occasion, but render such an interference of the Executive indispensably necessary. When these happen, and lenient & temporizing means have been used, and serve only to increase the disorder; longer forbearance would become unjustifiable remissness, and a neglect of that duty which is enjoined on the President. I can have no hesitation therefore, under this view of the case, to adopt such legal measures to check the disorderly opposition which is given to the execution of the Laws laying a duty on distilled spirits, as the Constitution has invested the executive with; and however painful the measure would be, if the Proclamation should fail to produce the effect desired, ulterior arrangements must be made to support the Laws, & to prevent the prostration of Government.

Were it not for the peculiar circumstances of my family, I would return to the Seat of Government immediately; at any rate I hope to do it in the early part of next month, or before the middle thereof.[2] With esteem & regard, I am &c.

                                        G: Washington

LB, DLC:GW.

1. GW issued his proclamation urging compliance with the federal excise tax on whiskey on Saturday, 15 September. GW received the countersigned proclamation from Jefferson at Mount Vernon on Friday, 21 Sept. (see GW to Hamilton, 21 Sept.), and Hamilton received it at Philadelphia on Tuesday, 25 Sept. (see Hamilton to GW, 26 September).

2. The critical illness of George Augustine Washington, GW's nephew and manager of Mount Vernon, and the illness of some of the servants who would travel with him to Philadelphia kept GW at home until 8 October. He arrived in the capital on 13 Oct. (see GW to Tobias Lear, 1 Oct., to Betty Washington Lewis, 7 Oct., and to Anthony Whitting, 14 October).

To Alexander Hamilton

(Private)

My dear Sir,   Mount Vernon Sepr 17th 1792[1]

Your private letter of the 11th, accompanying an Official one of the 9th came safe—as did your other private letter of the 9th. I feel myself obliged by the observations contained in the first, respecting the Proclamation.[2]

As the former Proclamations, on similar occasions, have been Countersigned by the Secretary of State, I have, for *that* reason, and for another which has some weight in my mind, thought best not to depart, in *this* instance, from the Precedent that has been set; and therefore, as it cannot (unless unforeseen delays happen) be with-held from you more than six days longer than if it had been returned by this days Post, I dispatched by express the Proclamation to Mr Jefferson for the purpose above-mentioned.[3]

I have no doubt but that the Proclamation will undergo many strictures—and, as the effect proposed may not be answered by it; it will be necessary to look forward in time to ulterior arrangements. and here, not only the Constitution & Laws must strictly govern—but the employing of the regular Troops avoided, if it be possible to effect order without their aid; otherwise, there would be a cry at once "The cat is let out; We now see for what purpose an Army was raised"—Yet, if no other means will effectually answer, and the Constitution & Laws will authorise these, they must be used, in the dernier resort.

If you remain in opinion that it would be advisable for the President to transmit the Proclamation to the Governors of North & South Carolina—and the Governor of Pennsylvania, I pray you to draught such letters to them, to be forwarded from hence (with the Proclamations which must also be sent to me) as you may think best calculated to produce the effect proposed.[4] I am always Your Affectionate

Go: Washington

ALS, CtHi: Oliver Wolcott, Jr., Papers; ADfS, DLC:GW; LB, DLC:GW.

1. On the receiver's copy of this letter GW wrote a "7" over the "6" previously entered on the dateline; both the draft and letter-book copy retain the 16 Sept. date.

2. On 15 Sept., GW issued a proclamation urging obedience to the federal excise tax on whiskey.

3. See GW to Jefferson, 15 Sept. 1792.

4. GW sent a circular letter dated 29 Sept. to North Carolina governor Alexander Martin, Pennsylvania governor Thomas Mifflin, and South Carolina governor Charles Pinckney.

From Alexander Hamilton

Sir,   Treasury Departmt 17th Septr 1792.

Representations have been made by the Collector of the Customs at Edenton, and the Inspector of the Revenue for the third Survey of North Carolina, that Thomas Davis Freeman Surveyor of the Port of Plymouth and Inspector of the Revenue for the same, has been absent from that Port since February last. As it is stated in those representations, that it is not known whither that Officer has gone, and that it is not believed he will ever return, there is great probability that the public service will continue to suffer, unless the President on a knowledge of the circumstances, shall think proper to appoint some other suitable person to perform the duties of those offices. The name of Mr Jno. Armistead having been mentioned by the Collector & Inspector, with a reference to the Honorable Mr Johnston of the Senate of the United States, of which Gentleman enquiry has been made: He represents Mr Armistead as bred to Navigation and acquainted with business—as an old Inhabitant of the place, of good character & competent property. In regard to qualifications he spoke of him not only as a suitable person for the offices to be filled, but the most so of any Inhabitant of Plymouth.[1] I have the honor to be &c.

Alexr Hamilton

LB, DLC:GW.

1. Thomas Benbury was the collector of Edenton and the inspector of the third survey in North Carolina (see Executive Order and GW to Hamilton, both 15 Mar. 1791). Tench Coxe had written Hamilton on 4 Sept. informing him of Freeman's absence from Plymouth, N.C., since February and that Senator Samuel Johnston had recommended John Armistead (b. 1757) "as bred to Navigation and acquainted with Business, as an old inhabitant of the place, of good Character and competent property" (DNA: RG 58, Letters Sent by the Commissioner of the Revenue and the Revenue Office, 1792–1807).

On 24 Sept., GW wrote Hamilton: "Under your statement of the conduct of Thomas Davis Freeman Surveyor of the Port of Plymouth and Inspector of the Revenue of the same, there can be no question with respect to the propriety of superceding him in Office; and from the character given of Mr John Armistead of that place by the Collector and Inspector, and more particularly by Mr Johnston of the Senate, there can be as little doubt of his fitness to fill it. I have no objections therefore to Mr Armistead's doing it accordingly—of which you may inform him, and that a Commission will be sent to him for this purpose as soon as circumstances will permit" (LB, DLC:GW). GW included Armistead's nomination in a list of appointments dated 19 Nov. 1792. This list was received by the Senate on 20 Nov. and approved the following day (*Executive Journal*, 1:125–26).

From Thomas Jefferson

Dear Sir　　　　　Monticello [Va.] Sep. 18. 1792. 2. oclock P.M.

Your express is this moment arrived with the Proclamation on the proceedings against the laws for raising a revenue on distilled spirits, and I return it herein inclosed with my signature. I think if instead of the words 'to render laws dictated by weighty reasons of public exigency & policy as acceptable as possible' it stood 'to render the laws as acceptable as possible' it would be better. I see no other particular expressions which need alteration. I am sincerely sorry to learn that such proceedings have taken place: and I hope the proclamation will lead the persons concerned into a regular line of application which may end either in an amendment of the law, if it needs it, or in their conviction that it is right.[1] if the situation of my daughter (who is in the straw) admits it, I purpose to set out about a week hence, & shall have the honour of taking your commands for Philadelphia.[2] I have now that of being with great & sincere respect & attachment, Dr Sir Your most obedt & most humble servt

　　　　　　　　　　　　　　　　　　Th: Jefferson

P.S. the express is detained but about twenty minutes.

ALS, DNA: RG 59, Miscellaneous Letters; ALS (letterpress copy), DLC: Jefferson Papers; LB, DNA: RG 59, George Washington's Correspondence with His Secretaries of State; LB (photocopy), DLC:GW. The ALS is addressed to "The President of the United States Mount-Vernon By mister William Gray express."

1. For the express carrying the proclamation that GW issued in response to opposition to the excise tax on whiskey, see GW to Jefferson, 15 September. For previous correspondence about the need for Jefferson's signature on the

document, see Hamilton to GW, 11 Sept., and GW to Hamilton, 17 Sept. (second letter). For the final wording adopted, see Proclamation, 15 Sept. 1792.

2. Jefferson's eldest daughter, Martha Jefferson Randolph, gave birth to her eldest son and second child, Thomas Jefferson Randolph, on 12 Sept. 1792. Jefferson left Monticello on 27 Sept. and stopped briefly at Mount Vernon on 1 Oct. to confer with GW (see Jefferson's Conversation with Washington, 1 October).

From Isaac Mansfield

Marblehead [Mass.]
May it please your Excellency, Sepr 19. 1792
I had the Honour of serving as a Chaplain in the late Army of the United States under your Command—I was introduced to the Regiment under the Command of Genl Thomas in October 1775.

The same Regiment commanded by Coll J. Bailey after Jan. 1. 1776 (which Coll J. Bailey had been Commandant under Genl Thomas) I was continued with, till they moved on from Roxbury to New York in March 1776.[1]

Directions were given in your general Orders in December 1775 that no Return was to be made of a Chaplain till further Orders; because, it having been proposed to Congress that each Chaplain should have the Charge of two Regiments with £10 pr Month they, the Congress had not advised you thereon.[2]

On Feb. 7. 1776 Directions were given in your general Orders in the Words following—"The Continental Congress have been pleased to order & direct that there shall be but one Chaplain to two Regiments, and that the Pay to each Chaplain shall be 33⅓ Dollars pr Calendar Month." Having never received my Pay, Application has been made to Congress; & after having laid before them the two last Sessions—the Settlement seems now to be referred to the Pay Master.

Notwithstanding a Commission from you with which I was honoured dated Apr. 1. 1776 & appointing me Chaplain to two Regiments speaks for itself, the Matter labours on this account I perceive; the Pay Master does not observe by any Resolve of Congress that the pay of Chaplains was augmented or their Service increased by an additional Regiment till July 1776.[3]

The Design of my addressing your Excellency at present is to request a Copy of the Directions in your general Orders beforementioned attested by your Secretary or authenticated in the usual way, which Copy I presume will answer as a sufficient Document.[4]

I have apprehended that there is an Arrearage in respect of Rations, but I perceive that the Pay Master is of Opinion that no Allowance is to be made on that account notwithstanding I have candidly pointed him to a Receit I once gave for some R⟨a⟩tion Money; if not too troublesome shall ⟨be⟩ very much obliged by your Advice thereon likewise.[5]

In the Close of 1776 Sir, I retired f⟨rom⟩ the more public Service of our Country & settled in the Ministry at Exeter in [New] Hampshire; having left that place b⟨y⟩ mutual Agreement I became an Inhabitant of this Town with a purpose, under the Direction of my late Father who was for many years before & since the Revolution a Practitioner at Law, to qualify myself for usefulness in the civil Line. I should now esteem it a very great Favour to be on the List of Candidates for any Appointment within your own Direction; & hope if honoured by any Appointment I should be able to recommend myself by Fidelity in the Discharge of its Duties.[6]

Wishing you the continued Care of that kind Providence which has guided & so eminently protected you thro' Life thus far, I conclude Your's with great Respect

Isaac Mansfield

ALS, DNA: RG 59, Miscellaneous Letters. Mansfield wrote "a Duplicate" near the bottom of this letter. The mutilated text in angle brackets is provided from Mansfield's original letter dated 11 June 1792 (ALS, DNA: RG 59, Miscellaneous Letters).

Isaac Mansfield (1750–1826), a Harvard graduate who had served as a chaplain to Massachusetts troops from the spring of 1775 to the summer of 1776, became the minister of the First Church of Exeter, N.H., in July 1776. Dismissed from his pastorate in August 1787, he returned to his hometown of Marblehead, Mass., in 1790, where he studied law with his father, Isaac Mansfield (1720–1792), before joining the Massachusetts bar in 1796. During his residence at Marblehead, Mansfield held a number of local offices, including justice of the peace and coroner.

1. Mansfield first served as a chaplain of the regiment commanded by John Thomas (1724–1776), whom the Continental Congress commissioned a brigadier general in June 1775 and gave command of the brigade stationed at Roxbury, Mass., during the siege of Boston in 1775–76. John Bailey (1730–1810), who was promoted to colonel in July 1775, assumed command of Thomas's regiment upon Thomas's promotion. Thomas, promoted to major general on

6 Mar. 1776, took command on 1 May 1776 of the American army laying siege to Quebec, only to die a month later of smallpox. Mansfield chose to remain with those troops left at Boston after the Continental army moved to New York in April 1776.

2. No such general order for December 1775 has been found, but GW wrote John Hancock, president of Congress, on 31 Dec. 1775 that as "frequent applications had been made to me, respecting the Chaplains pay," he had decided to recommend that there be "an advancement of their pay" and "that one Chaplain be appointed to two Regiments." Congress approved GW's recommendation on 16 Jan. 1776 (see *JCC,* 4:61).

3. For Mansfield's unsuccessful petition to Congress in December 1790, see *DHFC,* 3:634–35.

4. Tobias Lear replied to Mansfield on 29 Oct. 1792 from Philadelphia: "The President of the United States has received your letter of the 19th of september, requesting a copy of the general Orders relative to Chaplins, issued on the 7th of February 1776, and in obedience to his command I have the honor to enclose you an extract from those orders attested as you desired." Lear enclosed an extract from GW's general orders given at Cambridge, Mass., on 7 Feb. 1776: "The Continental Congress having been pleased to order & direct, that there shall be *one* Chaplain to *two* Regiments; & that the pay of each Chaplain, shall be *Thirty three dollars* and *one third* per kalender month; the &c." Lear attested that this extract was a "true Copy from the Records of General Orders now in possession of the late Commander in Chief of the Armies of the United States of America, & extracted therefrom by his direction" (DNA: RG 59, Miscellaneous Letters).

5. Mansfield wrote Tobias Lear on 16 April 1794 that he had received his back pay but still had not obtained any compensation for his rations. In that same letter Mansfield referred to Joseph Howell, Jr., the acting paymaster in the early years of GW's administration until Caleb Swan was appointed to that position on 8 May 1792 (DNA: RG 59, Miscellaneous Letters).

6. Mansfield did not receive any federal appointment.

From John Vaughan

Philadelphia 19. Sep. 1792

Mr Vaughan has the honor of transmitting to his Excellency President Washington a letter he received under Cover from England—The accounts from france are later than what are probably contained in the letter, & Not So Satisfactory as those Mr Vaughan recd by the same opportunity.[1]

L, DNA: RG 59, Miscellaneous Letters.

1. The enclosure has not been identified, but Philadelphia wine merchant John Vaughan may have enclosed a letter or other document received from his father, Samuel Vaughan, who resided in England at this time.

Letter not found: to Samuel Fraunces, 21 Sept. 1792. GW wrote Tobias Lear on 21 Sept. from Mount Vernon: "Not knowing what delays you may have met with on the Road, I have directed Mr Francis in a letter of this date, to engage Mr Page's Coach to be here, to accomodate our journey to Philadelphia."

To George Gale

(Private)

Dear Sir,   Mount Vernon Sep. 21st 1792

Your letter of the 4th Instt came duly to hand, but previous to the receipt of it I had been under the necessity of giving the Secy of the Treasury some direction for the Commd of the Revenue Cutter of Maryland, I am not less obliged however by the trouble you have been at to obtain the information you gave me on this point.[1]

I would thank you for relating, in as precise terms as you can recollect, what you told me (as I passed through Baltimore) Colo. Mercer had said of my Sentiments respecting his Speeches opinions & Conduct in Congress—and the manner in which he had come at or had understood them to be mine.[2] With much esteem I am—Dr Sir Yr Obedt Hble Servt

                                                        Go: Washington

ALS (photocopy), NjP: Armstrong Collection; LB, DLC:GW.

1. Gale's letter of 4 Sept., with its mixed recommendation of David Porter for the master commander of the Maryland revenue cutter *Active,* arrived after GW had decided to appoint Porter (see Hamilton to Otho H. Williams, 13 Aug. 1792, in Syrett, *Hamilton Papers,* 12:199). For GW's earlier request for Gale's opinion on Porter, see GW to Hamilton, 5 Aug. 1792. The appointment was effective 5 Aug. 1792 (see Tobias Lear to Jefferson, 26 Oct. 1792).

2. GW apparently saw Gale the previous July when he stopped in Baltimore during his return to Mount Vernon from Philadelphia (see Bartholomew Dandridge to Gabriel P. Van Horne, 14 July 1792, in Tobias Lear to Thomas Jefferson, 11 July 1792, n.2). For background on GW's disagreement with John Francis Mercer over Mercer's use of GW's name in his 1792 election campaign for Congress, see GW's Memorandum of a Statement to James Craik, 7 Sept., Mercer to GW, 15 Sept., and GW to Mercer, 26 Sept. 1792. Gale reported his recollections to GW in a letter of 23 Sept. from Baltimore: "As I have not an Opportunity of immediately recurring to the Gentleman from whom I had the confidential communication which I imparted to you (on your Way through Baltimore) I cannot at this Interval of Time State it as precisely as I could Wish. As well as I can now recollect I told you in general Terms I had been informed that Colo. Mercer had told two or three influential Characters in his district

that his Political Opinions and Conduct during the last Session were approved by you; that he had Assurances of it from some Character high in your family or Confidence and the impression of the Gentleman from whom I had it seemed to be that he meant the Secretary of State" (DLC:GW).

To Alexander Hamilton

Sir,   Mount Vernon Septr 21st 1792.
    Under cover of this Letter you will receive the Proclamation which is just returned to me with the counter signature of The Secretary of State. I have erased the words "dictated by weighty reasons of public exigency," & scored others with a pencil, which you are hereby authorised to take out or retain as you may think best.
    As the Instrument is drawn I could do no other than fill up one of the blanks with the name of the place at wch I *now* am; but, as it is to have a general circulation, you may decide upon the propriety of this, & alter or let it stand according to your judgment.[1] With esteem, I am &c.

                                    G: Washington

LB, DLC:GW.
    1. For background on the writing of the proclamation that GW issued urging compliance with the federal excise tax on whiskey, see Hamilton to GW, 1, 9 (second letter), and 11 Sept. 1792. For the final wording of this official document, see Proclamation, 15 Sept. 1792.

To Tobias Lear

Dear Sir,   Mount Vernon Sepr 21st 1792
    I have written but one letter to you since I came to this place[1] —I was on the point of writing a second when yours of the 5th of August came to my hands informing me of your intention to leave Portsmouth about the first of this month, and expectation of reaching Philadelphia (if no unforeseen delays happened) the 20th. This information arrested my intention, as it was uncertain at what place to direct to you—or, that the letter would reach your hands before it re-verberated back to that City.[2]
    I feel myself much obliged by the information contained in your letters of the 21st of July and 5th of August; but as I expect soon to see you I shall only take notice of that part of it which re-

spects a tutor for a few boys, and my ardent wish that you may have been able to succeed in your expectation of getting one. I am more & more persuaded of the utility of the measure; & that without it, the loss to Washington will be irreparable.[3]

I have nothing agreeable of a domestic nature to relate, and I go not abroad to Collect information of any other kind. Poor George! He is, I believe not far from that place, from whence no traveller returns. He is but the shadow of what he was; he has not been out of his room & scarcely from his bed these six weeks. At times he has intervals of ease which flatter a little, but I have little hope of his surviving the Winter. This adds not a little to my distress & perplexity on a subject you are already acquainted with— but no more of this—at least for the present.[4]

My family, and this part of the Country are more sickly than they have been since the recollection of the oldest of us; first with the flux (but that did not prevail in my family) and next with intermittant & remittant fevers. all the whites of it, however, have kept up, except William, whose fever is by an act of his own imprudence.[5]

Not knowing what delays you may have met with on the Road, I have directed Mr Francis in a letter of this date, to engage Mr Page's Coach to be here, to accomodate our journey to Philadelphia; for which place I expect to set *out* the 8th though I may not arrive in that City before the 13th or 14th of Oct.—The Stage however is to be at this place on the 7th at Night. If you should be in Philadelphia by the time this letter reaches it, I shall rely on your usual punctuality & exertion to effect this. If the Carriage should not be here before the 8th the case will not be altered, as I do not expect Mrs Washington will leave this place before the 9th—The Sale may require my remaining in George-Town one day.[6]

If this letter should find you in Philadelphia, let me know the result of your application to Mr Page by the first Post after it is received.[7] Our united and best wishes are offered for yourself Mrs Lear & the Child and with sincere & Affectionate regard I am always Your friend

Go: Washington

P.S. If Mr Page cannot send his Carriage some other equally convenient[,] if to be had[,] must be sent for our accomodation as it is thereon we depend.

ALS, CSmH.

1. See GW to Lear, 30 July 1792.

2. GW and Lear left Philadelphia in mid-July (see Lear to Knox, 10 July, and Lear to GW, 15 July). GW and his family returned to Mount Vernon for the summer, while Lear, his wife Mary, and his one-year-old son, Benjamin Lincoln Lear, visited family and friends in Lear's hometown of Portsmouth, New Hampshire. Both men and their families returned to Philadelphia in October, Lear on 7 Oct. and GW on 13 Oct. (see Lear to GW, 7 Oct., and GW to Anthony Whitting, 14 Oct. 1792).

3. For background on GW's earlier displeasure with the academic progress of Martha Washington's grandson, George Washington Parke Custis, at the academy of the College of Philadelphia, see Lear to GW, 3 April 1791, and note 2. For Lear's success in finding a tutor, see Lear to GW, 7 Oct. 1792.

4. Because of George Augustine Washington's illness, GW needed to arrange for someone else to take on the duties of Mount Vernon manager. Anthony Whitting, overseer of the Ferry and French's farms since 1790, gradually assumed more and more of the manager's duties. The "subject" with which Lear was familiar was whether GW should accept a second term as president. Lear used his trip to Portsmouth to survey public opinion about the new government and to determine if there was support for GW to serve a second term (see Lear to GW, 21 July and 5 August).

5. William Osborne, GW's valet de chambre, recovered sufficiently from his illness to accompany GW on the trip to Philadelphia. A relapse while on the road forced Osborne to delay his journey, and he arrived in Philadelphia a few days after the rest of GW's party (see Decatur, *Private Affairs of George Washington*, 183, 291). The administration of quinine for William's fever suggests that he had malaria (see GW to Lear, 1 Oct. 1792).

6. GW's letter to Samuel Fraunces, steward of his Philadelphia household, has not been found. GW hired a coach from Stephen Page of Philadelphia for the trip to Philadelphia, paying $7 per day for the use of coach, driver, and horses (16 Oct. 1792, Cash Memorandum Book H). As planned, GW left Mount Vernon on 8 Oct., and he stopped in Georgetown to attend the sale of lots in the Federal City before proceeding to Philadelphia (see GW to Betty Washington Lewis, 7 Oct., and Broadside: Sale of Lots in the Federal City, 8 October).

7. Lear replied on 7 Oct., the day that he returned to Philadelphia.

To John Lewis

Dr Sir, Mount Vernon Septr 21st 1792.

I have sent your brother Howell to Fredericksburgh to receive from you my moiety of the money which has been paid to you by Mr Cooper for the Land in Gates County No. Carolina.[1] I expect it will be fully paid; and a statement of the Accots rendered, by which I can here after settle with, and receive whatever may be due for my part, from Mr Cooper, without giving you any further trouble in the receipt of it. An exact statement of the Agreement, and of the account with him, therefore, becomes necessary in order to enable me to do this.[2] I am &c.

G: Washington

LB, DLC:GW; ALS, sold by Bangs, Merwin, & Co., *Catalogue of a . . . Collection of Autograph Letters, Documents, and Signatures,* item 416, 1 June 1874.

1. This tract of slightly more than 1,000 acres of Dismal Swamp land in northeastern North Carolina had been purchased jointly by GW and his brother-in-law Fielding Lewis in 1766. For background on the initial purchase and later the sale of this tract to Portsmouth, Va., merchant John Cowper after Fielding Lewis's death in 1781 and GW's attempts to collect payment from Cowper, see George Augustine Washington to GW, 7 Dec. 1790, and note 7, and Indenture with John Cowper, 17 May 1791, and note 1.

2. For a statement of GW's account with Cowper as of 3 Oct., see John Lewis to GW, 3 Oct. 1792, n.2.

To James McHenry

(Private)
Dear Sir,   Mount Vernon Septr 21st [1792].

Fearing some accident may have prevented my last (enclosing a letter for Mr Robt Smith) from reaching your hands, I take the liberty of giving you the trouble to receive this, requesting to be informed if this be the fact—and if not, what has been the result of your enquiries in the business Committed to you.[1]

I have had many applications in favor of Mr Hollingsworth as a fit character for the Attorney, and lately, one from the District Judge in his behalf. No answer has been given to any of them, awaiting to hear from you first.[2] With Sincere esteem & regard I am—Dear Sir Yr Affecte & Obedt Servt

Go. Washington

Copy (photocopy), DLC: James McHenry Papers; LB, DLC:GW.

1. For background on GW's search for a suitable candidate for appointment as the U.S. district attorney for Maryland, see GW to McHenry, 13, 31 Aug., and McHenry to GW, 16 Aug. 1792. For GW's letter to Robert Smith of 31 Aug., see GW to McHenry, 31 Aug., n.3.

2. For letters of recommendation for Zebulon Hollingsworth, including one of 18 Sept. from federal district court judge William Paca, see GW to McHenry, 31 Aug., n.1. McHenry replied to GW on 25 Sept. 1792.

From Alexander Hamilton

Sir,　　　　　　　　　　Treasury Departmnt Septr 22d 1792.

I have been duly honored with your Letters of the 7th and 17th instant, and perceive with much pleasure a confirmation of the expectation which your former communications had given that your view of the measures proper to be pursued respecting the proceedings therein referred to, would correspond with the impressions entertained here.

I flatter myself that the Proclamation will answer a very valuable purpose; but every thing, which the law and prudence will warrant, will be put in train, as circumstances shall indicate, for such eventual measures as may be found necessary. I do not, however, despair that with a proper countenance the ordinary course of legal coertion will be found adequate.[1]

The enclosed copy of a letter from the Inspector of Kentuckey to the Supervisor of Virginia, of the 12th of July last, and the copy of a letter from one of his Collectors to him of the 1st of June, contain interesting, and comparatively not discouraging matter respecting the state of things in that Survey.[2]

The Supervisor of Virginia in a letter to the Commissioner of the Revenue, of the 10th instant, expresses himself thus—"I can truly say that the Excise is now fairly on it's legs in this District—it rests on the good-will of the greater part of the people, and our Collectors are from no cause indisposed to the service, but the apprehension of too much business for too little compensation." A letter from Mr Hawkins (Senator) to Mr Coxe announces favorable symptoms in the part of North Carolina which is in the vicinity of his residence.[3]

On the whole, I see no cause of apprehension, but that the law will finally go into full operation with as much good will of the people as usually attends Revenue Laws.

You will be pleased also to find enclosed a letter from the Commissioner of Revenue to me dated the 12th instant, submitting an arrangement for compensating the Officers of Inspection for the period antecedent to the commencement of the permanent arrangement which you lately established; and the plan of an Act for that purpose to be passed by the President, if approved by him; together with an Estimate of the total expence of the proposed arrangement.

The law has made provision for the restrospective increase of compensation at the discretion of The President, and as the out-set of the business will have been of course the most perplexing and troublesome, nothing can be more equitable than such a retrospection, except in those particulars in which the encreased compensations would either be inapplicable or liable to abuse. It will have besides, the good effect of stimulating the zeal of the Officers by shewing a liberal attention to their past services, hith-erto defectively requited.

The Plan submitted is the result of previous consultation be-tween the Commissioner of the Revenue and myself, and appears to me an eligible medium.[4]

The Petition from the Keeper of the Rhode Island Lighthouse has been put in a course of enquiry, and the result will be made known.[5]

The Lighthouse in Virginia being nearly finished, a trusty keeper of it will be speedily necessary. A letter from David M. Randolph Esqr. to Governor Lee, which was transmitted by him to me, and is enclosed, recommends for the purpose the name of John Waller Johnson; but I have no other information con-cerning him. You will probably recollect, Sir, a person who some time since was recommended by Colo. Parker—a man who it seems was very active during the war and distinguished himself in some water-enterprises; but who appeared much addicted to liquor, a fault peculiarly disqualifying in such a station. I regret that I forgot his name—I believe he was disabled in one of his arms. No other Candidate has been brought forward. A letter has been written to Mr Newton, mentioning Mr Johnson to him and requesting him to communicate his opinion of him to you, and of any other character who might occur.[6]

Pursuant to the authorisation in your letter of the 7th instant, measures have been taken for discharging the Debts due to for-eign Officers. Upon a review of the tenor of the Certificates, in order to this, it appeared that the interest only was payable at Paris—the principal here. Had it been clear, that motives of ac-. comodation would render the payment both of principal and in-terest there desireable, there might have been difficulty in justi-fying the regularity of the proceeding, and of course hazard of blame, especially if any mistake or accident in the execution had happen'd. But it is very possible that payment in the United States will be most agreeable to the greatest number. The arrangement of course embraces the payment of Interest at Paris, of principal at the Treasury; but with an option to those who choose it to receive both at the Treasury, as will be more particularly seen by the enclosed copy of an Advertisement by the Treasurer.[7]

With the highest respect and the truest attachment, I have the honor to be &c.

Alexander Hamilton

P:S. I have the pleasure to transmit herewith a letter from Mr G: Morris which was handed to me by Mr R. Morris.[8] The Supervisor has been desired to forward to the Circuit Court at York town, such proof as he should be able to collect addressed to the Attorney General. It will I perceive be satisfactory to that Officer to receive your direction to proceed there. His presence is of importance, as well to give weight to what it may be proper to do, as to afford security that nothing which cannot be supported will be attempted. I submit the expediency of a line from you to him.[9]

A.H.

LB, DLC:GW.

1. See the proclamation that GW issued on 15 Sept. 1792 in response to opposition to the federal excise tax on whiskey.

2. Thomas Marshall was the inspector of the revenue for the new state of Kentucky, which was designated as the seventh survey in the District of Virginia. Edward Carrington was the supervisor of the revenue for the District of Virginia (see Executive Order, 15 Mar. 1791). The enclosed copies of these letters have not been identified.

3. Carrington's letter to Tench Coxe, commissioner of the revenue, of 10 Sept. has not been identified. Benjamin Hawkins resided in Warren County, which was in the fourth survey of the District of North Carolina. His letter to Coxe may have been the one of 12 Sept., an extract of which was printed in the *Gazette of the United States* (Philadelphia) on 22 Sept. 1792: "A correspondent from the western part of the state observes, that the people are generally anxious to take out licences for their stills during the season; but there is no county in which there is a person authorised to grant them, owing to the difficulty of executing the former law—that they are tolerably satisfied with the present modification, as better accommodated to their rights." For background on the federal excise tax on whiskey, see Hamilton to GW, 1 Sept., source note.

4. For Coxe's letter to Hamilton of 12 Sept., see the letter-book copy in DNA: RG 58, Letters Sent by the Commissioner of the Revenue and the Revenue Office, 1792–1807; see also the extract in Syrett, *Hamilton Papers*, 12:368. On 25 July, Coxe had sent Hamilton a draft proposal for changing the compensation rates for the supervisors, inspectors, and collectors employed in enforcement and collection of the excise tax on whiskey (see ibid., 85–98). Coxe's let-

ter of 12 Sept. included modifications to the 25 July proposal. Section 16 of "An Act concerning the Duties on Spirits distilled within the United States," of 8 May 1792, provided: "That the President of the United States be authorized to make such allowances for their respective services to the supervisors, inspectors and other officers of inspection, as he shall deem reasonable and proper" (1 *Stat.* 267–71). For GW's approval of Coxe's ideas, see GW to Hamilton, 1 Oct., and Orders to Revenue Officers, 29 Oct. 1792. GW included the revised compensation arrangement for revenue officers in his 22 Nov. report to Congress.

5. The petition from William Martin, keeper of the Rhode Island lighthouse on Conanicut Island, requesting an increase in his salary has not been identified (see Coxe to William Ellery, 30 Oct. 1792, DNA: RG 58, Letters Sent by the Commissioner of Revenue and the Revenue Office, 1792–1807). In the "List of Civil Officers of the United States, Except Judges, with Their Emoluments, for the Year Ending October 1, 1792," which Hamilton submitted to Congress on 26 Feb. 1793, Martin's salary is listed as $140 (see *ASP, Miscellaneous,* 1:68). Hamilton wrote GW on 22 June 1793 recommending that Martin's salary be increased to $160 per year, and GW approved the increase effective 1 July 1793 (see Tobias Lear to Hamilton, 18 July 1793, in Syrett, *Hamilton Papers,* 15:109–10).

6. The enclosed letter from David Meade Randolph, U.S. marshal for the District of Virginia, to Virginia governor Henry Lee, in which he recommended John Waller Johnston (Johnson; 1757–1832) for appointment as the keeper of the lighthouse currently under construction at Cape Henry, Va., has not been identified (see Henry Lee to Hamilton, 23 June 1792, ibid., 11:550–51). On 30 June 1792 Randolph wrote a letter of recommendation for Johnston addressed to Thomas Jefferson (DLC:GW), who forwarded it to GW on 7 July. Johnston, who was the deputy customs collector at Bermuda Hundred, Va., did not receive the appointment as the Cape Henry lighthouse keeper (see Johnston to James Madison, 1 Mar. 1792, *Madison Papers,* 14:239–41). Instead GW appointed William Lewis, inspector of the revenue for Fredericksburg, Va., to that position (see William Lewis to GW, 12 Nov. 1791, Lear to Hamilton, 13 Oct. 1792). When Lewis died in November 1792, Johnston reapplied for the job (see Thomas Jefferson to GW, 8 Dec. 1792, n.2). He again failed to receive the appointment, which went to Lemuel Cornick, who had overseen the building of the Cape Henry lighthouse (see Lear to Hamilton, 22 Dec. 1792, DNA: RG 26, Inventory NC-31, entry 16, Miscellaneous Records Relating to the Lighthouse Service; see also the extract in Syrett, *Hamilton Papers,* 13:356–57). Johnston moved to Spotsylvania County, Va., in 1793 and then to Nelson County, Ky., in 1794.

The person recommended by Virginia congressman Josiah Parker apparently was Capt. Thomas Herbert, who had lost his left hand in battle while serving as a captain in the Virginia navy during the Revolutionary War.

At Hamilton's request Coxe had written Norfolk merchant Thomas Newton, Jr., on 17 Sept. 1792 asking for his help in identifying suitable candidates for the lighthouse appointment and mentioning Randolph's recommendation of Johnston (DNA: RG 58, Letters Sent by the Commissioner of Revenue and the

Revenue Office, 1792–1807). For Newton's reply containing his opinions on Johnston and other candidates, see his letter to GW of 28 September.

7. For background on payment of the U.S. debt to foreign officers who served in the Revolutionary War, see Hamilton to GW, 27 Aug. 1792, and notes 1 and 2. The advertisement by Treasurer of the United States Samuel Meredith, dated 17 Sept. 1792, reads: "WHEREAS pursuant to the fifth section of the act of Congress entitled 'An act supplementary to the act making provision for the debt of the United States' passed the eight day of May last, provision has been made for discharging the debts due to certain foreign officers, on account of pay and services during the late war, the interest whereof as expressed in the certificates granted to the said officers, by virtue of a resolution of the United States in Congress assembled, is payable at the house of Mr. [Rodolphe-Ferdinand] Grand, Banker, at Paris.

"This is therefore to give notice, that provision has been and is made for the payment of the *Principal* of the said debt at the treasury of the United States at any time after the fifteenth day of October next, upon demand of the parties respectively to whom the said certificates were granted or their respective lawful representatives or attornies duly constituted and authorised, and the production of the certificates in each case granted; and also for the payment of the interest which shall be due upon the said certificates to the thirty first day of December next inclusively at Paris, in conformity to the tenor of the said certificates.

"Should there be any, who prefer receiving their whole dues, interest as well as principle at the treasury aforesaid, it shall be in their option so to do; but in this case all such who are not within the United States at the date hereof, must make known their election to the Minister Plenipotentiary of the United States at the Court of France, or to the person whom he shall appoint for that purpose, and must obtain from the said Minister Plenipotentiary, or from the person appointed by him, a certificate of his having made and communicated his election so to do.

"In consequence of the foregoing provision, interest, after the said last day of December next, will cease upon all such of the said debts, for the payment whereof, application shall not have been made pursuant to the tenor hereof, prior to the first day of January one thousand seven hundred and ninety-three" (*Federal Gazette and Philadelphia Daily Advertiser,* 19 Sept. 1792).

8. The letter from Gouverneur Morris, which apparently was delivered by Robert Morris, is probably his letter to GW of 10 June 1792 (see GW to Gouverneur Morris, 20 Oct. 1792).

9. For background on resistance in western Pennsylvania to the implementation of the excise tax on whiskey and the efforts of the federal government to indict members of this opposition at the U.S. Circuit Court for the Middle District, which met at York, Pa., on 11 Oct. 1792, see Hamilton to GW, 1 Sept. 1792, GW to Hamilton, 7 Sept., 1 Oct., Edmund Randolph to GW, 10 Sept., and GW to Randolph, 1 Oct. 1792. No letter from GW to George Clymer, supervisor of the revenue for the District of Pennsylvania, has been found for this period.

From Henry Knox

Sir.   War department September 22d 1792.

I have the honor to acknowledge the receipt of your letter of the 17th instant.[1]

I have now the honor to submit a copy of Major General Wayne's last letter dated the 14th instant No. 1 and my answer thereto No. 2.[2]

I have also the honor to submit a Copy of Brigadier Putnams letter of the 14th No. 3 and of Brigadier Wilkinson's of the 19th of August No. 4 with two enclosures one from Major Strong and another from Major Smith—these several letters will afford you a recent view of the situation of affairs North West of the Ohio.[3]

I hope daily to receive Governor Blounts communications which I flatter my self will be satisfactory.

Major Gaither had safely arrived at Charleston and sailed for Savannah—I believe every thing is in quietness in that quarter.[4]

I have also the honor to submit you a letter from Ensign Morgan No. 5. and my answer thereto of the 19th instant No. 6—The Court was assembled for the trial of Nineteen deserters whom I thought best to try and punish in preference to marching them in Irons through the Country.

I shall hope to receive your ultimate orders on this subject in the course of the next week.[5]

When the detachment shall arrive at Pittsburgh which marched hence yesterday, and also the troops mentioned in the letter to General Wayne to rendezvous at the great Kenhawa on the 25th instant, he will have received about One thousand nine hundred non commissioned and privates.

From the returns and estimates of the respective rendezvous there may be about Two hundred recruits not marched—If to this number we estimate five hundred additionals to be at Pittsburgh on or about the first of January it will make the number of recruits raised and marched this year about Two thousand six hundred—To this number is to be added the old troops of the First and Second Regiment and one company of Artillery amounting to one thousand two hundred & four, which will make the whole number of troops on the Ohio and its waters about Three thousand eight hundred & four.

But in all probability the recruiting service will be abundantly more successful in the autumn and Winter than it has been, so that hopes may be entertained of completing the establishment and having the recruits for that purpose at Pittsburg by the fifteenth of May next at farthest.

After all the desertions which have happened, it is my opinion that not more than twenty five or thirty have escaped—The prompt payment of ten dollars reward operates as a powerful inducement to apprehend them. I have the honor to be sir with the highest respect Your humble Servant

H. Knox

LS, DLC:GW; LB, DLC:GW. The closing of the LS is in Knox's handwriting.

1. This letter from GW is dated 16 September.

2. On 14 Sept., Wayne wrote Knox from Pittsburgh that both Arthur St. Clair, governor of the Northwest Territory, and the Seneca chief Geyesutha had visited him on 9 September. That same day ensign John Sullivan, Jr., Wayne wrote, "also arrived from Fort Franklin, which place he left two days later than *Geyesutha*—just before he set out, the Cornplanters *interpreter* came in, from the Nation, with intelligence, that he with the *New Arrow,* and other Indians, of influence from that town, had gone to accompany, about Five hundred of the Senekas, & Canada Indians, to visit the hostile Indians—and had set out from Buffaloe Creek a few days since, he also mentioned that the first *Messengers,* from the five Nations were put to death by the *Delawares,* that the Senekas or second Messengers, were saved, but had not yet returned—that the Cornplanter was very uneasy and said if any of his people were killed, he would immediately go to war with the hostile Indians—so much for Indian intelligence. . . . Permit me to ask a few interesting questions—1st Is there any certainty, of the posts on the Lakes being given up, in time for an early Campaign next Spring? 2d. If not—won't it be expedient for me to descend the Ohio with the troops in time, to cover them in *Hutts,* before the inclement season sets in? 3d. Will not a *desultory* expedition, composed of mounted Volunteers & some Regulars be adviseable (provided the Indians continue hostile) under cover of which, the head of the line may eventually be advanced to Genl St Clair's field of battle?" Wayne assured Knox that "every exertion in my power, has, and will be made, to perfect the troops, in discipline, & for the service, for which they are intended," and he described his training procedures. He estimated that the army would need 100,000 bushels of grain to support its horses, especially "should the war progress" (DLC:GW; see also Knopf, *Wayne,* 97–99).

Knox replied to Wayne on 21 Sept.: "I hope the six nations have gone forward to the hostile indians in the numbers mentioned by the Cornplanters interpreter. If so most probably peace would be the effect—It is to be very much desired that the *first* messengers of the five nations should not have been put to death, whom I take to be Captain Hendricks and his brother."

Knox disagreed with Wayne's estimate of the amount of grain needed and asserted that if "fifty thousand bushels of dry corn be now laid up," it should be sufficient until future events dictate additional purchases. "Your regular force this winter," Knox wrote, "will not probably exceed three thousand five hundred non commissioned and privates this may serve as data from which to estimate provisions—Although it is highly judicious to form abundant magazines both of provisions and forage; yet no small danger is incurred of damage and loss of various sorts by directing an excessive quantity without proper Store houses. If however you should foresee any obstacles to purchasing hereafter the full quantity of forage we may require for an early and vigorous campaign the next year, it will be perhaps the safest method to give the order now for an additional quantity of Twenty five thousand bushels, making in all Seventy five thousand bushels.

"In answer to your three interesting queries, I say, as to the first there is no certainty upon the subject, but the business at present rather has the aspect of being procrastinated beyond the time you mention.

"Secondly I believe the destination of your troops for the winter must be deferred until the arrival of the President of the United States, which will not be until the 12th of next Month. But in the mean time you will order the Quarter Master to make vigorous preparation of materials to cover the troops as mentioned in my last.

"Thirdly. As to a desultory expedition at present, it does not appear adviseable or consistent with good faith, until the determinations of the Indians shall be known—perhaps an expedition of that kind might during the Winter or very early in the Spring be undertaken with the most decisive good effect under the cover of which you might push the advanced posts of the line to the battle ground or to the Miami Village, provided the Indians have abandoned it, as all the information confirms—I have given you my opinions on your three queries, reserving further communications on the general conduct to be pursued until the President of the United State's arrival and his orders being taken thereon."

Knox estimated that recent recruitment efforts had raised an additional 555 troops, who were currently on their way to Pittsburgh. He promised to send the various articles requested in Wayne's letter of 13 Sept. (ibid., 92–94), including cloth, needles, thread, blank muster and pay rolls, and fine powder sieves, and he advised, "It is unnecessary to put the hand into the Calibre of the small howitzer to load them—to prove this some specimens of fixed ammunition shall be forwarded. Two thousand five hundred shells of a proper size have probably arrived, as they were forwarded by Colonel [Thomas] Procter— More howitzers have not been contemplated—But if they are necessary they may be cast. Baron Steubens blue book is out of print—but we will have one edition printed with all expedition" (DLC:GW; see also ibid., 100–105).

Knox enclosed in his letter to Wayne a copy of the letter that he wrote Pennsylvania governor Thomas Mifflin on 21 Sept., and he enclosed another copy of that letter in this letter to GW. Knox informed Mifflin that he had instructed Wayne that it was "essential that the frontier Counties should be amply protected" and that Wayne should "erect such stations or send such patroles as will afford all reasonable protection to the inhabitants and banish any well founded apprehensions from their minds" (DLC:GW).

3. Knox is referring to Rufus Putnam's letter to him of 16 Aug. from Fort

Washington, in which Putnam wrote that he was setting out for Vincennes the next day to meet with Indians in that region (DLC:GW; see also Buell, *Putnam Memoirs,* 321–24). For background on Putnam's peace mission, see Knox to GW, 26 Aug., nn.4–5, and GW to Knox, 3 Sept. (first letter), n.3.

James Wilkinson reported to Wayne from Fort Washington on 19 Aug. that "no material casualty has occurred, though my force is considerably diminished by the Escort furnished General Putnam, for his safe guard to Vincennes. . . . I am sorry to be obliged to inform that the forage arrived in very bad order, . . . On the subject of Hay, . . . I have now with infinite regret, to inform you that my force, did not justify a second attempt at Fort Jefferson, but that I have completed my first Crop at Fort Hamilton, computed by those who are called judges at 270 to 300 Tons which is secured by a Strong Stockade, the second Crop from sundry causes will not be considerable, but if the Season favors may turn out fifty or sixty Ton.

"Being at this moment totally uninformed as to the proposed operations of the season, or the arrangements for winter, it is not in my power to enter upon such measures as may hereafter be deemed necessary, and cannot at a late period be carried into execution with equal convenience, I shall however sir, at a hazard erect Stables for a body of Cavalry at Fort Hamilton, and will prepare Materials for Barracks to receive the Dragoons, I am obliged in this Case to proceed by inference & implication, which gives me much embarrassment & uneasiness, . . . The Security of this post, and the simplicity of the duty attending the command, induced me sometime since to move my Quarters to Fort Hamilton, in order that I may be at hand, and as near as possible to give my aid and personal directions in any exigency which might occur there at the advanced post, or, on the communication.

"I am now here on a visit to General Putnam, who sailed for vincennes yesterday morning, and shall return to Fort Hamilton in a day or two, where my presence hourly becomes more necessary.

"You will pardon me for an act of offensive hostility—I killed one and wounded two warriors on the 13th instant, a party had stolen eighteen horses from the Rifle Corps on the morning of the 12th instant about three quarters of a mile from Fort Hamilton, as soon as I got intelligence of the theft, I ordered Captain [Thomas] Barbee, with two suba[l]terns and fifty four men mounted, to take the trail of the Rogues, . . . and after a pursuit of about fifty miles on a N.E. course came up with them, in a very close and broken ground, killed one & wounded two out of Six, recovered every horse, and took six Rifles with their Blankets &c.

"As the season advances, the savages will increase the vigor of their depredations, they are now subsisted on Tassamanauge, and their Corn will soon be hard enough, to pull and dry in the ear; the enclosed copies from communications recently received, exhibit a menacing aspect on the part of the Enemy, who have within a few days killed one, & wounded two more at Dunlaps station on the Big Miami, and have killed taken & wounded several at Columbia, and the stations on the little Miami" (DLC:GW).

Maj. David Strong wrote Wilkinson on 15 Aug. from Fort Jefferson that "Since my last of the 9th instant to this date nothing worthy of notice has occurred. Yesterday morning about 10 oClock, a party of the Enemy, who, I suppose must have been in the neighbourhood some time, suddenly fired upon a few of our people who were watering at the Spring. . . . but I am happy to inform you without doing any further mischief than slightly wounding one man of Capt. [Jacob] Kingsbury's company in the thigh—as soon as they had discharged their pieces they betook themselves precipitately to flight. . . . their object may have been the Cattle—if so, I have hitherto and flatter myself will be enabled totally to disappoint any attempts they may think proper to make" (DLC:GW).

Maj. John Smith wrote Wilkinson, also on 15 Aug., from Fort St. Clair that on that morning "two Serjeants had permission to go out & shoot squirrels for the sick—they were about a half a mile from the Garrison when they received a fire from the Indians . . . the Enemy were in three parties, supposing to be fifty in number, I expect they are after our Cattle, which I hope it will be in my power to baffle their intentions" (DLC:GW).

4. Knox apparently received William Blount's letter to him of 31 Aug. a few days later because he enclosed a copy of it with his letter to GW of 29 September. Maj. Henry Gaither recently had been appointed commanding officer of the U.S. troops in Georgia (see Knox to GW, 23 Aug. 1792, n.3).

5. For background on the court-martial of John Morgan, see Knox to GW, 28 July, n.8, and 15 Sept., n.10. Morgan wrote Knox from Philadelphia on 19 Sept.: "Being this moment informed that a general court martial is sitting in this city, I beg in the most pressing manner to have my tryal brought forward—Excuse me Sir for reminding you of the Articles of War on the subject, they are too pointed surely to have escaped your notice; And with a full persuasion that you will not longer procrastinate my tryal as there is a court martial sitting where my supposed crimes were committed, I shall anxiously wait in expectation of a summons to appear before the court" (DLC:GW). In a subsequent letter to Knox of 20 Sept., Morgan corrected the date of this letter from that which appears on the dateline, 20 Sept., to 19 Sept. (see Knox to GW, 29 Sept., n.5).

Knox replied to Morgan's letter of 19 Sept. that same day: "I have just received your letter dated by mistake on the 20th instant, requesting you may have your trial before the Court Martial now sitting in this City." He informed Morgan that the current court-martial, which would finish its business on this or the following day, had only five members and that there were not enough officers in Philadelphia to form a court-martial of the size that Morgan's case required. The members of the current court-martial also were obligated to return to their previous assignments. Moreover, Knox wrote, "I have no power to revoke the orders of the President of the United States" for you "to repair to the Head Quarters of the Army for trial, allowing you reasonable time to collect your evidence. As your present letter is the first intimation of your being in readiness to undergo your trial your continuance in arrest therefore cannot be attributed to any of the public Officers. As the head quarters of the Army are now at Pittsburg, the sooner you repair there, the sooner you will have an opportunity of being tried before a full Court Martial" (DLC:GW). GW rejected Morgan's plea for a change of venue in his letter to Knox on 24 September.

From Alexander Hamilton

Sir   Philadelphia Sepr 23d: 1792

I have the pleasure of your private letter of the 17 instant.

I continue in opinion, that it will be adviseable to address a letter with the proclamation to each of the Executives of the States mentioned, and shall prepare a draft of one to be forwarded with the requisite number of copies.[1]

A letter from Mr King also of the 17 instant surprised me with the intelligence contained in the following extracts—"Burr is industrious in his canvass—Mr Edwards is to make interest for him in Connecticut—and Mr Dallas who is here, and quite in the circle of the Governor and the party, informs us, that Mr Burr will be supported as Vice President—in Pennsylvania. Nothing which has hitherto happened so decisively proves the inveteracy of the opposition. Should they succeed much would be to be apprehended."

Mr Burr was here about ten days since and every body wondered what was meant by it. It seems to be explained—Yet I am not certain that this is any thing more than a diversion in favour of Mr Clinton.[2]

I forbear any further comment on the event—But I thought it of importance enough to apprise you early of it. With the most respectful and affectionate attachment I have the honor to be Sir Your most obedient & humble servant

                                                    Alexander Hamilton

ALS, PHi: Gratz Collection; ALS (photocopy), DLC:GW. Both Hamilton's notation on the cover and GW's docket label this letter "Private."

1. GW's circular letter to the governors of Pennsylvania, North Carolina, and South Carolina of 29 Sept. enclosed a copy of the proclamation that GW issued on 15 Sept. 1792 in response to opposition to the federal excise tax on whiskey (see GW to Hamilton, 17 Sept. 1792 [second letter], and note 4).

2. New York senator Rufus King's letter to Hamilton of 17 Sept. is in Syrett, *Hamilton Papers*, 12:387. GW, King, and Hamilton were concerned about an effort by the nascent Republican party to replace John Adams as vice-president in the upcoming presidential election. Although Aaron Burr had support from men such as his uncle Pierpont Edwards (1750–1826), who was a prominent Connecticut lawyer and politician, and Alexander Dallas, who was the secretary of Pennsylvania, most Republicans preferred New York governor George Clinton.

From Tobias Lear

Sir,   Boston, September 23d 1792

I have the honor to inform you that I am thus far on my return from New Hampshire to Philadelphia. I have been detained at Portsmouth a fortnight longer than I expected to have been, in order to settle some matters that were interesting to me. I shall leave this place tomorrow and proceed to Philadelphia at the rate of about 30 or 35 miles per day.

I have neglected no opportunity of obtaining such information of the actual state of things in this part of the United States and the sentiments of the people respecting our public affairs as might be useful & proper to be known to you, and shall have the honor of communicating the same when I may be so happy to meet you in Philadelphia.[1]

Mrs Lear and our little boy are in the enjoyment of good health. She unites with me in sincere prayers for the health & happiness of Mrs Washington & yourself, and in se[n]timents of the purest respect & gratitude—to the children we present our love, and to our friends who are with you our best regards—with the truest respect & most grateful attachement I have the honor to be, Sir, Your most Obedient servant

Tobias Lear.

ALS, DLC:GW.

1. For more information about Lear's trip to Portsmouth, N.H., and his return to Philadelphia, see Lear to GW, 21 July, 5 Aug., and GW to Lear, 21 Sept., n.2.

From Aiguillon

                                      Zurich—[24 7bre 1792][1]
Sir,   the 4th year of french liberty

Permit a Frenchman, who loves liberty, and is forced to quit his Country—a prey to factions, to offer his homage to the respectable man who has given a free Constitution to America. Perhaps my name may have reached you. Perhaps you have sometimes heard me spoken of as the friend of Lafayette—faithful, like him, to the cause which he cherished[2]—and like him prosecuted by those who would substitute for despotism the horrors of Anarchy.

I thought it my duty to quit my Country when all the oaths which attached me to it were violated. See the motives which decided me. You will find them with this which I have the honor to address to you. It will be sweet for me to obtain your suffrage—and to know that my conduct is approved by you. the esteem of Washington will console me in my retreat, under the prosecutions which I have suffered & the misfortunes which surround me. I pray you accept the homage of my veneration & attachment

Richelieu [d]'Aiguillon

P.S. I set out for London. Perhaps circumstances may conduct me to the land of liberty where you dwell. If you do me the honor to answer this, will you have the goodness to address your letter to London—to be left in the Post Office.[3]

Translation, in Tobias Lear's hand, DLC:GW; ALS, in French, DLC:GW. The French text of the original receiver's copy appears in CD-ROM:GW.

Armand-Désirée Duplessis-Richelieu d'Agenois, duc d'Aiguillon (1761–1800), a French army officer and member of an influential and wealthy French aristocratic family, led the movement in the National Assembly of 4 Aug. 1789 to remove the traditional dues and services that a French peasant owed his manorial lord, and he challenged the tax exemptions that various corporations, towns, and individuals enjoyed. After the storming of the Tuileries on 10 Aug. 1792, Aiguillon fled to London. He eventually settled in Hamburg, where he remained until his death. For background on the events that led both Aiguillon and Lafayette to leave France in 1792, see Gouverneur Morris to GW, 23 Oct. 1792, and source note.

1. The date is taken from the original French manuscript. Lear mistakenly transcribed the date as "24 January [1]793." The original French manuscript also bears the notation in Lear's writing, "recd ⟨2⟩6 May 1793."

2. Lear made a loose translation from this place in the text to the end of the sentence. A more accurate translation would be: "and like him persecuted by those who tear apart France, and who will return her to despotism through the horrors of Anarchy." Here, as later in the letter, Lear erroneously translated the French word *persécution* as prosecution instead of persecution.

3. No reply from GW to Aiguillon has been found.

To Henry Knox

Sir, Mount Vernon Sepr 24th 1792

Your letter of the 15th instt, with its enclosures, came duly to hand.

It is exceedingly to be regretted that all the attempts of Government to bring the hostile Indians acquainted with the real designs of it—(so far as it respects the disputes with them)—should be so pointedly marked with misfortune, disappoint or delay. Captn Brants illness, and the sickness & delays of the other Chiefs of the Six Nations, are inauspicious of a favourable result; for much is not to be expected from the single attempt of Captn Hendricks however zealously he may labour in the Cause of humanity & Peace; and as prest appearances are so ominous of a continuation of the War, no pains, nor no expence within the bounds of moderation ought to go unessayed to ascertain the nature, extent and strength of the Confederation against which we are to contend; that our measures may be regulated accordingly. Without a competent knowledge of these facts we shall grope in the dark; and may meet disaster when danger is not expected. To this end General Wayne should be particularly instructed—and the Indian Agents also—Nor would it be amiss if some expedient could be devis'd to obtain intelligence from Detroit, that the British accts of these matters might be likewise known. From the nature, & circumstances of this War good information is scarcely to be obtained, at least not to be relied on, but from a comparison of the intelligence which is obtained through different channels.[1]

In your letter to Genl Wayne of the 7th instt, Copy of which is among the enclosures you have forwarded to me, he is informed, that you will "immediately write to the President of the U. States & request his orders on certain conditional Statements relatively to the proportion of Troops which may probably be necessary to retain in the upper parts of the Ohio." No such statement is yet come to my hands—of course I am unprovided with the means by which to form a judgment on this head; but under my present view of the matter, & the uncertainty in which we seem to be of the final & *positive* result of the grand Council of the Indians, holden at the Miami, the longer the decision is with-held the better; provided sufficient time is allowed the Troops to cover themselves comfortably for the Winter. And here, while it occurs, let me ask why the same kind of Huts, & mode of covering that was adopted by the army last War may not be again practiced, except *permanent* Barracks, for sufficient Garrisons, at the established Posts. If Scantling, Brick, &ca are to be provided by the Qr Master it will be attended with considerable expence, and if for a temporary purpose only will be thought injudiciously incurred; and besides, how can this be done, conveniently, before the dispos[it]ion of the Troops is resolved on?[2]

I am in sentiment with you, that Sub-Legionary Pay masters, and Sub-legionary Adjutants (the latter aided by the Sergeant Majors) are competent to their respective duties without Battalion Officers of this description—at any rate I conceive that the experiment ought to be made with the latter in the 1st inste. My observation on every employment in life is, that wherever, and whenever one person is found adequate to the discharge of a duty by close application thereto it is worse executed by two persons—and scarcely done at all if three or more are employed therein, besides, as you have very properly observed, the danger of money is encreased in proportion to the number of hands into which it is committed.[3]

As Major Fish declines the Office of Adjutant General, & Colo. Sproat who (I believe) is on the Spot, is willing to accept it, I have no objection to his entering on the duties; provided it is *known* that he is a man of liberal education and correct in his writings— *doubts* of these qualifications in Colo. Posey are the only obstacles to my giving him a preference to any other.[4]

I have no objections to Sergeants Dunn & Jones filling vacant Ensigncies if they have given sufficient evidence of their fitness; but as there have been some impositions already in people of this Class I recommend strict caution in future—Richardson Should be mentioned to Genl Wayne, that his behaviour may be noticed. A likely young man in Alexandria of the name of Turner, has been strongly recommended to me for an Ensigncy—It is said (among other things in his favor) that a number of young, country born men would enlist under *him*. I have answered, let him "ascertain *that* fact, and then apply with the list of them."[5]

If the Evidence in the case of Ensign Morgan is all given in, it becomes proper he should be ordered to the Army for his trial— & if it is necessary in *this* case, & will not be establishing an unusual, & bad precedent to do it in the name of the President, I have no objection to the measure. If discretion was a trait of this Officers character or fairness the view of his Advisers, I should hope he would abandon the idea of presenting a Memorial to be tried in Philadelphia or that he wd hesitate a moment to go where he is ordered; if, however, the latter should happen, it would be well, before it is reported to me to have him & his friends admonished in a friendly way of the consequences that must follow disobedience; for neither the Military or Civil government shall be trampled upon with impunity whilst I have the honor to be at the head of them. I have no objections to his being tried at Pittsburg, and if their is no reasons opposed to it (unknown to me) I wd advise it. That it cannot happen in Philadelphia is certain—military Propriety, the public Service[,] convenience, & the precedent such a measure would establish are so strongly opposed to it that it is wonderful, he should ever have sufferd the idea to enter into his mind. Why might not another Officer, if endulgence was granted in this instance, apply for a similar one—nay, why not to be carried to Boston, or Charleston as inclination on the expectation of benefits to be derived from it, might prompt.[6]

I perceive in the copy of General Wayne's letter to you beforementioned, that there has been some remissness on the part of the Contractors at Pittsburgh. This ought not to be suffered in the smallest degree, for one neglect or omission, is too apt to beget another, to the discontentment of the Troops & injury of the Service; whereas a rigid exac⟨tion⟩ in every case checks a departure on their par⟨t⟩ from the Contract in any and no indulgence is ever allowed by them to the p⟨ublic⟩. In a former letter led thereto by the observations of Mr Belli I requested that some consideration might be besto⟨wed⟩ on the mode suggested by him of supplying the Troops by means of a Commissary; but I have heard nothing from you on the Subject since.[7]

The Orders given to the Officer who commanded the Escort of money, and to Genl Wayne, respecting the Supervisor appear to have resulted from necessary precaution, and if war⟨r⟩anted by the Constitution & Laws, were undoubtedly proper; and of course are approved.[8] With esteem I am &ca

G. W——n

ADfS, DLC:GW; LB, DLC:GW. The mutilated text in angle brackets is supplied from the letter-book copy.

1. For an account of the various illnesses that delayed the peace process, see Knox to GW, 15 Sept., n.6. For the failure of Hendrick Aupaumut's peace mission, see Knox to GW, 16 Aug., n.4, and 6 Dec. 1792. Knox included GW's directives on gathering intelligence in his letter to Wayne of 28 Sept. (see Knox to GW, 29 Sept. [second letter], n.1).

2. For Knox's letter to Wayne of 7 Sept. 1792, see Knox to GW, 8 Sept. (sec-

ond letter), n.3. The grand council, held by members of the Indian confederacy hostile to the U.S. presence in the Northwest Territory, met between 30 Sept. and 9 Oct. at Au Glaize. Knox included GW's thoughts on winter quarters for the troops in his letter to Wayne of 28 Sept. (see Knox to GW, 29 Sept. [second letter], n.2). James O'Hara was the quartermaster from April 1792 until May 1796.

3. Wayne had suggested the desirability of appointing both sublegionary and battalion paymasters and adjutants in his letter to Knox of 7 Sept. (see Knox to GW, 15 Sept., n.2).

4. For Nicholas Fish's refusal of the adjutant general position and the subsequent failure of Ebenezer Sproat and Thomas Posey to accept the appointment, see Knox to GW, 15 Sept. 1792, n.11.

5. For the promotions of George H. Dunn and Abraham Jones to cornet, see Knox to GW, 15 Sept., notes 2 and 8. In his letter to Wayne of 28 Sept., Knox enclosed a copy of a letter of recommendation for Joseph Richardson written by a Mr. Sprigg to GW (see Knox to GW, 15 Sept., and note 8), and Knox instructed Wayne "to inquire into his conduct and report the same" (see Knopf, *Wayne*, 110). Turner has not been identified.

6. For background on the impending court-martial of John Morgan and his attempts to have the trial moved to Philadelphia, see Knox to GW, 28 July, and note 8, and 15 Sept., n.10.

7. For previous correspondence about supply problems, see Wayne's letter to Knox of 17 Aug., enclosed in Knox to GW, 26 Aug., and GW to Knox, 7 Sept. 1792. For the report from deputy quartermaster John Belli, see GW to Knox, 22 Aug., n.5.

8. For Knox's orders to the commanding officer of Fort Bedford to escort the army's pay and to General Wayne to protect George Clymer, supervisor of the revenue for Pennsylvania, see Knox to GW, 15 Sept. 1792, n.3.

To Henry Knox

(Private)

My dear Sir,   Mount Vernon Septr 24 92

I thank you for the information contained in your private letters of the 16th & 18th instt—From the contents of the last, it is probable Mr Hammond will be here to day, or tomorrow before Noon.[1]

I perceive by the Papers that Mr Penn & lady are arrived—and with them, Mr Andrew Hamilton & family. What, pray, has been the reception of the last mentioned Gentleman by the Officers of the State Government (particularly the Govr)—Mr Morris &ca? I wish to be pretty accurately informed of this before my arrival; because, as he is considered as *one* of the obnoxious characters of the State of Pennsylvania, a little circumspection on the part of the President of the U. States may be necessary.[2]

I hope Mrs Knox & your family were well when you last heard from them. My poor Nephew though a *little* better is scarcely able to walk—If he should recover strength enough to bear the ride it is recommended to him to spend the Winter in the lower parts of the State where the Weather is more temperate than it is at Mount Vernon. But the chances are much against this.[3]

I still hold to my resolution of leaving this for Philadelphia about the 8th or 9th of next month, if the Situation of my family & Servants does not absolutely prevent it; for, never since I have lived at this place has the remitting fever been so prevalent as it has this year.[4] Sincerely & Affectionately I am always Yours

Go: Washington

P.S. Since writing the foregoing, Messrs Hammond & Smith are arrived at this place.[5]

ALS, NNGL: Knox Papers.

1. British minister George Hammond and the Rev. Robert Smith from South Carolina arrived at Mount Vernon this day and left two days later (see note 5).

2. GW made a slip of the pen here by writing "Andrew Hamilton" instead of "Andrew Allen." The *Pennsylvania Gazette* (Philadelphia) reported on 19 Sept. 1792: "In the ship Amelia, [Capt. John] Hill, from London, arrived in this city, last Saturday [15 Sept.], John Penn, Esq; and his lady: also Andrew Allen, Esq; with his four daughters and three sons." John Penn (1729–1795), a grandson of Pennsylvania founder William Penn, had been lieutenant governor of that state before the Revolutionary War. Although Loyalist in his sympathies, Penn never took any overt action against the American cause, and except for some years abroad, he continued to live in Philadelphia or at his nearby country estate until his death. Penn married Ann Allen, the eldest daughter of William Allen (1704–1780), who was chief justice of Pennsylvania 1750–74. Andrew Allen (1740–1825), the second son of William Allen and thus Penn's brother-in-law, became attorney general of Pennsylvania in 1769. Although Allen was a founder of the First Troop Philadelphia City Cavalry in 1774, a member of the city's committee of safety in 1775, and a delegate to the Continental Congress in 1775 and 1776, he balked at independence, and after GW's defeats at Long Island and New York City in 1776, he fled from Philadelphia to British-controlled New York City, returning to Philadelphia only after British general Howe's forces entered the city in December 1777. Allen and his father eventually immigrated to England, and because he was a Loyalist, his property was confiscated and sold. Following his return to Philadelphia in 1792, Allen tried unsuccessfully for several years to recover some of his lost assets before returning permanently to England.

Although some Pennsylvania patriots might have harbored bitter feelings toward Andrew Allen, Knox reported that many did not. In his first letter to GW of 29 Sept. from Philadelphia, marked "Private," Knox wrote: "Mr Andrew Allen (who came out with Mr and Mrs Penn, and who is brother to the latter) has been well received. Previously to his return, a pardon, or the reversal of his attainder was obtained from the Governor, under the seal of the State. He appears to be esteemed and his former conduct entirely obliterated. I dined in company with him two days ago at a large party given by Mr [Isaac] Hazlehurst, specially I beleive to him and Mr Penn" (DLC:GW).

3. Knox, in his first letter to GW of 29 Sept., wrote that his wife, Lucy Flucker Knox, "was brought abed on the 16th instant with a daughter" (DLC:GW). George Augustine Washington left Mount Vernon in October to spend the winter in New Kent County, Va. (see Anthony Whitting to GW, 31 Oct. 1792).

4. GW and family left Mount Vernon on 8 Oct. and arrived in Philadelphia on 13 Oct. 1792 (see GW to Betty Washington Lewis, 7 Oct., to Anthony Whitting, 14 Oct. 1792). For further mention of the illnesses that afflicted various members of GW's household, see GW to Lear, 21 Sept. 1792.

5. When Hammond and Smith were preparing to leave Mount Vernon on 26 Sept., GW wrote a note introducing them to Andrew Ellicott, surveyor of the federal district: "Mr Hammond, Minister of Great Britain, and Mr Smith of South Carolina wish to pass through the Federal City to day, on their way to Bladensburgh [Md]. I pray you to attend on them, and shew the Gentleman such parts of it as their time and inclination may dispose them to view" (ALS, NjP: Straus Autograph Collection).

From Betty Washington Lewis

My Dear Brother　　　　　　　　　　　　Sepbr 25th 1792

My Indisposition for some time Past prevented my writing to you when Howell did,[1] finding my self better to day, I shall endeavour to answer your request of my takeing Harriot to stay with me this winter. I shall have no objection to her being with me, if she comes well cloath'd or Provided to get them, that she may appear tolerable for I can assure you it was not so while with me before, by which means she was prevented frequently from appearing in publick—when it would have been my wish she should.[2]

A Little money laid out in cloaths at this time may be an advantage—I am sorry it will not be in my Power to advance any, haveing at this time three of my Grandchildren to support, and god knows from every Account but I may expect as many more shortly, [(]Fieldings is so distrest that his Childrer would go naked if it was not for the assistance I give him)[3] I am happy to hear by Howell that you and my Sister keep in good health, I sincerely wish a continuance of it, I never had a more Sickly family in my life, than I have had this fall. I shall set out in a few day's to see my Daughter Carter in Albermarl, I think the change of air may be of service[.][4] I shall return in a few weeks, when I shall be glad to see Harriot Present my Love to my Sister and the rest of the family, and Except the sincere good wishis of your Affe⟨c⟩et. Sister

Betty Lewis

ALS, ViMtV.

1. This letter to GW from his nephew Howell Lewis has not been found. The last extant letter from Howell before 25 Sept. 1792 is dated 24 April 1792 and that from his mother, Betty Washington Lewis, is dated 14 May 1792.

2. For background on the care and education of Harriot Washington, see the source note for her letter to GW of 2 April 1790. Harriot moved to the Lewis home in Fredericksburg, Va., in early October (see GW to Betty Washington Lewis, 7 Oct. 1792).

3. Fielding Lewis, Jr. (1751–1803), Betty Lewis's eldest son, spent much of his life in dire financial straits. His extravagant lifestyle and careless handling of money were already evident at the age of 18 (see Fielding Lewis, Sr., to GW, 16 Sept. 1769, and note 3). By the time of his father's death in 1781 he was deeply in debt (see Fielding Lewis, Jr., to GW, 22 Feb. 1784). By 1790 Fielding had sold not only most of the land he had inherited but also most of his worldly goods such as livestock, books, and furniture. Still he could not pay his creditors, and he was incarcerated in debtors' prison in Winchester, Va., later that year (Felder, *Fielding Lewis*, 311).

4. GW's niece Betty Lewis (1765–1830) married Charles Carter (1765–1829), a son of Edward and Sarah Carter of Albemarle County, Va., in 1781, and their home in 1792 was Western View, located near Stevensburg, in Culpeper County, Virginia.

From James McHenry

Sir   Baltimore 25th Sepr 1792

My not writing has been owing to two causes. I was confined to my bed by a fever (remittent) the 5th instant, which left me there till the 20th. I had little hopes of a recovery but it has pleased god that I should get the better of it. I am now convalescent and may soon be as well as heretofore. The other reason is that I have only had Mr Hammonds answer which is against a removal. Mr Tilghmans I expect every day. I had written to both before my illness being very intimate with them.[1] This my dear Sir is the cause why

I have not sooner informed you of the state of the business you were so kind as to commit to my care.[2]

The merchts have again renewed their application to me to beg you to spend one day in Baltimore on your return, and with such instances of respect and attattchment to your person as to make me more desirous that it may be convenient. I told them that I thought the best way would be to concert matters with Grant, and when we got you here to keep you for the day.[3] With the most sincere attattchment and affection I am D. Sir, your Ob. hble st

James McHenry

ALS, DLC:GW; ADf, MdAA: James McHenry Collection.

1. The last five words of this sentence are not included in the draft.

2. In his letter to McHenry of 31 Aug., GW asked him to inquire of Maryland lawyers Nicholas Hammond and William Tilghman whether either would be interested in appointment to the recently vacated position of U.S. district attorney for Maryland, and if so, whether they would be willing to move to Baltimore in order to fulfill the duties of that office. In his first letter to GW of 4 Oct., McHenry enclosed Hammond's and Tilghman's letters, written to him on 12 Sept. and 3 Oct., respectively, in which they both declined the appointment because they were unwilling to move to Baltimore.

3. GW often stayed at Daniel Grant's Fountain Inn when he was in Baltimore. A notice in the *Baltimore Evening Post and Daily Advertiser* on 11 Oct. 1792 reported that GW arrived in Baltimore the previous evening "and this morning proceeded on his journey to Philadelphia, accompanied by his Lady."

From Alexander Hamilton

Sir,   Treasury Departmt Septr 26th 1792.

The Post of yesterday brought me your letter of the 21st instant, with the Proclamation enclosed, which was immediately published through the Secretary of State's Office, in Brown's Federal Gazette; and means will be taken to accelerate a general circulation of it.[1] I have the honor to be with the highest respect & truest attachment, Sir, Your most Obedient and humble servant

Alexander Hamilton

LB, DLC:GW.

1. For publication of GW's proclamation of 15 Sept. urging compliance with the federal excise tax on whiskey, see the 25 Sept. 1792 issue of Andrew Brown's *Federal Gazette and Philadelphia Daily Advertiser*.

Letter not found: from Henry Lee, 26 Sept. 1792. GW wrote Henry Lee on 30 Sept.: "I was favored with your letter of the 26th instt."

To John Francis Mercer

Sir,   Mount Vernon Septr 26. 1792.

Your Letter of the 15th inst: was presented to me by Mr Corbin, on his return from Philada.[1]

As my object in taking your Land near Monocasy (in payment of the Debt due from the Estate of your deceased Father to me) is to convert it into Cash as soon as possible *without loss,* I can have no other objection to an advantageous partition of the Tract than what might result from the uncertainty of the price that may be affixed to it, and the consequent possibility that the amount of a moiety may exceed the sum which is due to me by the last settlement of the Accots—thereby occasioning a payment of money, instead of receiving it. If these difficulties were removed, I have none other to your proposal of dividing the Tract into two equal parts, & fixing the property therein by lot. A mean of doing this, I will suggest. It is—if you have not heard the sentiments of the Gentlemen, or either of them, who were chosen to affix a *ready money* price on the Land (& I give you my honor I have not, and moreover that I have never exchanged a word on the subject with any one, except what I told you was Colo. Wm Deakins's opinion of it's worth)—I will allow you seven Dollars pr acre for a moiety; to be ascertained in the manner before mentioned. I name seven dollars for the following reasons—1st because I have been assured by the above Gentleman (who professes to be well acquainted with the Land) that, in his judgment, it would not sell for more than six Dollars Cash, or seven dollars on credit; & 2d because you have set it at Eight Dollars your self, without being able to obtain that price. Five hundred & fifty acres (if the tract contains 1100) would then be within the compass of my claim; & the surplus, if any, I would receive in young Cows, or full grown heifers from Marlborough at three pounds a head, if more agreeable to you than to pay the Cash[2]—Your answer to this proposal, soon, would be convenient to me, as I shall be on my return to Philada in a short time.[3]

I come now to another part of your Letter, and in touching

upon it, do not scruple to declare to you that I was not a little displeased to find by a letter from Captn Campbell, to a Gentleman in this neighbourhood, that my name had been freely used by you, or your friends, for electioneering purposes, when I had never associated your name & the Election together; and when there had been the most scrupulous & pointed caution observed on my part, not to express a sentiment respecting the fitness, or unfitness of any Candidate for representation, that could be construed, by the most violent torture of the words, into an interference in favor of one, or to the prejudice of another. Conceiving that the exercise of an influence (if I really possessed any) however remote, would be highly improper; as the people ought to be entirely at liberty to chuse whom they pleased to represent them in Congress. Having pursued this line of conduct *steadily*— my surprise, and consequent declaration can be a matter of no wonder. when I read the following words in the letter above alluded to—"I arrived yesterday from Philadelphia, since which I find Colo. Mercer has openly declared, that Mr Richd Sprigg junr informed him, that Bushrod Washington told him that the President in his presence declared, that he hoped Colo. Mercer would not be left out of the next representation in Congress; and added that he thought him the best representative that now goes, or ever did go to that Body from this State."[4]

I instantly declared to the person who shewed me the letter, "that to the best of my recollection, I never had exchanged a word to, or before Bushrod Washington on the subject of your Election—much less to have given such a decided opinion. That such a measure would have been incompatible with the rule I had prescrib'd to myself, & which I had invariably observed—of not interfering directly or indirectly with the suffrages of the People, in the choice of their representatives: and added, that I wished B. Washington might be called upon to certify what, or whether any conversation had ever passed between us on this subject, as it was my desire that every thing should stand upon it's proper foundation." Other sentiments have been reported as mine, that are equally erroneous.[5]

Whether you have, upon any occasion, expressed your self in disrespectful terms of me, I know not: it has never been the subject of my enquiry. If nothing impeaching my honor, or honesty, is said, I care little for the rest. I have pursued *one* uniform course for three score years, and am happy in *believing* that the world have thought it a right one—if its being so, I am so well satisfied myself, that I shall not depart from it by turning either to the right or to the left, until I arrive at the end of my Pilgrimage. I am, Sir, Your very hble Servt

G.W.

Df, DLC:GW; LB, DLC:GW. The draft's docket is in GW's writing.

1. The bearer of this letter may have been Francis Corbin, who represented Middlesex County in the Virginia house of delegates from 1784 to 1794.

2. Mercer and GW had agreed to hire Benjamin Jones and Francis Deakins, brother of William Deakins, Jr., to value the land located in Montgomery County, Md., that was to be transferred to GW in payment of a long-standing debt from the estate of John Mercer, the father of John Francis Mercer (see GW and John Francis Mercer to Francis Deakins and Benjamin Jones, 8 Aug., GW to William Deakins, Jr., 13 Aug., and William Deakins, Jr., to GW, 24 Aug. 1792). Marlborough, located on the Potomac River in Stafford County, Va., was the Mercer family estate.

3. GW left Mount Vernon on 8 Oct. and arrived in Philadelphia on 13 Oct. 1792 (see GW to Betty Washington Lewis, 7 Oct., and to Anthony Whitting, 14 Oct. 1792). For Mercer's reply, see his letter to GW of 5 November.

4. For background on GW's dispute with Mercer over Mercer's reported use of GW's name in his 1792 congressional election campaign, see John Francis Mercer to GW, 15 Sept., and note 2, and GW's Memorandum of a Statement to James Craik, 7 Sept. 1792. Richard Sprigg, Jr. (1739–1798), was a member of a politically influential Maryland family. His estate, Strawberry Hill, overlooked Annapolis and today is part of the U.S. Naval Academy's grounds. Sophia Sprigg Mercer (1766–1812), the eldest of his five daughters, married John Francis Mercer in 1785, and it was land she had inherited that was being surveyed for settlement of the Mercer debt to GW (Kelly, "Cedar Park," 42–47). According to GW's Memorandum of a Statement to James Craik of 7 Sept., the sentence quoted here is from a letter that Capt. William Campbell sent to Philip Richard Fendall.

5. GW is quoting from his Memorandum of a Statement to James Craik of 7 Sept. 1792.

Letter not found: to unknown recipient, 27 Sept. 1792. Sold by Leavitt, Strebeigh & Co., New York, item 501, 15–17 Mar. 1869. Listed as "A.L.S, 'G. W——n,' 1 p. 4to, Mount Vernon."

To Henry Knox

Sir,   Mount Vernon Sepr 28th 1792
    Your letter of the 22d Inst., & the enclosures, came to my hands by Wednesdays Post.

I adhere to my resolution of commencing my Journey for Philadelphia the 8th of next month if the condition of my Servts will admit of it, two of them (one a Postilion) having been extremely ill with remittant fevers which have not yet left them. My order for the Carriage from Philadelphia, to be here by the 8th for my accomodation back, is not countermd on that Acct.[1]

But, as my journey *may* be delayed something longer than was expected—and as the cold season is approaching, I shall, in addition to what I said on the subject in my last, give you, *in general terms,* my ideas for the disposition of the Troops for the Winter under the uncertainty in which we are of Peace, with the Western Indians.[2]

My first wish would be to keep the Army as compact as possible for the purpose of disciplining, and training the men to such kinds of manœuvres & firings as are proper for Indian Warfare—but, as this would involve one of two evils of magnitude namely, an exposed frontier, or an expensive Militia for its protection, this wish is scarcely attainable. How to dispose of the Troops then to the best advantage for defence &ca is next to be considered; and to do this properly, the ulterior movements of the Army must be held in view, & the period of their commencement also—There are two *principal* & one intermediate points on the Ohio which claim particular attention; to wit—Pitsburgh, or some place not far from it—Fort Washington—and Marietta. The grand movement, in the present train of things, must certainly proceed from Fort Washington, but it does not follow (unless circumstances should point to advantages to be derived from a Winter Campaign, when frost would prevent the descent of the Ohio), that the force ought necessarily to be assembled at that place until it was about to make a forward movement—1st because the enemies attention would be less fixed to it—2. because the Magazines of Provisions—Military stores & forage—would accumulate with more ease at that place by lessening the consumption there—and 3d because the River from Pittsburgh to that Post might be descended when the Waters were up, in six or eight days: and matters being previously arranged thereat the army might march as soon as the Junction should be formed: whilst the desultory movement which has been contemplated, might proceed (if from good intelligence it should be thought advisable) from big Beaver to Sandusky. Under this idea of the matter one Sublegion might be Posted under the Comd of Genl

Wilkinson at the Posts below; one at Marietta under the Commd of G. Putnam; & the other two in the upper part of the River under the Commander in Chief, with whom the intercourse would be easy from Philadelphia and his Orders quickly dispatched to the Subordinate parts of the Army below. Without being decided, I ask whether the upper division of the Army, (except the Garrison of Fort Franklin, and a sufficent one for the Stores &ca at Pittsburgh), had not better be hutted in a secure manner on some convenient Spot near the Mouth of, or some where on Big Beaver Creek? Keeping out (as ought also to be the case at the other Stations) a regular succession of Scouts to scour the Ctry above & below as well for defence as an essential part of their Tactics. Such a disposition of the force, if the real movements & plan of operations is kept secret, which they undoubtedly ought to be, would embarrass the enemy not a little; and more than probably be attended with solid advantages—I do not however convey these sentiments to you as an *order*, but give them rather as thoughts that have arisen from the incomplete state of our force & the incertitude of the result of the Indian Councils— and for free observations & remarks both by yourself and General Wayne if there was time to obtain them than from any other motive at present. Perhaps a sufficient Garrison might be better at Mariatte (as the intermediate Post) than a larger force; and *two* Sub-legionary Corps, (including the said Garrison and all others lower down, as the calls for Troops below are great, on acct of the Communication with the advanced Posts) be wintered in Hutts secured by Intrenchments or a fortified Camp at Fort Washington if there are not Barracks sufficient to contain them at that place.[3] I am &ca.

ADf, DLC:GW; LB, DLC:GW; copy, PHi: Large Miscellaneous Volumes. The copy at PHi is docketed "For M: Gen: Wayne."

1. GW received Knox's letter on Wednesday, 26 September. He left Mount Vernon on 8 Oct. despite the illness of William Osborne, his valet de chambre, and Richard Keating, the postilion (see GW to Lear, 21 Sept., and note 5, GW to Lear, 1 Oct., GW to Betty Washington Lewis, 7 Oct. 1792; Decatur, *Private Affairs of George Washington,* 252, 296). GW hired a coach from Stephen Page of Philadelphia for the trip from Mount Vernon to Philadelphia (see GW to Lear, 21 Sept. 1792, and note 6).

2. For GW's previous directives on a variety of military considerations, see GW to Knox, 24 Sept. (first letter).

3. For Knox's reply, see his letter to GW of 29 September. Knox relayed

GW's suggestions and enclosed a copy of GW's letter in a letter to Gen. Anthony Wayne of 5 Oct. (Knopf, *Wayne*, 112–14).

From Thomas Newton, Jr.

Sir   Norfolk [Va.] Sept. 28th 1792
    By request of Tench Coxe Esqr. I beg leave to inform you of
the persons who, have offerd as keepers of the Light house[.] [1]
Capt. William Lewis of Fredricksburg, Capt. Leml Cornick of
Princess Ann, Mr James of the same place & a Mr Thos Herbert
are all that I have known. Capt. Lewis & Capt. Cornick are men
that I am well acquainted with and proper persons to take charge
of so great a trust. Capt. Lewis I beleive you are acquainted, with,
his character. Capt. Cornick is a man of repute & property & has
conducted himself with great propriety as commissr of Wrecks,
is well acquainted with the Coast & vessels & I have no doubt but
either of these wou'd give general satisfaction. Mr James is reputed an honest man but I beleive not able to make such observations as may be necessary. Mr Herbert I cannot recommend as
a fit person. Mr Coxe mentiond a Mr Jno. W. Johnson, I am totally unacquainted with the Gentleman, but think seafaring men
are the most proper for the service.[2] The situation of the Light
house is dreary & disagreeable. the Sea & bay on one side & a
desart on the other & when the wind blows fresh the sand drifts
in such a manner that one is almost blinded by it, no inhabitant
within four five miles of the Light house no garden Spot near it
& no comforts, but in the fishing seasons, deer are plenty in the
desart but hard to get at. Under these circumstances I am of opinion that four hundred Dollars is not too great a compensation
for a good man to keep it.[3] Mr Coxe mentiond if the keeper was
a man of decernment he might be able to check illicit practices,
the situation is such, that a man well acquainted with vessels &
their customs, might probably give such information, as woud be
highly useful to the Revenue officers & be a means of detecting frauds.[4] I expect this night the Light house will be finished
& ready to be lit up, but judge some public information shou'd
be given before a permanent light is fixed. I have prepared the
minds of the Seamen that is nearly done & that a light might be
soon expected in it. I inclose a letter to Mr Coxe wherein I have

given every information that I am acquainted of & have only to observe that Mr McComb merits much in executing the work & running a wall to secure the Light & Dwelling houses, the price of which he leaves to be determind by you, the season was so far advanced that there was no time to be lost in executing it & if it had been left to another year it woud have cost double the sum to have done it.[5] I am respectfully Yr Obt Servt

Thos Newton Jr

Since writing the above Capt. Robt Baron a good man has also proposed himself for a keeper & I have heard that Mr Johson is a serious steady man.[6]

ALS, DNA: RG 59, Miscellaneous Letters.

1. Commissioner of the Revenue Tench Coxe wrote to Norfolk merchant Thomas Newton, Jr., on 17 Sept. 1792 asking him "to receive propositions from persons disposed and able to perform the duties of a keeper and that you will also make enquiries for such suitable persons, transmitting to the President at Mount Vernon all the names that occur and applications that shall be made, with your opinion of that one which shall appear to you most eligible. Honesty, Sobriety, regularity and health ought all to be kept in view, and as the service is a new one the person ought to be [a] man of discretion & plain Sense" (DNA: RG 58, Letters Sent by the Commissioner of the Revenue and the Revenue Office, 1792–1807).

2. For previous discussion about candidates for the position of lighthouse keeper at Cape Henry, Va., see Hamilton to GW, 22 Sept. 1792, and note 6. Although Lewis received the initial appointment, he died shortly thereafter, and Cornick succeeded him (see Lear to Hamilton, 22 Dec. 1792, DNA: RG 26, Inventory NC-31, entry 16, Miscellaneous Records Relating to the Lighthouse Service; see also the extract in Syrett, *Hamilton Papers*, 13:356–57). Mr. James of Princess Anne County, Va., was probably Henry James, a "native of the place, an old Seafaring Man," and a naval veteran of the Revolutionary War, who was appointed lighthouse keeper at Cape Henry in December 1794 (see Coxe to Hamilton, 26 Dec. 1794, in Syrett, *Hamilton Papers*, 17:482 and note 2; Gwathmey, *Historical Register*, 413).

3. GW approved an annual salary of $400 for the lighthouse keeper at Cape Henry (see Tobias Lear to Hamilton, 13 Oct. 1792).

4. Newton is paraphrasing a portion of the 17 Sept. letter he received from Coxe: "It is possible that the keeper of the light house, if an observing and discerning Man may be able to check illicet practices unfavorable to the Revenue of Impost" (see note 1).

5. The enclosed letter from Newton to Coxe has not been identified. For background on the construction of the Cape Henry lighthouse and the awarding of the building contract to John McComb, Jr., see Hamilton to GW, 5 Jan. 1791, source note, and notes 1 and 2.

6. Robert Barron (1748–1811), who had been an officer in the Virginia

navy during the Revolutionary War, served several years on the Norfolk common council before expressing an interest in the lighthouse position. Another candidate for the appointment, not mentioned in this letter, was George Wray, Sr. (see Jacob Wray to GW, 13 Sept. 1792).

Circular to the Governors of North Carolina, Pennsylvania, and South Carolina

Sir,   United States, September 29th 1792.

Inclosed you will find the Copy of a Proclamation, which I have thought proper to issue, in consequence of certain irregular and refractory proceedings which have taken place in particular parts of some of the States, contravening the Laws therein mentioned.[1]

I feel an entire confidence, that the weight and influence of the Executive of North Carolina, will be chearfully exerted, in every proper way, to further the object of this measure, and to promote on every occasion, a due obedience to the constitutional laws of the Union.[2] With respect, I am Sir, Your Excellency's Obt Servt

Go: Washington

LS, addressed to Alexander Martin, Nc-Ar: Governor's Papers; LS, addressed to Thomas Mifflin, PWacD; Df, in Alexander Hamilton's writing, DNA: RG 59, Miscellaneous Letters; LB, DLC:GW. The LS to Martin was posted at Alexandria, Va., on "1st Octr," with a notation in GW's writing: "President U.S." The dateline and docket of the draft are also in GW's writing.

1. On 15 Sept., GW issued a proclamation urging compliance with the federal excise tax on whiskey.

2. In his second letter to Alexander Hamilton of 17 Sept., GW asked him to prepare a draft of a letter to accompany the transmission of the proclamation to Thomas Mifflin, Alexander Martin, and Charles Pinckney, governors respectively of Pennsylvania, North Carolina, and South Carolina. The letter to Pinckney has not been found.

To the Commissioners for the District of Columbia

Gentlemen,   Mount Vernon Sepr 29th 1792

Your letter of the 1st instant from George Town came duly to hand.

The delay in acknowledging the receipt of it, has proceeded from a belief that if the orders were transmitted before the sale of lots (appointed to be holden on the 8th of next month) they would get to your hands in time.

Enclosed is an order from the President of the United States authorising the above Sale—and an another for disposing thereafter, of lots by private Sale, at such times, and on such terms as you shall deem best calculated to promote the growth of the Federal City, and the essential interests thereof.[1] With esteem I am —Gentlemen Your Most Obedt Servt

Go: Washington

ALS, DLC:GW; ADfS, DLC:GW; LB, DLC:GW. The ALS is docketed: "Recd 8th Octr 1792."

1. Both orders are dated 29 Sept. 1792. The first order reads: "The President of the United States doth hereby order & direct that any Lot or Lots in the City of Washington may, after the public sale to commence on the Eighth day of October, be sold and agreed for by the Commissioners or any two of them at private sale, for such price and on such terms as they may think proper" (copy, filed with the ADfS, DLC:GW; LB, DLC:GW). The second order reads: "The President of the United States doth hereby order and direct that the sale of Lots in the City of Washington, to commence the eigth day of October next, be of such Lots as the Commissioners, or any two of them shall think proper; that the same sale shall be under their direction, & on the terms they shall publish" (copy, filed with the ADfS, DLC:GW; LB, DLC:GW).

From Henry Knox

Sir   War department September 29th 1792

I have the honor to acknowledge the receipt of your favor of the 24th instant.

I have agreeably to your orders written to General Wayne in strong terms to take immediate measures to obtain a knowledge of the numbers and designs of the hostile Indians. I believe the Wabash is the principal channel through which this can be obtained—There is a person in this town lately from Niagara, from whom I am promised some information—this will be however british reports.[1]

I did not submit to you my statement for the ulterior disposition of the troops, as I conceive that some existing circumstances of the frontiers might render it expedient to wait your return.

The idea of hutting the troops has been suggested to General Wayne.[2]

His last letter, of the 21st instant, mentions nothing material;

he had given orders for an additional quantity of forage—and suggests an additional Officer to each company; the consideration of which will be deferred until your arrival.[3]

Colonel Sproat does not possess the requisite of a liberal education. He was considered a good Inspector of a division under the Baron Steuben. I submit a letter of his for your inspection.[4]

In order to show the improper conduct of Mr Morgan I enclose a copy of a letter of his written on the twentieth instant, to which I have given no answer.

As I am persuaded that he will consider the intimation of his memorial to you, a reason for his not obeying immediately any order I may give him, perhaps it will be best to suspend the ultimate order for him to repair to Pittsburgh until your arrival.[5]

I have the honor to submit a letter from General Pickens and another from Governor Blount since their return—Mr Allison has not arrived.[6]

It seems absolutely necessary that some person should be actually in the Creek Nation in order to prevent by persuasion and bribes the horse stealing and other depredations complained of—A War with the Creeks would generate all sorts of Monsters—It may be an easy matter to light it up but almost impossible to suppress it. I have the honor to be sir with the highest respect Your obedient Servant

H. Knox

LS, DLC:GW; LB, DLC:GW.

1. Knox wrote Wayne on 28 Sept.: "It is of the highest importance . . . that you should be possessed as accurately as possible of a knowledge of the numbers of your Enemies and of the tribes to which they belong. . . . You will therefore to the utmost of your power endeavor to ascertain these facts by all the ways you can devise as well from Detroit as by the way of the Wabash—let the channels be as diversified as possible so that by a comparison of one account with another a satisfactory result may be found" (Knopf, *Wayne*, 111).

2. Despite Knox's omission, GW outlined his opinion on the disposition of the troops during the upcoming winter in his letter to Knox of 28 September. GW expressed his views on quartering the army for the winter in his letter to Knox of 24 Sept. (first letter), and Knox included GW's thoughts in his letter to Wayne of 28 Sept.: "It is suggested by the President of the United States that it may be proper to hut the mass of the troops during the Winter excepting those which shall be destined to form the respective garrisons of the posts. The idea is mentioned that such tools as shall be proper for this business be seasonably provided by the Quarter Master General, if he shall not have a sufficiency on hand—the final position of the troops will be deferred until the arrival of the President about the fifteenth of next Month" (ibid., 110–11).

GW arrived in Philadelphia on 13 Oct. in order to prepare for the beginning of the second session of the Second Congress (see GW to Anthony Whitting, 14 Oct. 1792).

3. Wayne, in his letter to Knox of 21 Sept., wrote: "The principle,—if not the only defect (in my humble Opinion) in the Organization of the Legion & Sub Legions, is that of too few Commissioned Officers, in proportion to the Non Commissioned Officers & privates, considering the service, for which they are intended—perhaps a Captain Lieutenant with the pay of Lieutenant wou'd have a good effect, as in that case, the present Lieutenants might receive brevets of Captains—the Ensigns & Cornets that of Lieutenants, & Ensigns Appointed to each Company.

"At first view it may appear, a heavy additional expence, but in the end I am confident, it will be found both advantagious & Economical—you will have a choice of fine young fellows of education, who may be sent forward to the Legion as a Military school, whilst the recruiting Officers are completing their respective Corps; at all events the Majors ought to have Brevet Commissions of Lieut. Colonels so as not to be Commanded by Militia Lieut Colonels" (ibid., 106–7). Knox commented on Wayne's suggestions in his letter to Wayne of 28 Sept.: "Your ideas relatively to an increased number of Officers will be transmitted to the President of the United States—But I believe he will not approve the idea of brevet rank as he two or three Years ago expressed his disapprobation of that sort of rank" (ibid., 110).

4. The enclosed letter from Ebenezer Sproat (Sprout) has not been identified. During the Revolutionary War, GW had appointed Sproat inspector for Gen. John Glover's brigade on 29 Mar. 1778 and a subinspector under Inspector General Friedrich von Steuben on 11 Aug. 1779. Sproat wrote GW on 15 April 1792 asking for a military appointment, but he did not receive one at that time. For Sproat's current interest in the office of adjutant general of the army and his failure to acquire that position, see Knox to GW 15 Sept., and note 11. Sproat finally obtained a federal post when GW appointed him the inspector of the revenue for the second survey in the District of Ohio on 10 Dec. 1794 (see *Executive Journal*, 1 : 164–65).

5. For background on the court-martial of John Morgan and his attempts to have his trial moved to Philadelphia, see Knox to GW, 15 Sept., n.10, and 22 Sept. 1792, n.5. In his letter to Knox of 20 Sept., Morgan wrote from Philadelphia: "I was honored last evening with your answer to my letter in the morning, dated by mistake the 20th instead of the 19th requesting I might have my Tryal before the Court Martial now sitting in Philadelphia." He then rebutted paragraph by paragraph Knox's refusal of a change of venue, beginning with Knox's observation that there were not enough qualified officers in Philadelphia for a proper court-martial: "Suffer me Sir to ask you whether this Statement contains one single reason, or semblance of reason, for the refusal of my Request, after my having been upwards of two hundred days in Arrest? And more especially when there are at this moment, in this City, double the number of Officers necessary for my tryal; and four times the necessary number are at this moment, and to your knowledge, within two or three days Ride of it! And I believe scarce a day has passed since the day of my Arrest, when there

have been a lesser number! Permit me again to ask Sir, whether my particular Case is of less consequence to the Public, than the Case now under Consideration of the present General Court Martial. I believe I may venture to say it is not. You know Sir that the Rules and Articles of War declare 'No officer who shall be put in Arrest, shall continue so more than eight days, or until such time as *a Court* Martial can be established' And you know too, that I have been in Arrest more than two hundred days, during which time, one or more Courts Martial have been established in the City of Philadelphia, and yet I am refused my trial there, although my accuser is and has been on the Spot, or in its neighbourhood during the whole time! Is this Sir a wise measure? or is it a just one? . . . Your next Paragraph states that were it proper to detain all the officers now in the City of Philadelphia, they would amount to a *much less number,* than thirteen, *which the Articles enjoin when practicable;* and that my case *would seem* to require the highest number. To this I beg leave to answer; that for some days past there have been Ten officers in the City: Vizt Two Majors, four Captains, two Lieutenants, and two Ensigns, and there are many more in the neighbourhood; how then Sir do these amount to *a much less number* than thirteen?

"Permit me again to ask, Sir, whether it is not *practicable,* to order thirteen officers to assemble and constitute a General Court Martial in the City of Philadelphia; where my accuser resides, and where he has been ever since the date of my arrest, except when on some pleasurable excursions into the Country at his own Will? You know Sir that it is practicable. But let us suppose it were not. permit me to ask, ought this to deprive me of the right, to be tried by a lesser number, which the Articles of War give me, in the following Words. Article 1st Administration of Justice 'General Courts Martial may consist of any number of Commissioned Officers from five to thirteen inclusively.' And Article 16th 'No Officer or soldier who shall be put in Arrest or Imprisonment shall continue so for more than eight days or until such time as a Court Martial *can* be assembled.' I cannot but be of opinion that witholding this right from me is an Arbitrary and reprehensible breach of the Articles of War, and for which you are liable to Impeachment. . . . Permit me Sir to ask with due respect, what injury to the public service, can arise from my being tried at Philadelphia, instead of Fort Washington? Allow me to declare Sir, that I can refute every Argument which you or others can adduce on this Head. And I doubt not you know I have it in my power to do so. Your order dated the 29th of March last was, 'to repair *to Fort Washington,* for my trial, because as your orders express, there could not then be assembled at Philadelphia, a competent number of Officers to constitute a Court Martial' Whereas there were then more than treble the number of Officers necessary for the purpose, in the City, and its Vicinity, doing little, and *most of them* no Duty."

Morgan then disputed Knox's claim that he had not heard previously of Morgan's readiness to stand trial: "Have you forgotten Sir my repeated applications for a Court Martial for my Tryal? If you have, I beg leave to refer you to them, and they will convince you that you have had several intimations, and that I have made direct applications for a Court Martial for my Trial; and as none has been appointed, that you alone are the cause of my continuing in Arrest!

"Should you attempt to throw it on the President, my reply will be, that it was your duty to have informed him of the practicability of Assembling, at Philadelphia, a competent number of Officers to constitute a Court Martial."

Morgan reminded Knox that he intended to appeal to GW so that "a General Court Martial may be constituted for my Tryal at Philadelphia where the Parties are and all the evidences may be conveniently Assembled, And where the Gentlemen of approved abilities may be had as Judge advocate and Counsel. And this is the more incumbent on me, as it is expected by several of my brother officers who esteem your order for my going to Fort Washington as an unwise and arbitrary Punishment for a supposed crime before tryal, and tending to deprive me of the advice, and of the Evidence, I may require for my Justification. And especially too as this order, if submitted to without a remonstrance, may be drawn into precedent and some military tyrant may, at a future day, order a supposed offender from Georgia to the Lake of the Woods.

"As this Letter may be adduced as Testimony at my Tryal, permit me to remark, that it appears to me a little extraordinary, that the papers I called for out of the War Office so long ago as the 27th of March and my repeated application the thirtieth of March as necessary to my trial have never yet been furnished to me: I complain of this, because it was materially necessary to me, to have had them at that time. I beg leave now to repeat that request.

"Permit me also to say that so material an evidence as Major [Henry] Gaither being ordered to Georgia, has surprized me, but if his Testimony which Major [Thomas] Butler published in the Pennsylvania Federal Gazette No. [   ] proving that Major Gaither did actually report to General St Clair in the night of the 3d of November, can be admitted as testimony at my Court Martial, no Inconvenience can arise to me, but you know Sir, that the Testimony of an Officer, can not be admitted, before a Court Martial but in person.

"So long ago as the 3d of March, Captain [Jacob] Slough requested the public to suspend their opinion with regard to this Business and he pledged himself to prove by officers and Gentlemen of the Army, then at a distance, that what I said was false and that he did actually receive his orders from and make report to General [Richard] Butler; If there is no impropriety therein, I would ask the favor to be informed of the names of these *Officers and Gentlemen of the Army,* previous to my Court Martial; and that he may be officially reminded of his promise. As it has been reported that I have declined appearing before a Court Martial, or to that Effect, I shall take the necessary step to contradict the report.

"It is true that I have often declared his Excellency General St Clairs Arrest of me to be void, in as much as it was Arbitrarily illegal, and unmilitary: Illegal as a military officer on Furlough, is not liable to arrest, and unmilitary for want of the necessary form—But if it had been legal and in due Form. I am advised that it is now void, from the unjust studied delays and oppression I have experienced, as already stated in this Letter." In a postscript written the following day from Prospect, N.J., Morgan adds: "My being obliged to come into Jersey to consult my Papers as to dates of several Transactions mentioned in this Letter, is the cause of its not being sent the date it was written" (DLC:GW). No memorial concerning Morgan's court-martial from Morgan to GW has been found.

6. Andrew Pickens and William Blount had returned from a peace conference with the Chickasaw and Choctaw Indians on 7–11 Aug. (see *ASP, Indian
Affairs,* 1:284–88). Pickens, in his letter to Knox of 22 Aug. from Knoxville,
Tenn., wrote: "Agreeably to your request with Governor Blount I attended the
conference with the Chickasaws and Chactaws near Nashville for the proceedings of which I refer you to his report.

"No advices were received from General Wayne tho' the business was not
concluded before the 9th instant, hence no attempts were made to induce any
part of either of those Nations to join the Arms of the United States but from
private conferences with individuals there were good grounds to believe that
a part of both would, if they had been requested.

"But permit me to say that it is in my opinion best that they were not requested and that they may probably be used to more advantage against the
Creeks who from their conduct, as well since the Treaty of New York as before,
evince a determination never to desist from murdering and robbing the defenceless frontier citizens of the United States until they are chastized and restrained by the hands of Government" (DLC:GW).

Blount, in his letter to Knox of 31 Aug. from Knoxville, reported: "On the
10th instant the Conference with the Chickasaws and Choctaws ended, there
was a very full representation of the former but not of the latter, owing there
is reason to believe to the Spanish influence. the Minutes of which will be forwarded to you by Mr [David] Allison who leaves this in ten or fifteen days for
Philadelphia.

"During the conference General Pickens and myself received the strongest
assurances of peace and friendship for the United States from both Nations and
I believe they were made with great sincerity.

"With respect to any part of them turning out to join the arms of the United
States I refer you to General Pickens's letter of the 22d instant forwarded
herewith by Mr Tate [William Tait] and I beg leave to add that my opinion perfectly agrees with his respecting the Creeks.

"The Cherokees as well as the Creeks commit depredations and deserve to
be punished, that is the young and unruly part of them, for the Chiefs to a
Man, except *Double Head* who was a signer of the treaty, I have great reason to
believe most earnestly wish for peace and friendship, but to punish them with
a view to giving peace to the frontiers would be like lopping off a Bough from
a tree for the purpose of killing it, the root of the evil is the numerous and insolent Creeks and it is they who encourage and lead forward the too willing
young Cherokees to murder and rob. By Mr Allison I shall forward you a report upon the state of the four Southern Nations in which I shall be as particular as the information I am in possession of will allow.

"Annexed is a list of the killed and wounded in this territory since the date
of my last letter to you, and by Mr Allison I will forward a list containing the
whole number of killed wounded and made prisoners since January 1791, with
remarks shewing by what Nation.

"I have heard of some letters from your Office in care of Captain Springs who
is gone to Kentuckey but have not received one since that of the 22d of April.

"Mr Tate the Bearer is an Inhabitant of Nashville, a merchant, a man of ve-
racity and well informed as to the occurrences of this Country."

According to Blount's annexed list of those wounded and killed since 26 June, nine people had been killed, six "wounded and escaped," and thirteen made prisoners, of whom nine had been "regained by purchase made by their parents and friends" (DLC:GW). For the list of those killed, wounded, and taken prisoner in the Southwest Territory since 1 Jan. 1791, see *ASP, Indian Affairs*, 1:329–32.

From Edward Newenham

My Dear Sir   [Ireland] 29 Sepr 1792.

A Ship having announced her Departure in two or three Days, I have sent to Dublin to muster up Some of the Last Papers, as Every hour is pregnant with Important News.

Knowing those Virtuous Principles that adorn your Character, & which Justly render you the *First* Character of the Age, I venture to give my opinion—I was a Zealous & ostensible Supporter of the Revolution in France as settled in 1789, but that of the 10th of August, appears to me, as the most dreadfull Scene of Murder, Anarchy & Confusion, that Ever occurred in the annals of Ancient or Modern History—our Noble & Virtuous Freind Marquiss de La Fayette, has acted a Noble Part—if possible, he has Added to his Fame; I think, the Prussian & Austrian Generals, had no right to withhold him, as he travelld as a Stranger, & not as Deserter or an Emigrant—The Cheifs of the Reigning Power in France have amassed Vast fortunes, as they have purloind the Revenues—the amount of the Church Plate—the rent of the Absentees, the Profits of the Royal Forests—& the best Part of the forfeitures[1]—My fourth son, whom you will probably be acquainted with, has just arrived here; he was Captain in the National Guards untill the 10th of August; he left Marsailles on the 11th; bought a Coach, & Luckily arrived Safe here,[2] as the Mob were so furious, that it was Expected Every Englishman would be Massacred, for Reports were Spread that the English Fleet were saild to attack Brist[3]—these Kinds of reports are dayly Spread, as serving to Inflame & Keep alive the fury of the Mob & not leave them a moment for Recollections.

I fear this Ship will sail before we get the Papers of the 11th from Paris; we have now 5 Pacquets, to the 16th Instant due, & I think, when they arrive, that we must have some very Important News; If the whole of what is stated (350000) to Compose the ⟨d⟩ifferent Armies of France, is Collected & armed, an Enthusiastic Spirit may give them a Victory over the Combind Royal Armies, which are not more than 122000 Effective Men—it is thought, that the Russians will soon arrive to join them, & that the Kings of Spain & Sardinia will not any longer preserve a Neutrality.[4]

The Papists here, are Exerting Every Nerve to obtain the Elective Franchise—they are upwards of 3 & ½ to 1, & consequently if they obtain the Elective Franchise, they will return Every County Member, & also the Representatives for all Free Cities & open Boroughs, consequently the Elective Franchise would be useless to the Protestants—they have committed a most Barbarous Murder on a Protestant Farmer for declaring his sentiments; & I fear, that in the Course of next Session of Parliament, the Metropolis will Experience dreadfull Convulsions unless the Protestants take some strong & Decisive Measures to protect themselves—In America they are so few, that they cannot Change your Constitution or Interrupt your Happiness—I assure you, we go to Bed with fears of a Nightly rising, not a Protestant, but what is Doubly Armed—they have so Contrived Matters, that our Popish Servants report Every word that passes at our Table to their Committees.[5]

This moment I recived the Enclosed Paper, & as an Extract of your Letter has been published by Mr Frost the Companion of Mr Paine, I Enclose it in this Letter;[6] the Custom House officers have made a daring Breach of the Constitution, in opening Letters; this affair will undergoe a Very Serious Investigation.

Lady Newenham joins me in most Sincere & Respectfull regards to Mrs Washington & you—I have the Honor, to be, with the greatest respect—Dear Sir your Excellency's most obt & affte Humble Sert

　　　　　　　　　　　　　　Edward Newenham

I did not Know of the sailing of this ship (the Cardiff) untill this Morning, or I should have Collected more papers.

ALS, DLC:GW.

1. For the recent events in France, including the storming on 10 Aug. of the Tuileries, where Louis XVI and his family were living, the subsequent arrest of the king, and the capture and imprisonment of Lafayette by the coalition army of Austria and Prussia, see Gouverneur Morris to GW, 23 Oct. 1792, and source note and note 1. For background to the recent anticlerical policies of the French government, see Bouscat to GW, 17 May 1792, n.3.

2. Newenham, who was the father of eighteen children including five sons,

frequently mentioned his fourth son in his letters to GW without identifying him by name. Robert O'Callaghan Newenham was probably this son, but it is also possible that he was Burton Newenham. The eldest two sons were Edward and William, and another son, Charles, was an officer in the British navy. In 1786 Newenham wrote GW in an ultimately unsuccessful attempt to have his son Robert appointed the U.S. consul at Marseilles (see Newenham to GW, 12 Aug. 1786, and note 1). In his letter to GW of 24–27 July 1789, Newenham wrote: "my fourth Son, whom I bound to a Merchant at Marsailles, . . . enlisted as a Member of the Marsailles Corps."

3. Brest was the principal French navy base on the Atlantic. France and Great Britain were not officially at war until France declared war upon Britain on 1 Feb. 1793.

4. Contrary to Newenham's expectations, Russia did not join the Austro-Prussian alliance against France at this time. Sardinia, although currently defending its provinces from French aggression, officially did not join the alliance until 1793, when Spain, Great Britain, and the Netherlands also entered into what is known as the First Coalition. Charles IV was the king of Spain from 1788 to 1808, and Victor Amadeus III was the king of Piedmont-Sardinia from 1773 to 1796.

5. Although the Irish Parliament by this time had acquired a degree of legislative independence, it still represented the interests of the British Empire and the Anglican Church. The Roman Catholic majority was excluded from the franchise until 1793.

6. None of the enclosures have been identified. Attorney John Frost (1750–1842) was a founder and leader of the London Corresponding Society, a radical political group inspired by the French Revolution and the ideas found in Thomas Paine's *Rights of Man*. Frost was arrested by the British government in 1793 and found guilty of sedition for his public advocacy of the abolition of the British monarchy.

To Henry Lee

Dear Sir,   Mount Vernon Sepr 30th 92

I was favored with your letter of the 26th instt enclosing one from Arthur Campbell Esqr—For the perusal of which I thank you. The information contained in it is extremely agreeable for it has brought the supposed dead to life, and a valuable man back to his Country again.[1]

I congratulate you on your return to Richmond in good health. In a few days I shall commence my journey for Philadelphia.[2] Always—I am Yr Obedt & Affecte

Go: Washington

ALS, Bibliothèque Publique et Universitaire, Geneva; ADfS, DNA: RG 59, Miscellaneous Letters; LB, DLC:GW. The ALS is postmarked "Alex. 1 Octr."

1. Lee's letter to GW of 26 Sept. 1792 has not been found. The enclosed letter from Arthur Campbell, county lieutenant of Washington County in southwest Virginia, to Lee of 10 Sept. reads: "It is with pleasure I communicate the account of the return of Coll Hardin to Fort Washington. His narrative is concisely this—that he reached the Sandusky unmolested, but was there made a prisoner with the man that accompanied him, both of whom was condemned to death, and the Colonel had the affliction to be a Spectator when his fellow traveller was committed to the flames. The following day was allotted for his execution; but in the night, eight young men of the Wyandot tribe, stole him from his keepers—concealed him some days in a wood, and then set out with him for Fort Jefferson, where they all arrived safe.

"We are assured that the Illinois & Wabash Indians are disposed to treat with the United States for peace; but that the Miami's, Chippawa's, & the Shawanese & Delawares continue inveterate enemies—This intelligence comes from Post Vincennes.

"Governor Blount has had an interview with a number of the Cherokee Chiefs since his return from Nashville. He with warmth complained of the depredations of their disorderly young men, & added, his people would pursue & kill all that was met with, if an instant stop was not put to future attacks. An old Chief answered laconically that his people had Guns, & could shoot too. On our frontier northwardly, all is quiet since the affair in the New Garden" (PHi: Large Miscellaneous Volumes). Campbell's information concerning John Hardin's survival was erroneous (see Knox to GW, 16 Aug., n.3, and GW's Address to the U.S. Senate and House of Representatives, 6 Nov., n.2). GW sent a copy of Campbell's letter to Knox, with a brief covering letter written at Mount Vernon on 1 Oct. 1792, in which he wrote that Campbell's letter gives "some information with respect to Indian Affairs" (Df, DLC:GW; LB, DLC:GW; copy, PHi: Large Miscellaneous Volumes).

2. Lee had returned recently from an extended tour of the militia outposts in southwest Virginia (see Knox to GW, 15 Sept. 1792, n.7). GW left Mount Vernon on 8 Oct. 1792 (see GW to Betty Washington Lewis, 7 Oct. 1792).

From Charles Pinckney

Dear Sir   Charleston [S.C.], September 30th 1792.

I have the honor to enclose you copies of Letters from General Pickens[1] and Colonel Anderson on the subject of Indian Affairs[2]—To me I confess their intelligence is unexpected, for I thought the justice and friendship the United States had treated the Creeks and Cherokees with, had entirely secured their confidence and respect; and that notwithstanding the attempts of the northern and western Indians, the Spaniards, and perhaps the British, the Southern States would have been free from their hostility. To the enclosed Letters I refer you for a full statement

of their situation, and as the opinions of General Pickens and
Colonel Anderson on Indian Affairs are much more to be depended upon than any others I must submit to your better judgment the measures necessary to be pursued in this emergency,
assuring you that while I continue in office no exertions of mine
shall be wanting to carry your directions fully into execution. In
answer to that part of Colonel Anderson's letter which seems to
wish my authorizing an expedition immediately into the Indian
country, I have said, that having been always determined to make
the federal Constitution my guide, and the individual States being very properly restrained from commencing or undertaking
a war without the authority of the Union, I should not feel myself by any means justified in sanctioning a measure of that kind,
even from its necessity, because however properly it might be
done in this case, yet still if a precedent was once established no
doubt instances would frequently occur where the Union might
be involved in the most serious expenditures of blood and treasure by the unjustifiable or perhaps unprovoked and precipitate
measures of interested States or individuals—I informed him I
would however immediately submit the intelligence and opinions of General Pickens and himself to you, and I had no doubt
but proper measures would be adopted by the general government to support our Citizens and protect their rights—In the
interim I have ordered the frontiers of this Country to be put in
the best state of defence the situation of the militia will admit,
and have sent and mean to send them up such supplies of ammunition as the commanding Officer requires, and have directed Block houses to be built for the protection of the most exposed inhabitants of the frontier—The Regiments of Militia I
have ordered to hold themselves in readiness are some of them
on, others near, and none of them more than eighty miles distant
from the frontier—they consist of about 8000 men altogether,
of which I hope a sufficient number may be summoned if they
have notice to protect it, as I have desired them to raise a corps
of militia horse to each Regiment as soon as possible—I have
also requested General Pickens and Colonel Anderson to send
me their opinions on the subject and if they concur with me, I
shall endeavour to have a deposit of ammunition &c. established
in a situation sufficiently near to supply them with ease and at
the same time so distant as to be free from surprize—Our upper
Counties being covered in some degree by the more distant and

extensive frontier of Georgia and North Carolina I am hopeful the measures I have pursued may be sufficient to protect them until some general system is adopted by the Union with respect to the War which I assure you I am apprehensive will be much more serious than the northern one as the southern States are not numerous, the frontiers extensive and exposed, the scene of action at a great distance from the seat of the federal government and the hostile tribes strong and well supplied with arms and ammunition—Georgia will be the most severe sufferer— for if a general Creek war takes place which from these accounts seems unquestionable, I have very little doubt the greatest part of that Country will soon be overrun by them—I shall write you again in a few days by Mr Barnwell,[3] and remain with the highest respect & attachment—Dear sir, Yours truly

Charles Pinckney

LB, DNA: RG 107, Office of the Secretary of War, Letters Sent and Received, 1791–97; copy, DNA: RG 46, Second Congress, 1791–93, Senate Records of Legislative Proceedings, Reports and Communications; copy, DNA: RG 59, Miscellaneous Letters. The latter copy, which is docketed "Duplicate of A Letter by Burrough⟨s⟩," lacks a dateline and is filed under the date 25 Sept. 1792. Pinckney sent his letter by Edward Burrows, captain of the brig *Georgia Packet.*

Henry Knox, in a letter to Pinckney of 27 Oct., wrote: "The President of the United States has directed me to acknowledge the receipt of Your Excellency's letter of the 30th ultimo, with the enclosures therein contained, from General Pickens and Colonel Anderson, dated the 12th, 13th, and 20th of the same month" (*ASP, Indian Affairs,* 1:262; see also Knox to Tobias Lear, 27 Oct., n.3).

1. For background on Andrew Pickens's past military and diplomatic experiences with Indians, see Pinckney to GW, 8 Jan. 1792 (first letter), n.3. Pickens and William Blount, governor of the Southwest Territory, had recently returned from a meeting with the Chickasaw and Choctaw Indians (see Knox to GW, 29 Sept. [second letter], n.6). From Hopewell, his estate in South Carolina, Pickens wrote Pinckney on 13 Sept.: "Colonel Anderson I expect has written you fully on the state of affairs in this part of the country and the prospects there are of a war with the Creeks and some of the Cherokees, it might perhaps be well to give him some general orders in case our frontiers should be attacked and to make some necessary arrangements to prevent a surprize— Ammunition I know is very scarce in the frontier parts of this State and I find that circumstance very much discourages the people. Whilst I was in the western Country attending the treaties with Governor Blount I found that Country particularly Cumberland, in a most pitiable and distressed situation, almost continually harrassed by the Creeks and the four *lower towns of the Cherokees on the Tenessee*—just before we went there a small station was taken with about nineteen or twenty persons in it, all were killed or taken but three or four which made their escape, this was done by a party of Cherokees, Creeks and a few Shawanese, who had resided among the Cherokees for some years past sev-

eral others were killed and wounded in that Country while I was there. From the different accounts which I had from the Chiefs of the Chickasaws and Choctaws, in private conversation, as well as from persons from that Country, all agree that the Spaniards are using all their influence with the southern Indians to engage them against the United States—and I am clearly of opinion that the Creeks are on the eve of going to war with us as well as those four lower towns of the Cherokees—I believe there is no doubt but the Chiefs and a number of the warriors of the Creeks are now at Pensacola in treaty with the Spaniards, they are soon expected here with a large quantity ⟨of⟩ ammunition for the purpose of going to war, the same thing has been offered to those tribes we have lately been in treaty with, this the Chiefs told us in confidence—but the Chickasaws appear well attached to the interest of the United States, so did the Choctaws *who attended the treaty, but the Spaniards* have great influence over a great part of that nation—the cause of our misfortunes with the Indians in general is of an old date, and our misfortunes in the northern Campaign the two last years, and I fear our prospects the present expedition in that quarter are not favorable—all those things are against us and encourage our enemies; were I to venture an opinion respecting our southern country it would be this, make immediate preparation for the *defence of the frontiers, and as soon as possible carry a vigorous campaign into the Creek country, this would convince the southern Indians in general that we are able and determined to protect ourselves and would chastise their insolence, this might prevent the junction* of more tribes against ⟨us⟩ than perhaps is now expected, it is vain to attempt treaties with the Creeks or to make any offers to them until they are chastised by the arm of government." Pickens also reported that "Mr [Leonard] Shaw, an Agent from Congress has lately come in here and left the Cherokee nation, he thinks it unsafe at present to return, altho' a great majority of the Cherokees appear friendly to the United States" (DNA: RG 107, Office of the Secretary of War, Letters Sent and Received, 1791–97; the missing text in angle brackets is supplied from DNA: RG 59, Miscellaneous Letters).

2. Robert Anderson (1741–1812), who moved from his native Virginia to South Carolina in 1761, served as an officer in the South Carolina militia, beginning in 1775, and spent most of his military career during the Revolutionary War under the command of Andrew Pickens. After the war he became brigadier general of the South Carolina militia's 4th Brigade. Anderson served eleven terms in the state house of representatives and one term as lieutenant governor, 1796–98.

Pinckney enclosed two letters from Anderson, both probably written from his estate on the Keowee River. The first letter, dated Wednesday morning, 12 Sept., contains an extract of a letter that Anderson had just received from Pickens, which reads: "Mr Shaw agent from Congress to the Cherokees arrived here last evening. . . . He says the four lower Towns of the Cherokees in the Tennessee have declared for war—with John Watts at their head who was lately with the Spaniards at Pensacola. He says they were to set out in a body on the 4th instant, and to make a stroke at Cumberland or the settlements near Knoxville on the Holstein—He expects that their numbers will be from four to five hundred, the Creeks will no doubt make a part—He says the Creek Chiefs are not yet returned from Pensacola but are expected shortly with a large quantity of ammunition for the purpose of war—The other parts of the Cherokees from Eust⟨anury⟩ this way advised him to come down here, and sent a guard with him—As you are about writing to the Governor I have sent you this intelligence, as I wish you to write fully to him as I am well assured if some immediate measures are not taken to prevent, this Country will be in a distressed situation."

Anderson then gave Pinckney his own views on the situation: "Having previously conversed with the General, and having consulted my own reason on the present prospect of Indian affairs, my real sentiments were as communicated in the Letter, of the rectitude of which there is a strong confirmation. We can only expect now to hear of the perpetration of such acts of savage cruelty committed on the defenceless inhabitants in all quarters of an extensive frontier a circumstance which must be regretted by every feeling heart" (DNA: RG 107, Office of the Secretary of War, Letters Sent and Received, 1791–97).

The second enclosed letter from Anderson to Pinckney, which is dated 20 Sept., begins with a brief history of past attacks by the Cherokees upon the western portion of South Carolina. Anderson then wrote: "I have ordered the people to build Block houses where they are exposed and intimidated to fly to with their families, in case of alarm—I have frontier Block houses built, and building at suitable places along our frontiers at the distance of about 8 or 10 miles apart, five are on the way, some of which are nearly completed, but I believe another must be appointed to complete the chain—I have ordered trusty Spies to be constantly kept out at Toogalo and the Oconey mountain as they are the spots (in all appearance) which will be most exposed—I have ordered a few men from the more interior part of the Regiment to each of the frontier posts, but in some places there is a difficulty in providing them provisions, the settlements being thin on the frontier, the people poor, and their improvements and crops but small—I mention those matters to show what is done in the mean time, and to beg your Excellency's further orders and directions in those matters.

"Permit me to observe that we (having had so much experience in the ways of Indian warfare) are of opinion that it is very expensive, hazardous, and distressing to carry on a defensive war with Indians. . . . Experience has discovered it to be much the better way to carry the war immediately into their own country—they seem not to be so well calculated to oppose a spirited attack in their own country as they are to take sculking wolfish advantages of the defenceless in ours—a very speedy and spirited attack in their country might perhaps rid us of a war which might become very hazardous, and expensive in the long run. We think that if a party of men could possibly be marched through the peaceable Towns and into the disaffected Towns of the Cherokees, before the Creeks made a stroke, that it might check the Creeks, at least it might keep back their premeditated stroke until the clumsy wheels of government could be got turned. But we are well aware that if the Creeks do immediately break (of which there is but little room to doubt) and the United States are obliged to carry on a defensive war, if only till next June yet it will cost them much blood and treasure; perhaps double as much as would keep an army in their country during the time—these conclusions we are warranted to draw from past experience—I just returned home from reviewing the frontier parts of the Regiment. . . . But now Sir, you may rest assured, that the moment has arrived, when the most spirited exertions of Government are necessary, and I am truly sorry that the Citizens cannot be permitted to defend themselves in the best way without the approbation of Government—I mean by an offensive war—because I am of opinion that much could be done in the course of two months from this date, much blood and treasure might be saved, by a spirited exertion before they were aware, and I have no doubt but two or three thousand of the Militia from this State and Georgia could be immediately raised to march light into the Creek country—about 500 militia horse, the rest Infantry with pack horses—Two thousand more from the Western territory and N. Carolina in the same manner to march through and destroy the disaffected Cherokee towns, which would be just on their way and meet in the Creek country, destroy what they could and so return. . . . But if your Excellency would even consent to risque your approbation to such a plan and depend upon the necessity of the case to justify the measure in the eyes of the President and Congress, I have hardly any doubt but the western country people would do their part at all ventures, for they are well calculated for such enterprizes. But if any thing of the kind was attempted to be carried into effect, General Pickens must be appointed to the command in preference to every other man, for two reasons, first because the people have confidence in him and will chearfully turn out to go under his command—and in the next place because he is most equal to the task. . . . should an expedition into their country next Spring be approbated, we are very scarce of Flour in those Southern States, as the rust killed up the wheat generally. This is an unfortunate circumstance, but there is flour enough in the northern States, which could be shipped to Savannah in Georgia and brought up in Boats to Augusta, all those things must be done this winter, else no Campaign in the Spring—then we may as well dissolve the Union, as to pretend to hold together because Georgia will be ruined, perhaps this State and several others much injured—Indeed I am of opinion (if they see Congress tardy, or relax in their exertions, as they have been against the northern tribes) they will soon have Spain to contend with and perhaps one more of the European powers." Anderson concluded his letter by reminding Pinckney of an earlier, unfulfilled request for "arms and ammunition" (DNA: 107, Office of the Secretary of War, Letters Sent and Received, 1791–97).

3. Robert Barnwell, a rice planter from near Beaufort, S.C., was elected to the Second Congress in 1791. The previous year he had delivered to GW, on behalf of Pinckney, a sketch of an *Agave americana* (century plant) in bloom (Pinckney to GW, 6 Oct. 1791). Pinckney's next letter to GW was dated 14 Oct. 1792.

From Joseph Donaldson

Sir   Baltimore 1st Octobr 1792

After a labour of thirty years in this Country I am reduced to distress—My first place of residence was Fredericksburg—I removed from thence to York in Pennsylvania and acquired by industry a fortune—I came to Baltimore and by giving too extensive credit I lost my all, during the War my services in York County were not unprofitable to the cause of Liberty, I exerted myself in sending out men and my House and Purse were ever open to the friends of America.

I am now poor—a Wife and six children look to me for support—I am unable to give it My request to you Sir is to mention my name for any place which is or may become vacant in this Town the profits of which may maintain my family[1] and gratitude will ever exist in the breast of

Joseph Donaldson

ALS, DLC:GW; copy, DLC:GW.

1. Donaldson, a Baltimore merchant, wrote GW on 8 Aug. 1793 to apply, again unsuccessfully, for a federal appointment, this time for the position of surveyor of the port of Baltimore (DLC:GW).

To Alexander Hamilton

Sir,   Mount Vernon Octobr 1st 1792.

Your letter of the 22d ulto, with it's enclosures, came duly to hand.

Lest any *material* disadvantage should result from delay; I have signed the Act which has been drawn by the Commissioner of the Revenue & approved by you, for arranging allowances to the Supervisors &c.—and now forward it; but I would rather, if this is not likely to be the case, have it retained in your hands until my arrival in Philadelphia, as I wish for some explanations, which I have not the means of obtaining from the want of the former Act of the 4th of August; a copy of which I requested might be returned to me, but from a misconception of my meaning, a copy of my letter was sent in lieu thereof. I now request a copy of the Act of the 4th of Augt & of the present one also.[1]

Before any nomination, or appointment of a Keeper of the Lighthouse on Cape Henry takes place, it would be proper to examine the List of Applicants (& I think there are several) who have applied to me for this Office, & is to be found among my papers by Mr Lear. If the person recommended by Colo. Parker is intemperate in drinking, it is immaterial, whether you can recollect his name or not; for, with me, this would be an insuperable objection, let his pretensions & promises of reformation be what they may. I have been once taken in by the fair promises of Major Call to refrain, & the strong assurances of his friends that he would do it; but will not, knowingly, trust again to the like from any one.[2]

I have, by this Post, directed the Attorney General to attend the Circuit Court in York Town, & see that the Indictments are legally prosecuted & properly supported.[3] I am &ca

G: Washington

LB, DLC:GW.

1. For background on changes implemented in the compensation rates for the supervisors, inspectors, and collectors employed in enforcing and collecting the federal excise tax on whiskey, see Hamilton to GW, 22 Sept. 1792, and note 4. See also GW's Orders to Revenue Officers, 29 Oct. 1792. Hamilton erroneously had enclosed a copy of GW's letter to him of 5 Aug., rather than the 4 Aug. proclamation, in his letter to GW of 10 August.

2. For previous discussion of the candidates for lighthouse keeper at Cape Henry, Va., see Hamilton to GW, 22 Sept., and note 6, and Thomas Newton, Jr., to GW, 28 Sept., and notes 2 and 6. For problems with Maj. Richard Call, see GW to Knox, 19 Aug. 1792.

3. See GW to Edmund Randolph, 1 Oct. 1792, and note 1.

Thomas Jefferson's Conversation with Washington

Bladensbg [Md.] Oct. 1. [1792]

This morning at Mt Vernon I had the following conversation with the President. he opened it by expressing his regret at the resolution in which I appeared so fixed in the letter I had written him of retiring from public affairs.[1] he said that he should be extremely sorry that I should do it as long as he was in office, and that he could not see where he should find another character to fill my office. that as yet he was quite undecided whether to retire in March or not. his inclinations led him strongly to do it. nobody disliked more the ceremonies of his office, and he had not the least taste or gratification in the execution of it's function. that he was happy at home alone, and that his presence there was now peculiarly called for by the situation of Majr Washington whom he thought irrecoverable & should he get well he would remove into another part of the country which might better agree with him.[2] that he did not believe his presence necessary: that there were other characters who would do the business as well or better. still however if his aid was thought necessary to save the cause to which he had devoted his life principally he would make the sacrifice of a longer continuance. that he therefore reserved himself for future decision, as his declaration would be in time if made a month before the day of election. he had desired mister Lear to find out from conversations, without appearing to make the enquiry, whether any other person would be desired by any body. he had informed him he judged from conversations that it was the universal desire he should continue, & the expectation that those who expressed a doubt of his continuance did it in the language of apprehension, and not of desire. but this, says he, is only from the North, it may be very different in the South.[3] I thought this meant as an opening to me to say ⟨w⟩hat was the sentiment in the South from which quarter I came. I told him that as far as I knew there was but one voice there which was for his continuance. that as to myself I had ever preferred the pursuits of private life to those of public, which had nothing in them agreeable to me. I explained to him the circumstances of the war which had first called me into public life, and those following the war which had called me from a retirement on which I had determd. that I had constantly kept my eye on my own home, and could no longer refrain from returning to it, to as to himself his presence was important, that he was the only man in the U.S. who possessed the confidence of the whole, that government was founded in opinion & confidence, and that the longer he remained, the stronger would become the habits of the people in submitting to the government & in thinking it a thing to be maintained. that there was no other person who would be thought any thing more than the head of a party. he then expressed his concern at the difference which he found to subsist between the Sec. of the Treasury & myself, of which he said he had not been aware. he knew indeed that there was a marked difference in our political sentiments, but he had never suspected it had gone so far in producing a personal difference, and he wished he could be the Mediator to put an end to it. that he thought it important to preserve the check of my opinions in the administration in order to keep them in their proper channel & prevent them from going too far.[4] that as to the idea of transforming this government into a monarchy he did not be-

lieve there were ten men in the U.S. whose opinions were worth
attention who entertained such a thought[.] I told him there
were many more than he imagined. I recalled to his memory a
dispute at his own table a little before we left Philadelphia, between Genl Schuyler on one side & Pinkney & myself on the
other, wherein the former maintained the position that hereditary descent was as likely to produce good magistrates as election. I told him that tho' the people were sound, there was a numerous sect who had monarchy in contemplation. that the Secy
of the Treasury was one of these. that I had heard him say that
this constitution was a shilly shally thing of mere milk & water,
which could not last, & was only good as a step to something better. that when we reflected that he had endeavored in the Convention to make an English constitution of it, and when failing
in that we saw all his measures tending to bring it to the same
thing[.][5] it was natural for us be jealous: and particular when we
saw that these measures had established corruption in the legislature, where there was a squadron devoted to the nod of the
treasury, & doing whatever he had dir[e]cted & ready to do what
he should direct. that if the equilibrium of the three great bodies Legislature, Executive & Judiciary could be preserved, if the
Legislature could be kept independant, I should never fear the
result of such a government but that I could not but be uneasy
when I saw that the Executive had swallowed up the legislative
branch. he said that as to that interested spirit in the legislature,
it was what could not be avoided in any government, unless we
were to exclude particular descriptions of men, such as the hold-
ers of the funds from all office. I told him there was great difference between the little accidental schemes of self interest which
would take place in every body of men & influence their votes,
and a regular system for forming a corps of interested persons
who should be steadily at the orders of the Treasury. he touched
on the merits of the funding system, observed that was a difference of opinion about it some thinking it very bad, others very
good. that experience was the only criterion of right which he
knew & this alone would decide which opinion was right. that for
himself he had seen our affairs desperate & our credit lost, and
that this was in a sudden & extraordinary degree raised to the
highest pitch. I told him all that was ever necessary to establish
our credit, was an efficient government & an honest one declar-

ing it would sacredly pay our debts, laying taxes for this purpose & applying them to it. I avoided going further into the subject. he finished by another exhortation to me not to decide too positively on retirement, & here we were called to breakfast.[6]

AD, DLC: Jefferson Papers.

1. See Jefferson to GW, 9 Sept. 1792.

2. Maj. George Augustine Washington, manager of Mount Vernon for his uncle, was critically ill and died on 5 Feb. 1793.

3. Lear used his trip to Portsmouth, N.H., in the summer of 1792 to survey public opinion about the new government and to determine whether there was support for GW to serve a second term as president. For Lear's reports, see his letters to GW of 21 July and 5 August.

4. For GW's earlier attempts to curtail partisan quarrels between Jefferson and Hamilton, see GW to Jefferson, 23 Aug., and to Hamilton, 26 Aug. 1792.

5. Hamilton, who was a son-in-law of Revolutionary War general Philip Schuyler, had suggested the establishment of a government based on the English model during the Constitutional Convention in Philadelphia in 1787 (see Farrand, *Records of the Federal Convention*, 1:288, 299, 303, 308, 424). Jefferson's ally in the discussion was Thomas Pinckney, who had been confirmed in January 1792 as the U.S. minister to Great Britain and who spent the spring and early summer of 1792 in Philadelphia preparing for his mission and the ensuing journey to London (see Jefferson to GW, 16 May 1792).

6. Jefferson did not submit a letter of resignation to GW until 31 Dec. 1793.

To Tobias Lear

Dear Sir,   Mount Vernon. Octr 1st 1792

Expecting this letter will find you in Philadelphia—I wish you wd begin in time to compare *all* my Speeches in Congress with the subsequent Acts of that body; that I may see what parts of them have passed altogether unnoticed, or which have been only partially noticed; thereby enabling me to judge whether any, and what parts of them should be brought forward again. It is my request also, that you would note everything that may occur to you as fit subjects of information, or for recommendation at the opening of the Session—and such other matters as result from the Laws with wch it is proper to make the Legislature *or* the Senate acquainted. I want to have all the materials collected for my Communications previous to my arrival, that when the whole are before me I may select & digest into order, such as will be proper for my Speech.[1]

It is my present intention to commence my journey to Philadelphia on this day week; & to spend that, and part of the following day in George Town; but whether I shall be able to do it is not absolutely certain, as yet. William and Richard have both been confined to their rooms, and mostly to their beds for ten or twelve days with intermittant fevers; which, never before yesterday, was moderate enough to admit the Bark which makes it doubtful at this moment whether they will be in condition to undertake the journey if they keep well, & a return of the fever I am sure will prevent it.[2] As to poor George I shall say nothing—His fate is unquestionably fixed, and Fanny's, from prest appearances, is very unpromisg probably terminating in the same disorder. These occurrances throws my private Affairs into considerable embarrassment; But as they, especially the Major, is not likely to get better, and if they do will spend the winter at her fathers, I must leave them in it, as there is no remedy at present.[3]

The light house on Cape Henry, in this State, will soon want a Keeper, & if my memory serves me many have offered. Pray examine the characters and have them ready to be decided on by the time I arrive.[4]

Mrs Washington went up this Morning to bid Mrs Stuart (who has lately added a Son to the family) farewell[5]—My best wishes attend Mrs Lear yourself and the Child and I am—Dear Sir Your sincere friend and Affecte Servant

Go: Washingt⟨on⟩

ALS, CSmH.

1. Lear returned to Philadelphia on 7 Oct. after a trip to Portsmouth, N.H., and GW arrived in the capital on 13 Oct. (see Lear to GW, 7 Oct., GW to Anthony Whitting, 14 Oct. 1792). GW gave his address to the U.S. Senate and House of Representatives on 6 Nov. 1792.

2. Despite the illness of William Osborne, GW's valet de chambre, and Richard Keating, a postilion, GW left Mount Vernon on 8 Oct. for his return to Philadelphia. Osborne recovered sufficiently from his illness to accompany GW on the trip. A relapse while on the road forced Osborne to stay behind, and he arrived in Philadelphia a few days after the rest of GW's party (see GW to Betty Washington Lewis, 7 Oct. 1792; Decatur, *Private Affairs of George Washington*, 291, 296). The administration of quinine bark suggests that these servants were suffering from malaria. As planned, GW stopped in Georgetown to attend the sale of lots in the Federal City (see Broadside: Sale of Lots in the Federal City, 8 October).

3. George Augustine Washington, GW's nephew and manager of Mount Vernon, was ill with tuberculosis, and his wife Frances (Fanny) Bassett Washington apparently also had contracted the disease. G. A. Washington and his family

spent the winter at Eltham, the estate of his father-in-law, Burwell Bassett, where he died on 5 Feb. 1793 (see Anthony Whitting to GW, 31 Oct. 1792).

4. For background on the candidates for keeper of the lighthouse at Cape Henry, Va., see Hamilton to GW, 22 Sept., and note 6, and Thomas Newton, Jr., to GW, 28 Sept., and notes 2 and 6.

5. Eleanor Calvert Custis, widow of Martha Washington's deceased son John Parke Custis, had married Dr. David Stuart in 1783 and now lived at the Stuart estate Hope Park ten miles west of Alexandria in Fairfax County, Virginia.

To Edmund Randolph

Sir,   Mount Vernn Octr 1st 1792.

It is highly important that the proceedings in the Indictments of those who have opposed themselves, *unwarrantably,* to the Laws laying a duty on distilled spirits, should be placed on legal ground & prosecuted properly; it is my desire therefore that you will attend the Circuit Court at York Town, to be holden the [   ] of this Month and see that, that business is conducted in a manner to which no exception can with propriety be taken: and for the further purpose also of giving to this measure of Government a more solemn & serious countenance aspect.[1] I am &ca

                                    G. W——n

ADfS, DNA: RG 59, Miscellaneous Letters; LB, DLC: GW.

1. For background on the civil disorder in western Pennsylvania occasioned by opponents of the excise tax on whiskey and GW's response, see Alexander Hamilton to GW, 1 Sept., and notes, GW to Hamilton, 7 Sept., 1 Oct., and Randolph to GW, 10 Sept. 1792, and note 3. The grand jury of the U.S. Circuit Court for the Middle District, which met at York, Pa., on 11 Oct. 1792, indicted William Kerr and Alexander Berr, participants in the August 1792 attack on William Faulkner's tavern, in which John Neville, the inspector of the revenue, had established his office. On 13 Mar. 1793 GW wrote William Rawle, U.S. district attorney for Pennsylvania, instructing him to discontinue prosecution of the rioters.

From John Lewis

Dear Sir,   3 Octr 1792

Inclosd I send you a Coppy of Mr Cowpers Accot[1] according to the payments that were to have been made He has never paid (without it has been within a very few weeks past) more than between three & four hundred pounds. His bonds I have parted with except the one I send you wch was in part of the last payment. I had every reason to believe I shoud have been able by Howell to have sent you the full amount of the money due you (wth Cowpers Bond) But have been disappointed particularly in a Sum promissd me by Coll Fontain. yet have every reason to believe I shall get it shortly. On Saturday next I shall Certainly recd £50. I expected to have sent that sum more than I send you. Your or Maj: Washingtons order for that sum shall be paid on demand[.] It shall be but a few weeks sir you shall recd the full amount of the debt. Howell Brings you £212:6:5½ I shoud esteme it a favor you'd inform Majr Washington I did not know (till Howel Informed me) he had not recd the bond of £50 promissd by Doctr French. If is not paid in Ten days I can furnish him one of £57. which I hope will answer his purpose.[2] I am Dr Sir Your most Obdt Hum: Servt

John Lewis

ALS, ViMtV.

1. Portsmouth, Va., merchant John Cowper's account concerned land in North Carolina that he had purchased from GW and John Lewis, the eldest son of GW's deceased brother-in-law Fielding Lewis. For background on this land deal, see George Augustine Washington to GW, 7 Dec. 1790, n.7, and Indenture with John Cowper, 17 May 1791, and note 1. For earlier efforts by GW and George Augustine Washington to obtain GW's share of the money paid by Cowper to John Lewis, see GW to John Lewis, 20 July 1792, and notes. In late September, GW sent his nephew Howell Lewis to Fredericksburg to obtain his half of the money recently paid to Howell's half brother John Lewis in partial settlement of this debt (see GW to John Lewis, 21 Sept. 1792).

2. According to the enclosed account with John Cowper of 3 Oct. 1792, Cowper had paid £950 for the land, and as of 3 Oct. he still owed £140.5.8, which included £24.5.5½ in interest (D, DLC:GW). See also Ledger B, 354; Ledger C, 9.

William Fontaine (1754–1810), a veteran of the Revolutionary War who had served as a lieutenant colonel in the guards for the Convention Army prisoners from 1779 to 1781, lived in St. Martin's Parish in Hanover County, Virginia. George French (1751–1824), an immigrant from Scotland, was a physician and businessman who served eight terms as mayor of Fredericksburg, Va., between 1789 and 1813.

To James Mercer

Dear Sir,   Mount Vernon Oct. 3d 1792

It has long been in my mind to ask you, though I have never yet done it, if you could give me any information of a conveyance of the Lotts I purchased at Colo. Mercer's sale of Land in Frederick County in the year 1774.[1] I can find no Deeds for these Lotts amongst my land papers; but by recurring to Letters which have passed between you & me (in a settlement of Accts with your Brother Colo. Jno. F. Mercer in August last) it would appear as if this had been done through your Agency. If so, your memory (much better I am sure than mine) may furnish you with the fact, and with the circumstances attending it—or, if it should not, and you would be so obliging when in Richmond to examine the Clerks Office of the General Court to see if any Deeds from *you* to *me,* by way of re-conveyance (for this I think was the mode suggested) are on record, it would be doing me an acceptable favor. If none is to be found there nor in the Frederick Office, I am yet without a legal title to the Land, although the purchase money has been allowed in the Settlement before alluded to, with interest thereon agreeably to the tenor of the Sale.[2] With sincere esteem & regard I am—Dear Sir Your Affecte Servt

Go: Washington

ALS (photocopy), DLC:GW, ser. 9; ADfS, DLC:GW; LB, DLC:GW. The cover of the ALS is addressed to "The Honble James Mercer Esqr Fredericksbg" and includes the postal notation "Alex. 3 Octr."

1. In November 1774 GW bought two lots, totaling 571 acres, near present-day Berryville, Virginia. For background on GW's purchase of this land from the estate of George Mercer, eldest brother of James Mercer, and his subsequent difficulties in acquiring a clear title to the land, see GW's Statement concerning George Mercer's estate, 1 Feb. 1789, and note 3.

2. Mercer received this letter at his home in Fredericksburg on 6 Oct., and that same day he replied: "the Circumstances of the Deed you enquire after are full in my memory & I am certain they are of record in the General Court—this fact is the deeper impressed on my mind from the Circumstance of being obliged on a former consultation to devise the mode of perfecting this business by putting your Excellency to the trouble of attending purposely at Richmond—this hapened some years ago & I also remember you then convened the old members of the Dismal Swamp Compy[.] I mention these things hoping to recall the lease to yr own memory but as I go to Richmond on Monday next for a month I will take Care to remove yr Excellencys Suspense as soon as I reach that place—by writing you again & perhaps sending you the original Deed which I presume is yet in the office, not being called for you or yr agent." He concluded this letter with regret that recent illness had prevented his visiting Mount Vernon (PHi: Gratz Collection). Mercer soon found the missing deeds and sent them to GW (see GW to James Mercer, 1 Nov. 1792).

For GW's memorandum of 8 Aug. pertaining to his settlement with John Francis Mercer, see GW to Francis Deakins and Benjamin Jones, 8 Aug., source note.

From James McHenry

Sir. Near Baltimore 4th Octbr 1792.

I do myself the honor to inclose you Mr Tilghmans determination which I received only to-day. I had informed him that you had intimated to me a desire to appoint him to the vacant office of District Attorney if it could be ascertained that he would remove to Baltimore which the nature of the business made necessary. After visiting this Town to examine and investigate prospects *in the way of his profession* he told me he was satisfied that it would be to his interest to remove; but requested to have an opportunity to consult with his father whom he did not wish to disoblige. I said any delay would be embarrassing to me as the information you had required had been procrastinated already too long; however as my indisposition had chiefly occasioned it, the time he asked for might be placed to that account. I inclose you also Mr Hammonds answer. In every point of view either of these gentlemen would have been an acquisition to Baltimore. The law characters here who may still be unfriendly to the constitution are not sufficiently balanced by those we have of a different description. Hollingsworth belongs yet neither to one nor other or rather to both as the case may be.[1]

I shall send Mr Smith his commission to-morrow.[2] His brother the Col. and Mr Charles Ridgley are competitors for Congress. I hear Colonel Smith will succeed by a considerable majority, but that both Town and County seem to shew by their tardiness to vote no very strong inclination for either. One half of the Town, and this is the last day, have not voted and not one fourth of the County. Mercers election on tuesday night was not in a very favorable train.[3]

I have been only once in Town since my getting better. I am still very weak. With sincere prayers for your health so essential to us all I am Dr Sir most affectionately and truely Your Obt servt

James McHenry.

Gen. Williams has been very ill at Hagers Town, but is better.[4]

ALS, DLC:GW.

1. For earlier discussion of possible candidates for the position of U.S. attorney for the District of Maryland, see GW to McHenry, 13, 31 Aug., McHenry to GW, 16 Aug. 1792. William Tilghman, in the enclosed letter written to McHenry from Chestertown, Md., on 3 Oct., declined the position because the ill health of his father made the required move to Baltimore impossible (DLC:

GW). Nicholas Hammond, in the enclosed letter of 12 Sept., wrote James McHenry from Easton, Md., to withdraw his name from consideration, also citing his reluctance to move to Baltimore as his reason (DLC:GW).

2. GW had written McHenry on 3 Oct. from Mount Vernon: "If this letter shall have reached your hands before that which I addressed to Mr Robt Smith (under cover to you) has passed from them, I pray you to retain it until you see me, which will be, I expect, about the middle of next week on my return to Philadelphia (if I am not detained by the convalescent State of two of my Servants)—or, if that should happen, 'till you hear further" (ALS, CSmH; ADfS, PBbCald; LB, DLC:GW). McHenry in his second letter to GW of 4 Oct., written at "8 o'clock P.M.," replied: "I have this moment received your letter of the third and shall observe its directions" (DLC:GW). For GW's letter to Robert Smith of 31 Aug., see GW to McHenry, 31 Aug., n.3.

3. Col. Samuel Smith (1752–1839), a Revolutionary War veteran, was a wealthy Baltimore merchant who was elected to his first term in the U.S. House of Representatives in 1792. He served in the House 1793–1803 and 1816–22 and in the Senate 1803–15 and 1822–33. His opponent, Charles Ridgely, who was a member of another prominent Baltimore family, was described by McHenry in a letter to Alexander Hamilton of 16 Aug. 1792 as being "largely in the iron works a man of great wealth, without skill in public affairs" (Syrett, *Hamilton Papers,* 12:212–14). John Francis Mercer, who had been elected to a second term in the House of Representatives in 1792 from Maryland's second district on Tuesday, 2 Oct., was considered an opponent of Federalist policies.

4. Revolutionary War veteran Otho Holland Williams had declined a commission as brigadier general earlier this year because of ill health (see Williams to GW, 13 May 1792). Although Williams went to Barbados in 1793 in an effort to improve his health, he died on 15 July 1794 at the age of 45.

From the Commissioners for the District of Columbia

Sir   George-Town 5th Octr 1792

As we have not yet received your order for the Sales and the Time is near at hand, we think it proper (least it should have escaped you) to remind you of it[1]—A few of the Plans executed, in Boston have Arrived, which we have dispersed, we have some expectation, that tomorrows Post may bring us some of those executed in Philaa—We take the liberty to send you one of the former.[2] We are Sir &c.

Dd Stuart
Danl Carroll

LB, DNA: RG 42, Records of the Commissioners for the District of Columbia, Letters Sent, 1791–1802.

1. GW had enclosed his orders for the sale of lots in the Federal City in his

letter to the commissioners of 29 Sept. 1792, the receiver's copy of which is docketed "Recd 8th Octr 1792."

2. The enclosed plan, which has not been identified, was the *Plan of the City of Washington in the Territory of Columbia, Ceded by the States of Virginia and Maryland to the United States of America.* Samuel Hill of Boston completed his engraving of this plan in the summer of 1792. Samuel Blodget, Jr., enclosed prints from this engraving in his letter to Thomas Jefferson of 25 June 1792 (see *Jefferson Papers,* 24:119–20), and Jefferson forwarded them a short time later to GW, who noted the absence of "the soundings of the River & Branch," which would be "very satisfactory & advantageous to have done" (see Tobias Lear to Jefferson, 11 July 1792). Later this year Philadelphia engravers James Thackara and John Vallance finished their larger and higher-quality engraving, which included the desired soundings, but it was not printed until after the October sale of lots. Jefferson sent 500 prints made from the Thackara and Vallance engraving to the commissioners in November (see Jefferson to D.C. Commissioners, 13 Nov. 1792, *Jefferson Papers,* 24:612). For a reproduction of the print that Jefferson sent to the commissioners, see Reps, *Monumental Washington,* 23.

From Thomas Mifflin

Sir.   Philadelphia, 5th Octr 1792.

I have the honour to acknowledge the receipt of your Excellency's letter, inclosing a copy of a Proclamation, that you have issued, in consequence of certain irregular and refractory proceedings, which have taken place, in particular parts of some of the States, contravening the laws for raising a revenue upon Spirits, distilled within The United States: And it affords me the sincerest satisfaction to find, that you repose a just confidence in the exertions of the Executive of Pennsylvania, to further, in every proper way, the particular object of the measure, which you have, at this time, adopted, as well as, on every other occasion, to promote a due obedience to the constitutional laws of The Union.[1]

Previously to the publishing of your Proclamation, certain Rioters, of the county of Chester, who, in opposing the collection of the revenue upon Spirits, had committed an assault and battery on the officer, were indicted, convicted, and fined; and, I am informed, that the regular process had, likewise, issued against the perpetrators of a similar offence, in the county of Allegheny. Every other necessary step, which the law permits to be taken, I will cheerfully pursue, in order to prevent, or punish, the repetition of delinquencies, so hostile to the peace and happiness of the Community; for, independent of an earnest desire to contribute to the tranquility and honour of your administration, I am sensible, that the prosperity of every individual State, depends upon the prosperity of The Union; which can only be effected by a strict and faithful attention to our Federal obligations.[2]

Under these impressions, I have thought it proper to address a letter (a copy of which I take the liberty to inclose) to the Judges of the Supreme Court, and the Presidents of the courts of Common Pleas, requesting that they will inculcate the indispensable duty of obedience to the laws of The Union; and, particularly, as far as their jurisdiction extends, that they will charge the Grand Inquest convened in the several counties, to enquire into, and present, offences of the nature, to which your Proclamation refers.[3] I have the Honour to be, Sir, With perfect respect, Your Excellency's Most Obedt Hble Servt

Thomas Mifflin

LS, DNA: RG 59, Miscellaneous Letters. The closing is in Thomas Mifflin's hand.

1. See GW's circular letter to the governors of Pennsylvania, North Carolina, and South Carolina of 29 Sept. and his proclamation of 15 Sept. 1792.

2. For background on the opposition in western Pennsylvania to the excise tax on whiskey, see Hamilton to GW, 1 Sept., and notes. For the trial of the Chester County rioters, see Edmund Randolph to GW, 10 Sept., n.3. For the indictments in the U.S. circuit court of the middle district of rioters from Allegheny County, see GW to Randolph, 1 Oct., n.1.

3. In the enclosed copy of this letter of 5 Oct. from Philadelphia, Mifflin wrote: "The President has communicated to me a copy of a Proclamation, which he issued in consequence of certain irregular and refractory proceedings, that have taken place in particular parts of some of the States, contravening the laws for raising a revenue from Spirits distilled within the United States; and I am desirous, in every proper way, to manifest my disposition to further the object of the particular measure, which he has at this time adopted, as well as to promote on every occasion, a due obedience to the constitutional laws of The Union.

"Permit me, therefore, Gentlemen, to request, that you will take every official opportunity to inculcate the indispensable duty of obedience to the acts of Congress: and, particularly, that you will be pleased, as far as the jurisdiction of your court extends, to charge the Grand Juries of the several counties, to enquire into, and present, all offences of the nature, to which the proclamation refers.

"I am persuaded, Gentlemen, that you are convinced, with me, that the prosperity of the States individually, depends upon the prosperity of The Union, which can only be effected by a strict and faithful attention to our Federal obligations; and, viewing the vigilance and wisdom with which you discharge the other duties of your important station, I repose a perfect confidence in your exertions upon the particular subject, that I have now suggested" (DNA: RG 59, Miscellaneous Letters).

From the Citizens of Vincennes

Au Poste Vinçenne le 5 8bre 1792.
A Son Excellençe George Washinton Ecuier premier President des Etats unis de l'Amerique du nord. &c. suplie humblement.

Les habitants de ce district qui ont l'honneur de vous Exposer que vu les mauva⟨ises⟩ Guerres qu'ils onts Eües a soutenir pendant plusieurs Années avec les Nations Indiennes de Ces Contrées, ce qui a Causée la perte generale de touts les Citoïens jusqu'a leurs tués femmes Enfants et Animaux domestiques et les reduire dans la derniere Indigençe.

actuellement que le traité de paix a Eté fait avec ces mêmes nations l'on veut nous Imposer des droits sur toutes les marchandises Ce qui nous les fait païer un prix Exorbitant et nous Empêche de pouvoir Entretenir nos familles; nous ne pretendons pas Cependant opprimer[1] les Loix; mais l'Indigençe actuelle ou nous sommes nous obligent Connoissant votre Bonté d'y avoir Recours et nous vous supplions de rechef de Jetter un Regard favorable sur de pauvres Infortunés Citoïens qui ne desirent que le bien de l'etat et qui ne Cêsseront de prier dieu pour la Conservation & vos grandeurs.

Malgré notre pauvreté ont ne veut pas nous permettre de faire aucunes ventes ni traite qu'en païant des sommes Immenses et Il nous Est Impossible de pouvoir y Resister mais S'il nous Etoit possible d'avoir un Commerçe libre pendant quelques Année⟨s⟩ que les Etrangers ou autres purent nous apporter nos besoins nous pourions par la suite revenir a notre premier Etat et soutenir l'Endroit dans la paix et l'union Comme nous avons fait Ci devant, C'est ce que nous Attendons de vos Bontés ainsi que de Croire que nous sommes et seronts toujours vos tres humbles et obeissants serviteurs et Zelés Citoïens

P[ierre] Billet[2]

DS, DNA: RG 59, Miscellaneous Letters.

In this petition the residents of Vincennes in the Northwest Territory, now Vincennes, Indiana, sought the right of free trade and relief from duties on merchandise that they claimed had been imposed by the local Indians. GW's secretary Tobias Lear forwarded this document to Thomas Jefferson on 30 Jan.

1793 with a request from GW that "the Secretary will take into consideration and report to him his opinion on what ought to be done" with this petition (DLC: Jefferson Papers). A note written by Jefferson on the cover of the document reads: "Genl Sinclair knows of no duties on the merchandize of the petitioners unless they mean either our own Impost, or the duties imposed by the Spaniards down the river. by the paiment of immense sums on sales and bargains, he knows nothing which can be meant but that they are not allowed to trade with the Indians but on taking out a license which costs 100. d." Jefferson enclosed his reply of 21 Feb. 1793 to Pierre Billet in a letter to GW dated 22 Feb. 1793 (see *Jefferson Papers*, 25:249–50). For GW's approval of Jefferson's reply, see *JPP,* 62.

1. This word probably was meant to be "opprimer."

2. Additional signatures read: "[John] Darguilleur[,] Marie[,] Chal. Bounaure[,] Christopher Wyant[,] J. Bte Morel fils[,] N[icolas] Mayot." Vincennes residents whose marks and names appear on this petition are "Jean Toulon[,] Jean Mugnier[,] Laurent Bazadonne[,] Pierre Cartier pere[,] Vital Boucher[,] Jacque Cardinal[,] Pierre Gilbert[,] Alexandre Valé[,] François Baroi pere[,] Fr. Baroi fils[,] Jn Baptiste Arpin [Harpin,] Charle Villeneuve pere[,] Pierre Cournoier[,] Amable Baulon[,] Joseph Amelin[,] Jn Bte Vaudri[,] Antoine Bordeleau[,] Loüis Coder[,] Michel Neau[,] Francois Boier[,] Jn Bte Joial[,] Jacque la Trimouille[,] Etienne Pinsouneau." For a list of French residents in Vincennes as of 13 July 1790, see Carter, *Territorial Papers,* 2:285–87; see also "Grants to the Settlers in Vincennes and the Illinois Country," 17 Dec. 1798, in *ASP, Public Lands,* 1:84–88.

From the Citizens of Vincennes

[Vincennes, 6 October 1792]
To George Washington. President of The United States of America.

The Supplication of Laurence Bazadone, John Darguilleur, John Toulon, and Peter Troussereau; residing at Postvincents in the County of Knox. Most Humbly Sheweth.

That your Suppliants being reduced to the most Indigent circumstances, by the greatest stretch of usurped Power, conceive their only remedy to depend on your Patronage.

Their Case being unparalleled, they beg your attention to the following recital, in which they will state Facts.

Your Suppliants all born subjects to France, came from New-orleans with divers Merchandise in 1783. to this place, where the Ancient Inhabitants received them with their usual Humanity. And where they had every reason to be satisfied with their reception and prospects. In October 1786. a Body of armed men under the command of General George Clarke from Kentuck penetrated into this country in search of Indians, who having come to a conference eluded the Fury of those ravagers. Under pretence of preventing the Incursions of the natives to the settlements on the south side of the Ohio, General Clarke embodied a number of his followers, and stationed them at this place under the command of a John Holder; and compelling the Inhabitants to supply them with Provisions and Fuel; assuring them that the levy was made by the Authority of the Executive of the State of Virginia, and that their disbursements would be paid. But they did not stop here. Your Suppliants were arrested, and imprisoned on the 17th of October and their Effects seized by the said General George Clarke, John Holder and other officers, who at a Court-martial tried and condemned your Suppliants; forfeited their Effects to the United States and appropriated the whole as they thought most proper.[1] This they termed the right of retaliation on the subjects of Spain for real or supposed instances of the same nature, committed on one of the Citizens of the United States on the Mississippi.[2] It would be too much to trouble you with an enumeration of all the Indignities with which those Tyrants treated your Suppliants. The loss of all their Property rated at the current prices amounts to near Seventy Thousand Livres money of France; and has reduced your Suppliants to the greatest Misery. Sensible of the rights of every citizen your Suppliants have been encouraged to borrow Money to support an Action in the District of Kentuck, against the said Offenders who have hitherto rendered abortive the efforts of your Suppliants in the Courts of Justice. And having no further support nor the means of obtaining that Justice which we expect is due to the unfortunate, tho' indigent sufferer; Your Suppliants have taken the resolution to address themselves to you, to pray you would consider their Case, become their Patron and obtain for them from the United States such Relief as they in their Wisdom may find equitable.

Your Suppliants rely entirely on your Patronage and Bounty; and they expect the happy period of their Misfortunes will be the consequence of your Intercession to the United States in their behalf.

The extreme Poverty to which their misfortune has reduced your Suppliants compels them to the necessity of applying to the

Chief of the Kaskaskias Indian Tribe to present you this their Supplication.[3] In hopes of your approveing of their resolution, and of your obtaining from the United States the relief they stand so much in want of, they beg leave to subscribe their names, and marks in presence of Witness's.[4] at Postvincents the 6th day of October 1792.

Paul Gamelin

Pierre Gamelin[5]

Laurence X Bazadone

Jhon Darguilleur

John X Toulon

Peter X Troussereau

DS, DNA: RG 59, Miscellaneous Letters.

1. In the fall of 1786, residents of the District of Kentucky, then part of the state of Virginia, commissioned Revolutionary War veteran George Rogers Clark to lead a militia expedition against hostile Indians in the Northwest Territory. Clark marched his troops to Vincennes, and when expected provisions failed to arrive, he commandeered supplies from the local residents. After an excursion against the neighboring Indians, Clark attempted to form a garrison at Vincennes under Col. John Holder. Again private property was impressed. Clark not only ordered the property of several traders seized and confiscated, but he also court-martialed them for their failure to cooperate. Charges that Clark had acted illegally were filed with both the Virginia government and Congress, but restitution was never made by either government, nor was Clark punished for his actions (see *JCC*, 32:189–99; Alvord, *Kaskaskia Records*, 457–58; Green, *The Spanish Conspiracy*, 92–101).

2. In order to trade on the Mississippi River, these four French traders probably possessed trading licenses from the Spanish government of the Louisiana Territory, which apparently created some confusion about their nationality.

3. Two Kaskaskia chiefs were among the Indians who had signed the recent peace treaty negotiated at Vincennes by Gen. Rufus Putnam. Kaskaskia chief Ducoigne was among the delegation of chiefs who then accepted an invitation to visit GW at Philadelphia. For background on the Treaty of Vincennes and the Indian delegation's visit to Philadelphia, see GW to Henry Knox, 3 Sept. (first letter), n.3, James Wilkinson to GW, 1 Nov., n.1, and George Clendinen to GW, 11 Nov. 1792, and notes 2 and 3.

4. Tobias Lear forwarded this petition to Thomas Jefferson on 30 Jan. 1793 with a request from GW that Jefferson suggest an appropriate response (DLC: Jefferson Papers). Jefferson composed a reply addressed to Paul Gamelin on 21 Feb. 1793 (*Jefferson Papers*, 25:251), and he enclosed it in a letter to GW dated 22 Feb. 1793. For GW's approval of Jefferson's response, see *JPP*, 62.

5. On 3 July 1790 Pierre Gamelin had been appointed a judge of the court of common pleas, and Paul Gamelin had been made a justice of the court of general quarter sessions of the peace, both for Knox County in the Northwest Territory. Paul, who was appointed treasurer for the county on 3 Sept. 1792, died sometime before 30 Jan. 1793 (Carter, *Territorial Papers*, 3:316, 384, 405).

To Thomas Jefferson

Mount Vernon, 7 Oct. 1792. Forwards to Philadelphia Jefferson's papers that were "found in the Road" by one of GW's neighbors, except for a letter to Daniel Carroll of Rock Creek, Md., which has been sent to the Alexandria post office.[1]

ADfS, DNA: RG 59, Miscellaneous Letters; LB, DLC:GW.

1. Jefferson wrote to James Madison from Bladensburg, Md., on 1 Oct. that he had "unfortunately dropped" some papers "in the road between Mount Vernon and Alexandria" (see *Jefferson Papers*, 24:432–33, and note, which lists the dropped papers, including a letter of undetermined date from Madison to Carroll).

From Tobias Lear

Sir,   Philadelphia October 7th 1792

I arrived in this place this morning when I was honored with your kind letters of the 21st of September and 1st of October, which were put into my hands by Mr Fraunces. I was detained in Portsmouth ten days longer than I expected to have been when I had the hononor of writing to you last from that place, in order to settle some affairs for my mother which I happily accomplished in a satisfactory manner. Our journey to this city has been very favorable both as to weather and other circumstances, Mrs Lear, our little son and myself have returned in perfect health—we met with no accident, not even the breaking of a strap, from the time of our departure 'till our return to Philadelphia.[1]

I am happy to inform you that I found a person who is recommended by General Lincoln & several other respectable Characte[r]s as being completely qualified in every respect to take charge of and superintend the education of a small number of boys, and who is ready to come on here & engage in that business as soon as he shall be informed that his services are desired. I wrote to Colo. Hamilton on the subject before I left New England desiring him to inform me of the number of boys that might be calculated upon to form a School and the sum that an instructor might expect annually for his services—his answer (which I received in Boston) mentioned the number of twelve boys, and that six hundred dollars per Annum would be given in full for all services &c. &c.—This was communicated to the

Gentleman who had been recommended to fill the place and was accepted by him; and he now holds himself in readiness to come on here as soon as he is desired, which will be by the next post.[2]

I shall be particularly attentive to your directions respecting the speeches &c. and trust those matters which you desire will be in readiness by your arrival here.[3]

I was very glad to be informed by Mr Page that he had sent his Coach off on the 3d instant so that it will in all probability be in season at Mount Vernon; and I sincerely hope that you will not be prevented from commencing your journey at the time you propose by the cause which you apprehend may delay you.[4]

I am truly greived by the account which you give of the poor Major's situation, and the unfavorable appearances which you mention in his amiable partner render the account still more distressing. On these occasions I feel with poignancy but I cannot express my feelings. I am sorry to hear of the general unhealthiness of the season in your quarter, and am glad that the same cause of complaint does not exist here nor in that part of the Country from whence I have lately come. The small pox had rendered Boston an hospital at the time of our passing through it; but the disorder was not uncommonly malignant—near nine thousand persons had been inoculated in that town, and not more than seventy had died with the small pox including those who had taken it the natural way.[5]

I found every thing in good order at the house and was informed, much to my satisfaction, that peace & good order had prevailed in it since my departure. I shall this week take measures for securing our wood, hay & Oats for the winter.

I have been just informed that a Ship has now arrived in the River in 35 days from Ostend which brings most disasterous accounts of the French affair such as that the Marquis de la Fayette was taken by some Pesants, with eight other officers all in disguise, or rather without their Uniforms, supposed to be on their way to Ostend to embark for London, and were carried prisoners to Antwarp where they were delivered to the Austrians— that Count Dillon with 30 other Officers had deserted to the Enemy, and that the army lately commanded by the Marquis was in so mutinous & distracted a state that they must either fall a sacrifice to the combined Armies or do irreparable mischiefs to their own Country. The Ship which brings this account is called the Patsy Rutledge and belongs to Mr Ross of this City who was out of town when she arrived and the letters which she brought were sent out to him so that no further particulars could be yet collected.[6]

Mrs Lear unites with me in grateful & affectionate respects for Mrs Washington and yourself—in love and sincere regards for the Children and the family with earnest prayers that it may please God to restore the health of my good fri[e]nd the Major and make him a continued blessing to his family and friends. With sentiments of the truest and most respectful attachment, I have the honor to be Sir, Your grateful & Obedt Sert

Tobias Lear.

ALS, DLC:GW.

1. For background on Lear's visit to Portsmouth, N.H., with his family, see Lear to GW, 15 July 1792, source note. Lear last wrote GW from Portsmouth on 5 August. His next letter to GW, before returning to Philadelphia, was from Boston on 23 September.

2. Lear's search for a proper person to operate a small school in Philadelphia was prompted by GW's dissatisfaction with the academic progress shown by George Washington Parke Custis at the academy of the College of Philadelphia (see Lear to GW, 3 April 1791, and note 2, 5 Aug. 1792, GW to Lear, 21 Sept. 1792). Lear wrote Alexander Hamilton for advice on 27 Aug. 1792; Hamilton's answer of 6 Sept. has not been found (see Syrett, *Hamilton Papers*, 12:279–80, and note 2).

3. In his letter of 1 Oct., GW instructed Lear to collect all pertinent papers and information that could be used in drafting the address that GW would send to the U.S. House of Representatives and Senate on 6 Nov. 1792. He also asked Lear to review the qualifications of the candidates for lighthouse keeper at Cape Henry, Va., in preparation for GW's selection of a nominee.

4. GW hired a coach from Stephen Page of Philadelphia for his return from Mount Vernon to Philadelphia. As planned, GW left Mount Vernon on 8 Oct., and he arrived in Philadelphia on 13 Oct. (see GW to Lear, 21 Sept., to Betty Washington Lewis, 7 Oct., to Anthony Whitting, 14 October).

5. For the illness of George Augustine Washington and his wife Fanny, as well as that of other members of GW's household, including his servants, see GW to Lear, 21 Sept., notes 4 and 5.

6. According to the *Pennsylvania Gazette* (Philadelphia) of 10 Oct., the ship *Patsy Rutledge*, owned by merchant John Ross (1729–1800), arrived in Philadelphia on 7 Oct. bringing news of political upheaval in France and of Lafayette's misfortune. For a summary of recent events in France and the imprisonment of Lafayette, see Gouverneur Morris to GW, 23 Oct. 1792, source note. For additional information on Lafayette's imprisonment, see the marquise de Lafayette's letter to GW of 8 October. Count Arthur Dillon (1750–1794), a native of Ireland who held a series of commissions in his family's proprietary regiment in the Irish Brigade of the French army, served during the

Revolutionary War primarily in Admiral d'Estaing's naval campaigns in the West Indies. In the fall of 1779, Dillon led his regiment in the unsuccessful attempt by American and French forces to recapture Savannah from the British. He spent the remainder of the war in the West Indies, where he later held several governorships. Elected in 1789 to the French National Assembly as a deputy for the island of Martinique, Dillon resigned to rejoin the army in 1791 and won praise for his leadership during the French victory at Valmy in September 1792. Accused of pro-royalist sympathies and counterrevolutionary activities, Dillon was alternately suspended from and rehabilitated to military command until his arrest in the summer of 1793. He was executed on 14 April 1794.

To Betty Washington Lewis

My dear Sister,   Mount Vernon Octr 7th 1792.

As Mrs Washington and myself expect to set out to morrow for Philadelpa and the Majr & Fanny the day after if the Vessel which is to carry him to Colo. Bassets arrives in time, I have taken the advantage of the good opportunity afforded by Mr Robt Lewis of sending Harriot to Fredericksburg. It is done at this time (notwithstanding your proposed visit to Albemarle) 1st because it would be improper to leave her here after we are all gone; 2d because there would be no person to accompany her down afterwards; and 3d because it might be inconvenient for her to travel alone.[1]

She comes—as Mrs Washington informs me—very well provided with every thing proper for a girl in her situation: this much I know, that she costs me enough to place her in it. I do not, however, want you (or any one else) to do more by her than merely to admit her into your family whilst this House is uninhabited by a female white Woman, and thereby rendered an unfit place for her to remain at—I shall continue to do for her what I have already done for Seven years past & that is to furnish her with such reasonable & proper necessaries as she may stand in need of, notwithstanding I have had both her brothers upon my hands and been obliged to pay several hundred pounds out of my own Pocket for the board, Schooling & Cloathing &ca of them for more than the period above mentioned; their fathers Estate being unable to discharge the Executions as fast as they issued against it.[2]

Harriot has sense enough, but no disposition to industry nor to be careful of her Cloaths. Your example and admonition may, with proper restraints, overcome the two last—and to that end I wish you would examine her Cloaths and direct her in the use and application of them—for without this they will be (I am told) dabbed about in every hole & corner—& her best things always in use. Fanny was too easy, too much of her own indolent turn, and had too little authority to cause, either by precept or example, any change in this for the better & Mrs Washington['s] absence has been injurious to her in many respects—but she is young and with good advice, may yet make a fine woman.

If, notwithstanding the supposition that she is well provided with every thing (except a Cloak which was not to be had in Alexandria and may be got at Fredericksburg) a deficiency is found, & you will supply it, there need be no occasion for your laying in advance more than ten days, as I could at any time remit a bank note (in a letter) to you in four days after I was made acquainted with the amount. I do not mean by this to launch into expensiveness—She has no pretensions to it, nor would the state of my finances enable me to endulge her in them if she had.

Mrs Washington joins me in best wishes for the perfect restoration of your health & every other blessing and I am, &ca

Go: W——n

ADfS, NjP: de Coppet Collection; LB, DLC:GW.

1. George Augustine Washington and his wife Fanny spent the winter months at Eltham, her father Burwell Bassett's estate in New Kent County, Va., where G. A. Washington died on 5 Feb. 1793. For Betty Lewis's "proposed visit to Albemarle" and plans for Harriot Washington to live with her in Fredericksburg, Va., see Betty Washington Lewis to GW, 25 Sept. 1792.

2. For background on GW's support of his nephews George Steptoe Washington and Lawrence Augustine Washington, sons of his deceased brother Samuel Washington, see Francis Willis, Jr., to GW, 24 Sept. 1788, source note.

Broadside: Sale of Lots in the Federal City

[8 October 1792]

TERMS AND CONDITIONS declared by the PRESIDENT of the UNITED STATES, this seventeenth day of October, seventeen hundred and ninety-one, for regulating the Materials and Manner of the Buildings and Improvements on the LOTS in the CITY of WASHINGTON.[1]

1st. THAT the outer and party-walls of all houses within the said City shall be built of brick or stone.

2nd. That all buildings on the streets shall be parallel thereto, and may be advanced to the line ⟨of th⟩e street, or withdrawn therefrom, at the plea⟨sure⟩ of the improver: But where any such build⟨ing is⟩ about to be erected, neither the foundation or party-wall shall be begun without first applying to the person or persons appointed by the Commissioners to superintend the buildings within the city, who will ascertain the lines of the walls to correspond with these regulations.

3d. The wall of no house to be higher than forty feet to the roof in any part of the city; nor shall any be lower than thirty-five feet on any of the avenues.

4th. That the Person or persons appointed by the Commissioners to superintend the buildings may enter on the land of any person to set out the foundation and regulate the walls to be built between party and party, as to the breadth and thickness thereof. Which foundation shall be laid equally upon the lands of the persons between whom such party-walls are to be built, and shall be of the breadth and thickness determined by such person proper; and the first builder shall be reimbursed one moiety of the charge of such party-wall, or so much thereof as the next builder shall have occasion to make use of, before such next builder shall any ways use or break into the wall—The charge or value thereof to be set by the person or persons so appointed by the Commissioners.

5th. As temporary conveniencies will be proper for lodging workmen and securing materials for building, it is to be understood that such may be erected with the approbation of the Commissioners: But they may be removed or discontinued by the special order of the Commissioners.

6th. The way into the squares being designed in a special manner for the common use and convenience of the occupiers of the respective squares—The property in the same is reserved to the public, so that there may be an immediate interference on any abuse of the use thereof by any individual, to the nuisance or obstruction of others. The proprietors of the Lots adjoining the entrance into the squares, on arching over the entrance, and fixing gates in the manner the Commissioners shall approve, shall be intitled to divide the space over the arching and build it up with the range of that line in the square.

7th. No vaults shall be permitted under the streets, nor any encroachments on the foot-way above the steps, stoops, porches, cellar doors, windows, ditches or leaning walls; nor shall there be any projection over the street, other than the eves of the house, without the consent of the Commissioners.

8th. These regulations are the terms and conditions under and upon which conveyances are to be made, according to the deeds in trust of the lands within the city.

George Washington.

TERMS of SALE of LOTS in the CITY of WASHINGTON, the Eighth Day of *October,* 1792.

ALL Lands purchased at this Sale, are to be subject to the Terms and Conditions declared by the President, pursuant to the Deeds in Trust.

The purchaser is immediately to pay one fourth part of the purchase money; the residue is to be paid in three equal annual payments, with yearly interest of six per cent. on the whole principal unpaid: If any payment is not made at the day, the payments-made are to be forfeited, or the whole principal and interest unpaid may be recovered on one suit and execution, in the option of the Commissioners.

The purchaser is to be entitled to a conveyance, on the whole purchase money and interest being paid, and not before. No bid under Three dollars to be received.

Broadside, DLC:GW.

1. GW signed two orders on 29 Sept. directing the sale of lots in the Federal City (see GW to D.C. Commissioners, 29 Sept., n.1). For the results of this sale, see D.C. Commissioners to GW, 13 Oct. 1792. For the previous year's proclamation regulating lot improvements, building materials, and construction, see GW's proclamation of 17 Oct. 1791, n.1.

From the Marquise de Lafayette

(*Translation*)

Department of the upper Loire at Chavamac[1] near Brioude
Sir,   8t Octr 1792.

Without doubt you have learnt our misfortunes—You know that your disciple—your friend has not ceased to act in a manner worthy of you, and of liberty—You know that his unalterable attachment to the Constitution which he swore to maintain, drew upon him the hatred of a powerful faction which wished to destroy it—that, proscribed by this faction—and accused at the head of his Army; he, wishing to avoid adding a new crime to his Citizens, withdrew his head from the sanguinary fury which pursued the courageous friends of liberty—and was already on his way to gain a neutral Country, from whence he intended to go among you, and offer up his wishes that his ungrateful Country might find defenders who would serve it *with as much zeal & disinterestedness & love of liberty as him.* His wish was that I should go with all our family to join him in England, that we might go & establish ourselves together in America, and there enjoy the consoling sight of virtue worthy of liberty. but before he arrived to this desireable point—and even before he reached a neutral Country it was necessary for him to cross a small corner of the enemys territory. There he was met and taken prisoner on the 23d Augt. He is yet in their hands. He was at first carried to Namur —then to Nivelle—from thence to Luxembourg, from thence I learnt by the public papers, that on the 6th of Septr they carried him to Wezel a City of Westphalia, under the dominion of the King of Prussia—and that there they seperated him from 3 members of the Constituent Assembly, who had been partakers of his lot and carried him alone to the Citadel of Spandau between Berlin & Potsdam. The motives—the design of such strange & cruel conduct on the part of his enemies are too deep for me to penetrate. They have not permitted him to write a line. He was taken by the Troops of the Emperor altho it is the King of Prussia who retains him a prisoner in his dominions. And while he suffers this inconceivable prosecution from the enemies without—the faction which reigns within keep me a hostage at 120 leagues from the Capital—judge then at what distance I am from him.[2]

In this abyss of grief the idea of owing to the U.S. and to M. Washington—the life & liberty of M. Lafayette re-animates my heart with some hope. I hope every thing from the goodness of a people with whom he has set an example of that liberty of which he is now the victim—And shall I dare speak what I hope? I would ask of them, through you, an Envoy who shall go to reclaim him in the name of the Republic of the U.S. wheresoever he may be retained, and who may make, in their name with whatso[e]ver power he may be, the necessary engagements to emancipate him from his captivity, & carry him to their bosoms. If his wife & his Children could be comprised in this happy mission, it is easy to judge how sweet it would be to her and to them; but if this would retard or embarrass, in any degree, the progress or his success— we will defer the happiness of a reunion yet longer, and when we shall be near you we will bear the grief of seperation with more courage.[3]

May heaven deign to bless the confidence with which it has inspired me. I hope my request is not rash. Accept the homage of the sentiments which have dictated this letter to me, as well as that of attachment & tender respect with which I am

Noailles Lefayette

Translation, in Tobias Lear's writing, DLC:GW; two copies, in French and in John Dyson's writing, DLC:GW; copy, in French and in Dyson's writing, NjMoNP. The first of the two French copies in DLC:GW, which appears in CD-ROM:GW, includes at the end Dyson's notation in English: "I have written & shall send 2 Copies of the above lest by accident one of them Should miscarry." That copy apparently was the one that Dyson enclosed in his letter to GW of 8 Dec. 1792 from "Gunton near Lowestoft Suffolk [England]," in which Dyson wrote: "I am just arrived in England from the family of Monsr Lafayette where I have constantly resided these last twelve months, the following Letter was delivered me by Madame Lafayette with a desire of its being forwarded to you by the first occasion, her present Situation is truly affecting, Separated from her Husband without the means of hearing from him, herself in captivity under the Safe-guard of the Municipality She is anxiously expecting the decision of his & her own destiny—under these circumstances She relies on your influence to adopt Such measures as may effectuate their mutual freedom" (DLC:GW). The docket, in GW's writing, on Dyson's letter to GW reads: "From Mr John Dyson 8th December 1792 enclosing a letter from Madame de la Fayette 8th October 1792 recd Feb. 20th." Lafayette had brought Dyson from England earlier this year as his farm manager in order to introduce English cattle and swine into French husbandry.

Dyson's third copy of this letter, which is in NjMoNP, includes the following postscript, which solicits assistance for the men who were captured with Lafayette and which does not appear in Dyson's other copies or in Lear's translation: "Si les bontés des Etats Unis peuvent s'etendre aux compagnons d'infortune de M. Lafayette ce sera y mettre le comble, mais comme la haine ne semble pas les poursuivre avec tant d'acharnement, je ne crois manquer à aucune delicatesse en demandant pour eux comme pour moi et mes enfans & que le soin de leurs interêts ne retardent pas les Secours qu'exige la position de M. Lafayette.

"Messr Maubourg, M. Bureau de Puzy et M. la Colombe qui a l'avantage d'avoir servi les Etats Unis meritent d'être distingués parmi les Compagnons d'infortune. Messrs Romeuf, Pillet, Masson, Curmeer les deux jeunes frères de M. Maubourg sont au nombre des Prisonniers, et ont tout le droit possible, à l'interêt le plus tendre par leur attachement à Monsr Lafayette depuis le commencement de la Revolution."

1. This name was incorrectly transcribed by Lear from the original "Chava-niac" that appears on the French copy that GW received on 20 Feb. 1793 with Dyson's letter to him of 8 December.

2. For background on Lafayette's departure from France and his subsequent capture and imprisonment, see Gouverneur Morris to GW, 23 Oct. 1792, source note and note 1. Among those captured with Lafayette were three other former members of the National Assembly: Alexandre Lameth, César de La Tour-Maubourg, and Jean-Xavier Bureaux du Pusy.

3. For GW's efforts to aid Lafayette's family, see GW to Marquise de Lafayette, 31 Jan. and 16 Mar. 1793.

From the Merchants of Charleston, South Carolina

Charleston So. Carolina 8th October 1792.
To The Honorable President & Members of the Senate of the united States in congress assemble'd

The Petition of the Subscribers, Merchants residing in Charleston, in the State of South Carolina, humbly sheweth,

That by an act pass'd at the third Session of Congress, to regulate processes, in the Courts of the United States, "It is enacted that the same mode of proceedings shall be had, & the same fees exacted in each State respectively as are now us'd, or allow'd in the supreme courts of the same["];[1] whereby your petitioners are subjected to the same enormous fees & obnoxious mode of proceedings in the court of Admiralty of the United States, in this State, as were practis'd & receiv'd in a Court of similar jurisdiction before the revolution; The Legislature of this State having never made any regulations or alterations therein; Your petitioners have annex'd hereto, a bill of costs in the said court as tax'd by the Judge, a reference to which by your honorable house, they presume, will render it unnecessary for them to use any arguments to induce a reduction of such excessive costs.[2]

Your petitioners feel themselves bound to make honorable mention of the most numerous & respectable practitioners at the bar, in this city, who have invariably, when in their power, refus'd to practice in a court, become obnoxious to all reasonable men, by the great & enormous costs to which Litigants there are made liable.

Your petitioners beg leave further to shew, that by an act pass'd at the Second Session of Congress, to regulate Seamen in the Merchants service, Ships or Vessells & their appurtenences are made Liable to actions of trivial amount, whereby it often happens that your petitioners are compell'd to submit to the most unreasonable demands as a Lesser injury, rather than suffer the detention of their Vessells; an evil which your petitioners apprehend may be remov'd without injury or Loss to any one, by giving power to the Judge of the Court, to accept of other sufficient security where the sum in action does not exceed One hundred & Fifty dollars.[3]

Your petitioners therefore pray that your honorable house, will be pleas'd to pass a Law, restraining the proceedings & reducing the fees in the Court of Admiralty of the United States in this State, & admitting of other security being taken to the satisfaction of the Judge of the Court, in small & trivial causes brought by seamen or others against Vessells in the Merchants service, & Your petitioners, as in duty bound will ever pray.

DS, DNA: RG 46, Second Congress, 1791–93, Senate Records of Legislative Proceedings, Petitions and Memorials, Resolutions of State Legislatures, and Related Documents. Sixty-one signatures appear at the bottom of this petition and are on CD-ROM: GW.

This petition was presented, read, and ordered to lie on the table at the 6 Nov. 1792 meeting of the Senate (*Annals of Congress,* 2d Cong., 610). Section 8 of "An Act for regulating Processes in the Courts of the United States, and providing Compensations for the Officers of the said Courts, and for Jurors and Witnesses" of 8 May 1792 already had repealed the act of 18 Feb. 1791, and GW approved on 1 Mar. 1793 "An Act to ascertain the fees in Admiralty proceedings in the District Courts of the United States, and for other purposes" (1 *Stat.* 278, 332–33).

1. During its third session the First Congress passed "An Act to continue in force, for a limited time, an act passed at the first Session of Congress, intituled 'An act to regulate processes in the Courts of the United States,'" which GW signed on 18 Feb. 1791. Section 2 of the original legislation of 29 Sept. 1789 provided that "the forms and modes of proceedings in causes of equity, and of admiralty and maritime jurisdiction, (a) shall be according to the course of the civil law; and the rates of fees the same as are or were last allowed by the states respectively in the court exercising supreme jurisdiction in such causes" (see ibid., 93–94, 191).

2. The annexed bill of costs has not been identified.

3. During its second session the First Congress approved "An Act for the government and regulation of Seamen in the merchants service," which GW signed on 20 July 1790 (ibid., 131–35).

From George Walker

Sir!   Georgetown Octr 8th 1792

Confident of your extreme anxiety to execute faithfully, Such Laws of the Union as are revolved upon you, I hope you will pardon the freedom of claiming your attention, to the present Alarming manner of conducting the operations in the intended City of *Washington*.

When the proprietors of land, contiguous to GeorgeTown and the Easternbranch, ceded by Deed of *Trust,* one half of the lots arising from their respective quantities, to be applied in conjunction with the grants of the two Adjoining States, in erecting the Public-buildings, and other improvements within the City; no one whatever entertained the most distant Idea but that, the operation in the City, and the expenditure of the money in *trust,* would be conducted with the most rigid Justice & impartiality; especially, after the places for the two grand Edifices were known, and that consequently, nearly an equal number of lots, convenient to the Presidents house & GeorgeTown, and to the Capitol and the Easternbranch, would be brought forward to Sale at the Sametime, leaving it to purchasers to determine the Superiority of Situation.[1]

It was also expected that, the two grand buildings would be carried on as nearly as possible at the Sametime, and that when any other work, besides the two buildings, Should be carried on at one end of the City, one of nearly equal importance would be carried on at the other.

The proprietors between Goose Creek and the Easternbranch however, with much concern, last year observed, the chief operations carried on at the GeorgeTown end of the City, and to their great Surprise, found the whole of the Sale held there; while not one lot was offered to the Eastward of Goose Creek, by which Several Gentlemen were disappointed, who had come with an intention to purchase on the Easternbranch. With equal Surprise, they beheld the Commissioners, expending a very large Sum of Money in *Trust,* without the limits of the City, upon a Bridge and Causway in the town of GeorgeTown; while no work of any kind was thought of at the other end of the City, even within its limits. The materials for the Presidents house, even to the Stones, are

now prepared, and the building ready to be begun, with every appearance of an intention to carry it into effect; While at the place
for the Capitol only a few Solitary Stones are to be Seen, with a
few bricks lately made in a hurry, as if intended to hoodwink the
proprietors, by keeping up Some Small appearance of an intention to build.[2]

This year, instead of the laying out the City, commencing on
the Easternbranch and continuing there till in equal forwardness with the other, it again commenced at the GeorgeTown end,
which is now completed; while that adjoining the Easternbranch,
is seemingly left to be laid out, when nothing else remains to be
done. The Sale having been held last year entirely between the
Presidents house and Georgetown, Justice, Policy, and impartiality, necessarily require that, it should this year be commenced
between the Capitol and the Easternbranch; but to our great Astonishment! very little of the City is yet laid out upon the Easternbranch, and not the Smallest appearance of any intention to
Sell there; while almost the whole of the property arround the
Presidents house, and adjoining GeorgeTown, is now laid off into
lots, divided with the proprietors, and ready for Sale: hence
those who may have come from a distance, with an intention to
purchase on the Easternbranch, will again be deceived, and naturally conclude that, the Commissioners are not *"Desirous"* that
any City should ever be built to the Eastward of Goose Creek.

The preceding facts, have naturally given rise to a suggestion,
that has long existed, and now gains considerable belief, viz. that,
the Commissioners are entirely led and directed by Col. Deakins, with Some other influential Gentlemen in GeorgeTown,
and that, there is a Secret intention, of giving every encouragement to the GeorgeTown end of the City, to the ruin of the other.
This Idea is Strongly Supported, by their begining the Smallest
Edifice first, for if any preference in commencement is necessary, it ought certainly to be given to the largest. Besides, two impressions of the Plan of the City are now extant, neither of which
exhibit the Soundings and Channels of the Rivers adjoining the
City meanly concealling the excellence of the Easternbranch as
a harbour, while the plan itself, as far as it relates to the Easternbranch, is not only erroneous, but very much curtailled, mutu-
lated, and disfigured.[3]

Although, the Secretary of State informed me that, you were

no longer to interfere in the affairs of the City, yet its friends, and the people of America expect that, you will be pleased to keep in Appointment, Commissioners possessed of Ability, integrity, and impartiality; otherwise the Object must certainly fail. The general want of confidence throughout the Union, in the present Commissioners, I am affraid will be fatally evident at the approaching Sale. But having laid a deep Stake in the object, while it was conducted by your own Just, wise, and decisive Direction, I hope you will now forgive the liberty I have taken, in complaining of injuries, and requesting that equal Justice may be done to all concerned. These truths, requiring no Sanction of names, I have not even mentioned my intention of addressing you, to any of the proprietors affected. and wishing this to be shewn to the Commissioners.[4] With great Respect I am Sir Your Mo. Obt Servant

George Walker

P.S. It is Submitted to your consideration, whether in the present partial State of the two buildings and other preparations, a Notification from the President of the United States to the public, before the Sale, may not be Just—assuring that, you will immediately give orders that, the same preparations be made for the Capitol, that are now made for the Presidents house, before the walls of either are begun; and that, afterwards they Shall be carried on at the Sametime, Storey for Storey, while, in future, you will take care that, equal Justice is done to both ends of the City.

G.W.

ALS, DLC:GW.

1. For background on the creation of the federal district by Congress, the selection of the district's current site, the cession by Maryland and Virginia of land to the district, and GW's authority over the district, see GW to Thomas Jefferson, 2 Jan. 1791, editorial note and n.2. For the cession of property by landowners in the federal district, see Agreement of the Proprietors of the Federal District, 30 Mar. 1791, and source note, and D.C. Commissioners to GW, 30 June 1791, and source note.

2. For the previous year's sale of lots, see GW's proclamation of 17 Oct. 1791 and source note. Walker's land in the district comprised a narrow rectangle extending from the Eastern Branch across the eastern part of the Federal City from current 15th Street, S.E., to current H Street, N.E. Walker was not alone in his criticism of the commissioners. For a more detailed indictment of the construction of the bridge being built over Rock Creek, see Benjamin Stoddert to GW, 24 Oct. 1792.

3. For results of the October 1792 sale of lots, see D.C. Commissioners to GW, 13 Oct., and notes 1 and 2. Georgetown merchant William Deakins, Jr.,

served as the treasurer for the D.C. commissioners from 1791 to 1796. Walker was probably familiar with the map printed in the March 1792 issue of the *Universal Asylum, and Columbian Magazine* (Philadelphia), the first confirmed publication of a map of the proposed Federal City, and with Boston engraver Samuel Hill's *Plan of the City of Washington in the Territory of Columbia, Ceded by the States of Virginia and Maryland to the United States of America,* which was printed in the summer of 1792. When GW saw Hill's prints earlier this year, he noted the absence of "the soundings of the River & Branch" which would be "very satisfactory & advantageous to have done" (see Tobias Lear to Thomas Jefferson, 11 July 1792). The larger and better engraving, produced later this year by Philadelphia engravers James Thackara and John Vallance, included the desired soundings, but prints were not made from it until after the 8 Oct. sale of lots.

4. For GW's response to criticism by Walker and Stoddert, see his letter to David Stuart of 30 Nov. 1792.

From Henry Knox

Sir   War-department, 9th October 1792

I have the mortification to submit you, the copy of a Letter this day received by express from Governor Blount—The enclosures he mentions are too lengthy to be copied this day, but are such as to leave no doubt of the authenticity of the information.[1]

I have consulted with the Secretary of State and the Secretary of the Treasury on this disagreeable affair. Our unanimous opinion is, That as Governor Blount has been furnished heretofore with the most ample powers, to draw for the Militia of his government for its defensive protection—that all measures of an offensive nature be restrained until the meeting of Congress, to whom belong the powers of war.

It is to be exceedingly apprehended, that this unfortunate event may light up a pretty general Indian war to the southward. Under this impression, it will be of the highest importance that it should, if constrained by sad necessity, be a constitutional and legislative act.[2]

I have the honor to transmit you the copies of the Letters I have written to Governors Blount & Lee on this occasion[3]—With the highest respect I have the honor to be sir, Your most Obed. servt

H. Knox

LS, DLC:GW; LB, DLC:GW.

1. William Blount's letter to Knox of 11 Sept. from Knoxville, Tenn., enclosed copies of letters from "the little Turkey the chief of the Cherokees, The

Boot who was his immediate Representative at the treaty of Holston and the two Interpreters of the United States James Carey and John Thompson by which you will be informed that the five lower towns of the Cherokees have declared War against the United States, you will observe James Carey estimates the numbers who were to leave the towns on the 7th instant to make an attack on the settlements of three hundred." The letters were delivered to Blount by James Ore who reported "that the party was estimated at five hundred of whom one hundred were Creeks the whole commanded by John Watts and from the best information he could collect it appears their destination is against Cumberland or the Frontiers of Knox County."

Blount also enclosed a copy of a letter received from Gen. John Sevier "containing the same information with the addition of three hundred more than mentioned by Mr Carey a part of whom are mounted on horses, supposed to the number of one hundred, and I also inclose copies of three Letters from Mr [Leonard] Shaw all which serve to shew the design of those Indians against the United States.

"I have ordered the Regiment of the County of Knox into actual service for its defence for a few days until the destination of John Watts and his party is certainly known, and have dispatched an express to General [James] Robertson giving him the necessary information with orders to put the Brigade of that district in the best possible state of defence.

"I have also given orders to the Colonels of the several Counties of Washington district to be in readiness to march on the shortest Notice.

"This declaration of War was very unexpected, and has given great alarm to the Frontiers."

Blount anticipated that the attack would be on Cumberland where "the guards stationed for the protection thereof [are] no ways equal to the weight of so unexpected an Attack. Inclosed is a Copy of my Order to Major [Anthony] Sharpe of the 10th Ultimo, which will shew the force and destination of those Guards.

"I am apprehensive the numbers may be thought too few, but it was with great difficulty so many were turned out, difficult to myself lest I should be thought too extravagant, and equally difficult to get so many from the district of Washington to the district of Mero" (DLC:GW). For the enclosures in Blount's letter, see *ASP, Indian Affairs*, 1:276–79.

2. For the president's message concerning Indian hostilities in the Southeastern Territory, see GW's Address to the U.S. Senate and House of Representatives, 6 Nov. 1792. The "Information received relatively to the disposition of the Southern Indians, and the causes of the hostilities of part of the Cherokees and Creeks" that Knox presented to the House on 7 Nov. included copies of Blount's letter of 11 Sept. and its enclosures (see *Annals of Congress*, 2d Cong., 673; DNA: RG 46, Second Congress, 1791–93, Senate Records of Legislative Proceedings, Reports and Communications).

3. Knox replied to Blount on 9 Oct.: "It is with infinite regret I have perused your letter of the 11th Ultimo which I have this day received containing information of the declaration of War by the five lower Cherokee Towns against the United States.

"From the train of the negociations with the Cherokees the causes of such a conduct on their parts is involved in obscurity—and the affair is still rendered more perplexed by their being headed by John Watts, from whom you have heretofore expected such assistance.

"I beg leave to request as early as possible a statement of the alledged and actual causes of their violent conduct in order that it may be explained to Congress.

"As you have ample powers to call forth such portions of the Militia of your Government for its defensive protection as you shall judge occasions to require no further steps can be taken at this moment.

"The Congress which possess the powers of declaring War will assemble on the 5th of next Month—Until their judgments shall be made known it seems essential to confine all your operations to defensive measures—This is ⟨intended⟩ to restrain any expedition against the Indian Towns—but all incursive parties against your frontiers are to be punished with the greatest severity.

"It will be of an high degree of importance on your part to confirm all the well disposed part of the Cherokee nation, and to quiet their apprehensions against our attacks.

"Were it possible to make them the instruments to punish the revolted towns it would seem to be just as well as good policy.

"Will it not be possible for you to send a faithful and intelligent agent to the upper Towns of the Creeks to restrain the expedition of their banditti? such a measure is indispensible.

"Mr [James] Seagroves communications are it seems more with the lower than upper Creeks—the depredations upon Cumberland seem to be confined to the latter.

"The President of the United States will arrive here on Saturday next being the 13th instant—any further measures which he shall direct to be taken shall be communicated to you by the post who will commence his operations on the 15 instant.

"Mr [David] Allison has not arrived nor have I heard from him.

"I have received your letters and also one from Genl Pickens dated the 22d of August" (DLC:GW).

In his letter to Virginia governor Henry Lee of 9 Oct., Knox summarized the information contained in Blount's letter of 11 Sept., including the declaration of war made by "the five lower Towns on the Tennesee, headed by John Watts," and the defensive measures taken by Blount. Knox explained that since Congress will be meeting soon and since only its members "are invested with the powers of War," it was necessary to wait for its decisions before the federal government can take offensive measures. "In the mean time," Knox wrote, "your Excellency will be the Judge whether any further measures should be necessary for the defense of the South western parts of Virginia at the expence of the Union, of the nature and in addition to those before taken" (DLC:GW).

Letter not found: to Leven Powell, c.10–11 Oct. 1792. GW wrote Robert Townsend Hooe on 29 May 1793 from Philadelphia that "on my way to this City last October I wrote a letter to Colo. Powell," and Powell wrote GW on 15 June 1793: "On my return home from the [Virginia] Assem-

bly about the first of December last, I found your favor from Baltimore."
While traveling from Mount Vernon to Philadelphia in October 1792,
GW spent the night of 10 Oct. at Daniel Grant's Fountain Inn in Balti-
more (see James McHenry to GW, 25 Sept. 1792, n.3).

From Isaac Huger

Sir,   Charleston S. Carolina Octr 12th 1792.
    From the confidential hints given to me of the many essential
services rendered by Mr John Clark (formerly of Pennsylvania) to
the late Colo. John Laurens, who commanded the Light Troops
in the late American Southern Army, some months before the
British evacuated this City, who's services were afterwards explained to me by the Late Genl Greene, induces me from Justice
and Gratitude to recommend the said Mr John Clark to your
Excellency's particular notice. I had the Satisfaction of knowing him several years in this City; during which he has been employed in public Offices of the highest importance to this State;
and for three years past he has had the principal management
of the Late Shff's Office for Charlestown Distt; and has always
in these employments conducted himself with Strict probity—
these Services will, I presume incline your Excellency to view
him favorably—And pardon the Liberty I have taken to Address
you on the Occasion.[1] I am Sir, with respect yr obdt and very
hble sert

                                                    Isc Huger.

ALS, DLC:GW. The docket reads: "recd Decr 18th 1792."
    1. The previous year, after returning to his home state of Pennsylvania, John
Clark had applied unsuccessfully for appointment as U.S. auditor, citing his
experience as an auditor in the Continental army (see Clark to GW, 2 Sept.
1791, Thomas Hartley to GW, 7 Oct. 1791). Although Clark now had the recommendation of Huger, a prominent South Carolina planter, Revolutionary
War general, and the current federal marshal of South Carolina, he did not receive a federal appointment at this time. On 27 Sept. 1794 Clark wrote GW
from "York Borough," Pa., this time to offer his services as an aide-de-camp to
GW while the president led the army in its suppression of the Whiskey Rebellion (DNA: RG 59, Miscellaneous Letters). GW declined Clark's offer, imply-
ing that the necessity of remaining in Philadelphia while Congress met would
limit severely his own military activity and thus negate the need for Clark's services (GW to John Clark, 6 Oct. 1794, ALS, sold by Christie's, catalog FLAVIA
7286, item 258, 17–18 May 1991). See also Spangler, "Memoir of Major John

Clark," 77, 79–80, 85. Known as John Clark, Jr., during the Revolutionary War, he often is confused with John Clark (d. 1844), also from Pennsylvania, who was a major in the 1791 levies and in the 3d Sub-Legion in 1792, and who was promoted to lieutenant colonel commandant in 1793 (see GW to the U.S. Senate, 9 April 1792, 22 Feb. 1793 [first letter]).

From the Commissioners for the District of Columbia

Sir,   George-town 13th October—1792

Inclosed we send you a list of our Sales, which were closed yesterday.[1] Tho' the average price is not entirely equal to that of the first sales, yet, when it is considered, that the Company assembled, was by no means such, as might have been expected, from the unlucky intervention of several circumstances; and allso, that it was the Public opinion, that the first sales were too high; and that they would be considerably less this year, we think we have much reason to be satisfyed—It was evident, that many who had the strongest reliance on this opinion, were much surprised, if not disappointed; as they did not make a bid, tho' it was known they had come with intentions of purchasing—We observe with pleasure now, a contrary opinion gaining ground fast, that they will not sell so cheap hereafter. Several of our Mechanics were among the purchasors; who will probably be among the first improvers—You will observe, that in two instances, we set up a square for sale—It was contrary to our opinion, to sell by the square, in the vicinity of such situations as either the Capitol, or President's house—To gratify some, who declared a strong wish to buy by the square, near the Capitol, and to gratify the Proprietors allso at that quarter, we accordingly set up one—It was not our intention to have gone further in this mode; but Mr Davidson talked directly of our partiality to the other end of the City, and insisted on a square near the President's house being allso set up; which to remove all foundation for such charges was done the next day—The result, will we hope teach them to confide a little more in the judgement of the Commissioners in future—From the deep stake which Mr Blodget has in the city, we have thought it our duty to communicate freely with him. We accordingly instructed him not to let the squares go at an under value—In consequence of this, the square near the Capitol tho' bought by him, still rests with us—But as it will not be proper, that this circumstance should be known, or even suspected (tho' generally practiced at all sales) we shall make some arrangements with Mr Blodget for disposing of them on his own. From their very advantageous situation, he gives us much room to think, they will command, (as they certainly ought) a much superior price.[2]

He has some propositions to make to us, respecting the employment of an agent, to pass through the different States for the purpose of disposing of lotts in the course of next summer; which we have desired him to communicate to you when matured— Not only from the conversation we have had with him on this subject, but from similar ideas having been frequently suggested to us by gentlemen, who have come from a distance, we are induced at present, to concieve a very favourable opinion of such a plan.[3] A Mr Ford from Philadelphia, who purchased pretty freely last year, made us an offer of 35£ a lot for 500 lots—But, as it was done without any specification of the lots he would fix on, we came to nothing conclusive—He was informed generally, that it was much below what had ever been contemplated for lots in any eligible situation—As it is probable, he may have been employed by some moneyed people from Philadelphia, who did not chuse themselves to appear in such a speculation, we hope our conversation with him, will lead to a more just opinion of the value of the lots—It was strongly wished by several strangers, who did not however purchase, that there might be a sale in the Spring or early in the Summer—As we are entirely of the same opinion, we have given them every reason to believe there will be one[4]—We are Sir, with the greatest respect, Your most Obt Servts

Dd Stuart.
Danl Carroll

P:S: Our great hurry would not permit us to have a copy taken of this.

LS, in David Stuart's writing, DLC:GW.

1. The summary of the October 1792 "Sale of Lots from District of Columbia," which Stuart enclosed, reported 45 lots "sold seperately" averaging £91.14.10 per lot; 24 lots "in one square near the capitol, sold by the square," averaging £57 per lot; and 24 lots in "one square near the President's house sold by the square" averaging £85 per lot and bought by Samuel Davidson. Ac-

cording to Stuart's computations, the commissioners sold 93 lots at an average price of £80.0.9 per lot for a total of £7,536.10 (DLC:GW). For the results of the 1791 sale, see Stuart to GW, 19 Oct. 1791, nn.1–2, and D.C. Commissioners to GW, 21 Oct. 1791. For background on Georgetown merchant Samuel Davidson's financial interest in the sale, see D.C. Commissioners to GW, 3 April 1791, n.1, and Davidson to GW, 28 May 1792.

2. Samuel Blodget, Jr., already one of the largest landholders in the federal district, bought square 688 near the site of the proposed Capitol. According to a later affidavit, prepared on 21 Nov. 1794 by commissioners Daniel Carroll and David Stuart: "Mr Blodget at our desire bid for Square No. 688 near the Capitol which we considered as selling at a very under rate Mr Blodget in this manner became the purchaser of it on behalf of the public: after the Sales were finished, . . . Mr Blodget told us, that tho' he had become the purchaser of that Square on account of the public, he would with our approbation take it on himself and in consideration of the low rate at which he should have so important a Square, he would erect on it a handsome building which should be commenced in the course of the ensuing Summer After some consideration we consented to it induced by the proposition of building. . . . We certainly considered the price as by no means Sufficient for a Square—our principal inducement was certainly the building to be erected on it" (DNA: RG 42, Records of the Commissioners for the District of Columbia, Proceedings, 1791–1802).

3. On 5 Jan. 1793 the commissioners appointed Blodget the district supervisor and gave him the authority to sell lots in the federal district on their behalf (see D.C. Commissioners to Blodget, 5 Jan. 1793, DNA: RG 42, Records of the Commissioners for the District of Columbia, Letters Sent, 1791–1802, and D.C. Commissioners to GW, 5 Jan. 1793).

4. Philadelphia merchant Standish Ford (Forde) had purchased land costing £1,075 during the 1791 sale of lots, and along with his business partner John Reed, he continued speculating in federal district land over the next several years (see Arnebeck, *Through a Fiery Trial*, 70, 511). The next public auction of lots began on 17 Sept. 1793 (see GW to D.C. Commissioners, 16 Sept. 1793).

Tobias Lear to Alexander Hamilton

United States [Philadelphia] 13th Octor 1792
By the President's command T. Lear has the honor to inform the Secretary of the Treasury that the President has appointed William Lewis to be keeper of the Light-house on Cape Henry, with a salary of four hundred Dollars per annum. The President does not conceive that the circumstance of mister Cormicks being employed to oversee the building of the Lighthouse, tho' in

his favor, as sufficiently strong to recommend him as the most proper person to be Keeper of it.[1]

Tobias Lear. S.P.U.S.

T. Lear has mentioned to the president the Auditor's wish to go to Virginia, & he has no objection to his going.[2]

LB, DLC:GW.

1. For previous discussion of several candidates, including William Lewis and Lemuel Cornick, for appointment as lighthouse keeper at Cape Henry, Va., see Hamilton to GW, 22 Sept. 1792, and note 6. Hamilton wrote Lear from Philadelphia on 18 Oct. 1792: "Before a final step is taken respecting a Keeper of the Virginia Lighthouse, I wish it to be known to the President . . . that Mr Cornick was appointed by Colo. [Thomas] Newton to oversee the building of the Lighthouse, for which he will receive a *quantum meruit*. This is a circumstance in his favour tho' a very slight one, and such as may be overruled by any other consideration. Propriety, however, requires that it should be brought into the President's view" (DLC:GW). Cornick was appointed as keeper of the lighthouse at Cape Henry after Lewis died in November 1792 (see Lear to Hamilton, 22 Dec. 1792, DNA: RG 26, Inventory NC-31, entry 16, Miscellaneous Records Relating to the Lighthouse Service; see also the extract in Syrett, *Hamilton Papers*, 13:356–57).

2. For Hamilton's response to Richard Harrison's leave of absence from his position as auditor of the U.S. treasury, see Hamilton to GW, 19 Oct. 1792.

From Thomas Jefferson

[Philadelphia] Oct. 14. 1792.

Th: Jefferson presents his respects to the President & incloses him some letters for his perusal. those from G. Morris & mister Short require immediate notice, because there are vessels about to sail by which answers should be sent.[1] the President will see by mister Remsen's letter the peculiar misfortune of the dispatches to Carmichael & Short, of which, from their particular delicacy, it was thought best not to risk duplicates, because being put on board a vessel bound directly to Amsterdam, they seemed to run no other danger than of the sea. but it so turns out as to bring on them what is tantamount to a loss by the sea, and the possibility of their getting into other hands. this loss was not ascertained till yesterday. the clerks are now all employed in copying the dispatches over again to go by a vessel which sails for Amsterdam on Wednesday.[2]

AL, DNA: RG 59, Miscellaneous Letters; LB, DNA: RG 59, George Washington's Correspondence with His Secretaries of State; LB (photocopy), DLC:GW.

1. Gouverneur Morris's letter to Jefferson, written from Paris on 10 July 1792 and received by Jefferson on 6 Oct., contains news of political developments in France, including a veiled hint of the king's plans for escape from Paris and the increasing military presence of the Austrian and Prussian armies on French borders. Morris also reported that the French were interested in negotiating a new commercial treaty with the United States (see *Jefferson Papers*, 24:207–9). William Short's letters from The Hague of 20, 27 (two letters), and 31 July 1792, all received on 6 Oct., devote much attention to events in France and on the growing threat of a war against France (see ibid., 240–46, 260–61, 270–72). Jefferson replied to Morris's letter on 15 Oct. and to those from Short on 14 and 16 Oct. (see ibid., 482–85, 490–91).

2. Henry Remsen, Jr., former chief clerk of the State Department, wrote Jefferson from New York on 10 Oct. 1792 to report that "dispatches made up in February for Mr. Short" and Jefferson's letters to Short of 18 Mar. were placed on the brig *Sion*, captained by William Oliver, which set sail between 22 and 26 Mar. from New York. Unfortunately the ship sprung a leak in the midst of a gale, and "the Captain finding she could not be kept from sinking, went with his crew on board an English vessel which fortunately appeared . . . *taking with him the bag containing the letters.*" The English vessel "was bound to Newfoundland, and arrived there in safety, from whence the Captain of the Sion informs his owners, in a letter dated in April, that he purposes sending the bag of letters to Amsterdam by any vessel bound thither, or by the way of London" (ibid., 463–64). The ship preparing to sail for Amsterdam on Wednesday, 17 Oct., was the *Columbia*, captained by William Maley (see *General Advertiser* [Philadelphia], 12 Oct. 1792).

From Henry Knox

Sir   Philadelphia 14 October 1792

I have the honor with great diffidence to submit hints of points in the War department which appear necessary to be mentioned to the Legislature at their approaching session.

Arsenals are exceedingly wanted in the middle and southern states for the well ordering of the military stores—But as this is a ticklish subject it is omitted for the present.[1]

I have also the honor to submit a letter from Governor Lee of the 4th instant, with the draft of an answer thereto, which if it should receive your approbation may be transmitted by tomorrows post.[2]

I propose to set out early tomorrow Morning for the Eastward. I hope from circumstances to meet my family and return by Sunday or monday of the next week.[3] I have the honor sir to be with perfect Respect Your Obedient Servant

H. Knox

ALS, DLC:GW; ADfS, NNGL: Knox Papers; LB, DLC:GW.

1. On 3 Sept., GW had written Knox requesting his opinion about what to include in the address to the U.S. Senate and House of Representatives that GW presented on 6 Nov. 1792. No list of "hints" has been identified.

2. Henry Lee's letter to Knox of 4 Oct. 1792 has not been identified. Knox replied to Lee on 14 Oct. from Philadelphia that the president "has directed me to inform you that from his present view of the subject, he does not conceive any measures on the part of the Legislature of Virginia necessary for the defence of the frontiers. . . . the respectable force authorized by Congress during their late session, together with the militia which the laws authorize him to call into service, will prove adequate to the occasions which may arise.

"He has farther desired me to tender his thanks for your ideas relatively to the Block-houses, for the purpose of cutting off the communication between the Northern and Southern Indians, which he will take into his consideration" (*Calendar of Virginia State Papers,* 6:97).

3. Knox returned to Philadelphia from his trip to New York City sometime between Friday, 19 Oct., and Thursday, 25 Oct. (see Knox to William Duer, 19 Oct., and to Thomas Randall, 25 Oct., NNGL: Knox Papers).

From Charles Pinckney

(Private)

Dear Sir.   Charleston [S.C.] October 14: 1792

I have the honour to inclose you copies of my dispatches by Captain Burroughs lest any accident should have happened to him—not having recieved any Express since the first, I am not able to add to my former communications on that subject.[1]

As the *four years* for which I have been appointed to the office I hold will expire in December, and as by our Constitution I am *ineligible and* disqualified from serving for four years to come I embrace this opportunity of returning you my thanks for the polite attention I have recieved from you in my official situation and to assure you I shall ever retain a grateful sense of them. at the same time permit me to add that as my Education and pursuits have been entirely adapted to a public life, that whenever you may think proper to honour me with any appointment under the federal Government which I can with propriety accept considering the different situations I Have been in I shall with plea-

sure accept it—Emoluments of Office are not, nor have ever
been my aim, but I confess it always gives me pleasure to serve
the Public—when I can do it with honour and with respect to the
Appointments I have already held. If the entire confidence and
approbation of my public conduct of the state I live in, may be a
recommendation I think I may venture to say and I believe you
know I fully possess it—I have said this much to you, because I
am told you expect on occasions of this kind to be previously informed of the wishes of those whose situations or inclinations
may lead or entitle them to look up to public appointments—
but whether any proper Opportunity may offer or you should be
disposed or not to gratify my wishes I hope your friendship will
induce you to consider this communication as *entirely confidential*—I should not have made it, but I have been told that although my friend Colonel Laurens has mentioned me to you, &
I believe some others have likewise done so, yet upon these occasions it is considered as *more respectful* that the parties themselves should signify their inclinations.[2] I am with Respect & Attachment Yours truly

Charles Pinckney

ALS, DLC:GW.

1. For the letters sent originally by Edward Burrows, captain of the brig *Georgia Packet,* see Charles Pinckney to GW, 30 Sept. 1792, and notes 1 and 2.

2. Pinckney currently was finishing his second term as governor of South
Carolina. His father-in-law, Revolutionary War statesman Henry Laurens, had
written GW on 20 Aug. 1791 recommending Pinckney for a diplomatic position, but it was Pinckney's second cousin Thomas Pinckney who became minister to Great Britain later that year (see GW to the U.S. Senate, 22 Dec. 1791).
Charles Pinckney was elected governor of South Carolina for a third term in
1796, and in 1798 he was elected to the U.S. Senate, from which he resigned
in 1801 in order to accept an appointment by President Jefferson as minister
to Spain. Upon his return to South Carolina in 1806, Pinckney was elected
governor for a fourth term, and he served in the U.S. House of Representatives
from 1819 to 1821.

To Anthony Whitting

Mr Whiting,   [Philadelphia] Oct. 14th 1792.[1]

I arrived in this City yesterday afternoon, without encounter-
ing any accident except what you are acquainted with by the return of the Mare from George Town; and the indisposition of

Richard; who, with difficulty, was able to travel from Baltimore to this place, on acct of the fever wch returnd on him.[2]

Recollecting that it was my desire that you should send the Reports to the Post Office every Wednesday afternoon, & receive at the sametime my communications from thence; I shall now, to avoid the delay of a week, mention such things as have occurred to me since I left home, and were not communicated to you; or, if mentioned at all, were but slightly touched upon; from the hurried situation into which I had been thrown.

Having left the disposition of the Mansion House people to you, I wish to know how they are arranged; and think the sooner they are distributed to their permanent abodes the better. Those which I alloted to the Gardener, are neither to be idle themselves, nor to support him in idleness; but are to enable him to carry certain plans of mine into effect with more promptness; and in a better manner (under his immediate superintendance) than it otherwise could be, without withdrawing your attention more than it ought to be from matters of greater magnitude. The things which I want him to do with these people (aided by the Mansn Ho. Cart) are to complete the upper garden Walk, with gravel, taken from the nearest Pit wch is hid from view; & this I think may be found in a gully in the Clover lot, in front of the M: House. The gravel to pass through a wooden sieve, to take out Stones of too large a size. To gravel the Walks in the Pine labyrinths, on both sides of the Lawn West of the House. To plant fresh clumps as soon as the trees can be removed; in the Buck Wheat Lot; the two clover lots; &ca; & of the best, & most ornamental trees—quick in their growth. These clumps are not to be placed with regularity as they respect one another—nor the trees in each, individually. Nor are the clumps to cover (individually) half the ground those did which were planted out last fall, Winter, & Spring. In a word, the trees are to be so close together in each Clump as for the tops, in a little while, to appear as if they proceeded from one trunk. they can always be thinned if found too thick. Those clumps wch are already planted (if alive) may be thickened in the manner I have described, and with the same kind of trees; provided they do not stand in too formal a point of view, one to the other. The ever-greens must be removed when they can be taken up with a compact & solid body of frozen earth to the Roots, otherwise the labour will be lost, and another year will pass away without accomplishing my design; as abundant experience has incontestibly proved. The flowering ever-green Ivy, I want them to plant thick around the Ice house upper side[3]— not of the tallest kind, but of an even height: this should be taken up as above; & to insure its thriving, as well as barely living, there ought, I conceive, to be a bed of its natural soil prepared two or three feet deep, & as wide as the transplantation (six or eight feet at least) is intended. The like at the No. East of the same lawn, by the other Wall. and if beyond that Hah! Hah!—between it and the Path leading from the Barn to the wild Cherry tree in the Hollow, was pretty thickly strewed with them (of the lower sort) & intermixed freely with the bush honey suckle of the Woods, it would, in my opinion, have a pleasing effect. Besides these things, & keeping the Gardens (my small, as well as the others) —lawns—Shrubberies, and Ovals clean & free from Weeds and grass, I would have what is called the Vineyard Inclosure cleansed of all the trash that is in it, and got in perfect order for fruit trees —Kitchen vegitables of various kinds—experimental grasses— & for other purposes.[4] Perhaps after the trash & grubs are taken out, a good plowing with a strong team where there is nothing growing may be an essential preparatory operation for the work that is to follow. The old ditch & bank which splits this inclosure in two is to be levelled, & the trees, except here & there one, taken away; in these I do not comprehend fruit trees; After these things are accomplished—or in weather when they cannot be employed usefully in either of the works before enumerated, these (Negro) hands may be employed in cutting wood, or in other work with the Mansion House Gang.

I would have the Gardener also, with these people, if the Autumn is a proper Season for it, if not, without fail in the Spring, plant cuttings of the Weeping Willow, yellow willow, or Lombardy Poplar prefering the first & last mentioned, at the distance of a foot, or 18 Inches apart from the Smiths shop,[5] quite as the Post & Rail fence runs, around both these inclosures; and the Vine yard inclosure; also that lately sown in Lucern[6] from the Stercorary[7] to the river fence: that by entwining them as they grow up I may have a substitute for the fences that are now there. To do this, is of the utmost importance to my interest; as it also is in a more essential degree, to supply by hedges of this, or some other kind all my other fences; as well the exterior ones as those which seperate the different fields from one another. I have laboured to effect this latter point for years. I have pressed it, & pressed it again—but, strange to tell! the Season has either been suffered to pass away before it is set about; or it has either been set about improperly; or, no care has been taken afterwards to preserve & nourish the young plants so as to fit them for the purpose they were intended. Let me therefore in the strongest terms possible, call your attention to this business, as one, than which nothing is nearer, both to my interest and wishes; first, because it is indispensably necessary to save timber & labour; and secondly, because it is ornamental to the Farm, & reputable to the Farmer. If you want Honey locust seed, or any thing else from hence to enable you to effect these I will send them. About the Mansion House (and indeed in other cross fences; where Hogs cannot come) I think the Weeping Willow & lombardy poplar, which are quick of growth, is to be preferred. Save much of the Cedar Berries, and (after washing, & rubbing off the glutinous coating around the Seed) sow them in every place where you think they can be established to advantage. This might be done even, where you put the cuttings above mentioned (at the Plantations) as a more *permanent* fence than the other; which may yield, as the Cedars grow up, and are plashed.[8]

Let the hands at the Mansion House Grub *well*, & perfectly prepare the old clover lot at the Mansion House for whatever you may incline to put into it, preparatory for grass, with which it is to be laid down. When I say grub *well*, I mean that every thing wch is not to remain as trees should be taken up by the roots; so as that the Plow may meet with no interruption, and the field lye perfectly smooth for the Scythe. Let this, I earnestly request, be received as a general, & positive direction; for I seriously assure you, that I had rather have *one Acre* cleared in this manner, than four in the common mode; especially in *all* grounds designed for grass; & for the reasons which I have often mentioned to you. It is a great, & very disagreeable eye-sore to me, as well as a real injury in the loss of labour & the Crop (ultimately) and the destruction of Scythes, to have foul meadows. After this is done by the Mansion House people, let them begin at the Wharf, or rather at what is called hell hole,[9] and Grub as has been cleared

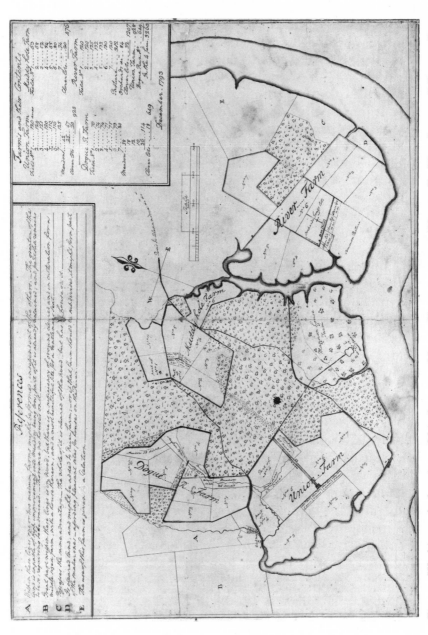

Fig. 1. Washington's drawing of his farms at Mount Vernon, 1793. (Henry E. Huntington Library, San Marino, Calif.)

all the under-growth, trimming the large from that place to the cross fence which runs down from the spring to the River fence, that I may, when the wet spots are made dry, & without plowing or breaking the ground more than a harrow would do, lay it down in grass—And when these two objects are accomplished, if nothing else *more* desirable should occur, to set them about, they might be employed in grubbing & preparing the ground I once (as you know) contemplated as a Corn field for the Muddy hole[10] people at the Mansion House.

It is my wish that no hogs may be put up for Porke that is not of sufficient size and age. I had rather have a little Porke that is good, than much bad.

I am persuaded your exertion, to get out your Wheat, will be commensurate to the necessity; that gathering of Corn (as soon as it can be with safety) may follow before the frosts may render it pernicious to run Carts over the Wheat, that is amongst it. Delay no time in getting up—threshing out—and measuring your Buck Wheat that I may know what is made. Nor in digging up the Potatoes at Dogue-Run. And I am persuaded you will begin your Autumn plowing as soon as circumstances will permit—remember that the season is now approaching fast when frosts will put a stop to this business.

The second Visto which I mentioned to you is but a secondary object, and yet I am anxious to know over what ground it will pass; but this may be done by a line of stakes in an avenue not more than Six feet wide.[11]

The Sooner the old Quarter is pulled down the better. Davis may then do up the Wall, and he ought, in time, to do the other Jobs I mentioned to you—to wit—the Chimney in the Neck—the Chimney at French's—& that at Bishops house[.] the Vault (burying place) also wants repair. After these he will, as late as the Weather will permit, proceed in painting; first finishing the Quarter—then the four Garden houses—then the Smoke house & Store—then the old Spinning house, Wash house, & Coach house with red roofs as the others have—After doing this work —or when obliged to quit it he will join the Carpenters. This Nuclus may do immediately; or as soon as all the Cedars, locusts, and other valuable Wood where Sam has been clearing, can be stripped of its limbs & brought to, & secured in, or at the Barn.[12]

As it is proposed that the hands at Muddy hole should obtain their Corn ground at Dogue run, parts of it that now are, or probably will be wet in the Spring, ought without loss of time to be ditched; that they may be thoroughly grubbed this fall, or in the Winter; and the middle meadow there are two places, I conceive, that will want main ditches, besides smaller cross ditches, viz.—the arm of the swamp running up towards the Spring—& the other arm leading to the outer fence. What Ditching may be wanting in the Mill swamp, above the present Corn field therein, I know not; one main ditch, however, will certainly be necessary, & more than probably one or two cross ones. But in this case, as in every other, it is my express desire that no more may be attempted than what can be compleatly, & effectually executed.

As I have already furnished you with a memorandum of the work marked out for the Carpenters, I need not, at this time, add any thing on that head; except a wish that the Well may be compleated agreeably to the model, that I may know whether it will answer or not. And, if it was not mentioned in my last, that the Qr may be taken down.[13]

Endeavor to provide Oyster Shells in the course of this Winter, that, in case I should resolve on it, there may be no let, or delay in building a Barn, or treading floor at Dogue-run to be in readiness for the next Wheaten Crop. I met with a Nephew of mine —Colo. Willm Augustine Washington—at George Town, who promised to engage some persons, if he could, to carry shells to Mount Vernon for me; if this should happen but do not depend upon it you must take what are brought, although you may have entered into other engagements; as it will be on my acct he sends them; they must be paid for on delivery; I do not suppose they will exceed 16/8 or 18/. the hundred bushels, but if they are engaged for me they must be taken if they do exceed this price.[14]

As I can get Iron as cheap, if not cheaper here than it is obtained from Alexandria, send me the sizes of the Bars, plates, &ca which you would have to compose a Tonn, and I will send it from hence before the frost sets in.[15]

Mrs Washington requested the Gardeners Wife—& she readily undertook it—to superintend, under your general direction, the care of the Spinners. This will also lessen the minutiæ of your business, & enable you to attend closer to the great, & important parts of it. Put her in a good & regular mode, & keep her to the exercise of it. An allowance will be made her for the trouble this business will occasion.[16] Tell the Gardener, it is my desire that he should raise Chesnut trees from the Nuts of those which grow on the front Lawn.

Although it is last mentioned, it is foremost in my thoughts, to desire you will be particularly attentive to my Negros in their sickness; and to order every Overseer *positively* to be so likewise; for I am sorry to observe that the generality of them, view these poor creatures in scarcely any other light than they do a draught horse or Ox; neglecting them as much when they are unable to work; instead of comforting & nursing them when they lye on a sick bed. I lost more Negros last Winter, than I had done in 12 or 15 years before, put them altogether. If their disorders are not common, and the mode of treating them plain, simple & well understood, send for Doctr Craik in time. In the last stage of the complaint it is unavailing to do it. It is incurring an expence for nothing.

I shall now briefly say, that the trust I have reposed in you is great, & my confidence that you will faithfully discharge it, is commensurate thereto. I am persuaded of your abilities, industry & integrity; cautioning you only, against undertaking more than you can execute *well,* under almost any circumstances; and against (but this I have no cause to suspect) being absent from your business; as example, be it good or bad, will be followed by all those who look up to you. Keep every one in their places, & to their duty; relaxation from, or neglects in small matters, lead to like attempts in matters of greater magnitude; and are often trials in the under Overseers to see how far they durst go. Have all the Tools collected from the scattered situation in which they are, and all that are not in use, put securely away; the loss, or abuse of Tools, though nothing to the Overseers—when they can ask more and obtain them, is a very heavy expence to those who have them to furnish & are to be at the expence of providing them.

I beseech you to be very attentive to the fires, keeping none in the yard except the one in your own room and another in the Kitchen—the latter to be under the particular care of Frank & his wife.[17] Let the Gates be locked—The gravel may be dropped at the back door of the Garden, as in any event, I believe, it must be wheeled in hand barrows. the same may, possibly be done by the gravel for the Pine labyrinths—that is, come in on the back side of them. I remain Your friend &ca

Go: Washington

P.S. Let me know when the Major left Mt Vernon, and how he was at the time.[18]

ALS, DLC:GW. Only part of this manuscript appears in the microfilm edition published by DLC.

1. GW inadvertently wrote "Mount Vernon" on the dateline, although he had left Mount Vernon on 8 Oct. for Philadelphia to prepare for the opening of the second session of the Second Congress (see GW to Betty Washington Lewis, 7 October).

2. For the illness of GW's postilion Richard Keating, see GW to Tobias Lear, 1 Oct., n.2.

3. GW's gardener at this time was German immigrant John Christian Ehlers (see Ehlers to GW, 24 June 1789, and source note). By "flowering ever-green Ivy" GW may mean *Kalmia latifolia,* the common laurel, which Americans at this time often called ivy. For the bushes and trees that GW purchased earlier this year for the landscape at Mount Vernon, see his March 1792 List of Plants from John Bartram's Nursery. The icehouse was at the southeast corner of the riverside lawn at the mansion.

4. GW's "small" or botanical garden, which he often referred to as "my little garden," was located a short distance west of the mansion between the upper garden and the north lane. Here GW conducted experiments in cultivating both ornamental and useful plants for his estate. Part of the 4-acre vineyard enclosure, south of the lower or kitchen garden, served as an orchard and fruit garden, while the other section was an experimental garden.

5. The blacksmith's shop was northwest of the mansion, on the other side of the north grove.

6. GW experimented with raising the perennial legume lucerne or alfalfa, *Medicago sativa,* on his estate.

7. For a description of the stercorary, or dung repository, see George Augustine Washington to GW, 8–9 April 1792, n.5.

8. To plash is to interweave branches or vines for a hedge or arbor.

9. The wharf was located near Hell Hole, a swampy area just downriver from the mansion.

10. Muddy Hole, one of five farms that comprised the Mount Vernon estate, was located north of the Mansion House farm, and just west of Little Hunting Creek. The other farms included Ferry and French's or United Plantations, later called Union, on the Potomac River west of the Mansion House farm; Dogue Run, northwest of the Mansion House farm, on the creek of the same name; and River, on Clifton's Neck between Little Hunting Creek and the Potomac River, east of the Mansion House farm. See fig. 1.

11. The second vista was the one seen beyond the Bowling Green on the west side of the mansion.

12. "Bishops house" refers to the house in which Thomas Bishop, GW's personal servant from 1756 to 1760, lived (see George Augustine Washington to

GW, 26 Mar. 1790, and note 10). Tom Davis, a dower slave, worked primarily as a stonemason and bricklayer. Nuclus, who usually appears in documents as Muclus, was also a bricklayer, and the 21–27 Oct. farm reports noted that "Nuclus" worked with Tom Davis one day, at Bishop's one day, and with the carpenters for four days that week (DLC:GW). Sam may be the man of that name recorded as a laborer at the Mansion House farm in 1786. On the 1799 slave list, 40-year-old Sam, described as "Passed Labour," was listed as a cook at the Mansion House farm (see Slave List, 18 Feb. 1786, in *Diaries,* 4:278, and Washington's Slave List, June 1799). For a description of the carpentry and other work assigned in the summer of 1791, some of which was still in progress, see GW to Tobias Lear, 26 June 1791, n.1.

13. No memorandum listing the desired carpentry work, other than the one mentioned in note 12, has been found. The old slave quarter was located north of the mansion just outside the upper garden wall.

14. For an example of GW's continuing difficulty in acquiring a sufficient supply of oyster shells, an important source of the lime needed for making the mortar used in bricklaying, see GW to Whitting, 17 Feb., 3 Mar. 1793, and to William Augustine Washington, 17 Feb. 1793. For GW's intention to build a new barn, with an interior treading floor, at Dogue Run, see the plan for a barn enclosed in his letter to Whitting of 28 Oct. 1792.

15. An entry in Cash Memorandum Book H for 10 Nov. 1792 records a payment of $96.14 for "a ton of Iron sent to Mt Vernon."

16. On 14 Mar. 1792 GW paid £15.4.10 for Catherine Ehlers's (c.1767–1827) passage from Bremen, Germany, to Alexandria, Va. (Ledger B, 337). Before the year was over she assumed not only supervision of the spinners but also of the knitters and the women making the slaves' clothing (see GW to Whitting, 18 Nov., 9 Dec. 1792).

17. Frank (Francis) Lee was purchased from Mary Smith Ball Lee in 1767 at the same time that GW bought William (Billy) Lee, his body servant during the Revolutionary War. Frank's obituary notice, which appeared in the *Alexandria Gazette & Daily Advertiser* on 30 July 1821, reads: "DIED. Lately at Mount Vernon, at a very advanced age, Francis Lee, Butler to that mansion in the days of its ancient master." Frank's wife was Lucy, a dower slave who worked as a cook at the mansion (see Cash Accounts, May 1768, Washington's Slave List, June 1799, and Slave List, 18 Feb. 1786, in *Diaries,* 4:277).

18. George Augustine Washington, GW's nephew, who was ill with tuberculosis, left Mount Vernon with his family in October to spend the winter at Eltham, the estate of his father-in-law, Burwell Bassett, where he died on 5 Feb. 1793 (see Whitting to GW, 31 October).

Tobias Lear to Samuel Hodgdon

Sir,   [Philadelphia] October 16th 1792

I have had the honor of laying before the President the enclosed extract of a letter which you put into my hands for that purpose,[1] and he has directed me to request that you would let him know the number & state of the arms & accoutrements which are under your care in this place, that he may be able to form a judgement whether it would be proper to spare the num[b]er wanted out of the public stores.

The President does not wish a formal return, but merely the number & their situation.[2] with much respect & esteem I am Sir, Your most Obedt Servt

Tobias Lear.

ALS, NjMoNP; ALS (letterpress copy), DNA: RG 59, Miscellaneous Letters; LB, DLC:GW.

1. The "extract of a letter" has not been identified.

2. Hodgdon, the current commissary of military stores, replied to Lear in a letter written from Philadelphia on 17 Oct.: "permit me to request you to inform the President that I have upwards of fourteen thousand new Arms under my care, & that every part of the Army is fully supplied. from this representation the President will judge of the propriety of sparing the number of Arms requested by the State of South Carolina.

"Nothing but Arms are mentioned in the requisition, nor indeed could we furnish Cartouch Boxes if requested, we have none on hand, every other Musket Accoutrement we have in abundance.

"The Arms if delivered, should value at fifty shillings, Pennsylvania Currency, each—a sum that would replace them in kind at a short notice" (DNA: RG 59, Miscellaneous Letters).

Lear responded to Hodgdon's reply in a letter written later that same day informing him that the president "consents to your furnishing six hundred stand of Arms (the number applied for) out of the public Stores under your care, on the terms which you observe will replace them in kind at a short notice" (ViU). For further description of the arms supplied to South Carolina, see Lear to Hodgdon, 18 Oct., n.2.

From Thomas Jefferson

Oct. 16. 1792.

Th: Jefferson has the honor to inclose to the President some letters just received.[1] Colo. Fay having sent him a paper of Sugar-Maple seed, Th: J., on his request, asks the President's acceptance of the within.[2]

AL, DNA: RG 59, Miscellaneous Letters; LB, DNA: RG 59, George Washington's Correspondence with His Secretaries of State; LB (photocopy), DLC:GW.

1. The enclosed letters were probably those written to Jefferson by William Short from The Hague on 6 Aug. and David Humphreys from Lisbon on 12 Aug. 1792. Jefferson recorded both letters as received on 16 Oct. 1792.

Short, the U.S. minister resident to The Hague, reported that Russia had intimidated Poland into conceding to its demands for territory and that it was uncertain how events in France would proceed. He wrote that he would set out the next day for Amsterdam "to sign the contract and bonds of the last loan" negotiated by the United States (*Jefferson Papers*, 24:280–81). For that loan, see GW's ratification statement of 5 Nov. 1792. Humphreys, U.S. minister to Portugal since early 1791 and former secretary to GW, reported on the changing fortunes of individual members in the Portugese royal court but found general political calm within the nation. He also observed that "the prospects of markets here for the produce of the U.S." were not as favorable as hoped and that there had been little progress in negotiating the release of U.S. prisoners held in Algiers (ibid., 287).

2. Jefferson delivered some of the seeds sent by Joseph Fay (c.1752–1803) of Bennington, Vt., to both GW and James Madison (see Fay to Jefferson, 8 Oct., and Jefferson to Fay, 4 Nov. 1792, ibid., 451, 575).

From Michael Rudulph

Sir   Octr 16th 92 in Camp at Pittsburgh

It is with extreme diffidence I ask a moment of your time, I have lately learned that the Collectors Office of Baltimore will be vacated by the dissolution of Genl Williams.[1]

I wou'd not ask for what my qualifications were not equal to, I have a family. they have became common adventureers with me from Georgia to maryland where they now are, I have no more to support them on than my persquisites under my present appointment this is a small pittance when divided as it must be, and under the disadvantage of supporting my family in maryland and me so distant from them, my attachment for the Army surpasses every other consideration, but that of having an amiable wife & three perhaps four little children depending on my life.

having been brought up to a life of hardship and a constitution to bear it, it might be argued that I ought to remain in the Army be my lott what it may I never will disgrace the character, which I value so highly. but Sir, my situation is beyond my own choice—I wou'd anxiously see the Issue of the next summer if I cou'd then be certain of a permanence in Cival or Military employ where I cou'd attend to, & sometimes participate with my family; but unless I cou'd command once the smiles of fortune so far as to influence something certain for me to depend on, I must give up my own inclination to the powerfull interest of family friends and all that is dear to me. I have the high honor to be sir, with all possible respect your very Hbl. & obdt Servt

Ml Rudulph Majr of Dragoons

ALS, DLC:GW.

1. Contrary to Rudulph's expectations, the ailing Gen. Otho Holland Williams did not resign his position as the collector of revenue at the port of Baltimore. Michael Rudulph (Rudolph; 1758–1795), a veteran of the Revolutionary War, failed to acquire a civil appointment. He remained in the army, and early in 1793 he was promoted to the dual position of adjutant and inspector general of the army (see GW to the U.S. Senate, 22 Feb. 1793), only to resign from military service on 17 July 1793.

From Thomas Jefferson

Sir   Philadelphia Oct. 17. 1792.

In a letter from Monticello I took the liberty of saying that as soon as I should return here, where my letter books were, I would take the liberty of troubling you with the perusal of such parts of my correspondence from France as would shew my genuine sentiments of the new constitution.[1] when I arrived in Philadelphia, the 5th inst. I found that many of my letters had been already put into the papers, by the gentlemen possessed of the originals, as I presume, for not a word of it had ever been communicated to me, and the copies I had retained were under a lock of which I had the key.[2] these publications are genuine, and render it unnecessary to give you any further trouble than to see extracts from two or three other letters which have not been published, and the genuine letter for the payment of the French debt.[3] pardon my adding this to so many troubles as you have. I think it necessary you should know my real opinions that you may know how to make use of me, and it is essential to my tranquillity not to be mis-known to you. I hope it is the last time I shall feel a necessity of asking your attention to a disagreeable subject, being with sincere wishes for your tranquility & happiness, & with perfect respect, Sir your most obedt & most humble servt

Th: Jefferson

ALS, DLC:GW; ALS (letterpress copy), DLC: James Monroe Papers.

1. The question of whether Jefferson had opposed ratification of the Constitution became an issue for public debate in 1792. This question reflected the growing political division within GW's cabinet over Alexander Hamilton's

financial policies and the animosity between Jefferson and Hamilton. For Jefferson's earlier denial to GW that he had written letters against ratification while the U.S. minister to France, see Jefferson's letter to GW of 9 Sept. 1792.

2. Although Jefferson did not challenge Hamilton or his policies openly in the public press, his political allies often did. James Monroe, assisted by James Madison, wrote six unsigned articles that used extracts from Jefferson's past correspondence to counter criticism of Jefferson that appeared in a series of essays published in the *Gazette of the United States* (Philadelphia) between July and December 1792 and written by Hamilton using various pseudonyms: "T.L.," "An American," "Amicus," "Catullus," and "Metellus" (see Syrett, *Hamilton Papers*, 12:107, 123–25, 157–64, 188–94, 224, 354–57, 379–85, 393–401, 498–506, 578–87, 613–17, 13:229–31, 348–56). Monroe's rebuttals appeared in the 22 Sept., 10, 20, 30 Oct., 8 Nov., 3, 31 Dec. issues of *Dunlap's American Daily Advertiser* (Philadelphia).

3. Jefferson enclosed several extracts, all of which are in DLC:GW. The first one was from his letter to Alexander Donald, written at Paris on 7 Feb. 1788: "I wish with all my soul that the 9. first conventions may accept the new Constitution, because this will secure to us the good it contains, which I think great & important. but I equally wish that the 4. latest conventions, whichever they be, may refuse to accede to it till a declaration of rights be annexed. this would probably command the offer of such a declaration, & thus give to the whole fabric, perhaps as much perfection as any one of that kind ever had. by a declaration of rights, I mean one which shall stipulate freedom of religion, freedom of the press, freedom of commerce against monopolies, trial by juries in all cases, no suspensions of the Habeas corpus, no standing armies. these are fetters against doing evil which no honest government should decline. there is another strong feature in the new constitution which I as strongly dislike. that is the perpetual re-elegibility of the President. of this I expect no amendment at present, because I do not see that any body has objected to it on your side the water. but it will be productive of cruel distress to our country even in your day & mine. the importance to France & England to have our government in the hands of a friend or a foe, will occasion their interference by money & even by arms. our President will be of much more consequence to them than a king of Poland. we must take care however that neither this nor any other objection to the new form produce a schism in our union. that would be an incurable evil, because near friends falling out never reunite cordially; whereas all of us going together, we shall be sure to cure the evils of our new constitution, before they do great harm."

The second extract was from Jefferson's letter to Edward Carrington of 27 May 1788, also written from Paris: "my first wish was that 9. states would adopt it in order to ensure what was good in it, & that the others might, by holding off, produce the necessary amendments. but the plan of Massachusets is far preferable, & will I hope be followed by those who are yet to decide. there are two amendments only which I am anxious for. 1. a bill of rights, which it is so much the interest of all to have, that I concieve it must be yielded. the 1st amendment proposed by Massachusets will in some degree answer this end, but not so well. it will do too much in some instances and too little in others.

it will cripple the federal government in some cases where it ought to be free, & not restrain it in some others where restraint would be right. the 2d amendment which appears to me essential is the restoring the principle of necessary rotation, particularly to the Senate & Presidency: but most of all to the last. re-eligibility makes him an officer for life, & the disasters inseparable from an elective monarchy render it preferable, if we cannot tread back that step, that we should go forward & take refuge in an hereditary one. of the correction of this article however I entertain no present hope because I find it has scarcely excited an objection in America. and if it does not take place ere long, it assuredly never will. the natural progress of things is for liberty to yeild, & government to gain ground. as yet our spirits are free. our jealousy is only put to sleep by the unlimited confidence we all repose in the person to whom we all look as our president. after him, inferior characters may perhaps succeed & awaken us to the danger which his merit has led us into. for the present however, the general adoption is to be prayed for, & I wait with great anxiety for the news from Maryland & S. Carolina, which have decided before this, & wish that Virginia, now in session, may give the 9th vote of approbation. there could then be no doubt of N. Carolina, N. York & N. Hampshire."

The third extract was from Jefferson's letter to John Brown Cutting, written at Paris on 8 July 1788: "the first vessels will probably bring us news of the accession of S. Carolina & Virginia to the new Confederation. the glorious example of Massachusets, of accepting unconditionally & pres[er]ving for future amendment, will I hope reconcile all parties. the argument is unanswerable that it will be easier to obtain amendments from 9. states under the new constitution, than from 13. after rejecting it.

"P.S. July 11. since writing this letter I recieve from America information that S. Carolina has acceded to the new constitution, by a vote of 149. against 72. I hope Virginia will now accede without difficulty."

Jefferson also included a "Quotation from Fenno's gazette of Sep. 19. 1792. a peice signed Catullus," which reads: "I proceed now to state the *exact tenor* of the advice which mister Jefferson gave to Congress, respecting the transfer of the debt due to France to a company of Hollanders. after mentioning an offer which had been made by such a company for the purchase of the debt he *concludes* with these extraordinary expressions 'if there is a danger of the public paiments not being punctual, *I submit whether* it may not be better that the discontents which would then arise should be transferred from a court of whose good will we have so much need, to the breasts of a private company.' the above is an *extract* which was made from the letter in Feb. 1787. the genuineness of the foregoing extract may be depended on."

This quotation was accompanied by what Jefferson called "an exact copy from the original letter" that he had written at Paris on 26 Sept. 1786 to John Jay: "It being known that M. de Calonne the Minister of finance for this country is at his wit's end how to raise supplies for the ensuing year, a proposition has been made by a Dutch company to purchase the debt of the U.S. to this country for 20. millions of livres in hand. his necessities dispose him to accede to the proposition. but a hesitation is produced by the apprehension that it might lessen our credit in Europe, & perhaps be disagreeable to Congress. I have been consulted hereon by the Agent for that company. I informed him that I could not judge what effect it might have on our credit, & was not authorised either to approve or disapprove of the transaction. I have since reflected on this subject. if there be a danger that our payments may not be punctual it might be better that the discontents which would thence arise should be transferred from a court of whose good will we have so much need to the breasts of a private company. *but* it has occurred to me that we might find occasion to do what would be grateful to this court & establish with them a confidence in our honour. I am informed that our credit in Holland is sound. might it not be possible then to borrow there the four & twenty millions due to this country, & thus pay them their whole debt at once. this would save them from any loss on our account; nor is it liable to the objection of impropriety in creating new debts before we have more certain means of paying them: it is only transferring a debt from one creditor to another, & removing the causes of discontent to persons with whom they would do us less injury. thinking that this matter is worthy the attention of Congress, I will endeavor that the negociation shall be retarded till it may be possible for me to know their decision, which therefore I will take the liberty of praying immediately."

The letter to Jay included the following observation: "Th: J. *mentions only* to Congress the proposition of a Dutch company to buy at a discount their debt, (which was already in arrears in part, and would be becoming due by large portions soon) and that it might perhaps be better, if the payments should not be punctual, to have a weak enemy rather than a strong one; and he believes that no man's morality or politics would oppose this making that choice between two adversaries. but instead of supporting this proposition, he *passes it by* and *makes another,* to go to Holland and borrow at once our whole debt & pay it, without discount, to our friends, who had saved us by their loans: which would retain the same advantage of giving us a weak instead of a strong enemy in the event of a want of punctuality: and would evidently give us other advantages, which it was not necessary for him to develope, because known to Congress: to wit, in making the new loan in Holland the lenders themselves would always insist that no part of it should be repaid under 10. or 15. years, & then by instalments. this would give time for us to get our government into a way of collecting money. there was also a possibility of a lower interest. but this writer suppresses the real proposition which Th: J. made, interpolates into that of the Dutch company the words '*I submit whether*' so as to make Th: J. propose the very thing he rejects. his proposition necessarily involved the obtaining longer time for payment; the one he is made to *submit* to Congress was to leave our friends under the loss of four millions of livres, and ourselves under the pressure of *immediate payments,* or dishonour. his whole correspondence would shew that he was constantly urging Congress, by new loans, to obtain further time, till the government could become able to levy money. this single letter has been selected, detached from the general correspondence, it's real proposition suppressed, & the one to which it gives the go-by, is interpolated so as to make him propose an acceptance of the Dutch company's offer."

Tobias Lear to Samuel Hodgdon

Sir,   Philadelphia October 18th 1792

The President wishes to know if the Vessel which has taken the Arms for So. Carolina has sailed if she has not, when she expects to sail, as [he] has letters prepared for So. Carolina which he wishes to send by the first vessel.[1] The President likewise desires to have an Acct of the number Arms furnished from the public stores for So. Carolina.[2] With great esteem, I am Sir, Your most Obedt Servt

Tobias Lear.

ALS (letterpress copy), DNA: RG 59, Miscellaneous Letters; LB, DLC:GW.

1. The word in square brackets is supplied from the letter-book copy. The letters sent by GW to South Carolina have not been identified.

2. Hodgdon replied to Lear later on this date: "You will please to inform the President of the United States, that the Vessell that takes the Arms for South Carolina will not sail until Sunday next. Another Vessell sails for that place to day or to morrow, in which, if the President choose, he may forward his Letters.

"Six hundred Muskets with Bayonets, in complete Order are to be delivered the State of South Carolina's Agent from the Public Stores, in consequence of the Presidents Order" (DNA: RG 59, Miscellaneous Letters). For earlier correspondence regarding South Carolina's request for arms, see Lear to Hodgdon, 16 Oct. 1792, and note 2.

To Thomas Jefferson

(Private)

My dear Sir   Phila. Octobr 18th 1792.

I did not require the evidence of the extracts which you enclosed me, to convince me of your attachment to the Constitution of the United States, or of your disposition to promote the general Welfare of this Country. But I regret—deeply regret—the difference in opinions which have arisen, and divided you and another principal Officer of the Government; and wish, devoutly, there could be an accomodation of them by mutual yieldings.[1]

A Measure of this sort would produce harmony, and consequent good in our public Councils; the contrary will, inevitably, introduce confusion, & serious mischiefs—and for what?—because mankind cannot think alike, but would adopt different means to attain the same end. For I will frankly, & solemnly declare that, I believe the views of both of you are pure, and well meant; and that experience alone will decide with respect to the salubrity of the measures wch are the subjects of dispute.

Why then, when some of the best Citizens in the United States —Men of discernment—Uniform and tried Patriots, who have no sinister views to promote, but are chaste in their ways of thinking and acting are to be found, some on one side, and some on the other of the questions which have caused these agitations, shd either of you be so tenacious of your opinions as to make no allowances for those of the other?

I could, and indeed was about to add more on this interesting subject; but will forbear, at least for the present; after expressing a wish that the cup wch has been presented, may not be snatched from our lips by a discordance of *action* when I am persuaded there is no discordance in your *views*. I have a great—a sincere esteem & regard for you both, and ardently wish that some line could be marked out by which both of you could walk. I am always—Yr Affecte

G. Washington

ALS, DLC: Jefferson Papers; LB, DLC:GW.

1. For the extracts and background on Jefferson's reason for sending them to GW, see Jefferson to GW, 17 Oct. 1792, and notes. For other recent correspondence regarding the political division between Jefferson and Alexander Hamilton, see Hamilton to GW, 9 Sept. (first letter), and Jefferson to GW, 9 Sept. 1792.

From Arthur Campbell

Sire Washington [County] V[a]. Octo. 20th 1792

An unexpected and important event has taken place, the late agression of the Creek and Cherokee Indians.[1]

Notwithstanding all that has happened, I cannot subscribe to the Plan, of immediately dispossessing them of their Country, and making sale of their lands. This may accord with the views of Georgia Purchasers; and their friends, but promises but little towards restoring peace, and a future good understanding: It would tend to affirm the declarations of Spanish Agents to the Indians.

The better way seems to be, for to religiously adhere to the stipulations of the Treatys of New-York and Holstein: and that the hostile acts of the Indians, be considered as an insurrection, and as much as possible, that the punishment fall on the leaders, and guilty individuals. To effect this, a force will be necessary, to move into the Indian Country, the ensuing Winter or early in the Spring. The Militia may do this service; but their leader ought to be a Man, whom the Indians already venerate that they may more readily submit, after receiving chastisement. This idea naturally leads me to think of General Pickens, as the most proper Man.[2]

To reap the fruits of victory, it will be necessary to establish two or more Posts, on the banks of the Tennesee, below the Cumberland Mounta⟨ins.⟩ The mouth of Duck-river, and near Nicojac seems the most eligible spots, the first to be convenient to keep up an intercourse with the Chickasaws, and the other to awe the lower Cherokees, and upper Creek Towns.[3]

Regular Troops will be necessary to Garrison these Forts.

You will excuse, Sir, my thus offering sentiments when assured, that it proceeds from an ardent desire, to promote the welfare of the United-States.[4] I have the honor to be, with the greatest resp⟨ect,⟩ Sir, Your most Obedient servant

Arthur Campbell

ALS, DNA: RG 59, Miscellaneous Letters.

1. For accounts of recent Creek and Cherokee aggression, see the report on "the attack . . . upon Buchanan's Station," Ky., of 30 Sept., the account of "Indian depredations in the district of Miro, and on the Kentucky road, from the 3d to the 14th of October, 1792," and the return of the number of "persons killed, wounded, and taken prisoners" in the Southwest Territory since 1 Jan. 1791, in *ASP, Indian Affairs*, 1:294–95, 329–32. GW enclosed these reports in his letter to the U.S. Senate and House of Representatives of 7 Dec. 1792.

2. The Treaty of New York, signed on 7 Aug. 1790, and the Treaty of Holston, signed on 2 July 1791, obtained land cessions from the Indians and established new boundaries between the United States and the Creek and Cherokee Indians, respectively, but violations of these borders threatened to incite a general Indian war in the Southwest (Kappler, *Indian Treaties*, 2:25–32). Particularly troublesome for federal officials were the activities of speculators and expansionists involved in the Yazoo Land Companies, to which Georgia, in 1789, had granted extensive lands in present-day Alabama and Mississippi that fell within Indian territory as defined in these treaties. For earlier efforts to curtail white encroachments on Indian lands and thus prevent an Indian war, see GW's proclamations of 14 and 26 Aug. 1790 and 19 Mar. 1791.

Andrew Pickens, a veteran of punitive military expeditions against hostile

Cherokees during the Revolutionary War and an experienced negotiator with the Indians, accompanied Gov. William Blount to a conference at Nashville on 7–11 Aug. with the Chickasaw and Choctaw Indians (see Council Proceedings, *ASP, Indian Affairs,* 1:284–88).

3. Henry Knox already had dismissed the idea of establishing a post on the Duck River, a tributary of the Tennessee River approximately sixty miles southwest of Nashville, in his letter to Blount of 22 April 1792, because "it is to be apprehended that starting a new object at the mouth of Duck river, would have the effect to excite suspicions and jealousies" among the Indians and "the risque of injury would far over balance any advantages, and therefore the attempt ought not to be made" (see Knox to GW, 21 April 1792, n.1).

Nickajack refers to a region along the Tennessee River near the Tennessee-Alabama border, west of present-day Chattanooga, where the major north-south trails used by Indians and traders intersected. The name of one of the Lower Towns of the Cherokee in that region, it was also the name of a large cave from which various bandits, both Indian and white, sometimes surprised travelers on the river.

4. From Philadelphia, GW replied on 24 Nov. to Campbell: "While I acknowledge the receipt of your letter of the 20th Ultimo, on the subject of Indian Affairs in your quarter, and thank you for the information it contains; let me assure you that I am always ready to receive any information that relates to the public welfare; and as my sole view is to promote thus to the utmost of my power and ability—I am ever open to the opinions of well informed persons in those matters with which their situation or circumstances may have given them an opporty of being well acquainted—and I shall consider such information & sentiments you may think proper to communicate on the occurrences which may take place in your quarter as a mark of attention" (Df, DNA: RG 59, Miscellaneous Letters; copy, MHi: Pickering Papers; LB, DLC:GW).

To Andrew Ellicott

Sir,   Philadelphia Oct. 20th 1792.

The Honble Mr Cushing one of the Judges of the Supreme Court of the U. States has some thought of passing through the Federal City in the Circuit he is about to make. Should this happen, I shall be obliged to you for shewing him such parts of it as he may incline to view.[1] I am Sir Your very Hble Servt

Go: Washington

ALS, DSI.

1. William Cushing, associate justice of the U.S. Supreme Court, was currently riding the middle circuit, which consisted of New Jersey, Pennsylvania, Delaware, Maryland, and Virginia. On 23 Oct. he wrote John Jay from Newcastle, Del., that he intended to go "from Easton in Maryland for Kent [Is-

land?], & thence across the Chesapeak an 8 or 9 mile ferry, to Annapolis, then to the federal city, perhaps buy a house lot there, & so onward to Richmond" (Marcus and Perry, *Documentary History of the Supreme Court,* 2:319).

To Thomas Jefferson

Dear Sir,   [Philadelphia] October 20th 1792.

The letters of Gouvr Morris give a gloomy picture of the Affairs of France. I fear with too much truth.[1]

If the order of Senate, dated the 7th of last May, is compleated, it may be with *all* Offices except the Judges.[2]

The Post Office (as a branch of Revenue) was annexed to the Treasury in the time of Mr Osgood—and when Colo. Pickering was appointed thereto, he was informed, as I find by my letter to him dated the 29th of August 1791, that he was to consider it in that light.

If from relationship, or usage in similar cases (for I have made no enquiry into the matter, having been closely employed since you mentioned the thing to me, in reading papers from the War Office) the Mint does not appertain to the Department of the Treasury I am more inclined to add it to that of state than to multiply the duties of the other.[3] I am always Yours

Go: Washington

P.S. The letters of Mr Seagrove to Genl Knox are a contin[uatio]n of the evidence of Spanish interference with the Southern Indians.[4]

ALS, DLC: Jefferson Papers; ADf, DNA: RG 59, Miscellaneous Letters; LB, DNA: RG 59, George Washington's Correspondence with His Secretaries of State; LB (photocopy), DLC:GW. The ALS is docketed: "recd Oct. 20," and only it includes the postscript.

1. For letters recently received from Gouverneur Morris, see Morris to GW, 10 June, and to Jefferson, 10 July, which Jefferson enclosed in his letter to GW of 14 Oct. 1792. For GW's reaction to recent events in France, see his reply to Morris of 20 October.

2. GW may be referring to "An Act for regulating Processes in the Courts of the United States, and providing Compensations for the Officers of the said Courts, and for Jurors and Witnesses," approved on 8 May 1792 (1 *Stat.* 275–79).

3. Samuel Osgood sent his letter of resignation to GW on 11 July 1791, and the following month GW appointed Timothy Pickering to succeed him as postmaster general. For GW's view that the post office was "a branch of the reve-

nue department," see Tobias Lear to Pickering, 29 Aug. 1791, at Pickering to GW, 27 Aug. 1791, n.2. Earlier in the year, in an attempt to decrease Alexander Hamilton's power in the federal government, Jefferson had suggested to GW that the post office should be transferred to the State Department (see Jefferson's Memorandum of Conversations with Washington, 1 Mar. 1792). When Congress established the Mint, it placed ultimate authority for the Mint with the president, assigning the Mint to neither the Treasury nor the State Department (1 *Stat.* 246–51).

4. The letters from James Seagrove to Henry Knox have not been positively identified, but they may have been Seagrove's letters to Knox of 8 and 13 Sept. 1792 (see DNA: RG 46, Second Congress, 1791–93, Senate Records of Legislative Proceedings, Reports and Communications; see also *ASP, Indian Affairs,* 1:310–11). Knox acknowledged these letters in his reply to Seagrove of 27 Oct. (see Knox to Tobias Lear, 27 Oct., n.3). Seagrove complained about Spanish intrigues in some detail in his letter of 8 Sept.: "I am happy in informing that no unfavorable change hath taken place in Indian affairs, notwithstanding the unremitting endeavours of the spanish agents to prejudice them against us. Scarce a day passes but I have additional proofs of the base conduct of the spanish agents in the Creek nation: They unquestionably are using every means to induce the four southern nations of Indians to take up the Hatchet against the United States. Every undue, unjust and villainous means is using by them, to bring these unfortunate people to act to their diabolical purposes—What the spaniards can promise themselves by such conduct I cannot discover—with all their promises, presents and threats, added to the exertions of McGillivray and Panton &c. I am hopeful they will not be able to prevail on the Creeks to join them, or even to attend their treaty at Pensacola this month. . . . Mr Olivar, the successor of McGillivray, hath lately been in the lower towns inviting them to Pensacola to receive arms and ammunition from the spaniards, and talks in the most insulting terms of the United States. . . . In my opinion remonstrance ought to be made to the Court of Spain against the House of Panton, Leslie & Co. british merchants residing in Florida. Panton (it can be proven) openly invited the Creeks and Cherokees to Pensacola to receive arms and ammunition to use against the Americans, and said he was authorized so to do by the spanish government and that if they entered into a war with us the spaniards stood ready with troops to assist them. He also advised the Indians to plunder and kill every american trader they found in the nation, declaring to them, that no one had any right or authority to be among them as traders, but such as Spain approved." For Seagrove's earlier reports on Spanish activities, see his letters to GW of 5 and 27 July 1792.

To Samuel McDowell, Sr.

Sir,   Philadelphia October 20th 1792
Your letter of the 6th of April, inclosing a copy of the Constitution formed for the State of Kentucky, did not get to my

hands 'till I was about leaving this place to go to Mount Vernon, and I embrace the earliest opportunity, after my return to the seat of Government, to acknowledge the receipt of it, and to thank you for the transmission.[1] I am Sir, with esteem Your most Obedt Servt.

Df, in Tobias Lear's writing, DNA: RG 59, Miscellaneous Letters; LB, DLC: GW. The draft is docketed: "To Colo. Saml McDowell."

Samuel McDowell, Sr. (1735–1817), a veteran of Braddock's expedition in 1755 and Dunmore's War in 1774, served two terms in the Virginia House of Burgesses and was colonel of a regiment from Augusta County, Va., during the Revolutionary War. After the war he moved to present-day Mercer County, Ky., and he subsequently served as a surveyor of public lands in the District of Kentucky, a judge of the first district court in Kentucky, and a judge in the first county court of Kentucky. An active proponent of Kentucky's independence from Virginia, he presided at the April 1792 convention that produced Kentucky's first state constitution, a copy of which he was instructed to deliver to the president. GW had appointed his son Samuel McDowell, Jr. (1764–1834), the federal marshal for Kentucky in 1789 and renewed the appointment in 1793 (see GW to the U.S. Senate, 24 Sept. 1789, 27 Dec. 1793).

1. McDowell's letter to GW of 6 April 1792 has not been found. GW had his secretary Tobias Lear send a copy of Kentucky's constitution to Thomas Jefferson on 1 Nov. 1792. "The President thinks," Lear wrote, "it would be proper for him to cause a Copy of this Consititution to be laid before each branch of the Legislature, and requests that the Secretary of State will have them prepared in his Office, unless something should occur to him to render the laying them before the Legislature improper or unnecessary.

"The President wishes that all papers which are to be laid before Congress by him may be ready to go in as soon as he has made his general communication to that body" (DLC: Jefferson Papers).

To Gouverneur Morris

(Private)
My dear Sir,   Philadelphia Octr 20th 1792.

Although your letter of the 10th of June, which I have received, did not paint the prospects of France in the most pleasing colours; yet the events which have since taken place give a more gloomy aspect to the public Affairs of that Kingdom than your letter gave reason to apprehend.[1]

A thousand circumstances, besides our distance from the Theatre of Action, make it improbable that we should have, in this

Country, a fair statement of facts & causes through the medium of the public prints; and I have received no other accounts than what have come in that channel. But taking up the most favorable of these—gloomy indeed appears the situation of France at this Juncture. But it is hardly probable that even you, who are on the spot, can say with any precision how these things will terminate; much less can we, at this distance, pretend to augur the event. We can only repeat the sincere wish that much happiness may arise to the French Nation & to Mankind in general out of the severe evils which are inseperable from so important a Revolution.

In the present State of things we cannot expect that any Commercial Treaty can now be formed with France; but I have no doubt of your embracing the proper moment of arrangement & of doing whatever may be in your power for the substantial interest of our Country.

The Affairs of the U. States go on well. There are some few Clouds in our political Hemisphere but I trust that the bright sun of our prosperity will disperse them.

The Indians on our Western & Southern frontiers are still troublesome, but such measures are taken as will, I presume, prevent any serious mischiefs from them; I confess, however, that I do not believe these tribes will ever be brought to a quiescent state so long as they may be under an influence which is hostile to the rising greatness of these States.

From the complexion of some of our News-papers Foreigners would be led to believe that inveterate political dissentions existed among us, and that we are on the very verge of disunion; but the fact is otherwise—the great body of the people now feel the advantages of the General Government, and would not, I am persuaded, do any thing that should destroy it; but this kind of representations is an evil wch must be placed in opposition to the infinite benefits resulting from a free Press—and I am sure you need not be told that in this Country a personal difference in political sentiments is often made to take the garb of general dissensions.[2]

From the Department of State you are, I am informed, furnished with such papers & documents, from time to time, as will keep you more particularly informed of the state of our affairs; I shall therefore add nothing further to this letter than assurances of being always & sincerely Yours

Go: Washington

ALS, NN: Washington Collection; Df, DLC:GW; LB, DLC:GW.

1. In addition to Morris's letter to him of 10 June, GW had read Morris's letter to Thomas Jefferson of 10 July that Jefferson had enclosed in his letter to GW of 14 October. For a brief summary of events in France during the summer and early fall of 1792, see the source note for Morris to GW, 23 Oct. 1792.

2. This paragraph is based on a draft prepared for GW by Jefferson on 4 Oct. that reads: "Foreigners would suppose from some of our newspapers that there were inveterate political dissensions among us, & even that we were on the eve of dissolving the Union. nothing is farther from the truth. the people are sensible of the blessings of the general government, & of the prosperous state of our affairs, nor could they be induced to any change. under a government like ours, personal dislikes often assume the garb of public dissension. it is one of the evils to be set off against the innumerable blessings of a free press" (DLC: Jefferson Papers).

To Edward Newenham

Dear Sir,   Philadelphia 20th October 1792

Where your Letter of the 21st of december last[1] has been travelling since it left you, I cannot tell; but it did not get to my hands 'till within a few weeks past, when I likewise received yours of the 15th of July introducing Mr Anderson.

I was sorry to see the gloomy picture which you drew of the affairs of your country in your letter of december; but I hope events have not turned out so badly as you then apprehended. Of all the animosities which have existed among mankind those which are caused by a difference of sentiment in Religion appear to be the most inveterate and distressing and ought most to be deprecated.[2] I was in hopes that the enlightened & liberal policy which has marked the present age would at least have reconciled *Christians* of every denomination so far that we should never again see their religious disputes carried to such a pitch as to endanger the peace of Society.

The affairs of this Country still wear a prosperous aspect. our agriculture, commerce & navigation are in a flourishing state. In some parts of the Country the crops of Indian corn (Maiz) have been injured by the drought in summer and early frosts in Autumn. We have, however, a happiness which is scarcely known in any other Country; for such is the extent of the U.S. and so great a variety of climate and soil do they embrace, that we never need apprehend an universal failure of our crops and a consequent famine.

I have spent part of the summer at Mount Vernon, & have but just returned to the seat of government, where I am so much engaged in attending to business which has accumulated during my absence—and in preparing such business as will be necessary to lay before the Legislature at their meeting early in next month, that I have but little time to attend to any affairs of a private or personal nature; I am therefore persuaded you will to these causes impute the shortness of this letter.[3] Mrs Washington unites with me in respects & best wishes for Lady Newenham & yourself. I am Dear Sir with great esteem Your most Obedt Servt.

Df, in Tobias Lear's writing, DNA: RG 59, Miscellaneous Letters; LB, DLC:GW.

1. The actual date of Newenham's letter is 22 Dec. 1791.

2. GW added the phrase "and ought most to be deprecated" to Lear's draft.

3. GW had returned to Philadelphia on 13 Oct. 1792 (see GW to Anthony Whitting, 14 October). See GW's Address to the U.S. Senate and House of Representatives, 6 Nov. 1792.

To William Davies Shipley

Philadelphia, 20 Oct. 1792. Acknowledged receipt of Shipley's letter of 23 May 1792, "together with the works of your late Right Reverend father, Lord Bishop of St Asaph," for whose "character & sentiments . . . I entertained the most perfect esteem; and have a sincere respect for his memory, now he is no more."

ALS, owned (1991) by Mr. Todd Axelrod, Las Vegas, Nev.; ADfS, MiU-C: Schoff Collection; LB, DLC:GW.

To John Sinclair

Sir,   Philadelphia Octr 20th 1792

I have received your letter of the 18th of May, enclosing the Pamphlet & papers which you had the goodness to send me.

While I beg your acceptance of my acknowledgments for the polite mark of attention in transmitting these things to me, I flatter myself you will be assured that I consider the subject therein recommended as highly important to Society, whose best interests I hope will be promoted by a proper investigation of them, and the happiness of mankind advanced thereby.

I have to regret that the duties of my public station do not allow me to pay that attention to Agriculture and the objects attached to it (which have ever been my favourite pursuit) that I could wish; but I will put your queries respecting Sheep into the hands of such Gentlemen as I think most likely to attend to them, and answer them satisfactorily; I must, however, observe that no important information on the subject can be expected from this Country where we have been so little in the habit of attending either to the breed or improvement of our Stock.[1] With great respect & esteem I have the honor to be Sir Your Most Obedt Servt

Go: Washington

ALS, British Library: Add MSS 5757; Df, DLC:GW; LB, DLC:GW.

1. Sinclair devoted much of his life to improving the science and practice of agriculture, and during the 1790s he became interested especially in the breeding of sheep for the production of the fine wool needed by the British woolen industry. In 1791 he founded the British Wool Society, and in 1793 he became the first president of the British Board of Agriculture, of which GW was made an honorary member in 1795 (see British Board of Agriculture to GW, 6 April 1795, DLC:GW). Because GW raised sheep on his own plantation, he discussed sheep, as well as a variety of other agricultural concerns, with both American and British correspondents, including Thomas Jefferson, Richard Peters, James Anderson, and Arthur Young. For letters in which the raising of sheep is mentioned by GW's correspondents, see James Anderson to GW, 3 Nov. 1792, and Arthur Young to GW, 17 Jan. 1793. For letters in which GW discusses sheep, see GW's letters to his farm manager Anthony Whitting of 4 Nov., 9 Dec. 1792, and 13 Jan. 1793, and to Arthur Young, 18–21 June 1792.

From Jonathan Williams

Mount Pleasant on Schuylkill [Pa.]

Sir.   Octob. 20. 1792.

A few copies of the inclosed memoir have been extracted for the purpose of private distribution.[1]

If my beleif be well founded, that an attention to the directions it contains, would prevent shipwreck, & consequently save many lives, you will not think this intrusion upon your valuable time an unjustifiable presumption. If it should appear that I am mistaken, I trust to your goodness for an excuse in consideration of the motive. I am with the most dutifull and most respectfull Regard Sir, Your obedient servant

Jona. Williams

ALS, DNA: RG 59, Miscellaneous Letters.

Jonathan Williams, Jr. (1750–1815), was the grandson of Benjamin Franklin's half sister Anne Franklin Harris. As a commercial agent in Nantes, France, during the Revolutionary War, he inspected the arms and other supplies being shipped to the American army. He returned to the United States in 1785 and became a successful merchant in Philadelphia. A member of the American Philosophical Society, he worked with Franklin on his later experiments. Considered an expert in the theory of fortifications, Williams was appointed by Thomas Jefferson as inspector of fortifications and superintendent at the military post at West Point in 1801, and upon the establishment of the U.S. Military Academy there the following year, he became its first superintendent.

1. Williams's *Memoir on the Use of the Thermometer in Navigation,* published in Philadelphia in 1792, was first presented to the American Philosophical Society at its 19 Nov. 1790 meeting. *Memoir* was an extract taken from the society's *Transactions,* which at this time were being prepared for publication (see Williams, "Memoir," in the 1793 volume of *Transactions of the American Philosophical Society*). Williams later published a book entitled *Thermometrical Navigation* (Philadelphia, 1799).

To Arthur Young

Sir,   Philadelphia Oct. 20th 1792

I must beg your acceptance of my best thanks for the book that accompanied your polite letter of the 9th of June which came duly to my hands.

I presume you have long before this received my letter which was committed to the care of Mr Pinckney, our Minister at the Court of Great Britain,[1] and shall be very glad if the contents of it afforded you the information which it was intended to communicate; for I am persuaded, that I need not repeat to you how sincerely I wish success to those laudable exertions which you are making to promote the important interest of Agriculture and the cause of humanity. With very great esteem I am—Sir Your Most Obedt Servt

Go: Washington

ALS, PPRF; Df, DLC:GW; LB, DLC:GW.

1. GW is referring to his letter to Young of 18–21 June 1792.

To the Alexandria, Virginia, Inspectors of Tobacco

Gentn   Philadelphia Octr 21st 1792.

In 1790 I had 13 Hhds of Tobo Inspected at the Warehouses in Alexandria—and in 1791, 12 more were also Inspected at the same place.[1]

Not meeting a price which I was disposed to take, they remain there still. My Nephew Majr Washington either before, or since your care of those Warehouses was allowed to stow them in a secure place, therein; but as it is now more than a year since this happened, and a good deal of Tobacco may, possibly, have been recd and delivered in that period, they may have been displaced —I have on the presumption of this directed Mr Whiting, my Manager, at such time as you shall please to appoint, to take some hands with him and again collect & well secure them.[2] I do not mean that they should be reinspected at this time; but to be placed only in a state of security. Before delivery, it will be necessary I presume to have the condition of the Tobo examined— or if the Law requires—or if any advantage would result from it, I have no objection to its being done now. I recollect to have been informed that the Tobo was put up dry, and that it was of a good sort & of superior quality; if so it will not have suffered from its age.[3] I am—Gentn Your's &ca

G. W——n

ADfS, DLC:GW; LB, DLC:GW.

1. In order to protect the quality of Virginia tobacco, all tobacco exported from the state had to be brought first to designated public warehouses for review by state-appointed inspectors. Tobacco that did not pass inspection could not be exported legally from Virginia (see Hening, 11:205–46).

2. As George Augustine Washington's health declined dramatically in 1792, Anthony Whitting, who had been hired as overseer of GW's Ferry and French's farm in 1790, gradually assumed management of Mount Vernon (see GW to Whitting, 14 April 1790, 14 Aug. 1791).

3. In late April 1793 GW reported 25 hundredweights of tobacco in the tobacco warehouses at Alexandria that he wanted to sell (see GW to John Fitzgerald, 28 April 1793).

To David Stuart

Dear Sir,   Philadelphia Oct. 21st 1792.

You informed me when I was at George Town on my way to this City[1] that Colo. Mercer, upon receiving, or being told of Colo.

Hamiltons letter to him requesting to know if the words with which he was charged by Major Ross as having uttered in his public harangues against the conduct of the Secretary of the Treasury were true expressed, if I understood you rightly much surprize at the application; as *he Colo. Hamilton* must be conscious of his having attempted to *bribe him Colo. Mercer* to vote for a further assumption of the State debts—and that this surprize was expressed at a public *Table* before many Gentlemen.[2]

This is a charge of so serious a nature that it is incumbent on Colo. Hamilton to clear it up—or for the President of the U States to take notice of it.[3] For this reason, before I communicate the matter to Colo. Hamilton, I beg to be informed whether I precisely understood the information you gave me—and, in that case, who were the persons that heard Colo. Mercer express himself to that effect.[4]

It was my intention to have asked this at the time you mentioned the matter—but I was diverted from it by something that occurred at the moment. and the variety of things which have been thrown in my way since I came to this place, have prevented it till now. With great esteem & regard I am Dr Sir Your Affectionate

G. W——n

ADfS, DNA: RG 59, Miscellaneous Letters; LB, DLC:GW.

1. During his journey from Mount Vernon to Philadelphia, GW stopped in Georgetown on 8 Oct. to attend the sale of lots for the Federal City (see GW to D.C. Commissioners, 29 Sept. 1792).

2. A prolonged dispute between Hamilton and John Francis Mercer began with the publication in the *Maryland Gazette* (Annapolis) on 20 Sept. 1792 of a letter by David Ross (1755–1800), a Revolutionary War veteran and member of the Continental Congress from Maryland 1787–89, in which Ross accused Mercer of falsely charging Hamilton with gross improprieties as secretary of the treasury. Hamilton wrote Mercer on 26 Sept. to ask "how far Mr. Ross's statement is accurate or otherwise—in other words what you did really say, upon the occasion alluded to." Mercer replied to Hamilton on 16 Oct. "that I never impeach'd your integrity as an Individual or public Officer (farther than that in the pursuit of public objects) without any other private view than that of encreasing your own influence and attaching to your administration a Monied Interest as an Engine of Government, your political principles differed from my own, may be so construed, in either a public address or private conversation" (Syrett, *Hamilton Papers*, 12:489–90, 574–75). Hamilton's attempted bribe allegedly occurred in the spring of 1792 during the congressional debate on "An Act supplementary to the act making provision for the Debt of the United States" (1 *Stat.* 281–83).

3. A much more serious charge of misconduct against Hamilton began to

emerge later this year with the first uncovering of a political scandal known as the "Reynolds Affair," in which Hamilton was accused of using his position as secretary of the treasury to buy the silence of James Reynolds, the husband of Hamilton's former mistress Maria Reynolds, by providing Reynolds with privileged information for speculation in government securities. Hamilton's involvement with James and Maria Reynolds threatened to become public knowledge when Oliver Wolcott, Jr., comptroller of the treasury, charged James Reynolds and Jacob Clingman, a former clerk for Representative Frederick A. C. Muhlenberg of Pennsylvania, with attempting to defraud the federal government. In return for information against other potential criminals, Wolcott released Reynolds and Clingman from prison in early December, but not before the two men had implicated Hamilton in statements made to Muhlenberg, Virginia senator James Monroe, and Virginia representative Abraham B. Venable.

The three men apparently decided to inform GW of the charges against Hamilton, and Monroe and Venable wrote GW on 13 Dec.: "We think proper to lay before you, some documents respecting the conduct of Colo. Hamilton, in the Office of Secretary of the Treasury. The inclosed will explain to you the particulars, and likewise, how they came to our knowledge. They appeared to us to be of such importance, as to merit our attention, and in further pursuit of the object, that the proper course was, to submit the whole to your inspection.

"What we have stated of our own knowledge, we are willing to depose on oath. We think proper, however, to observe, that we do not consider ourselves, as prosecutors, but as only communicating, for his information, to the Chief Majistrate, intelligence, it highly imports him to know. We were, however, unwilling to take this step without communicating it to the Gentleman, whom it concerns, that he might make the explanation, he has it in his power to give; we, therefore, informed Mr Hamilton of the step we now take.

"You will readily perceive, that light might have been thrown on this subject, by the several public officers, who have had any part in the transactions of the prosecution and enlargement of Reynolds. But as we apprehended, an application to these parties might contribute to make the subject public, which, in tenderness to the person interested, we wished to avoid, on that account we declined it" (ViU: John James Beckley Papers).

Before sending this letter, however, the three men visited Hamilton twice on 15 Dec., being joined on their second visit by Wolcott. They confronted Hamilton with the accusations against him, listened to his admission of adultery and denial of official impropriety, and left the final meeting apparently satisfied with Hamilton's explanation and unwilling to expose his personal indiscretion to public scrutiny. There is no evidence that the letter was sent to GW. Neither Hamilton's adulterous affair nor the accusations of illegal activity remained secret, however, and both became public knowledge through a series of pamphlets published by James Thomson Callender in June and July 1797. GW's reaction to the published accusations are absent from his extant correspondence for that time. For background on the personal and political aspects of this scandal, see James Reynolds to Hamilton, 15 Dec. 1791, and note 1, 13–15 Nov. 1792, and note 1, Oliver Wolcott, Jr., to Hamilton, 3 July 1797, and introductory note, in Syrett, *Hamilton Papers*, 10:376–78, 13:115–17, 21:121–

45. See also Hamilton's "Reynolds Pamphlet" of 25 Aug. 1797, ibid., 21:238–85, which was printed in Philadelphia that year under the title *Observations on Certain Documents Contained in No. V & VI of "The History of the United States for the Year 1796," in Which the Charge of Speculation against Alexander Hamilton, Late Secretary of the Treasury, Is Fully Refuted. Written by Himself.*

4. For Stuart's reply, see his letter to GW of 5 Nov. 1792.

Letter not found: to Anthony Whitting, 21 Oct. 1792. Whitting wrote GW on 31 Oct., acknowledging receipt of GW's letter "with the Bill of Scantling & List of plants from Norfolk." An ALS of this letter was offered for sale in 1926 in James F. Drake, *A Catalogue of Autograph Letters and Manuscripts,* number 177, item 357. According to the catalog entry, which provides the date of 21 Oct., this letter "gives explicit directions about how some plants are to be taken care of, some rare ones received from Jamaica, etc."[1]

1. The enclosed bill of scantling and list of plants have not been found. A second bill of scantling was sent in GW's letter to Whitting of 28 Oct. as a part of the enclosure entitled "Washington's Plan for a Barn." The list of plants is probably the one to which Tobias Lear referred in his letter to William Hilton of 2 December.

From the Earl of Buchan

Sir,   Dryburgh Abbey [Scotland] October 22. 1792.

I had the honour and pleasure of receiving your Excellency's Letter of the 20th of September having been forwarded to me on the 12th of that month by Mr Rutledge, but I have been so unfortunate as not to have received the letter of the first of May which yr Excellency mentions in your last but still entertain some hope of its coming safely tho so long a time has elapsed. If it were not too much trouble I would wish in case a copy was kept to have a duplicate in case of accident for I shall ever value what shall mark the intercourse of esteem that has taken place between us and shall be proud to preserve it not on account of yr celebrity so much as of your virtues.[1]

You have made an industrious honest man happy in countenancing the Bee the tendency of which is commendable & useful in our Scotland.[2]

Dr Anderson informs me that he is about to do himself the honour of addressing yr Excellency with the Ships and the sequel of yr volumes. He has expressd to me a wish to be chosen a correspondent member of yr Phil. Soc. at Philadelphia, and I think him worthy of that honour and that he may be useful to the institution by promoting agricultural and mechanical correspondence between the two Nations.[3]

I wish your America to be like a thriving happy Young family and to be little heard of in the great world of Politics and nothing seems so likely to produce this prosperity & happiness as agricultural & mechanical improvements accompanied by moderate desires and virtuous affectations enlightened and cherished by the dissemination of Science and literature in the mass of the people⟨.⟩ I have taken a pleasing interest in what concerns the States of America from their first institution and I loved the Country long before its political connection with Britain was dissolved because my great grand father Henry Lord Cardross was banished to America during the reign of Charles the II. of England and settled himself with a colony of his people from Perthshire & West Lothian in Carolina near Charles Town and was thrown out by the Spaniards when he was kindly assisted by many of the colonists.[4]

My Cousin Lord Fairfax too on whose district yr excellency resides gave my family an old connection with Virginia thro' the Colepeppers and I have enjoyed the friendship of Franklin and the correspondence of the Adams, Cushings and other men of probity and merit who have so much contributed to the happy state of yr Country and Nation which I sincerely pray long to continue & to be finally established on the Basis of republican Virtue and Publick credit.[5] I have the honour to be with great Esteem yr Excellency's most obedt humble Servant

Buchan.

ALS, DLC:GW. Because GW mistakenly docketed this letter "22d Oct. 1793," it is erroneously filed under that date.

1. Buchan appears to have made an error in dates. The letter recently received from GW was probably that written on 20 June 1792 in which GW expressed hope that Buchan has "received my letter of the first of May." GW enclosed a copy of the missing 1 May 1792 letter when he wrote Buchan on 22 April 1793.

2. GW had received volumes 1 to 6 of the *Bee, or Literary Weekly Intelligencer* in mid-June. For GW's thanks for and praise of this journal, see GW to Buchan and to James Anderson, both 20 June 1792.

3. Scottish economist James Anderson's letter to GW of 3 Nov. 1792 accompanied volumes 7 to 11 of the *Bee*. Both Anderson and Buchan were elected to membership in the American Philosophical Society on 18 April 1794 (see "Early Proceedings," 220).

4. Previously imprisoned for his religious dissension, Henry Erskine, third Baron Cardross (1650–1693), sailed to North America in 1683 with fellow Scottish dissenters and settled at Port Royal, South Carolina. Cardross did not stay long in South Carolina but relocated to the Netherlands before returning to England during the Glorious Revolution of 1688.

5. Buchan was noted among his contemporaries, somewhat derisively, for boasting about his ancestors and his correspondence with famous people, including GW (see Campbell, *Lives of the Lord Chancellors*, 8 : 316). Buchan's grandfather David Erskine, the ninth earl of Buchan, married Frances Fairfax, a distant cousin of Lord Thomas Fairfax, the sixth Baron Fairfax, who was the grandson and heir of Virginia's colonial governor Thomas Culpeper. Part of Fairfax's inheritance included the Northern Neck proprietary grant in Virginia that included all the land between the Potomac and Rappahannock rivers to their headwaters. Anne Fairfax, a daughter of Lord Fairfax's cousin and proprietary agent William Fairfax, married GW's half brother Lawrence Washington in 1743.

From Gouverneur Morris

My dear Sir,   Paris 23 October 1792

Yours of the twenty first of June is at length safely arriv'd. Poor lafayette. Your Letter for him must remain with me yet some Time. His Enemies here are virulent as ever and I can give you no better Proof than this. Among the King's Papers was found Nothing of what his Enemies wishd and expected except his Correspondence with Monsieur de la Fayette which breathes from begining to End the purest Sentiments of Freedom. It is therefore kept secret while he stands accus'd of Designs in Conjunction with the dethroned Monarch to enslave his Country. The Fact respecting this Correspondence is communicated to me by a Person to whom it was related confidentially by one of the Parties who examind it. You will have seen in my Letters to Mr Jefferson a Proposition made by Mr Short respecting Monsieur de la fayette with my Reply. I had very good Reason to apprehend that our Interference at that Time would have been injurious to him, but I hope that a Moment will soon offer in which Something may be done for his Releif.[1] In reading my Correspondences with Mr Short you must consider also that I wrote to the French and austrian governments as each would take the Liberty to read my Letters. You will have seen also that in my Letters to Mr Jefferson I hint at the Dangers attending a Residence in this City. Some of the Sanguinary Events which have taken Place and which were partial Executions of great Plans will point to a natural Interpretation thereof but these were not what I contemplated. Should we ever meet I will entertain you with the Recital of many Things which it would be improper to commit to Paper, at least for the present.[2] You will have seen that the King is accus'd of high Crimes and Misdemeanors, but I verily beleive that he wish'd sincerely for this Nation the Enjoyment of the utmost Degree of Liberty which thier Situation and Circumstances will permit. He wish'd for a good Constitution, but unfortunately he had not the Means to obtain it, or if he had he was thwarted by those about him. What may be his Fate God only knows, but History informs us that the Passage of dethroned Monarchs is short from the Prison to the grave.[3]

I have mention'd to Mr Jefferson repeatedly my Wish to have positive Instructions and orders for my Government. I need not tell you Sir how agreable this would be to me and what a Load it would take from my mind. At the same Time I am fully sensible that it may be inconvenient to give me such Orders. The United States may wish to temporize and see how Things are like to end, and in such Case leaving me at large with the Right reserv'd to avow or disavow me according to Circumstances and Events is, for the Government, an eligible Position. My Part in the Play is not quite so eligible, but altho I wish the Senate to be sensible of this, I am far from wishing that any precipitate Step be taken to releive me from it; for I know how contemptible is every private Consideration when compard with the public Interests—one Step however seems very natural viz. to say that before any new Letters of Credence are given it will be proper to know to whom they are to be directed because the Convention, a meer temporary Body, is to be succeeded by some fix'd Form & it may be a long Time before any such Form is adopted.[4] Mr Jefferson from the Materials in his Possession will be able to give you an accurate Account of the military Events. I discover three capital Errors in the Conduct of the Duke of Brunswic. First his Proclamation arrogated Rights which on no Construction could belong to him or his Employers, and contain Threats which no Circumstances could warrant, and which in no supposeable Success could be executed. They tended however to unite the Nation in opposing him, seeing that no Hope remain for those who had taken any Part in the Revolution, and the Conduct observd towards Monsieur de la fayette and his Companions was a severe Comment on the Cruelty of the Text: thus in the same Moment he wounded the Pride, insulted the Feelings, and alarmd the Fears of all France. And by his thundering Menaces to protect the royal Family he plung'd them into the Situation from which he meant to extricate them. The second Error was not to dash at Paris the Instant he receivd the News of the Affair of the tenth. He should then have advanc'd at all Hazards, and if in so doing he had declard to the several Generals and Armies that he expected their Assistance to restore their dethroned Prince and violated Constitution I am perswaded that he would have met with as much Support as Opposition. I learn within these two Days that the Delegates of Lorraine and Alsace had so little Hope, or rather were so thoroughly perswaded that those Provinces would join the Enemy, that they made unusual Haste to come forwarded lest they should be apprehended. Great Activity in that Moment would have done Wonders; but then he was not ready. The third great Error was that after waiting so long He came forward at all this Season. By menacing the Frontiers with great and encreasing Force vast Numbers of the Militia would have been drawn to the utmost Verge of the french Territory. The Difficulty of subsisting them there would have been extreme. By taking strong and good Positions his Troops would have been preserv'd in full Vigor; and the french wasted by Disease, tired of Inaction, and stimulated by their natural Impatience and Impetuosity of Temper, would have forcd their Generals to attack even if *they* had the Prudence to be quiet. The Consequences of such Attack, excepting always the Will of God, must have been a compleat Victory on his Part, and then it would have been next to impossible for them to escape—Then the Towns would have surrendered beleiving the Business to be over, and he might have come as far forward this Autumn as the needful Transportation of Stores would permit. Next Spring France would have found it almost impossible to subsist the Armies needful for her Defence in that Part of the Country which is most defensible, and of Consequence her Enemy would have reachd the Point from which he lately retreated without the smallest Difficulty.[5]

The Appearances are so vague and Contradictory that I cannot pretend to tell you whether the Alliance will or will not be preservd for the next Campaign. If I were to hazard Conjectures

on the present State of Things, it might cast Suspicions where I
have not sufficient Ground, and therefore I will bury them in my
own Bosom lest Accident should put this Letter into improper
Hands. France has a strong Ally in the Feelings of those Nations
who are subject to Arbitrary Power; but for that very Reason she
has a mortal Enemy in every Prince. If (as is very possible) the
League hold firm till next Spring it will then have gain'd considerable Auxiliaries and I am very much mistaken if this Nation will
make as great Efforts as those she is now making—The Characters of Nations must be taken into Consideration in all political questions, and that of France has ever been an enthusiastic
Inconstancy. They soon get tird of a Thing. They adopt without
Examination and reject without sufficient Cause. They are now
agog of thier Republic, and may perhaps adopt some Form of
Government with a Huzza; but that they will adopt a good Form
or having adopted adhere to it, that is what I do not beleive.
There is a great Body of Royalists in the Country who do not now
declare themselves because it would be certain Death, but a favorable Occasion would bring them out of their Holes. The Factions here are violent and among those who administer the Government there is not I am told that Degree of Character which
lays Hold of the Esteem and Respect of Mankind, but rather the
contrary. In their Opponents there is a nervous temper which
sticks at nothing which shrinks from Nothing, and if I see rightly
there is in the Current of their Affairs a strong Eddy or counter
Tide which may change materially both Men and Things. Yet let
what will happen I think it hardly possible that they should blun-
der as much as the Emigrants and I am prone to beleive that
in War and Politics the Folly of our Adversaries constitutes our
greatest Force. The future Prospect therefore is involved in Mist
and Darkness. There is but one Sovereign in Europe, the Em-
press of Russia, who is not in the Scale of Talents considerably
under Par.[6] The Emperor who it is said is consumptive and cannot live long is now much influenced by Manfredi a Statesman
of the Italian School who takes Insincerity for wisdom. The prussian Cabinet is far from strong. Lucchesini an able Man is said to
be rising in Influence there but there is such a Mixture of Lust
and Folly in the Chief that no one Man can keep Things steady.[7]
The Alliance with Vienna is disagreable to the Prussians and particularly to the Inhabitants of Berlin which may have some In-

fluence in destroying it and his Majesty has given three strong Proofs since his Accession that he is by no means nice on the Subject of public Faith. The Invasion of Brabant will I am perswaded alarm both Britain and Holland but whether they will confine themselves to Court Intrigue or come into the Field is doubtful.[8] Thus you will perceive Sir that Nothing can be predicated with tolerable Certainty respecting the Affairs of this Country either internal or external in the present moment. I am ever truly yours

Gouvr Morris

ALS, DLC:GW; LB, DLC: Gouverneur Morris Papers. Tobias Lear docketed the ALS as "recd Feby 12th 1793." A shorter version, in which the paragraphs are in a different order, is printed in Morris, *Diary and Letters of Gouverneur Morris*, 1:589–93, under the date 22 Sept. 1792.

Since Morris's last letter to GW, dated 10 June 1792, a number of important events had coalesced to create a reign of terror in France. Earlier, on 20 April 1792, France had declared war on the king of Hungary and Bohemia, Francis II, who also was the Holy Roman Emperor and ruler of Austria. An earlier alliance between Francis II and Frederick William II, the king of Prussia, meant that France also would be at war with Prussia. Shortly after declaring war, France sent three armies into the field, including one under Lafayette. The commander in chief of the coalition armies was the duke of Brunswick, Karl Wilhelm Ferdinand (1735–1806). In an attempt to intimidate the French government and to encourage the supporters of the monarchy, the governments of Austria and Prussia prepared a manifesto, dated 25 July 1792 and issued under Brunswick's signature, which threatened "total destruction" to anyone who opposed their efforts to restore the authority of Louis XVI. Its publication in the Paris newspapers led to violent protests in the streets of Paris. On 10 Aug. a mob stormed the Tuileries, where Louis XVI and his family were living, and massacred the Swiss Guard which protected the king. The insurgents forced the Legislative Assembly to suspend the monarchy and insisted on new elections for a national convention that would decide the now imprisoned king's fate and would write a constitution for a republican form of government. Shortly afterwards, the allied army invaded France, and the French suffered two humiliating military defeats with the capture of the fortresses at Longwy on 23 Aug. and Verdun on 2 September. News of these defeats fueled suspicions of plots against the new government and contributed to the September Massacres on 2–6 Sept., in which hundreds of prisoners, both political and criminal, were seized from their cells, hastily tried by improvised tribunals, and executed. The National Convention, elected by manhood suffrage, met on 20 Sept., and its first act was to abolish the monarchy. See also Morris's accounts of these events in Morris, *Diary of the French Revolution*, 2:414–548.

1. Morris was referring to GW's letter to Lafayette of 10 June 1792. After the storming of the Tuileries on 10 Aug., Lafayette's public opposition to the es-

tablishment of the new government resulted in his removal from his military command and his indictment by the government. On 19 Aug. he fled France, only to be arrested by Prussian forces on the French border. He was transferred to Austrian custody the following May and imprisoned at Olmütz until his release in September 1797. In a letter to Jefferson of 27 Sept. 1792, Morris enclosed an extract of a letter of 7 Sept. from William Short, minister to The Hague, in which Short asked Morris to consider joining with him and Thomas Pinckney, minister to Great Britain, in efforts at "reclaiming Mr de la Fayette in the name of the U.S. as a citizen thereof." Morris also enclosed an extract of his reply to Short of 12 Sept., in which he observed: "Supposing that M. de la Fayette were a natural born Subject of America, . . . I do not exactly see how the United States could claim him. He was not in their Service. . . . Can the United States interfere in an affair of this sort, without making themselves Parties in the Quarrel?" Morris cautioned that the United States needed to consider all possible actions carefully before doing something which could result in its being "drawn into a War." In spite of these hesitations, Morris concluded his letter: "If there was however any probability that a Demand on our part would liberate him, it might be well to attempt it. You may perhaps find out how that matter stands thro the Medium of the Court at which you are" (DNA: RG 59, Despatches from U.S. Ministers to France).

2. For Morris's hints of danger, see his letters to Jefferson of 22, 30 Aug., 10, 19, 27 Sept., in *Jefferson Papers*, 24:313–15, 331–35, 364–65, 404–5, 419–22.

3. After a trial before the National Convention, Louis XVI was executed on 21 Jan. 1793.

4. Morris remained the U.S. minister to France until his recall in 1794. He alone of the diplomatic corps remained in Paris during the various stages of the Terror from its beginnings in 1792 until its end in 1794. Contrary to Morris's prediction, the National Convention, in power from 20 Sept. 1792 until 26 Oct. 1795, was the longest-lived of the revolutionary assemblies.

5. Although the allied army had been victorious at Longwy and Verdun, the French army defeated Brunswick's forces at the Battle of Valmy on 20 Sept. 1792, halting the allied invasion and forcing Brunswick's army to retreat.

6. Although Catherine the Great, who ruled Russia from 1762 to 1796, was hostile to the ideals of the French Revolution, she did not join the Austro-Prussian alliance against France.

7. Leopold II, the former grand duke of Tuscany who became the Holy Roman Emperor in September 1790, died in March 1792 and was succeeded by his son Francis (1768–1835), who, as Francis II, reigned as emperor until 1806, when the Holy Roman Empire was formally dissolved. Federigo Manfredini (1743–1829), who studied at the college of Modena and at the military academy of Florence, became the tutor to Francis II and his brother Ferdinand (1769–1824) in 1776. When Ferdinand succeeded his father as the grand duke of Tuscany, he appointed Manfredini as his prime minister, and together they maintained Tuscany's traditional foreign policy of neutrality.

Although Girolamo Lucchesini (1751–1825) was a native of Italy, he spent much of his diplomatic career in the service of Prussia, and in 1792 he accompanied Frederick William II to the front during the Austro-Prussian campaign against France. After the French military victory at Valmy, Lucchesini helped negotiate an armistice and terms for the allied retreat. He later served as the Prussian minister to France from 1800 until 1806.

8. Early French efforts to capture Belgium (Austrian Netherlands), first in April and then in June 1792, failed. The third attempt, begun in October, proved more successful. The French victory at Jemappes on 6 Nov. was followed by their capture of Brussels, located in the duchy of Brabant, and by the end of the year, Belgium was under French control. Both Britain and the Netherlands joined the coalition against France in 1793.

From Benjamin Stoddert

Sir   Geo. Town 24 October 1792

I should apoligize for taking the liberty of addressing this letter to you, but the best apoligy I can make is to trespass as little as possible on your time; and though I have no doubt every person interested in the City of Washington would chearfully Join in the observations I shall make, I write alone considering it most respectful, as it will be less irksome to pass unnoticed the trifling opinions of an individual, than of many persons combined.

I beg leave to premise, that I have not the slightest enmity to either of the Commissioners—on the contrary, I esteem them all —and wanting neither contracts, nor employment under them and of course not being disappointed it affords me no pleasure to remark that the business of the City might certainly be better managed.[1] I know of but few things under their direction which go on so well as they might do—the Comrs who I am well satisfied have every disposition to do right, meet too seldom, & remain too short a time together, to obtain that kind of information, & intimate knowledge of the affairs of the City, so requisite to be possessed by those who have not only the general superintend⟨e⟩ncy, but the direction of the execution of every part of a business, requiring undivided & unremitted attention. Many facts could be adduced to shew the Justice of my observations, I will mention only one, & that, not as a charge against the Comrs, for I have no desire to be their accuser, particularly their secret accuser, but merely to prove that there is something wrong in the present system of management. and I believe would so continue, let who would be Comrs, until the gentlemen either reside on the spot, & each takes his particular department of the business, or until some person of Industry & talents is employed under their direction, to superintend in their absence & to bring before them at their stated meetings the proper objects, whose duty it should be to see, & to know every thing about the City. Something like this opinion, as to a superintendent, the Comrs took up at their last meeting, & in consequence wrote a letter to you Sir by Mr Blodget who was willing to be employed in this Character—they do not go into particulars, but refer to Mr Blodget, who from motives of delicacy I have reason to think will not go into the communications so freely as they expected—It is on that acct only, that I have taken the freedom to write this letter.[2]

The instance of mismanagement I mean to adduce respects the Bridge over Rock creek—It might have been completed by Novr—It will not be completed till the Spring. The Comrs preferred the plan of a single Arch because it appeared cheapest—after some progress had been made in the work—too much to admit of correcting the Error without delaying the completion of the Bridge, & incurring some additional expence, it was apprehended a single Arch would not vent the water of the Creek, & two more were in consequence agreed for—the mistake arose from the Comrs not Judging for themselves, from an accurate knowledge of the place where the Bridge was to be thrown over & all the attending circumstances—Whatever errors they have committed have proceeded from the same cause, want of sufficient attention to acquire the proper information—the fact is, that the Bridge of three arches with its appendages, is actually cheaper than one of one arch, with its appendages would be, and this either of the Gentlemen would have known, had it been *only his* duty to have known it. The money lost by getting right at last instead of at first, is not worth a thought—the delay occasioned, is in many accts of more importance.[3]

I beg to be permitted to add, that ⟨*mutilated*⟩ Public sales interested but very few persons who were not be⟨*mutilated*⟩ested in the fate of the City—and afforded no evidence of that diffusion of confidence so much to be wished for—Mr Blodget having authority from the Comrs sold 12 or 14 Public lots at private sale, during the few days he remained here, to four or five people from Phila. & the Eastward, one of whom, a man of property will move his Family here in the spring from Boston—and from Mr Blodgets General acquaintance, it is the opinion here he would be able to sell more lots in a few months, than the Comrs would in a year. I have communicated with Mr Deakins, who is the warm Friend of the Comrs & their officer; whose sentiments accord with mine—this I mention to remove from myself the suspicion of being actuated in what I have said, by any improper motive.[4] I have the honor to be with the greatest respect & esteem sir Yr most Obed. Servt

Ben. Stoddert

ALS, DLC:GW.

1. David Stuart, Thomas Johnson, and Daniel Carroll were the current commissioners for the federal district.

2. Stoddert, a Georgetown merchant, was not alone in his conclusion that the federal district needed a supervisor. GW expressed similar thoughts in his letter to the commissioners of 13 Nov. 1792. The commissioners appointed Samuel Blodget, Jr., to this position on 5 Jan. 1793 (see D.C. Commissioners to Blodget, 5 Jan. 1793, DNA: 42, Records of the Commissioners for the District of Columbia, Letters Sent, 1791–1802; to GW, 5 Jan. 1793).

3. On 30 Mar. 1792 the commissioners wrote Thomas Jefferson that "we determined on the immediate errection of a Bridge over Rock Creek," and on 5 April, Jefferson notified Baltimore builder Leonard Harbaugh that the "President of the U.S. has approved the contract of the Commissioners of the federal building with you, for erecting a bridge over Rock creek" (*Jefferson Papers,* 23:350, 379). Problems with the original one-arch design prompted the commissioners to conclude a second agreement with Harbaugh on 1 Sept. for construction of two additional arches (DNA: RG 42, Records of the Commissioners for the District of Columbia, Proceedings, 1791–1802).

4. For the results of the October 1792 sale of lots in the Federal City, see D.C. Commissioners to GW, 13 Oct., nn.1–2. For a list of buyers from "the Eastward," see David Stuart to GW, 10 Dec., n.3. Fellow Georgetown merchant William Deakins, Jr., served as treasurer for the commissioners from 1791 until 1796.

Letter not found: from Anthony Whitting, c.24 Oct. 1792. GW wrote Whitting on Sunday, 28 Oct. 1792: "By yesterdays Post I received a letter from you without date, but suppose from the contents it must have left Mount Vernon on Wednesday last," which was 24 October.

From Major Swiney

Harrisburg, Pa., 25 Oct. 1792. Writes that he left Ireland "to participate in the asylum your laudable and ever memorable conflict with the arbitrary enemy prepaired for us in America." He named his oldest son George Washington Swiney "in full hopes that some day . . . when he arrives at such an age as to be able to contemplate the character of the man he was named for, it will at least inspire him with a courage becoming a good Soldier; his situation in life will preclude him from emulating your Excellency in any other line." His two younger sons are named "Montgomery, & Frankland."[1]

ALS, DNA: RG 59, Miscellaneous Letters.
  1. Major Swiney has not been identified. A Montgomery Sweeny is listed on the 1820 Pennsylvania census as living in the town of Milton in Northumberland County (see *Pa. 1820 Census Index*, 357).

From Alexander Hamilton

[Philadelphia] 26. October 1792

The Secretary of the Treasury presents his respects to the President, and encloses him a letter received yesterday from the Supervisor of New York. The Secretary will have the honor of reminding the President of the subject when he has that of waiting upon him next.[1]

LB, DLC: GW.
  1. The enclosed letter from Richard Morris to Hamilton has not been identified. Morris apparently argued in this letter that he should not have to pay for certain job-related expenses out of his salary as supervisor of the revenue. In his letter to Hamilton of 10 Nov., Morris wrote: "I hope when the President Reconsiders this Business he will direct the Clk, the Stamper of Certificates, Office Rent, Fuel and the Expence of Guageg. and Marking the Stills in the Remote Counties to be paid as Contingencies" (Syrett, *Hamilton Papers*, 13:34).

Tobias Lear to Thomas Jefferson

United States [Philadelphia], October 26th 1792.

By the President's command T. Lear has the honor to inform the Secy of State, that the President desires Commissions to be made out for the following persons—and to bear the dates annexed thereto—viz.

John Adams, the first, and Benjamin Gunnison, second mate in the New Hampshire Cutter—June 30th 1792.

John Finley, second Mate in the New York Cutter—July 17: 1792.

David Porter, Master of the Maryland Cutter—Augt 5: 1792.

William Cooke, Master of the North Carolina Cutter, has lost his Commission by accident, the date of which was April 5th, 1791.[1]

John Armistead, Surveyor of the Port of Plymouth in No. Carolina, and Inspector of the Revenue, for the said Port—vice Thos Davis Freeman (superseded)—Septr 24th 1792.

Thomas Parker, Attorney for the United States in the South Carolina District; vice John J. Pringle—(resigned) October 25th 1792.[2]

Tobias Lear.
Secretary to the President of the United States.

ADfS, DNA: RG 59, Miscellaneous Letters; LB, DNA: RG 59, George Washington's Correspondence with His Secretaries of State; LB (photocopy), DLC:GW.

1. Alexander Hamilton recommended Adams, Gunnison, and Fenley for these appointments in his letter to GW of 26 July, and GW responded positively to those suggestions in his reply to Hamilton of 5 Aug. 1792. For correspondence concerning Porter's appointment, see GW to Hamilton, 5 Aug., and George Gale to GW, 4 Sept., and note 2. For background on Cooke's original commission, see GW to Cooke, 25 April 1791, and notes, and Lear to GW, 29 May 1791, n.3.

2. For recent reports of Freeman's unsuitability for his job and for recommendations of John Armistead as his replacement, see Hamilton to GW, 17 Sept. 1792, and note 1. Charleston lawyer Thomas Parker (c.1760–1820) served as district attorney for South Carolina until his death. Pringle wrote a letter of resignation to GW on 3 Sept. 1792. For GW's nomination of Armistead and Parker, see GW to the U.S. Senate, 19 Nov. 1792.

From Thomas Jefferson

[Philadelphia] Oct. 26. 92.
Th: Jefferson has the honor to send for the perusal of the President the inclosed letters just received from mister Barclay.[1]

AL, DNA: RG 59, Miscellaneous Letters; LB, DNA: RG 59, George Washington's Correspondence with His Secretaries of State; LB (photocopy), DLC:GW.

1. Jefferson received two letters from Thomas Barclay, U.S. consul to Morocco, on 26 October. Both letters were written from Gibraltar, the first one on 31 July and the second one on 22 Aug. 1792. In both letters Barclay reported on recent events in the Moroccan civil war, and in the 31 July letter he wrote: "The Americans at Algiers had not, in the beginning of this Month, received any part of the relief that was held out to them, their deplorable situation is Confirmed by a letter which I received open from the British Consul at Algiers

to the British Consul at Philadelphia, requesting hi⟨m⟩ to lay their sufferings before the legislatures of the United States, accompanied with one to my self partly on the same subject. Major Grey of the Queens regiment who was a Witness to thei⟨r⟩ wants, and I belive Contributed to relive them as far as prudently he Could do, Consulted me about the propriety of his writing to the President to procu⟨re⟩ them some attention from their Country, but I gave My opinion that it would not be necessary" (both letters are in DNA: RG 59, Consular Despatches: Gibraltar; extracts are in *Jefferson Papers*, 24:269–70, 312–13).

Letter not found: from Anthony Whitting, c.26 Oct. 1792. Whitting wrote GW on Wednesday, 31 Oct.: "The bill of Scantling I took to Alexa. on Friday and inform'd You the price & time it could be deliver'd if I could Get Your Answer this Week which occasioned my writing from thence."

From B. Francis

Sir,   New York, Oct. 27: 1792.

An inquiry into the mineral productions of this country, appeared to me an object of so much importance, that I was induced to take the liberty of writing to you on the business from Boston, I think in June, and had the honour of receiving your reply in this City. The motives that occasioned my former letter (& the only excuse I can plead for taking this freedom) were similar to what dictate the present, viz. The advancement of the public-Good.[1]

The advantages to a country, of inland water-carriage, have been demonstrated by so many happy experiments in England, and other parts of Europe, that new canals are projected almost daily; and so dextrous are they become in the execution of them in Great-Britain, having surveyors and workmen accustomed to the business, that an interruption or disappointment in the work is hardly ever known. In England they are enabled to execute these extensive designs with so much facility and correctness, by having at hand the best workmen for the purpose in the world, viz. Miners. The wages they give (but they generally agree with them at so much per yard, or fathom) are always something more than these men can earn in their mines, which soon procures as many as can, in almost any of those works, be conveniently employed. These Miners are from their childhood accustomed to labour in the earth, to handle the mattock, blast rocks asunder, &c. &c. and their early introduction, and perseverence in this rude occupation, disqualifies them for any other pursuit whatever: But 'tis to such hardy, untutord Men the British-Canals owe their stability.

The having, at call, workmen enow of the above description to execute that in a few months, which without such an advantage would require several years to perform, must have a very material effect not only on the expences of conducting such a work, but on the benefit expected to flow from it when compleated.

To undertake an extensive work of this kind, without having at hand the number of workmen proportionable, may produce expence & disappointment, but can hardly be expected to produce a navagable canal. When the channel of a canal is unoccupied by Water for any length of time, as it necessarily must when there are but few hands and much to be done, its banks exposed to the sun & rain fall in, and its course, in particular soils, is soon obliterated; for it appears, as well from the nature of the case, as from experience, that the preservation of the channel of a canal depends on its being constantly filled with water.

The scarcity of labourers in this country, is not the only difficulty that occurs in this business: perhaps a sufficient number might, by very extraordinary encouragement, be collected, but whether their services might be depended upon, and whether they could be kept together, and at their duty, in places remote from domestic accommodation, appears to me a matter of doubt. But the liberal wages given by individuals to industry, all over the country, will, I apprehend, keep sober steady labourers from list'ning to any proposals that may lead them from their homes.

That neither the country, nor those directly interested in these public-works may lose those years in the delay of their accomplishment, which seems unavoidable from the common mode of conducting them, and the scarcity of workmen, I beg leave to offer to your consideration, and if you think proper the consideration of Congress, a means whereby these or any works of the like nature may be facilitated, without being subjected to those obstructions which frequently arise from employing, and depending on, promiscuous hands.

There are in many parts of Europe remains of works (once of great importance) performed by the Roman Soldiers, the accounts of which have several times furnished me with hints how the Soldiers of this day might, in times of quiet, be usefully employed. The present circumstances of this country, and the magnitude of the public Designs, suggest very forcibly the utility of adopting in these States the practice of the Romans, and employing soldiers in the civil service of the community.

A Corps of Artificers might be of service to the Country in a Moral view. The licencious disposition that most commonly leads the illiterate to prefer a military life, would be most naturally & effectually corrected by labour and good discipline. I am, with the greatest Respect, Sir, Your most obedt & humb. Servt

B. Francis: Post-Office.

ALS, DNA: RG 59, Miscellaneous Letters. The cover is postmarked "N YORK OCT 28."

1. GW had referred Francis's earlier letter to him, written at Boston on 25 May 1792, to Thomas Jefferson to answer (see Jefferson to Francis, 22 June 1792, in *Jefferson Papers*, 24:109).

From Thomas Jefferson

[Philadelphia] Oct. 27. 92.

Th: Jefferson has the honor to inform the President that in a Madrid gazette of Sep. 14. is an article of Namur Aug. 23. which states circumstantially the capture of M. de la Fayette, and that he was carried from the place to Antwerp. it says that his intention had been to pass in the rear of the Austrian army, but ran foul of a picquet near Rochfort. there were 17 or 18. officers altogether.[1] Longwy had surrendered with a garrison of 2600 men on being invested by the Austrians.[2]

AL, DNA: RG 59, Miscellaneous Letters; LB, DNA: RG 59, George Washington's Correspondence with His Secretaries of State; LB (photocopy), DLC: GW.

1. On 19 Aug., Lafayette and twenty-two members of his general staff fled France only to be captured by Prussian army sentinels near Rochefort, Belgium. During his first year of imprisonment, Lafayette was transferred from one place to another, starting at Namur, Belgium. In May 1793 he arrived at Olmütz where the Austrians held him prisoner until September 1797. News of Lafayette's capture appeared in an "Extract of a letter from Namur, August 20" in the 31 Oct. 1792 issue of the *Pennsylvania Gazette* (Philadelphia);

this extract parallels the information in the 14 Sept. 1792 issue of the *Gazeta de Madrid,* to which Jefferson referred. For background on the events that led to Lafayette's flight from France, see Gouverneur Morris to GW, 23 Oct. 1792, and source note.

2. Longwy, a fortified French town near the Belgian border, surrendered on 23 Aug. 1792.

Henry Knox to Tobias Lear

Dr sir,   [Philadelphia] 27 October 1792.
   The statement relatively to the Cherokees shall be made to-morrow, or next day at furthest[1]—The intelligence received, this afternoon from Governor Blount renders alterations necessary. I submit this intelligence to the President in Governor Blounts Letter of the 7th instant, received at 3 oClock P.M.,[2] together with certain Letters which I have written in consequence, to the Governors of South Carolina & Georgia—and to Mr Seagrove & Major Gaither[3]—Two Vessels sail in the morning—One for Charleston and the other for St Marys.[4]
   If the President should direct any alterations or additions to the said Letters, I shall be glad to have them as early as possible.[5]
                                             H. Knox

LS, DLC:GW; LB, DLC:GW.

1. Knox presented a report on Indian affairs, "with sundry papers therein mentioned," to both houses of Congress on 7 Nov. 1792 (see *Annals of Congress,* 2d Cong., 611, 673). It included "A statement of the measures which have been taken to conciliate and quiet the Southern Indians" and "Information received relatively to the disposition of the Southern Indians, and the causes of the hostilities of part of the Cherokees and Creeks" (all in DNA: RG 46, Second Congress, 1791–93, Senate Records of Legislative Proceedings, Reports and Communications).

2. Blount's letter to Knox written from Knoxville on 7 Oct. 1792 enclosed recent accounts that warned about the increasing hostility of the Cherokees from the five Lower Towns and the Creeks. Blount reported that the "Militia are turning out with unusual alacrity" and that he hoped to receive Knox's orders "as speedily as possible" (DNA: RG 46, Second Congress, 1791–93, Senate Records of Legislative Proceedings, Reports and Communications; see also *ASP, Indian Affairs,* 1:292–94).

3. These letters, each of which is dated 27 Oct., are in *ASP, Indian Affairs,* 1:262–63. In his letter to South Carolina governor Charles Pinckney, Knox wrote: "The President of the United States has directed me to acknowledge the receipt of your Excellency's letter, of the 30th ultimo, with the enclosures

therein contained, from General Pickens and Colonel Anderson, dated the 12th, 13th, and 20th of the same month.

"Governor Blount, of the territory of the United States, south of the Ohio, has also transmitted similar information to that contained in your enclosures, relatively to the hostile designs of the five Lower Cherokee or Chickama[u]ga towns, on the Tennessee river.

"It would appear, that the five Cherokee towns, containing perhaps from three to five hundred warriors, and abetted by a number of individuals of the Upper Creeks, chiefly young men, are disposed for war; and their principal object appears to be the settlements on Cumberland river. A summary of this information is contained in the papers No. 1, 2, 3, and 4, this day received from Governor Blount.

"The information from Mr. Seagrove, agent to the Creek nation, dated at St. Mary's, on the 13th ultimo, appears to encourage the hope, that the Lower towns of the Creeks are favorably disposed for peace.

"The United States have existing treaties of peace and friendship with the four Southern tribes of Indians: no complaints have been made of the infraction of those treaties, nor does it appear that any of the Southern tribes have any just cause of war against the United States. Valuable presents have been given to all the said tribes, in the course of the present year, and the Creeks and Cherokees have, each of them, an annual allowance of one thousand five hundred dollars.

"The Chickasaws and Choctaws are friendly, and it would appear, so are the mass of the Cherokees and Creeks, the five towns of the former, and certain individuals of the latter, excepted; for it has not yet been made to appear that the conduct of the Creeks is the result of any deliberation of any assembly of chiefs, or of any particular towns.

"It has been said, that the sudden turn that the Indians have taken for war, has been dictated by the interference of a neighboring European Power; but the evidence on this head may be questioned.

"As Congress will be in session in a few days, the information on this subject will be submitted to them. The constitution has invested them with the right of declaring war. Until, therefore, their decision shall be made known, the Executive cannot authorize offensive measures; although, in the mean time, it may be necessary to make the most vigorous preparations for defensive, and eventually for offensive measures, by providing abundance of arms and ammunition.

"The President of the United States has commanded me to express his entire approbation of your Excellency's sentiments and orders on this head.

"The agent appointed by you, to provide six hundred arms in this city, being unable to purchase any that were suitable, the President of the United States directed that he should be furnished from the public arsenal, at the prices mentioned in the within schedule." For GW's directive, see Tobias Lear to Samuel Hodgdon, 16 Oct. 1792, and note 2.

Knox's letter to Georgia governor Edward Telfair contains information similar to that sent to Pinckney and questions "whether it would not be highly expedient that the militia should be well armed, and furnished with ammunition as soon as possible, so as to be ready for any events."

Knox's letter to Indian agent James Seagrove also reported that the "five Lower towns on the Tennessee . . . have probably decided for hostilities . . . and are aided by a number of banditti of the Upper Creeks, chiefly young men. It does not appear in evidence, that the conduct of the said Creeks is influenced by the result of any deliberations of any assembly of chiefs, or even of towns." Knox urged Seagrove to "strain every nerve, and make use of every possible expedient" to impress the various chiefs to restrain their young men from war with the United States, and he suggested that a visit by Seagrove to the Upper Creeks "might be the means of preventing a war." A visit with the Creek leader Alexander McGillivray might also "have a good effect."

Knox's letter to Maj. Henry Gaither, commanding officer of the U.S. troops in Georgia, instructed him "to be on your guard" and to observe, along with his troops, "the most soldierly vigilance," but Gaither also must "endeavor to avoid an air of suspicion to any friendly Indians; always treating them with frankness and kindness, and assuring them of the friendship of the United States."

4. A notice that the brig *Georgia Packet* "intended to sail the 27th" for Charleston appeared in the 27 Oct. issue of *Dunlap's American Daily Advertiser* (Philadelphia).

5. No alterations or additions have been identified.

Letter not found: from Henry Lee, 27 Oct. 1792. Henry Knox wrote Lee on 3 Nov. 1792 explaining that GW "has directed me to acknowledge the receipt of your Excellency's Letter to him of the 27th ultimo."[1]

1. For Knox's letter to Lee, see Knox to GW, 3 Nov. 1792, n.1.

From "A True Republican"

Sir,   Philada 27th October 1792.

By an Act of Congress passed 23d January last—the Powers of the Board of Commissioners, for settling the Accounts between the United States, and individual States, were prolonged, until the first day of July 1793[1]—now, Sir, why the Claims of those, who, escaped the Jaws of Death from the flying Camp, should be rejected is a thing that I cannot comprehend—certainly they formed a part of our Army—our Army was paid, why not pay them?[2] I think, Sir, you would do honor to your Country, and releive the distresses of many of our poor Brethern; if you were to cause the law to be put in force, that these (few existing)

Creatures might be releived. I have the honor to be Sir your most obedient humble Sert

A true Republican

L, DLC:GW.

1. See "An Act to extend the time limited for settling the Accounts of the United States with the individual States," signed by GW on 23 Jan. 1792, in 1 *Stat.* 229.

2. The Continental Congress created a flying camp, or mobile reserve, for the middle colonies on 3 June 1776 from militia forces raised in Pennsylvania, Delaware, and Maryland. Congress resolved on 5 June that "the militia, when in service, be regularly paid and victualled in the same manner as the continental troops" (*JCC*, 4:412–13, 5:418). The flying camp served with GW's troops during the New York campaigns of 1776, including the battles of Long Island and Harlem Heights, and at the defense of Fort Washington, during which many suffered death and captivity at the hands of the British (see GW to Joseph Trumbull, 9 June 1776, nn.1–2, General Orders, 31 Aug. 1776, n.3, Henry Knox and Rufus Putnam to GW, 6 Oct. 1776, n.1, GW to John Hancock, 18 Sept. 1776, n.2).

From Edmund Randolph

Sir   Philadelphia October 28. 1792

On revolving the subjects, with which I am officially connected, I discover none, deserving the notice of congress, except those, which are comprehended in the necessity of reforming our judicial system. The detail of them would be almost infinite; and certainly too minute for a communication from the executive: Nor can the congress forget the admonitions, which they have already received on this head. And yet I am so deeply impressed with the dangers to which the government is exposed from this quarter, that it would be a happy circumstance, if they could be stimulated to the discussion.[1]

Were I to indulge myself in a general review of our political situation, I should probably repeat without use topics, which have presented themselves to your own mind, or which have been suggested more accurately by others, to whose departments they belong. I confess indeed, that I feel at the present crisis these strong solicitudes: that the public be assured of stability in the *existing* fiscal arrangements; that the redemption of the public debt be commenced at no distant day; that the land office, if the hostility of the Indians will permit, be employed, as one of the in-

struments of redemption; that the state-governments be prohibited from intermeddling with the Indian tribes, to the utmost
limit of the constitution; that some temporary mode be provided
for the relief of many crippled soldiers, who must beg or starve,
until the schism between the legislative and judiciary shall be ad-
justed; and that the violence of the sanguine states, which may
be disappointed on the final settlement of their accounts with
the United States may in some manner or other be softened.

I cannot undertake to say, that these hints are capable of being carried into practice, or are intitled to your attention. But I
submit them, according to your instructions, without a comment;
as you will best know, how to appreciate them.[2] I have the honor,
sir, to be with the highest respect yr mo. ob. serv.

Edm: Randolph

ALS, DLC:GW.

1. GW asked his cabinet officers to suggest items that he should include in
his opening address to Congress when it assembled in November for its second
session (see GW to Thomas Jefferson, 23 Aug., to Alexander Hamilton, 26 Aug.,
and to Henry Knox, 3 Sept. 1792 [second letter]).

2. For the incorporation of Randolph's suggested topics in GW's message to
Congress, see GW's Address to the U.S. Senate and House of Representatives,
6 Nov. 1792. For GW's attention to Randolph's concerns about veterans' pensions and judiciary reform, see GW's second letter to the U.S. Senate and
House of Representatives of 7 November.

To Anthony Whitting

Mr Whiting   Philadelphia Oct. 28th 1792.

By yesterdays Post I received a letter from you without date,
but suppose from the contents it must have left Mount Vernon
on Wednesday last.[1]

The letter to Mrs Fanny Washington must be sent to me, because the purpose of it cannot be answered by sending it to her
below.[2]

The Mansion house surplus hands, may be disposed of as you
shall, upon a full view of all circumstances, conceive best; and
the Mule Cart (instead of the Oxe Cart) may be retained, with
the single horse Cart also at that place. Sinah may also remain
there until her Mother gets up again, although it is my intention
to substitute Anna in her place, as an assistent to Kitty. Sinah &

Patt may strengthen the Plantation which stands in most need of their aid.[3]

The scarcity of Timber in the Neck[4] for fences, & the distance it is to draw at other places, are evils I have long foreseen, and have endeavoured to guard against; but for reasons which I mentioned to you in one of my late letters it never has been accomplished—I hope, however, as I have, in as strong terms as I know how to use, impressed the necessity of raising live Hedges upon you, that I shall no longer have cause to complain of neglect on this score—Any thing, in the shape of a live hedge is desirable; and almost anything for partition fences (where there are no hogs) will suffice.[5] Mr Bartram, the Botanist whom I have seen since my return to this City, is of opinion that it was the Spring & Summer droughts that prevented the Cedar berries from vegitating; and that they may yet be expected; do not therefore let the ground where they were sown be disturbed without accurately examining the Berries to see if there be any hopes of their coming up. He also says that when Cedars are planted & laid down, that if the limbs next the ground are covered properly they will take root & send out a number of new shoots—this will be worth trying, if upon examination of the Cedar hedge rows in the Neck, you should think it advisable to lay them down.[6]

It is not to be wondered that the field No. 7 at the River Plantation should want a New Post & Rail fence when it is seen what kind my people make (in spite of all I can do to prevent it) that is, Posts when Morticed that a strong man would break across his knee—& rails so long, & so weak, as to warp, & be unable to bear the weight of a child in getting over them—This custom I hope you will get the better of.

The two Meadows at Dogue Run, that is, the middle & upper one, contain by actual measurement $51\frac{3}{4}$ Acres—the middle one $31\frac{1}{4}$—and the Wood between, if opened by a strait line from one Indenture of the field to the other, will add $8\frac{1}{4}$ Acres thereto but to do this ought not to be attempted until the present open ground is compleatly grubbed—ditched (where necessary[)] & put into perfect order for the Plow & smooth laying for grass—for I repeat it again, that I had rather have one acre in this order, than five in a slovenly way; which is not only disadvantageous in many points of view, but is a very great eye-sore to me.

I suppose it was owing to the hurry & distress in which Mrs Fanny Washington was at the time she left Mount Vernon that a little Wine &ca was not left out for extraordinary occasions; because I know it was intended—but not for sick Negros, unless it might be in particular cases which rendered it indispensably necessary; for Docr Craik never practiced any thing of this kind when Mrs Washington & my self were at home, or ever suggested it as necessary: Nor was it my intention to leave it for the purpose of entertaining travellers—because there is a striking impropriety in travellers making use of it as a house of convenience, knowing as they certainly must do, that neither my family, nor the Majors is there; & when it is far removed from the Post, or any other public Road. And if people were led there by curiosity as soon as that was satisfied, they would retire; without expecting, under the circumstances just mentioned, to be invited to lodge, dine, or spend their time there. However, as it may happen that characters to whom one would wish to shew civility—and others, that may have a line from me (as was the case the other day with the Honble Judge Cushing) may call there.[7] I shall, by a Vessel which will leave this according to the Master's Acct on thursday next, send you a little Wine, Tea & Coffee, along with the Iron & somethings which will accompany it.[8] When I recommended care of and attention to, my Negros in sickness, it was that the first stage of, & the whole progress through the disorders with which they might be siezed (if more than a slight indisposition) should be closely watched, & timely applications, & remedies be administered; especially in Pleurisies, & all inflamatory fevers accompanied with pain when a few days neglect, or want of bleeding, might render the ailment incurable. In such cases sweeten'd Teas—broths—and, (according to the nature of the complaint, & the Doctrs prescription) sometimes a little wine may be necessary to nourish & restore the patient; and these I am perfectly willing to allow when it is really requisite. My fear is, as I expressed to you in a former letter, that the under overseers are so unfeeling—in short viewing the Negros in no other light than as a better kind of Cattle, the moment they cease to work, they cease their care of them.[9]

I am very glad to hear that you think your young & soft Corn is out of danger; and wish upon further trial this may prove to be the fact, as I have been apprehensive of considerable loss from the backwardness of it.

You say in your letter, that the Ferry People have got out all their Wheat—and yet, by the Report of last week only 59½ bushls was sent to Mill; and by the Report of the preceeding week 182; If these two quantities with what was got out for seed, is all the crop that No. 1 at French's yielded, it is (if I recollect rightly what that was) a miserable turn out indeed—far short of the lower calculation that had been made of it. I wish you would, always, when the contents of a field is known enter it in the weekly report & let it come on—that I may be early advised.[10]

I perceive by the Report that you have been hauling the Buck Wheat from Mansion House to Muddy hole. I had no conception of this—but supposed you would have drawn it to the Brick yard, or some other naked piece of ground & there threshed & cleared it—putting the grain in the Green Ho. loft,[11] & retaining the straw for litter. I wish to know the quantity of the grain it has yielded—& what the appearence of grass is where the Buck Wheat grew.

I wish you would make old Jack and Frank, at their leizure hours, especially the latter, who I think must have many of them, open all the Springs that lye under the Hill, from the Bog (inclusive) by the Spring House onwards to the Wharf and let them, & the usual Spring, be thrown into one currt or channel and carried on a level or as nearly so as for the Water to run, along the Hill side until it is brought into that line which I was opening from the East front of the House (in a line with the Doors) to the River. If any aid from the Ditchers is wanting to accomplish this, it may be given—but I do not mean that any other ditch should be dug, where it can be avoided, than such as are used for side land meadows, and these you know are simple & small indeed.[12]

I shall make enquiry after linnen, and if I can get what is wanting upon reasonable terms, will send it by Captn Cahart; who, as I have before said talks of Sailing on thursday next. If I should not do this you will be informed thereof by the next Post.[13]

I have resolved to build a Barn & treading floor at Dogue Run Plantation, & to do it as soon as other more pressing work will permit; at any rate for the Wheat of next harvest. In my last, I sent you a Bill of such Scantling as I proposed to buy.[14] Now I give you a general Bill—and a Plan of the building—with such explanations and directions as I think Thos Green (to whom after you have perused it, it must be given) can be at no loss in the execution; and therefore shall add nothing more in this letter than to desire you will engage the Scantling marked to be purchased—provide Shells & the number of Shingles which may be deficient which, cannot be many as (for want of calculation) 10,000 were got for the Piaza and, I believe, less than 4,000 used—this small demand might, I should suppose be easily procured at Alexandria[15]—In general I shall depend upon you to provide what is wanted and to see that every thing is carried on properly. I am Your friend & well wisher

Go: Washington

ALS, DLC:GW.

1. Whitting's letter to GW, written c.24 Oct., has not been found.

2. Fanny Bassett Washington and her ailing husband left Mount Vernon in October to spend the winter at Eltham, the estate of her father, Burwell Bassett (see Whitting to GW, 31 October). The letter to Fanny, which was from GW, has not been identified (see GW to Whitting, 11 November).

3. Sinah and her mother, Kitty, who was identified as a spinner in 1786, were both dower slaves. If Sinah was transferred to another farm at this time, by 1799 she was working again at the Mansion House farm. Anna, another dower slave, was probably the daughter of Little Alice. Sinah and Anna were about 20 and 19 years old, respectively, at this time. Patt may be the slave identified in 1786 as the 11-year-old daughter of Doll, a laboring woman on the Ferry plantation. See Slave List, 18 Feb. 1786, in *Diaries*, 4:277–83, and Washington's Slave List, June 1799.

4. GW is referring to the River farm and the adjoining land located between the Potomac River and Little Hunting Creek on what was known as Clifton's Neck.

5. For GW's previous thoughts on the use of live hedges instead of wooden fencing, see his letter to Whitting of 14 October.

6. John Bartram, Jr., and his brother William Bartram, managed a well-known botanical garden on the west bank of the Schuylkill River three miles southwest of Philadelphia. See the List of Plants from John Bartram's Nursery that GW ordered in March 1792 and Directive to John Christian Ehlers, 7 Nov. 1792.

7. William Cushing, an associate justice of the U.S. Supreme Court, was currently riding the middle circuit, which consisted of the states of Pennsylvania, New Jersey, Delaware, Maryland, and Virginia. For Cushing's intention to visit the Federal City and other locations on his way to the circuit court session in Richmond, see GW to Andrew Ellicott, 20 Oct. 1792, and note 1. No letter from GW to Cushing relevant to Cushing's proposed visit to Mount Vernon has been found. For mention of Cushing's arrival at Mount Vernon, see GW to Whitting, 2 December.

8. The various articles, including the linen mentioned later in this letter, were shipped in November on Capt. William Carhart's ship the *President* (see GW to Whitting, 11 Nov. 1792).

9. For more of GW's thoughts on the proper care of his slaves, see GW to Whitting, 14 Oct. 1792.

10. The only farm report found for October 1792 is that for 21–27 Oct. (DLC:GW), which appears in CD-ROM:GW.

11. The greenhouse stood on the north side of the upper garden, a short distance west of the mansion.

12. The springhouse was on the hillside that slopes to the Potomac River, just south of the mansion. Frank was probably the 80-year-old man listed on the 1799 slave census at the Mansion House farm as "Past Labour." He was identified as a "Stock keeper" on the 1786 slave census and as "Old Frank," who worked six days "in care of Stock," on the farm report for 21–27 Oct. 1792. There were several Jacks included on both the 1786 and 1799 slave lists; "Old Jack" was noted as "attending Granary & taking out & drying Leather" for six days on the 21–27 Oct. 1792 farm report. See Slave List, 18 Feb. 1786, ibid., and Washington's Slave List, June 1799.

13. GW's next letter to Whitting was written on 4 Nov. 1792.

14. GW's previous letter to Whitting of 21 Oct. and its enclosed bill of scantling have not been found.

15. See the following enclosure entitled "Washington's Plan for a Barn," 28 Oct. 1792. Thomas Green, overseer of the carpenters at Mount Vernon, had worked for GW at least since 1783 (see GW to Green, 31 Mar. 1789, source note). For GW's previous purchase of 10,000 shingles for the piazza roof, see Tobias Lear to Lovell and Urquhart, 16 Dec., n.1.

Enclosure
Washington's Plan for a Barn

[28 October 1792]

The Plan of the building, as exhibited on the other Side;[1] The manner in which it is connected with the B: Yard; the possition of the outer door wch is to be 8 ft wide into the upper floor from the B. Yard & the entrance from thence into the Octogan or inner building between the braces after passing over the open or treading floor—The situation of the door into the floor below to be 4 ft—and in short every other thing necessary for information is so expressly & clearly explained in the details wch are given that it is scarcely necessary to give any further direction for the execution.[2] But that there may be no mistake on the part of Thos Green in laying the Work off—nor no unnecessary labour in digging the foundation I shall drop a few hints for his governmt and desire he will attend to them—viz.—first to lay of the

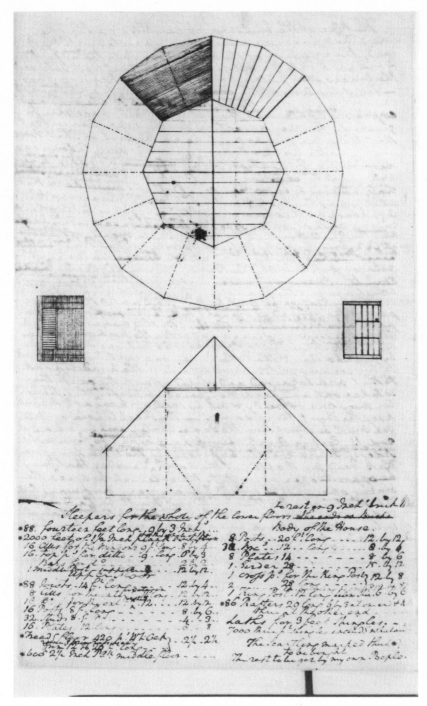

Fig. 2. Washington's plan for a barn, 28 October 1792, enclosed in GW to Anthony Whitting, 28 October 1792. (Library of Congress, Washington, D.C.)

Barn yard as described wch if I mistake not was originally intended to be 100 feet sqr.—But, if I am wrong in this let it run
as far back from the So. Wt & So. Et Corners of the Corn houses
as it is from one of the said Corners to the other & ranging with
the outer sides of both of them. Then half way along the line
O,O in the Plat, fix the angle, & center of the Barn door as at C &
Q—next from Q and the Center of the Barn Yard gate at P. and
runs in a line with the two objects, fix a stake 26 feet from the
Angle at C & Q for the Center of the Octagon, & of Course of the
Barn. From this Center form a Circle by a line or Rod as more
certain 26 feet long, which will give the Diameter of the Barn—
viz.—52. feet from out to out—then let the foundation be sunk
by this circular line until the highest part of the ground above,
& within the circle, is brought to the level of the lowest part of it
below & also within it. By this means there will be no unnecessary digging, and when the Wall comes to be built which it must
be of 16 equal sides 10 f. 3 Inchs each at the outer angle or as
near this as may ⟨illegible⟩ to be tried ⟨illegible⟩ there need be but
one face of it worked by plumb & line, & that the inner one, until it rises with in two courses of Bricks of the Cill of the Window
frame as all up to that will be raised and sloped off with the earth
that is taken out and must hereafter be paved; or turfed so as that
the water may run off freely, & not by settling against the wall
keep the lower floor damp. The Inner Circle, or Octagon must
be struck from the same Center by a line, or rod 14. feet in length.
& will have eight Pillars equal to form eight equal sides—one
of wch is to be parrallel with the line O.O. It will readily be perceived that the Door from the B. Yard must enter at the Angle
C.Q. in order that it may open opposite to the interval between
the braces. otherwise the entrance into the Octagon would have
a very aukward look nor will the door at this place look badly—
but have advantages from the cover tht will be over it⟨.⟩ All the
bricks for this building must be hard & good it would be well
therefore to have those that are on the spot assorted & counted
in time that if there be not a sufficiency of them. the best clay
from under the Barn may be laid aside for making the difficiency
early in the Spring. 30,820 I calculate a sufft number but this
supposes all to be good—perhaps 35, or even 40,000 wd not be
too many to provide.

Sleepers for the *whole* of the lower floors
To rest on 9 Inchs brick Wall[3]

*	88. [joists] fourteen feet long	9 by 3 Inchs
*	2000 feet of 1½ Inch plank for the whole of the lower floor.	
	16 Cills for the Windows 9 ft long	8 by 4
	16. top ps. for ditto 9 long	6 by 3
	["] Bars for do	2 by 2
	1 Middle Post—supporter 9	12 by 12.

Upper Floor

*	88 Joists—14 ft long	12. by 4
	8 Cills for the inter or octagon—14 long	12. by 12
	16 Do for the extr or skid—12	12. by 12
	16 Posts 8 f. long	8. by 6
	32. Studs 8. f. do	4. [by] 3
	16. Plates. 12. long	6. [by] 8
*	Treadg floor 420 ps. Wh. Oak runng progressively from 12 to 20 ft long	2½ [by] 2½
*	600 [square feet] 2½ Inch Plk middle floor	

Body of the House.

	8 Posts—20 ft long	12. by 12 Inch
	3⟨o⟩. Bra[ce]s—12 long	8. by 6
	8 Plates 14	8 by 6
	1. Girder 28	15. by 12
	1 cross ps. for the King Post 28 long	12. by 8.
	2 [do] 14. feet long to cross do	12. by 8
	1 King Post—12 long below shin[gle]s	6. by 6
*	86 Rafters 20 long 6 by 3 at one end & 4 by three at the other end	

Laths for 3 feet Shingles.
7000 three ft shingles includg what are on hand
The Scantling marked thus (*) to be bought
The rest to be got by my own People.

ADf, DLC:GW.

1. See fig. 2. For GW's earlier mention of his intention to build a "Barn & treading floor" at Dogue Run, see his letter to Tobias Lear of 26 June 1791, n.1.

2. The detailed instructions that GW outlined in the rest of this document refer to a second sketch of the barn, which has not been found but which evidently contained lettered points of reference at various architectural compo-

nents. For clarification of the instructions regarding the construction of the treading floor, see GW to Whitting, 4 November.

3. This list of supplies for building the sixteen-sided barn appears below the sketch in figure 2.

From Thomas Jefferson

[Philadelphia] Oct. 29. 1792.

The Secretary of State has had under consideration the Report of the proceedings of the Secretary of the Territory of the U.S. North West of the Ohio in the absence of the Governor from January the 1st to June 30th 1792. and

Reports to the President of the United States that there is nothing contained therein which requires any thing to be done on the part of the President of the United States.[1]

Th: Jefferson

ALS, DNA: RG 59, Miscellaneous Letters; ALS (letterpress copy), DLC: Jefferson Papers; LB, DNA: RG 59, George Washington's Correspondence with His Secretaries of State; LB (photocopy), DLC:GW; LB, DNA: RG 59, Reports of the Secretary of State to the President and Congress, 1790–1906.

1. Tobias Lear had sent this report to Jefferson on 28 Oct., acknowledging that it had been "received by the President yesterday" and conveying the president's request "that, if the Secretary of State should, in perusing the enclosed, find anything which requires the agency or particular notice of the President, he would report the same" (DNA: RG 59, Miscellaneous Letters). The report, which is in Carter, *Territorial Papers,* 3:360–80, originally accompanied Winthrop Sargent's letter to GW of 6 July 1792.

From Thomas Jefferson

[Philadelphia] Oct. 29. 1792.

Th: Jefferson has the honor of inclosing to the President a letter just received from Messrs Viar & Jaudenes, and will have that of waiting on him in the evening.[1]

AL, DNA: RG 59, Miscellaneous Letters; AL (letterpress copy), DLC: Jefferson Papers; LB, DNA: RG 59, George Washington's Correspondence with His Secretaries of State; LB (photocopy), DLC:GW; copy, DNA: RG 59, Notes from the Spanish Legation.

1. Jefferson enclosed his translation of a letter of 29 Oct. 1792, written to him in Spanish at Philadelphia, by Spanish ambassadors José Ignacio de Viar and José de Jaudenes. It reads: "Tho' the short time which has past since we had

the honor of informing his Majesty of the contents of your letter of the 11th of July of the present year, does not admit us to have received any acknolegement whereby we might convince you again of the just conduct of our court, & the good disposition which subsists to preserve friendship & the best correspondances with the U.S. nevertheless as we have recieved advices from the Governor of Louisiana, which on one part confirm the suspicions which we insinuated to you in our answer to the said letter, 'that doubtless the Commissioners of the U.S. insisted on fixing the limits where it is known clearly to be prejudicial to Spain, & opposed to the interests of the Creek Indians.' & on the other part manifest the efforts which the said Governor has used to restrain the Indians from committing hostilities against the U.S. as they had determined. we have now the satisfaction to inclose to you an extract of the advices of the said Governor, concerning this object, as a new confirmation of the assurances of the good disposition & friendship which we have several times had the honor to give to the U.S.

"We omit commenting on the insinuations from the Governor of Louisiana, because we are persuaded that your own good understanding will easily penetrate to the bottom of them, and that they will have much weight in your reflection.

"We are induced equally to make the present communication by the consideration that we observe from the public papers, & some conversations, that the opinion prevails that Spain encourages the Creeks, at this moment, to commit hostilities against the U.S. and that those who explain themselves in this sense do not take time to examine into the true causes, and from whence they derive their root; nor do they appear to distinguish between the acts of individuals & those of nations. moreover it appears to be our duty to guard our government from all charge & censure for the want of an amicable preadmonition, whatever disagreeable consequences may probably result, if the U.S. do not desist from fixing the limits where they propose, or suspend all demarcation until the point is determined between our court & the U.S. by means of the negociation on foot; using at the same time the most efficacious means to prevent the exasperation of the minds of the Indians with threats, and all usurpation of their lands.

"You will be pleased to inform the President of the U.S. of what we have here expressed, & we flatter ourselves that the measures which the government of the U.S. take will be such as may contribute to preserve the good harmony & friendship which has so happily subsisted hitherto, & which otherwise would be much endangered" (DLC: Jefferson Papers).

Jefferson also enclosed an extract of the letter that Louisiana governor Carondelet wrote to Viar and Jaudenes on 24 Sept. from New Orleans. Jefferson's translation of that letter reads: "The favorable situation in which (as you inform me) the matters are which are in treaty between our Court & the U.S. of A. has engaged me to restrain the hostilities which the Creek nation had resolved to commence against the state of Georgia, to recover the lands which it has usurped from them since the treaty of limits agreed to by McGillevray in the year 1790, but null in effect, as having been rejected by the nation from the time it was informed of it's contents, as not having been ratified & confirmed by the Chiefs which compose their Council, & finally forasmuch as that the chiefs having already contracted in the year 1784. with Spain, they could not conclude with the U.S. a new treaty of limits, without their participation, nor could they stipulate in the said treaty, without an infraction of the friendship which subsists between them & Spain, that 'the Creek nation acknoleges itself under the protection of the U.S. of A. & not under the protection of any other sovereign whatever.'

"I have engaged the Nation to await in peace the result of the negociations which are under treaty in Madrid: & I hope that the U.S. will take the same measure, & will suspend running the line of demarcation in that part until the conclusion of the negociations beforementioned: since on the contrary, & in the case that the Americans realize the menaces which they have thrown out against the said Indians, to destroy them in the autumn, it will indispensably kindle a very bloody war" (DLC: Jefferson Papers).

For the administration's immediate response to the information contained in these two letters, see Jefferson's "Notes of Cabinet Meeting on the Southern Indians and Spain," 31 Oct., in *Jefferson Papers,* 24:547–50, and GW to Jefferson, 1 Nov. 1792, and note 1.

Orders to Revenue Officers

Philadelphia 29 October 1792 [1]

By the President of the United States

In pursuance of the powers and authorities vested in me by the Acts of Congress (of the 3rd of March 1791, & of the eighth of May 1792) relative to the duties on distilled spirits and to the collection thereof, the following alterations & additions to the arrangement of offices & distribution of compensations made on the 15th day of March 1791. are hereby adopted and established, in relation to the year ending on the 30th day of June 1792. [2]

1st—The Commissions to be allowed to the Supervisors & Inspectors of Surveys shall be upon the whole amount of the duties collected within their respective Districts and Surveys upon Stills and spirits distilled in the United States which accrued before the first day of July 1792.

2dly—The Supervisors of New Hampshire Connecticut, New York, Vermont, New Jersey and Pennsylvania shall each be entitled to a Commission on the said amount of the Revenue in their respective Districts of one per centum, in lieu of the Commission of one half per centum before allowed.

The Supervisors of Maryland, North Carolina and south Carolina shall each receive a commission, in manner aforesaid, of one and an half per centum in lieu of one per Centum.

The Supervisor of Delaware shall receive a Commission, in the manner aforesaid, of two per centum in lieu of one per Centum.

The Supervisor of Georgia shall receive a commission, in manner aforesaid, of two per centum in lieu of one per Centum.

3dly—To the salaries of the following supervisors there shall be an addition as set against the names of their offices.

The Supervisor of Massachusetts an addition of 200. Drs ⅌ ann.
The Supervisor of Rhode Island   100.   ″
The Supervisor of New York   100.   ″
The Supervisor of Maryland   100.   ″
The Supervisor of Virginia   200.   ″
The Supervisor of South Carolina   100.   ″

4thly—The Collectors of the Revenue shall be entitled to receive the following commissions upon the Revenue on Stills & distilled Spirits, by them collected; that is to say, upon the revenue upon Spirits distilled from foreign materials, two per centum; upon the revenue upon Spirits distilled from domestic materials, and upon Stills employed upon the said materials in Cities, Towns or Villages, four ⅌ Centum; and upon the revenue on spirits distilled from native materials, duties by the gallon of their quantity and upon Stills not in Cities, Towns & Villages, five per Centum; which rate of commission of five per centum shall also be allowed for the collection of the Revenue on Spirits distilled from native materials in places other than Cities, Towns and Villages during the term contemplated in the Act of the President of the United States of the 4th of August 1792 relative to the compensations of the Officers of the Revenue.

5thly—There shall be allowed to the Officers of inspection who have legally signed Certificates to accompany each Cask of distilled spirits, the sum of two cents and one half for each & every cask of spirits distilled in the United States, which has been duly marked & certified.

6thly—There shall likewise be allowed to the Collectors of the revenue for measuring the capacity of each Still and marking the Still and head according to Law, the sum of fifty Cents.

7thly—There shall be allowed to the Officers of Inspection who have legally signed Certificates to accompany foreign distilled spirits, Wines and Teas, the sum of two Cents and one half for every cask or package of the Merchandize above mentioned, which hath been legally marked & certified.

8thly—And whereas inconveniences and injuries to the manufacturers of Spirits of the several kinds distilled in the United States are apprehended from a continuance of the manner & form in which foreign and domestic spirits have been heretofore severally certified, and it has therefore become expedient to revise and adjust accordingly the provision for that service, it is hereby ordered & directed that the Certificates for and to accompany all foreign distilled spirits of every denomination may be signed by the Supervisors of the Revenue, or by the Inspectors of the Revenue for any Survey of Inspection including a seaport, as either may be found expedient, and the compensation of two Cents & one half allowed in & by the Act of the President of the United States of the 4th of August last to those who shall actually sign such Certificates for foreign distilled Spirits shall be forthwith terminated; and in lieu thereof there shall be allowed to the Supervisor or Inspector of a survey who shall sign the same, the sum of one Cent for each Certificate, and to the Inspector of the Revenue for the Post within which the said foreign spirits shall be landed, the sum of one Cent & one half for checking and issuing each of the same.

Given under my hand at Philadelphia on the twenty ninth day of October in the year one thousand seven hundred & ninety two.

Go: Washington

LB, DLC:GW.

1. Although these orders are dated 29 Oct., GW received them as an enclosure in Hamilton's second letter of 31 October. For background on their preparation, see GW to Hamilton, 1 Oct. 1792, and note 1. The substance of these orders was incorporated in an abstract that GW submitted to Congress in November (see GW to the U.S. Senate and House of Representatives, 22 Nov. 1792, and note 1).

2. See "An Act repealing, after the last day of June next, the duties heretofore laid upon Distilled Spirits imported from abroad, and laying others in their stead; and also upon Spirits distilled within the United States, and for appropriating the same," 3 Mar. 1791, and "An Act concerning the Duties on Spirits distilled within the United States," 8 May 1792, in 1 *Stat.* 199–214, 267–71. For background on the adoption and implementation of the federal excise tax on whiskey, including "the subdivisions of the several Districts thereof into Surveys, the appointment of Officers, and the assignment of compensations," see GW's Executive Order of 15 Mar. 1791 and source note.

From Alexander Hamilton

Treasury Departmt Octr 31st 1792.

The Secretary of the Treasury has the honor respectfully to communicate to the President an authenticated copy of the Contract for the last Loan made in Holland, for three millions of florins, bearing date the 9th of August 1792, at a rate of four per cent interest, of which Contract a ratification of the President as heretofore, is required.[1]

Alexander Hamilton Secy of the Treasury.

LB, DLC:GW.

1. For the enclosed contract, see the contemporary translation from the Dutch in DNA: RG 59, State Department Letters, Accounts, and Contracts Relating to European Loans. For background on this loan, see Hamilton to GW, 27 Aug. 1792, and notes 1 and 2. Tobias Lear returned the contract to Hamilton on 1 Nov. and informed him "that as soon as he shall have prepared the form of the ratification, the President will execute it" (DLC:GW). See the Ratification Statement that GW signed on 5 Nov. 1792.

From Alexander Hamilton

[Philadelphia] Wednesday Morning 31st Octr 1792.

The Secretary of the Treasury presents his respects to the president of the U: States, encloses the arrangement for retrospective compensations to officers of the revenue, which, agreeably to the intimation of the president, has been retained.[1] Mr Hamilton will wait on the President between 12 & one to give the explanations desired.

LB, DLC:GW.

1. For the enclosed arrangement, see GW's Orders to Revenue Officers, 29 Oct. 1792. Hamilton had retained these orders in accordance with directions given him in GW's letter to him of 1 October.

From Thomas Jefferson

[Philadelphia] Oct. 31. 92.

Th: Jefferson has the honor to inclose to the President some letters just arrived by the Pigou.[1]

AL, DNA: RG 59, Miscellaneous Letters; LB, DNA: RG 59, George Washington's Correspondence with His Secretaries of State; LB (photocopy), DLC:GW.

1. Tobias Lear added "one from Mr Short & one from Mr Pinckney" to the receiver's copy of this letter. Thomas Pinckney, in his letter of 29 Aug. from London, informed Jefferson that the "whole corps diplomatique and all the heads of departments are in the Country; . . . All that I can collect . . . is that the wishes of the people in power are very adverse to the new order of things in France; whether these wishes will, if occasion should require, be converted into active operation comes within the line of conjecture." Lord Grenville's current residence in the country, Pinckney wrote, "has prevented me from bringing forward some matters of business on which I am desirous of conferring with him, particularly on the subject of impressment, for altho' I am not apprized of any instances having lately occurred here, yet the present state of Europe seems sufficiently unsettled to justify the apprehension that marine armaments may take place; and in all events it would be most advantageous to discuss such a subject while no immediate interest gives an unfavorable biass to either party" (*Jefferson Papers*, 24:329–30).

William Short, in his letter to Jefferson of 24 Aug. from The Hague, reported "the arrestation, massacre or flight of all those who should be considered as the friends and supporters of the late constitution in France with a monarch at its head," including the capture and subsequent imprisonment of Lafayette by the Austrians as he and fellow officers fled France to escape arrest by the new government (ibid., 322–25). Jefferson received a second letter from Short on 31 Oct., which also described the recent violence and political changes within France, but apparently Jefferson did not submit this letter to GW (see Short to Jefferson, 15 Aug., ibid., 298–99).

From Thomas Jefferson

[Philadelphia] Oct. 31. 1792.

Th: Jefferson has the honor to inclose to the President two letters just received from Mr Barclay.[1]

AL, DNA: RG 59, Miscellaneous Letters; LB, DNA: RG 59, George Washington's Correspondence with His Secretaries of State; LB (photocopy), DLC:GW.

1. The first of the enclosed letters from Thomas Barclay to Jefferson, written at Gibraltar, was that of 8 Sept., in which Barclay conveyed a detailed summary of the continuing civil war in Morocco, which he had gathered from recent conversations with Francisco Chiappe, an American agent in Morocco. "The Contest," Barclay wrote, "is very doubtful either with regard to the Person or the Time in which it may be determined," and "it would be highly improper" for the United States to approach either side about a treaty "untill matters are ended by the sword or by a Compromise." In the second letter, dated 10 Sept., Barclay outlined Chiappe's proposed claims against the American government for payment of expenses incurred while attending to American interests in Morocco (both letters are in DNA: RG 59, Despatches from Consular Offices and are extracted in *Jefferson Papers*, 24:345–46, 360). For back-

ground on Chiappe's role in U.S.-Moroccan relations, see Giuseppe Chiappe to GW, 18 July 1789, source note.

From Anthony Whitting

Honrd Sir   Mount Vernon Octor 31st 1792
Your Letter of the 21st I had the Honor to receive on Wednesday last with the Bill of Scantling & List of plants from Norfolk these the Gardener had plac'd in the Green House, The Sugar Maple seed (not knowing the time for sowing it) I persuaded the Gardener to sow a part of it imediately & keep the Other 'till Spring The bill of Scantling I took to Alexa. on Friday and inform'd You the price & time it could be deliver'd if I could Get Your Answer this Week which occasioned my writing from thence[1] The White Oak cannot be engag'd there, nor I believe in this Neighborhood I do not perfectly understand the progression mentioned in the Bill 425 ps. of White Oak runing progressively from 12. feet to 20 in length. I Guess may mean an equal Number 12 feet 13—14—15—16 and so on to 20 if it should not be so Should be Glad to be inform'd These as I before mentioned I think must be sawed here McIvir & McKenzie have engaged to deliver the pine Scantling & plank if you Sir approve of the price & time[2]—Boatswain & Charlotte have both had the flux but Charlotte very lightly Boatswain has been bad I sent for Docr Craik last Saturday who gave them Medecine which seemd to relieve them The Docr Orderd them Rice Water but I can find none in the House Charlotte had a sore throat he order'd her Honey & Vinegar of the former there is none likewise, He Scolded said medecine would not cure them if they had not things proper for them likewise He wish'd me to buy a Quantity of Rice says the people in Sickness Ought always to have of it of this I must wait Your direction a Gallon of Honey likewise he says is necessary—He informs me the Major took what honey there was in the House with him it being very proper for his complaint.[3]
We have several Old Horses that are not Worth keeping thro Winter One at Ferry has not done one days work these 18 months 2 at Muddy hole one a horse with the Pole evil[4] which I think will neve Get well the Other an Old Mare was not Capable of work last summer Likewise the Horses calld Old Chatham and the

Lame Horse that used to go in the Waggon now in a one horse Cart, If any thing could be Got for them it might be well but they are not worth keeping after Christmas.

I dont find any of our fields of Wheat turnd out equal to N. 6. frenchs, not even Dogue Run N. 6 (which I thought was an excellent field of Wheat) will not be equal to the above.

I have enclosed the Quantity of Clover seed wanting at the different plants. River plantation & I think Dogue run may be well worth sowing but as to the Others I dont expect much will come from them only the introducing it in the Grounds, Of this You Will please to Consider & let me know Clover seed is very expensive & none can with propriety be sav'd in this part of the Country we have of What was sent last season abt 2½ or 3 bushs. and Shall have (Growing last summer) as much Timothy seed as will be wanted.[5] I am Honrd Sir Your Obdt Servt

A. Whitting

P.S. By the Capn of the Norfolk packet I am informd Major Washington arriv'd at Colo. Bassetts on Wednesday Evening following the Sunday they left Mount Vernon he Continued very well during the passage and in Good Spirits.[6]

ALS, DLC:GW.

1. Whitting received GW's letter of 21 Oct. on Wednesday, Oct. 24. That letter and its enclosed bill of scantling and list of plants have not been found, but a similar list of scantling was in Washington's Plan for a Barn, enclosed in GW's letter to Whitting of 28 October. The letter that Whitting wrote at Alexandria circa Friday, 26 Oct., has not been found. For GW's recent acquisition of sugar maple seeds, see Thomas Jefferson to GW, 16 Oct., and note 2.

2. For GW's more detailed directions concerning the proposed lumber purchase, see Washington's Plan for a Barn, enclosed in his letter to Whitting of 28 Oct. 1792. The Alexandria firm of MacIver and McKenzie, owned by John MacIver and probably James McKenzie, specialized in lumber products (see Miller, *Artisans and Merchants of Alexandria*, 1:305–6).

3. For the absence of Maj. George Augustine Washington from Mount Vernon, see note 6. Charlotte was a seamstress at the Mansion House farm. Boatswain, identified in 1786 as a laborer and in 1799 as a ditcher, also was assigned to the Mansion House farm, as was his wife, Myrtilla (Matilda), a spinner (see Slave List, 18 Feb. 1786, in *Diaries*, 4:277–78; Washington's Slave List, June 1799).

4. Poll-evil is an inflamed or ulcerous sore between the ligament of the neck of a horse and the first neck bone.

5. In the enclosed list Whitting calculated the amount of clover seed required for each farm. He reported that GW would need a total of fourteen bushels of clover seed, but he added: "About 10 bushs of Clover seed I Could

wish to make do by sowing a little of Timothy," already at hand, with the clover seed at River and Dogue Run farms (DLC:GW). For GW's order of clover seed, see his letter to Whitting of 9 Dec. and note 5.

6. Suffering from tuberculosis, George Augustine Washington spent the winter months at Eltham, the New Kent County, Va., home of his father-in-law, Burwell Bassett.

Extracts of Correspondence on Indian Affairs

[October 1792]

General Wilkinson Fort Hamilton—6th Sepr 1792 [1]

Refers to a letter dated 31st Augt from Fort Jefferson— Marched that evening at 9 'Oclock with 26. mounted Infantry and 80 Rifle men, & reached Genl St Clairs field of Action next morning [2]—The road filled up in many places by the floods of last sprg and by Shrubs, grass, & weeds. Intended to reconnoitre as far as the confluence of the St Marys & St Josephs Rivers & to return by the most direct Rout—Prevented—Sent an Officer of the Rifle Corps Ensign Flin & 5 volunteers on this Service— Returned himself, & Party to the Incampment of Genl St Clair on the night of the 2d Novr. From hence made a detour E.S.E. & turned the head of the West bra. of the Big Miame River, and descended the same 20 miles abt So. E.—crossed & recrossed it several times & quitting it, on the left, struck it again abt 5 miles above Fort Hamilton where he arrived the 5th in the evening.

The party detached the first of Septr to the St Marys, arrived at Fort Hamilton & made a satisfactory Report the 6th—They discovered that Indian Road branched at the Militia Camp in front of Gen. St Clairs field of Battle—one path inclining West-ward—the other due North—the latter they took & in 4 Miles crossed the same Creek where the Battle was fought—12 Miles further, in the same course crossed the Creek again where it was 12 rod wide—all this distance the ground was high, firm & even; & the woodlands remarkably open. they then changed their course to No. 10 Et still following the Indian path & passed sevl flat Praries but on firm ground for 8 Miles—then went No. 10 Wt & for 3 Miles, grd the same as before. then crossed over a body of low wet land abt 9 Miles—then got upon firm grd & had a very brushy road for 2 Miles—After which the Country rose, be-came undulating and firm, free from Brush, Shrubs felled timber &ca for 5 Miles to the St Mary's where it was 15 or 20 pole wide & the grd at the Spot high & Commanding. Thence on the path down the same No. 25 Wt about 12 Miles, & at the sevl places where they came in view of the River found it free Rapids &ca— and the turnings not acute—Here they crossed the River, and in abt 2½ Miles No. Et course fell in with a Sugar Camp with which Ensign Flin was acquainted and is about 12½ Miles from the old Maumee Village.[3]

Genl Wilkinson thinks he has ascertained the following facts; with a considerable degree of certainty viz.—That the Creek on which Genl St Clair Encamped 5 Miles in front of Fort Jefferson is the *Main* west branch of the Big Miame—wch after runng to the No. Et abt 14 Miles without receiving any lateral branches makes a short and most extraordinary curve—running So. Et— That this branch is navigable to the bottom of this curve— within two Miles of wch it is 20 poles wide—& that from the circumstance of its taking its source in extensive ponds & Praries it is presumable that the waters of this branch keep up steadily during the Months & from the same cause, not subject to violent floods—never swelled above 12 feet perpendicular. That the Enemy had occupied the Banks of this River in many hunting Camps during the past Spring—& that at the most Northern part of the curve before mentioned they had erected a small Village of 12 Cabbins from which went 3 large paths—one No. No. Et—another So. So. Wt and the third running down on the River Bank. That the Course & diste from Fort Jefferson to the aforesaid Village is No. 51 Et 17 Miles—& from Fort Hamilton No. 6 Et 52 Miles over grd in genl level & free from bogs & Praries— That a due East line from Fort Jefferson will strike this branch at 18 miles distance, & that a due So. course, wch was actually run from the centre of this line will strike Fort Hamilton, at 41½ Miles—That the distance from the field of Battle to the St Marys River, is 34 Miles on a line due No. & by the Indn Path wch varies from No. 10 Et to No. 10 W. diste 35 M:—That the St Mary's River is navigable to large Boats, as high up as the point where it is intersected by the Indian path before mentioned—That if the genl course from Ensign Flins crossing of the St Marys, to the confluence of that River & the St Josephs to be No. 25 Et & the distance as is generally believed to be 14 Miles, then the direct course from the field of Battle to the Maumi Villages will be No. 2 Et &

the distance 59 Miles—and by the Road which varies its course from No. 25 Et to No. 25 Wt the distance will be found 61 Miles. That on the same principles the course from Fort Hamilton to the Maumi Villages will be about No. 5 Wt distance on a right line about 123 Miles—and by Genl St Clairs rout (the genl course of wch varies from No. 22½ Wt to No. 25 Et pursuing the Indn Path 140 Miles. Genl Wilkinson discovered in the Creek in front of Genl St Clairs field of Battle 2 pieces of brass Ordnance a Six & 3 pounder.

From the same—17th Sepr Ft W———n

Intended to have discharged all the Scouts employed at ⅚ of a dollar pr day but prevented by the letter from the Secretary at War—still thinks it ought to be done as soon as may be—The Northern tribes can have no idea of Peace—but believes a different Sentiment prevails among the tribes of the Wabash and Illinois Indians—He has no doubt of the Murders of Colo. Harden & Majr Trueman.[4]

The Vice of drunkeness is no more among the Officers who fall under his personal observation—and that the Troops are in a great degree reformed. The plan for the payment of the Troops if it can be carried into effect will cut up a most disgraceful practice of Speculation (or rather peculation) among some of the Company Officers—too long in Exercise.[5] The Infantry which were mounted in the Spring are quite naked—he will cloath them in the best manner he can with the remnant of the Levy Cloathing—hopes for approbation. His corrispondence in future agreeably to the suggestions given will be with the Commander in Chief.[6]

He conceives as that the sword alone can decide the dispute with the Indians— Offers a plan of operations—which is To effect an establishment upon the navigable waters of the St Mary's River before winter sets in, & to employ the inclement season in constructing Batteaux & other Craft suitable to the Navigation, & in such a manner as effectually to masque that measure from the Enemy. Thinks this object may be accomplished without loss of blood, by proper concert between 750 mounted Rifle men, & 9 companies of Infantry—and that a close chain of communication to Fort Jefferson may be established & supported. But the operation should commence as early as possible, & not later than the 1st day of November. The Infantry might insensibly be slipped forward to Forts St Clair[7] & Jefferson when the necessary stock of Provisions Stores & impliments should be accumulated, and every preparation being matured for the operation the Rifle men should be called from Kentucky, and by rapid Marches shd pass Fort Jefferson & attack the nearest Villages of the enemy on the Omee [Maumee]; the Infantry might safely March one day before the Rifle men reached Fort Jefferson, and in their progress, one complete Company should be left to erect a small post at the Creek 5 or 6 miles in advance of Fort Jefferson—another company for the same purpose, at Genl St Clairs Incampment on the 2d of November—a third Company at the 2d crossing of the Creek 4 miles in front of the field of Battle—a fourth Company, three Miles advanced of the 3d crossing of the same Creek—& 5 Companies would then remain for the Post on the St Mary's which might be brought to a state of perfect security against the enemy, on the 5th day after leaving Fort Jefferson: The Act of occupying so many points, almost in the same day, [w]ould tend under any circumstances to distract the Councils of the Enemy; but in this case, the Rifle men pressing forward, would attract their whole attention, and that Corps having ravaged the Settlemts on the Omee in the Vicinity of Au Glace, should file off to the right & marching up the River of that name wd intersect Genl Harmers Route abt 60 miles So. Et of the Maumi Villages, by which they might return to Fort Washington & be discharged;[8] This movement would naturally draw the enemy to that quarter, and would give time for the completion of the chain of Posts proposed to be established. It should be stipulated that the Contractors is to deposit five months provision on the ground where each Post is to be erected for the garrison of such Post—and on the day on which the erection thereof may be commenced—and as the Season will be rigorous & the Troops exposed to extreme hardships, a quantity of extra cloathing, should go forward, particularly shoes, Socks, Watch Coats & blankets—The Officer destined to Command in this enterprize should have discretionary powers, either to execute or abandon it at his will.

No Provision by the Act of the 5th of March is made for forage to the general Staff—nor Rations nor forage for the Adjt & Inspector Genl; the Surgeon Genl—the D.Q.M. Genl or the principal Artificer or his second.[9]

The Kentucky Mounted Rifle men under Captn [Daniel] Barbee (an Officer of merit) has this day (17th Sep.) been mustered to the 20th Instt & are discharged—He shall retain Ensign Flin and 15 of the Columbia Militia in Service until the arrival of the Corps which he expects from Kentucky to supply Mr Barbee's place. the activity of the enemy rendering this necessary for his communications until he is reinforced from Pittsburgh.

Mr Shaw Eustinale—20th June 1792.

Seems to condemn Govr Blount for not coming to the meeting at Coyattee at the time appointed.[10]

Proceedings at the same place—held the 26th June—1792. letter dated 4th July. Dissatisfaction expressed by the little Turkey in behalf of the 4 Nations of Indians to the Southward respecting the boundary lines between them and us—as fixed by treaty.[11]

They want the following line to be established "From Campbells line to the crossing of Cumberland River; and from thence to the big Savanna, called the Barrens of Cumberland; and to keep along the said Savannah on the dividing Ridge between Green and Cumberland Rivers a middle course to strike the River Ohio."—If they could obtain this they would give up all claim to the Big Island in Holstein although their claim to it is a just one.

The whole Nation (Cherokees) says the little Turkey are much disturbed at our Navigation of the Tennessee. & at the idea of our settling the Muscle Shoals. They object because it is the commn hunting ground of the 4 Nations. They likewise object to the sale of Occochappe or bears Creek Station as that is the common property of the 4 Nati[o]ns.[12]

The little Turkey in behalf of his Nation, recommends for compensation, a Magistrate of the name of Thos Gagg;[13] not only for past services but for services which he may yet be called upon to render Mr [Benjamin] Hawkins is well acquainted with him—and to his recommendation he would submit for a character.

The Cherokees promised at this meeting to give up the captives in their possession. and to compell a return of the horses stolen by their people.

Mr Shaw—Eustinalie—10th July 1792

Chinibie the great Natchie Warrior, gives assurances of his continued friendship; but wishes & hopes that the boundary line may be altered agreeably to the prayer of the Cherokees. and the desire of his own Nation (Creeks) being their common hunting ground also.[14]

Wishes the President of the U. States wd interfere in the Trade carried on in his Nation which they find exceedingly oppressive.[15]

Thinks Bowles was employed by the British—& when his papers were seen by the Spanish Govrs at New Orleans and the Havannah Was treated with respect.[16]

From the same person & place 23d July.

Intend to get all the half breed Indians to live in one town that their weight may be greater than it is in their present state of dispersion through the different towns.

The Indians will expect an answer to the proposed alteration of the boundary lines and if not complied with—the refusal softened as much as possible.

From the same person & place 29th Augt 1792 [17]

The Creek Indians steel, or take horses from the Cherokees.

Have killed & scalped a Mr Ramsay a respectable Trader by his own house in the Nation, & another person who had just arrived from Charleston.

They openly avow their intention to kill every white man they meet. Adding that such is their orders. The Spanish liberality in supplying them with ammunition is supposed to be the cause of the present disorders—together with their intreggues. hopes his conjectures may not prove true respecting the coalition between them and Bowles.

Thinks the greater part of the Cherokees wish for, & would maintain peace if the Creeks would let them alone.

From Mr Shaw—Hopewell 20th Sepr 1792.[18]

About the 25th of August the lower Town Cherokees held a talk & were but too unanimous for War.

When the News of it reached Eustinaulee the Indians there gave him notice that it was time for him to leave the Nation—& afforded him an Escort before which for a fortnight he had been confined to his House by the Creeks.

The Chiefs of the Cherokees sent a letter by him to Genl Pickins with assurances of their Attachment to the U. States & his own Person. as also of their entire disapprobation of the conduct of the lower Towns.

Mr Shaw thought it but reasonable to give them assurances of protection, provided they followed his advice.

Mr [James] Cary the Interpreter has been left in the Nation (as one of themselves) & is charged to give information of what is going forward to Governor Blount, Genl Pickens & himself.

He expects the Peaceable Cherokees will move towards the Hopewell frontier. Having the highest confidence in Genl Pickens & a great veneration for his character.

The lower town Cherokees will be assisted by the Creeks & about 40 Shawanees—the whole probable number abt 400.

They had determined to start the 4th instt (Sepr) but he has reason to believe they did not set off so Soon. Their object is either Cumberland or Powells Valley—both in the So. Western territory.

The causes of these hostile measures he ascribes to Spanish machinations—of this he has no doubt—A letter at one of the Public meetings of the Indians, upon the return of John Watts from Pensacola gave assurances of supplies of Arms and Ammunition to regain their former situation; for that the Spaniards took pity on the Indians.[19]

He cannot help thinking that their is a good understanding between the Spaniards and Bowles in the pretended Capture of the latter.

The Creek Chiefs were expected back from Pensacola about the 15th of Sep: when it was expected they wd generally commit hostilities. They boast of a general Confederacy of the Southern Indians but two thirds of the Cherokees are friendly at present.

Thinks a speedy & vigorous War necessary—& the sooner it is undertaken the better—because many are now Neuter that may hereafter be involved, & obliged to take an Active part against the U. States—and especially too while the content of the Spanish support is uncertain.

Letters from Govr Blount.[20]

Knoxville 31st Augt 1792

A full representation of Chicasaws at the Conference of Nashville—Not many Choctaws—attributed to Spanish Influence. Minutes of wch will be forwarded by Mr Ellison.[21]

Strong assurances of Peace & friendship from both were given.

The Cherokees as well as the Creeks commit depredations & deserve to be punished—that is the Young & unruly parts of them—the Chiefs to a man (except *double head*) want to live in peace & friendship with us[22]—The Creeks are at the bottom of the evil. He will forward a state of the 4 Southern Nations & will be as particular as his information will allow him—Sends a list of the Killed & wounded in his territory since the Month of Jany 1791.

From Govr Blount—[23]

To—The little Turkey—13th & 14th of Sepr 1792.

Assures him, that the Upper Cherokees, if they remain at home and do not join the lower Towns, may live in Peace, & securely.

That he is building Forts on our side of the line and desires the Indians may not come near them, for fear of Accidents. But, if any of them want to come in to the Settlements of the Whites, to do it along the great Road by Major Craigs.[24]

That he has heard of the war party being stopped by the Bloody fellow, Glass & Jno. Watts.[25]

To—The Glass—13th Sepr

Nearly to the above purpose—and, That he had never heard of the threat reported by Codeatoy to have been made by Genl Robinson [26]—but Genl Pickens did, & spoke to them both on the Subject—Codeatoy must have misunderstood the talk; but at any rate Genl Robinson was subject to his orders, & he ought to regard any talk that did not come from him—the Presidt of the U. States or the Secrety of War as he could not act without orders from one or the other of them or transact any business with the Indians but under such authority.

Explains the treatment the White Mankiller met with into a drunken frolic—& reconciliation afterwds.[27]

To—The Bloody fellow—13th Sepr

Expressive of the pleasure stopping the war party has given him.

Denies positively that any encroachment has been made on the Indian side of the line—or a single house built since the treaty entered into by him in behalf of the U. States.[28]

The White people are not as much to blame as the Cherokees—having killed no Indians except in defence of their persons & horses—whilst *he* knows how many of them have been killed and captivated—many of them helpless Women & Child⟨ren⟩ and the number of horses stolen, according to a long written Acct which he well send to the President—that he may judge who is to blame.[29]

requests the B: fellow would keep his people from Cumberland; and in that case he will answer that, no disturbance by words or Acts shall be given from that quarter to the Indian Settlements.

Forts will be built, & strongly garrisoned for defensive protection.

The White Mankiller, and the other person who lost horses have no cause to complain—reasons assigned.

He has told no body that he was displeased by the Cherokees having talks with the Spaniards—but expected that he—the bloody fellow—would have related what had passed at them. He & Watts were both invited to the Treaty at Nashville—but as the latter chose to attend the meeting with the Spaniards at Pensacola he certainly expected to know what passed at it.

Informatn given by the Red Bird a Cherokee[30]

To Major Craig—4th Septr—viz.—that 6 or 7 Indians were out in order to do mischief. part of them Shawanees & part Cherokees from running water or Nickajack.

A few days afterwards Cockran was shot at.[31] Reasons—and said that Jno. Watts had been to Pensacola—that he brought with him Seven horse loads of Ammn and as many Accoutremts as were sufficit to equip 200 horsemen—Swords, &c.—and that Watts was appointed to Command the Creek & the Cherokees who should be called into the field & be for war; and that the Creek Nation had met in Council & agreed to the appointment. By harrassing the frontiers near the upper towns of the Cherokees they meant to draw the White people on those towns & thereby engage them in the war contrary to their inclination.

That the Party who had Assembled for War was not stopped so much by the Bloody fellow, Glass & Jno. Watts as by Unanecata who returned from Knoxville just as they had Assembled. That the Headmen of the other towns sent talks to the 5 lower towns to suspend their hostilities until their Corn was ripe lest the White people should come & destroy it, and they, thereby be unable to stand both *hunger* & *cold*—But the Red Bird does not know whether this advice proceeded from policy to defer—or willingness to proceed at a more eligable season.

Willi[a]m Cockrans deposin

Gives an Acct of his being stopped by the call of a Man on horseback—a half-breed Indian—and then fired upon by three Indians—one Ball through his hat, & another thro' his Jacket.

Governor Blount—20th Sep.[32]

Encloses minutes of the Conference at Nashville with the Chicasaw & Choctaws. only 110 of the latter Chiefs included. The acct of Mr Foster will best explain this. Conduct of Mr Smith.[33] Choctaws might have been brought, had it not been for these disputes, to War against the Northern Indians—Might still be employed against their old enemies the Creeks if they were furnished with Arms and Ammunition—They are poor & have not the means of providing either—Do not like the Spaniards; but from their dependent situation are obliged to preserve the appearance of friendship towards them. Would be glad to have their Trade and Supplies from the U. States in preference.

Spanish Treaty by Govr Guioso at the Natches a relinquishment by the Choctaws of a large tract of Country beginning at the mouth of the Yazoo thence 10 miles up it—thence So. Et to a River which empties into lake Ponchartrain (he believes called Midway) and down that River. This made by the Indians in the Spanish Interest and highly disapproved by the rest.[34]

Both Nations (Chickasaws & Choctaws) gave at the Nashville conference, the strongest assurances of friendship for the U. States; & contentment for the goods they had received at that meeting.

The Piemingo party of the Chicasaw Nation, which is much the strongest, repeatedly assured him, & Genl Pickins, that if war took place between the U. States & the Creeks & Cherokees (wch they were sure would be the case) that they wd join the U. States —& that the Spaniards were urging those two Nations to acts of hostility agt this Country.[35] Enclosures.

Fosters Report. 29th July

The substance of this is related in the preceeding letter of Governor Blount's, except that when he first conversed with the Indians they seemed keen for war against the Northern Indians, but on their way to Nashville changed their tune.

The Conference[36]

Contained little more than assurances on both Sides of friendly dispositions—an explanation of boundary—and a dereliction on the part of the Indians to the establishment of a trading Post at the Mouth of Bear Creek. also want of Implimts.

Goverr Blount—22d Sep.

Enclosing the Petitions of Jane Brown & Margaret Gibson to have their Sons in captivity released.[37]

From the same 26th Sep.[38]

Encloses the information of Joseph Derague and Richd Findleston—which he thinks may be relied on[.] Letters from the Little Turkey, Chief of the Cherokees. The Boot, and the two Interpreters of the U. States—viz.—James Carey & Jno. Thompson. inform that the 5 lower towns of the Cherokees have declared war against the U. States.[39]

Carey makes the Party going to war 300—others 500, and some 600—including 100 Creeks to be commanded by Jno. Watts. Destination against Cumberland or the Frontiers of Knox County.

Genl Sevier makes the Numbers 600, part of whom are mounted on horses.[40]

The Regiment of the County Knox ordered into Service for its defence, for a few days, until the destination of the Indn force is ascertained—And General Robinson of Miro [Mero] district was ordered to put that Quarter in the best state of defence. And the Colonels of the sevl Counties of Washington district were ordered to be in readiness to march at the shortest notice.

He thinks the Stroke will fall on Cumberland District which is unable to bear it.

Orders to Majr Sharpe—the number there mentioned difficult to obtain from Washington to go to Miro.[41]

The Cherokees have never complained of a single infraction (on our part) of the treaty of Holstein.

Enclosures in the above letter—datd 2 Sepr

Little Turkey—The 5 lower towns will go to war the 8th of this month by themselves; without the consent of the Nation—You may know the good from the bad—do not come to war against the good.

The Spaniards have given them ammunition and Guns, Hatchets Knives &ca—and told them not to go to war, but to keep them in reserve by them. You may blame no body for all this but the Spaniards—We look on you to be our friend—we have done all in our power to keep the lower towns from War—but they threaten us if we write or give any information to strip & perhaps kill us—but I will give informn Notwithstanding—Let me know if we may remain in safety that are disposed for Peace.

Boots, or Chuleoah—2d Sep. 1792.

He, and all the good men have given out good talks & have endeavored to keep the bad ones from war, but are unable to do it—wants a gun, as a compensation for accompanying Mr Heth to the Creek Nation[42]—promises friendship and refers to the little Turkey for particulars.

James Carey—Estanaule. 7th Septr 1792.

Mr Thompson sent Express to him by the little Turkey to go to Govr Blount—but dare not for his life—sends an Indian to the Hanging Maws where he is to wait for an answer—give him two blankets.[43]

The five towns on the River have declared war against the U. States—This quarter of the Nation is entirely for Peace.

John Thompson—Turkeys town 2d Sepr 1792

The Indians on the Big River—or 5 lower towns will on the 8th of this month fall on the Settlements but what part he knows not—this is the truth—The bad Indians want the Whites to fall on the peaceable Indians & will endeavor to effect this—The Creeks will do their part. The Spaniards are to blame. They have given the Indians Guns, Hatchets & Knives, but not to go to War with, but to keep as a reserve.

The peaceable Indians want to know if they can with safety stay in their towns—It may be depended on these Indians will be at Peace if the Whites do not come against them. Wants to be ascertained of this matter.

Genl Sevier—Little River. 10th Sepr 1792

This moment arrived from the Cherokee Nation—Many of the Cherokee chiefs at Chota informed him that the 5 lower towns had, to the number of 600, actually gone to War against the U. States and were determined to give a severe blow somewhere. 100 of them well mounted Watts Comr of the whole. 100 Creeks included. Other parts of the Nation are disposed to Peace. Observe that the 5 lower towns, spoken of, on the Tennessee are composed of the 12 lower ones on it & in the vicinity. The P.S. explains this—into no more than five.

Governor Blount Knoxville 15th Sep.[44]

Esquaka—otherwise the Bloody fellow & Glass write on the 10th from the Lookout Town—that they & John Watts & other head men had prevailed on the Party that were going to War to disperse & go peaceably to their Hunting.

The above information induced him to discharge the Regiment of Knox, & to dispatch an Express to Genl Robinson of Miro District with orders to discharge such of his Brigade as may be in Service under his order of the 11th instt—but, still harbouring doubt of the good intention of the Indians, as mischief & murders had been committed he should order an additional Number of Militia into Service for a 3 Mo: tour.

James Alexander Douglass a Scotchman, a Jesuit bred, understands Spanish, and his lived many years among the Indians, is the Person he has engaged to attend the Meeting of the Indians & Spaniards at Pensacola—He has been a tutor in Genl Pickenss family & recommended by him.

Enclosures—

Bloody fellow—Lookout Mountain 10th Sep.

Is in bad health—Overtook the young Warriors—a long time before he & the other head men cd put a stop to their intended proceedings—Much pitied the helpless people that must have suffered on both sides had they proceeded.

Charges our people with building houses on their land contrary to the assurances given by the President—This is not what was agreed upon & what the sevl Governors were to be informed of.

Sees no reason why Govr Blount shd be displeased at their holding talks with the Spaniards their neighbours as they do not want to be at War with any body if they can avoid it.

Thinks it more the White People's fault than theirs that these disturbances happen, as they are constantly encroaching upon, & sending threatning talks to them.

Desires they may be restrained from doing the Indians injury. and that he would let the Cumberland people know that if they are annoyed it will not be by the Cherokees in future.

The White mankiller thinks it hard, his loosing his horses at their place—the other fellow also—send them to the hanging Maw.

From the Glass. 10th Septr 1792.

The Young men who had assembled for war & which he—the Bloody fellow &ca had stopped—were provoked to it by a threatning message from Genl Robinson; who had declared that, as numbers of People in the District of Miro had been killed, & he expected more would be so, that upon the next blood that should be shed, he would Sweep their Country clean. This threat was brought by Codeatoy from the Conference at Nashville and as they expected the Creeks would repeat their hostilities & they be involved they be the sufferers—their Young men had determined to strike.

They desire no more threatning talks may be sent to them. Nor, that our People may be suffered to go among them, except on business; and then to Estanaula only. If the Indians have Beaver or any thing else to dispose of, let them come to the Settlement with it.

The White Mankiller from the Turkeys Town has been while in the Inhabitants severely threatened. arrangements for the defence of the frontiers—Want of arms—Scarcity of Powder & Lead in Miro District. Wants arms &ca sent. Many valuable men (if War should be inevitable) may be raised in the District of Washington (Virginia)—In those of Salisbury & Morgan in No. Carolina and that of 96 in So. Carolina to serve as Militia under Genl Pickins—The lowest terms on wch he has been able to supply the Militia by contract is 12 Cents pr Ration.

Richd Finnelsons—Informn [45]

Is very minute—The substance of it is to shew the designs of the Spaniards to stimulate the 4 Southern Indian Nations to break with the united States, & to make war against them—the means they have made use of to accomplish this and the effect it has had upon the Creeks & Cherokees—with the preparations of the latter to invade our Settlements. Govr of New Orleans [Baron de Carondelet]—Commandant at Pensacola &ca all concurring.

Breath—or—Charley—15th Sepr [46]

Many parties of Creeks have passed through their Towns to war against the Cumberland Settlement—& several hundreds have crossed the River below—John Sevier &ca have threatned the Cherokees—this ought not to be unless he is in earnest.

Jas Carey—Eustanaule 15th Sep. [47]

Eight Creeks brot a boy Gallaspy to his Ho.—With much difficulty, & giving a horse £15 Sterlg and 250 lbs. of leather he had obtained him—The Big river (Tenessee) Indians are much taken with the Spanish talks—the Expedition, however, is put off as yet—Govr Blount in answr is glad Gallaspy is recovered but, not by purchase—The U.S. will take a difft mode to recover their prisoners.

Joseph Deraque's information—15th Sepr

He was in the Employ of a Mr Faget; who on the 16th of June left red river & proceeded down the Cumberland for New Orleans. [48]

Coming near Lance le Grace,[49] he, with the rest of the Boats Crew, were directed by Fagot to say, that the people of the U. States from Cumberland & Kentucke were preparing to Attack the Spanish Settlements—Fagot at this place recd a large Packet for the Baron de Carondelot at New Orleans—which, when he delivered, he told the same tale as to the hostile intentions, of the U. States' intention to attack them. He was sent from hence to desire the Southn Indians—more particularly the Creeks, Cherokees and Choctaws—to come to him and get Arms & Ammunition to war with the People of Cumberland & Holstein—that the land were theirs, & he would furnish them with means to defend it—to be active & unanimous in going to war. Between Pensacola & the Creek Nation he met about 300 of that Nation going to Pensacola for Arms &ca to go to war against the U. States— and that by the directions of the Spanish Officers—Oneal at Pensacola told him he had orders to excite the Creeks Choctaws Cherokees & Chicasaws to war against the U. States[50]—though he doubted whether the last would join—The Creeks when they arrived among them were found generally preparing for war only waiting the arrival of the Ammunition—Willstown was the first Cherokee Settlement he came to (the 2d instt Sepr) where at least 600 warriors were assembled for war[51]—Watts, Taylor, Tatlontiske, White Owl's Son[,] Dragging Canoe, the Glass & others at their head—but vehemently opposed by the bloody fellow— He was informed that a 1000 Creeks would be in acts of hostility this Moon.[52]

Fagot did not pay him his wages—He was promised 500 dollars & Finniston 400 for their services by the Baron de Carondelet.
Govr Blount[53]
In the character given by him of the Cherokee Indian Chiefs recites what had been their conduct—and what he supposes to have occasioned the change in it—to wit Spanish promises— presents, &ca.
Govr Blount—27th Sep.[54]
Has determined to call into the Service, for the protection of the Frontiers, in addition to the Troops mentioned in his letter of yesterday. Seven companies from the difft Counties—one for 3 Months & the others for 6 weeks—besides the Green County Troop of Cavalry making in the whole (all of the District of Washington) besides Sharpes Battn (whose times will expire on

the 11th of Octr) fourteen Companies of Infantry & the Troop above—with the necessary field Officers to be commanded by B: Genl Sevier.

Govr Blounts—dispatches[55]

He has had a meeting with hanging Maw, John Watts & Jno. Taylor (Cherokee Chiefs)—the two first unwilling to go to War against the Western Indians—the latter inclined to the measure—to be lieutt under Jno. McKee a Trader of Chota.[56]

He has promised Taylor the command of this Company if he can raise it. This was going too fast—and this appointments ought to be left to the arrangements of the Indians themselves—if they will adopt the plan.

He has written to the Little Turkey suggesting the idea of the young Warriors joining our Troops against the Western Indians, & requests a meeting with him and the other Chiefs of the Nation (principal chiefs) at nine mile the first of May (the house of Majr Craig's).

Proposes at this meeting, among other things, to pay them the 1000 dollars annuity—Is not this done already?

He ought to be Instructed not to attempt to extend the line that was established at the Treaty.

Persons killed in the district of Miro—other mischiefs done—supposed by Indians at Lan's legrace—Robinson, a Brigr Genl had written to the Spanish Commander there[57]—& proposes to Govr Blount that he should do so likewise.

Robinson wants to have the distribution of Spirits Ammunition to the Indians—and an Armourer to their Guns.

Treaty, or conference proposed to be held at Nashville with the Chicasaws in June next. at wch to obtain a cession of ground for a Post at the mouth of Duck Creek instead of Bear Creek.[58]

He could get an Officer who would raise twenty four men to Garrison it. Proposes to hold a Treaty with the Choctaws also at the place & time above mentioned.

He has submitted a plan of defence for protection of the frontiers of the So. Western territory and hopes it will be approved.

Majr Gen ⟨Wayn⟩e. 21st Sepr 1792[59]

Mr Butler is only 19 years of age. highly spoken of. Too few Officers in the establishment of the Legion—A Captn Lieutt with the pay of Lieutt is suggested—In that case the present Lieutts might receive brevets of Captns—the Ensigns & Cornets that of

Lieutts—and an Ensign appointed to each Company. this, at first view may appear a heavy expence, but &ca &ca. At *all events* the Majors ought to have Lieutt Col. brevets.

Genl Wayne. 28th Sepr.[60]

The complaint of the Lieutt of Westmoreland is idle. but all the Continental Troops would not answer, unless the people had Militia, & two or three distributed to each farm to assist at harvest, seeding &ca.

Lieutt Staats Morris appointed Dy Judge advocate & Captn Edwd Butler D. Adjt & Inspector—both Pro: tem.[61]

From the same—3d Octr[62]

Will not animadvert upon the change in the Sentiments & conduct of Captn Brant and the Six Nations or on the views of the British—but is sure we shall have no peace with the Indians until they are drubbed into it.

From the same 5th Octr

Has anticipated the order to ascertain as far as possible the strength of the confederated Indians and will continue his exertions to effect this desirable object.

He will be obliged to discharge many of the Men who never *were* nor never *will* be fit for Ser.

Sundry vacancies in the Legion in lieu of resignations.

Sergeant Torry recommended by Majr [Michael] Rudolph to fill a vacant Cornecy. Mr McLean a Volunteer recommended to him by some of the most respectable characters in New york for a Commn.[63]

There will be some difficulty before the Legion will be purged of characters who never were fit to hold Commissions in it.

From the same—12th Oct.[64]

Will give due consideration to the Presidents letter respecting the disposition of the Troops on the Ohio during the Winter;[65] & will, as desired give his sentiments thereon.

Gives a copy of his orders respecting the Supplies of Provisions & forage—and requires *explicit* directions on this head.

Sends a Copy of May's deposition wch he believes to be true and of the Genl Orders for promotion & appointment of Offic⟨er⟩s to vacancies.[66]

Deposition of Wm May 11th Oct. 1792.[67]

Sent out as a Deserter by Genl Wilkinson for intelligence from the hostile Indians, on the 13th of April last—Saw Freeman with the French baker & the other person who was sent as a flag and on whose trail he was directed to follow lying dead & scalped.[68] After which he fell in with 3 Mingos—& then elevn Chippawa's who made a prisoner of him and carrd him through Genl St Clairs field of Battle, threatned to kill him—Saw three field pieces and carried first to a little Village burnt by Genl Harmer 57. miles from the field of Action lying on the St Josephs—then struck across the Country 50 Miles, & fell in with a Delaware Town on the Tawa river—carried down by the side of it through several little Villages ten Miles to a trading town where many of the principal Trade⟨*mutilated*⟩ among whom are Messrs McKenzie, Donnals, W⟨*mutilated*⟩ and two of the name of Abbet. At this place the River Glaze forms a junction with the Tawa and is the principal Town, or Indian head Quarters—where there were 3,600 warriors—who draw daily rations to that amount & comes from Detroit.[69] That he was employed 3 Mos. in the transport Service on board a Schooner that carried about 160 barrls that he made a trip generally in from 8 to 12 days—That Alexr McGee is the principal Indn Agent and keeps his Stores at the Rapids 16 Miles above the Mouth of the River—which from Detroit is 108 Miles or 90 along the Lake & 18 up the River to Detroit. That Majr Trueman & his Servant boy Lynch's Scalps were carried to Detroit on board the Vessel on which he was after havg passed the hands of McGee—the manner of taking them he relates—that he was told Colo. Hardins Scalp was also carried to the place of Indian Rendezvous. That the Papers of both Truemn & Hardin were sent to Detroit.[70] That a Captn Brumley of the 5th British Regimt was in the Action—That Simon Girty told him there were 1200 Indians at the place—but 300 did not engage having cha: of their horses. that 300 more under Lt Silvy were coming up but had not joined[71]—That the hostile Indians say they are to be joined by 17 Nations in case of War. Among whom are now at the Glaze the Putawatamies, Shawanees, Miamies, Tawas, Wyendots, Delawares, Munseys, Attawas & Chippewas— That 10 chosen Indians were sent to accompany 3 Creeks to the Creek Nation with 17 Horses loaded with presents among which were a great many gold & Silver laced cloaths sent on board the Schooner from Detroit. That these Cks were in the late Action and it was expected a great number wd join the Northern Indns agt the U. States.

That it w⟨*mutilated*⟩mmon opinion and the common conversation, ⟨*mutilated*⟩ no peace would take place unless the Ohio was established as a boundary, between the Indians & Americans. Canada and all other Indns Assembled and Assembling at Au Glaze were unanimously of this opinion and that all the Indian Nations will confederate to effect this nor return till it was accomplished having brot their families from a distance for this purpose.[72] That the Cornplanter with about 300 Indns from Canada were at Fort Erie the 5th of Sepr 100 of them were Senecas —He dont think they will let the Cornplanter return unless he agrees to join them should they decide for War. That Captn Brant returned from Fort Erie to Niagara—said he was too sick to go on—that he did not look sick & is of opinion that he was affraid to go to the genl Indian Council. That Simon Girty was on the 25th of Sepr with 247 Wyendots & Mingos, & two guides, Darling of Captn Strongs Company, & Smally who went with Majr Trueman as an Interpreter to march in order to make a stroke at the Pack horses between Fort Hamilton & Fort St Clair; or, failing in that at the settlemt of Columbia and to do every mischief in his power. That Girty was sent on that business by Colo. McGee. That he (May) got a passport from the Commandant of Detroit and arrived at Fort Erie the 5th of Sepr—On the 9th he got another Passport from the Officer Comg at Niagara.[73] And on the 17th one from Genl [Israel] Chapin. The above taken at Pittsburg by Genl Wayne 11th of Octr.

AD, DLC:GW.

1. Neither James Wilkinson's letter of 6 Sept. nor his letter of 17 Sept., which GW also extracted in this document, has been identified. Both letters presumedly were written to Secretary of War Henry Knox.

2. Fort Hamilton was established in September 1791 on the east bank of the Miami River at present-day Hamilton, Ohio, about thirty-five miles north of Fort Washington at present-day Cincinnati. Fort Jefferson, built in October 1791, was about forty-four miles northwest of Fort Hamilton. Gen. Arthur St. Clair and his troops were defeated by a confederation of hostile Indians on 4 Nov. 1791 while encamped on the banks of the eastern branch of the upper Wabash River, at the present-day site of Fort Recovery, Ohio. For background on St. Clair's expedition and subsequent defeat, see William Darke to GW, 9–10 Nov. 1791, and source note; "Denny Journal"; Guthman, *March to Massacre*.

3. The "old Maumee Village" was probably Kekionga, located on the banks of the St. Joseph River, about one-quarter mile above its confluence with the St. Marys River. Kekionga and other nearby Indian villages had been destroyed by U.S. troops under the command of Gen. Josiah Harmar in October 1790 (see Guthman, *March to Massacre*, 198; Carter, *Little Turtle*, 90–91).

4. For background on the successful peace mission of Gen. Rufus Putnam

to the Wabash and Illinois Indians in September 1792, see GW to Knox, 3 Sept. (first letter), n.3. For the deaths of peace envoys Col. John Hardin and Maj. Alexander Trueman, see Knox to GW, 16 Aug. 1792, and note 3.

5. For difficulties with paying the army, see Knox's letter of 1 Sept. 1792 to Anthony Wayne in Knox to GW, 1 Sept., n.2.

6. Anthony Wayne was commander in chief of the U.S. Army. For his appointment as major general, see GW to the U.S. Senate, 9 April 1792.

7. Fort St. Clair, which was built in December 1791 on the St. Clair River near present-day Eaton, Ohio, was midway between Forts Jefferson and Hamilton.

8. For Josiah Harmar's unsuccessful expedition in the fall of 1790 against the hostile Indians of the Northwest Territory, see GW to Knox, 19 Nov. 1790, and notes. See also Guthman, *March to Massacre,* 173–98.

9. GW approved "An Act for making farther and more effectual Provision for the Protection of the Frontiers of the United States" on 5 Mar. 1792 (1 *Stat.* 241–43).

10. Indian agent Leonard Shaw's disapproval was directed toward governor of the Southwest Territory William Blount's delay in attending the conference with the Cherokee at Coyatee in May 1792. For the reason for Blount's delay, see the minutes of the Coyatee meeting in *ASP, Indian Affairs,* 1:267–69. Shaw's letter, written at Estanaula, has not been identified.

11. The minutes of the Cherokee national council that met at Estanaula from 26 to 30 June were enclosed in Blount's letter to Knox of 4 July (ibid., 270–73). During this council the Cherokee expressed their unhappiness with the boundary line established in the 1791 Treaty of Holston and claimed, along with the Choctaw, Chickasaw, and Creek Indians, that they "have not room to hunt." For the Treaty of Holston, see Kappler, *Treaties,* 2:29–32.

12. The Chickasaw ceded land surrounding the mouth of Bear Creek (Occochappo), a tributary of the Tennessee River, to the United States in the 1786 Treaty of Hopewell (see ibid., 14–16).

13. Thomas Gegg was one of the signers of the 1791 Treaty of Holston (ibid., 32).

14. Neither Shaw's letter of 10 July nor that of 23 July, which GW also extracted in this document, has been identified. "Chinabie, or the Great Natchez Warrior" was one of the signers of the Treaty of New York negotiated between the United States and the Creek nation in 1790 (ibid., 28).

15. For the Indian trade policy adopted by the U.S. government during GW's administration, see "An Act to regulate trade and intercourse with the Indian tribes," 22 July 1790; "An Act to regulate Trade and Intercourse with the Indian Tribes," 1 Mar. 1793; "An Act for establishing Trading Houses with the Indian Tribes," 18 April 1796; and "An Act to regulate Trade and Intercourse with the Indian Tribes, and to preserve Peace on the Frontiers," 19 May 1796 (1 *Stat.* 137–38, 329–32, 452–53, 469–74). See also GW to Knox, 19 Aug., n.6.

16. For background on William Augustus Bowles's intrigues among the Creek Indians and his arrest by Spanish authorities in late February 1792, see the Secret Article of the Treaty with the Creeks, 4 Aug. 1790, source note, enclosed in GW to the U.S. Senate, 4 Aug. 1790, and Knox to GW, 14 Nov. 1791, n.1. Contrary to Shaw's opinion, Bowles was imprisoned for five years in Spanish prisons in Cuba, Spain, and the Philippines before escaping in 1797.

17. See Shaw's letter to Blount of 29 Aug. in *ASP, Indian Affairs,* 1:278.

18. Shaw wrote this letter, which has not been identified, while at Gen. Andrew Pickens's estate of Hopewell in South Carolina.

19. Cherokee chief John Watts departed in late May "with ten pack horses" for a meeting with Spanish officials at Pensacola in West Florida. He returned home in late August with a large supply of arms and ammunition and promises of additional supplies and protection against American encroachment (see ibid., 327–28).

20. For Blount's letter to Knox of 31 Aug., see Knox to GW, 29 Sept., n.6. Blount's letter was presented to both houses of Congress on 7 Nov. (see GW's Address to the U.S. Senate and House of Representatives, 6 Nov., n.2). For an abbreviated version of Blount's letter and its enclosed list, see ibid., 275–76.

21. The exact date of David Allison's arrival in Philadelphia, with the minutes of the Nashville conference of 7–11 Aug., has not been determined, but he had not arrived by 9 Oct. (see Knox to Blount, 9 Oct., in note 3 of Knox to GW, 9 October). For the minutes, see ibid., 284–88.

22. Doublehead (Chuquilatague; d. 1807) was a leader of the Chickamauga, the Cherokee who had separated from the rest of the tribe during the Revolutionary War and had established what became known as the Lower Towns of the Cherokee—Nickajack, Running Water, Long Island, Crow Town, Lookout Mountain Town—located on or near the Tennessee River near the junction of the Alabama, Georgia, and Tennessee borders. He was known for his fierce opposition to and recurrent attacks on white settlers, both during and after the Revolutionary War. In June 1794 he accepted an invitation to visit GW in Philadelphia and while there agreed to a peace treaty, signed on 26 June, in which the Cherokee affirmed the 1791 Treaty of Holston and the 1785 Treaty of Hopewell and which raised the tribes' annuity from $1,500 to $5,000 (see *JPP,* 309–10; Kappler, *Indian Treaties,* 2:33–34; Heard, *Handbook of the American Frontier,* 1:94–95, 136–37).

23. The following extracts from Blount's speeches to various Cherokee chiefs and from the testimonies of Red Bird and William Cockran were enclosed in Blount's letter of 15 Sept. to Knox (see *ASP, Indian Affairs,* 1:279–82).

24. John Craig lived on Nine Mile Creek, south of Knoxville, at Craig's Station, now Maryville, Tenn. (see Pollyanna Creekmore, "Early East Tennessee Taxpayers," East Tennessee Historical Society, *Publications* 24 [1952], 125–54).

25. Chickamauga chief Glass (Tauquotihee; d. 1819) was a fierce opponent of American encroachment on Indian land during and after the Revolutionary War, but he adopted a more pacific attitude in 1794 when he signed the Tellico Blockhouse peace treaty. After efforts to halt white settlement on Cherokee lands failed, he became an advocate of Cherokee removal to lands west of the Mississippi (see Heard, *Handbook of the American Frontier,* 164–65, 355–56).

26. Cotetoy (Coteatoy) was a Chickamauga Indian (see Brown, *Old Frontiers,* 273). According to Glass's report to Blount of 10 Sept., which also was enclosed in Blount's letter to Knox of 15 Sept., Gen. James Robertson "said that there had been a great deal of blood spilt in his settlement, and that he would come and sweep it clean with our blood" (see *ASP, Indian Affairs,* 1:280).

27. White Man Killer, or Unacata, was a brother of John Watts and participated in the attack on Buchanan's Station on 30 Sept. 1792 (see ibid., 331).

28. Both Blount and Bloody Fellow were signers of the 1791 Treaty of Holston (see Kappler, *Indian Treaties,* 2:32).

29. See "A RETURN of persons killed, wounded, and taken prisoners, from the Miro District, since the 1st of January, 1791" in *ASP, Indian Affairs,* 1:329–31. For the presentation of this report to Congress, see GW to the U.S. Senate and House of Representatives, 7 Dec. 1792, n.2.

30. The Cherokee chief Red Bird was from the town of Chilhowee (Chilhowie) located on the Little Tennessee River in Tennessee (Brown, *Old Frontiers,* 277). His report is dated 15 Sept. (see *ASP, Indian Affairs,* 1:282).

31. GW extracted below William Cockran's deposition of 7 Sept. describing the shooting incident.

32. For Blount's letter to Knox of 20 Sept. and its enclosures, see ibid., 282–88.

33. GW extracted briefly below Anthony Forster's letter to Blount, written at Nashville on 29 July. The letter included an an account of Capt. David Smith's conduct.

34. Manuel Gayoso de Lemos (1747–1799), who was born in Portugal and educated in England, joined Spain's Lisbon Regiment in 1771. Appointed governor of the District of Natchez in West Florida in 1787, he arrived there in 1789, and he became governor general of Louisiana and West Florida in 1797. While serving in those positions, Gayoso fortified the Spanish frontier, concluded treaties with the southern Indians, and intrigued unsuccessfully for the western territories to secede from the United States. In the spring of 1792, Gayoso presided over a conference at Natchez with representatives from the Choctaw and Chickasaw nations, and he successfully negotiated the Treaty of Natchez, signed on 14 May, in which the Indians ceded a portion of their territory to Spain and pledged to "be the constant friends of the Spanish nation" (see *ASP, Foreign Relations,* 1:280).

35. Chickasaw chief Piomingo was pro-American and anti-Spanish in his outlook and actions after the Revolutionary War. He signed the 1786 Treaty of Hopewell ending Chickasaw hostilities with the United States, and in 1791 he led a contingent of Chickasaw warriors northward to join St. Clair's expedition against the hostile tribes of the Northwest Territory. Piomingo visited GW in Philadelphia in July 1794 and confirmed his loyalty to the United States while he was there (see Heard, *Handbook of the American Frontier,* 1:290–91; *JPP,* 312).

36. For an account of the conference held at Nashville from 7 to 11 Aug., see *ASP, Indian Affairs,* 1:284–88.

37. Blount's letter to Knox of 22 Sept. has not been identified. One of the enclosed petitions was probably from Jane Gillespie Brown, the widow of Revolutionary War veteran Col. James Brown (1738–1788). While moving from their home in Guilford County, N.C., to settle near Nashville in 1788, the Brown family was attacked near Nickajack by several Chickamauga Indians. Colonel Brown and two sons were killed, and Mrs. Brown and the five remaining children were captured and dispersed throughout the southern tribes. By 1790 all of them had been released or ransomed, except George Brown who remained a prisoner of the Creek Indians until 1798 (see Brown, *Old Frontiers,* 272–75).

38. For Blount's letter to Knox of 26 Sept. and its enclosures, see *ASP, Indian*

Affairs, 1:288–92. A copy of this letter was sent to Congress on 7 Nov. (see GW's Address to the U.S. Senate and House of Representatives, 6 Nov., n.2).

39. Richard Finnelson, part Cherokee, and Joseph Deraque (Derague), originally from Canada, recently had arrived at Nashville from New Orleans. Boot (Boots; Chuleoah, Chuleowee), a Cherokee chief, had accompanied Cherokee chief John Watts on his trip to Pensacola in the early summer of 1792 (see note 19). In the summer of 1794, Boot went to Philadelphia as a member of the Cherokee delegation that signed a treaty on 26 June confirming the boundaries established in the 1785 Treaty of Hopewell and the 1791 Treaty of Holston (see *JPP*, 309–10; Kappler, *Indian Treaties*, 2:33–34). GW extracted below the enclosed letters of 2 Sept. from Little Turkey, Boot, and John Thompson, and the 7 Sept. letter of James Carey. They are printed as enclosures to Blount's letter to Knox of 11 Sept. in *ASP, Indian Affairs*, 1:276–77.

40. GW extracted below John Sevier's letter of 10 Sept., which is printed under the date of 13 Sept. as an enclosure to Blount's letter to Knox of 11 Sept., ibid., 277.

41. For Blount's muster of militia forces, see his orders to Maj. Anthony Sharpe of 10 Aug. and his letter to Knox of 27 Sept., ibid., 279, 292. See also Blount's letter to Knox of 15 Sept., which GW extracted below.

42. Virginian John Heth, a captain in the 2d Infantry, had received orders in May from Henry Knox to deliver a letter to Alexander McGillivray, "the beloved chief of the Creek nation of Indians, and also, the sum of two thousand nine hundred dollars," the balance due on the annual payment and salaries promised by the United States in the 1790 Treaty of New York. For Knox's instructions to Heth and letter to McGillivray, both dated 31 May 1791, and the U.S. account with McGillivray and the Creek nation, see ibid., 125–27. Knox also wrote Blount that same day requesting him to "provide Mr. Heth guides, and a party of friendly and faithful Cherokees, to escort him" (ibid., 127).

43. Hanging Maw (Scholanuetta, Squollecuttah; died c.1794), a principal chief of the Upper Towns of the Cherokee, had signed both the 1785 Treaty of Hopewell and the 1791 Treaty of Holston.

44. For Blount's letter to Knox of 15 Sept. and its enclosures, see ibid., 279–82.

45. For Richard Finnelson's affidavit, see ibid., 288–91.

46. Breath, a Chickamauga chief from Nickajack, was killed during a militia attack against the Lower Towns on 13 Sept. 1794 (see ibid., 632). Charley, a Chickamauga from Running Water, may have been known as Fool Charles or Captain Charley (see ibid., 291). The report of Breath and Charley was enclosed in Blount's letter to Knox of 7 Oct. (ibid., 293).

47. James Carey's report of 15 Sept. has not been identified. For other accounts of the Gillespie boy's capture and return, see ibid., 294, 329. He may have been the Gillespie whom Blount reported as having been captured by the Creek Indians on 12 Sept. (ibid., 331).

48. Joseph Deraque's report was enclosed in Blount's letter to Knox of 26 Sept. (ibid., 291–92). André (Andrew) Fagot, a French merchant from St. Louis, carried on trade between New Orleans and the Nashville region.

49. L'Anse à la Graisse, on the west bank of the Mississippi River in present-

day Missouri, had been settled originally by French fur traders, but after Spanish rule was established in the upper Louisiana Territory, it became known as New Madrid.

50. Arturo O'Neill (1736–1814), a native of Ireland, joined Spain's Irlanda Regiment in 1752 but transferred the following year to the Hibernia Regiment in which he spent the remainder of his military career. In 1781 Lieutenant Colonel O'Neill participated in the Spanish victory at Pensacola that ended British sovereignty there. He became governor of West Florida a short time later and held that office until 1793, during which time he fortified the defenses of the region and cultivated the friendship and trade of the neighboring Indians. O'Neill then served as captain general of Yucatán and intendant of Tabasco and Laguna de Términos before returning to Spain in 1801. Promoted to lieutenant general in 1802 and appointed to the king's Supreme War Council the following year, he became the first marquis del Norte and viscount de O'Neill in 1805.

51. Willstown was a Cherokee town situated on the Cherokee trace that ran from Tennessee to Pensacola and New Orleans. Located at present-day Fort Payne, Ala., it was the home of Cherokee chief John Watts in 1792.

52. John Taylor, who was part Cherokee, often aligned himself with the Chickamauga. See Blount's favorable assessment of Taylor in his note of 26 Sept. 1792, ibid., 291. Tahlonteskee (d. 1819), a Chickamauga chief and brother-in-law of Doublehead, accompanied John Watts to the 1792 meeting with Spanish officials at Pensacola (see note 19). Although a fierce opponent of American expansion in 1792, Tahlonteskee later cooperated with U.S. officials in obtaining Cherokee land and peacefully accepted the Cherokees' removal west of the Mississippi in the early nineteenth century. Young Dragging Canoe, the son of a Chickamauga war chief of the same name who had died in March 1792, also accompanied Watts to the meeting with Spanish officials at Pensacola in 1792.

53. This section is probably an extract of Blount's note of 26 Sept., which he enclosed in his letter to Knox of that date (see ibid., 291).

54. For Blount's brief letter to Knox of 27 Sept., see ibid., 292. This letter was sent to both houses of Congress on 7 Nov. (see GW's Address to the U.S. Senate and House of Representatives, 6 Nov., n.2).

55. The original dispatches have not been identified.

56. Virginia native John McKee (1771–1832) attended Liberty Hall Academy, now Washington and Lee University. He received a commission from Blount in 1792 to negotiate the U.S. boundary line with the Cherokee in accordance with the 1791 Treaty of Holston (see Blount to Knox, 8 Nov. 1792, ibid., 326). McKee remained active in Indian affairs throughout his life, serving as an agent to the Choctaw and Chickasaw. In 1814 he organized a corps of Chickasaw and Choctaw volunteers to serve with Andrew Jackson's troops against the Creek Indians. One of his last public duties was as a commissioner for the 1830 Treaty of Dancing Rabbit Creek with the Choctaw Indians (see Kappler, *Indian Treaties*, 2:310–17). He also represented Alabama in the U.S. House of Representatives from 1823 to 1829.

57. Tomás Portell was the commandant at New Madrid (L'Anse à la Graisse) from 1791 to 1796.

58. For Knox's rejection of a post at Duck Creek, see Arthur Campbell to GW, 20 Oct. 1792, n.3.

59. For Wayne's letter to Knox of 21 Sept., see Knopf, *Wayne,* 105–7. See also Knox to GW, 29 Sept., n.3.

60. For Wayne's letter to Knox of 28 Sept., see ibid., 107.

61. Charles Campbell was the county lieutenant of Westmoreland County, Pa., in 1792. Staats Morris, a native of New York, who enlisted as a lieutenant in the artillery in 1791, was promoted to captain in 1795 and served until 1802. Edward Butler (1762–1803), a native of Pennsylvania who was a Revolutionary War veteran, served as a captain under General St. Clair in 1791. He was assigned to the 4th Sub-Legion in 1792 and served as its adjutant and inspector general from 18 July 1793 until 13 May 1794. Retained as a captain in the 4th Infantry in 1796, he transferred to the 2d Infantry in 1802.

62. Wayne's letters to Knox of 3 Oct. and 5 Oct., which GW extracted below, have not been identified.

63. For GW's instructions that Wayne gather intelligence about the strength of the hostile Indians in the Northwest Territory, see GW to Knox, 24 Sept., and note 1. In his second letter to the Senate of 22 Feb. 1793, GW nominated Daniel Torrey as a cornet in the cavalry. Torrey was killed on 30 June 1794 in the Battle of Fort Recovery. In his first letter to the Senate of 22 Feb. 1793, GW nominated Pennsylvanian Levi McLean as an ensign. McLean became a lieutenant in 1794 and was discharged on 1 Nov. 1796.

64. For Wayne's letter to Knox of 12 Oct., see ibid., 117–19.

65. A copy of GW's letter to Knox of 28 Sept. had been enclosed in Knox's letter to Wayne of 5 Oct. (see GW to Knox, 28 Sept., n.4).

66. For the general orders respecting promotion, dated 10 Oct., see Burton, "General Wayne's Orderly Book," 394.

67. GW submitted William May's deposition to Congress on 7 Nov. (see GW's Address to the U.S. Senate and House of Representatives, 6 Nov., n.2; the deposition is in *ASP, Indian Affairs,* 1:243–44). May was described in deserter John Smith's deposition of 4 April 1793 as a private in Capt. John Armstrong's company of riflemen in the 1st Sub-Legion who received a reward of "Thirty pounds" and a promotion to "Sergency in a Troop of light Horse" for his duplicity (Cruikshank, *Simcoe Papers,* 1:330). May continued to act as a spy for the U.S. Army until his capture by Indians on 18 Aug. 1794 and his execution the next day (see Carter, *Little Turtle,* 129, 134–35).

68. New Jersey native Isaac Freeman, accompanied by a man named Gerard, was sent as a U.S. peace envoy to the northwest Indians in April 1792. Both men were captured and killed by Indians (see Abraham Freeman to GW, 5 Sept. 1793; Knox to Wayne, 22 June 1792, in Knopf, *Wayne,* 22–23). According to the 22 Aug. 1792 issue of the *Pennsylvania Gazette* (Philadelphia), Freeman and Gerard may have been joined by Dominique Debartzch, a Montreal merchant and fur trader. The reference to "the French baker" may indicate the presence of a man named Perault who lived among the traders at Au Glaize and who supplied bread for the white residents there (see Tanner, "The Glaize in 1792," 25).

69. Au Glaize, the point where the Auglaize River flows into the Maumee (sometimes called the Tawa or Omee) at present-day Defiance, Ohio, was the

site of a French and English trading town and seven villages of various Indian nations. It was the central meeting place for the Indian confederacy that opposed American expansion in the Northwest Territory (see ibid., 15–36). Contrary to article 2 of the 1783 Treaty of Paris, the British retained possession of Fort Detroit at this time (Miller, *Treaties,* 97–98).

70. The papers carried by Alexander Trueman and John Hardin on their unsuccessful missions included "an Address from the President of the United States to all the Western Indians, signed & forwarded by Major General Knox." These papers were sent to Matthew Elliott, the British assistant superintendent of Indian affairs, whose headquarters was at Au Glaize and who forwarded these papers to the commandant at Detroit (see Richard England to Francis Le Maistre, 5 July 1792, in "Canadian Archives. Colonial Office Records: Michigan," 427). For GW's address and Trueman's instructions, see Knox to GW, 1 April 1792, n.2.

71. Joseph Bunbury (d. 1802) was a lieutenant in the 49th Regiment of Foot in early 1775 and probably accompanied his regiment to North America later that year. He was promoted to captain in 1782, and in 1785 he transferred to the 5th Regiment of Foot, which arrived in Canada in 1787. Three years later Bunbury and his regiment were assigned to Detroit where he began his involvement in Indian affairs. In 1796 he became the agent for Indian affairs in Lower Canada, but he returned to settle in England in 1798.

Lt. Prideaux Selby (c.1747–1813), who also was a member of the 5th Regiment of Foot at Detroit in 1790, became assistant secretary of Indian affairs in Upper Canada in 1792. Selby settled at York, Ontario, in 1807. He became a member of the executive council in 1808 and served as receiver general and auditor general until his death.

72. A grand council of members of the Indian confederacy hostile to the U.S. presence in the Northwest Territory was held between 30 Sept. and 9 Oct. at Au Glaize. For the minutes of this council, as recorded by British agent Alexander McKee, see ibid., 483–98; see also the journal of Stockbridge chief Hendrick Aupaumut, an American peace envoy, in Aupaumut, "Narrative."

73. Lt. Col. Richard G. England (c.1750–1812), a native of Ireland, was the commander at Fort Detroit. Having entered the British army in 1765, he arrived in the United States in 1773 as a captain in the 47th Regiment of Foot. Although he was wounded at the Battle of Bunker Hill in June 1775, England participated in the relief of Quebec early in 1776, and he served under General Burgoyne at the Battles of Saratoga in 1777, during which he was taken prisoner by the Americans. Promoted to lieutenant colonel of the 24th Regiment of Foot in 1783, England was sent to Canada in 1789. He was assigned to Detroit in 1792 and oversaw the British evacuation of that post in 1796 before he returned to England. Maj. John Smith of the 5th Regiment of Foot was transferred in the summer of 1792 from his command at Fort Detroit to the command of Fort Niagara, where he remained until his death in November 1795.

To Thomas Jefferson

[Philadelphia] 1st Novr 1792

The enclosed places matters on their true rounds; and in my opinion on a proper footing.[1]

G.W.

ALS, DLC: Jefferson Papers. Jefferson docketed this letter: "recd Nov. 1. 92."

1. Beneath GW's text Jefferson added "this was my answer of Nov. 1. to Viar & Jaudenes." Jefferson wrote the Spanish diplomats José Ignacio de Viar and José de Jaudenes in reply to their letter to him of 29 Oct. (see Jefferson to GW, 29 Oct. [second letter], and note 1). After observing that some parts of their letter "were truly unexpected," Jefferson defended the U.S. treatment of the Creek Indians: "On what foundation it can be supposed that we have menaced the Creek nation with destruction during the present autumn, or at any other time, is entirely inconcievable. Our endeavors, on the contrary, to keep them at peace, have been earnest, persevering and notorious, and no expence has been spared which might attain that object. With the same views to peace, we have suspended, now more than a twelvemonth, the marking a boundary between them and us which had been fairly, freely and solemnly established with the chiefs whom they had deputed to treat with us on that subject: we have suspended it, I say, in the constant hope that taking time to consider it in the councils of their nation, and recognising the justice and reciprocity of it's conditions, they would at length freely concur in carrying it into execution. We agree with you that the interests which either of us have in the proceedings of the other with this nation of Indians is a proper subject of discussion at the Negociation to be opened at Madrid, and shall accordingly give the same in charge to our Commissioners there. In the mean time we shall continue sincerely to cultivate the peace and prosperity of all the parties, being constant in the opinion that this conduct reciprocally observed will most increase the happiness of all" (*Jefferson Papers*, 24:552–53).

From Thomas Jefferson

[Philadelphia] Nov. 1. 1792.

Th: Jefferson has the honor to return the inclosed to the President.[1] the following are the only alterations he supposes might be proper.

pa. 4. line 2. & 3. he thinks it better to omit the passage marked with a pencil.

same page. three bottom lines. he sees no objection to the passage marked.

page 6. & 7. the six lines marked he thinks would be better omitted.

page. 11. line 16. perhaps the expression 'just state of our credit' would be better than 'high state of our credit.' our efforts & our circumstances authorize us to say that we are justly entitled to the credit in which we stand.[2]

AL (facsimile), Charles Hamilton, auction number 147, lot 146, 1 July 1982.

1. The enclosed draft of GW's address to the U.S. Senate and House of Representatives of 6 Nov. 1792 has not been found.

2. For GW's reaction to Jefferson's suggestions, see his letter to Jefferson of 3 November.

To James Mercer

Dear Sir,   Philadelphia Novr 1st 1792.

I pray you to accept my thanks for your obliging attention to my request respecting the conveyance of Lots which I purchased at the sale of Colo. Mercers Estate; and for sending the Deeds from Mr Muse to me. I see no occasion of a Copy of the re-conveyance of the above lots from you to me, as I am persuaded they were drawn with correctness; and because it appears by the Clerks certificate on the back of the Deed to you, that it was duly recorded.[1]

Permit me before I close this letter, to express my regret that want of health, or any other cause should have prevented you from making me the visit you proposed whilst I was at Mount Vernon; and to assure you that it will ever give me sincere pleasure to see you at that place. And I will also unite my regret to yours for the death of our old friend, & acquaintance Colo. Mason.[2] With Affectionate regard I am always—Yours

Go: Washington

ALS, DLC:GW; ADfS, NjMoNP: Smith Collection; LB, DLC:GW. The cover of the ALS is stamped "2 NO" and "FREE" and is addressed to "The Honble James Mercer Esqr Fredericksbg or Richmond."

1. In his letter to Mercer of 3 Oct., GW requested copies of the deeds for the land in Frederick County, Va., that he had purchased in 1774 from the estate of Mercer's eldest brother, George Mercer. Battaile Muse, GW's former land, or rental, agent may have been the conveyor of the missing deeds.

2. For Mercer's ill health and plans to visit Mount Vernon, see James Mercer to GW, 6 Oct., at Mercer to GW, 3 Oct., n.2. Virginia statesman George Mason died on 7 Oct. 1792.

From Samuel Meredith

Sir   [Philadelphia] Thursday Morng Novr 1st 1792[1]
The bearer will deliver agreeably to Mr Lears request 100 White Mulberry Trees taken out of Aspinwalls Nursery, they are untrimmed, as the other parts may be cut off when planted & stuck in the ground to produce Trees as well as the Main Standards,[2] he will likewise deliver half of the Double eared Wheat recd from the Agricultural Society.[3] I have the honor to be with Proper Respect Your Most humble Servt

                                              Saml Meredith

ALS, DLC:GW.

1. The date is taken from the letter's docket.

2. No written request from Tobias Lear to Meredith has been found. An article in the *Pennsylvania Gazette* (Philadelphia) on 13 May 1789 informed readers that "Mr. Nathaniel Aspinwall, full of the spirit of the silk culture, has for this end planted a nursery of fifty thousand trees in New-Haven [Conn.], and another in Kensington [Conn.], and is proceeding in this laudable work." The following year, Aspinwall and Peter DeWitt placed an advertisement in the 28 April 1790 issue of the paper, advising readers that Aspinwall's mulberry trees were available in the area: "THE inhabitants of Pennsylvania and New-Jersey, who wish to promote the agriculture and manufactures of their own country, are respectfully informed, that the subscribers are now ready to supply them with any quantity of young white Italian mulberry trees, from their Nursery, at Samuel Meredith, Esquire's place, or Mr. Robert Towers's, on the Ridge road and Poplar lane, about a mile and a half from the city of Philadelphia." GW shipped the trees by boat to Mount Vernon, and on 11 Nov. he sent instructions for their planting to his farm manager Anthony Whitting.

3. GW forwarded the double-eared wheat to Mount Vernon with instructions for its planting (see GW to Anthony Whitting, 4 Nov. 1792). GW was a corresponding member of two agricultural societies in Philadelphia: the Philadelphia County Society for the Promotion of Agriculture and Domestic Manufactures, to which he was elected in 1789 (see Philadelphia County Society for Promotion of Agriculture and Domestic Manufactures to GW, 4 May 1789), and the Philadelphia Society for Promoting Agriculture, of which he had been a member since 1785 (see Samuel Powel to GW, 5 July 1785).

From James Wilkinson

Sir   Fort Washington [Northwest Territory] Novr 1st 1792
Conceiving that the novelty of the thing may render it acceptable; I have presumed to offer to you, by the Hands of Capt. Prior, two Kegs of Salted Fish, which were taken in the Big Mi-

ami River.[1] And, with the most dutiful attachment to your Person, & the highest veneration for your exalted Station I have the Honor to be Your obliged & faithful Soldier & Servant

                                                                    Ja. Wilkinson

ALS, NIC. The docket reads: "recd Decr 29th 92."

1. Abner Prior (d. 1800), a New York native and Revolutionary War veteran, had been promoted to captain in the U.S. Army on 2 June 1792 (see GW to the U.S. Senate, 22 Feb. 1793). Prior attended the peace conference that Gen. Rufus Putnam conducted with the Wabash and Illinois Indians in September 1792, and he subsequently accompanied an Indian delegation from this conference to Philadelphia, arriving there on 26 Dec. 1792 (see Knox to the U.S. Senate, 8 Nov. 1792, *ASP, Indian Affairs,* 1:319; *Pennsylvania Gazette* [Philadelphia], 2 Jan. 1793). Prior later was wounded at the Battle of Fallen Timbers on 20 Aug. 1794.

From Thomas Jefferson

Sir,   Philadelphia Nov: 2. 1792.

I have the honor to inclose you copies of a letter I have received from the Governor of Virginia and of sundry papers which it covered on the subject of that part of the boundary between that State and the territory of the United States south of the Ohio, which has never yet been authoritatively settled, and to observe that an extension of the same line will form the boundary between the same territory and the State of Kentucky.[1] There being then three parties interested in the establishment of this line, it will rest with the wisdom of the Legislature to take such measures as they shall think best for establishing it by common consent or otherwise for instituting judiciary proceedings for it's establishment, according to the provision made in the constitution.[2] As the papers herewith transmitted will fully explain the case in question, I need not recapitulate their contents. I have the honor to be with sentiments of the most perfect respect and attachment, Sir Your most obedient, and most humble servant

                                                                    Th: Jefferson

LS (letterpress copy), DLC: Jefferson Papers; copy, DNA: RG 46, Second Congress, 1791–93, Senate Records of Legislative Proceedings, President's Messages; LB, DLC:GW; LB, DNA: RG 59, Domestic Letters. Jefferson added the words "The President of the U.S." at the end of the text of the letterpress copy. Jefferson signed the copy in DNA: RG 46.

In 1779 North Carolina and Virginia appointed commissioners to survey their common border west of the Allegheny Mountains along the 36° 31′ parallel. Disagreement between the parties led to the creation of two parallel lines two miles apart, Walker's line to the south and Henderson's line to the north. By the end of 1791 both states agreed to recognize Walker's line as the official boundary.

The creation of the Southwest Territory in 1790 from the western lands ceded to the federal government by the southern states, however, extended the controversy, and the admission of the state of Kentucky, a former district of Virginia, into the union in June 1792 further complicated the issue. The Treaty of Holston with the Cherokees in 1791 added to the confusion and conflicting claims. Virginia's boundary dispute with the Southwest Territory evolved into a dispute with the newly created state of Tennessee in 1796 and was not settled until 1803 when both states agreed to a line drawn halfway between Henderson's and Walker's lines. It was 1820 before Kentucky and Tennessee both accepted Walker's line as their common border. For more information, see Douglas, "Boundaries, Areas, Geographic Centers," 125–27, 129–34, 160–64.

1. Jefferson enclosed a copy of Henry Lee's letter to him of 24 Oct. from Richmond, in which Lee expressed concern about the "establishment of the boundary line" between North Carolina and Virginia. The copies of Lee's enclosed papers include the proceedings of the North Carolina legislature on 11 Dec. 1790; an undated committee report of the North Carolina legislature; "An Act concerning the Southern boundary" passed by the Virginia legislature on 7 Dec. 1791; a summons issued to Can Baily, Charles Wolf, James Anderson, and James Campbell on 18 June 1792 by a court in Sullivan County, Southwest Territory, for failure "to appear at the last General Muster"; a receipt for a fine paid by Charles Wolf to Sullivan County on 4 Aug. 1792; a letter from Gilbert Christian to Arthur Campbell of 8 Aug. 1792; an extract of a letter from William Blount, governor of the Southwest Territory, to Lee of 2 Sept. 1792 advising that he will continue to assert territorial control over the contested area until the federal government instructs him otherwise; depositions from Charles Wolf and James Campbell, both of 6 Sept. 1792, relating to fines imposed by the authorities of the Southwest Territory on residents living on the contested lands; and an undated copy of Joseph Martin's letter to Lee of 20 Oct. 1792 reporting that most of the families living in the disputed area wanted to remain in Virginia (see the letterpress copies of these enclosures in DLC: Jefferson Papers; see also Carter, *Territorial Papers*, 4:200–208, and *Calendar of Virginia State Papers*, 6:106).

2. GW submitted Jefferson's letter with its enclosures to the U.S. Senate and House of Representatives on 9 Nov. 1792.

From Thomas Jefferson

Sir,   Philadelphia November 2d 1792.
The letter of October 29th from messieurs Viar & Jaudenes, not expressing the principle on which their government inter-

ests itself between the United States and the Creeks, I thought it of importance to have it ascertained. I therefore, called on those Gentlemen, and entered into explanations with them. They assured me, in our conversation, that, supposing all question of boundary to be out of the case, they did not imagine their government would think themselves authorized to take under their protection any nation of Indians, living within limits confessed to be ours; and they presumed that any interference of theirs, with respect to the Creeks, could only arise out of the question of disputed territory, now existing between us; that, on this account, some part of our treaty with the Creeks had given dissatisfaction.[1] They said, however, that they were speaking from their own sentiments only, having no instructions which would authorize them to declare those of their Court: but that they expected an answer to their letters covering mine of July 9th (erroneously cited by them as of the 11th) from which they would probably know the Sentiments of their Court.[2] They accorded entirely in the opinion that it would be better that the two nations should mutually endeavor to preserve each the peace of the other, as well as their own, with the neighboring Tribes of Indians.

I shall avail myself of the opportunity, by a vessel which is to sail in a few days, of sending proper information and instructions to our Commissioners on the subject of the late, as well as of future interferences of the Spanish officers, to our prejudice with the Indians, and for the establishment of common rules of conduct for the two nations.[3] I have the honor to be, with the most perfect respect and attachment, Sir, Your most obedient and most humble servt

Th: Jefferson

LS, DNA: RG 59, Miscellaneous Letters; LS (letterpress copy), DLC: Jefferson Papers; LB, DLC: GW; LB, DNA: RG 59, George Washington's Correspondence with His Secretaries of State; LB (photocopy), DLC: GW; copy, DNA: RG 59, Domestic Letters; copy, DLC: William Short Papers. The original of the letterpress copy has not been identified. Jefferson signed the copy in the William Short Papers.

1. For the letter from Spanish diplomats Viar and Jaudenes to Jefferson of 29 Oct., see Jefferson to GW, 29 Oct. (second letter), n.1. For the Treaty of New York, which Alexander McGillivray and twenty-three other Creek chiefs signed with the United States on 7 Aug. 1790, see GW to the U.S. Senate, 4 Aug. 1790, and enclosure, and Proclamation, 14 Aug. 1790, nn.4–5.

2. For Jefferson's letter to Viar and Jaudenes of 9 July, see *Jefferson Papers*, 24:203.

3. See Jefferson to William Carmichael and William Short, 3 Nov. 1792, ibid., 565–67.

Letter not found: from Anthony Whitting, 2 Nov. 1792. GW wrote Whitting on 11 Nov. that he had received "your letters of the 2d and 7th instant."

From James Anderson (of Scotland)

Sir   Edinburgh [Scotland] 3d Novr 1792

I had the honour to receive your obliging favour of the 20th June last some time ago—since which time I have had no opportunities of sending any parcels from hence, which is the reason I have not sooner acknowledged that favour—I am highly flattered with the kind reception you have given to my little work *The Bee* the 7th, 8th, 9th—10th & 11th Volumes of which will accompany this. The former volumes were sent by the way of New york, to the care of Mr Samuel Campbell bookseller there, and I hope have come safe to hand[.]¹ Along with these I send a copy of the pamphlet on wool, which had been formerly mis sent, and have the satisfaction of assuring you that the reasoning in that pamphlet has been fully confirmed by our experience since it was published²—In consequence of selecting fine breeds of sheep we have been able to make broad cloth of the first quality *entirely of our own wool*—tho' it has been certain that for many years past it has been made altogether of Spanish wool without the smallest admixture of our own. The wool of this year is still finer than the last—And there can be no doubt, that with proper attention we shall be able to have finer wool than any that hath hitherto been brought to market in Europe.

I make no apology for stating these matters to *you* As I know your wishes for the prosperity of nations is not confined to one— I shall equally rejoice at hearing of the happiness and prosperity of America as of Britain. Indeed my sole aim in the little work I have attempted is to promote a friendly intercourse among all nations, and to augment the welfare of mankind, without any exception, as much as is in my power. Were my abilities equal to my inclination, this would be conspicuous in every page of the book—I hope you will find if ever you should honour any part of it with a reading that this is its general tendency.

We are distracted in this country at present by an excess of prosperity. From the imperfection of human nature this can in no case be born—and some wild spirits, under the pretexts of promoting, freedom, are, I am afraid preparing the seeds of slavery—I hope I shall not live to see the time, but without some reverse of fortune it will approach. I observe by the gazette of the united states that on your side of the Atlantic sensible people are not without the same apprehensions.[3] That these evils may be averted, and that your valuable life may be long preserved for a blessing to that country is the sincere prayer of Sir Your most obedient and Most Hue Servt

Jas: Anderson

I am not able to send any articles of importance respecting agriculture by this packet—Indeed I have rather avoided entering on that subject, tho' it has been my favourite pursuit all my life, fearing it might prove disagreeable to many of my readers—Dr Coventry, professor of Agriculture here, and myself—have it in contemplation to begin a small periodical work calculated to promote enquiries on that important subject alone—but we have not yet finally determined upon it.[4]

ALS, DLC:GW.

1. GW had received volumes 1 to 6 of the *Bee, or Literary Weekly Intelligencer* in June (see GW to the Earl of Buchan and James Anderson, both 20 June 1792). GW received volumes 7 to 11 on 18 April 1793 (see GW to the Earl of Buchan, 22 April 1793).

2. Anderson sent John Sinclair's *Address to the Society for the Improvement of British Wool*, of which three separate editions were published in Edinburgh, London, and Dublin, respectively, in 1791.

3. Anderson is referring to the *Gazette of the United States*, which was published in Philadelphia by John Fenno.

4. No subsequent publication on agriculture by Anderson in collaboration with Andrew Coventry (1764–1832) has been identified.

From Thomas Jefferson

Sir,   Philadelphia Novr 3d 1792.

In order to enable you to lay before Congress the account required by law of the application of the monies appropriated to foreign purposes through the Agency of the Department of State, I have now the honor to transmit you the two statements No. 1. & 2. herein enclosed, comprehending the period of Two Years preceding the 1st day of July last.

The first statement is of the sums paid from the Treasury under the act allowing the annual fund of 40,000 Dollars for the purposes of foreign intercourse, as also under the acts of March 3. 1791. c. 16 and May [8] 1792. c. 41. §. 3. allowing other sums for special purposes.[1] By this it will appear, that, except the sum of 500 Dollars paid to Colonel Humphreys on his departure, the rest has been all received in Bills of Exchange, which identical Bills have been immediately remitted to Europe either to those to whom they were due for services, or to the Bankers of the United States in Amsterdam to be paid out by them to persons performing services abroad. This general view has been given in order to transfer the debit of these sums from the Department of State to those to whom they have been delivered.[2]

But, in order to give to Congress a view of the specific application of these monies, the particular accounts rendered by those who have received them, have been analysed, and the payments made to them have been reduced under general Heads, so as to show at one view the amount of the sums which each has received for every distinct species of service or disbursement, as well as their several totals. This is the statement No. 2. and it respects the annual fund of 40,000 Dollars only, the special funds of the acts of 1791. & 1792. having been not yet so far administered as to admit of any statement.[3]

I had presented to the auditor the Statement No. 1. with the Vouchers, and also the special accounts rendered by the several persons who have received these monies, but, on consideration, he thought himself not authorized, by any law, to proceed to their examination. I am, therefore, to hope, Sir, that authority may be given to the Auditor, or some other person to examine the general account and Vouchers of the Department of State, as well as to raise special accounts against the persons into whose hands the monies pass, and to settle the same from time to time on behalf of the public.[4] I have the honor to be, with sentiments of the most perfect respect and attachment, Sir, Your most obedient, and Most humble servant

Th: Jefferson

LS (letterpress copy), DLC: Jefferson Papers; copy, DNA: RG 46, Second Congress, 1791–93, Senate Records of Legislative Proceedings, President's Messages; LB, DLC: GW; LB, DNA: RG 59, Domestic Letters. Jefferson signed the copy in DNA: RG 46.

1. GW submitted both of Jefferson's enclosed statements with his second letter to the U.S. Senate and House of Representatives of 7 Nov. 1792. The first of Jefferson's financial statements is titled "The Department of State in Account with the United States" (DLC: Jefferson Papers; see also *Jefferson Papers*, 24:570–71). According to this statement, the State Department had received and had disbursed $143,500 between 14 Aug. 1790 and 3 July 1792 in agreement with the legislation mentioned in Jefferson's letter.

On 1 July 1790 GW signed "An Act providing the means of intercourse between the United States and foreign nations," in which the president was "authorized to draw from the treasury of the United States, a sum not exceeding forty thousand dollars annually . . . for the support of such persons as he shall commission to serve the United States in foreign parts, and for the expense incident to the business in which they may be employed." According to "An Act making an appropriation for the purpose therein mentioned," of 3 Mar. 1791, Congress approved an appropriation of $20,000 "for the purpose of effecting a recognition of the treaty of the United States, with the new emperor of Morocco." In section 3 of "An Act making certain appropriations therein specified," of 8 May 1792, Congress directed that an additional sum of $50,000 "be appropriated to defray any expense which may be incurred in relation to the intercourse between the United States and foreign nations, to be paid out of any monies, which may be in the treasury, not otherwise appropriated, and to be applied under the direction of the President of the United States." See 1 *Stat.* 128, 214, 284–85.

2. GW and Jefferson entrusted David Humphreys in August 1790 with the secret delivery of instructions to William Carmichael, the American chargé d'affaires at Madrid, and Gouverneur Morris, the administration's agent in London. For background on Humphreys's mission, see Jefferson to GW, 8 Aug. 1790, and notes. Other recipients of State Department funds listed on this statement include Gouverneur Morris, Thomas Barclay, Thomas Pinckney, John Brown Cutting, and the Dutch banking firm of Willink, Van Staphorst & Hubbard.

3. Jefferson's second statement is titled "Analysis of the Expences of the U.S. for their intercourse with Foreign nations from July 1. 90. to July 1. 91. and from July 1. 91. to July 1. 92. taken from the accounts of Messrs [William] Short, [David] Humphreys, [Gouverneur] Morris, [Thomas] Pinckney & Willinks, Van Staphorsts & Hubbard given in to the Auditor" (DLC: Jefferson Papers; see also *Jefferson Papers*, 24:572). The expenses from 1 July 1790 to 1 July 1791 total $21,054.61 and from 1 July 1791 to 1 July 1792 total $43,431.90. For additional financial reports submitted by Jefferson, see his second letter to GW of 5 Nov. 1792 and notes.

4. Richard Harrison was the auditor of the U.S. Treasury in 1792. Congress responded positively to Jefferson's request for additional authority to facilitate payment of State Department expenses. On 9 Feb. 1793 GW signed "An Act to

continue in force for a limited time, and to amend the act intituled 'An act providing the means of intercourse between the United States and foreign nations.'" Section 2 of that act authorized the president to settle accounts "for the purposes of intercourse or treaty, with foreign nations" annually with treasury officials. Such monies were to "be accounted for, specifically, in all instances, wherein the expenditure thereof may, in his [the president's] judgment, be made public; and by making a certificate or certificates, or causing the Secretary of State to make a certificate or certificates of the amount of such expenditures, as he [the president] may think it advisable not to specify; and every such certificate shall be deemed a sufficient voucher for the sum or sums therein expressed to have been expended" (1 *Stat.* 299–300).

From Thomas Jefferson

[Philadelphia, 3 November 1792]
Th: Jefferson has the honor to inclose to the President three sets of the papers relative to the Spanish interference for the President & the two houses.[1]

AL, DNA: RG 59, Miscellaneous Letters; LB, DNA: RG 59, George Washington's Correspondence with His Secretaries of State; LB (photocopy), DLC:GW.
1. Jefferson's enclosures included copies of the 29 Oct. letter that he received from Spanish diplomats José Ignacio de Viar and José de Jaudenes, an extract of Louisiana governor Carondelet's letter to Viar and Jaudenes of 24 Sept., and Jefferson's reply to Viar and Jaudenes of 1 Nov. 1792 (see Jefferson to GW, 29 Oct. [second letter], and note 1, GW to Jefferson, 1 Nov., n.1). GW enclosed these papers in his first letter to the U.S. Senate and House of Representatives of 7 Nov. 1792.

To Thomas Jefferson

Dear Sir, Philadelphia Novr 3d 1792.
Your letter to Messrs Carmichael and Short (now returned) is full & proper. I have added a word or two with A pencil, which may be inserted or not as you shall think best.[1] The intention of them is to do away the charge of Sovereignty over more than are within our own territory.[2]

The erazures from the Speech—as you advise—are made, except exchange the word "high" for "just" If facts will justify the former (as I think they indubitably do) policy, I conceive, is much in its favor: For while so many unpleasant things are announced as the Speech contains, it cannot be amiss to accom-

pany them with communications of a more agreeable nature.[3]
I am always—Yours

Go: Washington

ALS, DLC: Jefferson Papers; ADfS, DNA: RG 59, Miscellaneous Letters; LB, DLC:GW.

1. Jefferson had enclosed a draft of his letter to William Carmichael and William Short in a brief cover letter to GW of this date (DNA: RG 59, Miscellaneous Letters). For Jefferson's final version, also dated 3 Nov. and including a revision made at GW's suggestion, see *Jefferson Papers,* 24:565–67, and note 2.

2. Both the draft and letter-book versions of this letter include the word "assumed" before "Sovereignty" and the words "of the Creeks" after "more."

3. For Jefferson's suggested changes to a draft of GW's message to Congress, see his letter to GW of 1 November. For the final version, see GW's Address to the U.S. Senate and House of Representatives, 6 Nov. 1792.

From Henry Knox

Sir,   War department November 3d 1792

I beg leave to submit to your consideration the draft of a letter to Governor Lee.[1]

I also beg leave to submit the draft of a letter to the Secretary of the Treasury relatively to the Magazines of Rations to be kept in advance.[2] I have the honor to be with the greatest respect Your most obedient servant

H. Knox

LS, DLC:GW; LB, DLC:GW.

Tobias Lear wrote Knox on 4 Nov. 1792 that his draft letters to Lee and Hamilton "have been submitted to the President, and . . . meet the President's approbation" (DLC:GW).

1. Tobias Lear had written Knox on 1 Nov. from Philadelphia: "By the President's Command T. Lear has the honor to transmit to the Secretary of War the enclosed letter from Governor Lee of Virga and to request that the Secretary will take the same into Consideration and report thereon to the President as soon as may be" (DLC:GW). Knox then wrote to Lee on 3 Nov.: "The President of the United States has directed me to acknowledge the receipt of your Excellency's Letter to him of the 27th ultimo., enclosing Resolves of the House of Delegates and the Senate of Virginia, relatively to the temporary defence of the frontiers thereof, and the Copy of a Letter from Colonel Arthur Campbell, dated the 13th of October.

"The Letters which have been written at various times, will enable you to take such steps with the militia for the temporary defensive protection of Virginia as you shall judge proper, but anything further or more permanent must result from such measures as Congress may please to direct.

"The inefficiency of a defensive protection against Indians must be well understood by your Excellency; if they, contrary to the desires of and from causes which the general Government cannot controul, are influenced to and decided for war, they must be made to feel the effects of our superiority before tranquility can be permanently established.

"If the present threatening aspect of affairs constrain a course of hostilities against the Indians, humanity may be pained, but the Justice of the United States cannot be impeached, even by the most malignant; For it has been the incessant endeavour of the President of the United States to satisfy every equitable demand of the Indians without the further effusion of blood.

"The last information from Governor Blount was dated on the 10th ultimo; the purport of which was, as I mentioned in mine of the 1st instant contained in the printed paper you transmitted, It is therefore to be expected that the information of Colonel Campbell may be premature" (*Calendar of Virginia State Papers*, 6:122–23).

2. Knox's letter to Hamilton has not been identified. In a letter to Anthony Wayne of 24 Nov. 1792, Knox wrote that "[Robert] Elliot and [Eli] Williams have engaged with the public to furnish *all the rations* which shall be required of them in the Year 1793 on due Notice. It is their object therefore and for which they are responsible with heavy penalties that the supplies shall be regularly furnished at such place as shall be ordered. It will be incumbent *on them* to provide such numbers of Beeves that the army shall not be in want of that article after the 15th of April and such quantities of flour in proper season so as to serve as well *after* the 15th of June as before that time if it be not then to be purchased." Knox then listed several instructions for the army contractors that are "in addition to the orders already given for the Magazines in consequence of my letter of the 3d. instant to the Secretary of the Treasury" (Knopf, *Wayne*, 139–40).

Letter not found: to John Christian Ehlers, 4 Nov. 1792. GW wrote Anthony Whitting on this date: "I have written, as you will see by the enclosed, long letters, both to Thos Green and the Gardner. . . . The letters are left open for your perusal & delivery."

Letter not found: to Thomas Green, 4 Nov. 1792. GW wrote Anthony Whitting on this date: "I have written, as you will see by the enclosed, long letters, both to Thos Green and the Gardner. . . . The letters are left open for your perusal & delivery."

Tobias Lear to Thomas Jefferson

sunday evening [Philadelphia] Novr 4th 1792
The President requests, that if Mr Jefferson intends writing to Mr Pinckney by the British Packet (the mail for which is to be

closed at New York on Wednesday) he will be so good as to transmit the enclosed letters to his care.[1]

AL, DLC: Jefferson Papers. Jefferson docketed this letter as being from "Lear Tob." and erroneously noted that it was "recd Oct. 4. 92."

1. The enclosed letters have not been identified, but they probably included GW's letters of 20 Oct. to his British correspondents Edward Newenham, William Davies Shipley, John Sinclair, and Arthur Young, and possibly his letter of the same date to Gouverneur Morris, the U.S. minister to France. For Jefferson's letter to Thomas Pinckney, the U.S. minister to Great Britain, of 6 Nov., see *Jefferson Papers*, 24:590.

Letter not found: from Alexander Robertson, 4 Nov. 1792. Tobias Lear wrote Robertson on 16 Dec. 1792: "Your Letter to the President of the United States dated the 4th of November, did not get to his hands 'till a few days ago."

To Anthony Whitting

Mr Whiting,   Philadelphia Novr 4th 1792.

I was very glad to receive your letter of the 31st ulto because I was affraid, from the account given me of your spitting blood, by my Nephews George & Lawrence Washington, that you would hardly have been able to have written at all. And it is my request that you will not, by attempting more than you are able to undergo, with safety & convenience, injure your self; & thereby render me a disservice. for if this should happen under present circumstances, my affairs in the absence of both the Major & myself, will be thrown into a disagreeable situation—I had rather therefore hear that you had nursed, than exposed your self. And the things which I sent from this place (I mean the Wine, Tea, Coffee & Sugar) & such other matters as you may lay in by the Doctrs directions for the use of the Sick, I desire you will make use of, as your own personal occasions, may require.[1]

I have written, as you will see by the enclosed, long letters, both to Thos Green and the Gardner; in hopes to impress them with the necessity, & to stimulate them to the practice of proper exertions during mine, & the absence of my Nephew. The letters are left open for your perusal & delivery; it is unnecessary therefore for me, in this letter, to repeat the contents of either of the others.[2]

By the Plan of the Barn & treading floor for Dogue run, which I sent you in one of my last letters, you will readily perceive by the mode in which the treading floor of 2½ Inchs square stuff is laid, what I meant by progressive lengths from 12 to 20 feet. The inner part of the double Sections, next the Octagon, is 12 feet only—the outer part is 20; consequently, every piece increases in length as it approaches the exterior line in a progressive ratio.[3]

The old horses may be disposed of as you shall Judge best for my interest. I am well aware that an old horse adds more to the expence than to the profit of a Farm.

I am very sorry to find that my prospect of a Wheaten Crop is lessening. I shall be anxious to learn the final result of its yield. and wish to hear how the Corn turns out upon being stripped of the shuck; and how your Potatoes yield; as I perceive you have been digging the latter, & husking the former? As it is proposed to cultivate field No. 4 at Dogue Run next year in Potatoes, would it not have been better if the Crop of this Root which grows there, could be well secured against damage & thefts, to let them remain at that place? for I question if many more will be made than what will be required for that field. Eight bushels, or thereabouts, is usually allowed to an Acre when planted in drills 3 feet apart—of course 74 acres will take near 600 bushels.

I am told by some of the Farmers in the vicinity of this City, that if the Apricot Potatoes are planted early, they will come off in time for Wheat; if so, and the ground be well worked during the growth of them, it must be in excellent preparation for the Seed.

I send you under cover with this letter, a little of the double eared Wheat. Plant it in drills as soon as you get it, some where in the Vineyard, where the soil is, or can readily be made, good. It is worth trying what it can be brought to.[4]

Let the Gardener put all the Seeds of the Sugar Maple in the ground this Fall; but not to cover them more than very slightly indeed, with Earth.[5] What kind of preparation, and what kind of a Crop Do you mean to put the clover lot (front of the house) into, in order to prepare it for Grass? Potatoes would be the best, but I do not expect you will have enough for Dogue Run & this place too. Let me again request that every thing that is not intended to remain, & live in that enclosure may be effectually eradicated; for reasons wch I have often enumerated. When this enclosure is prepared for Grass, let all the Brick bats in the Road which formerly led through it, be picked up & brought off. and let that part of it, towards the decline of the Hill, which is naked & bare, be broke up, improved, & sown, to give it a better appearance as the house is approached⟨.⟩ And it would be a pleasing thing to me if this entire Inclosure—from the present mowing ground on the height *quite* down to the Marsh, & wet ground of H—— Hole; from the Mouth up to Richards house,[6] could be most effectually grubbed & cleared (except such clumps or single trees, as one would wish to leave for Ornament[)]. What the quantity of it may be, I am unable to say; but if you conceive that the House gang, with such aids as you can derive from River Plantation, where I think the people, during Winter, can have very little to do, and from the Ferry & French's, where they cannot have much, I should be glad to have it undertaken; since the idea of clearing for Corn, for Muddy hole, without the Gates at Mansion house is relinquished. As the home house people (the industrious part of them at least) might want ground for their truck patches, they might, for this purpose, cultivate what would be cleared. But I would have the ground from the cross fence by the Spring, quite round by the Wharf, first grubbed, before the (above mentioned) is attempted.

It would be difficult for me, if I was ever so well disposed, to procure the full quantity of Clover seed mentioned in your memm; as it is (from such information as I have received) both scarce & dear in these parts.[7] but while I am on this subject, I beg that whatever you do sow (if covered at all) may be very slightly covered—Harrowing Clover Seed in, in the vicinity of this City is quite dis-used, and I never Saw better Clover any where than is about it—Five or Six lbs. of Seed, if they can depend upon its goodness, is all they allow to an Acre, and in no case more than 10 lbs., or as many pints. I mention these things for your government; & that, from experience they find no better Season for Sowing than towards the last of Winter, or opening of the Spring, on Winter grain—lea[v]ing it to the Snow, or Frosts to bury the Seeds.

I do not discover by your letters, or the Reports that your Porkers are yet up. It is high time this was done, and I desire that no Hogs, except such as are of sufficient age, & size may be fattened —I had rather have a little good, than much bad-Porke.

By your last Weeks Report, I perceive 80 Bushels of Wheat was sent from River Plantation to the Mill and 79 only received at it. detect, always, these differences as soon as they happen, & it will explain mistakes, and check many abuses which otherwise would be committed.[8] And I am sorry to find that scarcely any report comes to hand without mentioning the death of several Sheep. If the Overseers begin thus early to report deaths, what may I not expect to receive between this & May?

I think you had better turn Sam & George over to the Gardener—that their work may appear in his Report. And Davis & Nuclus in like manner to Green—Sims also if you think he had better remain with the Carpenters. This will simplify the Mansion house report greatly, and let me see more clearly what that gang are employed in. At present that head of the Report is swelled greatly and nothing hardly appears to be done by the people comprehended under it. If Peter does *any* work at all it is in the Gardening line—He therefore had better be turned over to him—though I believe he will do nothing that he can avoid— of labour.[9]

Supply Green & the Gardener with Paper that they may have no excuse for not giving in their Reports & see that they accompany your own every week. I am Your friend and Servant

Go: Washington

P.S. Doll at the Ferry must be taught to Knit, and *made* to do a sufficient days work of it—otherwise (if suffered to be idle) many more will walk in her steps. Lame Peter if no body else will, must teach her—and she must be brought to the house for that purpose.[10]

Tell house Frank I expect he will lay up a more plentious store of the black common Walnut than he usually does—Nor ought he to spend his time wholly in idleness.[11]

ALS, DLC:GW.

1. For GW's shipment of these items, see GW to Whitting, 28 Oct., and note 8.

2. The letters to Thomas Green, overseer of the carpenters at Mount Vernon, and John Christian Ehlers, the gardener, have not been found.

3. See Washington's Plan for a Barn, enclosed in GW's letter to Whitting of 28 October.

4. For GW's interest in double-eared wheat, see Samuel Meredith to GW, 1 Nov. 1792, and note 3.

5. For GW's recent acquisition of sugar maple seeds, see Thomas Jefferson to GW, 16 Oct., and note 2. For Whitting's receipt of these seeds, see Whitting to GW, 31 October.

6. In his memorandum to George Augustine Washington of 27 June 1791, GW ordered the removal of "Richards House in the Hollow to Muddy hole" (see GW to Tobias Lear, 26 June 1791, n.1).

7. For Whitting's estimate of the amount of clover seed needed for the estate, see his letter to GW of 31 Oct., n.5. For GW's order of clover seed, see Tobias Lear to William Shotwell & Co., 3 Dec., in note 5 of GW to Whitting, 9 Dec. 1792.

8. Whitting's most recent farm report was for 21–27 Oct. (DLC:GW).

9. For identification of the slaves Sam, Nuclus, and Tom Davis and their earlier work assignments, see GW to Whitting, 14 Oct., n.12. George was identified in 1799 as a gardener belonging to GW and as married to Sall Twine, a dower slave at the Dogue Run farm. Simms, a dower slave, appeared as a carter on the 1786 slave list and as a carpenter on the 1799 slave list. He was married to Daphne, a plower hired from Mrs. Penelope French. Peter may be the dower slave listed as a distiller on the 1799 slave list (see Slave List, 18 Feb. 1786, in *Diaries*, 4:277–83, and Washington's Slave List, June 1799).

10. There were several female slaves named Doll or Dolly employed on the Mount Vernon estate during GW's lifetime; this one was probably the dower slave identified as one of the "labourg. Women" at the Ferry farm in 1786 (see Slave List, 18 Feb. 1786, in *Diaries*, 4:281). Doll was described in 1799 as a 52-year-old dower slave at the Union farm, who was "Lame & pretds to be so" and therefore was "Passed labour" (see Washington's Slave List, June 1799). Lame Peter, another dower slave, was listed on both the 1786 and 1799 slave lists as a knitter.

11. "House Frank" is Frank Lee, the butler (see GW to Whitting, 14 Oct., n.17).

From Charles Barbier de La Serre

Baltimore, 5 Nov. 1792. Seeks employment in the U.S. military service, having decided to leave his native France. He cites his attendance at the French military school at Douaï, his eight years of experience in the French artillery, and his knowledge of fortification and the moving of convoys. Although he has forgotten the English that he once knew, he says that he will strenuously apply himself to relearning the language.[1]

ALS (in French), DLC:GW.

1. French artillery captain Nicolas-Marie-Charles Barbier de La Serre (1767–1841) fled France in 1789 and spent several years as a political refugee in the United States before returning to France to resume his military career in Napoleon's army. He later developed a system of silent military communication,

known as *écriture nocturne* (night writing), which used a combination of raised dots to represent the sounds of the French language and influenced the alphabet for the blind designed by Louis Braille.

From William Jackson

Philadelphia, 5 Nov. 1792: Declines "the honor of your nomination to the important office of Adjutant General of the Army of the United States."[1] Jackson assured GW "that no other consideration but an engagement of the heart, involving the happiness of a most amiable Woman, who is, as she ought to be, peculiarly dear to me, could prevent" acceptance of this position.[2]

ALS, DLC:GW.

1. For other candidates for the position of adjutant general, see Knox to GW, 28 Aug., 15 Sept. 1792, and note 11.

2. Jackson, a Revolutionary War veteran, had served as GW's secretary from 1789 until early 1792 (see GW to Jackson, 26 Dec. 1791, and note 1). George and Martha Washington attended Jackson's marriage to Elizabeth Willing of Philadelphia on 11 Nov. 1795.

From Thomas Jefferson

[Philadelphia] Nov. 5. 1792.

Th: Jefferson having had the honor at different times heretofore of giving to the President *conjectural* estimates of the expences of our foreign establishment, has that of now laying before him in page. 1. of the inclosed paper, a statement of the whole amount of the foreign fund from the commencement to the expiration of the act which will be on the 3d of March next, with the *actual* expences to the 1st of July last, & the *conjectural* ones from thence through the remaining 8. months, and the balance which will probably remain.[1]

Page 2. shews the probable annual expence of our *present* establishment, & it's excess above the funds allowed; and in another column the *reduced* establishment, necessary & most proper to bring it within the limits of the fund, supposing it should be continued.[2]

AL, DNA: RG 59, Miscellaneous Letters; AL (letterpress copy), DLC: Jefferson Papers; LB, DNA: RG 59, George Washington's Correspondence with His

Secretaries of State; LB (photocopy), DLC:GW; LB, DNA: RG 59, Domestic Letters.

Jefferson also wrote a brief cover letter to GW on this date noting that he was sending "the President 3 complete copies of the inclosed papers for himself & each house of the legislature, and a copy of the account to be lodged in the treasury" (DNA: RG 59, Miscellaneous Letters). On 7 Nov., Lear sent Alexander Hamilton "a statement of the administration of the funds appropriated to certain foreign purposes" (DLC:GW). The enclosed papers were the two documents described below. For earlier financial statements issued by Jefferson, see his first letter to GW of 3 Nov. 1792 and notes 1 to 3.

1. The first document was Jefferson's "Estimate of the fund of 40,000 Dol. for foreign intercourse, and it's application" from 1 July 1790 until 3 Mar. 1793, when "An Act providing the means of intercourse between the United States and foreign nations" of 1 July 1790 would expire. By that legislation Congress appropriated $40,000 annually for the support of U.S. diplomats and "for the expense incident to the business in which they may be employed" (1 *Stat.* 128). Jefferson reported "actual expences incurred" of $21,054 for 1 July 1790 to 1 July 1791 and $43,431.09 for 1 July 1791 to 2 July 1792. He estimated that from 1 July 1792 to 3 Mar. 1793 "the probable expences may be abt 26,300," leaving a surplus of $16,214.91 out of the $107,000 appropriated by Congress for the period (DNA: RG 59, Miscellaneous Letters; Jefferson erased the original date of 21 Oct. and replaced it with 5 Nov. 1792; see also *Jefferson Papers*, 584).

2. The second document was Jefferson's "Estimate of the ordinary expence of the different diplomatic grades, annually." Jefferson reported that the current annual cost for a minister plenipotentiary was $12,307.13, for a resident was $5,653.56, and for an agent was $1,650. The estimated annual expense for "Medals to foreign ministers" was $654.60. Jefferson concluded that to "support the present establishment would require" $42,229.54, but by demoting the resident at The Hague to an agent, the budget could remain within the $40,000 appropriated annually by Congress, leaving an annual surplus of $1,774.02. (DNA: RG 59, Miscellaneous Letters; Jefferson erased the original date of 21 Oct. and replaced it with 5 Nov. 1792; see also *Jefferson Papers*, 24:585).

On the reverse of the letterpress copy of this estimate is a letterpress copy of a draft of the first paragraph of GW's second letter to the U.S. Senate and House of Representatives of 7 Nov. (DLC: Jefferson Papers). The draft's introductory phrase "According to the directions of the law" was replaced by "In pursuance of the law."

From John Francis Mercer

Sir   Annapolis Nov. 5. 1792.

I shoud have taken a much earlier opportunity of replying to yours from Mount Vernon, but Mrs Mercer's extreme indisposition (and I have attended to the business) woud have rendered any arrangement to the completion of which her concurrence was so essential, altogether precarious—he[r] re-establishment altho' slow has been pretty certain for 10 days past, but in that time, I have had to communicate with Doctor [James] Steuart now living in Baltimore who was to sell that proportion of Land that woud complete one half of the whole Tract.

I have never had directly or indirectly the most distant hint from the persons appointed to value the Land, of any price proposed, & shoud apprehend that they have not proceeded as yet on the business, as in consequence of my proposition to sell you one half instead of one third, no division into three parts has been attempted & the three months have not yet (I beleive) expired after which these persons were to make an average value, without a division. At one word I am willing to sell you my third at Seven dollars, but Doctor Steuart not being under any other impulse to sell than the advantage of a division into two parts instead of three, as yet does not seem disposed to sell at this price —Seven dollars & an half seems to be the lowest he will take which is one half a dollar less than he has hitherto asked—this woud render the whole near 200 dollars dearer than your offer altho no advantage whatever to me—he may possibly change this opinion before I pass thro' Baltimore on my way to Philadelphia where I shall certainly attend as soon as the health of my family will permit & where I will immediately communicate his ultimate determination.[1]

The latter part of your Letter was the cause of uneasiness to me, as it evidently appeard that you were not satisfied with my explanation of the transaction to which it alludes[2]—this has led me to state the following particulars—I had been long appriz'd of reports not only generally propagated but credited of my inimical disposition to yourself—I had been inform'd that respectable persons, otherwise most friendly disposed towards me had taken a part against me in this principle for instance Mr [Henry] Rozier (who so explain'd his conduct to me in person)—the Mr Calverts, (by others) & many others who are considered as your particular acquaintance in this District[3]—to this I will add an Extract from a publication Signed "A Voter" thousands of which were circulated in this District in hand bills previous to the late Election—all which will serve to discover the nature of the impression that has been made here for more than 5 Years past, altho' the sentiments have been with truth altogether disavow'd by me—"I will not vote for Mr Mercer for another reason, he was educated under the late General Lee who hated General Washington & it seems Mr Mercer entertains the same Sentiments of his master to this hour & hates the President of the United States as much as General Lee hated General Washington"—then follows another infamous falsehood & the paragraph concludes "Nor will I ever give my Vote to an Enemy of the President of the United States"[4]—With such imputations so publickly made & countenancd by persons who were known to be frequently at, if not intimate at Mount Vernon, I must confess I felt myself much reliev'd when informed from an authority that I coud not doubt, that you had express'd yourself favorably of me—I was lead therefore to repeat before five of my intimate friends what I had heard as a proper means of refuting the inputations above describ'd, & I stated at the same time, that I had written to Mr Sprigg Junr from whom the communication to me came for the particulars—under such circumstances I expected that it wou'd not be promulgated untill I shou'd receive that answer from Mr Sprigg which I said I was expecting—It seems it was mentioned, & my Enemies made that infamous use of the circumstance, which the particulars you are already appriz'd of & those detaild in the enclosed publication in the Maryland Gazette will disclose[5]—a publication to which no reply has yet been made, but an apologetic letter from Capn [William] Campbell to Mr Sprigg—I hope that this statement will satisfy you as to my conduct in this business[.] I never intended to make any use of your name, (even when satisfied of the truth of the report) than merely to counteract that free use that has been made of it, against me—There is no other man living to whom I woud justify myself in any circumstances, much less then I have stated— & permit me to add that it is from the result of a knowledge that has caused a settled respect for your person & character, & that at any moment of my life even at that early period when I left the Northern Army not 19 Years of age have I ever entertain'd Sentiments or used expressions unworthy of that general esteem in which you are held by your Countrymen. I am Sir &c

John F. Mercer

ALS, DLC:GW.

1. Mercer is replying to GW's letter of 26 Sept. 1792. For background on GW's attempt to collect a long-standing debt from the Mercer family by acquisition of land belonging to Sophia Sprigg Mercer, the wife of John Francis Mercer, see GW to Mercer, 26 Sept., William Deakins, Jr., to GW, 24 Aug., and note 2, and Mercer to GW, 15 Sept. 1792. For the agreement reached between GW and John Francis Mercer concerning the price and division of this land, see GW and Mercer to Francis Deakins and Benjamin W. Jones, 8 Dec. 1792.

2. For background on GW's dispute with Mercer over Mercer's reported use of GW's name in his 1792 congressional campaign, see GW's Memorandum of a Statement to James Craik, 7 Sept., Mercer to GW, 15 Sept., and note 2, and GW to Mercer, 26 Sept. 1792.

3. In addition to Henry Rozer of Prince Georges County, Md., Mercer probably is referring to Maryland residents Edward Henry Calvert (1766–1846) and George Calvert (1768–1838), who were brothers of Eleanor Calvert Custis Stuart, the widow of Martha Washington's son John Parke Custis and now the wife of David Stuart.

4. During 1778 Mercer had served as an aide-de-camp to Gen. Charles Lee (1731–1782). Lee's disdain for GW's military abilities and his attempts to undermine GW's leadership culminated in his court-martial after the Battle of Monmouth of 28 June 1778. Lee was found guilty of disobeying orders, misbehaving before the enemy by making an unnecessary and disorderly retreat, and showing disrespect to the commander in chief in letters to GW. Mercer resigned his commission in October 1779 and returned to Virginia for a brief time before returning to military service in 1780. The enclosed extract has not been identified.

5. Mercer apparently enclosed the portion of the *Maryland Gazette* (Annapolis) for 4 Oct. 1792 that includes Richard Sprigg, Jr.'s 1 Oct. letter "To the CITIZENS of PRINCE-GEORGE's and ANNE-ARUNDEL counties, and the city of ANNAPOLIS," two affidavits of 1 Oct. signed by John Smith Brookes, and a 2 Oct. letter from John Kilty "To the PRINTERS of the MARYLAND GAZETTE," all of which address the GW-Mercer controversy.

Ratification Statement

[Philadelphia, 5 November 1792]

To all whom it may concern—Greeting

Whereas the Legislature of the United States of America, by their Acts passed on the fourth and twelfth days of August one thousand seven hundred and ninety, authorized the President of the United States to borrow on their behalf certain sums of money therein named, or any lesser sums, for the purposes therein stated, and to make Contracts respecting the foreign debt of the United States,[1] and the President thereupon gave to

Alexander Hamilton Esquire, Secretary of the Treasury of the United States, full powers by himself, or any person appointed by him, to carry the purposes of the said Acts into execution, and the said Alexander Hamilton in pursuance of the said powers having authorized William Short Esquire Minister Resident of the United States of America at the Hague in that behalf,[2] the said William Short hath accordingly entered into Contract with certain persons therein named for the loan of three millions of Guilders, Dutch Current money, which Contract was executed at Amsterdam in the United Netherlands on the nineth day of August in the year one thousand seven hundred and ninety two, and is in the words following, to wit,

(Here insert it)[3]

Now know ye, that the President of the United States of America having seen and considered the said Contract, hath ratified and confirmed, and by these presents doth ratify and confirm the same and every article thereof.

In Testimony whereof he has caused the seal of the United States to be affixed to these presents, and signed the same with his hand. Done at the City of Philadelphia the fifth day of November in the year of our Lord one thousand seven hundred and ninety two, and of the Independence of the United States of America the Seventeenth.

Go. Washington.

By the President
Th: Jefferson.

Copy, DNA: RG 59, State Department, Letters, Accounts, and Contracts Relating to European Loans, 1791–1805.

The notation "Recorded in Compts. Office from pg 136 a 140 Henry Kuhl," chief clerk of the comptroller's office in 1792, later was added to this document. Jefferson had the ratification statement sent to Tobias Lear for GW's signature on this date because, as state department clerk George Taylor, Jr., informed Lear, "the Secretary of the Treasury wishes to receive [it] to day to transmit by a vessel bound for Amsterdam to morrow" (see Taylor to Lear, 5 Nov., in DNA: RG 59, Miscellaneous Letters). Hamilton enclosed the statement in his letter to Wilhem and Jan Willink and Nicholaas and Jacob Van Staphorst of 5 Nov. (see Syrett, *Hamilton Papers*, 13:22–23).

1. See "An Act making provision for the (payment of the) Debt of the United States," 4 Aug. 1790, and "An Act making Provision for the Reduction of the Public Debt," 12 Aug. 1790, in 1 *Stat.* 138–44, 186–87.

2. For Hamilton's authorization, see GW to Hamilton, 28 Aug. 1790, and

note 1. For William Short's authorization to seek a loan on behalf of the United States, see Hamilton to Short, 21 Mar. 1792, in Syrett, *Hamilton Papers*, 11:165.

3. A contemporary English translation of the contract made with Dutch bankers Wilhem and Jan Willink, Nicholaas and Jacob Van Staphorst, and Nicholas Hubbard, which was to have been inserted here, is in DNA: RG 59, State Department Letters, Accounts, and Contracts Relating to European Loans. For background on this loan, see Hamilton to GW, 27 Aug. 1792, and notes 1 and 2. The loan was acquired at a rate of 4 percent interest, to be paid "within the Space of fifteen years after the first day of June 1792." The principal was to be redeemed in five annual payments of 600,000 guilders each, beginning in 1803.

From David Stuart

Dear Sir,   Ge town 5th Novr 1792

I recieved your letter of the 21st ulmo a few days ago, but deferred answering it, 'till I could again see Mr Bayly, & Mr [Daniel] Carroll of Duddington, my informants respecting Coll Mercer's speech[1]—Inclosed, I send you Mr Bayly's certificate of what passed—Mr Carroll tho' he agrees with Mr Bayly, that Coll Mercer expressed himself as stated, has I know not for what reasons declined sending me his certificate, as he promised.[2] The conversation happened at dinner at Marlborough, in the presence of many and I have heard it spoke of by many since, and with but little variation—Mr Samuel Hanson among others, informed me as I passed through Alexa., that his Brother Coll Thomas Hanson, who heard Coll Mercer, at the same time with Mr Bayly, had given him the same idea of Coll Hamilton's having offered Coll Mercer a bribe, as is certifyed by Mr Bayly[3]—From my acquaintance with Mr Bayly, and his general character, I think him as much to be depended on, as any man in the State of Maryland—And, if it is thought proper to investigate the charge, I am satisfyed, Mr Bayly's certificate can never be done away.[4] I am Dr Sir, with the greatest respect Your most Obt Servt

                                          Dd Stuart

ALS, DLC: Hamilton-McLane Papers.

1. For background on the prolonged dispute between John Francis Mercer and Alexander Hamilton, see GW to Stuart, 21 Oct. 1792, and note 2; Hamilton to Mercer, 26 Sept. 1792, and introductory note, in Syrett, *Hamilton Papers*, 12:481–90.

2. William Bayly (Bailey, Bayley; c.1742–1824), a merchant and planter who lived in Prince Georges County, Md., provided a certificate concerning a bribe that Hamilton allegedly offered Mercer in exchange for his vote in favor of "An Act supplementary to the act making provision for the Debt of the United States," 8 May 1792 (1 *Stat.* 281–83). The enclosed copy of Bayly's statement has not been identified, but a signed certificate of 4 Nov. 1792 in DLC: Hamilton Papers reads: "On Tuesday the 2d Day of the Election at Upper Marlbro, after I had got there, I heard that Colo. Mercer had said, that Mr Hambliton the Secretary had Offered him, Money if he wou'd Vote for the Assumption, I asked Colo. Mercer if he had said so, he Answered Yes, by God he had, Mr Walter Bowie who was sitting by Colo. Mercer, said it was in a Jocular way, I then ask'd Colo. Mercer if he thought Mr Hambliton was Serious or Jesting, he Answered, that he had a Right to take it either way—I Repeated the same Question, to which he made the same Answer, but said he wou'd tell me how it was, He then said, he had been Down at Mr Hamblitons Office, in Order to settle some Accounts, or to receive some Money that was due to him, from the United States, but that Mr Hamblitons Clerks, or Understrappers, wou'd not pay it— & on Colo. Mercers Return from the Office he met Mr Hambliton who Observed to him, if he wou'd Vote for the Assumption—he Mr Hambliton wou'd pay the money."

3. Samuel Hanson (c.1752–1830), a merchant who currently was the inspector of the port of Alexandria, Va., and his brother Thomas Hawkins Hanson (1750–1810), who lived at Oxon Hill in Maryland across the Potomac River from Alexandria, were longtime acquaintances of GW (see Samuel Hanson to GW, 2 Oct. 1788, source note, and GW to the U.S. Senate, 6 Mar. 1792).

4. Sometime in April 1793 Hamilton apparently decided it was time to end the charges and countercharges that had dominated his relationship with Mercer for the past year, and on his "Statement on Remarks by John F. Mercer," he wrote: "This matter is dead. I will not revive it" (Syrett, *Hamilton Papers,* 14:361–63).

Address to the United States Senate and House of Representatives

United States [Philadelphia] November the 6th 1792.
Fellow-Citizens of the Senate, and House of Representatives.

It is some abatement of the satisfaction, with which I meet you on the present occasion, that in felicitating you on a continuance of the National prosperity generally, I am not able to add to it information that the Indian hostilities, which have, for some time past, distressed our North Western frontier, have terminated.

You will, I am persuaded, learn with no less concern than I communicate it, that reiterated endeavours, towards effecting a pacification, have hitherto issued only in new and outrageous proofs of persevering hostility on the part of the tribes with whom we are in contest. An earnest desire to procure tranquillity to the Frontier—to stop the further effusion of blood—to arrest the progress of expense—to forward the prevalent wish of the Nation, for peace, has led to strenuous efforts, through various channels, to accomplish these desireable purposes: In making which efforts, I consulted less my own anticipations of the event, or the scruples which some considerations were calculated to inspire, than the wish to find the object attainable; or if not attainable to ascertain unequivocally that such is the case.

A detail of the measures which have been pursued, and of their consequences, which will be laid before you, while it will confirm to you the want of success, thus far, will, I trust, evince that means as proper and as efficacious as could have been devised, have been employed. The issue of some of them, indeed, is still depending; but a favourable one, though not to be despaired of, is not promised by anything that has yet happened.[1]

In the course of the attempts which have been made, some valuable citizens have fallen victims to their zeal for the public service. A sanction commonly respected even among Savages, has been found, in this instance, insufficient to protect from massacre the emissaries of peace. It will, I presume, be duly considered whether the occasion does not call for an exercise of liberality towards the families of the deceased.[2]

It must add to your concern, to be informed, that besides the continuation of hostile appearances among the Tribes North of the Ohio, some threatening symptoms have of late been revived among some of those south of it.

A part of the Cherokees, known by the name of Chickamagas, inhabiting five villages on the Tenessee River, have long been in the practice of committing depredations on the neighbouring settlements.

It was hoped that the treaty of Holston made with the Cherokee Nation in July 1791, would have prevented a repetition of such depredations. But the event has not answered this hope. The Chiccamagas, aided by some Banditti of another tribe, in their vicinity, have recently perpetrated wanton, and unprovoked hostilities upon the citizens of the United States in that quarter. The information which has been received on this subject will be laid before you.[3] Hitherto defensive precautions only have been strictly enjoined, and observed.

It is not understood that any breach of treaty, or aggression whatso[e]ver, on the part of the United States, or their Citizens, is even alledged as a pretext for the spirit of hostility in this quarter.

I have reason to beleive that every practicable exertion has been made (pursuant to the provision by law for that purpose) to be prepared for the alternative of a prosecution of the war, in the event of a failure of pacific overtures. A large proportion of the troops authorized to be raised, have been recruited, though the number is still incomplete. And pains have been taken to discipline, and put them in condition for the particular kind of service to be performed. A delay of operations (besides being dictated by the measures which were pursuing towards a pacific termination of the war) has been in itself deemed preferable to immature efforts. A statement, from the proper department, with regard to the number of troops raised, and some other points which have been suggested, will afford more precise information, as a guide to the legislative consultations; and among other things will enable Congress to judge whether some additional stimulus to the recruiting service may not be adviseable.[4]

In looking forward to the future expence of the operations, which may be found inevitable, I derive consolation from the information, I receive, that the product of the Revenues for the present year is likely to supersede the necessity of additional burthens on the Community, for the service of the ensuing year. This, however, will be better ascertained in the course of the Session; and it is proper to add, that the information alluded to proceeds upon the supposition of no material extension of the spirit of hostility.[5]

I cannot dismiss the subject of Indian Affairs, without again recommending to your consideration the expediency of more adequate provision for giving energy to the laws throughout our interior frontier; and for restraining the commission of outrages upon the Indians; without which all pacific plans must prove nugatory. To enable, by competent rewards, the employment of qualified and trusty persons to reside among them, as agents, would also contribute to the preservation of peace and good neighbourhood. If in addition to these expedients, an eligible plan could be divised for promoting civilization among the friendly tribes, and for carrying on trade with them, upon a scale equal to their wants, and under regulations calculated to protect them from imposition and extortion, it's influence in cementing their interests with our's could not but be considerable.[6]

The prosperous state of our Revenue has been intimated. This would be still more the case, were it not for the impediments, which in some places continue to embarrass the collection of the duties on spirits distilled within the United States. These impediments have lessened, and are lessening in local extent; and as applied to the community at large, the contentment with the law appears to be progressive.

But symptoms of increased opposition having lately manifested themselves in certain quarters; I judged a special interposition on my part, proper and adviseable, and, under this impression, have issued a proclamation, warning against all unlawful combinations and proceedings, having for their object or tending to obstruct the operation of the law in question, and announcing that all lawful ways and means would be strictly put in execution for bringing to justice the infractors thereof and securing obedience thereto.

Measures have also been taken for the prosecution of Offenders: And Congress may be assured, that nothing within constitutional and legal limits, which may depend on me, shall be wanting to assert and maintain the just authority of the laws. In fulfilling this trust, I shall count intirely upon the full co-operation of the other departments of the Government, and upon the zealous support of all good Citizens.[7]

I cannot forbear to bring again into the view of the Legislature the subject of a Revision of the Judiciary System. A representation from the Judges of the Supreme Court, which will be laid before you, points out some of the inconveniencies that are experienced. In the course of the execution of the laws, considerations arise out of the structure of that system, which, in some cases, tend to relax their efficacy. As connected with this subject, provisions to facilitate the taking of bail upon processes out of the Courts of the United States, and a supplementary definition of Offences against the Constitution and laws of the Union, and of the punishment for such Offences, will, it is presumed, be found worthy of particular attention.[8]

Observations on the value of peace with other nations are unnecessary. It would be wise however, by timely provisions, to guard against those Acts of our own Citizens, which might tend to disturb it, and to put ourselves in a condition to give that satisfaction to foreign nations which we may sometimes have occasion to require from them. I particularly recommend to your consideration the means of preventing those aggressions by our Citizens on the territory of other Nations, and other infractions of the law of Nations, which, furnishing just subject of complaint, might endanger our peace with them. And, in general, the maintenance of a friendly intercourse with foreign powers will be presented to your attention by the expiration of the law for that purpose, which takes place, if not renewed, at the close of the present Session.[9]

In execution of the authority given by the Legislature, measures have been taken for engaging some artists from abroad to aid in the establishment of our Mint; others have been employed at home. Provision has been made of the requisite buildings, and these are now putting into proper condition for the purposes of the establishment. There has also been a small beginning in the coinage of half-dismes; the want of small coins in circulation calling the first attention to them.[10]

The regulation of foreign Coins, in correspondency with the principles of our national Coinage, as being essential to their due operation, and to order in our money concerns, will, I doubt not, be resumed and completed.[11]

It is represented that some provisions in the law, which establishes the Post-Office, operate, in experiment, against the transmission of News-papers to distant parts of the Country. Should this, upon due inquiry, be found to be the fact, a full conviction of the importance of facilitating the circulation of political intelligence and information, will, I doubt not, lead to the application of a remedy.[12]

The adoption of a Constitution for the State of Kentucky has been notified to me. The legislature will share with me in the satisfaction which arises from an event interesting to the happiness of the part of the Nation, to which it relates, and conducive to the general order.[13]

It is proper likewise to inform you, that since my last communication on the subject, and in further execution of the Acts severally making provision for the public debt, and for the reduction thereof, three new loans have been effected, each for three millions of florins—One at Antwerp, at the annual interest of four and one half per Cent, with an allowance of four per Cent in lieu of all charges, and the other two at Amsterdam, at the annual interest of four per Cent, with an allowance of five and one half per Cent in one case, and of five per Cent in the other, in lieu of all charges. The rates of these loans, and the circumstances under which they have been made, are confirmations of the high state of our Credit abroad.

Among the Objects to which these funds have been directed to be applied, the payment of the debts due to certain foreign Officers, according to the provision made during the last Session, has been embraced.[14]

Gentlemen of the House of Representatives.

I entertain a strong hope that the state of the national finances is now sufficiently matured to enable you to enter upon a systematic and effectual arrangement for the regular redemption and discharge of the public debt, according to the right which has been reserved to the Government. No measure can be more desireable, whether viewed with an eye to its intrinsic importance, or to the general sentiment and wish of the Nation.

Provision is likewise requisite for the reimbursement of the loan which has been made of the Bank of the United States, pursuant to the eleventh section of the act by which it is incorporated. In fulfilling the public stipulations in this particular, it is expected a valuable saving will be made.[15]

Appropriations for the current service of the ensuing year, and for such extraordinaries as may require provision, will demand, and I doubt not, will engage your early attention.

Gentlemen of the Senate, and of the House of Representatives.

I content myself with recalling your attention, generally, to such objects, not particularized in my present, as have been suggested in my former communications to you.

Various temporary laws will expire during the present Session. Among these, that which regulates trade and intercourse with the Indian Tribes, will merit particular notice.

The results of your common deliberations hitherto, will, I trust, be productive of solid and durable advantages to our Constituents; such as, by conciliating more and more their ultimate suffrage, will tend to strengthen and confirm their attachment to that Constitution of Government, upon which, under Divine Providence, materially depend their Union, their safety and their happiness.

Still further to promote and secure these inestimable ends, there is nothing which can have a more powerful tendency, than the careful cultivation of harmony, combined with a due regard to stability in the public Councils.

Go: Washington

DS, DNA: RG 46, Second Congress, 1791–93, Senate Records of Legislative Proceedings, President's Messages; copy, DNA: RG 233, Second Congress, 1791–93, House Records of Legislative Proceedings, Journals; LB, DLC:GW.

Alexander Hamilton, Thomas Jefferson, Henry Knox, and Edmund Randolph submitted suggestions or draft messages to GW for use in composing this address. For Knox's and Randolph's suggestions, see their letters to GW of 14 and 28 Oct., respectively. See also Hamilton's draft address of 15–31 Oct. in Syrett, *Hamilton Papers*, 12:558–66. For Jefferson's suggestions, see notes 9 and 10.

1. On the following day GW "laid before the Senate a Letter from the Secretary for the Department of War, on the subject of Indian affairs, with sundry papers therein mentioned." These papers also were presented to the House of Representatives on that date (*Annals of Cong.*, 2d Cong., 611, 673). Knox's letter to the U.S. Senate of 7 Nov. groups these papers under five headings: "1st. A statement of the measures taken and the overtures made, to procure a peace with the Indians North west of the Ohio." These papers consisted of copies of the following items, all written in 1792 unless otherwise indicated: Knox to Samuel Kirkland, 20 Dec. 1791, 9 Jan., 25 Feb., 7 Mar., to Cornplanter and other Seneca chiefs, 7 Jan. (see Knox to Tobias Lear, 21 Jan., n.1), to Peter Pond and William Steedman, 9 Jan., and to Waterman Baldwin, 10 Feb. (see Knox to GW, 9 Jan., n.1), to New Arrow, Cornplanter, Big-Log (Big Tree), and other Seneca chiefs, 10 Feb., to Joseph Brant, 25 Feb. (see GW to Knox, 25 Feb., n.1), 23 April, 27 June, GW to the Five Nations, 23 Mar., 25 April, Knox to Alexander Trueman, 3 April (see Knox to GW, 1 April, n.2), 22 May, to the Sachems and Warriors of the Tribes in the Northwest Territory, 4 April (see Knox to GW, 1 April, n.2), to Israel Chapin, Sr., 23 (see Knox to GW, 21 April, n.2), 28 April, 8 May, 27 June, to Deodat Allen, 25 April, Timothy Pickering to the Sachems and Chiefs of the Five Nations, 30 April, Knox to Pickering, 3 May, to Hendrick Aupaumut, 8 May, to John Heckenwelder, 18, 21 May, to Rufus Putnam, 22 May (see GW to Knox, 3 Sept., n.3), 7 Aug. (see Knox to GW, 7 Aug., n.3), to Israel Chapin, Jr., 27 June, and to George Clinton, 27 June. These documents are in *ASP, Indian Affairs*, 1:226–38.

Knox's second heading was "Information received relatively to the pacific overtures, and the dispositions of the Indians North west of the Ohio." The letters, with their enclosures, that Knox submitted on this subject were: Putnam to Knox, 5 (see Knox to GW, 5 Aug., n.3), 22, 26 July, 16 (see Knox to GW, 22 Sept., n.3), 21 Aug., Israel Chapin, Sr., to Knox, 17 July (see Knox to GW, 7 Aug., n.5), 14 Aug., 24 Sept., Affidavit of William May, 11 Oct., Report of Reuben Reynolds, 19 Oct., Brant to Knox, 27 Mar. (see GW to Knox, 25 Feb., n.1), 26 July. For these documents, see ibid., 238–45.

Knox's third heading was "A statement of the measures which have been taken to conciliate and quiet the Southern Indians." The documents, with their enclosures, that Knox submitted under this heading were: Knox to William Blount, 31 Jan. (see Charles Pinckney to GW, 8 Jan., [first letter] n.3), 16 Feb., 31 Mar., 22 April, 15 Aug. (see Knox to GW, 5 Aug., n.5, and 16 Aug., n.6), 9 Oct. (see Knox to GW, 9 Oct., n.3), to Alexander McGillivray, 17 Feb., 29 April, 11 Aug., to Leonard Shaw, 17 Feb., with Knox's messages of 17 Feb. to the Creek, Choctaw, and Chickasaw nations, to James Seagrove, 20 Feb., 11, 29 April, 11, 31 (see Knox to GW, 31 Aug. [second letter], n.2) Aug., 24 Sept., 27 Oct. (see Knox to Lear, 27 Oct., n.3), to Andrew Pickens, 21 April, 15 Aug., to Joseph Ellicott, 29 April, 11 Aug., to Henry Lee, 16 May, 30 June, 11 July, 9 (see Knox to GW, 9 Oct., n.3), 11, 14 (see Knox to GW, 14 Oct., n.2) Oct., to Edward Telfair, 11 July, 31 Aug. (see Knox to GW, 31 Aug. [second letter], n.1), 27 Oct., to Charles Pinckney, 27 Oct. (see Knox to Lear, 27 Oct., n.3, and Pinckney to GW, 30 Sept., n.2), to Henry Gaither, 27 Oct. 1792 (see Knox to Lear, 27 Oct., n.3). For these documents, see ibid., 245–63.

Knox's fourth heading was "Information received relatively to the dispositions of the Southern Indians, and the causes of the hostilities of part of the Cherokees and Creeks." Knox submitted the following documents, with their enclosures, for this category: Blount to Knox, 20 Mar. (see Knox to GW, 21 April, n.1), 5 (see John Stagg, Jr., to Lear, 4 June, n.2), 16 (see Knox to Lear, 28 June, n.1) May, 2 June (see Knox to GW, 12 May, n.2), 4 July (see Knox to GW, 15 Sept., n.7), 31 Aug. (see Knox to GW, 29 Sept., n.6), 11 (see Knox to GW, 9 Oct., n.1), 15, 20, 26, 27 Sept., 7 (see Knox to Lear, 27 Oct., n.2), 10 Oct., Seagrove to Knox, 21 April, 24 May, 14 June (see Seagrove to GW, 5 July, n.1), 5, 27 (see Seagrove to GW, 27 July, n.8) July, 4 Aug., 8 (see GW to Jefferson, 20 Oct., n.4), 13 (see GW to Jefferson, 20 Oct., n.4) Sept., 17 Oct. (see GW to Knox, 19 Aug., n.7), Seagrove to GW, 5, 27 July, McGillivray to Knox, 18 May, Charles Pinckney to GW, 30 Sept. 1792. For copies of these letters, with their enclosures, see DNA: RG 46, Second Congress, 1791–1793, Senate Records of Legislative Proceedings, Reports and Communications, and ibid., 263–318.

Knox's fifth heading was "A statement of the Troops in the service of the United States," dated 6 Nov. 1792 (see ibid., 318).

"It is humbly suggested," Knox advised at the end of his letter, "that the public good requires, that a number of these papers be considered as confidential" (DNA: RG 46, Second Congress, 1791–93, Senate Records of Legislative Proceedings, Reports and Communications).

2. By "An Act making provision for the persons therein mentioned," on 27 Feb. 1793, Congress approved annual allowances of $450 and $300, respectively, for seven years, to the families of Col. John Hardin and Maj. Alexander Trueman, who had been killed while on a peace mission to the hostile Indians of the Northwest Territory. In "An Act to make further provision for the children of Colonel John Harding, and Major Alexander Trueman, deceased," approved on 14 May 1800, Congress allotted an annual sum of $100 for each child until the age of 21 (6 *Stat.* 12, 41).

3. See Knox to GW, 7 Nov., and note 3. For the Treaty of Holston, 2 July 1791, see Kappler, *Indian Treaties*, 29–33.

4. See "An Act for making farther and more effectual Provision for the Protection of the Frontiers of the United States," 5 Mar. 1792, in 1 *Stat.* 241–43.

5. See Hamilton's "Report on the Receipts and Expenditures of Public Monies to the End of the Year 1791," 10 Nov. 1792, and the "Report on Estimates of the Expenditures for the Civil List of the United States for the Year 1793," 14 Nov. 1792, in Syrett, *Hamilton Papers*, 13:34–114, 118–47. Hamilton submitted both reports to the House of Representatives on 12 and 14 Nov. 1792, respectively.

6. The first act "to regulate trade and intercourse with the Indian tribes" had been approved on 22 July 1790, and the second such measure, which incorporated GW's suggestions, was signed by the president on 1 Mar. 1793 (1 *Stat.* 137–38, 329–32).

7. See GW's proclamation of 15 Sept. 1792, which urged citizens to comply with the federal excise tax on whiskey. For the prosecution of Pennsylvania citizens William Kerr and Alexander Berr for their violent opposition to this tax, see GW to Edmund Randolph, 1 Oct., and note 1.

8. See GW to the U.S. Senate and House of Representatives, 7 Nov. (second letter), and notes.

9. This paragraph was taken from Jefferson's memorandum of 1 Nov. in which Jefferson revised an earlier paragraph submitted to GW on 15 Oct. (see Jefferson's memoranda to GW of 15 Oct. and 1 Nov., both in DLC: Jefferson Papers; see also *Jefferson Papers*, 24:486, 552). For background on the subject matter of this paragraph, see Jefferson's "Opinion on Offenses against the Law of Nations," 3 Dec. 1792, and notes, and "Edmund Randolph's Opinion on Offenses against the Law of Nations," 5 Dec. 1792, ibid., 693–96, 702–3.

10. GW adopted this paragraph, with minor changes, from Jefferson's memorandum to him of 15 Oct. (DLC: Jefferson Papers; see also ibid., 486). For Jefferson's involvement in the establishment of the U.S. Mint and the production of U.S. coins, see GW to Jefferson, 20 Oct., and note 3, and Jefferson to GW, 16 and 28 Nov., and notes. For Jefferson's critique of a draft address that GW submitted to him, see Jefferson to GW, 1 November. The draft address has not been found.

11. See the House of Representatives to GW, 29 Nov., and note 1.

12. See section 22 of "An Act to establish the Post-Office and Post Roads within the United States," 20 Feb. 1792, in 1 *Stat.* 238.

13. See GW to Samuel McDowell, 20 Oct. 1792, and note 1.

14. For the legislation on foreign loans, see "An Act making provision for the (payment of the) Debt of the United States," 4 Aug. 1790, "An Act supplementary to the act making provision for the reduction of the Public Debt," 3 Mar. 1791, and "An Act supplementary to the act making provision for the Debt of the United States," 8 May 1792 (1 *Stat.* 138–44, 218–19, 281–83). For the Dutch loan of 1791, see Ratification of the Holland Loan, 1 Sept. 1791, and notes. For the Antwerp loan of 1791, see William Short to Hamilton, 8 Nov. 1791, n.4, in Syrett, *Hamilton Papers*, 9:481–82. For the Dutch loan of 1792, see GW's ratification statement of 5 Nov. 1792 and notes.

15. See section 11 of "An Act to incorporate the subscribers to the Bank of the United States," 25 Feb. 1791, in 1 *Stat.* 196.

Letter not found: to John Christian Ehlers, c.7 Nov. 1792. In his letter to Anthony Whitting of 11 Nov., GW refers to his "last post to the gardener."

Directive to John Christian Ehlers

[Philadelphia] Novr 7th 1792.

List of Trees, Shrubs &c. had of Jno. Bartram to supply the place of those of his Catalogue of Mar: 92. which failed.[1]

No.

—feet high

E. d. 2 Ulex europeus   grows from 3 to 4
  embellished with sweet scented flowers of a fine yellow colour. [Furze]

a. 3. Hypericum kalmianum   3 to 4.
  profusely garnished with fine gold coloured blossoms 2 plants. ["Shrub St. John's wort"]

4. Hyperi: Angustifolium   3 to 6.
  Evergreen, adorned with fine yellow flowers.

e. 5. Taxus procumbens   3 to 6.
  Evergreen—of a splendid full green throughout the year— red berries. [Yew]

E 6. Buxus aureus   3 to 10.
  Elegant, called gilded box.

E. 7. Daphne mezerium [*mezereum*]   1 to 3.
  an early flowering sweet scented little shrub. [Mezereon, paradise plant]

8. Calycanthus floridus   4 to 8.
  Odoriferous, it's blossoms scented like the Pine Apple. ["Sweet Shrub of Carolina," Carolina allspice][2]

E. 10. Æsculus hippocastanum.   20. 40. to 50.
  a magnificent flowering and shady *tree.* [Horse chestnut]

11. Euonimus atrapurpurius.   6 to 8.
  It's fruit of a bright crimson in the autumn (*burning bush*) 3 plants. [*Euonymus atropurpureus*]

13. Franklinia [*alatamaha*].   3, 15 to 20.
  flowers large, white and fragrant. Native of Georgia. [Franklin tree]

16. Kalmia angustifolia. 　　　　　　　　　　　1 to 2.
　　Evergreen. garnished with crimson speckled flowers. 4 plants.
　　["Thyme leav'd Kalmia," lambkill, sheep laurel]

24. Halesia tetraptera [or *carolina*]. 　　　　　4, 10 to 15.
　　flowers abundant. white, of the shape of little bells. [Carolina
　　silverbell] [3]

25. Viburnum opulifolium. 　　　　　　　　　　　3 to 7.
　　of singular beauty in flower & fruit

27. Viburnum alnifolium— 　　　　　　　　　　　3 to 6
　　handsome flowering Shrub. [*Viburnum lantanoides;* hobble
　　bush]

E. 29. Sorbus Sativa [4] 　　　　　　　　　　　10, 15. 30.
　　It's fruit pear & apple shaped, as large & well tasted when
　　mellow.

31. Sorbus aucuparia. 　　　　　　　　　　　　8. 15 to 30.
　　foliage elegant: embellished with umbells of coral red berries.
　　[European mountain ash]

e. 36. Stewartia malachodendron 　　　　　　　　5 to 8.
　　floriferous. the flowers large and white, embellished with a
　　large tuft of black or purple threads in their centre. [Silky
　　stewartia or stuartia]

38. Styrax grandifolium. 　　　　　　　　　　　3 to 10.
　　a most charming flowering shrub blossoms snow white, & of the
　　most grateful scent. (call'd Snow-drop tree.) [Snowbell, storax]

E 39. Philadelphus coronarius 　　　　　　　　　4. 6. 10.
　　a sweet flowering shrub (called mock Orange).

40. Philadelphus inodorus 　　　　　　　　　　　5. 7. 10
　　his robe a silver flowered mantle.

e. 41. Pinus Strobus 　　　　　　　　　　　　　50. 80. 100
　　magnificent! he presides in the ever green Groves. (White Pine)
　　—*4 Plants.*

*E 42. Pinus communis 　　　　　　　　　　　　20. 40. 60.
　　a stately tree, foliage of a Seagreen colour; and exhibits a good
　　appearance whilst young. [5]

*E 43. Pinus Larix 　　　　　　　　　　　　　　40 to 60.
　　Elegant figure & foliage. ["Larch Tree"]

45. Robinia villosa. 　　　　　　　　　　　　　1. 2. 3. 5. 6.
　　a gay shrub enrobed with plum'd leaves and roseat flowers.
　　3 Plants. ["Peach Blossom Acacia"]

52. Prunus chicasa.   6. 8. 10.
Early flowering, very fruitful; the fruit nearly round, cleft, red,
purple, yellow of an inticing look, most agreeable taste &
wholesome (chicasaw Plum.).

57. Æsculus alba.   1. 4. 6.
The branches terminate with long erect spikes of sweet white
flowers.

E 58. Juniperus sabina.   1. to 5.
Evergreen. [Savin]

54. Æsculus pavia.   6. 8. 10. 12. 15.
It's light and airy foliage crimson & variegated flowers, present
a gay and mirthful appearance; continually, whilst in bloom,
visited by the brilliant thundering Huming-bird. *The root of the
tree is esteemed preferable to Soap, for scouring & cleaning woolen
clothes.* (*2 plants*) [Red buckeye]

c. 63. Myrica gale   2 to 4.
possesses an highly aromatic, and very agreeable scent.
(*3 Plants*). ["Bog gale," sweet gale, bog myrtle]

69. Mespilus pubescens   2. 3. 4.
an early flowering shrub of great elegance, produces very
pleasant fruit.[6] (*2 Plants*)

E. f. 72. Colutia [*Colutea*] arborescens   3. 6: 10.
Exhibits a good appearance; foliage pinnated, of a soft pleasant green colour, interspers'd with large yellow papillionacious
flowers in succession. [Bladder senna]

77. Prunus Divaricata   6. 8.
diciduous, flowers white in raumes [racemes], stems diverg-
ing & branches pendulous. [*Prunus cerasifera divaricata;* cherry
plum]

78. Hydrangia [*Hydrangea*] arborescens   3. 5 to 6.
Ornamental in shruberies flowers white in large corymbes:

79. Andromeda exilaris [*axillaris*].   1 to 3.
Evergreen. [Bog rosemary]

80. Acer pumilum; s, montanum.[7]   4 to 8.
handsome shrub for coppices. foliage singular, younger shoots,
red. [Dwarf maple]

84. Rubus odoratus   3 to 7.
foliage beautiful; flowers of the figure, colour & fragrance of
the rose. [Flowering raspberry, thimbleberry]

E 92. Laurus nobilis   10. 20. 30.
   Sweet bay; a celebrated evergreen—leaves odoriferous. ["Red
   Bay," bay laurel, sweet bay]
c. 101. Arundo donax   5. 6. 8.
   Maiden Cane.

                  In addition to the above,
                                    October. 30th 1792.

No. 1. Mespilus pyracantha.[8] Evergreen Thorn. a very beautiful flowering shrub; in flower & fruit. evergreen in moderate cli-
mates, and not to be exceeded in usefulness, for hedges Fences
&ca. [*Pyracantha coccinea;* firethorn]

                                    October 30th 1792.

   The following Letters in the margin serve to explain the natural soil & situation of the Trees, Shrubs, &c.
   a   rich, moist, loose or loamy soil, in shade of other trees.
   b.   rich deep soil.
   c   wet moorish soil.
   d   Dry indifferent soil.
   e   A good loamy moist soil in any situation.
   f   Any soil and situation.
   E.   Exoticks.

             Directions for disposing of the Trees, Shrubs
                &ca, mentioned in the aforegoing list.
   The intention of giving the heights to which they may grow, is,
that except in the centre of the Six Ovals in the West Lawn; and
at each end of the two large Ovals; none of the tall, or lofty growing trees (ever-greens) are to be planted. But this I would have
done in all of them, whether any thing occupies these particular
spots, or not: removing them if they do, to some other parts of
the aforesaid Ovals. ⟨A⟩t each end of the 4 Smaller Ovals, trees
of midling growth (for instance those which rise to 15, 20, or
even to thirty feet) may be planted. My meaning is, that in the
Centre of every Oval (if it is not already there) one of the lofty
growing trees should be planted; and the same done at each end
of the two large Ovals; and at the ends of the 4 Smaller ones,
trees of lesser size to be planted. The other parts of all of them
to receive the Shrubs—putting the tallest, always, nearest the
middle, letting them decline more into dwarfs towards the outer
parts. This was my intention when they were planted in the Ovals

last Spring—but I either did not express my self clearly—or the directions were not attended to.[9] I now hope they will be understood, and attended to both. The two trees marked thus (*) in the Margin, I would have planted by the Garden gates opposite to the Spruce Pines. I believe common pine are now in the places where I intend these, but they may be removed, being placed there merely to fill up the space. If any of these tall growing trees are now in any other part of the Ovals, except those here mentioned (and that you may be enabled better to ascertain this, I send you a list of what went from Bartrams Garden last Spring) I would have them removed, so as to conform to these directions; and if there be more with what are now sent, than are sufficient to comply with these directions, there may be one on each side of the two large Ovals making five in each. You will observe that the Pinus Strobus (or white Pines) are the loftiest of all the Tall trees which now are, or have been sent; and that it is these which are to form your centre trees—and the end trees of the two large Ovals.

I must request also, that except the large trees for the Centre & sides no regularity may be observed in planting the others in the Ovals—This I particularly desired last Spring, but found when I got home it was not attended to.

When you have disposed of all the trees & Shrubs agreeably to these directions return this Paper, and the general list which accompanies it, back again to me; as I may have occasion for them in procuring plants in future.

Note—If there are now growing in the Ovals, as many as 4 of the Hemlock Spruce (sent last Spring)[10] let them be taken up when the ground is hard & deep frozen in the Winter, & placed on the sides of the two large Ovals instead of the White Pines, wch you might have put there in consequence of the aforegoing directions.

D, DLC:GW. The "List of Trees" is in Bartholomew Dandridge's writing, while the "Directions for disposing" is in GW's writing. This document was probably an enclosure in GW's letter to John Christian Ehlers, c.7 Nov., which has not been found.

For the meaning of the letters that precede the plant names, see the list of symbols following the list. For ease of reading, all such letters, regardless of original position, have been placed to the left of the botanical classifications. Common names for each plant (when missing from the descriptive entry), modern classifications (if different), alternative classifications, and corrected spellings are given in square brackets. Common names within quotation marks are from John Bartram's *Catalogue of American Trees, Shrubs, and Herbacious Plants: Most of Which Are Now Growing, and Produce Ripe Seeds in John Bartram's Garden, near Philadelphia. The Seed and Growing Plants of Which Are Disposed Of on the Most Reasonable Terms* (Philadelphia, 1784).

1. For GW's original order, see List of Plants from John Bartram's Nursery, March 1792.

2. In May 1786 GW planted six of these shrubs "in my Shrubberies, on each side the Serpentine walks on this (or East) side of the Garden gate" (*Diaries*, 4:321).

3. Bartram offered "Halesia or Silver Bells 2 varieties" in his 1784 catalog.

4. This tree is probably *Sorbus domestica*, the service tree.

5. This tree was identified on the March list as "Scotch Fir." The Scotch pine is classified today as *Pinus sylvestris*.

6. This description is less detailed than that given on the March list.

7. The phrase "s, montanum" does not appear on the March list.

8. This plant appears as item 74, with a shorter description, on the March list.

9. See George Augustine Washington to GW, 8–9, 15–16 April 1792.

10. See item 47 on the March list of plants.

From Henry Knox

Sir.   War-department, Nov: 7th 1792.

I have the honor to submit to you, the pleasing information of a treaty with the Wabash indians; and which appears to have been a general one. After you shall have perused them, they shall be copied, to be laid before the two houses.[1]

Mr Bradshaw says, there were upwards of seven hundred indians present[2]—He came by the way of Kentucky, and says that he understood that about twenty people had been killed by the indians at their late several attacks—That they were repulsed at another station, besides Buchannans—that the celebrated John Watts, the indian leader, was shot through both thighs, and the Shawanese warrior was killed, with several other indians.[3] I have the honor to be Sir, with very great respect, Your most obedt Servt

H. Knox secy of War

LS, DLC:GW; LB, DLC:GW.

1. The enclosed documents are identified in Knox's letter to the Senate of 8 Nov.: "The President of the United States has directed me to inform the Honorable the Senate, that yesterday afternoon an Express arrived with information from Major Hamtramck, dated at post Vincennes on the 4th of October—that Brigadier General Putnam who then was sick, had on the 27th day of September concluded a treaty of peace with the Wabash and Illinois Indians, consisting of the following tribes—to wit: Eel river indians, Ouittananons, Pattewatimas of the Illinois River, Musquitons, the Kickapoos of the Wabash,

Piankishaws, Kaskaskias, and Perorians—and that Brigr General Putnam was to forward to the hostile Indians, by certain Chiefs of the Wabash, the Messages, of which copies are herewith submitted.

"Lieut. Prior, also writes, on the sixteenth ultimo from Louisville on the Ohio, that he has arrived there with sixteen Chiefs of the Wabash Indians, who are proceeding to Philadelphia by the way of Pittsburg" (DNA: RG 46, Second Congress, 1791–93, Senate Records of Executive Proceedings, President's Messages—Indian Relations). For the treaty of 27 Sept. 1792, see *ASP, Indian Affairs*, 1:338. For background on this treaty, see GW to Knox, 3 Sept. (first letter), and note 3. GW submitted the treaty, which was never ratified, to the Senate on 13 Feb. 1793. For Lt. Abner Prior's escort of an Indian delegation to Philadelphia, see James Wilkinson to GW, 1 Nov., n.1.

2. Gen. Rufus Putnam recorded that a total of 686 Indian men, women, and children from the various tribes attended the conference at Vincennes (see "Number of Indians Present at the Treaty of Vincennes," [September 1792], OMC: Putnam Papers).

3. According to an account enclosed in William Blount's letter to Knox of 10 Oct., "On the 30th September, about midnight, John Buchanan's Station, four miles south of Nashville, (at which sundry families had collected, and fifteen gun-men) was attacked by a party of Creeks and Lower Cherokees, supposed to consist of three or four hundred." The Indian attackers maintained a "very heavy and constant firing upon the station, (blockhouses, surrounded with a stockade) for an hour, and were repulsed with considerable loss, without injuring man, woman, or child, in the station" (*ASP, Indian Affairs,* 1:294). Blount's letter to Knox of 8 Nov. reported that the attacking Indians consisted of 400 to 500 Creeks, 200 Cherokees, and 30 to 40 Shawnees, "of whom, three were killed, and seven wounded." The dead incorrectly included "the Shawanese warrior" Tecumseh (d. 1813), and Cherokee chief John Watts was among the wounded, "with a ball through one thigh, and lodged in the other . . . now on recovery" (ibid., 331).

To the United States Senate and House of Representatives

United States [Philadelphia] November 7th 1792. Gentlemen of the Senate, and of the House of Representatives,

I lay before you copies of certain papers relative to the Spanish interference,[1] in the execution of the Treaty entered into, in the year one thousand seven hundred and ninety, between the United States and the Creek nation of Indians[2] together with a letter from the Secretary of State to the President of the United States, on the same subject.[3]

Go. Washington.

Copy, DNA: RG 233, Second Congress, 1791–93, House Records of Legislative Proceedings, Journals; LB, DLC:GW.

1. The presented papers included a letter to Thomas Jefferson of 29 Oct. 1792 from Spanish diplomats José Ignacio de Viar and José de Jaudenes and an extract of Louisiana governor Carondelet's letter to Viar and Jaudenes of 24 Sept. (see Jefferson to GW, 29 Oct. [second letter], n.1). Also included was Jefferson's reply to Viar and Jaudenes of 1 Nov. (see GW to Jefferson, 1 Nov., n.1). For background on these letters, see Jefferson's "Notes of Cabinet Meeting on the Southern Indians and Spain," 31 Oct., in *Jefferson Papers*, 24:547–49.

2. For the 1790 Treaty of New York with the Creek Indians, see GW's proclamation of 14 Aug. 1790, nn.4–5, and Kappler, *Indian Treaties*, 25–29.

3. See Jefferson's second letter to GW of 2 November.

To the United States Senate and House of Representatives

United States [Philadelphia] November 7th 1792.
Gentlemen of the Senate, and of the House of Representatives:

In pursuance of the law, I now lay before you a statement of the administration of the funds appropriated to certain foreign purposes, together with a letter from the Secretary of State, explaining the same.[1]

I also lay before you

A Copy of a letter and representation from the Chief Justice and Associate Judges of the Supreme Court of the United States, stating the difficulties and inconveniencies which attend the discharge of their duties according to the present Judiciary System.[2]

A Copy of a letter from the Judges attending the Circuit Court of the United States for the North Carolina District in June last, containing their observations on an act passed during the last Session of Congress, entitled "An Act to provide for the settlement of the claims of Widows and Orphans, barred by the limitations heretofore established, and to regulate the claims to Invalid Pensions"[3]—and

A Copy of the Constitution formed for the State of Kentucky.[4]

Go: Washington

LS, DNA: RG 46, Second Congress, 1791–93, Senate Records of Legislative Proceedings, President's Messages; copy, DNA: RG 233, Second Congress, 1791–93, House Records of Legislative Proceedings, Journals; LB, DLC:GW.

1. See Thomas Jefferson to GW, 3 Nov. (first letter), and notes 1 and 3. For Jefferson's draft of this introductory paragraph, see Jefferson to GW, 5 Nov., n.2.

2. See the Supreme Court Justices to GW, 9 Aug. 1792, and note 1. For the attorney general's suggestion that GW bring the "necessity of reforming our judicial system" to Congress's attention, see Edmund Randolph to GW, 28 October.

3. See James Iredell and John Sitgreaves to GW, 8 June 1792. For the earlier legislation of 23 Mar. 1792 concerning the "the Claims of Widows and Orphans" and "the Claims to Invalid Pensions," see 1 *Stat.* 243–45. This act was modified by Congress in "An Act to regulate the Claims to Invalid Pensions," which GW signed on 28 Feb. 1793 (ibid., 324–25). Randolph also had suggested in his letter to GW of 28 Oct. that the problem of providing "some temporary mode" for "the relief of many crippled soldiers" merited GW mentioning the subject to Congress.

4. See GW to Samuel McDowell, 20 Oct. 1792, and note 1.

Letter not found: from Anthony Whitting, 7 Nov. 1792. GW wrote Whitting on 11 Nov. acknowledging receipt of "your letters of the 2d and 7th instant."

From Joseph Jones

S⟨i⟩r   Fredericksburg [Va.] 8th Novr 1792.

I understand Capt. Wm Lewis has undertaken the management of the Light-house on our Cape, whereby the Surveyors place is vacant and of course a new appointment necessary to supply the vacancy.[1] Mr [   ] Moffat formerly a merchant of this Town who intermarried with Dr Chs Mortimer's daughter, and has been resident here ever since, is I am told desirous of being appointed to the office, and is I think well qualified to discharge the duties [of] it. I have my information of Mr Moffats willingness to serve from the Doctor, to whom I have no doubt the appointment would be a gratification but a matter of convenience to Mr Moffats family—these considerations however do not determine me to recommend Mr Moffat for public employment—I am induced to mention His pretensions from a conviction in my own mind, and from a knowledge of his activity and vigilance which qualify him for the office, that he will do the duties of it as well if not better than any other person here, who could be selected and at the same time willing to undertake the business—He has been trained in the merchantile line, and is capable of keeping and rendering regular accounts of his transactions in office[2]—with great respect I am S⟨ir⟩ yr most obt Servt

Jos: Jones.

ALS, DLC:GW.

1. For the appointment of William Lewis as the lighthouse keeper at Cape Henry, see Tobias Lear to Alexander Hamilton, 13 Oct. 1792.

2. Thomas Moffat's recommendation from Joseph Jones, a judge of the Vir-

ginia general court, and his marriage to Maria Mortimer, the only daughter of Charles Mortimer, the late Mary Ball Washington's personal physician, apparently helped him in his search for federal employment. On 19 Nov., GW sent Moffat's nomination for surveyor of the port of Fredericksburg to the Senate, which approved his appointment on 21 Nov. (see *Executive Journal*, 1:126).

From Lebrun

Translation,   Paris the 8⟨th⟩ November 1792.
                                            The first year of the Republic.
P. Le Brun, Minister of Foreign Affairs for the Republic of France, to George Washington, President of the United States of America. Health, Peace and Liberty.[1]

The return of Colo. Smith to the free Country of North America,[2] furnishes me with an opportunity of presenting to George Washington the homage of my esteem, and my veneration for his civic virtues. I thank Heaven for it.

When the French helped to free your happy Country from the yoke which threatened to oppress it, they were themselves slaves; but the principles of liberty were in their hearts: they have since developped themselves; and the French are free—they are Republicans. These new Relations cannot but draw closer the bands which have for a long time united them with the American People. Let me be permitted to renew the assurances of the friendship & fraternity of the French. These sentiments will undoubtedly become more durable. May they extend themselves to all the people of both hemisphers! May the sacred principles of liberty & equality become the happy lot of all the world, as it is already of the people of America & France!

Colo. Smith is charged to communicate to George Washington plans worthy of his great Love.[3] The Government of the Republic of France will be pleased that the Colonel should be charged with our Report as well as with your answer, your approbation—and the means of execution which you shall judge in your wisdom to be more convenient.

                              The Minister of Foreign Affairs Le Brun

Translation, DLC:GW; LS, in French, DNA: RG 59, Communications from Heads of Foreign States, Ceremonial Letters; Df, in French, Arch. Aff. Etr. The original receiver's copy, in French, appears in CD-ROM:GW.

1. Pierre-Henri-Hélène-Marie Lebrun (c.1753–1793), known previously as

the abbé Tondu, abandoned his early ecclesiastical career for the French army, from which he deserted after two years of service to become a printer and journalist in Liège (Belgium), where he founded the *Journal Général de l'Europe* in 1785. Lebrun's political philosophy led him to return to revolutionary France where he received an appointment as the French foreign minister on 10 Aug. 1792. Arrested on 2 June 1793 under suspicion of monarchist sympathies, he was guillotined on 27 Dec. 1793.

2. Col. William Stephens Smith, the son-in-law of Vice-President John Adams, had resigned as supervisor of the revenue for the District of New York effective 1 Mar. 1792 and had traveled to London and Paris in pursuit of a private business venture (see GW to Smith, 10 Feb. 1792, and note 1). Smith sailed for the United States on 23 Dec. and arrived in New York City on 7 Feb. 1793 (see Smith to Thomas Jefferson, 8 Feb. 1793, in *Jefferson Papers*, 25:161–62).

3. In early November 1792, shortly before Smith left Paris, the French Provisional Executive Council authorized Smith to "procure to the republic not only the reimbursement of what remains due from the United States, although not yet payable, but for the application of it, either for supplies for the army, or wheat, flour, and salted provisions, in augmentation of our internal supplies." The Washington administration, however, refused to negotiate with Smith (see the second report on the American debt, from Gaspard Monge, comte de Péluse, to Lebrun, 4 Jan. 1793, in *ASP, Foreign Relations* 1:144–46; Jefferson's Conversations with George Washington and William Stephens Smith, 20 Feb. 1793, in *Jefferson Papers*, 25:243–45; the Cabinet to GW, 2 Mar. 1793).

The translation of the French word *âme* should be spirit or soul and not "Love."

Letter not found: from Lovell and Urquhart, 8 Nov. 1792. Tobias Lear, in his letter to Lovell and Urquhart of 16 Dec., referred to "your letter to him [GW] of the 8th of Novr."

From the United States Senate

[Philadelphia] November the 8th 1792.
To the President of the United States—

Accept, Sir, our grateful acknowledgments for your address at the opening of the present Session.[1] We participate with you in the satisfaction arising from the continuance of the general prosperity of the nation, but it is not without the most sincere concern that we are informed, that the reiterated efforts which have been made to establish peace with the hostile Indians have hitherto failed to accomplish that desired object: hoping that the measures still depending may prove more successful than those which have preceded them, we shall, nevertheless concur in every necessary preparation for the alternative; and should the Indians on either side of the Ohio persist in their hostilities, fidelity to the Union, as well as affection to our fellow citizens on the frontiers will insure our decided co-operation in every measure, which shall be deemed requisite for their protection and safety.

At the same time that we avow the obligation of the Government to afford its protection to every part of the Union, we cannot refrain from expressing our regret that even a small portion of our fellow Citizens in any quarter of it should have combined to oppose the operation of the law for the collection of duties on spirits distilled within the United States—a law repeatedly sanctioned by the authority of the Nation, and at this juncture materially connected with the safety and protection of those who oppose it—should the means already adopted, fail of securing obedience to this law, such further measures as may be thought necessary to carry the same into complet operation cannot fail to receive the approbation of the Legislature, and the support of every patriotic Citizen.

It yields us particular pleasure to learn that the productiveness of the Revenue of the present year, will probably supersede the necessity of any additional tax for the service of the next.

The organization of the Government of the State of Kentucky being an event peculiarly interesting to a part of our fellow Citizens and conducive to the general order affords us particular satisfaction.

We are happy to learn that the high state of our Credit abroad has been evinced by the terms on which the new loans have been negociated.

In the course of the Session we shall proceed to take into consideration the several objects which you have been pleased to recommend to our Attention; and Keeping in view the importance of Union and Stability in the public Councils, we shall labor to render our decisions conducive to the safety and happiness of our Country.

We repeat with pleasure our assurances of confidence in your administration, and our ardent wish, that your unabated zeal for the public good may be rewarded by the durable prosperity of the Nation and every ingredient of personal happiness.[2]

John Langdon, President, pro tempore, of the Senate

LB, DLC:GW; Df, DNA: RG 46, Second Congress, 1791–93, Senate Records of Legislative Proceedings, President's Messages.

This message, approved by the Senate on 8 Nov., was delivered to GW at 11:00 A.M. on 9 Nov. (see *Annals of Congress*, 2d Cong., 611–13), and the letter-book copy in DLC, although dated 8 Nov., is recorded under the date of 9 November.

1. See GW's Address to the U.S. Senate and House of Representatives on 6 Nov. 1792.

2. GW replied briefly on 9 Nov.: "I derive much pleasure, Gentlemen, from your very satisfactory address. The renewed assurances of your confidence in my Administration, and the expression of your wish for my personal happiness, claim and receive my particular acknowledgements. In my future endeavour for the public welfare, to which my duty may call me, I shall not cease to count upon the firm, enlightened and patriotic support of the Senate" (LB, DLC:GW).

From Jonathan Dayton

Sir,   Philadelphia Novr 9th 1792

Having delivered to the Secretary of the Treasury, pursuant to the 2nd Section of the Act of Congress entitled "An Act authorizing the grant & conveyance of certain lands to John Cleves Symmes & his associates," military warrants sufficient to pay for One hundred & six thousand eight hundred & fifty seven acres of land, I am prepared, as Agent for, & the associate of, said Symmes to carry into effect the Act before mentioned, as well as the one previously passed, entitled "An Act for ascertaining the bounds of a tract of land purchased by John Cleves Symmes," so far as the same depends on me.[1]

As Mr Ludlow, the surveyor of the Ohio company and Miami purchases is now in town on his way to the western territory, & as his aid will be very useful, if not necessary, in defining the lines of boundary, I submit it to your consideration sir, whether it would not be adviseable to have him detained a few days for that purpose.[2] I have the honor to be sir with the greatest respect & attachment Your most obedt servt

Jona: Dayton

ALS, DNA: RG 59, Miscellaneous Letters.

1. In 1787 Congress authorized the sale to New Jersey resident John Cleves Symmes of a two-million-acre tract of land in the Northwest Territory between the Miami and Little Miami rivers. A final contract with the Treasury Department, however, was not signed until 15 Oct. 1788 and then only for one mil-

lion acres (see *ASP, Public Lands,* 1:75–77). That same year, on 19 Feb., Congress appointed Symmes one of the judges of the newly established Northwest Territory. The indefinite boundary lines of the Miami, or Symmes, Purchase, in addition to delays and inaccuracies in surveying lots and poor record keeping, led to the sale of lands outside Symmes's grant, disputed property claims, and conflict with territorial governor Arthur St. Clair (see Jefferson to GW, 10 Nov. 1791, n.1, for earlier letters and reports about problems with the Symmes Purchase). The various complaints led to "An Act for ascertaining the bounds of a tract of land purchased by John Cleves Symmes," 12 April 1792, and "An Act authorizing the grant and conveyance of certain Lands to John Cleves Symmes, and his Associates," 5 May 1792 (6 *Stat.* 7–8; 1 *Stat.* 266–67). Under the terms of these two acts, GW issued a patent on 30 Sept. 1794 for the 311,682 acres for which Symmes had completed payment. For the patent to John Cleves Symmes of 30 Sept. 1794, see the copies in ViLxW, DLC: Short-Harrison-Symmes Families Papers, OHi: Charles E. Rice Collection, and Vi; see also Carter, *Territorial Papers,* 2:496–98.

On 5 Nov. 1792 Dayton, a congressman from New Jersey and a business associate of Symmes, delivered to Alexander Hamilton "warrants sufficient to pay for 106,857 acres, making in all 248,540 acres, exclusive of a complete township to be given in trust for the establishing of an academy and public schools," in accordance with the requirement set forth in section 3 of the legislation passed in May (see Dayton to Symmes, 19 Nov. 1792, in Bond, *Correspondence of Symmes,* 272). For the administration's response to Dayton, see Tobias Lear to Dayton, 9 Nov. 1792, and note 1.

2. In 1787 Thomas Hutchins, the current surveyor general of the United States, appointed New Jersey native Israel Ludlow to survey the Symmes Purchase, and Ludlow began his work in the fall of 1788 with the town of Cincinnati. After various problems delayed completion of the survey, Ludlow received additional instructions to establish the boundaries of the Symmes Purchase from Secretary of the Treasury Hamilton on 20 Nov. 1790, but the surveyor reported to Hamilton on 5 May 1792 that continued Indian hostilities in the Northwest Territory had frustrated his efforts. Hamilton, therefore, reissued his orders on 25 Nov. 1792, and Ludlow notified Hamilton on 10 July 1793 that the task finally was complete. Ludlow later surveyed the boundary line established between the United States and Indian territory under the 1795 Treaty of Greenville (see Teetor, *Life and Times of Col. Israel Ludlow,* 7–22, 49; Syrett, *Hamilton Papers,* 8:362, n.2, 11:361–63, 13:233, 15:81–82).

Tobias Lear to Jonathan Dayton

Sir,   Philadelphia Novr 9th 1792

In reply to your letter of this date, the President of the United States directs me to inform you, that he is ready to do, at any time, whatever may depend on him towards completing the "grant and conveyance of certain lands to John Cleves Symmes and his associates," in conformity to An Act of the Legislature passed during the last session of Congress. But as the President understands that there are certain things in that business which may require legal investigation, he thinks it proper that it should come to him through the Attorney General of the United States.[1] I have the honor to be very respectfully Sir, Your most Obedt Servt

Tobias Lear.

Secretary to the President of the United States.

ALS (letterpress copy), DNA: RG 59, Miscellaneous Letters; LB, DLC:GW.

1. For background on the Symmes Purchase, see Dayton to GW, 9 Nov. 1792, and note 1. Dayton replied to Lear the next morning, Saturday, 10 Nov.: "I wish to speak with you on the subject of your letter to me of yesterday in reply to mine of the same date to the President. I shall remain at the Hall of the House of Representatives until the hour of adjournment, or if it be inconvenient for you to come here, I will call upon you at the President's to ask an explanation of a part of your answer" (DNA: RG 59, Miscellaneous Letters, docketed as 10 Oct. 1792; the dateline is "Saturday morning").

On 19 Nov., Dayton wrote Symmes from Philadelphia that Attorney General Edmund Randolph agreed with GW and Alexander Hamilton that "we must be confined to the original boundaries in the contract until you or your agent and associate duly authorized for that purpose, have applied and agreed, as mentioned in the first act [of 12 April 1792], to alter the contract agreeably thereto. They think my letter of agency insufficient for the purpose." The attorney general, Dayton reported, "will decide on the fullness and sufficiency of the powers you may send me." Dayton concluded his letter by suggesting several actions that Symmes might take to facilitate the issuance of a new patent (Bond, *Correspondence of Symmes,* 271–75).

Lear wrote Dayton again on 20 Nov. 1792 from Philadelphia: "In obedience to the President's command, I have the honor to enclose for you, a copy of a letter from the Attorney General of the United States, on the subject of your letter to the President, of the 9th instant" (DNA: RG 59, Miscellaneous Letters). The letter from Randolph has not been identified.

To promote his interests and remove various obstacles to acquiring a new patent, Symmes visited Philadelphia in the summer of 1793. He did not return to the Northwest Territory until after GW issued him a land grant on 30 Sept. 1794 (ibid., 163–67). For the 1794 patent, see Dayton to GW, 9 Nov. 1792, n.1.

To the United States Senate and House of Representatives

United States [Philadelphia] November 9th 1792.

Gentlemen of the Senate and of the House of Representatives;

I now lay before you, a letter from the Secretary of State, covering the copy of one from the Governor of Virginia, with the several papers therein referred to, on the subject of the boundary between that State, and the territory of the United States, south of the river[1] Ohio. It will remain with the Legislature to take such measures, as it shall think best, for settling the said boundary with that State, and at the same time, if it thinks proper, for extending the settlement to the State of Kentucky, between which and the same territory, the boundary is, as yet, undetermined.[2]

George Washington.

Copy, DNA: RG 233, Second Congress, 1791–93, House Records of Legislative Proceedings, President's Messages; LB, DLC:GW; Df (letterpress copy), in George Taylor, Jr.'s writing, DLC: Jefferson Papers. The date of "Nov. 8. 1792" on the letterpress copy of the draft is in Jefferson's writing.

1. The word "river" does not appear in either the letter-book copy or the draft.

2. For the letters of Thomas Jefferson and Virginia governor Henry Lee, and the several affidavits and reports that were enclosed in Lee's letter, and for background on the Virginia and Kentucky boundary disputes, see Jefferson to GW, 2 Nov. 1792 (first letter), and source note and note 1.

Letter not found: from Anthony Whitting, 9 Nov. 1792. GW wrote Whitting on 14 Nov.: "Your letter of the 9th came to my hands last night."

From the United States
House of Representatives

Sir,   [Philadelphia] Saturday the 10th of November, 1792.

The House of Representatives, who always feel a satisfaction in meeting you, are much concerned that the occasion for mutual felicitation, afforded by the circumstances favorable to the national prosperity, should be abated by a continuance of the hostile spirit of many of the Indian tribes; and particularly, that the reiterated efforts for effecting a general pacification with them, should have issued in new proofs of persevering enmity, and the barbarous sacrifice of citizens who, as the messengers of peace, were distinguishing themselves by their zeal for the public service. In our deliberations on this important department of our affairs, we shall be disposed to pursue every measure that may be dictated by the sincerest desire, on one hand, of cultivating peace, and manifesting by every practicable regulation, our benevolent regard for the welfare of those misguided people: and by the duty we feel, on the other, to provide effectually for the safety and protection of our fellow citizens.

While with regret we learn, that symptoms of opposition to the law imposing duties on spirits distilled within the United States, have manifested themselves, we reflect, with consolation, that they are confined to a small portion of our fellow-citizens. It is not more essential to the preservation of true liberty, that a government should be always ready to listen to the representations of its constituents, and to accommodate its measures to the sentiments and wishes of every part of them, as far as will consist with the good of the whole, than it is, that the just authority of the laws should be steadfastly maintained. Under this impression, every department of the Government and all good Citizens must approve the measures you have taken, and the purpose you have formed, to execute this part of your trust with firmness and energy; and be assured, Sir, of every constitutional aid and co-operation which may become requisite on our part. And we hope, that while the progress of contentment under the law in question, is as obvious as it is rational, no particular part of the community may be permitted to withdraw from the general burthens of the Country, by a conduct as irreconcileable to national justice as it is inconsistent with public decency.

The productive state of the public revenue, and the confirmation of the Credit of the United States abroad, evinced by the loans at Antwerp and Amsterdam, are communications the more gratifying, as they enforce the obligation to enter on systematic and effectual arrangements for discharging the public debt, as fast as the conditions of it will permit; and we take pleasure in the opportunity to assure you of our entire concurrence in the opinion, that no measure can be more desireable, whether viewed with any eye to the urgent wish of the community, or the intrensic importance of promoting so happy a change in our situation.

The adoption of a Constitution for the State of Kentucky, is an event, on which we join in all the satisfaction you have expressed. It may be considered as particularly interesting; since, besides the immediate benefits resulting from it, it is another auspicious demonstration of the facility and success with which an enlightened people is capable of providing, by free and deliberate plans of government, for their own safety and happiness.

The operation of the law establishing the Post-Office, as it relates to the transmission of news-papers, will merit our particular enquiry and attention; the circulation of political intelligence through these vehicles, being justly reaconed among the surest means of preventing the degeneracy of a free government, as well as of recommending every salutary public measure to the confidence and co-operation of all virtuous Citizens.

The several other matters which you have communicated and recommended, will, in their order, receive the attention due to them. And our discussions will in all cases, we trust, be guided by a proper respect for harmony and stability in the public councils, and a desire to conciliate, more and more, the attachment of our Constituents to the Constitution, by measures accommodated to the true ends for which it was established. Signed by Order, and in behalf of the House

                                        Jona. Trumbull, Speaker.

Attest. John Beckley, Clk

Copy, LB, DLC:GW; LB, DNA: RG 233, Second Congress, 1791–93, House Records of Legislative Proceedings, Journals.

This address is a response to GW's Address to the U.S. Senate and House of Representatives of 6 Nov. 1792. Approved by the House on 10 Nov., it was delivered to GW on 12 Nov. (see *Annals of Congress*, 2d Cong., 677–79). The letter-book copy in DLC is recorded under the delivery date.

GW replied to the House's message on 12 Nov.: "It gives me pleasure to express to you, the satisfaction, which your Address affords me. I feel, as I ought, the approbation, you manifest, of the measures, I have taken, and the purpose, I have formed, to maintain, pursuant to the trust reposed in me, by the Constitution, the respect, which is due to the laws—And the assurance, which you, at the same time, give me, of every Constitutional aid and co-operation, that may become requisite, on your part.

"This is a new proof of that enlightened solicitude for the establishment and confirmation of public order, which, embracing a zealous regard for the principles of true liberty, has guided the deliberations of the House of Representatives: a perseverance in which can alone secure, under the divine blessing, the real and permanent felicity of our common country" (Copy, DNA: RG 233, Second Congress, 1791–93, House Records of Legislative Proceedings, Journals; LB, DLC:GW).

From George Clendinen

Sir,   Kanhawa County Virginia November the 11th 1792
    permit me to Introduce to your particular favr and Respect Our Brother Batis. Dequan, The Kascaska chief, who So early as

the Year eighty One, made his personal appearance with offers Of his decided and determinate Friendship and Affection to the United States, to which he as ever Since adheard with all his nation and those In Alliance with him[1]—King dequan Informs me that he has prevaild upon the Chiefs Of Many Nations to Travel With him to you; with The United Belt of piece To present you, Hoping that we may all become the Same people, Firmly United to Each Others Interests, In the Strictest Tyes Of Friendship Unalterable for ever, Saying That the Americans The French Nation and All the Nations Of Red Men Are the Same people Or that their Receprocal Interest Out to be the Same,[2] King Dequan, will perhaps be Introduced to you by the Honorable Thomas Jefferson Secretary Or prime Minister, to the United States, with whom he Contracted A most Friendly Acquaintance In the Year Eighty One, when he was Governor Of Virginia—Your Excellency will Find very Little Occasion for this my letter of Introduction after being Acquainted with he who is the Subject of It as his person and Behaviour truely Represent the Greaces and Philantropy Of his mind.[3]

In his endeavours for peace may God of his Infinite Mercy promote, as our Frontiers at present Groan Under the Hard hand of War and Opp[r]ession. I have the Honr to be with great Respect and Esteem your Obt Humble Sevt

Geo. Clendinen

ALS, ViMtV: Storer-Decatur Collection.

1. County lieutenant George Clendinen (Clendenin), one of the founders of Kanawha County and the city of Charleston in present-day West Virginia, served several terms in the Virginia general assembly, 1781–89, 1791, and 1793–95. GW earlier had sought Clendinen's assistance in disposing of his holdings along the Kanawha River (see GW to Clendinen, 21 Feb. 1791).

Kaskaskia chief Jean-Baptiste Ducoigne (died c.1832) had visited Thomas Jefferson at Monticello in June 1781 (see Jefferson to Ducoigne, 1 June 1781, and source note, in *Jefferson Papers*, 6:60–64).

2. Ducoigne was one of two Kaskaskia chiefs who signed the Treaty of Vincennes on 27 Sept. 1792 (Names of Signers of the Treaty of Vincennes, OMC: Putnam Papers). At the end of the negotiations, Gen. Rufus Putnam issued an invitation for a delegation of chiefs, including Ducoigne, to visit GW at Philadelphia. For background on this treaty, see GW to Knox, 3 Sept. 1792, and note 3.

3. The Indian delegation arrived in Philadelphia in late December, and Ducoigne met with Jefferson shortly thereafter (see *Pennsylvania Gazette* [Philadelphia], 2 Jan. 1793; Jefferson to Martha Randolph Jefferson, 31 Dec. 1792, *Jefferson Papers*, 24:806). GW formally addressed the chiefs on 1 Feb. 1793,

and Ducoigne was one of the chiefs who replied that same day on behalf of the delegation (see *JPP,* 40; Speech from the Wabash and Illinois Indians, 1 Feb. 1793).

To Anthony Whitting

MR. WHITING,   Philadelphia, 11 November, 1792.

Since my last, I have received your letters of the 2d and 7th instant, and shall notice such parts of them as require it, and give such directions respecting my business, committed to your management, as may occur to me.[1]

I shall again express my wish, and, as the raising of corn at the Mansion-House is given up, will also add my anxiety, to have all the ground (except single trees and clumps here and there) cleared, and well cleared, as mentioned in a former letter, between the old clover lot and the sunken ground quite from the wharf to Richard's house and the gate; but, previously, do what has been desired from the cross fence by the spring, to the wharf. In clearing the whole of this ground, let all the ivy and flowering trees and shrubs remain on it, over and above the clumps, and other single trees where they may be thought requisite, for ornament.[2] The present growing pines within that enclosure might be thinned, and brought more into form. When this is done, and all the low land from the river up to the gate laid down in grass, it will add much to the appearance of the place, and be a real benefit and convenience, as it will yield an abundance of grass.

All the hands, that can be conveniently spared, may be kept steadily at this work until it is accomplished, or till they are called off for other essential purposes. The ditchers too, when not employed about more essential work, may aid in this. And it will be necessary for you to think of some crop for the new part of the ground, that will require cultivation through the summer; otherwise the clearing of it will be labor in vain, as in a year or two, without cultivation, it will be as foul as ever.

By a vessel called the *President,* Captain Carhart, you will receive, I hope, the articles contained in the enclosed invoice and bill of lading. The linen, I expect will be cut out and used to the best advantage. You will perceive there are two prices; let that, which bears the lowest price, be given to the boys and girls, and the highest price and best, to the grown and most deserving men and women, and the surplus (for there is more than you required) be put away securely.[3]

The mulberry trees may be planted about in clumps, as mentioned in my letter by last post to the gardener. They are not trimmed, because, as I am informed, these trees may be propagated by cuttings from them, and save me the trouble and expense of sending more from this place. With respect to the shrubs from Mr. Bartram's botanical garden, directions at the foot of the list are given so fully, as to render it unnecessary to add aught concerning them in this letter; but the grapes the gardener must take particular care of, as they are of a very fine kind.[4]

I send you, also, under cover with this letter, some seeds, which were given to me by an English farmer from the county of Essex, in England, lately arrived in this country to settle, and who appears to be a very sensible and judicious man, and a person of property. He also gave me a pamphlet upon the construction of the kind of plough, which he has used for many years; and the principles for putting the parts together, to make it work true and easy, which I will send to you so soon as I shall receive it from a gentleman to whom I lent it.[5] The plough is simple in its make. The oats, which he gave me as a sample, exceed very little, if any, what I have grown myself. They may, however, in the spring be put into the ground by single seeds, to try what can be made of them. The cattle cabbage may also be tried.

Mr. Lambert, the name of the farmer from whom I had these things, says that the land, on which he and his father before him have lived for fifty or sixty years, is a stiff white clay; and, being at a distance from any source of manure, besides that which is made on the farm, they have pursued a different mode of cropping from that which is usually followed in England; and by so doing, with the aid of the internal manure of the farm, they have brought their poor, stiff land, which originally did not yield them more than five or six bushels of wheat to the acre, and other grain in proportion, to produce very generally from twenty-five to thirty of wheat, and from forty to fifty of barley. Their method has been to keep the arable land always perfectly clean, and alternately in crop or fallow; that is, to take a corn crop from it one year, and have it under the plough in a naked fallow, by way of preparation for the next crop, the next year; beginning this fallow in the autumn, when the ground is dry, again in the spring, as soon as it becomes dry, and three or four times after, before seeding for wheat (if wheat is the crop); never ploughing it wet, which is the cause, he says, of its running. He seems to understand the principles as well as the practice of husbandry, being a sensible man, and inured for a number of years (I suppose he is sixty) to the labor and practice of it. He has travelled a good deal about this country, and is of opinion that our great error lies in not keeping our arable land clean, and free from weeds. I observed to him, that the people of this country are of opinion, that naked fallows under our hot sun are injurious. He will not by any means admit the principle or the fact; but ascribes the impoverished state of our lands and bad crops to the weeds which he everywhere sees, and which both exhaust and foul it. By constant ploughing, these, he says, are eradicated; and when the fields come to be laid in grass, which is sown, the hay will be pure and unmixed with any thing hurtful to it.

The giving way of the post-and-rail fencing proves, in a strong point of view, the necessity of seeing that all which is made hereafter be of a more substantial kind; that is, the posts larger, and the rails shorter; and it proves, too, the necessity of what I can never too often nor too strongly impress upon you, and that is, to begin and make a business of rearing hedges, without the loss of a single season; for really there is no time to lose. Set about it effectually. I am sure every plantation is now of sufficient force to spare labor for this purpose; not merely to scratch a little trench along the banks of the ditches, and therein put a few seeds, or cuttings, among weeds, briars, and every kind of trash, which will prevent their coming up, or choke them if they do. I would wish to have the seeds or cuttings of any thing tried, rather than that the attempt should be delayed, as it has hitherto been, from one season to another.[6]

Desire Thomas Green to date his reports. That of the week before last I send back for explanation of his measurement of the sawing. I fancy it will puzzle him to make out 508 feet in the twenty-four plank there set down; for, as plank, length and breadth only could be measured. This would amount to no more than 296 feet. As scantling, length and side and edge would be measured, and this would give only about 310 or 312 feet. If he goes on at this rate, he will, in appearance, amend their work, though it will not in reality be any better. But, admitting that the true admeasurement was 508 feet, this would make but a miserable quantity for the time they were about it. That these people (sawyers I mean) may have no pretence for such idleness, not only get them two saws, but let them be of the largest and best kind. I have already told you, that the oak scantling is to be got on the estate, and the place where.[7] Let Thomas Green, while he is in the Neck, repair the overseer's house, as well as it can be done at this season.[8] The scantling that is to be bought, should be got as soon as possible, that the carpenters may be framing it in the winter, or early in the spring.

Direct the miller to report every week the state of his manufactory of the wheat; as well as the receipts and delivery of the grain into and from the mill, that I may see how he proceeds in that business, and what flour he has on hand, that I may govern my directions accordingly.[9]

I am very well satisfied with the reasons you assign for opening my letter to Mrs. Fanny Washington. It might, as you observe, have contained a request, which, as she was gone, you might have complied with.[10]

You have never mentioned in any of your letters what has become of the mare I left at Georgetown, and which was to have been sent to Mount Vernon. I hope she got there safe, and is now well; in that case you may, occasionally, ride her; keeping her in good order against I may call for her.[11]

How does your growing wheat look at this time? I hope no appearance of the Hessian fly is among it. On Patuxent, not far from you, I am told it is making such havoc amongst the growing wheat, as to render it necessary to sow over again.[12] I am sorry to find No. 1, at French's, turn out so poor a crop of wheat, and that the fields at Muddy Hole have yielded still worse. How much wheat at that place came off the lot by the overseer's house?[13]

In ploughing fields No. 3 and No. 4, Dogue Run, let them be so begun as that the rows when planted may run north and south, or as nearly so as the situation of the fields will admit.

In making your weekly reports, instead of referring to the preceding week or weeks, for the state of your stock of different kinds, enumerate the number of each. I shall have it in my power then to see at one view the precise state of it without resorting to old accounts. And let me entreat, that you will examine them yourself, frequently, as a check upon the overseers; without which, rather than be themselves at the trouble of counting them, they will make you that kind of general report.

The coffee and tea, that I sent you some time ago, you are very welcome to use, and it is my desire you should do it.[14]

The sheriff's bill for the taxes, which you paid while I was at home, cannot here be got at, as it is filed amongst my papers; but, as I want a copy of it for a particular reason, I should be glad if you would procure one from the sheriff, and send it to me exactly as it was handed in and paid. I want no receipt annexed to it. The account only is all I desire, containing the whole items of charges.[15] I am your friend and well-wisher,

GEORGE WASHINGTON.

P. S. In clearing the wood, mark a road by an easy and graduated ascent from the marsh or low ground, up the hollow which leads into the lot beyond the fallen chestnut, about midway of the lot; and leave the trees standing thick on both sides of it, for a shade to it. On the west side of this hollow, if I recollect rightly, there was an old road formerly, but not laid out agreeably to the directions here given. It would look well, and perhaps might be convenient, if there was a road on both sides of this hollow, notwithstanding the hill-side on the east is steep. At any rate, trees where the road would go, if made, might be left for future decision, as they might also be along the side of the low land at the foot of the hill quite from the wharf to the gate by Richard's house.[16] If that meadow should ever be thoroughly reclaimed, and in good grass, a walk along the edge of it would be an agreeable thing; and leaving trees for this purpose may not be amiss, as they may at any time be removed, although time only can restore them if taken away in the first instance. And this would be a good general rule for you to observe in other parts of the same ground; as, if too thick, they can always be thinned; but, if too thin, there is no remedy but time to retrieve the error.

Sparks, *Writings*, 12:354–58.

1. The letters from Whitting to GW of 2 and 7 Nov. have not been found. GW's previous letter to Whitting was dated 4 November.

2. Compare with GW's instructions in his letter to Whitting of 4 November.

3. The invoice and bill of lading have not been found. For GW's shipment of various items needed at Mount Vernon, including linen, wine, tea, and coffee, see GW to Whitting, 28 Oct., and note 8.

4. GW's letter to John Christian Ehlers circa 7 Nov. has not been found, but

a probable enclosure in that letter was GW's Directive to John Christian Ehlers of 7 Nov. 1792, in which GW listed the plants recently ordered from John Bartram, Jr.'s botanical garden near Philadelphia. For GW's purchase of 100 white mulberry trees, see Samuel Meredith to GW, 1 Nov. 1792.

5. GW had lent Richard Peters his copy of John Lambert's *A Letter on the Construction and Use of the Improved Foot Plough,* which had been published in London in 1784 (see Richard Peters to GW, 30 November). Lambert's pamphlet was in GW's library at the time of his death (see Griffin, *Boston Athenæum Washington Collection,* 117). GW enclosed this pamphlet, along with Peters's comments on it, in a letter to Whiting of 2 December. John Lambert (1746–1823) later published a brief essay entitled *A Short and Practical Essay on Farming: Being the Experience of a Farmer, of About Sixty Years of Age; Near Forty Years of Which Were Spent in England, Essex County, on Land Where Farming Is Done in Greatest Perfection: and Near Seven Years on Three Hundred and Twenty Acres of Worn Out Land in Pottsgrove and Alloway Creek, in Salem County, West Jersey . . .* (Philadelphia, 1798).

6. GW frequently urged his managers to work on developing hedges to replace the rotting wood fences. See, for example, GW to Whiting, 14 Oct., 18 Nov. 1792.

7. Green's carpentry report has not been found. For GW's earlier instructions on various carpentry projects, see GW to Whiting, 14 Oct., and notes 12 and 13. GW's instructions about the oak scantling may have been included in the missing bill of scantling enclosed in his letter to Whiting of 21 Oct., which has not been found. For further instructions on the use and purchase of scantling, see Washington's Plan for a Barn, enclosed in his letter to Whiting of 28 October.

8. The overseer at the River farm on Clifton's Neck was William Garner (see Articles of Agreement with William Garner, 10 Dec. 1788).

9. For background on miller Joseph Davenport's association with GW, see Robert Lewis & Sons to GW, 5 April 1785, and note 2, and Davenport's Proposal to GW, 18 Mar. 1792, and source note.

10. For GW's letter to Fanny Bassett Washington, see GW to Whiting, 28 Oct., and note 2.

11. For GW's problems with several horses on his July journey from Philadelphia to Mount Vernon, see Tobias Lear to Thomas Jefferson, 11 July, and GW to Lear, 30 July. GW mentioned this mare in his letter to Whiting of 14 October.

12. The Hessian fly, *Phytophaga destructor,* is a fly or midge, the larvae of which are very destructive to wheat. It was named after the Hessian troops hired by the British during the Revolutionary War because Americans thought that it had accompanied them to the United States. For earlier discussion about the problems caused by this pest, see GW to Edward Newenham, 22 June. The Patuxent River rises in central Maryland and flows about one hundred miles south and southeast into the Chesapeake Bay.

13. The dower slave Davy, who previously had been the overseer at the River farm, moved to the Muddy Hole farm as overseer about June 1791 and was still there at the time of GW's death in 1799. Davy was married to Molly, a dower

slave also at the Muddy Hole farm (see GW to Tobias Lear, 26 June 1791, n.1; Slave List, 18 Feb. 1786, in *Diaries*, 4:279; and Washington's Slave List, June 1799).

14. For GW's shipment of coffee and tea from Philadelphia, see GW to Whitting, 28 Oct., and note 8.

15. On 17 Sept. 1792 GW paid Fairfax County sheriff Jesse Moore £38.5.1 in full for "my Specie Tax in the Parishes of Truro & Fairfax, due for 1791," and on 27 Sept. he paid Jesse Simms £28.8.9 "for 4 Hhds Tobo to discharge Parish & County Levies of the year 1791—at 15/6 ⅌ ⟨Ct⟩" (Ledger B, 344, 346). Whitting enclosed the sheriff's account in his letter to GW of 22 Nov., which has not been found, and GW enclosed a copy of this report in his letter to Arthur Young of 2 December.

16. For similar instructions regarding land near Richard's house, see GW to Whitting, 4 November.

From Thomas Jefferson

[Philadelphia] Nov. 12. 92.

Th: Jefferson has the honor to inclose to the Presidt a letter from mister Pinckney.[1] he will have that of waiting on him to-day to know what to say to the Commrs of the Federal seat about the order for money on Virginia.[2]

AL, DNA: RG 59, Miscellaneous Letters; LB, DNA: RG 59, George Washington's Correspondence with His Secretaries of State; LB (photocopy), DLC:GW.

1. Jefferson had received the previous day a letter from Thomas Pinckney, the U.S. minister to England, written from London on 8 Sept. 1792, in which Pinckney wrote that he had declined a request from fellow American Stephen Sayre to be "appointed my secretary (if only nominally) whereby he would be entitled to the privilege of freedom from arrest and urged it as a protection due from the Minister of the United States to a man suffering on their account" (*Jefferson Papers*, 24:346–48). The British briefly had imprisoned Sayre, a banker in London at the beginning of the Revolutionary War, for his active support of the colonies. After the war, and upon his return to London, the authorities jailed him again, this time for failure to pay his debts. Sayre repeatedly petitioned Congress for compensation for his various activities on behalf of the United States during the war, and in 1807 Congress granted him payment for his time as secretary to diplomat Arthur Lee while in Berlin.

2. The Virginia legislature had approved on 27 Dec. 1790 a grant of $120,000 for the construction of public buildings in the federal district, to be made in three equal payments (see Hening, 13:125). After meeting with Jefferson, GW sent a letter to Virginia treasurer Jaquelin Ambler on 13 November, in which he requested payment of Virginia's second installment. Jefferson enclosed a copy of GW's letter to Ambler in his next letter to the D.C. commissioners, also dated 13 Nov. (see *Jefferson Papers*, 24:612–13).

From Thomas Jefferson

[Philadelphia] Nov. 12. 92.

Th: Jefferson has the honor to inclose to the President Judge Turner's answer.[1] his office has been thoroughly searched, and no copy exists there of the act of Virginia giving money for the federal buildings: that of Maryland only is there. he is in hopes it may be among the President's papers.[2]

Dr Barton, a learned & very ingenious gentleman of this city, mentioning to Th: J. that he had never had the honour of being presented to the President, asked to be presented.[3] if the President has no objections Th: J. will take that liberty tomorrow at three aclock.[4]

AL, DNA: RG 59, Miscellaneous Letters; LB, DNA: RG 59, George Washington's Correspondence with His Secretaries of State; LB (photocopy), DLC:GW.

1. GW recently had received a letter dated 6 July from Winthrop Sargent, secretary of the Northwest Territory, in which Sargent complained about the long absence from their duties of George Turner and John Cleves Symmes, two of the three territorial judges. At GW's request Jefferson wrote Turner on 9 Nov. 1792 to urge him to repair to the Northwest Territory in order to carry out his responsibilities there. The enclosed reply of 11 Nov. from Turner to Jefferson has not been found (see *Jefferson Papers*, 24:604).

2. Jefferson was searching for a copy of the act passed by the Virginia legislature on 27 Dec. 1790 granting $120,000 "towards erecting public buildings" in the federal district. The Maryland legislature in its November session of 1790 had approved a similar grant of $72,000. Each state's contribution was to be made in three equal payments (see Hening, 13:125; *Laws of Maryland, Made and Passed . . . in 1790*). Virginia governor Beverley Randolph had sent GW a copy of Virginia's law in a letter dated 15 Feb. 1791, but GW could not find his copy at this time (see note 4). Jefferson wrote Virginia treasurer Jaquelin Ambler on 13 Nov. 1792 asking for a copy of the Virginia act (see *Jefferson Papers*, 24:612). GW also wrote Ambler on 13 Nov., requesting payment of Virginia's second installment of its grant.

3. Benjamin Smith Barton was a noted Philadelphia physician and naturalist, and his work *New Views of the Origin of the Tribes and Nations of America* (2d rev. ed.; Philadelphia, 1798), in which he inscribed "For General Washington, with the most respectful compliments of his very obedient and very humble Servant &c.," was in GW's library in 1799 (see Griffin, *Boston Athenæum Washington Collection*, 17). For Benjamin S. Barton's earlier correspondence with GW, see William Barton to GW, 29 July 1790, and notes 2 and 3.

4. Tobias Lear, at GW's request, replied to Jefferson later on this date: "The President returns Judge Turner's letter which The Secretary of State submitted to his perusal. The President has no copy of the Act of Virginia giving

money for the federal buildings. The President requests that the Secretary of State will at all times introduce such Characters to him as he may think proper to be introduced" (DLC: Jefferson Papers).

From Rodolph Vall-travers

Rotterdam, Haring's-Vliet, 9ber—12th 1792.
boarding at Mrs Anna Hamilton's.

May it please Yr Excellence! Sir!

An official Letter, dated the 2d of April, recieved but a few Weeks ago, from Thos Jefferson, Esqe Secretary of State for your united american Republics, in answer to Part of the Contents of four of mÿ Letters to Yr Excellence, claims my humble and thankful Acknowledgments.[1] I hope a fifth Letter of mine, dated the 10th of June last; transmitted, with a new Supply of instructive Materials for my worthy, ingenious and laborious Friend, John Churchman, the american Geographer; and entrusted to the special Care of Mr C. Maÿer, Agent of Adrian Valck Esqe of Baltimore, sailing from this City to Baltimore, on Board the Wachtsamkeit, freighted with 400. german Emigrants; came likewise safe to Hand: which I shall be glad to hear.[2]

It is with Joy I observe; considering the Multiplicity of political Objects, which so gloriously engross Yr Exc.'s chief Cares; that my humbly tendered Services, of an œconomical, philosophical and literary Nature, have been, most judiciously, referred to the peculiar Attention of the illustrious American Academical Society for promoting useful Arts & Sciences. The very great Honor conferred on me by my ensued Adoption into that learned Body of american Worthies, adds a new Spur to my strenuous Exertion of my poor Abilities, in promoting their beneficent Pursuits, to the utmost Extent, not of mÿ manÿfold Opportunities, but of mÿ too limited Powers.[3]

As a true American Fellow-Citizen, not only by my universal Philanthropy, and peculiar Esteem and Attachment to the happiest, wisest, freeest & most respectable Nation on Earth; but even by several Grants of Land made me, whilst in England, in Georgia, Carolina, and Newengland: maÿ I presume to offer Yr Excellence some Services also in the political Line, which may occasionally occurr on this Continent?

The ten Provinces of the austrian Netherlands, together with the Bishopric of Liege; now invaded by the french Assertors of civil & religious Liberty, very likely soon rescued from the grasping Claws of the twoheaded Monster of the imperial Eagle, and restored to their antient Liberties & Independence will, undoubtedly be happy, to enter into a close Alliance of Friendship, Protection & Commerce with your united States, on the same Principles, as France and Holland, their contiguous Sister-Republics. The Ports of Ostend & Antwerp will readily recieve, on moderate reciprocal Duties, yr Rice, Tobacco, Furs, newbuilt Ships, Irons, Sugar, dried & Salt Fish, Bee's Wax & Spermaceti—Candles, dried Fruits of all Sorts, Timber &c. and you may recieve in Return all Sorts of Linnen, Sail-Cloths, Cordage, Threads, Hosierÿ-Goods, Hardwares &c. with a large Ballance of Cash. So beneficial & mutually desirable a Connection I shall be proud to bring about, with the powerful Influence of my Friends at Brusselles, Antwerp, and Ostende, as soon, as duly authorised thereto. In that Case, I wou'd shift my Residence from this Place to Brusselles, to act, first, as your Consul, or, as ÿr Resident, with an adequate Power & Salary.[4]

Shou'd the U. S. have Occasion for anÿ further Supplies of ready Money, for their public Services, those very Netherlands, especially the wealthy Clergy thereof, wou'd, I am sure, be ready to lend almost any Sum, especially at this Juncture, on your public Security; even at 5. pr Ct with an additional 3. pr Ct annually, as a sinking Fund for the total Extinction of the whole Capital and Interest, in less than thirty Years. Shares of a hundred Dollars each, cou'd be sold at Bruxelles, at Antwerp, at Liege, and at Amsterdam, and halfyearly Interests paid, by the most capital Bankers: Mess[r]s Fred: Romberg & Son, at Brusselles & Ostende; Mess[r]s Earlborn [F. E. van Ertborn] & Co: At Antwerp; Mess[r]s Pankouke [Panckoucke] & Co. at Liege; and Mess[r]s Staphorst & Hubbard, at Amsterdam, ÿr Agents; allowing them 1. pr 1,000. for their Commissions. Even So, Millions of Dollars wd soon be subscribed for. Mess[r]s Fontain & Van Dooren, merchants of this City, with a corresponding Part of their House at Amsterdam, offer likewise their Services, in similar Operations, as Co-Agents to the United States; whose Solidity, credit, and Reputation, will give full Satisfaction on an impartial and fair Enquiry.

Give me Leave, most worthy Sir, to Subscribe myself, with infinite Veneration of your eminent public and private Virtues—Your Excellence's Most sincerily devoted humble Servant:

J. Rodolph Vall-travers.

P.S. The News, just now recd from Flanders import: that Du-Mourier, the french General, after having gained an obstinate Battle, and taken Mons, has capitulated with the Austrian Commander in chief, the Duke of Saxe-Teschen, Governor of the austrian Netherlands, & granted the following Articles. *1st*) The whole german Army to evacuate all the Netherlands, with their Arms, a Fieldpiece to each Regimt & their Bagage[.] *2nd*) to declare all the A. Netherlands, free & independent, under the Protection of the Republic of France, and at full Liberty, to chuse their own Form of Government.[5]

Roterdam, 9ber 12th at Night.

P.S. DuMou⟨r⟩ier is said, to have written ⟨a⟩ peremtory Letter to their h⟨i⟩gh mightenesses, the States of the Seven united Provinces of this Republic,[6] insisting:

1st) That all the french Emigrants shou'd be banished from their Territories.

2.) That the Republic of Fran⟨ce⟩ shall be avowed & acknowledged, as an independed State.

3.) That the Treaty of Friendship & Alliance made with their former King, shall be confirmed & ratified with the present french République.

4.) That all the Magistrates established since the Revolution, by a prussian Army, shall be deposed, and the former magistrates, antecedent to the said Revolution, be restored to their former Places;

5.) And all the exiled Dutch Patriots recalled.

ALS, DLC:GW.

1. For background on Vall-travers and his propensity for writing lengthy and apparently unwelcome letters to GW, see Vall-travers to GW, 20 Mar. 1791, and source note. For Jefferson's letter to Vall-travers, see *Jefferson Papers*, 23:366–67. No letter from GW to Vall-travers has been found. Vall-travers, nevertheless, continued to write to GW, at least until 15 June 1796, the date of his last extant letter to GW (DLC:GW).

2. Vall-travers's "fifth" letter to GW was dated 6 June. For GW's earlier forwarding of materials sent by Vall-travers in 1791 for Maryland cartographer John Churchman, see Churchman to GW, 5 Sept. 1792, n.4.

3. Vall-travers had been elected to membership in the American Philosophical Society on 20 Jan. 1792.

4. Although earlier French efforts to capture Belgium (Austrian Netherlands) had failed, the invasion begun in October proved more successful. The French victory at Jemappes on 6 Nov. was followed a short time later by the capture of Brussels, and by the end of the year Belgium was under French control. Vall-travers never received any appointment from the American government either in Belgium or elsewhere.

5. Vall-travers is referring to the French army's victory, under Gen. Charles-François du Périer Dumouriez (1739–1823), at Jemappes on 6 Nov. against the Austrian forces led by Albert, duke of Saxe-Teschen, who had positioned his army on the heights of Jemappes, just outside Mons on the Belgian frontier.

6. William V (1747–1806), prince of Orange-Nassau and the hereditary stadholder of the Republic of the Seven United Provinces (the Netherlands), was married to Wilhelmina (1751–1820), sister of the Prussian king Frederick William II. On 1 Feb. 1793 France declared war on the Netherlands.

To Jaquelin Ambler

Sir   Philadelphia Nov. 13. 1792.
Be pleased to pay to Messrs Johnson, Stuart & Carrol Commissioners of the Federal buildings on the Patowmac, or to their order, or by the order of any two of them, the second instalment of the monies granted by the state of Virginia towards the said buildings.[1]

Go: Washington

LS, in Thomas Jefferson's writing, Vi; L (letterpress copy), DLC: Jefferson Papers; copy, DNA: RG 59, Miscellaneous Letters; LB, DLC: GW. All are addressed to the "Treasurer of Virginia."

Jefferson enclosed this letter in his letter to the D.C. commissioners of 13 Nov. 1792. He also enclosed a separate letter that he had written to Ambler earlier on this date, in which he explained that the president's request did not specify the sum of the expected payment because "no copy of the act granting the money is possessed here" (*Jefferson Papers*, 24:612–13). The Virginia legislature on 27 Dec. 1790 granted $120,000 for the construction of public buildings in the federal district, payable in three equal installments (see Hening, 13:125). For both Jefferson's and GW's acknowledgments that they did not have a copy of the pertinent legislation among their papers, see Jefferson to GW, 12 Nov. 1792 (second letter), and note 4.

Jaquelin Ambler (1742–1798), a 1761 graduate of the College of Philadelphia, was a successful planter and merchant in Yorktown, Va., before the Revolutionary War. During the war he left his Yorktown home and mercantile business and began a career in public service, eventually settling in Richmond where he served as a director of public buildings from 1784 to 1791 and supervised the construction of the new capitol. Ambler served as Virginia's state treasurer from 1782 until his death.

1. On the verso of the receiver's copy of this letter, David Stuart wrote, "Pay the within contents to Coll Willm Deakins on order," and both he and fellow D.C. commissioner Daniel Carroll signed that order. Deakins acted as the commissioners' treasurer. Also on the verso, John Hopkins, commissioner of continental loans for the state of Virginia and a Richmond banker and merchant, wrote and signed the following receipt: "May 6th 1793 Recd a Warrant on the Treasury of Virga for Fifteen Thousand dollars in part of the within." Ambler had made an earlier payment of $10,000 on the second installment on 10 Dec. 1792 (see Tobias Lear to Thomas Jefferson, 20 Dec., n.1).

To the Commissioners for
the District of Columbia

No. 13.

Gentlemen,   Philadelphia Novr 13th 1792.

I have duly received your letter of the 13th of October, enclosing a list of the sale of lots in the federal City; with the prices of which I am more gratified than I am by the number which have been disposed of. I am pleased to find that several of your Mechanics were among the purchasers of lots, as they will not only, in all probability, be among the first improvers of them, but will be valuable citizens.

I agree with you in opinion that the ground in such eligible places as about the Capitol and the President's House, should not be sold in squares; unless there are some great and apparent advantages to be derived from specified buildings—immediate improvement—or something which will have a tendency to promote the advancement of the City.

The circumstances under which Mr Blodget bid off the square near the Capitol, were such as occur at almost every public sale, and in that instance, his having done so, appeared very proper for the interest of the public: I agree, however, with you, that it would be best for the circumstance not to be generally known.

How far the idea which Mr Blodget suggests of having an Agent to pass through the several States, to dispose of lots, might be beneficial or not, I am unable to say; but it appears to me, that if a respectable and responsible Character, in the principal town of each State, could be authorized to dispose of the public lots, as purchasers might appear; provided the matter could be so arranged that no confusion or inconvenience should arise from the same lot being disposed of by two or more agents, (which might possibly be done by monthly returns being made from the several Agents to the Commissioners, ascertaining the day—and even hour of each sale, to be by them confirmed previous to any payment: a small per Centum to be allowed the Vender—and all private sales to cease a month before every public sale) it would be a means of accommodating persons in different parts of the Union, and would expedite the sale of the lots. But this, as well as Mr Blodgets suggestion (which rather appears to me to be hawking the lots about) must be weighed and determined upon according to your best judgement and information.[1]

I think that a further public sale in the spring, or early in the summer, would be advantageous. For it is desireable that every opportunity which could be made convenient, on account of the season and other circumstances, to dispose of lots in this way, should be embraced.[2]

In proportion as numbers become interested in the federal City, and the public works advance, a constant attendance at the spot will be more and more requisite on the part of those who superintend or direct the business thereof; and I am of opinion it will be found necessary, as neither of the Commissioners reside there, that some active and competent character, vested with proper authority by them, should be constantly on the ground to superintend the business carrying on there. But who this person shall be, is altogether with yourselves to chuse—and the various and essential qualifications requisite in him will readily occur to you. With great esteem, I am, Gentlemen, Your most Obedt Servt

Go: Washington

LS, in Tobias Lear's writing, DLC:GW; L (letterpress copy; dated 17 Nov. 1792), DLC:GW; LB (dated 13 Nov. 1792), DNA: RG 42, Records of the Commissioners for the District of Columbia, Letters Sent, 1791–1802; LB (dated 17 Nov. 1792), DLC:GW. The letter-book copy in DNA: RG 42 indicates that the letter was received on 3 Dec. 1792.

1. The commissioners appointed Samuel Blodget, Jr., the district supervisor on 5 Jan. 1793. They also authorized him to sell lots in the federal district on their behalf (see D.C. Commissioners to Blodget, 5 Jan. 1793, DNA: RG 42, Records of the Commissioners for the District of Columbia, Letters Sent, 1791–1802, and D.C. Commissioners to GW, 5 Jan. 1793).

2. The next public auction of lots began on 17 Sept. 1793 (see GW to D.C. Commissioners, 16 Sept. 1793).

To Thomas Jefferson

Tuesday [Philadelphia, 13 November 1792]
I am glad the detention of the Ship gives you an opportunity of forwarding the enclosed.[1] Yours

G. W———n

ALS, DLC: Jefferson Papers. Jefferson docketed the letter: "Washington Presidt recd Nov. 13. 92."

1. Jefferson added a notation below the text in which he identified the enclosure: "it was my letter of Nov. 13. to mister Pinckney. London." In that letter Jefferson wrote that the "ship New Pigou still remaining in port," he was able to respond to Pinckney's letter of 8 Sept. 1792, which Jefferson had enclosed in his first letter to GW of 12 Nov. 1792. Jefferson informed Pinckney that he could not find any claims submitted by Stephen Sayre requesting compensation for services during the Revolutionary War. "Nevertheless," Jefferson wrote, "if he has any regular claim against the U.S. they are willing and able to meet them. In the mean time you have done perfectly right in refusing him the protection of an appointment under you." According to Jefferson the additional papers that he enclosed would show Pinckney that "our prospects with the Indians, both Northern and Southern, are better" (*Jefferson Papers*, 24:615–16). For background on Sayre's claims, see Jefferson to GW, 12 Nov. (first letter), n.1.

Tobias Lear to Henry Knox

United States [Philadelphia] Novr 14th 1792
By the President's command T. Lear has the honor to return to the Secretary of War the dispatches from Mr Seagrove, which were submitted to the president yesterday.

The President thinks there are some parts of these communications which should be laid before Congress, and requests that the Secretary will select such as may be proper & have them communicated accordingly.[1]

Tobias Lear
Secretary to the president of the United States.

ALS (letterpress copy), DLC: GW; LB, DLC: GW.

1. James Seagrove wrote Knox on 28 Oct. 1792 from St. Mary's, Ga., and enclosed a letter of 9 Oct. from Creek leader Alexander McGillivray, a letter of 15 Oct. from Indian interpreter James Durouzeaux, and a letter of 15 Oct. from John Galphin, a son of Creek native Metawney and George Galphin, trader and former Indian commissioner for the Southern District during the Revolutionary War. Based on the information contained in these enclosures, Seagrove reported that "The greatest part of the [Creek] chiefs, and many of their

people" were on their way to meet with him. Seagrove was optimistic that the boundary line between the Creeks and the United States, agreed upon in the Treaty of New York on 7 Aug. 1790, could be surveyed "this winter" if the "underhand machinations" of McGillivray were not too great. Although Seagrove complained about McGillivray's duplicitous behavior, he conceded that some of the problems with the Indians derived from "the intrusions" of white settlers on the frontier. "It is to be lamented," Seagrove wrote, "that the insatiable rage which our frontier brethren have for extending their limits, could not be checked, and kept within the bounds set them by the General Government. The United States, like most other countries, is unfortunate in having the worst class of people on her frontiers, where there is least energy to be expected in her civil government; and where, unless supported in the early stages of settlement by military force, civil authority becomes a nullity.

"I am extremely sorry to hear that the Cherokees are likely to be hostile to the United States. I am happy to say that I cannot discover a trace of disaffection or backsliding in the Creeks, in consequence of the commotions among the Cherokees. No endeavors on my part shall be wanting to keep them apart.

"Should the Cherokees have the audacity to take up arms against the United States, I fondly hope that not a moment will be lost in chastising them in the most exemplary manner. If they are allowed to proceed any length, and are successful, the infection will unquestionably spread among the other Southern tribes, and when, or where it may end, God only knows. Permit me to suggest the idea of a spirited, powerful volunteer expedition, from the three Southern States, being immediately sent into their country, and break them up" (*ASP, Indian Affairs,* 1:320–22). Knox presented Seagrove's letter and its enclosures to both houses of Congress on 15 Nov. 1792 (see *Annals of Congress,* 2d Cong., 615, 690).

From John Nicholson

sir,   [Philadelphia] Novr 14th 1792.

I was at a loss whether first to offer the subscription herewith that your name might grace the head thereof—or to be detered by the consideration that in your office it may be deemed if not an interference of our government, yet of the highest administrators thereof which may give offence to some other Nations, but I considered that of this you could best Judge And that if the presenting it to you was improper you would excuse it when you knew the Motives.[1] With the highest respect And Esteem I have the honor to be your Most obedt servant

Jno. Nicholson

ALS, DNA: RG 59, Miscellaneous Letters.

1. The enclosed subscription from Pennsylvania comptroller general John Nicholson has not been identified. For a discussion of the many and varied

economic pursuits of this prominent land speculator and financier, see Arbuckle, *Pennsylvania Speculator and Patriot.*

From St. Hilaire

Monsieur   A new-york ce 14. Novembre 1792
    je fus de tous tems l'ami des gens de génie; C'est pourquoi
Monsieur Cointeraux m'a envoÿé de Paris les papiers, que je vous
adresse, avec prière de vous les remettre en main propre; mais la
maladie, qui m'a attiré dans Ce salubre Continent, m'empêche
de remplir à la lettre sa Commission et me prive du plaisir de
vous assurer de vive voix du profond respect avec le quel j'ai
l'honneur d'être, Monsieur Vôtre très-humble et très-obéissant
serviteur,
                        Lerpaud-Tencin-de-Saint-hÿlaire

P.S. Daigner, Monsieur, m'accuser la réception, à new-york,
poste restante, de ce paquet, afin que je puisse écrire à Monsieur
Cointeraux, que vous avez reçu selon ses desirs, son placet.

ALS, DNA: RG 59, Miscellaneous Letters.
    French émigré St. Hilaire, "formerly Captain in the Regiment of Besançon, of the Corps of Royal Artillery," had written GW on 12 April 1792 seeking employment. His letter of this date accompanied papers that the French architect François Cointeraux had asked St. Hilaire to forward to GW. Cointeraux's papers have not been identified. For the content of those papers, see Thomas Jefferson to GW, 18 Nov. 1792.

To Benjamin Stoddert

Sir,   Philadelphia Novr 14th 1792[1]
    Your favor of the 24 Ulto came duly to hand, but the variety of
important matters which pressed between the receipt of it, and
the meeting of Congress, allowed me no time to give it an earlier
acknowledgment: and now, I pray you to consider what I am
about to say, as coming from me in my private capacity.
    It has always been my opinion, & still is so, that the Administration of the Affairs of the Federal City ought to be under the
immediate direction of a judicious & skilful superintendant, appointed by, & subject to the orders of the Commissioners (who,
in the eye of the law, are the responsible characters)—One in

whom is united knowledge of Men & things—industry, integrity impartiality and firmness. And, that this person should reside on the Spot. This, I believe, is also the opinion of the Commissioners. and if they think Mr Blodget possesses these qualifications (I know very little of him myself, and after what has happened shall be cautious in recommending) or, that he is the *most* competent character that presents who is willing to undertake, & ready to enter upon the duties of such an Office; their appointment of him will meet my entire approbation.[2]

I can readily conceive, Sir, that the motives to your communication were pure & laudable, & shall give you credit for them accordingly—On my part, permit me to add, that I have a mind open to information, and a disposition always to correct abuses (that shall come properly before me) as far as I am able; but I am sure it is unnecessary to remark to a person of your observation, that from the two great interests which divide the Federal City, & the lesser ones into which these are branched, it will be found difficult if not impossible for any set of Commissioners whatsoever to steer clear of censure.[3] One wants this thing—another wants that thing—and all, or most of them perhaps want things which our resources are incompetent to the accomplishment of. You will excuse my candour therefore, my good Sir, for observing that there is in my judgt but one line of conduct proper for these Gentlemen to pursue & that is to take a comprehensive view of the trust reposed in them—the general expectation of the community at large—and the means to effect it—form their plans agreeably thereto upon sound and just principles; & see that they are carried into effect by whomsoever they shall employ in the Execution thereof. without regard to any local concern or interest whatsoever. Such a conduct will meet general approbation, and of none, I am persuaded more than your own. With esteem I am Sir—Yr Most Obedt Servt

Go: Washington

ADfS, DLC:GW; LB, DLC:GW.

1. On the draft manuscript GW first wrote a "3" over a "1" and then a "4" over the "3," changing the date from 11 to 13 to 14 November. The letter-book copy is dated 14 November.

2. GW had expressed his support for the appointment of a district supervisor in his letter to the D.C. commissioners of 13 November. On 5 Jan. 1793 the commissioners appointed Samuel Blodget, Jr., to that position (see D.C. Commissioners to Blodget, 5 Jan. 1793, DNA: RG 42, Records of the Commission-

ers for the District of Columbia, Letters Sent, 1791–1802; and D.C. Commissioners to GW, 5 Jan. 1793).

3. The "two great interests" were the landowners and businessmen in Georgetown such as Stoddert, and those in Carrollsburgh (see GW to David Stuart, 20 Nov. 1791).

To Anthony Whitting

Mr Whiting,   Philadelphia Novr 14th 1792

Your letter of the 9th came to my hands last night, and though I am much hurried, will briefly observe, that I had rather repair my Seins, and fish myself, than hire the landing with the Negros. If a good price could be obtained for the Landing without the Negros, and an express prohibition of Waggons coming thither, I should like, & would prefer that. But at any rate repair, & keep the Seins dry and out of the way of Mice, that you may have an alternative. In the mean while, give it out, and make it as public as you can, that the landing alone, or landing and Boat, (with the prohibition above) is to be Rented; but that the Person renting is to furnish me with a certain quantity of Shad & Herring, to be specified, in the early part of the Season. Or if the Boat is reserved, I could easily catch what fish I should want at the landing by Bishops House; which used to be, and no doubt still is, a good fishery. If after giving this notice, and enquiring what Colo. Mason used to receive for his *best* landing, and what others, on both sides of the River get for theirs, you should have an Offer from a person of good character, & in whom confidence could be placed, similar to what is given for the best—I would advise you to take it. and either secure the fish wanted for my own use from them—or reserve the Boat, & catch for yourself at the Mansion House.

It will no doubt occur to you, when you are making enquiry into the Rent received by Colo. Mason & others, whether the Landings are furnished with convenient & secure houses, as mine is, for securing and preserving the Fish; and make the difference in the price if they are not, which these are entitled to.

It is not in my power to fix a Rent or hire for the Landing, because I do not know the usual price of the best, with the conveniences mine have; and this I must take, or not Rent. Take care, if you should hire it, to stipulate that the person hiring shall have nothing to do with the Shore after the Shad & Herring Season is over—nor with the Houses beyond a limited time; otherwise, I might sustain unexpected inconveniences.[1]

I presume, it would be better for me to take £25 for the Stallion than have him to Winter & therefore consent to its being done.[2]

Among other reasons for not hiring my hands with the Shore is, that I do not want to take them so long from the ground I wish to get in prime order in, and between the Old Clover lot and H—— Hole.[3] I am Your friend & well wisher

Go: Washington

ALS, DLC:GW.

1. Whiting's letter to GW of 9 Nov. has not been found. GW's main fishery was at the Ferry farm, on the Potomac River near the mouth of Dogue Run. George Mason owned fisheries on Occoquan Creek and on the Potomac, and his "best" landing was probably Baxter's (Simpson's) Bay at the mouth of the Occoquan (see Copeland and MacMaster, *The Five George Masons*, 66–67). For GW's further thoughts on renting out his own fishery, see his letter to Whitting of 6 Jan. 1793. On 12 Dec. 1793 GW wrote Arthur Young that his fishery was "well supplied with various kinds of Fish at all Seasons of the year, and in the Spring with the greatest profusion of Shad, Herring, Bass, Carp, Perch Sturgeon &ca." Nevertheless, neither GW nor Whitting had been successful in renting it by that date.

2. In his letter to Whitting of 4 Nov., GW had agreed that Whitting should dispose of old horses.

3. See GW's instructions in his letters to Whitting of 4 and 11 Nov. that this land be cleared and grubbed.

Letter not found: from Anthony Whitting, 14 Nov. 1792. GW wrote Whitting on 18 Nov. that Whitting's letter of the "14th instt came duly to hand."

To Thomas Jefferson

[Philadelphia] Thursday Eveng 15th Novr 1792

The letter enclosed, intended for Govr Blount, appears to me to be very proper.[1]

Go: Washington

ALS, DLC: Jefferson Papers. Jefferson docketed the letter: "Washington Presidt recd Nov. 15. 92," and he noted below the text that "it was my letter of Nov. 14. 92."

1. In a note to GW of 14 Nov. 1792, Jefferson had submitted his letter to William Blount of that date and "the correspondence on which it is founded"

for GW's approval (DNA: RG 59, Miscellaneous Letters). The enclosures included the letters to Jefferson of 24 Aug. and 4 Oct. 1792 from North Carolina governor Alexander Martin and the letter to Jefferson of 12 Nov. 1792 from Attorney General Edmund Randolph (see *Jefferson Papers*, 24:321–22, 439, 609). The subject of this correspondence was the legitimacy of certain land grants made by North Carolina in territory that the state recently had ceded to the federal government, which, according to Blount, was included in the Southwest Territory, of which he was governor. For Blount's original complaint to Jefferson, see his letter of 23 April 1792 (*ibid.*, 23:443–44). The dispute involved differing interpretations of a clause in the Act of Cession of 22 Dec. 1789 (see Carter, *Territorial Papers*, 4:5–6 and note 12). Martin in his letter to Jefferson of 4 Oct. conceded that the subsequent Treaty of Holston of 2 July 1791 reserved the disputed area for the Cherokee Indians, and he issued a proclamation prohibiting further land grants in that region. Randolph wrote in his letter to Jefferson of 12 Nov. that legal action would be necessary to negate grants already made, but that the "management of this business" might be left for Blount to conclude. Jefferson replied to Blount on 14 Nov. that "in order to avoid the appearance of wishing to harrass the people, it might suffice, where the grantee is not in *actual possession*, to warn him against taking possession and to see that he does not. Where they have come to the lands, . . . and remain in possession of them, it is difficult to say at this distance and with only our information, whether any and which of their cases have any equitable circumstances which should induce a permission to continue, on their giving an acknolegement that they hold subject to the future pleasure of the government of the U.S. This is submitted to your discretion, with an entire confidence that you will secure the right of the U.S. with as little trouble and injury to the intruders and grantees as you can" (*Jefferson Papers*, 24:617–18).

Memorandum from Thomas Jefferson

[Philadelphia, 15 November 1792]
Department of State, to wit:

The requisites of the Law having been complied with on the part of the Ship *Canton* fitted out from the port of Philadelphia, on a voyage to India, Hugh Alexander Makee Master thereof became entitled to a passport in the usual form, which was this day granted.

(N.B. The above passport is one of the six which were signed by the President previous to his departure for the southward.) [1]

Certified to the President of the United States this 15 day of November 1792.

Th: Jefferson

DS, DNA: RG 59, Miscellaneous Letters; LB, DNA: RG 59, George Washington's Correspondence with His Secretaries of State; LB (photocopy), DLC:GW.

The DS is docketed: "Certificate for a Sea Letter granted to the Ship Canton Novr 15th 1792."

1. GW had left Philadelphia on 21 Mar. 1791, stopping at Mount Vernon before his 7 April departure for a two-month journey through Virginia, the Carolinas, and Georgia. For details regarding GW's Southern Tour, see *Diaries,* 6:99–163. On 24 Nov. 1792 Jefferson sent GW the "2d" passport, issued for "the Brigantine, *Columbia,* fitted out from the Port of Philadelphia, on a voyage to the Isle of France, John Green, Master." On 28 Dec. 1792 Jefferson certified the "3rd" passport, for "the Ship *Washington,* fitted out from the port of New York, Thomas Randall Master," and on 15 Mar. 1793 he certified the "4th" passport, for "the Ship *Sampson,* fitted out from the port of Philadelphia, John Rossiter Master" (all are in DNA: RG 59, Miscellaneous Letters). The fifth and sixth passports have not been identified.

Letter not found: from the Ohio and Monongalia, Va., representatives, c.15 Nov. 1792. Tobias Lear sent under cover of his letter to Henry Knox of 21 Nov. a "letter which the President has received from the Representatives of the frontier Counties in the Gene[r]al Assembly of Virginia."

From George Cabot

Sir   Philadelphia Novr 16th 1792

I have thought it my duty to lay before the President of the United States the letter herewith enclosed,[1] which was brought me by this day's post together with several others of similar import from individual Gentlemen, all of them recommending Mr Joy as a Person eminently qualified to serve those the care of whose interests is the immediate object of the application.[2]

In addition to the reasons expressed by the Merchants of Massachusetts for a consular establishment in India, it is believed that a Gentleman of public character residing at Calcutta, if of competent abilities, might procure admission for our Ships into the ports of one Nation when excluded from those of others, an injury to which that commerce is too much exposed; for although the Vessels of all Nations are permitted to trade at the principal European Settlements in Bengal, yet this is a priviledge held by a very precarious tenure & requires to be secured by some permanent interest, if any such can be created in those Settlements, & by availing ourselves as much as possible of the competition which naturally exists among them.[3]

the testimony of the Gentlemen trading to India from Massachusetts is so respectable that I can add nothing to its weight, yet justice demands of me to confirm their sentiments in favor of Mr Joy & will induce me to give more ample evidence if required. with the highest degree of respect I have the honor to be Sir your most humble & obedient Servant

George Cabot

ALS, DNA: RG 59, Miscellaneous Letters.

1. Several Massachusetts merchants had signed the enclosed letter written from Boston to George Cabot on 1 Nov. 1792 recommending for appointment as the first U.S. consul in India Benjamin Joy (c.1757–1829), a Newburyport, Mass., merchant "who is shortly going to India," and in whose abilities they had confidence. The letter was signed by Thomas Russell, Stephen Higginson, John C. Jones, John Codman, Patrick Jeffrey, Elias Hasket Derby, Joseph Barrell, David Sears, and Joseph Russell, Jr. Tobias Lear endorsed the letter: "Note. there are about 40 Vessels trading beyond the Cape of Good Hope from the State of Massachusetts" (DNA: RG 59, Miscellaneous Letters).

2. The other letters to Cabot recommending Joy's appointment have not been identified. Benjamin Lincoln, however, had written to GW from Boston on 9 Nov. 1792: "You will soon be informed of the wish of a number of Merchants, here, trading to the East-Indies, other than to Canton, that a Consul might be appointed to remain in that country—If the measure shall meet your Excellencys approbation and you should cast your eyes this way for a person to fill the office, and if in that survey Mr Benjamin Joy, who has been, & is returning to the Indies should arrest your notice he will prove himself, I doubt, not a gentleman of information & probity and do honour to the confidence placed in him" (DLC:GW).

3. On 17 Nov. 1792 Lear, at GW's request, forwarded to Jefferson "letters relative to appointing a Counsul for the United States to reside in India; and to request, that, if the Secretary on considering the subject sees no objection to such appointment, he would prepare a message to the Senate therefor" (DNA: RG 59, Miscellaneous Letters). Jefferson's letter to GW of 19 Nov. 1792 enclosed "the form of nomination," which was dated 19 Nov. and nominated Joy as the U.S. consul "at Calcutta and other ports & places on the coast of India in Asia" (the letter and its enclosure are in DNA: RG 59, Miscellaneous Letters). GW sent Joy's nomination to the U.S. Senate on 19 Nov. 1792. Joy wrote GW from Newburyport on 9 Dec. 1792 to express his "gratitude for the confidence you have been pleased to repose in me, and for the honor you have done me by appointing me to that office" (DNA: RG 59, Despatches from Consular Offices, Calcutta, India, 1792–1906). Joy arrived in Calcutta in April 1794 to find that British officials refused to recognize his consular authority, although they allowed him to reside there as a commercial agent. By late 1794 continuing health problems convinced Joy to return to the United States. He arrived in Massachusetts in late 1795 and resigned his consulship in January 1796 (see Joy to Edmund Randolph, 24 Nov. 1794, and to Timothy Pickering, 24 Jan. 1796, DNA: RG 59, Despatches from Consular Offices, Calcutta, India, 1792–1906).

From Thomas Jefferson

[Philadelphia] Nov. 16. 1792.

Th: Jefferson has the honor to inform the President that the papers from Johanna Lucia Henrietta Hinrichsen, a Danish subject, state that she is entitled to inherit from her brother Daniel Wriesburg deceased two tracts of land in New Jersey & New York and she petitions Congress, & the states of New Jersey & New York to have justice done her, offering, if they will pay her the reasonable rents during her life and an indemnification for the detention hitherto, that she will cede to them the remainder after her death for the establishment of a charitable institution for the benefit of poor military persons, the plan of which she leaves to the President of the U.S. to settle.[1]

Th: Jefferson is of opinion that the incompetence of the General government to legislate on the subject of inheritances is a reason the more against the President's becoming the channel of a petition to them: but that it might not be amiss that Th: J. shou⟨l⟩d inclose to the Governors of New Jersey & N. York the petitions addressed to their states, as some advantages are offered to them, of which they will take notice, or not, at their pleasure. if the President approves of this, & will return the petitions they shall be inclosed accordingly.[2]

Th: Jefferson

ALS, DNA: RG 59, Miscellaneous Letters; ALS (letterpress copy), DLC: Jefferson Papers; LB, DNA: RG 59, George Washington's Correspondence with His Secretaries of State; LB (photocopy), DLC: GW.

1. The papers from Johanna Hinrichsen have not been identified, but she wrote GW on 3 May 1794 to express her dissatisfaction with the response to the representation that she had sent "last year" to the "Governor and Council" of New York. According to a contemporary translation of that letter, Hinrichsen's brother Conrad Daniel Wrisberg had been a lieutenant in the British army during the French and Indian War. When he retired from the army in 1763, he remained in the American colonies. Although he received a "grant of 2000 Acres of uncultivated land in New York," he apparently settled in New Jersey, and at the time of his death in 1774 he owned an ironworks at Mount Hope, New Jersey. "At his death," Hinrichsen wrote, "he left a very handsome estate; and, inasmuch as he died unmarried, he left no other heirs but myself—his only sister of the blood." She sought GW's assistance and hoped that he would "support my representation in the court of New York; to the end, that, after so many distressing delays, I may finally be placed in the possession, of the inheritance which has fallen upon me" (DNA: RG 59, Miscellaneous Letters).

Hinrichsen wrote a similar letter to GW on 9 Dec. 1794 (DNA: RG 59, Miscellaneous Letters). No reply from GW to either letter has been found.

2. On this date, on behalf of the president, Tobias Lear returned Hinrichsen's petitions "to the Governments of New York and New Jersey" to Jefferson for forwarding to the governors of those states, George Clinton and William Paterson, respectively (DLC: Jefferson Papers).

From Thomas Jefferson

[Philadelphia] Nov. 16. 92.

Th: Jefferson has the honor to submit to the inspection of the President a set of copper promisory notes, & coins, made by Boulton, the superiority of which over any thing we can do here, will fully justify our wish to set our mint agoing on that plan. they are obscured by the sea-air.[1]

AL, DNA: RG 59, Miscellaneous Letters; LB, DNA: RG 59, George Washington's Correspondence with His Secretaries of State; LB (photocopy), DLC: GW.

1. For background on the federal government's efforts to establish a mint and the attempt of British entrepreneur and engineer Matthew Boulton to profit from those efforts, see John Bailey to GW, 17 April 1790, n.1. On 2 April 1792 GW signed "An Act establishing a Mint, and regulating the Coins of the United States," which specified that the coinage was to include "CENTS—each to be of the value of the one hundredth part of a dollar, and to contain eleven penny-weights of copper" and "HALF CENTS—each to be of the value of half a cent, and to contain five penny-weights and half a penny-weight of copper" (1 Stat. 246–51). GW subsequently assigned the Mint to the jurisdiction of the State Department (see GW to Jefferson, 20 Oct. 1792, and note 3). It probably was at GW's direction that Jefferson wrote Thomas Pinckney, the newly appointed U.S. minister to Great Britain, on 14 June 1792, asking his "assistance in procuring persons" with the necessary skills and knowledge to aid the United States in producing its own coins. "Mr. Bolton," Jefferson wrote, "had also made a proposition to coin for us in England, which was declined.—Since this the act has been passed for establishing our mint. . . . I am therefore to request that you will endeavor, on your arrival in Europe to engage and send us an Assayer, . . . and a Chief-coiner and Engraver, in one person, if possible, acquainted with all the improvements in coining, and particularly those of [Jean-Pierre] Drost and Boulton" (*Jefferson Papers*, 24:74–76). For Pinckney's difficulty in securing appropriate artisans, see his letter to Jefferson of 13 Dec. 1792 (ibid., 738). For the permanent appointment as chief coiner and engraver of Henry Voight of Pennsylvania, who had been serving temporarily in this position, see Tobias Lear to Jefferson, 30 Jan. 1793 (DLC: GW); see also Voight to GW, 13 April 1792, and note 1. Former New Jersey resident Albion Cox, who currently was living in his native England, was hired as the assayer in May 1793 (*JPP*, 141, 297).

From Elizabeth Willing Powel

My dear Sir [Philadelphia] November 17th 1792

After I had parted with you on Thursday, my Mind was thrown into a Train of Reflections in Consequence of the Sentiments that you had confided to me.[1] For tho' they were not new, yet I had flattered myself that a nearer View of the Consequences that would probably ensue upon your quitting a Trust, upon the proper Execution of which the Repose of Millions might be eventually depending, would have pointed out to you the Impropriety, or to use a stronger Word, the Impracticability of carrying your Intentions into Effect—Regard for you and Anxiety for the Wellfare of our common Country, have determined me to submit to your Consideration the Thoughts which have occured to me on this Subject, and which, I think, it would be inconsistent with my Friendship for you to withold. That you have obtained the Love, Respect and Confidence of the Citizens of the United States is a Fact as well substantiated as any that we are in Possession of; and, be assured, that I am as superior to the Meanness of Adulation as you are incapable of receiving it with Pleasure. Your honest Mind is not a Soil for it to take Root in, nor are your Ears attuned to listen, with Delight to the Syren Song of Flattery; nor, on the other Hand, do I mean to give you Pain by wounding your feelings. I well know your invincible Diffidence, and your Sensibility with respect to public Opinion; on the last therefore I must lay some Stress. Be assured that a great Deal of the well earned Popularity that you are now in Possession of will be torn from you by the Envious and Malignant should you follow the bent of your Inclinations. You know human Nature too well not to believe that you may have Enemies. Merit & Virtue, when placed on an Eminence, will as certainly attract Envy as the Magnet does the Needle. Your Resignation wou'd elate the Enemies of good Government and cause lasting Regret to the Friends of humanity. The mistaken and prejudiced Part of Mankind, that see thro' the Medium of bad Minds, would ascribe your Conduct to unworthy Motives. They would say that you were actuated by Principles of self-Love alone—that you saw the Post was not tenable with any Prospect of adding to your Fame. The Antifederalist would use it as an Argument for dissolving the Union, and would urge that you, from Experience, had found the present System a bad one, and had, artfully, withdrawn from it that you might not be crushed under its Ruins—that, in this, you had acted a politic Part. That a Concurrence of unparralelled fortunate Circumstances had attended you—That Ambition had been the moving spring of all your Actions—that the Enthusiasm of your Country had gratified your darling Passion to the Extent of its Ability, and that, as they had nothing more to give, you would run no farther Risque for them—that as Nature had not closed the Scene while your Carreer was glorious you had, with profound Address, withdrawn yourself from a Station that promised nothing to your Ambition, and that might eventually involve your Popularity. The Federalists consider you as their own and glory in the Possession. They gave what a great and generous People might offer with Dignity and a noble Mind receive with Delicacy. They made no Oblation on the Altar of Idolatry or Vanity; their Offering was the Effect of Gratitude, Respect, Affection and Confidence to the Man that had, materially, assisted them in rearing and establishing the glorious Fabric of Liberty. Will you withdraw your Aid from a Structure that certainly wants your Assistance to support it? Can you, with Fortitude, see it crumble to decay? or, what is still worse behold the Monster Licentiousness, with all his horrid Attendants, exalted on its Ruins? I know you cannot you will not. But you will say that there are Abilities and Virtues in other Characters equall to the Task; admitting the Fact, it does not prove the Expediency of the Inference you have drawn from it, If there is not a Confidence in those Abilities and that Integrity they cannot be beneficially applied. I will venture to assert that, at this Time, you are the only Man in America that dares to do right on all public Occasions. You are called to watch over the Welfare of a great People at a Period of Life when Man is capable of sustaining the Weight of Government. You have shewn that you are not to be intoxicated by Power or misled by Flattery. You have a feeling Heart, and the long Necessity of behaving with Circumspection must have tempered that native Benevolence which otherwise might make you too compliant, the Soundness of your Judgement has been evinced on many and trying Occasions, and you have frequently demonstrated that you possess an Empire over yourself. For Gods sake do not yield that Empire to a Love of Ease, Retirement, rural Pursuits, or a false Diffidence of Abilities which those that best know you so justly appreciate; nay your very Figure is calculated to inspire Respect and Confidence in the People, whose simple good Sense associates the noblest qualities of Mind with the heroic Form when it is embellished by such remarkable Tenets of Mildness and calm Benevolance—and such I believe was the first Intention of Nature. You love philosophic Retirement; convince the World then that you are a practical Philosopher, and that your native Philanthropy has induced you to relinquish an Object so essential to your Happiness. To do this I am certain that you need only give free Exercise to those Sentiments of patriotism and Benevolence which are congenial to your Bosom. Attend to their Verdict—Let your Heart judge of its Truth—Its Decrees will be confirmed by Posterity. That you are not indifferent to the Plaudits of the World I must conclude when I believe that the love of honest Fame has and ever will be predominant in the best the noblest and most capable Natures. Nor is the Approbation of Mankind to be disregarded with Impunity even by you. But, admitting that you could retire in a Manner exactly conformable to your own Wishes and possessed of the Benediction of Mankind, are you sure that such a Step would promote your Happiness? Have you not often experienced that your Judgement was fallible with Respect to the Means of Happiness? Have you not, on some Occasions, found the Consummation of your Wishes the Source of the keenest of your Sufferings? God grant that your Mind may be so enlightened that you may, on this Occasion, form a true Judgement and may the eternal Disposer of human Events watch over your welfare. May the Remnant of your Days be happily and actively employed in the Discharge of those Duties which elevate and fortify the Soul. And may you, till the extremest old age, enjoy the pure Felicity of having employed your whole Faculties for the Prosperity of the People for whose Happiness you are responsible, for to you their Happiness is intrusted. Adieu believe me as I ever am Your sincere affectionate Friend

Eliza. Powel

ALS, DLC:GW; ADfS, ViMtV. The date on the draft is not clear. Mrs. Powel, however, docketed it: "To the President of the United States on the Subject of his Resignation November the 4th 1792."

Elizabeth Powel and her husband Samuel Powel, former Philadelphia mayor and current speaker of the Pennsylvania senate, were close friends of GW during his presidency.

1. On the draft manuscript the word "last" follows the word "Thursday,"

which would have been 1 Nov. according to the docket date on the draft or 15 Nov. according to the date on the ALS.

From the Quakers

[Philadelphia, 17 November 1792]
To the President, Senate and house of Representatives of the United States. The address of the people called Quakers.

It was the exhortation of the Apostle Paul that supplications, prayers, intercessions and giving of thanks be made for all men, for Kings and for all that are in authority, that we may lead a quiet and peaceable life in all godliness and honesty, for this is good and acceptable in the sight of God our Saviour.[1] Conformable whereto our minds have been brought into a religious concern that the Rulers of this Land may pursue such measures as may tend to the promotion of the peace and happiness of the people.

We are sensible that the Lord's judgments are in our Land and being deeply affected with the distressed situation of the Frontier inhabitants, we desire a solid and careful inquiry may be made into the cause, and are firmly persuaded that if the counsel and ⟨direction⟩ of the holy Spirit is waited for and followed, the Divine blessing will crown the labours of those who uprightly engage in the work of Peace.

The disposition which has appeared in the government to promote pacific measures with the Indians hath we believe been generally acceptable, and as it is consistent with our religious principles, so it has been our uniform care to admonish and caution our members against settling on Lands which have not been fairly purchased of the original owners, and as far as our influence extends we mean to maintain this our ancient testimony inviolate, which from experience has been found effectual to the preservation of Peace with the Natives, who with great hospitality cherished and assisted our Fore-fathers in their early settlement of this Country.

We feel cautious not to move out of our proper line, but being interested in the welfare of this Country, and convinced of the expedience of further endeavours being used to encourage the Indians to come forward with a full representation and statement of their grievances, and that every just cause of uneasiness in their minds may be fully investigated and removed, we apprehend it our duty again to address you on this affecting and important occasion, under a belief that nothing short of strict justice will ever be a basis of solid and lasting peace.[2]

We respectfully submit these things to your serious considerat⟨ion,⟩ earnestly desiring that through the influence of Divine wisdom on your Councils, you may be made instrumental to prevent the further effusion of human blood, and that the Inhabitants may long enjoy the blessing of a righteous government.

Signed in and on behalf of a Meeting appointed to represent our religious Society in Pennsylvania, New Jersey, Delaware, and part of Maryland and Virginia, held in Philadelphia the 17th day of the 11th month 1792.

Warner Mifflin

DS, in Warner Mifflin's writing, DNA: RG 59, Miscellaneous Letters; DS, DNA: RG 46, Second Congress, 1791–93, Senate Records of Legislative Proceedings, Petitions and Memorials, Resolutions of State Legislatures, and Related Documents. The text in angle brackets is provided from the Senate's copy.

This petition, signed by prominent Quaker abolitionist Warner Mifflin and fifty-two other Quaker leaders, was presented to each house of Congress on 19 Nov. 1792, when it was read and ordered to lie on the table (*Annals of Congress,* 2d Cong., 615, 690–91). The additional signatures appear in CD-ROM:GW.

1. The biblical reference is to 1 Timothy 2:1–3.

2. A similar petition from the Quakers to GW, signed on 16 Dec. 1791, had been presented to the House of Representatives on 22 Dec. 1791 (ibid., 278).

From Thomas Jefferson

[Philadelphia] Nov. 18. 1792.

Th: Jefferson has the honor to inform the President that the papers from Monsr Cointeraux of Paris contain some general ideas on his method of building houses of mud, he adds that he has a method of making incombustible roofs and cielings, that his process for building is auxiliary to agriculture, that France owes him 66,000 livres, for so much expended in experiments & models of his art, but that the city of Paris is unable to pay him 600. livres decreed to him as a premium, that he is 51. years old has a family of seven persons, and asks of Congress the expences of their passage & a shop to work in.[1]

Th: Jefferson saw M. Cointeraux at Paris, went often to examine some specimens of mudwalls which he erected there, and which appeared to be of the same kind generally built in the neighborhood of Lyons, which have stood perhaps for a century. instead of moulding bricks, the whole wall is moulded at once, & suffered to dry in the sun, when it becomes like unburnt brick. this is the most serious view of his papers. he proceeds further to propose to build all our villages incombustible that the enemy may not be able to burn them, to fortify them all with his kind of walls impenetrable to their cannon, to erect a like wall across our whole frontier to keep off the Indians, observing it will cost us nothing but the building, &c. &c. &c.

The paper is not in the form of a petition, tho evidently intended for Congress, & making a proposition to them. it does not however merit a departure from the President's rule of not becoming the channel of petitions to that body, nor does it seem entitled to any particular answer.[2]

Th: Jefferson

ALS, DNA: RG 59, Miscellaneous Letters; ALS (letterpress copy), DLC: Jefferson Papers; LB, DNA: RG 59, George Washington's Correspondence with His Secretaries of State; LB (photocopy), DLC:GW.

1. Tobias Lear had written Jefferson earlier on this date to ask him to "run over the enclosed papers," which Jefferson identified below the text of Lear's letter as "Cointeraux' proposition to come over with his family of 7. persons to shew us how to build houses with mud walls & incombustible roofs & cielings, if we would pay their passage & give him a shop" (DLC: Jefferson Papers). Cointeraux's papers originally were enclosed in French émigré St. Hilaire's letter to GW of 14 Nov. 1792.

François Cointeraux (1740–1830), an architect from Lyons, dedicated his career to the development and promotion of the pisé, or rammed-earth, method of construction, in which mud is placed in large wooden molds to form the components of fire-resistant buildings. Jefferson already was familiar with Cointeraux and his ideas, having first received a letter and promotional material from him in 1789. Cointeraux later sent Jefferson a copy of his book on the pisé method, *Ecole d'architecture rurale*, published in Paris, 1790–91 (see *Jefferson Papers*, 15:184–86).

2. No correspondence from GW to Cointeraux has been found.

To Anthony Whitting

Mr Whiting,   Philadelphia 18th Novr 1792

Your letters of the 9th & 14th instt came duly to hand. To the first I hastily replied the morning after it was received, and shall add nothing further on that subject, in this letter, respecting the Fishery.[1]

If the Mansn house people are permanently distributed to the plantations, to which they are destined; or, as soon as they are so; let all the Overseers know that they are no longer to look to the House gang for any assistance: on the contrary, that the work of every sort & kind whatsoever, is to [be] performed by the hands which are entrusted to them; Ditching alone excepted—and even this, when it is accompanied with a Post fence, they are to dig the holes for those Posts with their own people; for so long as they derive this *extra* assistance, and are helped out of every difficulty, they never will exert their own force to the best advantage; and the case invariably will be, that the House gang will be little more than an encouragement to their idleness instead of performing some settled work of their own, which will count, and tell something.[2] I am sure, that every plantation is abundantly stocked with hands, fully adequate to all the purposes of it; except ditching; which they could not perform to *advantage,* although their *force* might be competent to it. There is but one case in which I can see any propriety in aiding of them; and that is, in work that can only be done at a *particular* season, or under *particular* circumstances, whe⟨n⟩ their own strength cannot effect it in the time limited by that season; or by those circumstances. For instance, clearing, or breaking up, a piece of ground which cannot be touched after it is absorbed with water: which reminds me to tell you, that if those spots in the Mill meadow, which could not be got into corn last Summer, is not broke up before the ground gets too wet this fall, you will not reclaim it in the course of next year; which will be a *real* injury to that lot, & a grievous eye-sore to every one that looks into it. This also is the case with the lot below it, and is the reason why I earnestly desire that no more may *ever* be attempted than can be *compleatly* accomplished; for I repeat, and repeat again; that I should be better satisfied in having *one* acre of Corn land, or meadow ground, well prepared & cultivated, than *two* Acres imperfectly done—In a word, these things are *never* really done if they are not *well* done.

After having given you these ideas so fully, & so strongly, it is hardly necessary to add, as my desire, that what will remain as the House gang, properly, may be kept *steadily* to work at that place; under Will, or some other, if he cannot keep them to their business.[3] The work to be done there, has been pointed out in more letters than one; and as there is a good deal of wood to be taken off the ground proposed to be cleared; and which may serve for Coal wood, fire wood, &ca; and is very convenient. I have no doubt but your Axe-men belonging to the place I mean will *all* be employed therein, instead of going into the great-Wood, & generally, as far out of sight as they can get, to cut Wood for the House.

All the young Cedars between the fence by the Spring, & the Wharf, that are of a size to be removed with safety, may, at a proper time, be taken up, & form a fence from the style (leading to the Spring) along the Post and Railing of the Lucern Inclosure; and from the Corner of the Vineyard inclosure downwards, and parallel to the last. But my opinion is, that to insure there living, they ought not to be remov'd until the ground is hard froze, when they can be taken up with a large block of frozen earth adhering to their Roots. The efficacy of this I have proved most clearly. You did well to desire the Gardiner to preserve the Damson [s]cions, if there be enough of them to form one side of the fence to the vineyard Inclosure; otherwise it would have too much the appearance of patch work to insert them there at all: And as that enclosure will contain fruit principally, which is subject to great depridations; I have thought that the best live fence for that, except the side marked above for Cedar, and I hesitate even there too, had better be of the Honey locust; the seed of which not to be put more than Six Inches apart; that when they get to any size they may be so close, stubborn, & formidable, as to prevent an escalade[;] indeed I know of nothing that will so effectually, & at so small an expence, preserve what is within the Inclosure, as this plant.

The Gardener, I presume, ought to be acquainted with the proper Seasons for taking off, & setting out, the cuttings of the Lombardy Poplar, & those of the Weeping, & yellow Willow. If therefore you both agree that this is a proper one, I would have it set about fully, & compleatly; as there is nothing I have so much at heart as to introduce live fences around *every* Inclosure where Hogs are not Suffered to be: and this is the case of all the inner Inclosures at the Mansion house, and division fences at the Plantations. One Inclosure, may be fenced with the cuttings of one thing, and another with another, according to your means; and the ground which seems best adapted to this, or that kind of

Tree. Let me know what qty of the honey locust seed you have on hand—& take care to secure all those which may be on the Trees which grow by Johnstons Spring, at the River Plantation.[4] Let the ground wherein these cuttings or Seeds are to be deposited, be well prepared for the reception of them; for they were *absolutely* thrown away last year; and the labour, whatever it might be, has turned to no account. I do not perceive by any of the Reports that you have got any Cedar Berries, to (manage &) Sow as I directed. I fear it is now too late; as they were falling (and in the greatest abundance) about the time I left Mount Vernon.[5]

You have entirely mistaken my idea respecting the conducting of the Water from the *present* Spring, and those I desired might be opened (to see what a body of it I could collect).[6] Instead of carrying it to the Wharf, my intention was to carry the whole, as high up the side of the Hill as the level of it would admit when the whole should be united at, or below the Spring (according as the level would allow) until it was brought as far, & right opposite to, the River front of the Mansion House (that is to the Vista in a line with the two doors which I had opened whilst I was at home, by stakes which I suppose may be standing there yet.)[7] I wanted to see how high up the side of that hill I could carry the water, and what advantage I might hereafter turn it to: it was for this reason I wanted the Springs opened when they were low; and gums or half (old) barrels put into them; that a judgment might be formed of the quantity, &ca—and it was for this reason also I added, that the Ditchers might assist in conducting it. There will be some difficulty, I am sensible, in taking it over the sunken place East of the Spring House; but a trough would remove it: after which, the water would go on a level, as in the case of Sideland Meadows to the place I have in view—What banks there are to cut through between the Spring house, & the most westerly Spring that would be worth opening, at, or beyond the Hound kennel; or whether they lye as high as the Spring that is now used, if the level was traced, my memory is unable to inform me; but Water by cutting through, or winding round banks, may always be conducted to its own level—This, & carrying the aggregate quantity of what could be obtained, to the front of the House, was the objects I had in view.

I had like to have forgot to tell you that the Lombardy Poplars,

& Weeping Willows in the Serpentine Walks, may, as well as any others, be stripped to furnish you with cuttings, if necessary.

If the French furze is a fit thing for Hedging, and you have reason to believe the seed is good, I am very glad you bought it. Whether it is best to sow the Seed where it is intended to remain, or in beds to transplant, you must decide for yourself; but that you may not be deceived by bad Seed, try a certain number of Seeds in a hot bed, or any other method which will force them, to see what proportion of them will come up: do the same by the Clover seed you have, that I may know what dependence to place on its goodness.

There is a plant or two which went from Bartrams Garden last Spring, which he recommended in strong terms as valuable for hedging. make the most you can of the one you say is living.[8]

I am very glad to hear that your growing Wheat has a good appearance. Will the first Sowed, & thin Wheat, ever appear thick enough, especially in No. 7 in the Neck? It was not the getting of Fodder, generally, that injured the Corn: Stripping the blade I believe did, and said so at the time; but the great evil proceeded from its backwardness (occasioned by the long drought in Summer) and want of heat after the rains fell, to mature it.

Have you taken measures to save what Turnip Seed you may want next year? The purchase of these things ought, by all means to be avoided.

Inform me in your next how many Hogs you have up for Porke, at each place. The Robberies which all your letters relate, must be stopped by some means or another; or the consequences will inevitably be those I have mentioned in my last. It is growing worse & worse every day; and if a good deal of pains is not taken to discover the thieves, and the receivers, there is no telling where the evil will end. I am willing to be at the expence of Sheep-bells, but this will prove but a partial remedy: the evil must be probed deeper than that.

The dificiency of Stockings is another instance of the villainy of those I have about me; for, as you justly observe, it is impossible that lame peter & Sarah's work could amount to no more than 60 pair—The Gardeners Wife must *now* see that there is a just return of all that is given out & taken in—and when the work is handed over by her, to you, I am persuaded it will be safe. Let the Gardeners wife give work to, & receive it from, lame Peter as well as others; & then the whole will come under one head.[9] Their reports ought to be dated.

What painting has Tom Davis done; and what paints have you now on hand?

Mrs Washington desires you will order the ashes to be taken care of, that there may be no want of Soap.

The note, at the foot of the last River plantation return, is by no means such as I expected, or would wish to see again;[10] because it gives no idea of the real state of facts, as it respects the increase, & decrease of the Stock. My idea of this business is, that every change that takes place in the Stock in the course of the week, should be reported; that is—every lamb that falls, and every one that dies, ought to be *accurately* reported; how else am I to form any opinion of the care taken of these, & other things; or to form any tolerable opinion of my business, if the reports are not from the *actual* state of things, but from what they *may* be, according to contingencies.

From the present appearance of things, I think it highly probable that in the course of the Winter, or Spring, Flour will bear a good price. I would have none of mine therefore sold without directions from me—but it might not be amiss, now and then, for you to give me some account of the Alexandria price of this Article, least the disposal of it should escape m⟨e⟩. In the meanwhile, if you should want money for any particular purpose, & have it not, advise me thereof, and it shall be sent to you. The price of Tobacco, and for the same reason, may also be mentioned to me. I am—Your friend & well wisher

Go: Washington

P.S. As occasions may occur when Tea & other Spoons (better than Pewter) may be wanted in the absence of my family & the Majors at Mount Vernon—I do by this conveyance, send half a dozen of each; The hurry, & distress in which Mrs Fanny Washington left Mount Vernon, occasioned omissions of many things, which otherwise would not have been the case.[11]

ALS, NNPM.

1. Whitting's letter to GW of 9 Nov. has not been found. For previous mention of the fishery, see GW to Whitting, 14 November.

2. For the work assignments of some of the Mansion House slaves, see GW to Whitting, 14, 28 Oct., and 4 November. For the number of slaves assigned

to each farm, see Slave List, 18 Feb. 1786, in *Diaries*, 4:277–83, and Washington's Slave List, June 1799.

3. Will was GW's former body servant, William Lee. This paragraph and the following two paragraphs deal with work to be done on the Mansion House farm.

4. Johnston's spring was near the old Clifton, or Johnston's, Ferry on the Potomac River.

5. GW left Mount Vernon for Philadelphia on 8 Oct. (see GW to Betty Washington Lewis, 7 October).

6. For GW's previous instructions regarding the springs at Mount Vernon, see his letter to Whitting of 28 Oct. and note 12.

7. The vista opened earlier was from the doors on the river side of the mansion.

8. The March 1792 List of Plants from John Bartram's Nursery included *Mespilus pyracantha*, or firethorn, "a beautiful flowerg shrub, evergreen, in mild seasons." In the 7 Nov. Directive to John Christian Ehlers, the following information is added: "not to be exceeded in usefulness, for hedges Fences &ca."

9. For Catherine Ehlers's other supervisory duties, see GW to Whitting, 14 Oct., and note 16. Sarah may have been the woman of that name recorded as one of the "labourg. Women" at the Muddy Hole farm in 1786 and identified as the dead mother of Isbel, at the Muddy Hole farm, on the 1799 slave list. The only knitter listed at the Mansion House farm on the 1799 slave census, besides Lame Peter, was a dower slave named Alla (see ibid., 282, and Washington's Slave List, June 1799).

10. The report has not been found.

11. Maj. George Augustine Washington and his wife Fanny left Mount Vernon in October to spend the winter in New Kent County, Virginia. The need for a supply of better spoons may have arisen from the prospect of visitors to Mount Vernon in GW's absence. See the mention of a proposed visit by Supreme Court justice William Cushing in GW's letter to Whitting of 28 October.

From Alexander Hamilton

Sir   Treasury Department November 19th 1792

I have carefully reflected on the applicati[o]n of mr Ternant, for an additional supply of money for the use of the Colony of St Domingo on account of the Debt due to France; which I regard more and more as presenting a subject extremely delicate and embarrassing.

Two questions arise 1 as to the ability of the U. States to furnish the money, which is stated at about 326000 Dollars, in addition to the sum remaining of the 400000 dollars some time since promised 2 as to the propriet⟨y⟩ of doing it on political considerations.[1]

With regard to ability, I feel little doubt that it will be in the power of the Treasury to furnish the sum; yet circumstanced as we are, with the possibility of more extensive demands, than at present exist, for exigencies of a very serious nature, I think it would not be desirable to be bound by a positive stipulation for the intire amount.

With regard to the propriety of the measure on political considerations more serious difficulties occur. The late suspension of the King, which is officially communicated, and the subsequent abolition of Royalty by the Convention, which the News papers announce with every appearance of authenticity, essentially change for the moment the condition of France.[2]

If a restoration of the King should take place, I am of opinion, that no payment which might be made in the Interval would be deemed regular or obligatory—The admission of it to our credit would consequently be considered as matter of discretion, according to the opinion entertained of its merit and utility. A payment to the newly constituted power, as a reimbursement in course, or in any manner, which would subject it to be used in support of the change, would doubtless be rejected.

An advance, however, to supply the urgent necessities of a part of the French Empire, struggling under the misfortune of an insurrection, of the nature of that which has for some time distressed, and now exposes to the danger of total ruin by Famine the Colony of St Domingo is of a different complexion. Succours furnished in such a situation, under due limitations, would be so clearly an act of humanity and friendship, of such evident utility to the French Empire, that no future government could refuse to allow a credit for them without a disregard of moderation and Equity—But the claim for such credit would not be of a nature to be regularly, and of course valid; consequently would be liable to be disputed.

The condition in which the Colony has lately placed itself, by espousing the last change which had been made in France, operates as a serious difficulty in the case and may be made a ground of objection to any aid which may be given them.

There is even a question whether there be now any organ of the French nation which can regularly ask the succour—whether the Commission to mr Ternant be not virtually superseded.

It is also an objection, (in the view of regularity and validity), to the supply asked, that the Decree of the National Assembly, on which it is founded, contemplated a negotiation between the Executive Power in France and our Minister there—The Channel has not been pursued and no substitute has been provided. The business wants organization in every sense.[3]

From these premises, I deduce, that nothing can be done without risk to the United States—that therefore *as little as possible* ought to be done—that whatever may be done should be cautiously restricted to the single idea *of preserving the colony from destruction by Famine*—that in all communications on the subject care should be taken to put it on this footing, & even to avoid the explicit recognition of any regular authority in any person.

Under these cautions and restrictions (but not otherwise) I beg leave to submit it as my opinion, that succours ought to be granted; notwithstanding the degree of risk which will attend it. That they should be effected by occasional advances, without previous stipulation, and with only a general assurance that the United States disposed to contribute by friendly offices to the preservation of an important portion of the French empire and to that of French Citizens from the calamity of Famine will endeavour from time to time as far as circumstances shall permit to afford means of sustenance.

According to a statement of Mr De la Foret the provisions desired to be shipped in the course of November would amount to 83.800 Dollars, including the total supply of Fish & Oil. Towards this he computes the application of 50000 Dollars out of the remainder of 400000 Dollars heretofore promised which would leave a deficiency of 38.800 Dollar[.] This Sum or in round numbers 40000 Dollars can be engaged to be furnished—and in December if no future circumstances forbid a further sum can be engaged to be supplied payable at a future short period.[4] It will be proper that the most precise measures should be taken to ascertain from time to time the investment of the monies supplied in purchasing and forwarding provisions from this Country to the Colony in question.

It has been heretofore understood that the ballance of the sum some time since stipulated was to be furnished which accordingly has been & is doing.[5]

Engagements for supplies have been entered into upon the basis of that stipulation & payments to as great if not a greater amount are becoming due in which the Citizens of the U. States are materially interested.

The caution which is deemed necessary has reference not only to the safety of the U. States in a pecuniary respect but to the consideration of avoiding a dangerous commitment, which may even prove a source of misunderstanding between this Country and the future Government of the French Nation—From all that is hitherto known there is no ground to conclude that the Governing Power by the last advices will be of long duration.

ADf, DLC: Hamilton Papers; LB, DLC: GW; copy, DLC: Jefferson Papers; copy, DNA: RG 233, Second Congress, 1791–93, House Records of Legislative Proceedings, President's Messages. The closing on the copy in the DLC: Jefferson Papers is in Hamilton's writing.

1. For French minister Jean-Baptiste, chevalier de Ternant's earlier request for American aid following the slave revolt that began in Saint Domingue on 22 Aug. 1791 and for the American response, see Samuel Wall to GW, 16 Sept. 1791, n.1, Alexander Hamilton to GW, 22 Sept. 1791, and notes, Henry Knox to GW, 22 Sept. 1791, and notes. For Ternant's more recent appeal for an additional $400,000, see Hamilton to GW, 8 Mar. 1792, and notes. Ternant presented his latest application for assistance to Thomas Jefferson in early November, and the secretary of state then forwarded the request to Hamilton (see Hamilton to Jefferson, 17 Nov. [first letter], Jefferson's "Notes on the Legitimacy of the French Government, with Addendum," 18–19 Nov., Jefferson to Ternant, 20 Nov., and notes, Jefferson to Hamilton, 21 Nov., and notes, in *Jefferson Papers*, 24:627, 632–33, 652–54).

2. For background on the current political turmoil in France, see Gouverneur Morris to GW, 23 Oct., and source note. News of the abolition of the monarchy by the newly elected National Convention appeared in the 14 Nov. issue of the *Pennsylvania Gazette* (Philadelphia).

3. For the decree issued by the Legislative Assembly on 26 June 1792, see *Archives parlementaires*, 45:594–95. For Hamilton's earlier conversation with Jefferson on the wisdom of making payments on the American debt while France was governed by the National Convention and for a similar discussion between GW, Knox, Hamilton, and Jefferson, "about the 1st. week in Nov.," see Jefferson's "Notes on the Legitimacy of the French Government, with Addendum," 18–19 Nov., in *Jefferson Papers*, 24:632–33.

4. Hamilton obtained these figures from the 12 Nov. estimate of Antoine-René-Charles Mathurin de La Forest, the French consul general, entitled "Etat des subsistances et approvisionnemens nécéssaires, pour les troupes employées à St Domingue, pendant les Mois de Décembre 1792, Janvier et Fevrier 1793, establi d'après celui adressé par les administrateurs, calculé pour 4 mois à commencer de Novembre" (DLC: Jefferson Papers), which Jefferson had enclosed in his letter to Hamilton of 21 Nov. (ibid., 24:654). La Forest (1756–1846) was a member of the French legation and consulate in the United States from 1778 to 1793. After a brief recall to France, he returned to the United

States in February 1794 as the French consul general. He continued his successful career as a diplomat after his return to France in 1795. Under the Napoleonic regime La Forest held ambassadorships to Prussia, Russia, and Spain, and in 1825, during the royalist restoration, he was appointed the French minister of state.

5. For recent payments made from the earlier grant of $400,000, see Ternant to Hamilton, 22 Aug., 8 Oct., and 15 Nov., in Syrett, *Hamilton Papers*, 12:264, 528–29, 13:150.

To Thomas Jefferson

Dear Sir,   Philadelphia 19th Novr 1792.

I have run over the four numbers of Genl Green's letters to Congress—herewith returned—and find nothing contained in them, unmarked by you, which ought, in my opinion, to be withheld from the Public. Even those of the 3d of Novr 1780—tho' quite unnecessary, might pass with an explanatory note on the *then* value of our paper currency.[1]

It probably is best to [leave] out the scored part of No. 1, page 14, although, I am persuaded, it is no more than a statement of a fact, and not an unimportant one. In No. 4, latter part of page 57. nearly the same sentiment as that erased is conveyed.[2] I am always Yrs &ca

Go: Washington

ALS, DLC: Jefferson Papers; ADfS (facsimile), *Parke-Bernet Catalogue, Public Auction of the Collection of Emil Edward Hurja*, item 241, 27 April 1954; LB, DLC:GW. Jefferson docketed the ALS as "recd Nov. 19. 92." and added a note at the bottom of the letter that reads: "Cary was permitted to make from the Secretary of state's office a selection of state papers for publication particularly those of the commander in chief, & of the Generals commanding in separate departments. he submitted his selection to me to see if it contained any thing which ought not to be published. I marked a very few passages & stated them to the President. the above is his answer." The text in square brackets is supplied from the draft and the letter-book copy.

1. John Carey (1756–1826), brother of Philadelphia publisher Mathew Carey, arrived in the United States from his native Ireland about 1789. He solicited Jefferson on 30 June 1792 for permission to examine official papers in the office of the secretary of state in order to produce "an abridgment of the *Journals of the old Congress*" (*Jefferson Papers*, 24:140). Although that book never was published, Carey published in London in 1795 a two-volume edition of *Official Letters to the Honorable American Congress, Written, during the War between the United Colonies and Great Britain, by His Excellency, George Washington, Commander in Chief of the Continental Forces, Now President of the United States. Copied by*

Special Permission, from the Original Papers Preserved in the Office of the Secretary of State, Philadelphia. For the letter of 3 Nov. 1780 from Gen. Nathanael Greene to Samuel Huntington, president of the Continental Congress, see *Greene Papers*, 6:461.

2. The other letters reviewed have not been identified.

From George Skene Keith

Sir   Keith-hall by Aberdeen [Scotland] 19th Novr 1792
I had the Honour of your Excellencys Letter of the 22d of June, which I shall carefully preserve for the sake of the subscription. I received at the same time your Secretary's Letter of the 7th of May; both Letters bearing the Edinburgh Post mark of the 12th of September.[1]

The best return I can make for the distinguishing honour of a Letter from your own Hand is [t]o send you some information on the Subject of Weights and Measures, an Uniformity of which as you justly observe, would be attended with the most beneficial effects to Commerce.

There are *two things,* either of which may be done by the Legislators of America—They may either establish such a standard as the nations of Europe will probably adopt; or they may concert with the different Courts of Europe, about establishing a connexion between some of the principal weights and measures presently in use, and a Standard taken from nature. I beg leave to send you two papers, which I have compressed into as little Room as possible—One of them contains some Observations on the Report of the Committee of Senate of the United States on this subject; and the other has sketched out the Outlines of a proposed application from the United States to the different Courts of Europe about establishing an Uniformity of Weights & Measures. They have cost me some labour in drawing up and compressing them⟨.⟩ And I have no view in sending them but to be useful to mankind.[2]

Therefore I make no Apology to your Excellency for the form in which they are drawn up, excepting this that they would have been much longer in describing, and going round about every little circumstance, than by exhibiting them in the form a corrected report of the Committee of your Senate, and of an application from the States of America to the Courts of Europe.

To one of your elevated Mind Compl⟨i⟩ments are empty and Apologies unnecessary—I therefore request your Excellencys attention to the two first and the last pages of *the Observations on the Report* of the *Committee of Senate,* and to the first and last pages of the Outlines *of the proposed application* to the Courts of Europe— The mathematical information in other parts of these papers you can submit to those who have particularly studied the Subject.

I have only to request your forgiveness for the Liberty I take in writing your Excellency, and for sending my papers to be forwarded by your Minister Plenipotentiary at the Court of London, that they may not be so long, as my last communication was in reaching America.[3]

May God Almighty prolong your useful and valuable Life to a very remote period, for the good of those States, among whom your important services, your abilities and your virtues, give you a greater and a better influence, than may ever fall to the Lot of any of your Successers.

I beg offer of my best acknowledgements for your goodness in sending my Letter to my Aunt Mrs [Rachel] Barclay. I have the honour to be with the highest Esteem and Veneration for your Character, independent of the Respect due to your Rank Sir Your Excellencys most Obedient and most Humble Servant

Geo: Skene Keith

ALS, DNA: RG 59, Miscellaneous Letters. The docket indicates that the letter was "Recd Feby 14th 1793."

1. For background on the Washington administration's interest in establishing a uniform system of weights and measures and Keith's earlier correspondence with GW and Thomas Jefferson on the subject and for Tobias Lear's letter to Keith of 7 May 1792, see Keith to GW, 1 July 1791, and source note and notes 1 and 2. See also Jefferson to GW, 14 June 1792, n.2, and GW to Keith, 22 June 1792.

2. Keith enclosed two papers, both dated 19 Nov: "Observations on the Report of the Committee of the Senate of the United States of America, on the Subject of Weights and Measures" and "Outlines of a proposed application from the United States of America to the Courts of the different trading nations of Europe, in regard to establishing an Uniformity of Weights, Measures and Coins."

In the first two pages of his "Observations," Keith wrote: "If the American States propose only to establish a national standard of Weights and Measures, and have no view to this Standards being adopted by any nation of Europe, what the Committee of Senate have proposed, may, with some alterations, to be afterwards mentioned, sufficiently answer the purpose. Only it will add *one* more to the *too great number of national* standards, which are already established in different countries.

"But, (as the worthy President of the United States observes in a Letter, with which he honoured the Author of these remarks) 'if any Uniformity of Weights and Measures could be established upon a proper foundation through the several nations of Europe, and in the United States of America, its advantages would be great indeed.['] It is to be hoped that the American States will not lose sight of this Uniformity.

"If the Legislators of America wish to establish a Standard of Weights and Measures, which the nations of Europe will probably be inclined to adopt, then that which is proposed by the Committee of Senate must be laid aside, or it must be divided in a different manner from what is mentioned in the Report.

"The Length of the Standard Rod, proposed to be established in America, is already known probably within *one four thousandth* part of the truth. That length is 58.65 English inches. One fifth part of this length is 11.73 inches, *the proposed unit of measure of length,* in the United States being nearly $\frac{1}{43}$ part less than the *English,* and $\frac{1}{12}$ part less than the *Paris* foot. It is obvious by looking at the figures, and comparing them with the foot measures of Europe, that the proposed Unit or Foot does not correspond with any European measure [Keith's footnote placed here reads: "Perhaps the reason of adopting of this *foot measure,* was that it corresponded nearly with, the English Foot and Avoirdupois ounce. But in fact it does not correspond with either of these"], excepting the Swedish national foot and the provincial foot of Strasbourg, which nearly correspond with this Standard.

"As a Standard of weight the proposed foot contains very nearly 934 Avoirdupois Ounces of Rain water, of a moderate temperature, in a cube of its dimensions. The pound weight derived from this would consequently be $9\frac{1}{3}$ Ounces Avoirdupois, or nearly 4086 English Troy grains. There is not a nation in Europe which has so small a Pound as this, which is about one half of the provincial Pound of Rouen in Normandy. Therefore no European nation would probably adopt this Standard.

"It might farther be mentioned that the Superficial and Solid measure proposed by the Committee of Senate, do not correspond with *any* of those used by the different nations of Europe. But if the weights and lineal measures had corresponded this would have been of less importance. At the same time it ought not to be altogether overlooked, that the Standards proposed by the Committee of Senate do not correspond, with the Superficial and Solid measures, any more than with the Weights and Lineal Measures which are generally used in Europe.

"Nor should it pass unnoticed, that though the Coins [Keith's footnote here reads: "The American States ought to have fixed upon their weights and measures, before they fixed upon their Coins—The Eagle then should have been an Ounce of Gold, or the dollar an oz. of silver"] of the United States do correspond pretty nearly with the proposed weights and measures, none of these correspond with the majority, or indeed with any considerable number of the various Coins of the different trading nations of Europe.

"On these accounts the proposed Standard foot, and the other weights and measures proposed by the Committee of Senate, should be set aside by the Legislators of America, if they wish to establish weights and measures, which Europe would probably adopt.

"At the same time the *proposed Standard Rod* of Iron, which vibrates seconds of mean time in a moderate temperature and middle latitude, *may still be retained.* Only the Unit of all measures of length must be *two thirds* instead of *one fifth part* of the length of this Rod.

"The true length of pendulum in a cylindrical rod, is not the whole length of that Rod, but the length from the point of Suspension to what Philosophers call the center of oscillation in that Rod: And were it not for the resistance of the Air, and the weight and thickness of the rod (which occasion a small alteration in its measure) the length of the pendulum would be exactly two thirds of the length of the rod.

"Instead therefore of the 4th Article of the Report of the Committee of Senate, let it be proposed that the standard Rod shall be divided into three parts, two of which parts, or two thirds of the whole length of the rod, to be called a Standard Yard, shall be the Unit of measures of length for the United States, and shall be decimally divided into palms or handbreadths, digits, and lines.

"By adopting this alteration the Standard of Weights, Measures and Coins, adopted by the American States, would probably be imitated by the nations of Europe.

"As a Standard of length it corresponds almost exactly with the Vara of Madrid, and the Half-canna of Rome, Avignon, Provence and Mont Pelier, which measure is the standard used in all the Southern provinces of France, & different parts of Spain and Italy."

On the last page of his "Observations," Keith concluded: "The Legislators of America have *Much less Mind,* than the writer of this paper believes them to possess, if they need any Apology for the form, in which a Man who once thought of Spending his Life in America, conveys instruction, which he thinks may be useful to mankind.

"If any man of Science takes offence at this Author, for offering corrections on his plan which the Committee of Senate have adopted; and if he wish, from a false pride, to retain any article which is here shewn to be improper, let him stand on the banks of the Potowmac, and beholding the Alligany mountains on the one side, and the Atlantic Ocean on the other; let him learn to speak and act with liberality, when he approaches the most sublime object and elevated Mind in America—George Washington!

"P.S. The Author of these Observations, having bestowed more labour on the subject of Weights and Measures, than perhaps any man existing has done, shall be happy to receive instruction, and is ready to give all the information he can, to any Senator, Representative, Philosopher, Merchant or Citizen of the United States, on this important subject" (DNA: RG 59, Miscellaneous Letters).

On the first page of his "Outlines," Keith observed: "The United States of America have it in contemplation to establish within their own territories a Standard of Weights, Measures and Coins, which shall be taken from Nature, and may be rectified by an Observation taken from nature at any distance of time. But they wish to establish such a Standard as other nations will probably adopt; and even to concert with the different courts of Europe about establishing an Uniformity of Weights, Measures and Coins, which would be attended with many and great advantages to Commerce.

"With this view they wish to connect some of the principal weights, measures and coins, presently in use among trading nations, with a Standard taken from nature. For it fortunately happens that though the different Standards of Europe are arbitrary, yet many of them do very nearly correspond with philosophical Standards: And it is certainly better to retain some of the weights, measures and Coins, which are in present use, than to establish such as are not used by any nation of the earth.

"Farther, By adopting the Standards used by other nations, instead of establishing one of their own, the United States of America hope to induce the different Courts of Europe, to part at least with some of their *national* Standards, for the purpose of obtaining an Uniformity of Weights, Measures and Coins.

"The most unexceptionable Standards, in the opinion of philosophers, are those which are taken from the circumference of the earth, or from some part of that circumference, which can be accurately measured: or those which are taken from the length of a pendulum, or from the length of a cylindrical rod, which makes a certain number of vibrations in a solar or sidereal day, and under a certain parallel of latitude.

"The principal weights, measures and coins of Europe are those which are established in Great Britain, France, Spain and the Seven United Provinces—They are here called the principal ones, because they are most generally used, & best known even where they are not established."

On the last page of his "Outlines," Keith concluded: "When Rome carried her conquests over the earth, the Roman weights and measures were established, wherever the Roman arms prevailed—When Charlemagne had extended his Sceptre over a great part of Europe, he established *one weight* through all his dominions. And this was the old weight of Rome, with this difference, that the Roman Pound contained 12, and that of Charlemagne 16 Ounces. It is *this Pound* which is in *by far the most general use in the trading world.* And the Tun weight or 2000 of these Pounds, by a most fortunate accident corresponds very nearly with a Standard taken from nature in the 7th or last mentioned one.

"The United States of America are ready however to adopt any one of the above Standards, or any Standard whatever which shall be taken from nature by a new experiment, and which shall be agreeable to the majority of trading nations.

"As not only the Weights and Measures, but also the Coins of Europe are various it would be of consequence that money were coined in Ounces, drams and scruples of gold and silver, and that the value of the Coin in the national denominations of different countries were marked on one side of the coin, and the weight & fineness on the other side—By this means the various coins of different nations, by whatever name they were called in the country in which they were coined, would have a general value, known to all merchants, as the language of China and Japan though differently spoken, is written in the same character, and as the 9 Arabic figures and cypher, now used in Arithmetic, though differently pronounced in speaking the different languages, have the same value over all the world.

"If the different trading nations would only agree in fixing on a Standard for their *foreign trade,* and oblige all merchants to put up goods in the standard weights & measures, and charge their price in ounces of gold or Silver, it is highly probable that these would soon become universal: at any rate great advantage would arise to the commercial intercourse of mankind that they bought and sold at a known price, a known quantity of goods in every part of the world.

"The Author of the above Outlines respectfully hopes, and expects from the liberality of mind possessed by that great and good man who presides over the United States of America, that the *form* in which [it] appears will not give any offence, if the matter contained in it be useful to the Legislators of America" (DNA: RG 59, Miscellaneous Letters). The Senate report on weights and measures was read in the Senate on 5 April 1792 (see *Annals of Congress,* 2d Cong., 117–18).

3. Thomas Pinckney was the U.S. minister to Great Britain.

From J. R. Robinson

[c. 19] Nov. [1792].[1] Petitions for a military appointment, citing his experience as "an officer in the Sarvice of the united Stat⟨es⟩" during the Revolutionary War.[2]

ALS, DLC:GW. Although the letter states that the petition is for "Joseph Robinson," the docket identifies the sender as "John Robinson." The letter is signed "J. R. Robinson."

1. The docket reads: "Novr 19th 1792."
2. The petitioner may be Lt. Joseph Robinson (1743–1829) of South Carolina.

To the United States Senate

United States [Philadelphia]

Gentlemen of the Senate   November 19th 1792

I nominate the following persons to fill the Offices annexed to their names respectively, to which they have been appointed during the recess of the Senate.

Zebulon Hollingsworth to be Attorney for the United States in the Maryland District; vice Richard Potts, resigned.[1]

Copland Parker, to be Surveyor of the Port of Smithfield in Virginia; vice James Wells, resigned.[2]

James Gibbon, to be Inspector of Survey No. 4. in Virginia; vice Thomas Newton Junr resigned.[3]

John Armistead, to be Surveyor of the Port of Plymouth in North Carolina; vice Thomas Davis Freeman, superseded.[4]

Thomas Parker, to be Attorney for the United States in the South Carolina District; vice John J. Pringle, resigned.[5]

I likewise nominate

Thomas Moffat, to be Surveyor of the Port of Fredericksburg in Virginia;[6] vice William Lewis, who is appointed Keeper of the Light House lately erected on Cape Henry[7]—and—

Benjamin Joy of Massachusetts, to be Consul for the United States of America at Calcutta, and other Ports and places on the coast of India in Asia.[8]

Go: Washington

DS, DNA: RG 46, Second Congress, 1791–93, Senate Records of Executive Proceedings, President's Messages—Executive Nominations; LB, DLC:GW.

1. For background on Zebulon Hollingsworth's appointment, see GW to James McHenry, 31 Aug. 1792, and notes.

2. Although Copland Parker's brother Josiah Parker had written a letter to GW on 1 July 1789 recommending him for a surveyor's position in the new federal government, he did not receive any appointment that year. In that letter Josiah also wrote, "Colonel James Wells of the Militia of Isle of Wight requests to be appointed Surveyor at Smithfield." GW nominated Wells to the desired position on 3 Aug. 1789, and the Senate approved the appointment the next day (see *Executive Journal,* 1:11, 14). When Wells resigned his surveyor's position in 1792 following his election to the Virginia general assembly, GW appointed Copland Parker to succeed him (see GW to the U.S. Senate, 6 Mar. 1792 [third letter], n.6).

3. See James Gibbon's letter of application to GW of 17 July 1792. Gibbon's nomination was omitted in the letter-book copy.

4. For background on Thomas Davis Freeman's removal from office and John Armistead's appointment, see Hamilton to GW, 17 Sept. 1792, and note 1.

5. See John J. Pringle's letter of resignation to GW of 3 Sept. 1792.

6. See Joseph Jones's recommendation of Thomas Moffat in his letter to GW of 8 Nov. 1792.

7. For background on William Lewis's appointment, see Hamilton to GW, 22 Sept. 1792, and note 6.

8. For background on Benjamin Joy's nomination, see George Cabot to GW, 16 Nov. 1792, and notes. Tobias Lear notified Thomas Jefferson on 21 Nov. that all these nominations had been approved by the Senate on that same date, noting that Copland Parker and John Armistead were "ex officio, Inspectors

of the Revenue for the same ports" as those for which they were surveyors (DLC:GW). For the Senate's approval of these nominations, see *Executive Journal,* 1:126.

To the United States Senate

United States [Philadelphia]
Gentlemen of the Senate　　　　　　　November 19th 1792
The following appointments have been made in the Army of the United States, during the recess of the Senate; and I now nominate the following persons to fill the Offices annexed to their names respectively.[1]

Artillery　Peter L. Van Alen to be Lieutenant; vice [Dirck] Schuyler, resigned; to take rank from 6th Septr 1792.[2]

Infantry　Alexander Gibson to be Captain vice William Lewis declined.

Howell Lewis[3] to be Captain vice [Hugh] Caperton declined.

William Preston[4] to be Captain vice [William] Lowder declined.

John Cummin[g]s to be Captain vice [William] Powers declined.

Jonathan Taylor to be Ensign vice [Baker] Davidson declined.

Andrew Shanklin to be Ensign vice [James] Hawkins declined.[5]

Go: Washington

ADS (facsimile), sold by R. M. Smythe & Co., Inc., catalog 164, item 347, 12 June 1997; LB, DLC:GW.

1. Earlier on this date Henry Knox sent GW a list containing these nominations (DLC:GW).

2. For events leading to Dirck Schuyler's resignation and Peter L. Van Alen's appointment, see Knox to GW, 28 Aug. 1792, and note 3.

3. This nominee was probably Howell Lewis (b. 1759) of Goochland County, Va. (see Sorley, *Lewis of Warner Hall,* 445–47, 483–84).

4. William Preston requested such an appointment in his letter to GW of 10 May 1792.

5. The Senate approved these nominations on 21 Nov. 1792 (see *Executive Journal,* 1:126), and on that date Tobias Lear sent Knox notification of the Senate's confirmations (DLC:GW).

Tobias Lear to Henry Knox

United States [Philadelphia] Novr 21st 1792

By the President's command T. Lear has the honor to return to the Secretary of War the enclosed letter from the Governor of Virginia, which has been submitted to the President;[1] and to transmit a letter which the President has received from the Representatives of the frontier Counties in the Gene[r]al Assembly of Virginia.[2] The President requests that the Secretary will take the subject of the enclosed letters into consideration and report to him his opinion thereon.[3]

Tobias Lear.
Secretary to the president of the United States.

ALS (letterpress copy), DLC:GW; LB, DLC:GW.

1. Knox enclosed in a brief note to Lear of 20 Nov. 1792 a letter for GW's consideration that was "just received from the Governor of Virginia" (DLC: GW). The letter of 14 Nov. from Henry Lee has not been identified, but Knox wrote Lee on 20 Nov. 1792 that he would "lay [it] before the President" (see *Calendar of Virginia State Papers*, 6:154).

2. The letter from the Ohio and Monongalia representatives to GW of c.15 Nov. has not been found. In a letter to Henry Lee of 15 Nov., these representatives wrote: "We have Inclos'd to your Excellency a letter to the president of the United States. If you think proper may forward the same" (see Thomas Wilson et al. to Lee, 15 Nov. 1792, ibid., 151). In a letter to Anthony Wayne of 24 Nov., Knox wrote, "The representatives of that part of Virginia which lies upon the Ohio from the Pennsylvania line to the great Kenhawa and called the Monongahela district have applied for a protection of their own Militia during the Winter" (Knopf, *Wayne*, 141). GW assigned Knox the task of replying to the Virginia delegates, and by 24 Nov. Knox had written a letter to Thomas Wilson and the other representatives (see Lear to Knox, 24 November). Knox's letter has not been identified.

3. For Knox's submissions to GW, see Lear to Knox, 24 Nov. 1792. Knox conveyed GW's thoughts on the role of the federal government in protecting the Virginia frontier from hostile Indians to Lee in a letter of 24 Nov.: "It is his opinion that although small garrisons stationed in Block-Houses or other fortifications will secure probably whoever may be therein; yet they are entirely inadequate to protect a line of frontier against incursive parties of savages." Instead GW believed that "the patrols, termed scouts, formed of the most active, bold, and experienced hunters, are of the highest service in order to discover the approach of Indians, and alarm the inhabitants."

The cost for "a reasonable number of these scouts will be readily paid by the General Government, even at the high rate of pay hereafter allowed, which has been five-sixths of a dollar per day. . . . But if in addition to these means, one, or at most two companies of Rangers, should act upon the line of the Southwestern frontier of Virginia, it would appear to be entirely adequate to any probable demands. The pay and rations as fixed by law of such companies, the President consents shall for the present be defrayed by the United States. But, he considers that the expence of the six companies ordered out by the Executive of Virginia, in pursuance (it is supposed) of the resolves of the General Assembly of the 16th ultimo, would not form a proper charge against the general Government.

"It is, however, always to be understood upon an invasion, or an immediate threatening danger thereof, so as to render necessary the calling out the force of the country, that in such a case the United States will be responsible for the expenses, according to the nature of the circumstances. . . . The last intelligence from Governor Blount was dated on the 10th ultimo. . . . If the Chickamaygas continue their depredations, it is difficult to conceive any other mode of insuring future tranquility, but that of chastising them severely and desolating their Towns. But offensive measures must arise from such acts as the Congress may think proper to pass on the occasion."

General Wayne's troops, Knox wrote, will be posted "a little above the Big Beaver creek, and probably continue therein until March next. He is directed in the mean time to encrease the force at Galliopolis, below the great Kenawha, and at the Muskingum, to such a degree as to afford considerable and constant patroles along the line from Galliopolis to his Camp, and thence to Fort Franklin. These patroles it is conceived in addition to the scouts, which all the exposed Counties will be permitted to have during the winter, will prevent the necessity of ordering any of the militia of Monongahalia district into Service for the present, as suggested in your letter" (*Calendar of Virginia State Papers*, 6:155–57).

Letter not found: from Anthony Whitting, 21 Nov. 1792. GW wrote Whitting on 25 Nov.: "Your letter of the 21st instant enclosing the Reports of the preceeding week was received yesterday."

From James Mulryne

Worthy Sir,   Georgia November 22nd 1792

If I err by writing to the great it is not by wanton forwardness—but purely from a sincere wish for the welfare of my country—The ignorant per chance may utter a stroke of wisdom—which when cultivated by the wise may become permanent—therefore sir I humbly offer you my simple opinion on so important a Subject as concerns the peace of America (Georgia particularly) with the indians.

Great sums of money are yearly expended in presents to those tribes at large. they are like us Some from indolence and other

excuses omit attending at the place of distribution and such are
not apt to impute their folly but the disappointment adds ran-
cour and jelousy which causes altercation among themselves until the p⟨h⟩ilonium dies in oblivion as if no such gift ever existed
for the nature of an indian is such no longer He enjoys the present no longer will he acknowledge the favor.

Britain on our northward line makes it an object to encourage
their merchants to establish a commerce with those people—the
merchant finds it to his account to do so[.] Spain on our South
line (tho' contrary to her common policy) sees it necessary to
give the firm of Panthon Leslie & Co. all the protection in her
power and this house finds it to their advantage to supply those
people therefore these powers act by a political principle and
the individual encouraged from interest.[1]

At this time none but America makes presents (united States)
and at this day none are under such contentions it is equally
demonstrated to me with a certainty all this may be put an end
to without risque of life by arms or even expend the enormous
sums of money that is yearly exhibited.

If Merchants (of us) are encouraged to establish Stores for the
conveniency of those people we then will be no better off than
British or Spaniard as they will have equal power to attract—but
let us extend on a more liberal principle. let Stores be established
by Government for the indians with Such as may be necessary
and those entrusted to be considered as mere agents by certain
directions under penal Bonds & Security for their performance
—those Goods to be dealt out at 20 ℔ cent on the cost or so much
as will answer the exportation to those Stores &c. in payment take
the indians furr skins &c. by this means you please the idea atracts
the indian and in time he becomes naturalized.[2]

Permit me sir, to offer the following Questions and answers
which naturally occurs—will the British and Spanish import
Goods from Europe risque his life and property in a desolate
wilderness and sell those Goods at 20 percent—will an Indian
purchase, be friends or attach himself to any but those he finds
it his interest to be so with—does America want any profit from
this political adventure or wish any thing at present from the indians but peace—and will the British or Spanish Merchant encourage a trade of this nature or under any other idea but his
2 & 3 Ct ℔ Ct on the cost of his Goods exclusive of his ℔ Ct on

the returns of his furrs &c. the[se] and many more can be answered truly in the negative.

Can we offer more to the indian for his furrs, Skins &c. than the foreign merchant will not these furrs, Skins &c. circulate in our Country add to its wealth and manufactures—will not this mode of trade put a Stop to the petty traders who flew from the fangs of our laws by his transgression from some part of our dominion Settled among these people who are the instruments of our disputes by encouraging the Stealing of our Negroes and horses on both Sides—will not then America have the whole trade to herself obtain every end that can possibly be expected in that point of view—loose no lives, Sink no money if She makes none these and many others can be as easy answered in the affirmative.

In this case it would be political to advise a continuance of our usual poll tax 2/4 Sterling, this Year ½ Georgians will pay the former without demur—for it is natural to ask who would on such liberal principles when the reversion is offered by proclamation to the importer of Emigrants for the redemption of their passage that may come to our Country for the terror of bondage to the Stranger is horrid and the idea of this alone prevents the poor of other Countries (who would Cultivate ours) from Coming, if such modes as these are adopted in Six or Seven years our frontiers will be compleatly Settled by which means our monies withdrawn from this kind of commerce (if deemed necessary to our treasury[)]—and the indian must resign upon such terms as may be proposed for the idea of defence by arms to him would be vague.

If what I say can be of no use pardon me Great Sir for taking up so much of your time—to my weak head the idea is forcible and probable—the offer may be serviceable and if I should be honored with Call in consequence of this information—for the Georgia department—I will chearfully resign my own commerce Situated on my own plantation at South Newport in Liberty County to negociate so important a scheme for the interest of my Country and as to integrity and security for the performance of such business I believe I may be found equal to the demand.[3] I am Great Sir with sincere obedience Your very Humble servant

James Mulryne

ALS, DNA: RG 59, Miscellaneous Letters.

1. Contrary to the peace treaty of 1783, the British still occupied a number of forts within the northern border of the United States, including forts Niagara, Detroit, and Michilimackinac, which were major trading centers for the Indians. The Spanish authorities had granted the Bahamian trading house of Panton, Leslie, & Co., owned by British citizens William Panton and John Leslie, a trade monopoly in Florida with Indians under the Spanish sphere of influence.

2. For the Indian trade policy adopted by the U.S. government during GW's administration, see "An Act to regulate trade and intercourse with the Indian tribes," 22 July 1790, "An Act to regulate Trade and Intercourse with the Indian Tribes," 1 Mar. 1793, "An Act for establishing Trading Houses with the Indian Tribes," 18 April 1796, and "An Act to regulate Trade and Intercourse with the Indian Tribes, and to preserve Peace on the Frontiers," 19 May 1796 (1 *Stat.* 137–38, 329–31, 452–53, 469–74).

3. Mulryne did not receive any federal appointment, and no reply from GW to Mulryne has been found.

To the United States Senate and House of Representatives

United States [Philadelphia] November the 22d 1792
Gentlemen of the Senate, and of the House of Representatives.

I send you herewith the abstract of a supplementary arrangement which has been made by me pursuant to the Acts of the third day of March 1791 and the eighth day of May 1792 for raising a Revenue upon foreign and domestic distilled Spirits, in respect to the subdivisions and officers which have appeared to me necessary, and to the allowances for their respective services to the Supervisors, Inspectors and other officers of Inspection; together with estimates of the amount of compensations and charges.[1]

Go: Washington

DS, DNA: RG 46, Second Congress, 1791–93, Senate Records of Legislative Proceedings, President's Messages; LB, DNA: RG 233, Second Congress, 1791–93, House Records of Legislative Proceedings, Journals; LB, DLC:GW.

1. See "An Act repealing, after the last day of June next, the duties heretofore laid upon Distilled Spirits imported from abroad, and laying others in their stead; and also upon Spirits distilled within the United States, and for appropriating the same," 3 Mar. 1791, and "An Act concerning the Duties on Spirits distilled within the United States," 8 May 1792 (1 *Stat.* 199–214, 267–71). For background on the reports submitted with this letter, see GW's proclamation of 4 Aug. 1792, and note 2, and GW to Hamilton, 1 Oct. 1792, and note 1. The enclosed abstract consisted of GW's 22 Nov. restatement of the

4 Aug. proclamation and his orders to revenue officers of 29 Oct. 1792 (DS, DNA: RG 46, Second Congress, 1791–93, Senate Records of Legislative Proceedings, President's Messages). The other two enclosures were financial reports submitted by Tench Coxe. Report A, dated 12 Sept. 1792, was "An Estimate of the Compensations for, and contingent Expences on, the collection of the Revenue, On domestic distilled Spirits for one year following the 30th June 1791, to which are added the compensations for, and expences of the Inspection of foreign Distilled Spirits, Teas, and wines, for the same term, by the Officers of the Revenue, pursuant to Law," and report E, dated 25 July 1792, was "An Estimate for the Compensations for and Contingent expences on the Collection of the Revenue on domestic distilled Spirits for one year following the *30th* June *1792* to which are added the Compensations for and expences of the Inspection, marking and certifying Teas and Wines for the same by the Officers of the Revenue, pursuant to law" (both estimates are in DNA: RG 46, Second Congress, 1791–93, Senate Records of Legislative Proceedings, President's Messages). All three enclosures and GW's letter to Congress of 22 Nov. comprise a printed report in DNA: RG 233, Second Congress, 1791–93, House Records of Legislative Proceedings, Journals. See also *ASP, Finance,* 1:171–75.

Letter not found: from Anthony Whitting, 22 Nov. 1792. GW wrote Whitting on 2 Dec. acknowledging "Your letter of the 22d of Novr enclosing the Sheriffs account."

Tobias Lear to Thomas Jefferson

United States [Philadelphia] November 23d 1792

T. Lear has the honor to transmit to the Secretary of State the Commissions which were sent to the President for his signature, which they have received.[1]

T. Lear begs leave to observe that in the Commission of Mr Joy, it is expressed: *"He demanding and receiving no Fees or Perquisites"*— which appears to be contrary to the fourth Section of the Act passed during the last Session of Congress, entitled, "An Act concerning Consuls and Vice Consuls." If the matter should strike the Secretary in the same light as it does T. Lear, it will undoubtedly be rectified.[2]

AL (letterpress copy), DNA: RG 59, Miscellaneous Letters; LB, DNA: RG 59, George Washington's Correspondence with His Secretaries of State; LB (photocopy), DLC:GW.

1. For the commissions returned to Jefferson with GW's signature, see GW to the U.S. Senate, 19 Nov. 1792 (first letter).

2. Jefferson wrote Benjamin Joy on 21 Nov. enclosing his commission as "Consul at Calcutta and other ports and places on the Coast of India" (DLC:

Jefferson Papers). According to section 4 of "An Act concerning Consuls and Vice-Consuls," 14 April 1792, consuls could charge fees, as established by Congress, for specific consular services, and Joy's final commission was modified to reflect this privilege (see 1 *Stat.* 255–56; a copy of Joy's commission of 21 Nov. 1792 is in DNA: RG 59, Inventory No. 15, entry 777, Permanent and Temporary Consular Commissions). For background on Joy's appointment, see George Cabot to GW, 16 Nov., and notes.

Henry Knox to Tobias Lear

Dr Sir [Philadelphia] 23 Novr 1792
Please to submit the enclosed letters from M. Genl Wayne to the President of the United States.[1] When he shall have perused them, I pray they may be returned, with any remarks he may think proper, as I must answer them this day.[2] Yours sincerely,
H. Knox

ALS, DLC:GW; LB, DLC:GW.

1. "Your letters of the 14 and 16 instant," Knox wrote Wayne on 24 Nov., "have been received and submitted to the president" (Knopf, *Wayne,* 139). Wayne's letter of 14 Nov. has not been identified. His letter to Knox of 16 Nov. included a review of the provisions needed for the army in 1793 and of past difficulties in obtaining and distributing provisions, which had induced Wayne "to order the deposits of provision in advance." Wayne also wrote: "we have a report that the Cornplanter has returned from the Council of the Hostile Indians at Au Glaize—& that he is expected at Fort Franklin about this time in consequence of which I immediately dispatched Mr. Rosecrantz to meet & invite him with the New Arrow & red Jacket to visit Philadelphia agreably to your desire in a former letter" (ibid., 133–135). For Knox's instructions to invite the Seneca chiefs to Philadelphia, see his letter to Wayne of 12 Oct. (ibid., 114–16).

2. Lear returned Wayne's letters later on this date with Washington's Observations on General Wayne's Letters of 23 Nov. 1792. For Knox's reply to Wayne, see his letter of 24 Nov. (ibid., 139–42).

Tobias Lear to Henry Knox

United States [Philadelphia] November 2[3]d. [1]792[1]
T. Lear has the honor to return to the Secretary of War the two letters from Major General Wayne, with their enclosures, which have been submitted to the President, whose remarks thereon are herewith enclosed.[2]

Tobias Lear.
Secretary to the president of the United States.

ALS (letterpress copy), DLC:GW; LB, DLC:GW.

1. Lear wrote over his original date of 22 Nov. on the letterpress copy to change it to 23 November. Lear's docket reads "23d Nov. 1792," and the letter-book copy also is dated the "23d."

2. For the letters from Wayne, see Knox to Lear, 23 Nov. 1792 (first letter), n.1. For GW's "remarks thereon," see the following enclosure, Washington's Observations on General Wayne's Letters, 23 Nov. 1792.

Enclosure
Washington's Observations on General Wayne's Letters

[Philadelphia] Novr 23d [1792]
Observations

On Majr Genl Waynes letter of the 14th Instt[1]

It is unfortunate, & very extraordinary, that he should have suspended h⟨is⟩ opinion with respect to the disposition of the Army for the Winter, from a vague report of Mr H—⟨s⟩— declaration concerning the Western Posts. If this had been founded, he oug⟨ht⟩ to have looked for it from a better source, ⟨or⟩ to have disregarded it altogether.[2]

Now, I presume, it is too late to worry what *would*—(had he not been unde⟨r⟩ false impressions) have been *his* plan into execution. But I think he ought to be cha⟨r⟩ged in strong, & explicit terms, to run ⟨the⟩ public to no more expence in the Barrack⟨s⟩ he is about to build, than what is *indispensably* necessary to cover & secure the Officers & Soldiers from the weather—avoiding *all decorations,* and *as much as possible all conveniencies*—considering themselves, as it were, under marching orders, to remove *during Winter* or in the *Spring* according to events & circumstances.[3]

On the letter from D[itt]o dated 16th Novr[4]

The difficulty, and as He (G.W.) calls it, the impracticability of providing Flour after the 15th of June, is *New information,* which if it had been given before, might have induced the authorisation of a larger Magazine of this Article: and now, if it does not militate with the arrangement made with the Secretary of the Treasury I should have no disinclination towards increasing the quantity.[5] Of the Meat kind, after a sufficient quantity of that which is salted, is stored; the dependence ought surely to be on live Cattle—Stalled or Grass fed; As the expence of transportation in Carriages, or on Pack horses, would be immense—As flour must always be carried, there may, & I think ought to be exertion used to get it forward in the best mode & time that can be embraced to the advanced Posts—for reasons which are too obvious to be mentioned.

G. W——n

ADS (letterpress copy), DLC:GW; LB, DLC:GW.

1. Wayne's letter to Knox of 14 Nov. has not been identified.

2. Knox incorporated GW's observations in his letter to Wayne of 24 Nov., in which Knox referred to "a Vague report of Mr. H——s declaration of the posts of Detroit and Niagara being relinquished to us in the spring," but which is "not corroborated by his official declarations" (Knopf, *Wayne*, 139–42). "Mr. H." was probably George Hammond, British minister to the United States.

3. In his letter to Wayne of 24 Nov., Knox wrote, "your fortified camp near the Big Beaver is to be regarded, as a position for two or at most three Months," and then he delivered GW's instructions for construction of the barracks (ibid., 139). The new Legionville camp was located in western Pennsylvania near the confluence of Beaver Creek and the Ohio River. For GW's earlier thoughts on the type of winter quarters needed for the army, see GW to Knox, 24 Sept. (first letter).

4. For Wayne's letter to Knox of 16 Nov., see ibid., 133–35.

5. The arrangement for supplying flour to the army was contained in a letter, which has not been found, that Knox wrote Hamilton on 3 Nov. "relatively to the Magazines of Rations to be kept in advance" (see Knox to GW, 3 Nov., and note 2).

From Warner Mifflin

Philada 23d 11 Mon[th]: 1792

To the President, Senate and House of Representatives of the United States—

"He that ruleth over men must be just, ruling in the fear of God"—2d Sam: 23.3.

Having for a long time felt my mind impressed with a religious engagement on your account, and a belief that if measures are not taken to redress the wrongs, and alleviate the sufferings and oppression of the African race in these states, the Almighty will manifest his displeasure in a more conspicuous manner than has yet appeared: The consideration whereof excites me in his fear, earnestly to sollicit and solemnly to warn you, to exert your power and influence, that right and justice may be done in this important case.[1]

I have been also affected with the following declaration of the prophet, Vizt Ezek. 3.20. "When a righteous man doth turn from his righteousness, and commit iniquity, and I lay a stumbling block before him, he shall die; because thou hast not given him warning, he shall die in his sins, and his righteousness which he hath done shall not be remembred; but his blood will I require at thine hand.["]

21. "Nevertheless if thou warn the righteous man, that the righteous sin not, and he doth not sin, he shall surely live, because he is warned; also thou hast delivered thy soul."

Now, I cannot view the declaration made by the first Congress, in substance to amount to any thing short of a solemn covenant, entered into with the God of Heaven and the whole earth; Vizt We hold these truths self evident, that all men were created equal, that they were endowed by their Creator with certain unalienable rights, among which are life, liberty &ca; and which remains obligatory on the present Congress so to consider—How then have those rights become alienated, that Americans shall be permitted to continue to ravage the coast of Africa, thereby promoting murder, pillaging, plundering and burning its towns, and inslaving its inhabitants;[2] and in the United States, while some of those very men, who perhaps with their own hands subscribed the aforesaid declaration, remain in the Supreme Legislature,[3] that avaricious men shall be permitted to pass through the country, steal, buy, traffick, barter and exchange the blacks, as though they were indeed brute beasts, separating husband from wife, parents from children, even mothers from infant babes; yea, from all that is dear to men in this world except life, and indeed that also, as there are divers instances of their being murthered;[4] others in iron fetters, huddled into jails till the number wanted is collected, then stowed into vessels for transportation to foreign parts, and sold into perpetual slavery; not permitting a parting leave between the nearest ties of nature. My soul now revolts at the infernal crime committed against innocent persons without provocation. Oh! let me now beseech you, not to think it too much degradation for you to reflect, was this the lot of one of your beloved, delicate wives, your tender babes, or near relatives, how then would you feel?

Do not you with me believe that there is a God of Justice, who will finally recompence unto all men according to the fruit of their doings, and that he doth at one view, by his all-penetrating eye, behold the actions of men over the face of the globe; if so, how do we think he will look on the rulers of this land, when he beholds many of them faring sumptuously every day, living in ease and fulness, at the very time that they are inventing unto themselves instruments of music, and spending their precious time in vain theatrical and other amusements, and remember not the afflictions of their suffering African brethren; who in this country may be loaded with irons, under all the pangs of sorrow the human heart can be capable of enduring, for no crime whatever, but because it pleased God to suffer them to come into the world with a black skin; will not this make him your enemy, who is a God that is no respecter of persons.

I crave your serious attention to this important subject, and that while you may feel an animated warmth to fill your minds, when engaged respecting the natives of this land, you suffer a turn of thought respecting the conduct of Americans in Africa, and in this country also, towards Africans; and see if any savage cruelty of the natives, can exceed that of the white people towards the Africans, considering our superior advantage of civilization under the Light of the Gospel. Let us consider we are informed that the measure we meet to others is to be meted to us; and likewise that we may so conduct as never to feel the effects (in the full extent) of the declaration of the Almighty formerly delivered to a highly favoured people, in failure of complying with their covenants and engagements, Vizt—34.17. "Behold, I proclaim a liberty for you, saith the Lord, to the sword, to the famine, and to the pestilence."[5] Is there not reason to acknowledge that we have seen in some measure fulfilled a part of the first; are there not traces of the second, and do we not acknowledge that all three are subservient to Almighty Power; and has not our nation falsified its covenant? Oh! my countrymen and fellow-citizens, be serious on this subject, and allow me the liberty of a free expostulation with you; I feel for the welfare of my country, and my fellow-citizens; every one of whom I love; and believing myself every way equally interested with the largest part of your body in the welfare of my country, I hoped you would allow me freely, thus far to relieve my pained heart, who feel so much on account of the barbarous cruelties exercised on an unoffending people, which I am persuaded you generally have not a full conception of, that under an apprehension of duty I have attempted in this manner to address you.[6] Being with sincere desires for your welfare Your real friend

Warner Mifflin

ALS, DNA: RG 59, Miscellaneous Letters; ALS, DNA: RG 46, Second Congress, 1791–93, Senate Records of Legislative Proceedings, Petitions and Memorials, Resolutions of State Legislatures, and Related Documents.

1. For an earlier letter to GW on the same subject from this Quaker abolitionist, see Mifflin to GW, 12 Mar. 1790.

2. Even if GW and other federal leaders agreed with Mifflin's criticism of the African slave trade, Article 1, Section 9, of the U.S. Constitution says: "The Migration or Importation of such Persons as any of the States now existing shall think proper to admit, shall not be prohibited by the Congress prior to the Year one thousand eight hundred and eight."

3. Signers of the Declaration of Independence serving in the House of Representatives in November 1792 were Elbridge Gerry, Mass., and Abraham Clark, N.J., while those in the Senate were Roger Sherman, Conn.; Robert Morris, Pa.; George Read, Del.; Charles Carroll of Carrollton, Md.; and Richard Henry Lee, Virginia.

4. The copy sent to Congress has the word "murdered" at this place in the text.

5. The source of this biblical quotation was written in the left margin as "Jerem: 34.17." The verse taken in its entirety from the King James version of the Bible reads: "Therefore thus saith the Lord; Ye have not Hearkened unto me, in proclaiming liberty, every one to his brother, and every man to his neighbour: behold, I proclaim a liberty for you, saith the Lord, to the sword, to the pestilence, and to the famine; and I will make you to be removed into all the kingdoms of the earth."

6. On 28 Dec. the House of Representatives voted to return Mifflin's petition to him (see *Annals of Congress*, 2d Cong., 730–31). For further correspondence on this subject, see Mifflin to GW, 12 Dec. 1792.

From Alexander White

[Philadelphia] Nov. 23d 1792.

A. White having received the enclosed from his Friend General Wood, could devise no method so effectual to inform the President of General Martins wishes and merits as by communicating the letter of General Wood.[1]

AL, DLC:GW.

1. The enclosed letter from James Wood, lieutenant governor of Virginia, to Virginia congressman White has not been identified. General Martin is probably Joseph Martin, a Revolutionary War veteran and former Indian agent for

North Carolina, Virginia, and the United States who currently was a member of Virginia's general assembly.

From Thomas Jefferson

[Philadelphia] Nov. 24. 92.

Th: Jefferson returns to the President mister Cooper's pamphlet which he has perused with much satisfaction, & is thankful for the opportunity of perusing it, furnished him by the kindness of the President.[1]

AL, DLC:GW.

1. Jefferson apparently enclosed the pamphlet that had been written recently by British native Thomas Cooper (1759–1839), who traveled to France in the spring of 1792 to lend support to the radical faction of the French Revolution. A denunciation of Cooper by Edmund Burke led to Cooper's publishing in London later this year *A Reply to Mr. Burke's Invective against Mr. Cooper, and Mr. Watt, in the House of Commons, on the 30th of April, 1792.* Cooper's call for reform of Britain's political, economic, and social systems in this pamphlet and other writings resulted in persecution that convinced him to depart for the United States in 1794. He practiced law in Pennsylvania for several years before settling permanently in South Carolina in 1820 as a professor of chemistry and later president of South Carolina College. Cooper's political sympathies lay with Jefferson's Democratic followers, and he was tried in 1800 for libel under the Sedition Act of 1798 for his criticism of President John Adams. Found guilty, he was sentenced to six months in jail and fined $400.

Tobias Lear to Henry Knox

United States [Philadelphia] Novr 24th [1]792

By the President's command T. Lear has the honor to return to the Secretary of War the letter to Govrnor Lee—to Thomas Wilson Esq. & others[1]—and the Copy of a letter to Genl Wayne,[2] which have been submitted to the President & to inform the Secretary that their contents meet the ideas of the President.

T.L.
S.P.U.S.

ADfS, DLC:GW; LB, DLC:GW.

1. For Knox's letters to Henry Lee and to Thomas Wilson, see Lear to Knox, 21 Nov. 1792, and notes 2 and 3.

2. For background on Knox's letter to Wayne of 24 Nov., see Knox to Lear, 23 Nov., and note 1, and Lear to Knox, 23 Nov. 1792, and the accompanying

enclosure of that date, Washington's Observations on General Wayne's Letters, and notes. For the text of Knox's letter to Wayne, see Knopf, *Wayne,* 139–42.

From John C. Ogden

Sir   Portsmouth [N.H.] Novr 24th 1792

During times of war it is the duty of every individual to send that intelligence to head quarters, which may concern the honor or safety of the country. Such I conclude is the duty of citizens in days of peace. and that the President of the United States ought to be informed of every thing, in every part of the country, which concerns their religious or civil interests.

Deeply impressed with these ideas, which are collected from long observation, and undoubtedly are founded in the policy of government to know and attend to—I am led to transmit this, which more immediately is connected with my profession, and a trust reposed in me as a member of, and Secretary to a body, who have the care of a very valuable and extensive Church property.[1]

Your Excellency is no Stranger, to the grant of the former British administration, of certain lands in many towns in New Hampshire and Vermont, to the Church of England and Society for propagating the Gospel, for supporting religious worship and instruction in those settlements which are more immediately on and near the banks of Connecticut river. The Society in England about four years since, quit-claimed their title in said Land to certain Gentlemen in this State and Massachusetts, as trustees for carrying the original design into effect.[2]

Various frauds have been committed, and injuries done to this property, by which the original purpose is injured wantonly from the missdoings of the dissenting party. Trespassers have entered, and settled upon them, and many sources of controversy, and causes of action before civil courts aris⟨e.⟩ We once appealed to the Legislature for an act of incorporation, of our Trustees—but, from the *violent* opposition of The Honble John Langdon Esqr. then President of the State,[3] and his council, we were oblidged to withdraw our petition—no one appeared as our friend but The Honble Mr Pickering, the present worthy Chief Justice of the Superior Court.[4] The Lower house of assembly were in our favor. No time since has presented that favorable opportunity, when we might renew our application. Under this embarrassment we have no present remidy, but as Attorneys for the Society in England, by an appeal to the Federal Courts. The indisposition of my countrys friend, Judge Sullivan, and the expectation of Mr Woodbury Langdons friend⟨s⟩ that he will succeed to the place of District Judge alarm our cares, and awake a solicitude, for the interest of the Church, which is necessary.[5] The cause of this is, Mr Woodbury Langdon, has unjustly entered upon, and keeps possession of a valuable property, belonging to the Church in Portsmouth, which his *brother* and every other man in the State, say he has no honest equitable title to. He once attempted with others to obtain a seizure or forfeiture of the whole of these Church Lands, on the Grants (so called) into the treasury of The State, this failing they endeavored to lead the College to apply for a gift of this property to that institution, but without success.[6] A few weeks since I was informed that a plan once had been concerted by individuals, to prevail on the State to seize those Lands for vacant, and sell them to individuals, to enrich the Treasury. This was the plan of the dissenting party, at which those Mr Langdons are at the head.

Mr John Langdon, had even wished to divide them among the dissenting meetings by act of government.

For a Clergyman to say any thing on the subject of civil appointments, may in general be improper. but when the rights and property of his religion are concerned, he will be excused for giving information relating to those particulars.

Many leading Churchmen press me to inform your Excellency on the subject—that we may shew our county—the Church and Posterity, that we have attempted to ward off dangers in a prudent and quiet manner.

What will further evince, not only the mad policy, but intolerant injustice of seizing the Church Land is—that they are appropriated to the teaching of religion in a county newly settled, by hardy industrious emigrants, from Towns, where they enjoyed the public worship of their maker—and schools for their children. Great numbers of these emigrant⟨s⟩ were american soldiers —who after the peace, & the loss of their final settlement securities, obtained deeds on mort[g]age of lots, built huts—married wives—have cleared farms—and now have large families (in a prolific country), of fine promising children. They mourn the want of means to instruct them in religion and useful knowledge. The first settlers have sold generaly the school right of three hundred acres which was intended as a perpetual fund. To that six hundred acres only remain in most of those Towns, and these are church property—Many of these settlers are actualy Churchmen—They have paid road, town, and other taxes, during their residence, have virtuously submited to many hardships with the hope of doing good for their families and yet enjoying their religion. I have visited them, have eat, drank, and lodged in their houses during the summer past. I have heard their complaints—know their wants, and find a resentment raising against those who would deprive them of the benefit, which the Church, would long since have afforded them by sending Clergymen, among them—(Could we obtain an act of in corporation for our trustees)—This has been hither to prevented by the party under the influence of The Mr Langdons connections in New Hampshire. This State of facts is also known by the Bishops and Clergy, as well as by leading Lay-Churchmen through the States—It was my duty to inform them.

The nature of this letter will not require an answer—far be it from me to lead your Excellency into a correspondence on ecclesiastical subjects.[7]

Altho I have seen a great want of due caution on the part of Dissenters, as to the religious rights of Churchmen, I wish not to draw Churchmen into any thing which is not just—peaceable prudent & proper. I remain Sir Your Excellencys devoted Servant

John Cosens Ogden Rector
of St Johns Church in Portsmouth—N: Hampshire

ALS, DNA: RG 59, Miscellaneous Letters.

1. For background on the contentious relationship that Ogden, rector of St. John's Episcopal Church in Portsmouth (Queen Anne's Chapel before February 1791), had with members and clergy of the Congregational church and for his defense of the Episcopal church's glebe lands against seizure by local governments throughout New England, see Ogden to GW, 9 Jan. 1791, n.1.

2. The expansion of settlement in New Hampshire during the mid-eighteenth century provided opportunities for Gov. Benning Wentworth and his successor, John Wentworth, who served 1741–66 and 1767–75, respectively, to promote actively the interests of the Anglican church and the missionary endeavors of the Anglican-based Society for the Propagation of the Gospel in Foreign Parts (SPG). In approving over one hundred grants for new townships, Benning Wentworth set aside in each town one share for the SPG,

one share for "the First Settled Minister of the Gospel," and one share for "a Glebe for the ministry of the Church of England." This practice was continued by his nephew and successor, John Wentworth (see Kinney, *Church & State*, 67–72, 83–85).

3. Former New Hampshire governor John Langdon, an ardent patriot and a signer of the U.S. Constitution, served two terms as president of New Hampshire, 1785–86 and 1788–89, before being elected to the U.S. Senate in the fall of 1788. Chosen as the Senate's first president pro tempore on 6 April 1789, Langdon counted the first electoral votes for president and vice-president of the United States. He was reelected to that position on 5 Nov. 1792, and Samuel A. Otis, secretary of the Senate, so informed Tobias Lear on 8 Nov. (DLC:GW). Elected to a second Senate term, Langdon served until 1801. He was governor of New Hampshire from 1805 to 1809 and from 1810 to 1812.

4. Portsmouth resident John Pickering (c.1738–1805) studied law after graduating from Harvard College in 1761, and he was active in state and local politics during and after the Revolutionary War. Appointed chief justice of the New Hampshire superior court of judicature on 7 Aug. 1790, Pickering served in that position until February 1795 when the Senate confirmed his appointment as the U.S. district judge of New Hampshire to replace Revolutionary War general John Sullivan, who died on 23 Jan. 1795. Pickering's deteriorating mental health and inattention to his judicial duties prompted articles of impeachment by the U.S. House of Representatives in 1803 and a Senate vote for his removal from office on 12 Mar. 1804.

5. Woodbury Langdon, older brother of Gov. John Langdon, served as a justice on the New Hampshire superior court from 1785 to 1791, when he was forced to resign following his impeachment the previous summer for dereliction of duty. GW appointed Woodbury Langdon in December 1790 as one of three "Commissioners for settling the Accounts between the United States and individual States" (see GW to the U.S. Senate, 23 Dec. 1790).

6. For the efforts by Dartmouth College to obtain glebe lands in Vermont, the former New Hampshire Grants, see Chase, *History of Dartmouth*, 1:590.

7. No reply from GW to Ogden has been found. In his next letter to GW on 16 Jan. 1793, Ogden urged GW to appoint John Pickering to succeed John Sullivan on the U.S. district court and disparaged the character of Woodbury Langdon (DNA: RG 59, Miscellaneous Letters).

To Edmund Randolph

Sir,   United States [Philadelphia] November 24th 1792

It appears to me necessary,[1] that processes should issue without further delay upon the Indictments found at the last Circuit Court held at York Town in the Commonwealth of Pennsylvania, in reference to the laws laying a duty on Spirits distilled within the United States[2]—and proper, that they should be served by the Marshal of the District of Pennsylvania, in person. I am to desire, that the requisite arrangements, with the Attorney & marshal of the before mentioned District,[3] may be taken for these purposes; in doing which, you are authorised to signify to the latter,[4] my expectation of his immediate agency in the business.[5]

Df, in Tobias Lear's writing, DNA: RG 59, Miscellaneous Letters; Df, in Alexander Hamilton's writing, DNA: RG 59, Miscellaneous Letters; LB, DLC:GW. Lear apparently received Hamilton's draft, copied it over, and then decided, or was instructed by GW, to make changes, which he noted on both his own copy and Hamilton's draft.

1. At this place in his draft, Hamilton struck out the word "proper" and inserted the word "necessary." Lear retained Hamilton's change.

2. For background on the resistance in western Pennsylvania to the excise tax on distilled spirits and the subsequent indictments against William Kerr and Alexander Berr by the U.S. circuit court that met at York on 11 Oct. 1792, see Hamilton to GW, 1 Sept., and notes, GW to Hamilton, 7 Sept., and note 2, Edmund Randolph to GW, 10 Sept, and note 3, GW to Randolph, 1 Oct., and note 1, and GW's proclamation of 15 Sept. 1792.

3. Lear inserted the phrase "with the Attorney & marshall of the before mentioned District," before the words "may be taken" on Hamilton's draft, but his interlineation of this phrase on his own draft does not indicate its precise placement, and it appears after "may be taken" in the letter-book copy.

4. Although Lear substituted the word "and" in place of "in doing which" on Hamilton's draft, he did not do so on his own draft, nor does this substitution appear on the letter-book copy. Lear replaced "Marshall" on his own draft and on Hamilton's draft with the word "latter," which also appears on the letter-book copy.

5. For Clement Biddle's reluctance to perform his duties as U.S. marshal of Pennsylvania and GW's insistence on his cooperation, see Biddle to GW, 27 Nov., and notes. On 13 Mar. 1793, GW instructed William Rawle, U.S. district attorney for Pennsylvania, to dismiss the indictments against Kerr and Berr.

Tobias Lear to Henry Knox

United States [Philadelphia] Novr 25th 1792

By the President's Command T. Lear has the honor to return to the Secretary of War General Sevier's letter, which the President has refused,[1] and to inform the Secretary that the President observes, that the Secretary will in his answer to Genl Sevier let him know that by accounts from the Superintendent of Indian Affairs to the Southward, the disposition of the Creek nation is very different from what it is represented to be in General Sevier's letter, and that as to his acting offensively the Secretary will give him such reply as is proper.[2]

Tobias Lear.
Secretary to the president of the United States

ALS (letterpress copy), DLC:GW; LB, DLC:GW.

1. The letter-book copy reads "perused."

2. Knox enclosed John Sevier's letter to him of 25 Oct. for GW's review in a brief note to Lear written earlier on this date (DLC:GW). Neither that letter nor Knox's reply to Sevier has been identified. On 26 Nov. 1792 Knox wrote William Blount, governor of the Southwest Territory: "I have received a letter from Brigadier General Sevier dated the 25th of October, by which it would appear that he was in actual service at that period; and his letter seems to indicate an apprehension of a general Southern Indian War. The direct reverse of this picture is presented by Mr Seagrove as it relates to the Creeks; and your information of all the Cherokees, excepting the lower Towns, corroborates the general peaceable dispositions of that Tribe" (Carter, *Territorial Papers*, 4:224). For the latest information available to Knox and GW from Indian agent James Seagrove, see Lear to Knox, 14 Nov. 1792, n.1.

From Fulwar Skipwith

Sir   Portsmouth [Va.] 25 Novemr 1792

In the present urgency and peculiar hardship of my situation I am led with some persuasion of success to call a moment of your Excellencys attention to a short history of my distress, and to hope, that if I may be found to possess merit or talents sufficient to fit me for any little employment under Government, your Excellency may be induced to confer on me the honor of a future and second recommendation.[1]

Under an impression that the one, which favoured me with my appointment of Consul from the U. States for the Island of Martinique and its dependencies, would have also induced Government to make some provision for its support, I was tempted with what little property I had to leave my native Country in August 1792, when I arrived at Mtque at the moment of the commencement of its civil troubles. these disorders have continued with more or less abatement ever since, and have precluded me from opportunities of gaining a livelyhood in business, which I might have promised myself, from a more settled state of things. The ignorance of the french Colonial Governments of any Treaty or Convention which authorises the U. States to establish Consuls among them has destroyed every hope or prospect of my being acknowledged as one thus, from long delay and fruitless attention, I have been obliged to leave the Island in indigence.[2] Conscious that my endeavour, and intentions of Serving my Country cannot, in return, deserve distress; and resting much of my hope in the benevolence of your Excellency's heart, I do not altogether despair of your future notice.

Having never been honored with a personal acquaintance with your Excellency farther than that of a bare introduction, I flatter myself that Mr Jefferson, [Tobias] Lear, [John] Langdon, or any one of the Virginia delegation, to whom I have the pleasure of being known, would venture to give a favourable opinion of my deserts.

Sincerely wishing your Excellence the full enjoyment of all earthly happiness I have the honor to remain Your Excellencys Most Ob. and Most Hb. Servant

Fulwar Skipwith

ALS, DLC:GW. The cover is postmarked "PORTSMOUTH Novem. 27."

1. The appointment of Virginia merchant Fulwar Skipwith (1765–1839) in June 1790 as consul for the island of Martinique included responsibility for the nearby islands of Cayenne, Saint Lucia, and Tobago (see GW to the U.S. Senate, 4 June 1790; *Jefferson Papers*, 16:560). Skipwith remained in that position until 1795 when GW appointed him the consul general to France, a position that he held for only a year (see *Executive Journal*, 189, 191). Skipwith served as the commercial agent in Paris from 1801 to 1808 and again as the consul to France from 1814 to 1815.

2. Skipwith arrived in Martinique in the summer of 1790 shortly after his appointment, and he immediately encountered difficulties. Skipwith wrote Thomas Jefferson on 30 Aug. 1790 that he could not obtain the necessary exequatur because the French government had not sent notification of the Franco-American Consular Convention of 1788 to the island's governor, Claude-Charles de Damas (see *Jefferson Papers*, 16:561n). For background on problems with differing French and American interpretations of this consular convention, see Jefferson to William Short, 26 July 1790, 25 April 1791, ibid., 17:280–81, 20:254. The emerging civil war and nascent rebellion that Skipwith encountered on Martinique in 1790 was a much greater obstacle to the success of his consulship and his hopes of using his position for personal economic gain. For Skipwith's descriptions of the political and social unrest on the island, see his letters to Jefferson of 18 Sept. and 10 Oct. 1790, ibid., 17:510–11, 585–90.

Skipwith had left Martinique in the summer of 1791, leaving Nathaniel Barrett, nephew of New Hampshire senator John Langdon, to represent the United States. Congress's failure to provide financial support for its consuls, combined with the island's continued civil unrest and Skipwith's own lack of authority, contributed to his decision in 1791 and again in 1792 to return to the United States. Despite these problems Skipwith resumed his duties in Martinique in March 1793 (see Skipwith to Jefferson, 1 May, 20 July 1791, and Jefferson to Vicomte de Rochambeau, 6 Mar. 1793, ibid., 20:342, 655, 25:321). Skipwith was not the only U.S. consul to find the lack of remuneration a problem (see Jefferson to Sylvanus Bourne, 14 Aug. 1791, ibid., 22:40; Jefferson to GW, 19 Aug. 1792, n.2).

To Anthony Whitting

Mr Whiting,   Philadelphia Novr 25th 1792.

Your letter of the 21st instant enclosing the Reports of the preceeding week was received yesterday; but the Sheriffs acct of taxes was not, though mentioned, among the papers which were sent to me.[1]

As you think (as I do also) that the new part of the old Clover lot at the Mansion house had better be in Potatoes, Perhaps it would be well, to apply those you have, to this purpose; & instead of cultivating field No. 4 at Dogue run in this article, let it lay over; and in lieu thereof, fallow (with Buck Wheat for manure) No. 1 at that place, for Wheat. This is the rotation I had marked out for that plantation before you suggested Potatoes for No. 4, next year. By this alteration the last mentioned field will, as was intended, come in to Corn in 1794; succeeding No. 3, which will be in that article next year; and succeeded by No. 5 the year following; that is, in 1795 and so on—bringing them all on, with Corn, in the order of their numbers. And this, considering you have not a sufficiency of Potatoes for both purposes (and I find it too expensive, and too much unlike a Farmer to be always upon the purchase of my Seeds), and that by the *double* dressing with Green manure No. 1 may be got in fine order for Wheat if you can prepare & sow it with Buck Wheat early in the Spring, to be plowed in before harvest when seed enough is ripe to bring forward a second Crop for plowing in timously for Wheat Seeding—I feel more inclination for the adoption of this plan, than I do for planting No. 4 at Dogue run with the Potatoes you have: especially as the quantity on hand are inadequate to the demand of that field, & because they are at the Mansion house in readiness for the other purpose[.] If more than sufficient for which (allowing about 8 bushels to the Acre) the residue, instead of

Turnips, may be planted in the old part of the same (Clover) lot or elsewhere as you may conceive best—Besides the reasons I have just mentioned, there are others which influence me to this change (which, as I do not perceive by the Reports that any work has yet been done in No. 4, can be made without any loss of labor) and these are, that No. 1 is running very much into *furrow gullies,* which will, in a little time, if not stopped, be of magnitude; and very injurious to it; but by being contiguous to the Corn fields, you have the means now at hand, to fill & smooth them for the plow with very little labour, wch might not, & certainly would not, be the case another year after the Corn stalks, (than which nothing can be better calculated for filling these gullies) are removed & destroyed; & by altering the fence between the said No. 1 & the meadow (in the manner made known to you) it will place things as they ought to be without delay; and will more-over give No. 4 a year's more rest, which will be no disservice to it; whilst every thing in the rotation line will work more system-atically by means of it. There is another thing, equally necessary, wanting in this field; and that is, assistance to the poor & washed parts of it: for these can receive no benefit from Buck Wheat, be-cause none will grow on them: & to recover them before they get *quite* lost, is prudent & essential; as well for appearance as profit. The hedge row along the old race will be to be cleared, & the bank levelled: in doing the first, leave here & there a tree, or clump, for shade & ornament.

If Plants of the Drumhead & Cattle Cabbage can be raised in time, you might perhaps, find some part of the addition to the old clover lot very proper for them; & as they would require to be well cultivated, very proper also for the grass which is (as soon as the new part of the ground is fully reclaimed & cleansed) to follow.

I am very willing—nay desirous—that part of the Vineyard In-closure should be appropriated to raising *any* & *all* kind of plants fit for hedging, or to repair hedges. Those of the most valuable & scarcer kind of plants for this purpose, may receive nourish-ment in my little Garden; as the Firze, for instance.[2] But I am of opinion that all such hedges as are to be raised from the Seed— for instance—Cedar—Honey locust—White thorn—Sycamore —&ca—&ca—had better be sown in the places where they are to remain, having the ground *well* prepared previous to the reception of it, and well attended to afterwards, for I have been very unsuccessful in all my transplantations.

The quantity of Grain received into the Mill weekly; the quantity of Meal, flour, Bran, &ca delivered from it; & the quantity, and kind of flour that is packed in the course of it, & actually there; is all the report I want; that I may see at one view what *goes in,* what *comes out,* and what is *actually in the Mill;* barraled up of different sorts of flour; for I presume, as well to avoid dust, as petty robberies, the flour is packed as fast as it is ground—and that the Bran is brought away. This being the case there can be no difficulty, nor trouble in makg the Report; as I do not want the Wheat (after it gets in to the Garner) a second time measured, nor (supposing as above) any thing said of the unpacked flour.[3]

If your growing Wheat is cut off, are you not able to discover by what insect it is done so as to describe it?[4] Keep an attentive eye towards it, and let me know from time to time how this disaster progresses, and what the general appearance of your different fields is, & promises to be.

I wish to know, as soon as you can conveniently ascertain it, what the quantity of Buckwheat is, that you have made; what grd you mean to sow with it; and what quantity it will take to seed it (including No. 1 at Dogue run): and if your own stock shd fall short, enquire at what price it could be obtained, delivered at Alexandria—& let me know the result. Let me know also, as soon as your Corn is measured, the total quantity made; what each field produced; and how much has been used up to the period of rendering me the acct of the New Corn.

I perceive by the last report that 8 Sheep are missing; but that it is not known whether taken from Dogue Run or the Ferry & Frenchs. This confirms what I observed to you in my last, or one of my last letters—viz.—that the Overseers know very little of what relates to their own Stock; giving in the number from *old reports* instead of from *actual weekly* counting; by which means half my Stock may be stolen, or eaten, before they are missed: whereas, a weekly, or even a more frequent Count of the Sheep, & inspection of the Hogs (articles most likely to be depredated upon) would prevent, or if not prevent, enable them to pursue while the scent was hot these atrocious villainies; and either bring them to light, or so alarm the perpetraters of them, as to make them less frequent. As the Overseers, I believe, conduct matters, a Sheep, or Hog or two, may, every week, be taken without suspicion of it for months. An enquiry then comes too late; and I shall have to submit to one robbery after another, until I shall have nothing left to be robbed of.

I see alterations have been made in the Wheel, or Wheels of the Well, by the Quarter. How does it work now; what quantity of Water will it draw up in a given time; & what force is required to do it? that is to say, can the Children, or weak people about the Quarter, draw for themselves?[5]

Mrs Washington expected two barrels of *good* Shad would have come round with the things which were sent from Mount Vernon; but as this did not happen, take the first opportunity of forwarding them to this place; & I believe Captn Ellwood is, at this moment, or soon will be, at Alexandria.[6]

It is now, I believe, ten or 12 months ago, since I desired that ten or 12 Shoots might be put into a Stye, as soon as they were weaned, & well fed; to see what they could be brought to at a year old (keeping an exact acct of the expence) but whether it was ever done, or what the result if it was, I know not. I wish however that directions of this kind may be always duly attended. Few things will bear delay, but those of experiment worst of all; as it defeats the ascertaining of facts which might be of infinite importance; as in this very instance; for as the case now is, I am raising Hogs to a certain age for others; not for myself; Whereas if this method would succeed, a stye by a house could not be robbed, & fewer Sows would raise more hogs; &, I believe, at infinite less expence. I am—Your friend—& well wisher

Go: Washington

ALS, DLC:GW.

1. Whitting's letter of 21 Nov. and the enclosed reports have not been found. For GW's request for a copy of his tax bill, see GW to Whitting, 11 Nov., and note 15.

2. For GW's "little," or botanical, garden and the vineyard enclosure, see GW to Whitting, 14 Oct., n.4.

3. For GW's request that miller Joseph Davenport file weekly reports, see GW to Whitting, 11 November. The gristmill was located on the Dogue Run farm, at the head of navigation of Dogue Creek.

4. For earlier concern about the possibility that the Hessian fly had invaded nearby Maryland wheat fields, see GW to Whitting, 11 Nov., and note 12.

5. For the construction and location in the upper garden of a new well op-

posite the center of the greenhouse and near the new slave quarters, see George Augustine Washington to GW, 8–9 April, and GW to Whitting, 1 July.

6. Capt. John Ellwood (Elwood), Jr., made regular runs between Philadelphia and Alexandria, Virginia. The 13 Dec. issue of the *Virginia Gazette and Alexandria Advertiser* reported the arrival of his sloop *Nancy* in Alexandria.

Clement Biddle to Tobias Lear

Dr Sir   [Philadelphia] Nov: 26. 92.
 The prices of Stocks for Cash in this City on the 1st August last were for

6 ℔ Cts 21/4
3 ℔ Cts 12/6
deferred 13/4

these I find by reference to my books & they may be called the same on this day with difference of one penny less on 6 ℔ Cts being now 21/3. I am with great regard Dr Sir Yr ms. Obed. Serv.

Clement Biddle

ALS, owned (1992) by Mr. Ned W. Downing, Philadelphia.

From Andrew Ellicott

Sir,   City of Washington Novr 26th 1792
 With this you will receive an Almanac for the year 1793, which I calculated, and compiled, during my sickness last September. The astronomical part is adapted to the latitude, and meridian of the City of Washington.[1]

My design in this work, was merely to assist other (laudable) endeavours, in bringing the City of Washington into Public notice: and if it should be so fortunate as to meet your approbation, I shall think myself amply rewarded.[2] I am Sir your Hbl. Servt

Andw Ellicott

ALS, DNA: RG 59, Miscellaneous Letters.

1. The enclosed almanac was *Ellicott's New-Jersey, Pennsylvania, Delaware, Maryland and Virginia Almanac, and Ephemeris, for the Year of Our Lord 1793* (Baltimore, [1792]).

2. On behalf of the president, Tobias Lear wrote Ellicott on 3 Dec. offering GW's thanks for the almanac (DNA: RG 59, Miscellaneous Letters).

Benjamin Hawkins to Tobias Lear

No. 37

N. Carolina 26 novr 1792

On the same day you applied to me, I had a conference wth Mr Johnston and the representatives from N. Carolina[1] the result of which this day is that Thomas Overton of More County or Henry Waters of [New] Hanover is equal to the appointment contemplated by the President.

Overton was I believe of the rank of Major in the line of the late Army, and of the State of Virginia, he removed into N. Carolina since the termination of the War, and has resided in the County where he now is in the district of Fayette, he is Lt Colo. Commandant of the cavalry of that district, and has been a member of the Legislature, and has supported a very fair and upright character.[2]

Mr Waters is a native of North Carolina, of respectable connections, he is a young man of probity, the only advantage he has over Mr Overton is his being a native, but perhaps that is more than counterballanced by the others being publickly known, and for some years respected in that part of the Country.[3] I am with sincere regard sir, yr ob. servt

Benjamin Hawkins

ALS, DLC:GW.

1. Lear's letter to North Carolina senator Benjamin Hawkins has not been identified. The other senator from North Carolina was Samuel Johnston, and the current congressmen were John Baptista Ashe, William Barry Grove, Nathaniel Macon, John Steele, and Hugh Williamson.

2. Thomas Overton (1753–1824), a native of Virginia, began his Revolutionary War career as a second lieutenant in the 9th Virginia Regiment in 1776 and served to the end of war, rising to the rank of captain in the 4th Continental Dragoons. He moved to Moore County in the Fayette district, N.C., shortly after the war and soon became a leading citizen of the county, serving five terms in the state senate, 1787–90 and 1792. Overton was appointed a colonel in the county militia in 1788. GW sent Overton's nomination for "Inspector of the Revenue for Survey No. 1 in the District of North Carolina" to the U.S. Senate on 28 Jan. 1793.

3. Hawkins may be referring to Henry Hyrne Waters, who was born c.1770 in Wilmington, North Carolina.

From Thomas Jefferson

[Philadelphia] Nov. 26. 1792.
Th: Jefferson has the honour to inclose to the President the copy of a Report on the petition of John de Neufville referred to him by the house of Representatives, which he proposes to send in tomorrow.[1]

AL, DNA: RG 59, Miscellaneous Letters; LB, DNA: RG 59, George Washington's Correspondence with His Secretaries of State; LB (photocopy), DLC: GW.

1. On 11 April 1792 the House of Representatives referred the petition of former Amsterdam banker Jean de Neufville to Jefferson for examination (see *Journal of the House*, 4:180). For background on Neufville's prolonged attempt to receive reimbursement for money expended in support of the Americans and for losses sustained as a result of his efforts to secure a treaty between the Netherlands and the United States during the Revolutionary War, see GW to Leonard de Neufville, 29 June 1789, source note.

Jefferson reviewed the petition and its accompanying documents, and after summarizing the various claims, he concluded in his report that "no part of it ought to be granted" (DNA: RG 59, Miscellaneous Letters). The House read Jefferson's report on 27 Nov. and tabled it (ibid., 5:26). After Neufville's death in 1796, his family continued to press his claims, and in 1797 Congress granted them $3,000 in partial compensation, but final settlement was not made until 1851 (6 *Stat.* 29; 9 *Stat.* 814). For Jefferson's report in its entirety, see *Jefferson Papers*, 24:665–67.

From the Vicomte de Rochambeau

[le] Cap [Saint Domingue]
Sir,   26th 9ber 1792. 4th year of Liberti.
I have the honour to informe your Excellency that I have been invested the Governement of St Domingo. The desire to Serve a second time the noble cause of Liberty has imposed to me the Duty to Cross the Atlantic Ocean again, and to Vow the rest of my Life, to the Service of my own Country. The pleasure to be nearer the seat of the glory of your Excellency, and to be in measure in my Correspondance to assure him of my everlasting respect, Was also among the reasons Which determined me to accept this dangorous Commission, in the very odd Circumstances under Which we Lie in Europe.[1]

Capne Keating w[h]o will deliver this Letter goes to north

america to recoverer his health: I recommend this officer to your Excellency.[2] I have the honour to be Sir, of your Excellency—the most humble and obedient Servant

the Governor g[ener]al of Sainto Domingo
Dtn Rochambeau

ALS, DNA: RG 59, Miscellaneous Letters.

1. Donatien-Marie-Joseph de Vimeur, vicomte de Rochambeau (1755–1813), was a veteran of the Revolutionary War and the son of Jean-Baptiste-Donatien de Vimeur, comte de Rochambeau, the commander of the French forces sent to aid the Americans. In 1792 he was appointed lieutenant general in command of the Windward Islands, which included Martinique. Prevented from establishing his headquarters in Martinique by the rebellion there, he settled in Saint Domingue and was elected governor general on 23 October. Rochambeau spent most of the remainder of this decade and the beginning of the next one in the West Indies, often in military action against the British. In 1803 he was captured at sea by the British and was imprisoned in England until 1811. Rochambeau reentered active military service in 1813 and was fatally wounded during the Battle of Leipzig in October of that year (see Weelen, *Rochambeau*, 284–85).

2. Irish native John Keating (1760–1856), a captain in France's Irish Brigade, served in the West Indies between 1780 and 1783 and returned in 1792 with the 92d Regiment sent to quell the insurrection in Saint Domingue. Keating resigned his commission in November 1792 and immigrated to the United States, arriving in Philadelphia in late December. He settled first in Wilmington, Del., and later moved to Philadelphia, where he resided for the rest of his life. He was an agent for the unsuccessful Asylum Company, which attempted to establish a town for French refugees in northeast Pennsylvania (see Murray, *The Story of Some French Refugees*, 104–11).

From Clement Biddle

Sir,   Philada Nov: 27. 1792.

Mr Randolph communicated to me your Orders that I should in person serve the process on the two men indicted for a riot in Washington County.[1]

A Sense of Duty and earnest desire to execute it in such manner as would be most conformable to your desire, would make me undertake the Service in person but I am apprehensive that I may be lay'd up in the Attempt, as I have not only had repeated attacks of the Gout for several months past, but have been Afflicted with another Complaint which has prevented me from riding any distance on horseback.

From these Considerations I had prevailed on Captain Jonas Simonds formerly an Officer of Artillery and at present of the Customs, a man of respectability on whose firmness and prudence I could rely, to undertake the business and he was preparing to set off whenever I should be called on for the purpose.[2]

If you should not, under these Circumstances, approve of this Arrangement I will however attempt to execute the business in person.[3] I have the honour to be, with the greatest respect, Your most Obedient and very humble Servant

Clement Biddle
Marshall in & for the Pennsylvania District

ALS, DNA: RG 59, Miscellaneous Letters.

1. For background on Attorney General Edmund Randolph's instructions to Biddle to serve papers on William Kerr and Alexander Berr, who had been recently indicted for their violent resistance to the federal excise tax on whiskey, see GW to Randolph, 24 Nov. 1792.

2. Jonas Simonds, a Massachusetts native, began his military career in 1775 as a second lieutenant in Richard Gridley's Massachusetts artillery regiment and then served in other Continental artillery regiments until he retired in January 1783 with the rank of captain. At the time of Biddle's letter Simonds was a customs inspector in Philadelphia.

3. GW consulted Alexander Hamilton about Biddle's response, and Hamilton advised the president in a letter of 27 Nov.: "The execution of the process by the Marshal himself is, for many reasons, so important that it does not appear possible to dispense with it. If there should be any failure in the Deputy it would probably furnish a topic of censure and a source of much embarrassment. The impediment in point of health is to be regretted, but, it would seem, must be surmounted" (DLC:GW).

That GW agreed with Hamilton is apparent in Tobias Lear's letter to Biddle of 28 November. "In obedience to the command of the President of the United States," Lear wrote, "I have the honor to inform you, that while the President sincerely regrets the cause which prevents you from *immediately* executing in person the service which is required, relative to the process issued at the Circuit Court against the persons indicted for a riot in Washington County; yet so strongly is he impressed with the propriety of this business being executed by the marshall in person, and so much does he rely on your judgemt & zeal in the discharge of this duty that he considers the inconveniences which might be occasioned by a small delay in the matter, as being less than the disadvantages which might result from its being executed by a deputy. The President is therefore willing that the execution of this service should be postponed for a short time in hopes that your health will then be so well established as to enable you [to] perform it in person" (DNA: RG 59, Miscellaneous Letters).

Memorandum from Thomas Jefferson

[Philadelphia, 28 November 1792] [1]

Gentlemen of the Senate [and] H. of Representatives

I now lay before you, for your further information, some additional advices, lately received, on the subject of the hostilities committed by the Chuckamogga towns, or under their name and guidance.

The importance of preventing this hostile spirit from spreading to other tribes, or other parts of the same tribe of Indians, a considerable military force actually embodied in their neighborhood, and the advanced state of the season, are circumstances which render it interesting that this subject should obtain your earliest attention.

The Question of War, being placed by the Constitution with the legislature alone, respect to that made it my duty to restrain the operations of our militia to those merely defensive: & considerations involving the public satisfaction, & peculiarly my own, require that the decision of that Question, whichever way it be, should be pron⟨o⟩unced definitely by the legislature themselves.

AD (letterpress copy), DLC: Jefferson Papers. The manuscript is partly overwritten in a later hand.

1. The date is taken from Jefferson's Summary Journal of Public Letters, in which he described this document as a "draught of Message to Congr. on Chuckamogga aggressions" (DLC: Jefferson Papers). Compare this memorandum with the letter of 7 Dec. that GW eventually sent on this subject to the U.S. Senate and House of Representatives.

From Thomas Jefferson

Sir   Philadelphia Nov. 28. 1792.

The rise in the price of copper, & difficulty of obtaining it from other quarters, has induced the Director of the Mint (as I had the honor of mentioning to you yesterday) to turn his attention to Sweden, as the country from which according to his information it may be obtained on the best terms. he wishes that some means could be adopted of importing some on the public account. there is so little direct commerce between this country & Sweden that we shall be obliged to resort to some intermediate port, & I have imagined that (our resident in Holland being absent) our Minister in London would be the best person to confide the business to for the present occasion. you will see by mister Rittenhouse's letter inclosed that he proposes an importation of 30. or 40. tons from Sweden at present. the former quantity, by his estimate will cost between nine & ten thousand dollars.[1] if you approve of this mode & quantum of supply, a bill from the Treasury of 10,000 Doll. on our Holland bankers payable to mister Pinckney, would be convenient for the Director of the mint, and mister Pinckney shall be desired to adopt the best means he can of having 30. tons of copper shipped from Sweden for the Mint.[2] I also inclose the Director's letter of yesterday asking a supply of 5000. D. for the current purposes of the mint,[3] & have the honor to be with the most perfect respect & attachmt Sir Your most obedt & most humble servt

Th: Jefferson

ALS, DNA: RG 59, Miscellaneous Letters; ALS (letterpress copy), DLC: Jefferson Papers; LB, DNA: RG 59, George Washington's Correspondence with His Secretaries of State; LB (photocopy), DLC: GW; LB, DNA: RG 59, Domestic Letters. On both ALS manuscripts Jefferson first wrote "27" for the date, but he later changed the second digit to an "8"; the letter-book copies are dated 28 November.

1. For Director of the Mint David Rittenhouse's calculations that 30 or 40 tons of copper would be sufficient, "at least at first," to mint the number of copper coins required, "supposing the number of families in the United States to be 400,000," see his letter to Jefferson of 28 Nov. in *Jefferson Papers,* 24:671–72.

2. GW wrote Treasury Secretary Alexander Hamilton on 29 Nov. 1792, instructing him "to have a bill" for $10,000 "drawn on the Bankers of the United States in Holland," Willink, Van Staphorst, and Hubbard, "payable to Mr Pinckney" (LB, DLC: GW). At GW's direction Tobias Lear wrote Jefferson on that date to inform him "that a bill for ten thousand dollars will be drawn by the Treasury of the U.S. on our Holland Bankers payable to Mr Pinckney, for the purpose of obtaining Copper for the Mint. The President, however, suggests, that it would not perhaps be best to confine Mr Pinckney strictly to Sweeden for the purchase of the Copper, but to leave it to his discretion to obtain it where it can be had on the most advantageous terms, after calling his attention to Sweeden, for the reason mentioned in the letter from the Director of the Mint to the Secretary of State" (DLC: Jefferson Papers). In light of the anticipated absence of William Short from his duties at The Hague, Jefferson subsequently wrote Thomas Pinckney, the U.S. minister to Great Britain, on 30 Dec. 1792, with instructions to procure "a quantity of copper to be brought us from Sweden" (*Jefferson Papers,* 24:803).

3. Rittenhouse wrote Jefferson on 27 Nov. that the $10,000 granted in July "for paying for the House and Lot for the Mint and for purchasing Copper, except 900 Dollars, And Considerable Expences having since arisen for Additional Buildings, Furnaces[,] Horse-Mill and Machines of various kinds I find it necessary to apply for another warrant for the Sum of Five Thousand Dollars" (ibid., 668). For background on the original grant of $10,000 to pay for the cost of establishing the U.S. Mint, see Jefferson to GW, 9 June, GW to Rittenhouse, 9 July, and GW to Hamilton, 10 July 1792.

GW wrote Hamilton on 28 Nov. instructing him to pay Rittenhouse $5,000 for the current expenses of the U.S. Mint (LB, DLC:GW). Lear, at GW's direction, wrote Jefferson on that date to inform him that GW had "drawn the enclosed order for five thousand dollars to be applied to the purposes of the mint agreeably to the Director's letter of the 27th inst. to the Secretary.

"And that the President will take an opportunity of making an arrangement with the Secretary of the Treasury on the other subject mentioned in the Secretary of State's letter to him of this date" (DLC: Jefferson Papers). See also GW to Hamilton, 29 Nov. 1792, in note 2.

Letter not found: from Anthony Whitting, 28 Nov. 1792. GW wrote Whitting on 9 Dec.: "Your letter of the 28th of Novr . . . did not arrive until the 4th."

From Alexander Hamilton

[Philadelphia] Thursday Nov: 29th 1792

The Secretary of the Treasury presents his respects to the president; has the honor to transmit for his consideration the draft of a report pursuant to two references of the House of Representatives, concerning which he will wait upon the President on Saturday, being desireous of sending in a Report on Monday.[1]

LB, DLC:GW.

1. The House of Representatives resolved on 21 Nov. "That it is the opinion of this committee that measures ought to be taken for the redemption of so much of the public debt as by the act entitled 'An act making provision for the Debt of the United States' the United States have reserved the right to redeem; and that the Secretary of the Treasury be directed to report a plan for that purpose." On 22 Nov. the House resolved "That the Secretary of the Treasury be directed to report the plan of a provision for the reimbursement of the loan made of the Bank of the United States, pursuant to the eleventh section of the act, entitled 'An act to incorporate the Subscribers to the Bank of the United States'" (*Annals of Congress*, 2d Cong., 711, 723; for the acts mentioned in these resolutions, see 1 *Stat.* 138–44, 196). Hamilton submitted his "Report on the Redemption of the Public Debt," dated 30 Nov. 1792, to the House on

Monday, 3 Dec. 1793. The enclosed draft has not been identified. For the text of the report, see Syrett, *Hamilton Papers*, 13:261–75.

From the United States House of Representatives

Sir, United States [Philadelphia] the 29th of Novr 1792.

In obedience to the Order of the House of Representatives, I do myself the honor to transmit to you, their Resolution of this date, on the subject of an assay of foreign Coins.[1] With the most perfect consideration, I am Sir, Your most obedient, and very humble Servant

Jona: Trumbull Speaker.

LB, DLC:GW.

1. The House of Representatives resolved on 29 Nov. "That the PRESIDENT OF THE UNITED STATES be requested to cause assays and other proper experiments to be made, at the Mint of the United States, of the gold and silver coins of France, England, Spain, and Portugal; and a report of the quantity of fine metal, and of alloy, in each of the denominations of the coins, to be laid before this House" (*Annals of Congress*, 2d Cong., 732). GW referred the House resolution to Thomas Jefferson, under whose jurisdiction the Mint had been placed. Jefferson received the results of the assays of foreign coins from Mint Director David Rittenhouse on 7 Jan. 1793 and submitted the assay report to the House the following day after sending a copy to GW earlier that day (see Jefferson to GW, 8 Jan. 1793, and note 1).

From Richard Peters

30 Nov. 1792

R. Peters's respectful Compliments to The President & returns the Pamplet on the Foo⟨t⟩ Plough with Thanks for the Perusal.[1] R.P. thinks there are many good & useful Observations in the Book, but he cannot prefer the Plough to the Bar Share Plough in Use among good Farmers here. The Idea of accomodating one Plough to many & different Operations may be well executed. But he would rather have different Ploughs for different Works. No Chip Share Plough can be kept in Order with the same Expence or Facility with the Bar Shares. The Friction is greater & the Weight encreased by the Dirt they carry with them. The Mode of fixing the Draft is good but not uncommon & that of altering the Plough so as to take more or less Land is better than commonly practised but similar in a great Degree to the Mode used in the Dutch Plough—The Length in the Ground including the Spit & Share may make it run steady, but it seems to R.P. too long. The Plan of altering the Mould Board & the Cutter is ingenious but he fears our common Plough Men would soon disorder it.[2]

AL, DLC:GW.

1. For John Lambert's pamphlet on the foot plow, see GW to Anthony Whitting, 11 Nov., and note 5.

2. Peters, the current federal district judge for Pennsylvania, shared GW's interest in improving agricultural practices in the United States and carried out his experiments at Belmont, his estate near Philadelphia. Peters was one of the founding members and the first president of the Philadelphia Society for Promoting Agriculture. His published works, *Agricultural Enquiries on Plaister of Paris* (Philadelphia 1797) and *A Discourse on Agriculture* (Philadelphia, 1816), stress the need for scientific farming.

To David Stuart

Dear Sir,   Philadelphia Novr 30th 1792

Knowing that tomorrow is the time appointed for the monthly meeting of the Commissioners at George Town, I had intended to have written you a line or two on a particular subject by Wednesday's Post; but one thing or another put it out of mind until it was too late. I now set down to do it, as the letter in the common course of the Post will reach George Town on Monday—probably, before you shall have left that place.[1]

You will consider what I am now about to say as a *private* communication; the object of which is only to express *more* freely than I did in my last letter to the Commissioners,[2] the idea that is entertained of the necessity of appointing a Superintendant of the execution of the plans & measures wch shall be resolved upon by the Commissioners of the federal City. one who shall always reside there. and being a man of skill & judgment—of industry & integrity, would, from having a view of the business constantly before his eyes, be enabled to conduct it to greater advantage than the Commissioners can possibly do unless they were to devote their *whole* time to it. Instances of this are adduced by some of the Proprietors; particularly in the alteration which has taken place in the Bridge, the delay consequent thereof—&ca. It is remarked by some of (the best disposed of) them, that although you meet monthly—spend much time to-gether—and are truly anxious to forward this great object; yet, from the nature of the thing, you cannot acquire at those meet-ings the minute information which a proper character always on the spot would do; and which is indispensably necessary to do in order to avoid mistakes, and to give vigor to the undertaking. And besides, add they, a man of fertile genius, & comprehensive ideas, would, by having the business always before him, seeing, shewing to, & conversing with Gentlemen who may be led, either by curiosity or an inclination to become adventurers therein, to view the City, obtain many useful hints, by means of which, and his own reflections, might suggest many useful projects to the consideration of the Commissioners at their *stated* (say) quar-terly meetings, or at such occasional ones as he might, in cases of importance and immergency, be empowered to call.[3]

But where, you may ask, is the character to be found who pos-sesses these qualifications? I frankly answer I know not! Major L'Enfant (who it is said is performing wonders at the new town of Patterson) if he could have been restrained within proper bounds, and his temper was less untoward, is the only person with whose turn to matters of this sort I am acquainted, that I think fit for it. Th⟨ere⟩ may, notwithstanding, be many others al-though they are unknown to me, equally so.[4]

Mr Blodget seems to be the person on whom many eyes are turned, & among others who look that way, are some of the Pro-prietors. He has travelled, I am told, a good deal in Europe; & has turned his attention (according to his own Account) to Ar-chitecture & matters of this kind. He has staked much on the is-sue of the Law establishing the permanent residence; and is *cer-tainly* a projecting genius, with a pretty general acquaintance. To which may be added, if he has any influence in this Country, *it* must be in a quarter where it is most needed; and where, indeed, an antitode is necessary to the poison which Mr F——s C——t is spreading; by insinuations, that the accomplishment of the Plan is no more to be expected than the fabric of a vision, & will vanish in like manner.[5] But whether with these qualifications, Mr Blodget is a man of industry & steadiness, & whether (as soon as it is necessary) he would take up a settled abode there, are points I am unable to resolve.[6] As an Architect, Mr Jefferson has a high opinion of Mr Hallet, but whether Mr Hallet has qualities, & is sufficiently known to fit him for general superintendancy I cannot *pretend* even to give an opinion upon.[7] If Mr B⟨l⟩odget is contemplated for this office would it not be well to be *on* or *off* with him at once. [I] hear he is held in suspence on this head.[8]

Have you yet decided on a Plan for the Capitol? Mr Carroll talked of their being sent hither—Is any thing done towards the foundation of the Presidents house?[9] What number of lots are bona fide sold? In what squares do they lye? Let your Clerk send me a list. Do you receive offers to purchase at private Sale? If you have fixed on a time for another public Sale, ought not notice thereof to be *immediately* given; & measures adopted to make the thing known in Europe as well as in this Country; Inserting advertisements in the Gazettes of the latter at intervals between this & the Sale, by way of remembrancer. A little expence in these would be profitably incurred. How does [Andrew] Ellicot[t] go on?[10] I am always, & Affectly Yours

Go: Washington

ALS, sold by Christie's, 1993; ALS (letterpress copy), DLC:GW; LB, DLC:GW. The text in angle brackets is taken from the letterpress copy.

1. Since GW had missed the post for Wednesday, 28 Nov., he now hoped that this letter would reach Stuart on Monday, 3 December. Commissioner Thomas Johnson did not join the other commissioners, David Stuart and Daniel Carroll, when they met at Georgetown from 3 to 6 Dec. (DNA: RG 42, Records of the Commissioners for the District of Columbia, Proceedings, 1791–1802). Contrary to GW's expectations Stuart did not receive GW's letter until 8 Dec. (see Stuart to GW, 10 Dec. 1792).

2. See GW to D.C. Commissioners, 13 Nov. 1792.

3. For recent criticism of the commissioners, see George Walker to GW, 8 Oct., and Benjamin Stoddert to GW, 24 Oct. 1792, in which Stoddert criticized the construction of the bridge over Rock Creek and called for the appointment of a superintendent for the district.

4. For background on events leading to the dismissal in February 1792 of architect and engineer Pierre L'Enfant as surveyor general and supervisor of the construction of the new capital, see L'Enfant to GW, 21 Nov. 1791, editorial note; see also GW to L'Enfant, 28 Feb. 1792. L'Enfant was hired in July 1792 by the Society for Establishing Useful Manufactures to direct the construction of a manufacturing complex at the falls of the Passaic River, to prepare a plan for bringing water to the respective works, and to lay out the town of Paterson, N.J. (see "Draft Minutes of a Meeting of a Committee of the Directors of the Society for Establishing Useful Manufactures," 1 Aug. 1792, in Syrett, *Hamilton Papers*, 12:140–43).

5. For GW's earlier doubts about Francis Cabot, Jr., see his letter to Stuart of 8 Mar. 1792.

6. The commissioners appointed Samuel Blodget, Jr., the district superintendent on 5 Jan. 1793 (see D.C. Commissioners to GW, 5 Jan. 1793).

7. Although the commissioners did not select Stephen Hallet's design for the Capitol, they hired him in the summer of 1793 to revise the plan chosen for the building and to supervise its construction (see D.C. Commissioners to GW, 23 June 1793, and GW to Thomas Jefferson, 30 June 1793).

8. The preceding three sentences were inserted at this place in the text, by GW on the receiver's copy and by Tobias Lear on the letterpress copy.

9. The plan for the Capitol was not selected until early April 1793. The commissioners had selected James Hoban's architectural plan for the President's House in July 1792, and they subsequently hired him to supervise its construction (see D.C. Commissioners to GW, 19 July 1792).

10. For David Stuart's response to these various questions, see his letter to GW of 10 Dec. 1792.

From Paul Boughman

Sir   Wilmington Delawar December 1st 1792

Pleas to Except of one Barrel of apples[1] from one of your houner's old Soldiers who Enterd Early in the Caus of freedom, and Received Two Wounds wich now makes me labour under many Defiquelties as I haveig no Traid but am Exposed to wet and Cold.[2]

The Reason of my wrighting thus is to let you Know Sir that I having applied to Congress for Som Relief but Could obtain none becaus I Did not make applic[a]tion in the time limmetted by Congress as I Never knew of any limitation[3] Pleas Sir to let me know weather I am Entitled to be plased on the pension list I Did not Serve to the End of the war but Served five years in the bgining Sir I gave in a petition to land memoriel to Congress but Recived not any answer[4] So no more at present but I Remain your humbel Servent at Command

                              Paul Boughman

ALS, DLC:GW.

1. Tobias Lear docketed this letter: "From An Old Soldier with a bbl. of apples wh. however, never came to hand."

2. Paul Boughman (Bowman; c.1757–fl.1837), who had enlisted on 14 Aug. 1776 as a private in Capt. Thomas Kean's company of foot in the Delaware battalion of flying camp commanded by Col. Samuel Patterson, eventually attained the rank of sergeant (see *Delaware Archives*, 1:68–69, 3:1215).

3. Boughman is referring to the Continental Congress's resolution of 11 June

1788 which restricted eligibility for invalid pensions to veterans who applied before 11 Dec. 1788 (*JCC*, 34:210).

4. The House of Representatives on 25 Feb. 1791 referred Boughman's petition and those of other veterans asking to be placed on the "list of pensioners, in consideration of wounds received" to Secretary of War Henry Knox for examination (*Journal of the House*, 3:82–83). Section 5 of "An Act to provide for the settlement of the Claims of Widows and Orphans barred by the limitations heretofore established, and to regulate the Claims to Invalid Pensions," 23 Mar. 1792, specifies that "all non-commissioned officers, soldiers and seamen, disabled . . . during the late war" who had not applied to be placed on the pension list until after the deadline previously set by Congress were now to be put on the pension list (1 *Stat.* 243–45). Knox on 3 April, therefore, returned the petitions, including Boughman's, to the House, where they were read and tabled (*Journal of the House*, 4:161). Boughman eventually succeeded in his efforts to be placed on the pension list (see *Delaware Archives*, 3:1215). Boughman apparently also had applied for a land grant under resolutions passed by the Continental Congress on 16 and 18 Sept. 1776, which offered land to officers and soldiers who had served in the Continental army (*JCC*, 5:763, 781).

From Charles Carroll (of Carrollton)

Dear Sir   Annapolis 1st Decemr 1792
By an act of this Legislature, passed yesterday, Mr Thomas Harwood, who is treasurer of this Shore, will be obliged to resign his place of Commissioner of loans, the duties of which have in fact been performed by his brother Mr Benjamin Harwood.[1]

Mr Thomas Harwood has requested me to recommend to you his brother, and wishes that he may be appointed Commissioner of loans. I assure you, Sir, you could not select from the whole State a person better qualified to execute that office; Mr Secretary Hamilton can inform you with what method and accuracy Mr Harwood keeps his accounts.[2]

The same Law vacates my seat on the Senate of this State, unless I give up my seat in the Senate of the United States within fifteen days from its passage; indeed as Congress and this Legislature sit at the same time, the duties of the two Stations are become incompatible and therefore I have resigned my seat in the Senate of the United States. On Tuesday next the Assembly will choose my Successor; if the person talked of (Mr Richard Potts) should be chosen, and he will accept the trust he is really (I speak it not from false modesty) much better qualified to discharge it, than I am.[3]

I beg my respectful compliments to Mrs Washington and remain with Sentiments of the most perfect esteem Dear Sir, Yr most obedt hum. Servant

Ch. Carroll of Carrolton

ALS, DLC:GW, postmarked "ANNAPOLIS, Dec. 3."

1. Carroll is referring to "An act to prohibit members of congress, or persons in office under the United States, from being eligible as members of the legislature or council, or holding offices in this state" of 22 Dec. 1792 (*Laws of Maryland, . . . 1792*). As a result of this act, Thomas Harwood chose to remain treasurer for Maryland's Western Shore, a state office that he held until 1804, in lieu of his federal job as commissioner of loans for Maryland.

2. For Benjamin Harwood's letter of application, other letters recommending him, and GW's nomination of him as Maryland's commissioner of loans, see Harwood to GW, 3 Dec. 1792, and note 1.

3. As Carroll predicted, the Maryland assembly chose Richard Potts, Maryland's former federal district attorney, to fill the state's vacant seat in the U.S. Senate. Potts served from 10 Jan. 1793 to 24 Oct. 1796.

From Alexander Hamilton

[Philadelphia] 1st Decemr 1792.

The Secretary of the Treasury presents his respects to the President has the honor to submit to him the enclosed communications concerning which he will wait upon The President on Monday.[1]

LB, DLC:GW.

1. The enclosed papers that Hamilton wished to discuss on Monday, 3 Dec., have not been identified.

To Thomas Jefferson

[Philadelphia, 1 December 1792]

Mr Hammond starts three to one against you.[1]

AL, DLC: Jefferson Papers. Jefferson docketed this letter: "Washington President recd Dec. 1. 9⟨*mutilated*⟩."

1. For background on Jefferson's negotiations with George Hammond, British minister to the United States, see Jefferson's notes on two conversations with Hammond later this month, c.10 Dec. and c.12 Dec. 1792, and editorial notes, in *Jefferson Papers*, 24:717–21, 728–30.

From Thomas Jefferson

[Philadelphia] Sat. Dec. 1. 92.

Th: Jefferson has the honor to submit to the President the inclosed draught of a clause which he has thought of proposing to the committee to whom the President's letter with the accounts of the Department of state are referred.[1] he will have the honor of waiting on the President at one aclock, as well to explain any parts of it as to take his pleasure on the whole matter.

AL, DNA: RG 59, Miscellaneous Letters; LB, DNA: RG 59, George Washington's Correspondence with His Secretaries of State; LB (photocopy), DLC:GW.

1. For background on this letter and its enclosure, see Jefferson to GW, 3 Nov. 1792 (first letter), and notes, and GW to the U.S. Senate and House of Representatives, 7 Nov. 1792 (second letter).

Enclosure
Memorandum from Thomas Jefferson

To the bill which shall be brought in for continuing the act of July 1. 1790. c.22. 'providing the means of intercourse between the U.S. and foreign nations' it is proposed to add the following clause.[1]

And be it further enacted that where monies have issued, or shall issue, from the Treasury, for the purposes of *intercourse* or *treaty* with foreign nations, under the authority of the said act,[2] or of the present or any preceding act,[3] the President shall be authorized to refer the settlement & delivery of Vouchers, for all such parts thereof as in his judgment may be made public to the Auditor of the U.S., and for all other parts, to such person as he shall appoint, presenting for their government such rules as the nature of the case shall in his opinion require.[4]

AD, DNA: RG 59, Miscellaneous Letters.

1. For the act of 1 July 1790, see "An Act providing the means of intercourse between the United States and foreign nations" (1 *Stat.* 128).

2. Jefferson's first of two footnotes written in the left margin indicates that this act is that of "July 1. 1790. c.22." (see note 1).

3. Jefferson's second footnote reads: "to wit, 1791. Mar. 3. c.16 [and] 1792. May. 8. c.42.§.3[.] note the acts of 1790. & 1792. use the terms '*intercourse* with foreign nations[']; the act of 1791. is expressly for *a treaty* with the emperor of Morocco." The act of 3 Mar. 1791 is "An Act making an appropriation for the purpose therein mentioned," that is, the appropriation of a sum not exceeding $20,000 "for the purpose of effecting" a treaty with the new emperor of

Morocco (ibid., 214). Jefferson erred in referring to the appropriate act of 8 May 1792. He meant to cite chapter 41, "An Act making certain appropriations therein specified," section 3 of which appropriates $50,000 to "defray any expense which may be incurred in relation to the intercourse between the United States and foreign nations" (ibid., 284–85).

4. The substance of the clause proposed by Jefferson was incorporated in section 2 of "An Act to continue in force for a limited time, and to amend the act intituled 'An act providing the means of intercourse between the United States and foreign nations,'" approved on 9 Feb. 1793 (ibid., 299–300).

Henry Knox to Tobias Lear

My dear Sir   [Philadelphia] 1 Decr 1792
    Be pleased to submit the enclosed letter to the President of the United States from Colonel Willet which I have just received.[1]
Yours sincerely

                                                   H. Knox

ALS, DLC:GW; LB, DLC:GW.
    1. The enclosed letter from Marinus Willett has not been identified.

Henry Knox to Tobias Lear

Dear sir.   [Philadelphia] 1 Decr 1792
    Be pleased to submit to the President of the United states, the enclosed from Genl Wayne.[1] Yours sincerely

                                                   H. Knox

ALS, DLC:GW; LB, DLC:GW.
    1. In his letter to Anthony Wayne of 1 Dec., Knox acknowledged receiving on the previous day "your letter of the 23d November with the enclosures of a letter from Capt. Hughes and your correspondence with the Contractors" (Knopf, *Wayne,* 143). Wayne wrote in his letter that the enclosed letter from Thomas Hughes, commander of Fort Franklin, reported "the terms upon which peace is to be *granted* to the United States," and those terms "are such as to exclude us from the Waters of the Lakes, & in other respects, if literally agreed to, it must be at the expence of National Character, as well as Interest." Wayne cautioned, however, that "we have nothing Official" (ibid., 137). The enclosed letter of 18 Nov. 1792 from Wayne to the contractors Robert Elliott and Eli Williams concerned the arrangements for supplying rations at the advanced military posts (ALS, sold by Joseph M. Maddalena, *Profiles in History,* catalog 7, item 9, 1989).
    In his letter of 23 Nov., Wayne assured Knox that the rations would be deposited in accordance with Knox's previous instructions, and he wrote that

because the waters of the Allegheny and Monongahela rivers had risen sufficiently, "I will embark the troops to first Clear day & descend the river to Legion Ville—(the name of our new encampment)." Wayne then reminded
Knox that there was a "want of Clothing" for many of the men (ibid., 138).

Tobias Lear to William Hilton

Sir,   Philada 2d December 1792.
The President of the United States has received at his seat in
Virginia, a number of plants from the Island of Jamaica, which
were accompanied with a particular description of the plants
sent, and a catalogue of the plants in the Jamaica public Garden.[1]
As there was no Letter received with the plants, the President
would not have known to whose politeness he was indebted for
this mark of attention, nor where to have made his acknowledgements, had not the Memo[randu]m accompanying the plants &
Catalogue pointed out the name of Mr Hilton: he has therefore
directed me to beg your acceptance of his best thanks for the
plants as well as for the polite offer to supply him with any others he might name, which are contained in the Catalogue. I have
the honor to be &c.

T. Lear.

LB, DLC:GW.
   1. At the time of GW's death, the *Catalogue of Plants, Exotic and Indigenous, in
the Botanical Garden at Jamaica,* published at Saint Jago de la Vega in 1792, was
in the library at Mount Vernon (see Griffin, *Boston Athenæum Washington Collection,* 557; later editions are entitled *Hortus Eastensis: or A Catalogue of Exotic
Plants*). The accompanying description has not been found. GW's letter to his
estate manager Anthony Whitting of 21 Oct. 1792 and its enclosed directions
for the care of these plants have not been found.

To Anthony Whitting

Mr Whiting,   Philadelphia Decr 2d 1792
Your letter of the 22d of Novr enclosing the Sheriffs account
has been duly received; but no letter nor Report was receivd
from you yesterday, as usual; which makes me fear that you are
sick, or that some accident has happened; as I have never missed
before, receiving on Saturday the letter and reports which you
send to Alexandria on Wednesday.[1] I am always anxious to hear

once a week from home; & to be informed by the letter & Reports how my people are, and how my business is going on; & I am more desirous of it *now* when it remains to be told what the Crops of Wheat, Corn, & other things will turn out, than common.

You were perfectly right in discharging Jones. He always appeared to me to be incapable of the management of a Plantation from his want of capacity; but for his in⟨d⟩olent or wilful neglects there can be no excuse; and he would meet with no more than his deserts if he was made to pay for the damage my Wheat fields have sustained: for he had sufficient warning from myself, before I left home, to guard him against this evil. It is to such inattention, & want of exertion, together with the opportunities that are given to my Negros, that Robberies have got to the height they are. If some of the Nights in which these Overseers are frolicking, at the expence of my business, & to the destruction of my horses, were spent in watching the Barns—visiting the Negro quarters at unexpected hours—waylaying the Roads—or contriving some devise by which the receivers of Stolen goods might be entrapped & the facts proved upon them; it would be no more than the performance of a duty which I have a right to expect for the wages they draw from me; and it wd redound much more to their own credit and reputation as good & faithful Overseers than runng about. I wish, however, that the Season may not be too far advanced for you to get a person to supply the place of Jones that will, in any wise, be competent to such a trust as must devolve on him, in the management of so important a Plantation.[2]

I thought you had made it the particular duty of Old Matt to attend to the Fences?[3]

By Post of the 18th Ulto, I sent you Tea & other Spoons for the use of the house; & expected that *they,* the Tea, Coffee, Sugar & Wine would have been at Mount Vernon before the day on which you say judge Cushing called at that place.[4]

Wheat & flour are rising fast, & must bear a high price during the Winter & Spring; I again desire, therefore, that none of mine may be sold without particular directions from me; but keep me advised of the Alexandria prices of the Superfine, fine &ca that I may be able to decide on the time for disposal. In the meanwhile, let the Miller exert himself to get *all* the Wheat Manufactured as soon as he can, that it may be ready when a price shall offer that would induce me to part with it. Wheat is now at 8/4, & flour forty odd shillings, & rising. In the Mill Reports, the weight of the Wheat ought always to be mentioned as well as the quantity received there; without this there can be no accurate acct of this business kept with the Miller—and that he should receive no more Toll Wheat & Corn than what is mentioned in the weekly returns, is really unaccountable. The Toll of my own Corn, which is ground there, amounts to nearly the whole of his credit: and of Wheat, rarely more than a bushel or two is brought to the credit of the Mill.[5]

I have seen no account in any of the Reports, of the number of Bricks at Dogue run. I desired in a letter sometime ago that these might be counted, & assorted; that if they fell short of what were wanting for the Barn intended to be built at that place,[6] the earth might be taken from the foundation of it this fall, to ameliorate by the Spring. That you may never forget directions that are given, it would be well to extract them from my letters, and place them in a pocket Memorandum book, that they may be easily & frequently resorted to; without this they may, when a letter is laid by go out of your mind, to my disappointment—and I would have nothing left undone which is required to be done, without being informed of it, & the reasons assigned; that I may judge of their weight. The Springs under the hill, which I requested should be opened, that I might, whilst they were at their *lowest,* see what water could be collected from the whole of them, cannot be done well when the weather is cold and freezing; nor will it ascertain the fact I wanted to know, after the Autumn and Winter Rains have filled the earth with water; for then, Springs may appear that would be entirely dry in the Summer; & that is the Season I should want the Water. Speaking of this, I had rather the water from these Springs should be carried *round* any little risings wch may be between the most westerly ones (which are worth opening) and that by the Dairy, than to have a deep ditch cut *through* them. In short, I want the water carried on its level to the front of the Mansion house, as it is done in Watered Meadows; that I may, if I should hereafter want to water any, or all of that ground, or to make a pond on the level, directly in front, along the Visto that was opened in a line between the two doors, that so much of the work may be done to my hands.[7] Before I left home, I desired you to mark out another Visto on the West front of the Mansion house, merely to see over what ground it would go, that I might thereby be enabled to decide, whether to open it or not; but as you have mentioned nothing of it in any of your letters, I suppose it is not yet done.[8]

As I keep no copies of letters wch I write to you & always write in great haste (one thing or another always pressing upon me) it is more than probable I often repeat things over & over agn to you; but this I have preferred doing to remaining in Suspence of having done it at all—especially as you will consider it as a strong evidence that things *so repeated* are such as I am anxious about. In one of my last letters, I think I desired (I know I intended to do it) that you would, after you had finally designated the Mansion house gang, keep them steadily at work at that place—suffering them on *no* occasion, (unless very immergent ones) to be sent to any of the Plantations to work; for besides loosing much time in marching & counter marching, it weakens the exertion, & destroys the ambition of the different Overseers to excel one another in the good condition of their respective Plantations, when by extranious force they are relieved from difficulties which, more than probable, their own idleness has been the cause of.[9] I can conceive nothing, except Ditching (which is a kind of trade) that the hands of every plantation are not competent to, & should be made to execute. Hedging—setting out cuttings for it—Planting, or sowing the Seeds according to the nature of them—&ca &ca as well as other things is to be done by them; under (where skill, & attention is necessary) the immediate eye of the Overseers. And as I have often, & often declared, this business of hedging must not be considered in the light of a secondary, or trifling, or an occasional thing; but on the contrary, as one of the first magnitude, & to be entered upon with as much serious intention to execute it well, as to prepare for planting Corn, or sowing Wheat—and the wheat I am *more* anxious to accomplish.

I now send you Mr Lamberts Pamphlet, with the observations of Mr Peters upon it, to whom it was lent, & who I think one of the most judicious farmers in this part of the Country. If there are any hints in the Pamphlet worth improving on, you will not, I am persuaded, suffer them to escape you. Sinking the point of the beam below the parrallel line of the spit, or share, is a very material deviation from the common mode of setting a plough;

and certainly ought to be tried by the rules & principle he has laid down. And this I conceive may be done with one of the bar shear plows which are now in use, as well as by a plow in all respects like the plate.[10] I am Your friend and well wisher

Go: Washington

P.S. Perhaps you may not know, that if the Thursdays Post (which leaves Alexanda before day) is missed, no letter if sent to the Office even half an hour afterwards, will reach this place before Tuesday afternoon. Tuesdays Post from that place reaches this on Thursdays—Thursdays come in on Saturdays—and Saturdays not till Tuesdays, on account of Sundays intervening. You will see by this the necessity of sending up your Reports in time always on Wednesdays. It is more convenient for me to receive them on Saturdays than any other day; because between that & the departure of the Post on Monday, which gets into Alexandria on Wednesdays I can write with less interruption than at any other time.

ALS, DLC:GW.

1. Neither Whitting's letter of 22 Nov. nor the enclosed sheriff's report has been found. The anticipated letter, which was dated Wednesday, 28 Nov., and not received until Tuesday, 4 Dec., has not been found. For a copy of GW's tax bill, see GW to Arthur Young, 2 Dec. and note 2.

2. Henry Jones, overseer for the Dogue Run farm, had been employed at Mount Vernon since the previous December (Ledger B, 351). For his replacement, see GW to Whitting, 9 Dec., n.9.

3. A dower slave named Matt appears on GW's 1786 slave list as a laborer at the Dogue Run farm, but he is not on the 1799 list, having presumedly died in the meantime (see Slave List, 18 Feb. 1786, in *Diaries,* 4:280, and Washington's Slave List, June 1799).

4. For William Cushing's visit to Mount Vernon and for the shipment of tea, coffee, sugar, and wine, see GW to Whitting, 28 Oct., and notes 7 and 8. For the lack of quality spoons to use in case of visitors to Mount Vernon, see GW to Whitting, 18 November.

5. For similar instructions on the reports expected from miller Joseph Davenport, see GW to Whitting, 25 November.

6. See Washington's Plan for a Barn, enclosed in GW's letter to Whitting of 28 October.

7. GW had given Whitting instructions regarding the springs and vista on the river side of the mansion in his letter of 18 November. The dairy was located a short distance southwest of the mansion, near the kitchen.

8. For GW's previous mention of opening another vista, see GW to Whitting, 14 October.

9. For these instructions, see GW to Whitting, 18 November.

10. GW had loaned John Lambert's pamphlet on the foot plow to Richard Peters (see GW to Whitting, 11 Nov., and note 5). For Peters's observations, see his letter to GW of 30 November.

To Arthur Young

Sir,   Philadelphia Decr 2d 1792.

I must begin this letter with an apology—no apology ought to be so satisfactory as the truth—and the truth is—that not receiving the account of the taxes of a Virginia Estate for which I had written (before I left this City during the recess of Congress) as mentioned in my letter to you of the 18th of June, the promise I then made of forwarding it to you in my next, had escaped me altogether, until I was reminded of it, lately, by a circumstance too trivial to mention.[1]

A copy of the account is now annexed—the name of the Proprietor of the Estate is not inserted—but on the authenticity of it you may rely.[2] That you may understand the principle on which the Land tax in Virginia is founded, it will be necessary to inform you, that by a law of that State, the Inhabitants of it are thrown into districts—say Parishes—in each of which, or for two, or more of them united, Commissioners are appointed to assess the value of each man's land that lies within it—on which a certain per centum is uniformly paid.

No Negros under twelve years of age are taxed—nor are any under Sixteen subjected to the payment of County, or Parish levies. Horses, at present, are the only species of Stock, in that State, which pays a tax. Carriages were, when I left Virginia, and I believe still are, subject to a tax by the Wheel. It was then if I recollect rightly, about five dollars each wheel—but whether it is more or less now; or whether there be any at all, is more than I am able with certainty to inform you. With very great esteem & regard I am—Sir Your most Obedt & much obliged Servt

Go: Washington

ALS, PPRF; LB, DLC:GW.

1. In a letter of 11 Nov. 1792 GW had instructed his estate manager Anthony Whitting to obtain a copy of "the sheriff's bill for the taxes, which you paid while I was at home."

2. The tax account is for GW's estate.

"Dr—For Public taxes—& for County & Parish levies

In Truro Parish—1792

Tax on 6320 acs. of Land for 1791			£13. 8. 7
114 Negros	@ 2/6		14. 5. 0
87. Horses	@ 6d.		2. 3. 6
107. County & Parish levies @ 29 lbs. of Tobo each	3013		

Fairfax Parish (adjoining)

Tax on 3420 acres of Land [1791]			6. 6. 3
24 Negros	@ 2/6		3. 0. 0
15. Horses	6d.		7. 6
23. County & Parish levies @ 29 lbs. Tobo each	567		
	3670 &		£39.10.10
3670 lbs. Tobo at 15/. p. Ct [wt].			27.10. 6
Total—Dollars—	@ 6/		£67. 1. 4

Note, There ought to have been in the above account, a discrimination in the charge for County & Parish levies. The first is for building & repairing Court Houses—Goals—&ca—Criminal processes &ca—The latter is for the support of the Poor, and other Parochial charges" (AD, PPRF). The text within square brackets is taken from the letter-book copy (DLC: GW).

From Alexander Hamilton

Treasury Departmt 3d Decr 1792.

The Secretary of the Treasury has the honor to submit to the President a communication of the 30th of Novemr relating to some additional objects which have been executed towards the completion of the Lighthouse Establishment on Cape Henry.[1]

The Secretary, according to the best information in his possession, considers them as necessary objects, and respectfully submits it as his opinion that it will be advisable to confirm the Contracts which have been entered into by Mr Newton, in the first instance.

The Secretary, from experience, entertains a confidence in the discretion & judgment of that Gentleman which induces a reliance on the view taken by him of the subject on the spot, with the advantage of a knowledge of local, which cannot be possessed by any person here. A submission to arbitration might not be altogether free from hazard of an increased allowance and it is so apparent that the *whole work* has been accomplished upon such moderate terms, & so probable that it may not even have afforded a due degree of benefit to the Undertaker, as to create a claim on the liberality of the Government in regard to collateral Contracts.[2] All which is humbly submitted

Alexander Hamilton Secy of the Treasury.

LB, DLC:GW.

1. Commissioner of the Revenue Tench Coxe wrote Hamilton on 30 Nov. to report "the completion of the light House, Keepers house, oil Vault, and platform on Cape Henry in the state of Virginia." The "additional objects" involved two unapproved contracts between John McComb, Jr., the builder of the lighthouse, and Thomas Newton, Jr., one of the Virginia commissioners who had been appointed a trustee for the site. Newton, Coxe said, had decided that the project needed a platform constructed "to prevent injury to the foundations from the blowing away of the sand and frequent inconvenience, attended with labor and expence in removing it from the passages to the doors of the dwelling house, Vault and light house." The contract for construction of the platform and another contract for the extension of the foundation in depth and width were in addition to the original contract for the lighthouse (DNA: RG 58, Letters Sent by the Commissioner of the Revenue and the Revenue Office, 1792–1807). In the supplementary contract of 29 July 1791 for the extension of the foundation, McComb agreed "that in case his demand agreeably to an Estimate hereunto annexed, should appear too high in the opinion of the President, That the Extra work shall be determined by three disinterested persons to be mutually chosen" (DNA: RG 26, Lighthouse Deeds and Contracts, 1790–1812). For background on the construction of the Cape Henry lighthouse and the awarding of the original building contract to McComb, see Hamilton to GW, 5 Jan. 1791, source note, and notes 1 and 2.

2. For GW's approval of the additional construction costs, see Tobias Lear to Hamilton, 6 Dec. 1792.

From Benjamin Harwood

Sir   Annapolis December 3d 1792

Thomas Harwood Esquire the present Commissioner of Loans of this State having resigned, I beg leave to Offer myself for that appointment, having acted with him in that Office from it's commencement, I flatter myself I am qualified to fill that Station, not being personally known to you, I am favor'd with Letters upon the subject in my behalf, shou'd I meet your approbation to the appointment, it shall be my constant study not to forfeit the confidence and trust reposed in me.[1] Sir I have the honor to be with great respect your obt Servt

Benjamin Harwood

ALS, DLC:GW. This letter is identified as "No. 100 Maryland."

1. For background on the resignation of Thomas Harwood, Benjamin Harwood's brother, see Charles Carroll of Carrollton's letter to GW of 1 Dec. 1792, and note 1. Carroll's letter was one of three letters written to GW recommending Benjamin Harwood's appointment as Maryland commissioner of loans. Maryland governor Thomas Sim Lee recommended Harwood in a letter to GW of 1 Dec. 1792, in which he wrote: "A Considerable share of the business of that Office has been under the conduct of this Gentleman, & he has acquitted himself with such marked regularity, diligence and integrity, that I might venture to assert, that a Character, better qualified to fill the office . . . is not to be found in Maryland" (DLC:GW). U.S. Senator John Henry of Maryland recommended Harwood in a letter to GW of 10 Dec. in which he described Harwood as "a man of mild manners, punctual and attentive, with an accurate knowledge of the Business" (DLC:GW). GW sent Harwood's nomination to the U.S. Senate on 11 Dec. 1792 (LB, DLC:GW), and the Senate approved the nomination the following day (see *Executive Journal*, 1:126). At GW's request Tobias Lear on 12 Dec. sent Thomas Jefferson official notification of Thomas Harwood's resignation and Benjamin Harwood's appointment (DLC:GW).

Tobias Lear to John Lamb

Philadelphia December 4: 1792.

I was this day honored with your letter of the 30th ultimo, enclosing one for Mrs Washington, the receipt of which she requests me to acknowledge, and beg your acceptance of her best thanks for the nuts and Apples which you have had the politeness to send to her, & which have come safe to hand.[1]

The Box, which was at the same time sent to the President, and which you mention to have arrived from London in the Ship Betsy, contained two Charts of the Sea-Coast of North America, sent to the President for his acceptance by John Hamilton Moore, Esqr. of London, the executor of them. No account of the price of these Charts was sent and as I do not know of any of the same kind being imported or sold here I cannot form an opinion of their cost; but if it can be hereafter ascertained by any means you shall receive an acct of it.[2] I have the honor to be very respectfully Sir Your most Obedt Sert

Tobias Lear.

ALS (letterpress copy), DNA: RG 59, Miscellaneous Letters; LB, DLC:GW.

1. Former Revolutionary War officer John Lamb was currently the collector of customs at New York City. His letter to Lear of 30 Nov. has not been identified. The enclosed letter to Martha Washington, dated 30 Nov., covered a re-

ceipt for "the delivery of two Barrels Apples, and one Barrel Nuts, which, I have put on board the Schooner Dolphin" (DLC:GW). For Lamb's earlier gifts of apples to Mrs. Washington, see Lamb to Lear, 22 Mar. 1792, n.1.

2. The two charts that the British hydrographer John Hamilton Moore sent GW were *Chart of Navigation from the Gulf of Honda to Philadelphia* and *Chart to Bay of Fundy*. Both were in GW's library at the time of his death (see Griffin, *Boston Athenæum Washington Collection,* 561). For GW's letter to Moore of 2 Dec. 1792 thanking him for the charts, see Alexander Spotswood to GW, 4 Dec. 1791, n.2.

From John Small

[4 December 1792][1]

The Petition of John Small[2] Humbly sheweth, that your Petitioner is a native of the State of Virginia, and born in the County of Princess Ann, and from the Port of Norfolk served a regular Apprentiship to the Seas, which calling, as Commander of a Vessel, he has since followed: but from an unavoidable accident, on board the Ship Governor Livingston, (in which he acted as first Lieutenant) on her Passage from France with warlike Stores, for the State of Virginia, in having three of his Ribs, his Thigh and Coller Bones broken, he is rendered too infirm and lame to pursue that laborius occupation for the maintenance of himself and numerous family.[3] And as the Gentleman who was appointed Manager of the Light-House on Cape Henry in this State is since dead, your Petitioner, convinced of the willingness of your honourable Body, to assist those who in the support of our Rights and Liberties have been rendered unable to support themselves and families, is induced to offer himself a Candidate to fill that important Office[4]—And from his long services in the American War, in which he suffered greatly, as well as a particular attention to the management of Light-Houses, many of which your Petitioner has often frequented, and an acquaintance with Governor Johnson, to whom your Petitioner begs leave to refer your honours for his Character he humbly hopes that you will be pleased to honour him with that appointment[5] and should he meet with your Approbation, he assures your honours, that the greatest assiduity and strictest attention shall be used, to merit your approbation, and fully to accomplish the laudable purposes for which the said Light-House was erected, And your Petitioner as in duty bound shall ever pray &c. &c.

AL, DLC:GW; identified as item "No. 124 Virga."

1. The date is taken from the docket.

2. The heading on this petition reads: "To his Excellency the President and the honourable the Members of the American Congress."

3. The date of Small's accident has not been determined, but he may have been on the *Governor Livingston* that arrived at York, Va., on 22 July 1779 from Nantes, France, with military supplies for the state of Virginia (see John Gilbank to John Hancock, 23 July 1779, DNA:PCC, item 78).

4. William Lewis died in November 1792, shortly after receiving his appointment as keeper of the Cape Henry, Va., lighthouse (see Alexander Hamilton to GW, 22 Sept., n.6).

5. Despite his acquaintance with Thomas Johnson, a former Maryland governor and currently an associate justice of the U.S. Supreme Court, Small did not receive the desired appointment, which went to Lemuel Cornick (see Lear to Hamilton, 22 Dec. 1792, DNA: RG 26, Inventory NC-31, entry 16, Miscellaneous Records Relating to the Lighthouse Service; see also the extract in Syrett, *Hamilton Papers*, 13:356–57).

From the United States House of Representatives

United States [Philadelphia]

Sir,   the 4th of december, 1792.

In obedience to the Order of the House of Representatives, of this date, I have the honor to inclose your their Resolution respecting certain estimates from the department of War, for the year one thousand, seven hundred and ninety three.[1] With the most perfect respect I am, Sir, Your most obedient, and very humble Servant

Jona. Trumbull,

Speaker of the House of Representatives.

LB, DLC:GW.

This message from the House Speaker and its accompanying resolution were recorded in the letter book under the date of 5 Dec., which was the date it was "laid before the President."

1. The enclosed resolution of 4 Dec., copied for Trumbull from the House journal by its clerk John Beckley, reads: "Resolved, that the President of the United States be requested to cause to be laid before the House an estimate of the contingent expenses of the department of War, for the year one thousand seven hundred and ninety three, and of the items, upon which the report of the Secretary for the department of War states certain estimates, called conjectural, are founded, specifying, as distinctly as may be, the heads of such articles." Tobias Lear added the following note beneath the letter-book copy of the resolution: "N.B. In pursuance of the foregoing Resolution the President

directed the Secretary of War to make out a statement, conformable thereto & lay it before the House; which was accordingly done on the 12 of december 1792" (DLC:GW). Lear wrote Henry Knox on 5 Dec., at GW's request, asking Knox to provide the required information (DLC:GW). The House read Knox's report on 12 Dec. (see *Journal of the House*, 5:37).

From Matthew Flannery

[Philadelphia, 5 December 1792] [1]

The Memorial of Matthew Flannery Humbly sheweth; that your Memorialist came to this Country in expectation to get employed as Clerk in a Compting House or in a Publick Office, and during three Months residence in the City of Philadelphia, he has not met with the least encouragement, his Money being now expended, and being no longer able to support himself out of Business, being destitute of Friends who may lend him the least Assistance, and having no other resource whatsoever, obliges him with the greatest submission, to take the liberty of soliciting your Excellency for some Employment suitable to his Abilities⟨.⟩ He hopes from your Benevolent disposition towards the Distressed, that your Excellency will take his Case into consideration, and extricate him out of his present distressed situation by puting him into some Employ, as he can provide the most unblemished Character. And your Excellency will confer an everlasting favor on your Memorialist who will be during life in duty bound to pray &c.

AL, DLC:GW. A note on the cover identifies this letter as "No. 21 Foreign Applicatn."

1. The date is taken from the docket, which reads: "of Mathew Flannery for some employment 5 Decr 1792."

Letter not found: from Anthony Whitting, 5 Dec. 1792. GW wrote Whitting on 9 Dec. that his letter "of the 5th came yesterday."

Tobias Lear to Alexander Hamilton

United States [Philadelphia] Decr 6th 1792

By the President's command, T. Lear has the honor to return to the Secretary of the Treasury, with the President's approbation affixed thereto, the Contract entered into by Thomas Newton jur on the part of the U.S. with John McComb junr to execute certain additional objects specified in said Contract, to the Lighthouse lately erected on Cape Henry: And to inform the Secretary that the President approves of the sum of six hundred and fifty Dollars being paid to said McComb for building a certain Wall & laying a platform at the said Lighthouse, agreeably to a proposal for that purpose made in a Letter from sd McComb to said Newton, which letter has been submitted to the President.[1]

Tobias Lear S.P.U.S.

LB, DLC:GW.

1. Following Hamilton's instructions, Commissioner of the Revenue Tench Coxe had written Lear on this date to inquire "whether the President has formed his determination in regard to the two additional Objects (the platform and the extension of the foundation) in Mr McCombs account." Hamilton was anxious for GW's decision because John McComb, Jr., the contractor for the new lighthouse at Cape Henry, Va., had been in Philadelphia since "the Thursday in last week [29 Nov.]" and "has urgent business at home" (DNA: RG 59, Miscellaneous Letters). For background on the "additional Objects" and the question about paying McComb for work not included in the original contract, see Hamilton to GW, 3 Dec., and note 1. A copy of the supplemental 29 July 1791 contract for extending the depth and width of the foundation, which was signed by McComb and by Thomas Newton, Jr., who acted "for Alexr Hamilton," and McComb's estimate of the cost are in DNA: RG 26, Lighthouse Deeds and Contracts, 1790–1812. Neither the second supplemental contract, for building the platform, nor the letter from McComb to Newton has been identified. McComb's estimate for the foundation of 29 July 1791 proposed that "in case his demand agreeably to an Estimate hereunto annexed, should appear too high in the opinion of the President, That the Extra work shall be determined by three disinterested persons to be mutually chosen" (DNA: RG 26, Lighthouse Deeds and Contracts, 1790–1812).

Henry Knox to Tobias Lear

Dear Sir.   [Philadelphia] Dec: 6th 1792

Please to submit to the President of the United States, the enclosed letters, from Brigadier General Wilkinson and John Belli deputy quarter master—dated Oct: 4th and 8th 1792; which I have just received.[1] Yours sincerely,

H. Knox secy of war

LS, DLC:GW; LB, DLC:GW.

1. The enclosed letters from James Wilkinson and John Belli have not been identified.

From Henry Knox

Sir.   War-department, December 6th 1792.

In explanation of the speeches from the chiefs of the six nations herewith submitted, it may be proper to observe that Jasper Parish who is a temporary interpreter to those tribes[1] informs verbally that the said chiefs returned from the hostile tribes to Buffaloe Creek about the last of October—That they immediately sent a runner to General Chapin the temporary Agent to the six Nations, and who resides at Canandarqua, about ninety or one hundred miles distant—That he being absent, his son and the interpreter repaired to Buffaloe Creek, where they received the said speeches.

Besides the papers transmitted by Mr Chapin, the interpreter says, that a list of the tribes which composed the council, at the Au Glaize, on the Miami river of Lake Erie, was taken by Mr Chapin, but he omitted to transmit it.[2]

He was informed by the chiefs of the Six Nations, that at the council of the hostile indians, which was numerous, but the numbers not specified, no other white person was admitted but Simon Girty, who they considered as one of themselves.[3]

That the chiefs of the Shawanese were the only speakers, on the part of the hostile indians, and Red Jacket the Seneka chief, the only speaker on the part of the friendly indians.[4]

That Captain Brant did not arrive at the Au Glaize until after the council had broken up, which probably by a comparison of circumstances happened about the 10th or 12th of October.[5]

That Captain Hendricks the chief of the stockbridge indians had proved unfaithful, having delivered the message, belt, and map with which he was entrusted for the hostile indians, to Mr McKee, the british Indian Agent, and that the said Hendricks did not repair to the council at all.[6]

The said Jasper Parish also adds that Red Jacket was exceedingly desirous of repairing to Philadelphia in person, but Mr Chapin apprehending the expences persuaded him to the contrary—

This circumstance is exceedingly to be regretted, as further information and explanations would be highly desireable at this moment, in order to judge with greater precision of the meaning of the speeches, which may have suffered in the translation, as well as in other respects.[7] I have the honor to be, Sir, with the highest respect, Your obedient and humble servt

H. Knox secy of war

LS, DNA: RG 46, Second Congress, 1791–93, Senate Records of Legislative Proceedings, President's Messages; LB (dated 5 Dec.), DLC:GW; copy, PHi: Large Miscellaneous Volumes.

1. Jasper Parrish (1767–1836) had been captured in 1778 by the Delaware Indians and had been taken the following year to Fort Niagara, where he was sold for £2 to a Mohawk Indian. Released from captivity after the Revolutionary War, Parrish rejoined his family at Goshen, N.Y., and began a career as an Indian interpreter.

2. During a visit to Philadelphia in the spring of 1792, a delegation of Iroquois chiefs agreed to send emissaries to the western Indians in an effort to restore peace between those tribes and the United States. The Iroquois representatives attended the grand council that met between 30 Sept. and 9 Oct. at Au Glaize.

In the enclosed letter to Knox of 22 Nov., Israel Chapin, Jr., wrote: "There was a number of Gentlemen from Niagara who attended the Council at Buffaloe Creek, amongst which was Colonel [John] Butler the Indian Agent under the British Government, who in some of his hours express'd himself that unless proper means was taken that a lasting peace could not take place, but if the United State's proposals are honorable he would give every assistance in his power, but if otherwise he should prevent a peace taking place.

"Major Littletrates [Edward Baker Littlehales] who represented Governor [John Graves] Simcoe assured me it was the disposition of the Governor to give every assistance in his power to procure peace on equitable terms."

The enclosed speech, given to Chapin and Parrish at Buffalo Creek, N.Y., on 16 Nov., reads: "Brothers people of the United States & Kings people take notice, last winter the president took us by the hand and led us to the Council fire at Philadelphia there they made known to us their friendship, and requested of us to proceed to the westward, and to use our influence to make peace with the hostile Indians—we went accordingly and made known to them our agreement.

"When we returned from Philadelphia to Buffaloe Creek, the Chiefs that remained at home on their seats was well pleased with what we had done at Philadelphia, and after we had determined to proceed on our journey some of our Chiefs was detained on account of sickness.

"Broth⟨e⟩rs people of the U.N.S. & Kings people after we arrived at the westward we met with an agreeable reception, they informed us we was their oldest Brothers and appeared as the Sun risen on them, as they always looked to them for advice.

"It is now four years since we have heard your voices, and should be happy now to hear what you have to relate to us.

"The Six nations then requested of the western Indians what they had to relate to them, as they kindled the Council fire.

"The western Indians replied, about four years since your voices came to us, desireing us to combine ourselves together as we was the eldest people of this Island and all of one Colour, that our minds may be one.

"This they informed us they had attended to, and exhibited a large bunch of wampum to prove the same, from each nation.

"To confirm it still further they informed us we sent them a pipe, which passed through all the nations at the west and southward, all smok'd out of it both women and Children, and as this pipe has been through the nations and all smoked out of it, they then returned it to us and bid us to smoke out of it ourselves.

"Brothers listen once to your eldest Brothers—Our fore fathers have handed down to us that we are one people of one colour on this Island, and ought to be of one mind, and had made our minds strong and had become as one people in peace and friendship.

"This being done our Chiefs agreed to hand it down to future posterity, and the same combination to continue down to them.

"The nation called the unions took a brand from our fire and kindled it, and became a people with us—then we considered ourselves as one people, combined together.

"And now there is a white people on this Island who are watching our conduct—but let us attend to our own concerns, and brighten the Chain of friendship with our nations: and as our minds are one, let us consider future posterity, and not consider those young warriors who are in the prime of life and so much engaged in the pursuit of Land &c: which is the cause of so much difficulty at present.

"Brothers consider your Country which is good, and conduct yourselves in such a manner as to keep it, to yourselves and posterity.

"Now Brothers you present us the pipe you say your oldest Brothers sent you, you say your head Chiefs all smoked out of it, and returning it to us again all took it and smoked out of it ourselves in friendship. Now as we are thus combined together we are able to lift a heavy burden.

"Shawany nation—Our eldest Brothers we have heard what you have related, we have heard it with attention—we consider it as if you delivered it from the outside of your lips, although you consider us your younger Brothers, your seats are not at such a distance, but what we can see your conduct plainly, these are the reasons why we consider you to speak from the outside of your lips, for whenever you hear the voice of the United States, you immediately take your packs & attend their Councils.

"We see plainly folded under your arm the voice of the United States—wish you to unfold it to us, that we may see it freely and consult on it, speaking on a string of wampum of three strings, throwing it across the fire to us, instead of handing it in a friendly manner.

"Then we proceeded to relate the instructions of Congress which is too tedious to relate, and which they already know, but when we first related it, we failed for Interpreters so that they had not a proper idea of it, they appeared to be very much ruffled in their minds and adjourned the Council to the next day—then it was interpreted properly to them and they appeared easy in their minds.

"Eldest Brothers, you desire us to consider our Country and property, we will accept of your advice and proceed accordingly.

"Six nations—Let us look back to the time of white people coming into this Country, very soon began to traffic for land, Soon after Sr Wm Johnson was sent as an Agent from the King, and he began to purchase at the Treaty at Ft Stanwix—and purchased all, East of the river Ohio.

"A few years after this purchase, the people of the States and the King's people broke apart, and we being persuaded to take the Kings part became very bad for us—after a few years the King was beat, then the States took possession of all the Land the English formerly took from the French.

"You tell us we come with the voice of the United States, we do together with the advice of the King—He tells us not to throw our minds on either side, but to listen to reason &c. and remain a people confederated.

"Shawany nation[—]Now eldest Brothers, you come to us with your opinion and the voice of the U.N.S., it is your mind to put an end to all hostilities—Brothers, now we will relate what took place last Fall in our Country—General Washington sent an army into our Country which fell into our hands; their orders was thus to proceed into our Country as far as the Miami Towns, to the Glaze—thence to Detroit—but not to molest the Kings people, and if the army should meet any people that appeared friendly, to leave them behind their backs without harm.

"The president of the United States must well know why the Blood is so deep in our paths, we have been informed he has sent Messengers of peace on these Bloody roads, who fell on the way—and now as he knows that road to be bloody, no communication to take place through that Bloody way, as there is a path through the six nations Country, which is smooth and easy. If he wants to send the voice of peace, it must pass through this road.

"Eldest Brothers, We have been informed the President of the U.N.S. thinks himself the greatest Man on this Island, we had this Country long in peace before we saw any person of a white skin—we consider the people of a white Skin the younger.

"Brothers, you inform us it is the wish of the white people to hold Council with us, General Washington being the head Man—We will consent to treat with them—We desire you our older Brothers to inform General Washington we will treat with him, at the rapids of Miami next Spring, or at the time when the Leaves are fully out.

"We consider ourselves still the proper Owners of some Land on the East side of the Ohio.

"But we will deliver up that, for money that has been paid to some individuals, for Land on the west side of the River Ohio.

"Brothers, you have given us a Dish and one Spoon desiring the whole combination to eat with them; we accept of them & shall do accordingly.

"We are now about to complete the business you came on, when you return you will make known to the President what we have done, it may be he will not consent to what we have proposed, and if he will not, we must call on you to assist in the heavy burden which will lye on us—we have opened a path for them and pointed out a way, and if he will not walk in it, we must have your assistance.

"Now our eldest Brothers—when the president come to you, he took you aside to hear what he had to say, He desired you to come to us and deliver the Messages, you have delivered them, & we desire you to deliver the Messages we have given you to deliver to him, and desire him to send a Message back what he will do respecting what we have done and concluded on, to forward it to you, and you to us—We will lay the bloody Tomahawk aside until we hear from the President of the U.N.S., and when this Message come to us we will send it to all the different nations. Speaking on three strings of wampum." For other contemporary accounts of the grand council at Au Glaize, see "Canadian Archives. Colonial Office Records: Michigan," 468–74, 483–98, and Aupaumut, "Narrative," 115–30.

Chapin also enclosed the speech of 16 Nov. to GW from the Six Nations at Buffalo Creek: "You sent us on to the westward with a message of peace to the hostile Indians.

"We proceeded accordingly to your directions, and was protected going and coming by the Great Spirit.

"We give thanks to the Great Spirit that we have all returned safe to our seats.

"While we was at the Westward we exerted ourselves to bring about peace, the fatigues we underwent are not small—Now it is our desire for your people on the Ohio, to lay down their arms, or otherwise it is all in vain what we have done.

"Now if you wish for peace, you must make every exertion and proceed through this path we have directed for you. If peace does not take place the fault must arise from your people.

"We now desire you Brs. to send forward agents who are men of honesty, not proud Land jobbers but men who love & desire peace, also desire they may be accompanied by some Friend or Quaker to attend the Council.

"Wish you to exert yourselves to forward the Message to the western Indians as soon as possible—and we are taken by the hand, and have agreed next Spring to attend the Council at the rapids of Miami, when we shall hear all that takes place there.

"Hostile Indians to Governor Simcoe—Brothers, we have been informed the late Govr is a good man—we desire you that you will take the Governor by the hand, and lead him to the Council next Spring—Exert yourselves to get him up that he may not be backward, that he may sit side & side wth the Americans at the time of the Council. and when you take him by the hand, desire him to furnish us with provisions necessary for the Treaty.

"Six Nations to the Governor—Brothers, now we have laid all our proceedings before you which took place at the westward. You have heard the request of your western Brothers, therefore wish you to exert yourself to grant their requests.

"You informed us to listen to the voice of peace wherever we might hear it—now we hear the voice of peace—We call on you for assistance that we may obtain peace through this Island.

"Brothers, we now sit here together—you are the man who represents the United States—we have discerned that too great a degree of pride has subsisted between the two Governments—we desire that it may be laid aside.

"When the Agents from the U.N.S. come forward to the Council, we desire they may bring forward all records, plans, maps and documents that any way respect to Lands purchased from the Indians.

"Fish Carriers Speech—Desiring this degree of pride which has heretofore subsisted may be done away, and that each Government will mutually consent and agree on terms of peace.

"Cornplanter's Speech—He informs that he has always attended treaties that has been held and has always wished for peace, and has done all in his power for peace, that he has not advised any hostilities to commence on either side, and now wishes each Government to lay aside all pride and prejudice and to use their endeavours for peace.

"After the Council was over Major Littletrates who represented Governor Simcoe on that occasion, answered the Indians as follows.

"Brothers, I shall lay before the Governor your requests and respecting his furnishing you with provisions &c: I doubt not but he will do it agreeable to your wishes—and also to procure all Records, plans & Documents which shall be thought necessary—and to do every thing in his power to bring about a peace so interesting to the United States, as well as to the British Government." For another contemporary account of the November meeting at Buffalo Creek, see "Canadian Archives. Colonial Office Records: Michigan," 509–16. Copies of Chapin's letter and of both enclosed speeches are in DNA: RG 46, Second Congress, 1791–93, Senate Records of Legislative Proceedings, President's Messages, and they are identified as "true copies, from the originals on file in the War-Office of the United States, December 5th: 1792"; see also *ASP, Indian Affairs*, 1:323–24.

3. Pennsylvania native Simon Girty (1741–1818) was captured with his family by Indians in 1756 and spent the next three years as a captive among the Senecas who lived in the Ohio River Valley. After his release in 1759, he remained in the Ohio region as a trader, occasionally acting as an interpreter for the British and colonists at nearby Fort Pitt. During the early years of the Revolutionary War, Girty served as an interpreter for the Americans, but by 1778 he had transferred his loyalties to the British and had fled the Fort Pitt region for the British post of Fort Detroit. Girty subsequently was hired as an interpreter to the Six Nations by the British Indian Department, a position he continued to hold after the war.

4. Seneca chief Red Jacket (c. 1758–1830) was renowned for his oratorical abilities, and his political skills ensured his inclusion among the Indian leaders with whom the Americans conducted their diplomatic negotiations. For the visit of Red Jacket and other Iroquois leaders to Philadelphia in the spring of 1792 and for American overtures to the Iroquois for their assistance in the U.S. peace efforts in the Northwest Territory, see Timothy Pickering to GW, 21

Mar., GW to the Five Nations, 23 Mar., and source note, Henry Knox to GW, 2 April, n.1, 22 April, n.1, GW's Message to the Five Nations, 25 April 1792.

5. Knox and GW had hoped that diplomatic intervention by the Mohawk leader Joseph Brant would help to produce a peaceful settlement of U.S. differences with the western Indians. For an account of the illness that prevented Brant from reaching Au Glaize until after the council's conclusion, see Henry Knox to GW, 15 Sept., n.6.

6. Knox was wrong in his assessment of Stockbridge chief Hendrick Aupaumut. For Aupaumut's account of his peace mission to the western Indians in 1792, see Aupaumut, "Narrative." Alexander McKee, a deputy agent in the British department of Indian affairs, had entered that department in 1760, had married a Shawnee woman, and had pursued a career in the Indian trade, gaining considerable influence among the Indians north of the Ohio River. Sympathetic to the British cause, McKee had moved from the Fort Pitt area in 1778, eventually settling among the British at Detroit, where he used his considerable influence among the Indians against the American forces in the Ohio Valley during the remainder of the Revolutionary War. After the war McKee strongly supported the western Indians' resistance to American advances in the Ohio Valley.

7. For Knox's invitation to Red Jacket to visit Philadelphia, see his letter to Israel Chapin, Sr., of 12 Dec. in Tobias Lear to Knox, 11 Dec. 1792, n.2. GW sent Knox's letter of 6 Dec. and its enclosures with a cover letter to the U.S. Senate and House of Representatives on 6 Dec. 1792.

To the United States Senate and House of Representatives

United States [Philadelphia] December the 6th 1792.
Gentlemen of the Senate, and of the House of Representatives.

The several measures which have been pursued to induce the hostile Indian Tribes, North of the Ohio, to enter into a conference or treaty with the United States, at which all causes of difference might be fully understood, and justly and amicably arranged, have already been submitted to both Houses of Congress.[1]

The Papers herewith sent will inform you of the result.[2]

Go: Washington

DS, DNA: RG 46, Second Congress, 1791–93, Senate Records of Legislative Proceedings, President's Messages; copy, DNA: RG 233, Second Congress, 1791–93, House Records of Legislative Proceedings, Journals; LB, DLC:GW.

1. See GW's Address to the U.S. Senate and House of Representatives, 6 Nov. 1792, n.2.

2. For the enclosed papers, see Henry Knox to GW, 6 Dec. 1792, and note 2.

To the United States Senate and House of Representatives

United States [Philadelphia] December 7th 1792
Gentlemen of the Senate, and of the House of Representatives.[1]

I lay before you two letters with their enclosures, from the Governor of the south western territory, and an extract of a letter to him from the department of War.[2]

These, and a letter of the ninth of October last, which has been already communicated to you from the same department, to the Governor,[3] will shew, in what manner, the first section of the Act of the last Session, which provides for the calling out the militia, for the repelling of Indian invasions, has been executed.[4] It remains to be considered by Congress, whether, in the present situation of the United States, it be adviseable, or not, to pursue any farther or other measures, than those which have already been adopted. The nature of the subject does, of itself, call for your immediate attention to it; and I must add, that, upon the result of your deliberations, the future conduct of the Executive will, on this occasion, materially depend.

Go: Washington

Copy, DNA: RG 233, Second Congress, 1791–93, House Records of Legislative Proceedings, Journals; LB, DLC: GW.

1. Compare this letter with the memorandum of 28 Nov. that Thomas Jefferson prepared on the subject of Indian hostilities in the Southwest Territory for GW to send to Congress.

2. The following memorandum appears at the end of the letter-book copy in DLC: GW: "The letters &c. alluded to [in] the foregoing Message were copied at the War-Office, where the Originals are deposited and are as follows.

"A letter from Govr Blount, dated, Novr 12th 1792. giving an account of an attack made by the Indians on an house within 8 miles of Knoxville, where they were repulsed.

"A letter from ditto—dated Novr 8th 1792. stating the causes of the hostility of the Cherokees & Creeks against the U.S. and enclosing—No: 1—Minutes of Information given to Governor Blount, by James Cary, one of the Interpreters of the U.S. in the Cherokee Nation—dated Novr 3d 1792. No: 2. A Return of the persons killed, wounded, or made Captives in the Territory of the U.S. south of the Ohio since the first day of January 1791—No. 3—Governor Blounts Account of the number of Indians who made the attack upon Buchanans Station, their loss & particulars. No: 4—An Account of Indian Depredations in the District of Mero, and on the Kentuckey Road from the 3d to the 14th of October 1792. and No. 5—Governor Blount's instructions of the 7th of October to David Campbell, Chs MClury and John McKee, Commissioners

&c." William Blount's letters to Henry Knox of 8 and 12 Nov. and the five enclosures described above are in *ASP, Indian Affairs,* 1 : 325–32.

The enclosed extract may have been taken from Knox's letter to Blount of 26 Nov., in which he wrote: "All your letters have been submitted to the President of the United States. Whatever may be his impression relatively to the proper steps to be adopted, he does not conceive himself authorized to direct offensive operations against the Chickamaggas. If such measures are to be pursued they must result from the decisions of Congress who solely are vested with the powers of War." GW's address of 6 Nov., Knox reported, has brought "this subject . . . fully . . . to the view of Congress and the two Houses have been much occupied in reading the various communications relatively to the Indian department, what result the business will have it is not proper or possible for me to conjecture.

"I can however with great truth assure you that the extension of the Northern Indian War to the Southern Tribes would be a measure into which the Country would enter with extreme reluctance. They view an Indian War in any event of it as unproductive either of profit or honor, and therefore to be avoided if possible. . . . In this event Sir, you could not do a more acceptable service to the Government or more enhance your own reputation than by terminating the affair with the said Chickamaggas without further conflict. . . . The number of Militia which you appear to have called into service might probably at the moment of danger have appeared to be necessary and justifiable by the occasion—But Sir it is of the highest importance that they should not have been retained in service any longer than circumstances rendered indispensible. The great expence to the public attending so considerable a body of Militia together with the extreme injury to Individuals so called out will render the measure intolerable unless supported by the most conspicuous emergency and necessity—This is a point to which I am directed to request your serious attention." Knox concluded his letter with a review of the strategy, troops, and military supplies approved for the defense of the Southwest Territory (Carter, *Territorial Papers,* 4 : 220–26).

3. For Knox's letter to Blount of 9 Oct., see Knox to GW, 9 Oct., n.3. GW submitted a copy of this letter to Congress on 7 Nov. (see GW's Address to the U.S. Senate and House of Representatives, 6 Nov., n.2).

4. See "An Act more effectually to provide for the National Defence by establishing an Uniform Militia throughout the United States," 8 May 1792 (1 *Stat.* 271–74).

George Washington and John Francis Mercer to Francis Deakins and Benjamin W. Jones

Gentlemen, Philada 8th Decembr 1792.

Since the Letter which we addressed to you, requesting your valuation of a certain tract of Land in Montgomery County, another arrangement has taken place with regard thereto.[1] It is now agreed that the price of seven dollars per acre shall be fixed & the whole tract divided into two equal parts, with respect to quantity, quality & value. In giving effect to this agreement, we must still rely on your good offices to make the necessary division, which when certified to us will enable us to determine by Lot the possession. Your attention to this request, as early as your conveniency will permit, will greatly oblige,[2] Gentlemen, Your mo: obt hble Servts

G: Washington
John F: Mercer.

LB, DLC: GW.

This letter was enclosed in Mercer's letter to GW of this date from Philadelphia. "I have executed a Letter enclosed," Mercer wrote, "authorizing & requesting Mr Deakins & Mr Jones to divide the Land in Montgomery, which if you approve of, you will be pleased to sign & forward as you think proper" (DLC: GW).

1. In a letter to Deakins and Jones of 8 Aug. 1792, Mercer and GW had asked for an evaluation of a parcel of land that Mercer's wife, Sophia Sprigg Mercer, had inherited, in anticipation that this parcel would be used to settle a debt that the Mercer family owed GW. For GW's earlier efforts to collect the money due him from the estate of John Mercer, the father of James and John Francis Mercer, see GW to James Mercer, 18 Mar. 1789, and note 1, and 4 April 1789, and to John Francis Mercer, 5 April 1789, 30 June and 23 July 1792. For more recent attempts to reach an agreement, see John F. Mercer to GW, 15 Sept., 5 Nov., and GW to John F. Mercer, 26 Sept. 1792.

2. Deakins and Jones sent GW their assessment of Sophia Mercer's land on 20 Dec. 1792.

From Thomas Jefferson

[Philadelphia] Dec. 8. 1792.

Th: Jefferson has the honor to inclose to the President a letter from the Commissioners of Washington.[1]

Also begs leave to add to the list of candidates for the light house of Cape Henry, the name of John Waller Johnson, who has hitherto served in the Customs under Colo. Heath. he is recommended as a person of worth by a mister Waller Lewis of Spotsylvania, who is himself a man of worth. he has been a voyage or two to sea coastwise, which is all the knowlege he has of the distresses of that element.[2]

AL, DNA: RG 59, Miscellaneous Letters; LB, DNA: RG 59, George Washington's Correspondence with His Secretaries of State; LB (photocopy), DLC:GW.

1. In their letter to Jefferson written on 5 Dec. at Georgetown, commissioners David Stuart and Daniel Carroll acknowledged receipt of "the Presidents order on the Treasurer of Virginia for the second instalment due from that State. The plans are also received, and we shall have them distributed for sale immediately, at the price you have rated them." They asked Jefferson to inform GW that at their next meeting they would consider the advisability of hiring Samuel Blodget, Jr., to act as a land agent for the district. In regard to previous land sales, the commissioners wrote: "We are sorry to inform you that there has not only been a great want of punctuallity among those who purchased at the first sale, in their second payments; but even among those who were purchasers at the last, of their first advance. They have all been written to pressingly." After briefly discussing possible technical innovations for cutting stone and problems in recruiting "Mechanics from Scotland," the commissioners wrote that they had learned that William Thornton had a suitable plan for the Capitol, and that "as we expect by our next meeting, Mr. Hallets plan will be ready to send on to the President, we have desired him to lay his before you, for the President's inspection, in the first place, that he may have an opportunity of judging of their comparative merits." They also stated that "the outlines of the Territory are nearly completed" and that they expected to send GW their report on that subject in January (*Jefferson Papers,* 24:699–700).

2. John Waller Johnston (Johnson), the former deputy customs collector under William Heth at Bermuda Hundred, Va., had been unsuccessful in an earlier attempt to secure the position of lighthouse keeper at Cape Henry. The first appointee, William Lewis, died in November, but Johnston again failed to obtain the appointment, which went to Lemuel Cornick (see Alexander Hamilton to GW, 22 Sept. 1792, n.6). For Johnston's 8 Dec. application to Jefferson, which was accompanied by a letter of recommendation from Waller Lewis (1739–1818), see *Jefferson Papers,* 24:707.

Henry Knox to Tobias Lear

War-Office [Philadelphia] Dec: 8. 1792
General Knox presents his compliments to Mr Lear, and begs the favor that he will submit to the President of the United States, the enclosed letters just received from the Governor of Georgia and Major Gaither.[1]

L, DLC:GW; LB, DLC:GW.

1. The enclosed letter from Georgia governor Edward Telfair was one that he wrote to Knox from Augusta on 20 Nov. 1792. "With respect to some late outrages committed on the Cherokees," Telfair wrote, "I have to transmit the following certified documents, viz: 1st. A Proclamation. 2d. A Talk to the head-

men and warriors of the Cherokee nation. 3d. The Executive order of the 15th instant, to the Law Department. 4th. A communication to Major Gaither.

"From all which, it will evidently appear, that there can be no doubt of the mal-conduct of certain citizens of this State, who have murdered some friendly Indians, and committed other depredations.

"You will perceive that the necessary steps have been taken, to bring to justice those offenders, as well as to preserve a continuation of amity.

"I have to remark, that, from the very short crops of grain last season, no period has ever been more unfavorable for war than the present; and this, among other considerations, ought to be of great weight to preserve peace with the neighboring tribes. Should my endeavors prove unsuccessful on the score of peace, it will be necessary to be prepared; and for this purpose I have to call for the establishment of magazines of provisions, without which, it will not be possible to keep that number of militia in the field, which will be necessary to give confidence to the frontier settlers to keep their ground, should even war be avoided.

"From what I can learn, this violence on the part of the offenders has proceeded from the circumstances of four whites having been killed, horses stolen, and other depredations committed by the Cherokees; whatever palliating point of view this may be considered in, it cannot interfere to prevent the offenders from abiding the due execution of the laws." Telfair's letter and its four enclosures are in *ASP, Indian Affairs,* 1:333–34. Knox, following GW's orders, presented this letter and its enclosed documents to the Senate on 10 Dec. 1792 (ibid., 333; *Annals of Congress,* 2d Cong., 619). The letter from Henry Gaither, commanding officer of the federal troops in Georgia, has not been identified.

To Charles Carroll (of Carrollton)

Dear Sir,   Philadelphia Decr 9th 1792

In acknowledging the receipt of your letter of the 1st inst. and expressing my sincere wishes that your personal happiness may be promoted by the election you have made to continue in your State Legislature, I cannot but regret the loss of your services to the United States in your Senatorial Capacity. I am persuaded, however, that your endeavours to serve your Country will be no less exercised in the station which you have chosen to hold, than they have been heretofore in that which you have relinquished.[1]

It gives me pleasure to find that Mr Benj'n Harwood has accompanied his application for the appointment to the Loan Office with those respectable & strong recommendations which have been forwarded in his behalf—as I find a great relief in discharging this part of my duty (which is not the least embarrassing) when the opinions of respectable & worthy Characters unite in testifying to the merits, integrity & ability of the Candidate.[2]

Mrs Washington unites in best wishes for your health & happiness with Dear Sir Your most Obedt Sert.

Df, DNA: RG 59, Miscellaneous Letters; LB, DLC:GW.

1. Carroll served in the U.S. Senate from 1789 to 30 Nov. 1792 and in the Maryland senate from 1777 to 1800. For the Maryland law that forced Carroll to resign from his federal position, see Carroll to GW, 1 Dec., n.1.

2. For Benjamin Harwood's letter of application, for letters of recommendation in addition to Carroll's letter to GW of 1 Dec., and for GW's nomination of Harwood as Maryland's commissioner of loans, see Benjamin Harwood to GW, 3 Dec. 1792, and note 1.

To Thomas Sim Lee

Dr Sir,   Phila. Decr 9th 1792

I have to acknowledge the Receipt of your Excellency's letter of the 1st Inst. recommending Mr Benj'n Harwood to be Loan Officer for the U.S. in Maryland, and to express the satisfaction which I always feel in finding respectable & dignified Characters united in testifying to the merits & ability of those Candidates for office where I have not had an opportunity of being personally acquainted with their merits or pretensions.[1] I have the honor to be with great esteem Your Excellency's Most Obedt Set.

Df, DNA: RG 59, Miscellaneous Letters; LB, DLC:GW.

1. For background on Benjamin Harwood's appointment as the federal commissioner of loans for Maryland and for Maryland governor Lee's letter of recommendation, see Harwood to GW, 3 Dec. 1792, and note 1.

Letter not found: from Thomas Newton, Jr., 9 Dec. 1792. GW wrote Newton on 25 Dec., referring to "your Letter to me of the 9th instant."

To Anthony Whitting

Mr Whiting,   Philadelphia Decr 9th 1792

Your letter of the 28th of Novr, which ought to have been here the first day of this month, did not arrive until the 4th; that of the 5th came yesterday, at the usual time.[1]

I thought I had, in a former letter, desired that all the large

Cedars in the Lucern lot might be left standing; as they could, at any time, be thinned after I had seen them, free from other things. This is the footing I would have them remain on, at present; the young one's, as has been mentioned to you are to be taken up so soon as they can be removed with a large block of frozen Earth; and planted from the stile downwards, thick, so as to make a formidable hedge.[2] Let all the trees, large or small (unless very large indeed) that are taken out of either the lucern, or old clover lots, be grubbed up by the roots. It will, I am sensible, render this clearing more tedious; but it will be the means of saving much labour hereafter; besides giving a more agreeable appearance to the ground in the first instance. I will endeavor to procure seeds from the honey locust, & send you, but I question whether I shall get many, if any, as there are very few pods on the trees in the neighbourhood of this City, this year. I entirely approve, as I have mentioned to you in one or two letters lately, of establishing large Nurseries of every kind of plant that is fit for hedges; but then, I would do it (of the common plants) more for the purpose of repairing, than for raising hedges by transplanting the plants in the first instance, from these Nurseries.[3] For, as you know many thousands of the honey locust were transplanted from the Vineyard to the Ferry & French's, under the care of Mr Bloxham; whom, one would have thought, would have known how to manage them: but where are they now?[4] Indeed this question might be asked with respect to the Honey locust seeds which were planted there & elsewhere; and both be answered, justly perhaps, by saying that the ground was not properly prepared for either, nor the plants attended to after they were removed, or had come up from the Seeds. Indeed I am so anxious to get these hedges razed as soon as possible, that I would spare no expence of labour, or pains to facilitate the measure by trying both methods, with every thing you can devise as fit for it.

By the time this letter will have got to your hands, I expect 655 lbs. of Clover Seed at 1/5 pr lb., will be in Alexandria (from New York) for me, consigned to Mr Porter; to whom, if you should not do it to the Captn, the freight (not more I suppose than 8/ or 10/) must be paid. The Seed, as it is furnished by a person who is careful in the choice, I hope will prove good: the distribution of it, together with that which you have, I shall leave to yourself; but request, if harrowed at all, it may be done with nothing heavier than a light bush, as I am well persuaded that the thinness of my clover proceeds, as much as any thing, from the Seeds being buried too deep.[5]

Have you made any use of the Plough I sent from this place, & with three horses?[6] I hope both the old Clover lot, & the Brick yard lot will be well prepared for the Crops, & Seeds which are to be put into them. And if you could get some of the true Plaster of Paris or Gypsum, and sow the Lawns on both sides of the Mansion house, it would be of Service; as they begin to want dressing: about 5 or 6 bushels to the Acre is the usual allowance.[7] Put long litter against the Cellar Windows; Frank knows how, & should be made to do it, as well as other things; otherwise he will be ruined by idleness. And can Lucy find sufficient employment in the Kitchen? It was expected her leizure hours, of which I conceive she must have very many from Cooking would be employed in Knitting—of which both Peter & Sarah do too little. I expected Sinah was one of those who would have been sent to one of the Plantations: whether she remains at the Mansion house, or not, it is my desire that when Kitty is unable to attend the Dairy alone, that Anna may be the assistant.[8] The other, besides idling away half the day under that pretence, never failed, I am well convinced, to take a pretty ample toll of both Milk & butter.

I hope the Overseer you have got from Boggess[']s will answer your expectations, but I have no opinion of any recommendation from that person; and besides, a stayed, elderly man for such an important plantation as Dogue run would have been to be preferred to a young one, although the latter should be a married man. but I am sensible any one would be better than Jones, and that the Season was too far advanced to look for many to chuse from.[9] When do you expect the successor of Garner? If he does not come over before Christmas, he may not be able to do it before Spring, on account of Interruption by Ice.[10]

As soon as your Corn is all measured, and the Grain all threshed, give me an Acct of the *whole* Crop in one view; and what each field has produced of the several species; viz.—Corn, Wheat, Buckwheat, Oats, Potatoes, &ca—and as your apprehensions of a short Crop of Corn seems to be great, I beg that every possible œconomy may be attended to in the use of it; and to prevent waste & embezzlement; as the same Spirits which attack my Wheat, Hogs, & Sheep, will not spare the Corn, if means can be found to get at it; and this is often given by the Overseers entrusting the Keys of the Corn houses to those who want grain for their work horses, &ca—Do not bestow *too* much Corn on your fatting Hogs, unless it can be applied to no other use; I mean that which is soft, for it will not keep long without turning bitter, yellow, & becoming rotten: and if laid in bulk, will (I know from experience) be utterly ruined. For every purpose therefore to which soft Corn can be applied usefully, & œconomically, let it be & be the first consumed. I do not, by calling for this *general* return of *all* the Crops, mean that the individual ones, or parts of them, should go unreported as usual. My object is, that I may have the whole in one view, without resorting to the weekly ones.

I do not know what quantity of Wheat is yet to go to the Mill, but wish it may not fall short of your expectation of 5000 bushels in the whole, for market. It appears to me that the Miller must have been very inattentive to his duty, to have manufactured only 102 Barrls of flour besides 15 barls of midlings & 19 of Ship stuff out of 2387½ bushls of Wheat which has been delivered into the Mill.[11] I wish he may not have forgot what is usual for all Millers to do & what I am sure he must have done himself—and that is, to grind of Nights, as well as days when the water, & seasons will admit—a little time more & the frosts will stop the Mill—and in a little time after the frosts are over, the droughts will stop it, & my grain will remain unground. He has, it must be acknowledged, a fine time of it. Whether he works at night, or not, I hope particular charge will be given him respecting fire. The loss of the Mill, & its contents, would be too heavy for me to support; and I find the accident of fires is already begun. The loss sustained by which, & how it happened at the Hound Kennels ought to have been more particularly detailed than by the simple mention of it in the report, as if it was a thing of course.[12]

I did not expect that Buck Wheat could be had short of Loudoun. I wished to know whether it could be had from thence, & at what price, delivered in Alexandria; that I might be enabled to determine (if more than you have should be required) whether it would be best to buy there, or send it from here. For this reason it is, I have asked once or twice what you have made; as soon as the quantity is ascertained, let me know it—what ground you propose to sow with it & how much seed (more than you have) is wanting.

If it is the Hessian fly that has injured your Wheat, the insect will be found between the blade & the stem, at the lower joint. The Clumps, as marked by the Gardener are very well designed but if there had been *more* trees in them, they wd not have been the worse for it.

I presume Davis has painted the Windows & Cornice of the Green house & New Quarters white. I directed him so to do— Let me know what painting he has yet to do, & the quantity of paints on hand. What does the Gardeners wife in her report mean by Trowsers? She is not making them longer than common breeches I presume. This wd be a great consumptn of Cloth.[13]

If you will send me the size, & length of the well rope, I will endeavor to have a proper one made, & sent to you.[14]

You ask directions from me, respecting your conduct in the building of my poor Nephew, Major Geo: A. Washington's House. From every Acct we receive, his disorder is at a crisis, and must so (if that is not the case already) change for the better, or terminate in his speedy dissolution & as the latter is most likely to happen, I think you had better not (until further orders) procure any more scantling; especially such as must be cut to waste. It may be proper for Gunner to continue throwing up Brick earth; & for the Majors two men to be preparing plank for the floors; because these (especially the latter) cannot be lost. A very few weeks (before the end of the ensuing hollidays) will enable him or his friends to decide more accurately on the measures necessary to be pursued.[15] I am your well wisher & friend

Go: Washington

P.S. In the Reports, let the quantity of Super fine flour be distinguished from the fine, that the quantity of every kind may be known, & seen at one view.

ALS, DLC:GW.

1. For the schedule of postal deliveries from Alexandria, Va., see the postscript to GW's letter to Whitting of 2 December. Neither of Whitting's letters has been found.

2. See GW's instructions regarding the cedars in his letter to Whitting of 18 November.

3. In his letter to Whitting of 25 Nov., GW directed that part of the vineyard enclosure be used to raise plants "fit for hedging, or to repair hedges."

4. James Bloxham came from England in 1786 to serve as GW's farm manager, but four years later he returned to his native country.

5. At GW's request, Tobias Lear wrote the New York City merchant firm of

William Shotwell & Co. on 17 Nov. 1792 asking for the price of clover seed. In a reply dated 22 Nov., William Shotwell informed Lear that clover seed "may be purchased @ 1/6 ℔ lb. of a Superior quality—Inferior @ 1/3 & down to 1/—Are uncertain how long it will continue at this price the demand being considerable." Lear placed an order with Shotwell & Co. on 3 Dec.: "If there should be a Vessel to sail from Nw York to Alexandria by the middle of the present month—or at any time when she may probably reach that place before the river is closed, the President wishes you to put on board 600 wt of the *best* Clover seed, unless in your opinion that of the 2d or 3d quality would be better according to the prices. If you should ship the above Seed to Alexandria, let it be directed to Thomas Porter Esquire of that place, and your Accot be sent to me when it shall either be paid here, or the amount remitted to you, as you may wish. You will be so good as to let me know in the course of the present week, whether there is a prospect of sending the Seed from Nw York to Alexa. or not; for if there should not be a prospect of it's being sent from Nw York, we must procure it here & send it on, as a part of it will be wanted to sow on the snow early in the Spring, probably before the river opens to admit of it's being sent then." Shotwell informed Lear on 5 Dec. that "there is a Brig sails tomorrow for Alexandria & having purchased 600 wt good red Clover seed, propose shipping it by her." The next day Shotwell wrote Lear that the seed was being sent on the *Peggy* under Captain Starbuck, but that the "Casks happening to hold just 655 lb. We thought best to have them filled tho' it is a small deviation fro⟨m⟩ the quantity desired." On 10 Dec., Lear sent William Shotwell & Co. "four thirty dollar bills of the Bank of the United States, and one quarter of a dollar in silver—amounting to £48.2.0.," receipt of which Shotwell acknowledged on 12 Dec. (all the Lear-Shotwell correspondence is in DLC:GW). For Whitting's estimate of the amount of clover seed required, see Whitting to GW, 31 Oct., n.5.

6. For the Dutch plow that GW had sent from Philadelphia to Mount Vernon in May, see Enoch Edwards to GW, 1 May, and note 1. An entry in Cash Memorandum Book H recorded payments of 1s. 6d. on 15 May for "drayage of a plough to the river" and £3.15.10 on 12 June "for a plough for the Presidt sent to Mt Vernon."

7. See GW's letter to Whitting of 16 Dec. in which he wrote that he was sending plaster of Paris from Philadelphia.

8. For earlier mentions of the work assignments for these slaves, see GW to Whitting, 14 Oct., and note 17, and 28 Oct., and note 3.

9. Henry McCoy (McKay) replaced Henry Jones as the overseer of the Dogue Run farm. McCoy's agreement with Whitting, signed on 17 Dec. 1792, indicates that he was to be employed from 1 Jan. 1793 to 1 Jan. 1794 for an annual salary of £30 Virginia currency, 300 lbs. of pork, 200 lbs. of beef, 5 barrels of corn, 150 lbs. of middling flour, a milch cow, and permission to keep fowls for his own use (DLC:GW). Robert Boggess's letter of recommendation of 27 Nov. 1792, which probably was addressed to Whitting, is filed with McCoy's employment contract. Although Boggess wrote that McCoy was "very Capeble" and "very Industorous," GW complained often about McCoy's lack of energy and failure to obey instructions (see GW to McCoy, 23 Dec. 1793, and to William Pearce, 10 May 1795, AL, ViMtV).

10. William Garner was hired as an overseer at the River farm in December 1788 (see Agreement with William Garner, 10 Dec. 1788). For some reasons why GW dismissed Garner, see GW to Whitting, 13 Jan. 1793. William Stuart became the next overseer of the River farm.

11. Middling flour was a coarse, middle-grade flour, containing some bran. Ship stuff was the lowest-quality flour, containing much bran.

12. The kennels apparently were located a short distance south of the mansion, near the river (see GW to Whitting, 6 Jan. 1793). The report that mentioned the fire has not been found.

13. Catherine Ehlers's report has not been found. Trousers were ankle-length, while breeches came only to the bottom of the knee.

14. The rope was probably for the well mentioned in GW's letter to Whitting of 25 November.

15. In a letter to George Augustine Washington of 25 Oct. 1786, GW had informed his nephew that he was planning to leave in his will his land on Clifton's Neck, including the River farm, to George Augustine and his wife, Fanny, and GW encouraged the young couple to build a house on that property (see GW's Last Will and Testament, 9 July 1799, and note 30). Gunner, a laborer belonging to GW at the Mansion House farm, was described in 1799 as "Passed Labour" at 90 years of age. He was married to Judy, another of GW's slaves, at the River farm (see Washington's Slave List, June 1799). The major's two men were carpenters Gabriel and Reuben (see GW to Whitting, 3 Mar. 1793). After his nephew's death from tuberculosis in February 1793, GW, with Fanny's acquiescence, instructed Whitting to halt any further work on the house (see GW to Whitting, 24 Feb., 3 Mar. 1793).

Letter not found: from Lovell and Urquhart, 10 Dec. 1792. Tobias Lear wrote Lovell and Urquhart on 16 Dec., replying to "your Letter of the 10th inst: to the President of the United States."

From David Stuart

Dear Sir,   Hope-Park [Fairfax County, Va.] Decr 10th 1792

Your letter of the 30th of last month, which I ought to have recieved in Ge: town, I only got on Saturday on my return from thence in passing through Alexandria. It will therefore be impossible for me to comply with your request at present, in sending you a list of the lots which have been actually sold. But it shall be done at the next meeting.[1] If I was not setting off tomorrow for New-Kent [Va.], I would have gone to Ge: town for that express purpose. Your ideas respecting a Superintendant living on the spot coincide perfectly with those entertained by the Commissioners. From our conversation with Mr Blodget on this subject, we expected as soon as it was known how far it met with your approbation to have heard from him. It was at his request, we mentioned it to you, to give him an opportunity of explaining himself more fully to you, than his time would permit him to us, when at Ge: town. There were some accts at our late meeting, that he was expected down with his family to settle at Ge: town, and we attributed our not hearing from him to this determination. That he would be the most agreeable person to the Proprietors, there can be no doubt. From the little opportunities I have had of judging of him, he appears to me to be well fitted for the office, both in point of temper, and fertility of genius. Tho' he may not be so thorough an Architect as some others, he has certainly turned his attention much to that subject, and may I think be justly allowed to have a very pretty taste for it. And more perhaps is not so very necessary, if Mr Hallet is employed in the same line for the execution of the Capitol, in which Hoben is for the President's house; which I should suppose very proper— I believe he fully deserves the high opinion Mr Jefferson entertains of him—If this is done, I cannot but think that Mr Blodget will be found to possess the other qualities necessary for a Superintendant, in a higher degree than Major L'Enfant—For the Major, besides the objection to his temper, has no turn for œconomy, and no acquaintance with accounts, which are both indispensably necessary. Besides, he could not have the same influence with the Eastern people, which tho' it may be considered as an adventitious circumstance, is certainly very desirable.[2]

We are well apprized of Mr F: Ct[']s attempts: But from the light in which we are informed, he is considered by his Countrymen, have no doubt but he will be disappointed: particularly since Mr Templeman and his Companions from Boston, who became purchasers in the city, will join most heartily in counteracting his misrepresentations. It seems when the Gentlemen arrived at Ge: town, he gave them a most unfavourable account, both of the works carrying on in the City, and the Potowmac Canal. After viewing both places, they expressed the highest satisfaction; mentioning to Mr Blodget, what a different representation Ct had given them. Templeman has bought a house in Ge: town and means to be down early in the Spring with his Family.[3] Mr Hallet informs us, his plan will be ready by our next meeting, when we propose to send it up to you. From the judgement I could form of it, in it's unfinished state, I entertain very sanguine hopes that it will meet with approbation. You will have I expect by this time, a plan of Doctor Thornton's sent to you. Nothing further has been done towards the foundation of the President's house, than Laying the first corner stone. No Masons were to be got, 'till very lately. There are at present about fifteen at work on the Acquia stone, polishing and preparing it against the next Spring. These have come chiefly from the Northward. Mr Williamson tells us, that two or three drop in every week from thence. But I fear we shall not be able to get the number to be wished for, by the Spring.[4]

Excepting a fiew lots to our workmen, we have made no sales since the public one. At that time we had an offer from a Mr Ford of Philadelphia, to buy 500 at 30£. a piece. As many of these were to have been water lots, and in very eligible situations, we thought it much too low. This too was the opinion of Mr Blodget, with whom we communicated freely on the subject. It was besides I think, unaccompanied with any conditions to improve any part of them, in a short and reasonable time, which is certainly very important.[5]

We have not yet fixed on the time for another sale, but shall do it at the next meeting.[6] As a preparatory step towards it, we ordered our Secretary at the late meeting, to put an advertisement in the papers, calling on the Proprietors of lots in Carrolsburg & Hamburg to come in, & subscribe, otherwise, we should proceed according to law—It appears to me that the 20th of June will be the most convenient time, to fix on; the crops of all kinds being by that time fixed—In our late letter to Mr Jefferson, we informed him that we expected to be able at the next meeting, to send in our report respecting the outlines of the territory. Our authority for this, depends on verbal information from Mr Ellicot. We are much in the dark, as to every thing which concerns this department, which has been, and must be very expensive, as long as it continues—Tho' we entered into a resolution early in the Summer, that reports should be made to us monthly of the progress, we have never had but one and that very unsatisfactory, consisting of only about three lines. By his own acct, he is up by star light every morning. Allowing him to be so it is I think, to but little purpose. How to remedy it I know not. Perhaps, some hints from Mr Jefferson, whom he considers as a great Mathematician, and good judge of such kind of business, as he is engaged in, might be of use.[7]

We had information at our late meeting, from Messrs [Benjamin] Stoddert & Threlkeld, members of the Assembly at Annapolis, that a motion had been made, in the House that Maryland should withhold her future payments on her donation; 'till Virginia should pay up hers; taking it for granted, that Virginia had been applied to, and refused—It is probable I think, that Mr Corbin's idle talk gave rise to this belief—But idle and extraordinary as it was, it only failed by 13.

We are likely to have a dispute with the Proprietors, respecting those squares which tho' not appropriated to any particular purposes, are nearly cut up by the intersection of different streets. They contend that the streets terminate at the commencement of the squares. We think, that as the streets run in different directions through the squares, still bearing their respective names, they must be fairly comprehended, in the exception they have made in their deeds, of recieving no consideration for streets. Mr Burns has allready given us information, that he will sue us, for his land in that situation—I have proposed, that if upon more mature consideration, it still continued to be our opinion that they were not entitled to be paid for such ground, as not being an appropriation, to leave it to reference. I have reason to believe, they will all be satisfyed with this, except Burns, who is a weak and troublesome man. By an inspection of the squares thus situated in the plan, I expect you will readily comprehend the nature of the dispute, tho' I may have failed in explaining my meaning.

Thus Sir, you see, we have upon the whole, a most vexatious time of it, and have full as much cause to pray for a Superintendant, as any of the Proprietors. I am with the greatest respect Your Affecte Serv:

Dd Stuart.

ALS, DLC:GW.

1. Stuart received GW's letter on Saturday, 8 December. The commissioners for the federal district next met in Georgetown between 1 and 8 Jan. 1793. For an account of those meetings, see DNA: RG 42, Records of the Commissioners for the District of Columbia, Proceedings, 1791–1802. Stuart enclosed a list of lots sold in his letter to GW of 7 Jan. 1793.

2. The commissioners notified Samuel Blodget, Jr., of his appointment as the district superintendent in their letter to him of 5 Jan. 1793 (DNA: RG 42, Records of the Commissioners for the District of Columbia, Letters Sent, 1791–1802). For the employment of Stephen Hallet and James Hoban to supervise, respectively, the construction of the Capitol and the President's House, see GW to Stuart, 30 Nov., notes 7 and 9. For background on Pierre L'Enfant's dis-

missal in February 1792 as surveyor general and supervisor of the construction in the federal distict, see L'Enfant to GW, 21 Nov. 1791, editorial note, and GW to L'Enfant, 28 Feb. 1792.

3. For earlier concerns about the activities of Francis Cabot, see GW to Stuart, 8 Mar., 30 Nov. 1792. The commissioners wrote Thomas Jefferson on 5 Nov. that since the public sale of lots in the Federal City in October, "we have sold by private bargains fifteen lots at one Hundred pounds each." They enclosed a list of those fifteen lots and the names of the purchasers, whom they described as "Men of large property and from the Eastward." Besides Samuel Blodget, Jr., the listed buyers were John Templeman, Nathan Bond, Mr. Kellond, Peter Gilman, Thomas Mitcalf (Metcalf), and Benjamin Blodget. Most of those lots were in the vicinity of the site designated for the President's House. John Templeman, who became a prosperous shipping merchant in Georgetown and a leading investor and proponent of development in the federal district, served as a director of the Potomac Company, and in 1793 he and Samuel Blodget, Jr., were among the founders of the Bank of Columbia, the second bank established in the district. In 1800 Templeman built a house on lot 8 of square 253, one of the lots purchased in 1792, slightly east of the President's House, at present-day 1333 F Street, N.W. This house was home to James Madison during his service as secretary of state in the Jefferson administration. See *Columbia Historical Society Records*, 8:10–11, 10:100, 15:179, 184; Harris, *William Thornton*, 538, 560; *Madison Papers, Secretary of State Series*, 2:44–46, 3:341–42.

4. Although Hallet by this time had submitted several designs for the proposed Capitol, neither GW nor the commissioners were satisfied with his plans. Despite Hallet's continued efforts to produce a suitable design, the commissioners and GW eventually decided upon a plan submitted by William Thornton, an amateur architect residing in Philadelphia.

The cornerstone of the President's House was laid on 13 Oct. 1792 (see 13 Oct. 1792, DNA: RG 42, Records of the Commissioners for the District of Columbia, Proceedings, 1791–1802). On 29 Aug. 1792 the commissioners signed an agreement with Collen Williamson (1727–1802), a Scots mason and builder, to "superintend the Stone cutting . . . the laying the same Stone" and to assist in "hiring stone-cutters and adjusting their accounts, and in general in promoting and conducting the work" (see 30 Aug. 1792, DNA: RG 42, Records of the Commissioners for the District of Columbia, Proceedings, 1791–1802). The sandstone was mined at quarries on Aquia Creek, about thirty-five miles down the Potomac River from the federal district (see D.C. Commissioners to GW, 21 Dec. 1791, and notes 1 to 3).

5. For previous discussion of Standish Ford's offer, see D.C. Commissioners to GW, 13 Oct., and note 4.

6. The commissioners set 17 Sept. 1793 for the next public auction of lots (see 7 Jan. 1793, DNA: RG 42, Records of the Commissioners for the District of Columbia, Proceedings, 1791–1802).

7. The secretary for the commissioners was Georgetown attorney John Mackall Gantt (1762–1811), who also served at this time as clerk for recording land deeds in the district. Gantt and Thomas Beall of George (1735–1819) were trustees of the Maryland lands conveyed from the original proprietors to the United States in 1791 (see Agreement of the Proprietors of the

Federal District, 30 Mar. 1791). The proposed advertisement, as approved by the commissioners at their 5 Dec. 1792 meeting, reads: "Constant attendance will be given by the Commissioners of the Federal buildings or by a person properly authorized by them at their office in George Town from the first day of April to the first day of May next to execute assignments and allotments of lands in the City of Washington—The proprietors thereof whose lands have been conveyed in Trust or subjected by the 'act concerning the Territory of Columbia and the City of Washington' to the Terms and conditions of the Deeds in Trust are requested to attend that allotments may be made by agreement for the Commissioners after that time will proceed to make allotments agreeably to the directions of the above recited act of Assembly—The other proprietors are hereby informed that process will issue under the said Act after the first day of May next to have their lands valued if the same shall not be conveyed on the usual Terms before that time—For the convenience of such proprietors, deeds will be left at Annapolis with Mr Thomas Buchanan, at Baltimore with Mr Archibald Robinson, at Upper Marlbro with Mr David Craufurd and at George Town with Jn M. Gantt Clk to the Comrs" (DNA: RG 42, Records of the Commissioners for the District of Columbia, Proceedings, 1791–1802). The Maryland legislation to which this advertisement alluded was the act of 19 Dec. 1791 in which the Maryland assembly established an office for the recording of deeds within the district and authorized the commissioners to appoint a clerk in charge of that office.

For the commissioners' letter to Thomas Jefferson of 5 Dec. 1792, see *Jefferson Papers*, 24:699–700. Although the commissioners were dissatisfied with Andrew Ellicott, he finally produced the long-awaited survey of the federal district for the commissioners to review at their 1 Jan. 1793 meeting (DNA: RG 42, Records of the Commissioners for the District of Columbia, Proceedings, 1791–1802).

From Rodolph Vall-travers

Amsterdam, December 10th 1792.

May it please Your Excellency!

The gracious Answer officially transmitted to me, in your Name, by your worthy Secretary of State, Thos Jefferson Esqe, in Reply to my Several Addresses to Your Excellency, kindly countenancing my sincere old Zeal & Attachment to the Welfare of your prosperous Commonwealth, emboldens me to extend my best Exertions, under your approbation, not only to Objects of Arts and Sciences, (: as in Duty bound by my very honorable Election into the laudable philosophical Society for promoting useful Knowledge, established in Philadelphia, by my immortal Friend, Dr Bn Franklin; :) but likewise to those of a political Nature; especially relative to Industry, Commerce, public Economy & Finances.[1]

A gradual Introduction of useful Hands to agriculture & manufactures of its Products into Articles of primary Importance, requiring, perhaps more adequate means, than may be within the Reach of patriotic Individuals & Societies, tho' ever so well intentioned, & liberal in their Encouragements, will be considerably accelerated, and the Fruits thereof more abundantly reaped, even by the present Generation, when countenanced and well assisted by national Power.

The present general Ferment, towards assisting the just natural Rights of Men, in final Opposition to endless Usurpations of selfish Despotism, prevailing all over Europe, threatened with many a bloody struggle, affords now to your pacific Republics the happiest Opportunity for offering a Safe Asylum to all the Europeans endowed with useful Talents, but vexed in their Liberties, Properties, and even their Persons, and for acquiring, by proper Encouragements, very valuable Additions to your Population, Industry, Strength and Prosperity.

When stationed at Bruxelles, the Capital of ten austrian Provinces, now rescued by the Arms of France, and likewise restored to their Option of Liberty and Independence;[2] a central Situation between Holland, France, Gr. Britain, and Germany; and when graciously authorised thereto, as Agent, Consul, or Resident of your united States, by Your Excellency's appointment in some public Character:[3] it will then be in my Power, to persuade & to engage whatever Description of Subjects may be wanted, for establishing, enlarging, and improving any Sort of Trade or Manufacture particularly wished for. The inclosed Letter, with Proposals and Paterns in the Hemp Branch of Business, adressed to your honble Society for promoting & establishing all Sorts of useful Arts and Manufactures, all over your united States, may serve as a Specimen of the Objects in View.[4]

As to a sufficient Fund for executing the various public spirited Plans in agitation, prompted by your worthy Patriots; (: Such, as high Roads, Bridges, navigable Canals of Communication, deepening Rivers, removing their Obstructions, draining Marshes, erecting public Buildings, raising all Sorts of Minerals, forwarding the Capital Residence of the U.S. in Congress, providing Arsenals, Dock-Yards, a Navy, and other Necessaries for your De-

fence and Protection; As likewise public Libraries, Schools of polite arts; Premiums for a Variety of proper Encouragements; and
for discharging the Remainder of the Debt contracted in 1784.
in Circumstances of the most urgent Necessity, & consequent
great Disadvantage :), Shou'd the two Loans since obtained, on
more reasonable Terms, by Mess[r]s Staphorst, Hubbard, and
Willink, prove short of those main Purposes:[5] Mess[r]s Beerenbroek & Van Dooren, a capital-House of this City, of known
Honor & Activity engage to raise immediately, for the Use of the
united States, in Bonds of no less than one hundred Dollars, or
two hundred Florins, Dutch Currency, up to the Summ of Ten
Millions, if required and duely authorised; at 2.½ . per Cent half
yearly Interest, or five per Cent per Annum. The last Sums raised
at 4. pr Ct are already 2. pr Ct under Pair, and require a somewhat better Intt, Considering the enormous Terms extorted by
Necessity & granted for the first borrowed Million of Dollars,
8. Years ago; to the no small Detrimt of their public Credit, in
Europe; which may still have some Influence, & impede larger
Loans, less profitable to the Subscribers. A sinking Fund of 3. pr
Ct annually, added to the annual Interest of 5. pr Ct would ex-
tinguish, both Capital & Intt in the Space of 22. or 24. Years; by
a very evident Plan, to be laid fortwith before Your Excellcy for
the Perusal of Congress, and of the U.S. as soon, as ordered.

The Circumstances of Time, (: England preparing for War,
and Holland being now at the Mercy of France :)[6] bid fair to facilitate Such an Operation, by the gradual Rise of Credit gained
by your just and wise Government, far superior to any, as yet, in
Europe. So favorable a Juncture, to be seized by the Forelock,
urges the speediest Measures.

Whatever Commands, relative to these Objects, Congress may
be pleased to impart, shall most faithfully and punctually be
obeyed, by the abovementioned reputable House, either Separately, or jointly with Mess[r]s Staphorst, hubbard, and W. Will-
ingk your Agents.

No Words can express the high Veneration I bear to Your Excellency's exalted Merits.

Rodolph Vall-travers

Directed to the Care of Mess[r]s Beerenbroek & Van Dooren; At
Amsterdam.

ALS, DLC:GW; ALS (duplicate copy), DLC:GW; ALS (third copy), DLC:GW. The cover of the first ALS indicates that it was sent "By the Sally, Fregate, Captn Thos Kennedy Commander." The duplicate copy contains minor differences in wording. The third copy, which is dated 29 Dec. 1792, includes an additional introductory paragraph and minor differences in composition.

1. For Vall-travers's earlier letters to GW and for Jefferson's reply to him on behalf of the president, see Vall-travers to GW, 12 Nov., and note 1. Vall-travers had been elected to membership in the American Philosophical Society on 20 Jan. 1792.

2. The French army's victory at Jemappes on 6 Nov. was followed a short time later by the French capture of Brussels, and by the end of 1792 Belgium, or the Austrian Netherlands, was under French control.

3. GW did not appoint Vall-travers to any position.

4. The enclosed letter has not been identified, but it may have been addressed to the New York Society for the Promotion of Agriculture, Arts, and Manufactures, founded in 1791.

5. For a description of the Dutch loans of 1791 and 1792, see, respectively, Ratification of the Holland Loan of 1 Sept. 1791 and notes and GW's Ratification Statement of 5 Nov. 1792 and notes.

6. On 1 Feb. 1793 France declared war on the Netherlands and Great Britain.

Tobias Lear to Thomas Jefferson

[Philadelphia] Decr 11th 1792

By the President's Command T. Lear has the honor to transmit to the Secretary of State the Draft of a Proclamation, which the President requests may be prepared for his signature.[1] The President likewise wishes the Secretary's opinion whether this Proclamation should be published in the papers here, or whether it would be proper to send it to Georgia only for publication.[2]

AL, DLC: Jefferson Papers. Jefferson's docket reads: "Lear Tobias recd Dec. 11. 92."

1. See GW's Proclamation on Recent Crimes against the Cherokees issued on 12 Dec. 1792. The enclosed draft has not been identified.

2. The proclamation was published in the *National Gazette* (Philadelphia) on 15 Dec. 1792.

Tobias Lear to Henry Knox

United States [Philadelphia] Decr 11th 1792

By the President's command T. Lear has the honor to return to the Secretary of War the Speeches to the Chiefs of the Six Nations and to the hostile Indians which have been submitted to the President, and to inform the Secretary that their contents embrace the President's ideas on that subject.[1] The President observes that the Secretary will write to General Wayne respecting Corn Planter, and to Genl Chapin respecting Red Jacket as he intended.[2]

Tobias Lear.
Secretary to the president of the United States

ALS (letterpress copy), DLC:GW; LB, DLC:GW.

1. The enclosed speech to the chiefs of the Six Nations has not been identified. In his speech of 12 Dec. 1792 "To the Sachems, Chiefs & Warriors of the Wyandots, Delawares, Ottawas, Chippewas, Pottawatamies, Shawanese, and Miamis and the Head men of all the other Tribes in alliance with them," Knox acknowledged receipt of their messages suggesting a conference with U.S. commissioners the following spring. "The President of the United States, embraces your proposal," Knox wrote, "and he will send Commissioners, to meet you at the time and place appointed, with the sincere desire of removing all causes of difference, so that we may be always hereafter good Friends and Brothers." The United States would send "a full supply of Provisions" for use during the treaty. "We shall prevent any of our Parties, going into the Indian Country, so that you may with your Women & Children, rest in full Security; and we desire, and shall expect, that you call in all your Warriors, and prevent their going out again. It will be in vain to expect peace, while they continue their depredations on the frontiers" ("Canadian Archives. Colonial Office Records: Michigan," 518–19).

2. Knox's letter to Anthony Wayne of 15 Dec. expressed the hope that the Seneca chief Cornplanter had complied with Wayne's invitation to visit him. "If any thing should prevent his coming to you," Knox wrote, "I pray you to send him an invitation afresh, and urge him to come to this place." Cornplanter was needed, Knox said, to help explain "facts contained in the communications of the six Nations" that Knox recently had received. "Persuade him to come here as soon as possible—as an inducement you may hold forth to him reasonable rewards" (Knopf, *Wayne*, 151).

Knox wrote Israel Chapin, Sr., on 12 Dec.: "Your Son will have explained to you the conference which he had with the Senecas and others of the six Nations at Buffaloe Creek in November, and informed you of the purport of messages received from the hostile Indians through the Six Nations. And you will observe how the said Speeches have been received and treated by the messages, to the said hostile Indians, and the six Nations, which are in charge of Mr Jasper Parrish.

"It is now important that the message to the hostile Indians should be forwarded by some trusty Senekas as soon as possible. You will therefore repair to Buffaloe Creek and urge the departure of the Messengers and Speeches.

"It is also necessary that Red Jacket and one other of the Chiefs should repair to this City as soon as may be. It is understood that it was his desire to come personally with the message from the hostile Indians, but that your Son waved the measure on account of the expence. Although economy in general be essential to be observed, yet it was never less proper than in the case alluded to, as additional information to the speeches forwarded is indispensible.

"In order that there shall be no embarassments to the measures herein directed for want of means, I have issued my warrant in your favour for five hundred dollars for which you will be held accountable and which will be delivered to you by the said Jasper Parrish" (NHi: Henry O'Reilly Collection). Despite Knox's invitation Red Jacket did not visit Philadelphia that winter. Instead six other Seneca chiefs, identified by Knox in his letter to Anthony Wayne of 26 Jan. 1793 as "the farmers Brother, the Young King, the Infant, the Shining Breast plate, and two inferiors," arrived in Philadelphia on 20 Jan. 1793 (Knopf, *Wayne*, 178; *JPP*, 31).

For the speeches from the Six Nations and the hostile Indians of the Northwest Territory, see Knox to GW, 6 Dec. 1792, and note 2.

To John Singleton Copley

Sir,   Philadelphia Decr 12th 1792.

Through the hands of the Vice-President of the United States —Mr Adams—I received a few days ago your acceptable present of the Print, representing the death of the Earl of Chatham. This work, highly valuable in itself, is rendered more estimable in my eye, when I remember that America gave birth to the celebrated artist who produced it.[1] For the honor you have done me in this mark of your attention, I pray you to accept my best thanks, and the assurances of my being, Sir, Your most Obedient and obliged Hble Servant

Go: Washington

ALS, Trinity College Library, Cambridge: Lyndhurst Papers; ADf, DNA: RG 59, Miscellaneous Letters; LB, DLC:GW.

1. When he left Massachusetts for London in June 1774, Boston native John Singleton Copley (1738–1815) was a well-established portraitist, recognized for his superior talent both at home and in England. From Great Britain he traveled first to Paris and then to Italy where he studied and painted for several months. By the time Copley returned to London in the fall of 1775, his wife and children had left besieged Boston with other Loyalist refugees and had settled in London, where Copley established his studio, remaining in England for the rest of his life.

Copley's residence in England paralleled a new facet in his artistic career as he devoted more attention to historical events as the subjects of his paintings. Copley finished *The Death of the Earl of Chatham* in 1781, and ten years later Francesco Bartolozzi completed his engraving of it. On 10 April 1792 Copley sent two prints from the engraving to John Adams, one for Adams and the other for GW, which Adams delivered after his return to Philadelphia in November (see John Adams to Copley, 16 Nov., in MB). The print was in a "large gilt frame" at Mount Vernon at the time of GW's death (see Prussing, *Estate of George Washington*, 412).

Letter not found: from Thomas Jefferson, 12 Dec. 1792. An ALS, sold by Anderson Galleries, Howard K. Sanderson Sale, lot 471, 1–3 May 1916. According to the catalog entry, this letter asks GW to call at Jefferson's house, when riding out, to see Samuel Mulliken's model of a machine for sawing stone.[1]

1. The commissioners for the federal district had brought Samuel Mulliken and his saw for cutting stone to Jefferson's attention in their letter to him of 5 Dec. (see *Jefferson Papers*, 24:699–700). GW apparently responded positively to Jefferson's invitation because Jefferson's short note written to GW later on 12 Dec. reads: "Th: Jefferson presents his respectful compliments to the President & will take care to be at home tomorrow morning at 10. aclock" (DLC: GW). For GW's visit the next day to view Mulliken's invention, see Jefferson's notes on his conversation of 13 Dec. with GW.

From Warner Mifflin

Kent [County, Del.]

Respected Friend,   the 12th Day of 12 mo. 1792

I trust it will not be accepted by thee as flattery, when I mention what may in some respect appear like a repetition tho with some addition to what I communicated to thee both Verbally and in writeing heretofore; when I say from my heart, That I have real sincear respect for thy person and station.[1]

And that on serious reflection in my mind this day, I tryed the subject fully and found clearly I could in truth from the Heart say, I know of no man in the world, that I could wish to be put in thy place, And if it lay to me entirely to Elect a president, and I took such a matter on me thou art the Man I should Elect.

This revived many feelings, I have at diferent times had respecting thee, and such freedom would arise that I thought if I knew thee to do wrong and I found it my duty I could tell thee of it as soon as any other man, & this felt pleasant to me—Now I will just Venture to hint to thee what revived in my mind on my way from the City I thought of ahabs expression to Jehoshuphat when 400 Prophets had prophecied, King Jehoshuphat asked if there was no other prophet of the Lord they might enquire of Ahab answer'd there is Micajah but I hate him for he doth not prophecy good concerning me but evil.[2]

I wished no disposition like this might ever get possession of the Presidents mind against me nor my friends For our plainess of expression at any time, I thought it felt that evening we were with him as if he was a little hurt by somthing; I concluded it might be in part oweing to some anonimous publications respecting the Indian war that he might think our address to the general goverment might rather strengthen;[3] and which I did endeavoure to do away in some measure then, I was at that time much hurt on account of our Not accompanying that address to thee, it was my mind At first we should, that would have given thee an oppertunity of opening thy mind to us, and our giving thee our reasons, divers of our Committee were sorry after, and I hope thou wilt accept it that we did not intend any blame on thee or reflection on thy Conduct, But I was much pleased with the freedom thou used with us, it gave me much satisfaction, and I believe has been of use to many since my return home, as it gave an oppertunity for me to satisfy divers respecting the intentions of goverment, who had mistaken Idies on this subject of the war, and the intentions of Goverment relative thereto—For altho I am fully satisfy'd the Natives have been greviously imposed on, and unjustly dealt by—Yet it affords great satisfaction to find our rulers so generally disposed to favour them—and I have all along had much expectation from thee in this business relying on thy certain Knowledge off them, and disposition toward them—which induces me to hope somthing permanent may be fixed on; can thou but devise means to keep in order the Lawless whites.

I hope thou will not view our proceedings as improper medling, I believe it proceeded from a real religious concern, and to manifest we were willing to do what we could consistant with our principles for the aid of our Country, and the promotion of peace and good will towards all men—And wherein I have no doubt this Country will find some day we are right let southern blasts storm as they may and insinuate what they will respecting the Affricans, I remain of the very same sentiment made known to thee hereto-fore.[4]

And therefore have again to request which I think but a reasonable one that if our proceedings in a society or Individual Capacity at any time give thee uneasiness that thou wilt be so kind as to communicate the same to us, that thou may understand fully the ground we move on, for I may tell thee truly as far as I know and that is pretty generally the Sentiments of our members are favourable toward thee, and that I consider it an Offence against our dicipline if any of our members should be guilty of publishing under Anonimous signatures tending to the prejudice of rulers, I believe it unbecoming the Christian— "Thou shalt not speak evil of the ruler of thy people" Acts 23:3.[5]

And yet I can say I wish with all my heart that thou wert not a slave holder this does hurt the feelings of some of thy best friends, even such as are so, without any desire for either post Or pension from goverment—This is certainly somthing of a spech.

However my craveings for thee are that the Almighty may be mercifully pleased to afford thee such a portion of his divine Grace as may enable thee to go in and out before this so great People, and Hear them amidst the adverse winds in such manner as may be pleasing to him who rules in the army of Heaven, and amongst the Nations of the Earth who can turn and overturn Kingdoms and empires at his pleasure, set up and put down whom he will—May the a[s]piration of thy soul be to him, day and Night, That thou may be thereby continu'd a bles⟨si⟩ng in his holy hand to this Nation to the latest period ⟨of⟩ thy life and at the final close with thee on this se⟨a of⟩ glass,[6] thou might be fitted and prepared for a Cro⟨wn⟩ immortal in that State of existance that I believe unchangable and Eternal, in the Mansions of rest & peace, with the spirrits of Just men made perfect ⟨is⟩ the Unfeigned desire for thee, of thy sincear Friend

Warner Mifflin

Kent 10th of 12 mo. 1793[7]

P:S. since I wrote the Above I have been in Philadelphia and passing the street met an Acquaintance, who stopt me and qu⟨e⟩ried about the debates in Congress respecting my address respecting the Affricans[8]—Ah said he you deserve no better, you were very fond of addressing the President, and shew'd so much being wrapt up in the President and goverment that you deserved no better, This was a person who had a right of membership, at the time we prepared an Address to thee or just before, but he was one of the regimental kind of Quakers—finding his disposition I said little to him—and I now mention this to thee, that if any such information comes to thee through another chanel thou may understand he is none of us, he may say as much before some who may take him to be a Quaker.[9]

ALS, DNA: RG 59, Miscellaneous Letters.

1. For Mifflin's previous letter to GW, see Mifflin to GW, 23 Nov. 1792.

2. For Mifflin's biblical reference, see 1 Kings 22:6–8.

3. See the Quakers' petition to GW of 17 Nov. 1792, which Mifflin and fifty-two other Quakers from Pennsylvania, New Jersey, Delaware, Maryland, and Virginia had signed.

4. For Mifflin's views on the African slave trade and slavery in the United States, see his letter to GW of 23 November.

5. The correct citation for this biblical quotation is Acts 23:5.

6. Mifflin's use of "sea of glass" is probably a reference to the final judgment day and other events described in the New Testament book of Revelation (see Revelation 4:6 and 15:2).

7. Mifflin erred in dating the postscript. The docket of this letter reads: "From Warner Mifflin 12th Decr 1792 recd through the hands of Mr Bassett 13th Feby 1793." Richard Bassett (1745–1815), U.S. senator for Delaware, probably was the person who delivered Mifflin's letter to GW.

8. Mifflin's petition "on the subject of Negro slavery" was discussed in the House of Representatives on 28 Nov. 1792 (see *Annals of Congress*, 2d Cong., 730–31). Between 1783 and 1797 Mifflin, a noted abolitionist, helped write or present various petitions against slavery and the slave trade to Congress. He published in Philadelphia *A Serious Exposition with the Members of the House of Representatives of the United States* in 1793 and *The Defence of Warner Mifflin against Asperions Cast on Him on Account of His Endeavors to Promote Righteousness, Mercy, and Peace, among Mankind* in 1796.

9. At some point Mifflin decided to enclose a letter that he had written to GW on 20 Feb. 1791 but did not send at that time. The introductory paragraph to this enclosure, which probably was written on 20 Dec. 1792, reads: "some years back I wrote a letter to the present Arch-Bishop of Canterbury [John Moore] on the subject of the Affrican Slave Trade, since which, a friend of mine, on an interview with the Bishop, Queried, if he had any exceptions against the contents of said letter? The Bishop reply'd, 'We never take exceptions to things well meant.'

"In full confidence I am now addressing a personage of as generous principles, induces me to transcribe a letter, wrote at the time of the date thereof, which has been held back through difidence, and is as follows, To witt."

In his letter to GW of 20 Feb. 1791, Mifflin wrote: "I trust it is with all due respect to thy person and Station that I approach thy presence with this address, thereby opening a religious concern that has impressed my mind for some time, and has been lately revived by seeing thine to the two branches of the Legislature at the opening of the present sessions, feeling I believe real desires for thy Temporal tranquility, and eternal felicity in particular, and which concern is not confined there, but opens to the general welfare of mankind the world over; and therein have felt an engagement of heart that thy talents might be improved to a general good, in promoteing the Glory of God, Peace and good will amongst the inhabitants of the Earth. I sometimes have a hope from some sensations that have accompany'd my mind both sleeping and wa⟨k⟩ing respecting thee, that a measure of the favour of the Almighty was yet toward thee; and as I sat in a religious Meeting the other day labouring in the secret of my mind to perform that worship to Almighty God that might be acceptable to him, thou was presented to my View, and secret breathings of soul I believe I may say took place for thee, that thou might be animated with a disposition to do all in thy power that the Almighty might design thee as an instrument for, that thou might be sincerely given up to discharge the duty as in his sight, faithfully according to the measure of Light that he may be graciously pleased to illuminate thee with; that so thou might at least have this testamony given off thee that it was in thy heart to prepare Materials for forwarding the Lords in the Earth, as of David formerly respecting the building the Hou⟨se⟩ yet was not allow'd to build because as it was said 'Thou hast shed much blood in my sight' if this was an impediment under that dispensation, I think its as likely under the present to prevent ⟨such⟩ from being the most bright shining instruments in the Lords hands of spreading so generally, and establishing that peacable gov⟨er⟩ment, wherein Nation shall not dare to lift against Nation the d⟨e⟩vouring sword, Nither devise instrument of War, and shall be e⟨ver⟩ Asshamed of learning the Military art—When the people shall come to confide in the Holy fear of God Almighty; placeing their trust and confidence in him, respecting these outward tabernacles, dureing the little time he may be pleased to permit their residence in this World; without any desire for protection from those murderous weapons, as they most generally manifest a willingness to do, respecting the caretaking and disposition of the more Noble part that will endure to all Eternity, [(]more especially the military part) which if men were sufficiently concerned about would remove much of those fears about temporals.

"And as I firmly believe it is sacredly determined that the goverment of the Prince of Peace shall spread and prevail in the Earth, perhaps more generally in the present generation than in any former Age of the world—I should rejoice to see us as a Nation of people, taking the lead therein, believing the less a Martial spirit is encouraged by the Nation the more will the Protection and favour of Heaven be towards it; let other Nations do as they will I could wish that an apprehended Political expediency might Never sway the minds of our rulers to push into things of this Nature, Necessity may, or might never compel them to.

"Let it be remembred that if a mans ways please the Lord he maketh even his Enemies to be at Peace with him, and is it not reasonable to conclude, that if the ways of a Nation please him he will also make the enemies of that Nation dwell in concord with them—Have we not faith to believe, that he can keep it out of the heart of the enemies of ⟨*mutilated*⟩ a Nation even to desire to invade them; or if they should throug⟨h⟩ ⟨*mutilated*⟩stigation of the enemy of righteousness attempt so to do, cannot h⟨*mutilated*⟩ them without the breath of his mouth, Yea my faith is that he will yet ⟨*mutilated*⟩ these things—Therefore may we as individuals and as a Nation, be concerned that our ways please him, which will no doubt procure his favour and Protection; and in order thereto I firmly believe it does deeply concern us as individuals and as a Nation, to inspect our ways and Conduct toward the Natives of this Land, the Indians, and also the oppressed Affricans; should this be ommitted, it is in his power who hath all power in his hands, to Chastize us by those very people yet—Altho we may have at present so much the ascendency over them: and I much believe he will if we are not more careful—and then, can we but acknowledge that it is just—I was sorry when I heard there was an expid[it]ion on foot against the Indians, I felt sorrow of heart, but I hoped thou would not permit it but, from what to thee appeared Necessity; Yet, when I reflect who it is that brings thee information, the sorrow remains; I mean respecting their conduct—and it will not be surpriseing to me, if we should be sevearly chastized, in as much, that almost as barberous treatment is exercised in diferent parts by whites on Indians and Negroes, as any I have yet heard off by Indians toward whites; and all this done in the sight of him who is a *God of Justice:* have we not the most cogent reason to expect, that the measure we meet out to others shall and will indeed be Measureed to us: there is Undoubtedly a power that is able to do this, let us fortify our selves as we will, And I feel a concern solemnly to warn thee to do thy duty in those respects. remember that 'he who rules over men must be just ruleing in the fear of God,' and in the Judgment not be affraid of the Face of Man, for the Judgment is Gods. should the rule be other ways I believe he will yet do as he has done, pull the lofty from their seats.

"And in the Establishment of a Militia Law, there is especial need of care that no encroachment should be on the prerogative of the Almighty, especially in this day of so great favour in the extention of Civil and Religious Liberty—*Great Favour indeed.* Now let me beg thee to remember and I believe the Witness for God in thy Conference bears Witness thereto; that there are whom he hath enjoined to stand with a testamony against War in the very ground; and that not only at the risk of their Property, but also their lives; of which proof has been given; who dare not yield personal service, nor pay an equivalent in lieu thereof, let that be set as low as it may; and fines forfeitures, and Penalties on such consciencious persons is persecution in the full signification thereof; and which I do conceive will be a disgrace to America at this day and time, also an ⟨*mutilated*⟩ against the Majesty of Heaven, and such an One as he will not al⟨*mutilated*⟩ bare with; that his Servants cannot comply with his Royal ⟨*mutilated*⟩ and pleasure without incuring Penalties therefor from the governments of men—In this address as a real friend of thine I deal plainly with thee, and feeling a flow of Love toward thee, removes all fear of offending; believing thou art capable of discriminating between the friend and the flatterrer—I have indeed abundant Charity for thee considering how the Contrary interest Center in thee, and the tryall that must ensue.

"May God Almighty of his Manifold Grace and Mercy be pleased to Vouchsafe to thee such a portion of wisdom and Understanding as that thereby thou may be enabled so to conduct in his sight as to have his Royal Approbation, that thy Presidency and rule may be to his Honour the good and Welbeing of the People, and finally when the Undeniable messenger may be sent and no further respite of the summons allow'd that thou may be then admitted into the Ma⟨n⟩sions of Everlasting rest and unceasing Joy is the sincear desire & earnest prayer of Thy Friend" (DNA: RG 59, Miscellaneous Letters).

From William Vans Murray

Sir,   81 South 3d [Philadelphia] 12 Decr 1792.

As an Inspector of the Eastern Shore Survey of Maryland is, I am informed, speedily to take place[1] I beg leave as the only representative of that Shore now in Congress to place the names of Colonel William Richardson of Caroline county[2] & of Colonel John Eccleston of Dorchester county,[3] before you—Either of these gentlemen whether considered in point of weight of character⟨,⟩ merit of past services, centrality of situation or official qualifications would probably be found superior to most who could be brought to view. They are both much respected—men of firmness & very decided character—& who could in any situation to which their the official duties might be Placed act with a very deciding influence.[4] I have the honour to be Sir with great deference & respect Yr mo. obt sert

W. V. Murray.

ALS, DLC:GW.

William Vans Murray (1760–1803), an attorney and a loyal Federalist from Cambridge, in the Eastern Shore district of Maryland, served in the House of Representatives from 1791 to 1797, when GW appointed him U.S. minister to the Netherlands. Murray held that post until 1801. He also was a member of the diplomatic mission that negotiated the Convention of Mortfontaine of 3 Oct. 1800, which ended the Quasi-War with France.

1. GW issued a proclamation on 4 Aug. 1792 announcing modifications to the "arrangement of Offices and distribution of compensations" in the federal revenue service. One change was the increase of the surveys in Maryland from two to three, thus creating a new inspector of revenue position for a new third survey, which included all the counties on the Eastern Shore of the Chesapeake Bay.

2. William Richardson (1735–1825), a prominent merchant in Caroline County, Md., served in the lower house of the Maryland assembly until he accepted a colonel's commission in the 4th Maryland Brigade of the flying camp in 1776. He continued in active military service until October 1779, after which he held a number of state and local offices, including associate justice of the state's fourth district court, 1791–93. He had been a member of the state's ratifying convention in 1788.

3. John Eccleston of Dorchester County, Md., was a veteran of the Revolutionary War who had been commissioned a second lieutenant in Barrett's Independent Maryland Company in 1776 and subsequently served in the Continental army until the end of the war, rising to the rank of major. Tench Coxe described Eccleston in a letter to Alexander Hamilton of 14 Dec. 1792 as "a man of pure and extensive public Esteem, [who] lives in the distilling Country, and the centre of the Survey, [and who] has been recently sherriff of the County with great satisfaction to the bar, which evinces his punctuality and office talents. He has served in popular offices, but has had nothing lucrative in the executive line" (Syrett, *Hamilton Papers*, 13:322).

4. Former Maryland governor John Eager Howard and the current governor, Thomas Sim Lee, wrote letters of recommendation to GW for Talbot County planter William Perry, on 19 and 20 Dec., respectively. Howard described Perry as "a Gentleman well qualified to discharge the duties of Supervisor" (DLC: GW), while Lee wrote that Perry "is very much respected, both in his public & private Character" (DLC:GW). William Perry (1746–1799) represented the Eastern Shore district in the Maryland senate from 1781 until his death. James McHenry also had recommended Perry in a letter to Alexander Hamilton of 18 Nov. (Syrett, *Hamilton Papers*, 13:157).

GW already had decided to nominate William Richardson before Howard and Lee composed their letters. Hamilton wrote GW a brief note on 18 Dec. 1792, informing him that the title of the new appointment was "Inspector of the Revenue for Survey No. 3. of the District of Maryland" (DLC:GW), and GW sent Richardson's nomination to the U.S. Senate later on that date (LS, DNA: RG 46, Second Congress, 1791–93, Senate Records of Executive Proceedings, President's Messages—Executive Nominations; LB, DLC:GW). Following the Senate's approval on 19 Dec., Tobias Lear notified Thomas Jefferson of Richardson's appointment in a letter of that date (DLC:GW; see also *Executive Journal*, 127).

Proclamation on Recent Crimes against the Cherokees

[Philadelphia, 12 December 1792]
WHEREAS I have received authentic information, that certain lawless and wicked persons, of the western frontier, in the state of Georgia, did lately invade, burn and destroy, a town belonging to the Cherokee nation, altho' in amity with the United States, and put to death several Indians of that nation; and whereas such outrageous conduct, not only violates the rights of humanity, but also endangers the public peace; and it highly becomes the honor and good faith of the United States to pursue all legal means for the punishment of those atrocious offenders; I have therefore thought fit to issue this my proclamation, hereby ex-

horting all the citizens of the United States, and requiring all officers thereof, according to their respective stations, to use their utmost endeavours, to apprehend and bring those offenders to justice.[1] And I do moreover offer a reward of Five Hundred Dollars, for each and every of the above named persons,[2] who shall be so apprehended and brought to justice, and shall be proved to have assumed and exercised any command or authority among the perpetrators of the crimes aforesaid, at the time of committing the same.

In testimony whereof, I have caused the seal of the United States to be affixed to these presents, and signed the same with my hand. Done at the city of Philadelphia, the twelfth day of December, in the year of our Lord, one thousand, seven hundred and ninety-two, and of the Independence of the United States the seventeenth.

Go. Washington.

By the President,
Th. Jefferson.

National Gazette (Philadelphia), 15 Dec. 1792.

1. For background on this proclamation, see Henry Knox to Tobias Lear, 8 Dec. 1792, and note 1.

2. Tobias Lear, at GW's request, on 11 Dec. sent a draft of this proclamation to Thomas Jefferson for his comments. Tench Coxe wrote Jefferson on 14 Dec. to call his attention to an error in the wording of the document. Coxe pointed out that a $500 reward was "offered for 'the above *named* persons,' altho no persons have been previously mentioned by *Name*" (*Jefferson Papers*, 24:741–42).

Letter not found: from James Seagrove, 12 Dec. 1792. Seagrove wrote GW on 17 Mar. 1793: "When I had the honor of addressing you on the 12th of December from Savannah, I considred all matters between the United States, and the Creek people on a favourable footing."

Letter not found: from Anthony Whitting, 12 Dec. 1792. GW wrote Whitting on 16 Dec.: "Your letter of the 12th with its enclosures came duly to hand."

Thomas Jefferson's Conversation with Washington

[Philadelphia, 13 December 1792]

1792. Dec. 13. the President called on me to see the Model & drawings of some mills for sawing stone.[1] after shewing them he in the course of subsequent conversation asked me if there were

not some good manufactories of Porcelaine in Germany, that he
was in want of table china & had been speaking to mister Shaw
who was going to the East Indies to bring him a set, but he found
that it would not come till *he should be no longer in a situation to
want it.* he took occasion a second time to observe that Shaw said
it would be 2. years at least before he could have the china here,
before which time he should be where he should not need it.[2] I
think he asked the question about the manufactories in Germany merely to have an indirect opportunity of telling me he
meant to retire, and within the limits of two years.

AD, DLC: Jefferson Papers.

1. For background on GW's visit to view the mill for cutting stone that
Samuel Mulliken had designed, see Jefferson to GW, 12 Dec. (first letter), and
note 1. For a "Drawing of a Mill for Sawing and Polishing Stone," see *Jefferson
Papers,* 24:732.

2. Although GW apparently did not place an order for china with Samuel
Shaw, the U.S. consul at Canton, he did acquire a new "sett of China" from
Philadelphia merchant John Bringhurst, for which he paid $211 on 18 June
1793 (Presidential Household Accounts). For a description of the china acquired by GW during his residence in Philadelphia, see Detweiler, *George Washington's Chinaware,* 139–58.

Thomas Mifflin to Tobias Lear

Philadelphia, 13 Dec. 1792. Writes that he cannot dine with GW, "agreeably to Invitation," because he must remain "at Home this Afternoon
to receive a Committee of the Legislature of the State."

ALS, NNGL.

From James Madison

[Philadelphia] Decr 14. 92

Mr Madison presents his respectful compliments to the President, and informs him that Mr Johnson⟨,⟩ the candidate for the
light-house appointment, having left the City yesterday morning, it cannot now be ascertained how far he is apprised of the
limited provision annexed to the place.[1]

AL, DNA: RG 59, Miscellaneous Letters.

1. For background on John Waller Johnston's unsuccessful attempts to obtain an appointment as the lighthouse keeper at Cape Henry, Va., see Alexander Hamilton to GW, 22 Sept., n.6, and Thomas Jefferson to GW, 8 Dec. 1792,

and note 2. The salary for the Cape Henry lighthouse keeper was $266.66 in 1792 (see *ASP, Miscellaneous,* 1:68).

From Ezekiel Scott

[Philadelphia, 14 December 1792]

Proposition by Ezekiel Scott of Farmington Connecticut that for the purpose of obtaining and Commeunicating Intelligence from time to time to the Executive of the United States, of the temper & designs of the Indians and of the plans & measures of the British Connected with them, as they may respect the United *States* a seuitable person be stationed at Detroit a man in w[h]om the United States can place entier confidence in, and who at the Same time is well known to and respected by the British officers and Agents &C. and that to Conceal his real object, he assume the character of an Indian trader and take with him a proper assortment of goods, that he be a person who has heretofore acted in that capasity and formerly an Indian trader in Detroit, So as to have formed acquaintance & connections there & with the western Indians, it will better premote the design. that if found expedent, that he purchase a house lot thare, and in due time take his family with him. that he employ two Confidential persons as a Clark & Servant, by whom or by him-self, all important intelligance may be personally conveyed to Executive of the United States that these Stocks of goods be taken on his own accomst and from time to time the proceuring of goods and Supplies will furnish a reason for making jurnies to the United Stats or at least to Niagara from Whence the Communication would be easy to the Superintendant of Indian affairs at Canandarqua the amarican prisners that may be another object interesting to humanity and especially beneficeal to the United States, the preposer begs leve to add that he r[e]ceided in detroit as an Indian trader part of the time from 1767 to Septer 1774 and with the Indians west, and had oppertunity of contracting and Did Contract acquaintance & connections with both indians and white people, and if in ether respect he Shall be Judged a fit person to be employed in the preposed plan he would undertake it.[1]

AL, DNA: RG 59, Miscellaneous Letters. The docket reads in part: "Decr 14t 1792."

Connecticut native Ezekiel Scott (born c.1760) served as a captain in the 2d Connecticut Regiment under Col. Samuel Wyllys in 1775 and in Wyllys's 22d Continental Regiment during 1776. He continued under Wyllys's command, at least through 1780 when he was listed on the 24 Dec. 1780 payroll for the 7th Company of Wyllys's 3d Connecticut Regiment (see *Lists and Returns of Conn. Men,* 194). Scott was living in Wayne County, N.Y., in May 1830 when he applied for a military pension (see White, *Genealogical Abstracts,* 3:3044).

1. GW did not appoint Scott to any federal position despite the enclosed recommendations from Connecticut senators Roger Sherman and Oliver Ellsworth of 12 December. "I have not much personal Acquaintance with him," Sherman wrote from Philadelphia, "but have heard him Spoken of as a Gentleman of Integrity and a good Citizen." Ellsworth described Scott as being "reputed friendly to the interests of his Country" and "of an active & adventrous turn of mind, & from the course of his business of late years, has had occasion repeatedly to be at Niagara" (both enclosures are in DNA: RG 59, Miscellaneous Letters). For another opinion on Scott's qualifications and for Henry Knox's submission of this letter and the enclosed recommendations, see Knox to GW, 15 Dec. 1792.

Alexander Hamilton to Tobias Lear

Dr Sir,   [Philadelphia] 15th Decr 1792.

The Supervisor of Massachusetts is desirous of permission to come to Philadelphia on *urgent private business.* I believe the permission may be given him without injury to the service. Will you mention the matter to the President and inform me by a line whether permission may be notified to him or not.[1] Your's &ca

A: Hamilton

LB, DLC:GW.

1. Commissioner of the Revenue Tench Coxe wrote Nathaniel Gorham on 18 Dec. that the president was "disposed to permit your absence from the District . . . provided no injury is likely to arise to the public service" (DNA: RG 58, Letters Sent by the Commissioner of the Revenue and the Revenue Office, 1792–1807).

From Henry Knox

Sir   December 15th 1792[1]

I submit certain papers relative to a Capt. Scott. I have conversed with Colonel Wadsworth concerning him; the result of which is that Scotts discretion for the object proposed cannot be depended upon—As he however has mentioned that he had an audience of you I have thought it my duty to submit the papers.[2] I also submit Genl Waynes letter.[3] I am with perfect respect Your humble servant

H. Knox

ALS, DLC:GW; LB, DLC:GW; copy, NNGL: Knox Papers. Knox's retained copy is marked "Private."

1. Neither the dateline nor the address to "The President of the United States" on the cover of the receiver's copy is in Knox's writing.

2. See Ezekiel Scott to GW, 14 Dec. 1792, and notes. Jeremiah Wadsworth of Connecticut, who had been a commissary general during the Revolutionary War, served in the Continental Congress in 1788 and then in the U.S. House of Representatives from 1789 to 1795.

3. Knox received on this date Anthony Wayne's letter to him of 6 Dec. from Legionville, Pa., Wayne's newly established headquarters on the Ohio River twenty-two miles below Pittsburgh (see Knox to Wayne, 15 Dec., in Knopf, *Wayne*, 151–52). Wayne wrote: "The Patroles from Pittsburgh & big beaver to fort Franklin &c have been established more than three months since; as also from big beaver to Yellow and two Creeks on the N.W. side of the Ohio, covering all the frontiers of Ohio County in Virginia.

"But a patrole from this post or big beaver to Marietta, is rather out of the question. . . . I have put the spies or Guides of Ohio & Washington Counties under the Command of Capt. [Samuel] Brady, who frequently traverses the Country, from Yellow Creek towards the head waters of Muskingum & the settlement of Marietta: in addition to this, all the men belonging to Captain [John] Crawfords company of rifle men remain at Wheeling, about one hundred miles below this place on the south side of the river under & subject to the orders of Major [William] McMahon, who has heretofore been charged with the protection of the district you mention on the frontiers of Virginia; and who has been out for some time with a detachment of sixty men on the waters of Muskingum.

"In fact, every thing has already been done for the protection of the frontiers that can be reasonably expected or, devised with the force we have. and permit me once more to observe, that if an army of fifty thousand men, *regular troops* were strung along the N. W. side of Ohio; they would not be sufficient to quiet the minds of those people—unless you employ their *Militia*. . . . Capt. [Abner] Prior, with the Wabash & Illinois Chiefs arrived at this place on the 4th. instant. . . . Every necessary order has been issued for their accomodation & protection to your City." Wayne concluded his letter by reporting that the barracks for the men at Legionville and the "chain of redoubts & lines of defence are nearly completed" and that he had not received any "account as yet from the Cornplanter" (Knopf, *Wayne*, 145–48).

Tobias Lear to Lovell and Urquhart

Gentlemen,   Philada 16th Decr 1792.

In reply to your Letter of the 10th inst: to the President of the United States, I have to inform you, that upon receipt of your letter to him of the 8th of Novr, the sum of £25—10— Virginia Currency was paid to Messrs John Field & son agreeably to your desire expressed in said Letter—and their receipt therefor, dated the 16th of Novr is taken upon the Letter.[1]

As it was presumed that Messrs Field & son[2] would have advised you of this payment having been made, it was not thought necessary to do it on the part of The President. I am Gentlemen &c.

T. Lear.

LB, DLC:GW.

1. The letters to GW of 8 Nov. and 10 Dec. have not been found. An entry in Cash Memorandum Book H for 16 Nov. 1792 reads: "The President's private Acct—pd John Field & Son by order of Mess[r]s Lovel & Urquert, for 10,000 three feet shingles del[ivere]d at Mt Vernon by [John] Cowper & [Isaac] Sexton @ 51/ Virga Cy per M.—25⟨£⟩ Virga Cury" for a total of $85. Thomas Newton, Jr., earlier this summer had ordered these shingles, which were hewn from cypress trees in the Dismal Swamp, for shipment to Mount Vernon, and he had sent GW an invoice for £25.10, dated 28 June at Nansemond County, Va. (ViMtV). In his letter to Anthony Whitting of 28 Oct., GW wrote that 10,000 shingles had been obtained for the piazza roof.

2. The bill had been paid to the Philadelphia merchant firm of John Field & Son located at 22 South Front Street (*Philadelphia Directory, 1793,* 44).

From Debby Morris

Garlick Hall Myomensing township [Pa.]

Respected Sir   Decbr 16th 1792

In the Memorable Contest between America and Great Britain —My Father—Anthony Cadwallader Morris—had the honor of serving as Volunteer in the Cause of the former—in the year 1777—he untill that time possessed an handsome independency in the township of Haverford where he resided—but which by a train of Misfortunes attendant on his great republican Spirit— he was obliged to part with—having previously lost a large Stock —and every house-hold article—Except tables and chairs—that he possessed by his inhuman Enemies—I was at that time an in-

fant in arms—and am therefore unable—from my own knowledge to Sketch our Misfortunes—but a repitition of the sad tale
from my dear unfortunate parents enables me to perform the
disagreable task—for Events so Strikingly wretched are too apt
to dwell on Sensible Minds.[1]

My father had the honor of being desired by yourself to attend
a reconnoitreing party—to within a few miles of home—the Enemy approaching he desired his Companions to fly and leave
him to his fate—for his horse, through fatigue or infirmities being unable to proceed fast—they did so. he was immediatly
attacked by two of the Enemy—but dismounting and fixing his
back against the horse—resolved to defend himself as became an
American—but finding himself overpow[er]ed by numbers, he
yielded himself a prisoner, and desired to be treated as a Gentleman—at that instant their inhuman Commander—a Major Ca-
rew—came up and with Many Excorations—My Soul recoils at
the Idea—ordered him to be Split down—blows from his own
hand—followed his words—and my Father fell under Eight and
twenty wounds—a victim to british insatiate Cruelty—the cause
of this Excessive inveteracy—was the resort of Numbers of our
principal officers to our house—Some of whom had made it
their head quarters—and which was by the British calld the rebel
house—and my Father was particularly distinguished by the title
of rebel—think my respected Sir—What Must have been the
feelings—the Sufferings—of my poor Mother—who had been
tenderly Educated under an indulgent Father—at the sight of
her Husband in a small open house where he had crept after the
barbarous treatment he received—four Small children crying
for bread—and not even a bed to repose them on—Straw being
the only Substitute for them and my wounded Father for Several
Weeks in the coldest Season—indeed I believe few Suffered as
much—Either in mind—person—or property—as my afflicted
parents[2]—I find my pen inadequate to the descriptive task—and
will no longer trouble you with the recital of woes which perhaps
never reached your ears—all I have further to Say is to solicit an
office for a person who thinks the honor of Serving his country
a sufficient recompence for all his sufferings—pardon me—my
dear Father—your child cannot think So—or She would not
without your knowledge address our beloved President in your
behalf.

we are now on a farm—the property of my Mothers truly respectable Father—but I observe with regret—a State of dependency but ill agrees as with an independent Mind—and with due deference to the opinion of our honored president—and my dear Father—I think something ought to be done—remember my dear respected Sir—it is not the parent—it is the child—the daughter—that solicits for—-without the knowledge of her Father—my Mother approves of my proceeding—nay pressd me to address you as my Heart Should dictate for an aged parent— it wounds her peace of Mind to See my Father uneasy in dependence—we appeal to the humanity we rely on the goodness of the President—for the object is deserving—it may appear strange that I should write thus—without the approbation of my Father—and indeed—I could not reconcile the undertaking to myself—if I did not think the happiness of Seeing him independent—would Compensate for his Momentary Displeasure—being a young petitioner and unhackneyed in the ways of the world —I Scarcely know the form of a petition—but have adhered to Simple truth in reciting our troubles—I can with propriety say— in the School of adversity was I Educated together with Six Sisters and one Brother—Without any of those advantages derived from a knowledge of the polit world—as a child would address her Father—I address the President—and beg that the imperfections of my Stile may be imputed to the want of proper knowledge—and not to the overforwardness of youth to age[3]—I remain with respect your Sincere Well wisher

Debby Morris

ALS, DLC:GW. This letter is docketed erroneously as being written on 16 Dec. 1794, and it is filed in DLC:GW under that date.

1. Anthony Cadwalader Morris (1745–1798), who lived in Haverford, Delaware County, Pa., at the beginning of the Revolutionary War, had married Mary Jones (d. 1832), the daughter of prominent Philadelphia Quaker William Jones (b. 1723), in April 1770. At the time of this letter, Morris and his family lived at Moyamensing in Philadelphia County.

2. Morris's capture and mistreatment by Capt. Richard Crewe of the British army's 17th Regiment of Light Dragoons were portrayed graphically in an extract of a 12 Dec. 1777 letter printed in the *Pennsylvania Gazette* (York) on 20 Dec. 1777. According to that account, "All the fingers of one hand are nearly cut off, and the rest are so bad that Dr. [Jonathan] Morris was obliged to take one off; his upper lip is split, a piece cut out of his nose, both cheeks cut. . . . [and] several wounds on the head, some of which went through his scull." Morris was treated so brutally because Gen. Nathanael Greene had es-

tablished his headquarters at Morris's house (see Greene to GW, 14 Nov. 1777, and note 1).

3. No reply from GW has been found.

Tobias Lear to Alexander Robertson

Sir,   Philada 16th December 1792.

Your Letter to the President of the United States dated the 4th of November, did not get to his hands 'till a few days ago;[1] and in reply thereto the President commands me to inform you, that it is not at present in his power to give a decided answer to the request which you make for him to employ your brother in the management of one of his farms. Even if he was in immediate want of such a person as you describe your brother to be, it would be necessary to have certain points settled previous to his giving him encouragement to come over—such as, complete evidence of his being well qualified to manage the affairs of a farm in this Country, which is different from the management of a farm in England, & especially where the labour is performed by blacks: and a knowledge of the terms upon which your brother would be willing to engage in this business. But as the President has not immediate occasion for the services of such a person he can only observe, that the usual mode of engaging overseers of farms & plantations in Virginia where his Estate lays, is to give them a share of the Crop as a compensation for their services— for instance, if there should be on a plantation *ten* working hands —the crop is divided into eleven shares, one of which belongs to the Overseer: if a greater or less number of hands is employed, the Overseer's share is in proportion thereto. But the President having deviated from the common mode of cultivation practiced in that part of the Country, has been under the necessity of paying his overseers annual wages instead of giving them a share of the Crop; and the wages given to those whom he employs, as well as by other gentlemen in his vicinity who give annual wages instead of a share to the Overseer, vary from 80 to 130 Dollar ⅌ year, according to the extent of the farm to be superintended, & the skill of the person in managing the business of it. to these wages are added, a comfortable dwelling House on the farm, and a stipulated quantity of provisions, adequate to the support of the Overseer. In mentioning these terms, it must be observed that the President speaks only of his own Estate, & those in it's neighbourhood where he has had an opportunity of knowing the terms upon which Overseers are engaged on them. What may be given in other parts of the Country he cannot tell; & as the skill which you say your brother possesses in gardening & survey-ing, would not be likely to be called into exercise in overlooking such farms as the President's, they could not be taken into the account in making a compensation for his services as an Over-seer; but if they were found useful to a person who might employ him, in conjunction with his duties as Overseer or Manager, an extra compensation wou'd undoubtedly be made for them. I am Sir &c.

Tobias Lear.

LB, DLC:GW. This document was entered in the letter book under the head-ing: "Mr Alexander Robertson—Morristown, Nw Jersey."
   1. Robertson's letter to GW of 4 Nov. has not been found.

To Anthony Whitting

Mr Whiting,   Philadelphia 16th Decr 1792.
   Your letter of the 12th with its enclosures came duly to hand, and under cover with this letter you will receive Invoice & Bill of lading for somethings which went from hence yesterday.[1]

   I thought it best to send you, ready prepared, the Plaster of Paris from hence. March or April will be time enough to spread it (at the rate of 5 or 6 bushls to the acre) on the Lawns before each door; if there be more than enough for this purpose spread the remainder on the Lucern—or new Clover lot (poorest parts of it) as far as it will go. It ought to be done when it is drizzling, at any rate when the atmosphere is moist & giving, & when there is very little wind; otherwise the fine particles of the Gypsom will evaporate—blow away, and be lost. All the honey locust Seeds I could get before the Vessel Sailed are sent; if more are to be had I will send them. The fruit trees wch accompany them may be planted where the Gardener shall think it best they shd stand; & desire him to be careful of the Seeds you got from Mr Hunter; taking care to preserve the names of them, that the plants may be thereby known.[2]

   If (or whenever) you can obtain a good price for the Midlings

or Ship-stuff in Alexandria, I would have you sell them to raise
Cash for such purposes as indispensably call for it; but I earnestly
exhort you to buy nothing you can either make within yourselves,
or can do well without. The practice of running to Stores &ca for
every thing that is wanting, or thought to be wanting, is the most
ruinous custom that can be adopted and has proved the destruction of many a man before he was aware of the pernicious
consequences. There is no Proverb in the whole catalogue of
them more true, than that a penny saved, is a penny got. I well
know that many things must be bought, such for instance as you
have enumerated in your letter; but I know also, that, expedients
may be hit upon, & things (though perhaps not quite as handsome) done within ourselves, that would ease the expences of
any Estate very considerably. Before the navigation is closed it
might be prudent to make this Sale; or to have the Ship-stuff and
Midlings stored in Alexandria in readiness for it; otherwise you
will be unable to do it, or have it to Waggon, which will be not
only a drawback from the price, but may be attended with much
inconvenience.

I observed to you in my last, that I thought the Miller was very
negligent, & inattentive to his duty in not having more Wheat
manufactured than what appeared by the Report of the preceeding week;[3] and I now desire you will let him know that I am by no
means well pleased at the delay. I fear he makes so large a portion
of flour superfine, as to endanger, or at least to impoverish the
fine, this will not be good policy for either kind: and I perceive he
makes the Wheat weigh only 58 lbs. pr Bushel. I wish you would
now & then see a load tried. 58 is less than I have heard of any
Wheats weighing this year. Tell Davenport it is my desire that he
would immediately try with 100 bushels of Wheat (carefully measured, and as it is received at the Mill) what quantity of Superfine, fine, midlings, Shipstuff and Bran will come from it. This
100 bushels of Wheat (after it is measured & weighed) is to pass,
as usual, through the Mill Screen & Fan. My object you will readily perceive is to compare the prices of the Wheat before and after it is manufactured, together, that I may be enabled to form a
precise judgmt of the value of each: He must therefore be very
careful that no mistake is made, & the experiment such as he can
be responsible for. It is for this reason I have directed the Wheat
to be measured & weighed before it goes through the Mill oper-

ations for cleaning. A similar experiment to this was made last year, but I want another, & to have it done without delay, & with great exactness.

If Isaac had his deserts, he wd receive severe punishment for the House, Tools & Seasoned stuff which has been burned by his carelessness. He must have left the fire in a very unjustifiable situation, or have been a fine time absent from it, for such an accident to have happened before it was too late to have extinguished it. I wish you to inform him, that I sustain injury enough by their idleness—they need not add to it by their carelessness. The present work-shop (Barn) will do very well; at least 'till there is more leizure for altering that, or erecting another.[4]

I am sorry to find your Crop of Corn is likely to fall so short of expectation: I hope, however, that great care will be taken of what is made; & that every advantageous use will be made of the Soft Corn—It will not, with all the care that can be taken of it, keep long—& if you lay it in heaps it will inevitably spoil, & be fit for no use in a very short time.

I am not less concerned to find that I am, forever, sustaining loss in my Stock of Sheep (particularly). I not only approve of your killing those Dogs which have been the occasion of the late loss, & of thinning the Plantations of others, but give it as a positive order, that after saying what dog, or dogs shall remain, if any negro presumes under any pretence whatsoever, to preserve, or bring one into the family, that he shall be severely punished, and the dog hanged. I was obliged to adopt this practice whilst I resided at home, and from the same motives, that is, for the preservation of my Sheep and Hogs; but I observed when I was at home last that a new set of dogs was rearing up, & I intended to have spoke about them, but one thing or another always prevented it. It is not for any good purpose Negros raise, or keep dogs; but to aid them in their night robberies; for it is astonish to see the command under which their dogs are. I would no more allow the Overseers than I would the Negros, to keep Dogs—One, or at most two on a Plantation is enough. The pretences for keeping more will be various, & urgent, but I will not allow more than the above notwithstanding.

I hope your New Overseer will turn out well—his age (although he now has, or soon may get a wife) is much against him for a large concern, in my estimation; but the Season made it al-

most Hobson's choice, him or none.[5] I have engaged an elderly
man who may probably be with you on Sunday next to look after
the home house gang.[6] He is an Irishman, & not long from that
Country. According to his own, and the Accounts given of him
by others he is well practiced in both farming and grazing—He
is old enough to be steady, & to have had much experience in
both these branches—though old, & clumsey withall, he promises that activity shall not be wanting—nor obedience to any directions you may give him. I have agreed to allow him Seventy
dollars for the ensuing year, & have told him that further encouragement, either in an augmentation of wages, or removal to
a better place, will depend altogether upon his own conduct and
good behaviour. If he is such a man as is represented, he may be
useful to me; having it is said a perfect knowledge in Horses, and
Stock of all kinds. I should have prefered, if the Major had not
occupied the room over the Kitchen as a Store, to have put his
bed in that; but this being the case, he must go into the house
opposite to the Store; as the Servants Hall must be kept for that
purpose unappropriated to any other uses.[7] I have informed Mr
Butler (that is his name) that sobriety, industry & honesty, are
such indispensible qualifications in my eyes, that he will remain
but a short time with me if he is found deficient of either. and I
request you, not only in his case, but with all the other Overseers
likewise, to pass over no faults without noticing and admonish-
ing them against the commission of the like, or similar ones; for
in this, as in every thing else, it is easier to prevent evils than to
apply remedies after they have happened. One fault overlooked
begets another—that a third—and so on—whereas a check in
the first instance might prevent a repetition, or at any rate cause
circumspection.

I thought I had desired you, before I left home, to make some
enquiry respecting the person who lives in my house in Alexandria, & to Rent it upon the best terms you could to him or any
other; but as you have never mentioned the matter in any of your
letters, I presume I intended to do so, but did not—and therefore now request it may be done.[8]

I would have you open the second Visto 20 feet wide, as far as
muddy hole branch, and let me know whether the hill on the
other side of it is high or low; and whether it will require much
work to open it to the full width 'till you pass it; for as to open-

ing it beyond the hill I conceive it to be as unnecessary, as it was
in the first Visto, after you descend into the flat beyond it.[9]

If proper care and attention has been paid to Cilla's child, it is
all that humanity requires, whatever may be the consequence;
these I would have bestowed on all.[10] What is Boatswains complaint? I find he is still in the house; as Charles also is.[11] Let me
know the quantity of Water you are likely to draw together, from
the different Springs below the Lucern lot[12]—and inform me
what numbers of the fields will be united at the Ferry & French's
plantations, and what will be the numbers of them when this is
done: without this knowledge I shall be at a loss when you are
speaking of the different fields how to distinguish them.[13]

If Mr Hartshorn does not take the Stud horse—nor you should
not have disposed of him to any other, deliver him to Mr Robert
Lewis, or his order if he should send for him.[14] I remain Your
friend & Well wisher

Go: Washington

ALS, DLC:GW.

1. Neither Whitting's letter nor its enclosures have been found. The invoice
and bill of lading sent by GW have not been identified, but they probably included the purchase and shipment of the fruit trees mentioned later in this
letter.

2. Whitting may have purchased seeds from Alexandria merchant William
Hunter, Jr.

3. For GW's earlier criticism of Joseph Davenport's productivity, see his previous letter to Whitting, dated 9 December. For GW's instructions on the type
of report he expected from the miller, see GW to Whitting, 25 November. Davenport's most recent report has not been found.

4. In his letter of 9 Dec., GW refers to a fire at the dog kennel, but the fire
mentioned here appears to have been at a workhouse on the Mansion House
grounds. Isaac was one of the carpenters at the Mansion House farm (see Slave
List, 18 Feb. 1786, in *Diaries*, 4:278; Washington's Slave List, June 1799).

5. The new overseer at the Dogue Run farm was Henry McCoy (see GW to
Whitting, 9 Dec., n.9).

6. GW engaged James Butler to be the overseer of the Mansion House farm
(see GW to Whitting, 19 December).

7. The servants' hall and storehouse were a short distance northwest of the
mansion.

8. GW's house in Alexandria was built on one of two lots that he had purchased from John Alexander, Jr., in 1764. In 1769 GW hired Richard Lake
(Leake) and Edward Rigdon to build a small house on the lot at Pitt and
Cameron streets. The house was rented to various tenants over the years, but
during the presidency GW seems to have lost track of who the tenants were. In

compliance with GW's instructions, Whitting rented the house to a young couple. In the fall of 1793, however, GW decided to renovate the house for its use by newly widowed Fanny Bassett Washington. For a detailed history of the Alexandria house, see GW's Last Will and Testament, 9 July 1799, n.1.

9. For earlier instructions regarding the second vista and its location, see GW's letters to Whitting of 14 Oct., 18 Nov., and 2 December.

10. Silla appears on the 1786 Slave List as a "Labourg." woman at the Dogue Run farm with two children named Sophia and Sabra, aged 3 years and 6 months, respectively (see Slave List, 18 Feb. 1786, in *Diaries*, 4:281). On Washington's Slave List of June 1799, Sylla of the Dogue Run farm is listed as the wife of Slamin Joe, a ditcher at the Mansion House farm, and as the mother of five children at the Dogue Run farm, including Sophia (14 years old) and Savary (13 years old). She is probably the same person as the 36-year-old woman named Priscilla who in 1799 belonged to GW at the Dogue Run farm.

11. For an earlier identification of Boatswain and a mention of his illness, see Whitting to GW, 31 Oct., and note 3. Charles was identified as a laborer at the Muddy Hole farm on the 1786 Slave List and a ditcher at the Mansion House farm on Washington's Slave List of June 1799. His wife, Fanny, was listed as a dower laborer at the Ferry farm in 1786 and at the Union farm in 1799 (ibid., 282). Whitting's farm reports for 21–27 Oct. and for 30 Dec. 1792–5 Jan. 1793 show Charles and Boatswain out sick for the week; Charles was listed as "Lame" (both reports are in DLC:GW).

12. For the attempt to combine all the springs near the river, see GW to Whitting, 28 Oct., 18 Nov., and 2 December.

13. French's and Ferry farms had been combined under the same overseer for several years, but on 27 Jan. 1793 GW wrote Whitting that in the future these farms should be designated "Union Farm, or Plantation," instead of Ferry and French's farm.

14. In a letter to his nephew Robert Lewis of 23 Dec., GW offered the horse Sampson as a gift if the horse had not been sold already. Alexandria merchant William Hartshorne apparently declined buying the horse; Whitting wrote GW on 9 Jan. 1793 that he had sent the horse to Lewis that morning.

From Frederick A. Muhlenberg and Other Citizens of Pennsylvania

Reading Berks County [Pa.] Decr 17th 1792

We the Subscribers being well acquainted with John Witman junior of the Borough of Reading in the State of Pennsylvania recommend him to your Excellency as a man of Integrity whose Capacity activity and Attention to Business point him out as a fit Person to execute the Office of an Inspector of the Revenue for this District—He was formerly the Excise Officer for Berks County and is at present the Collector of the Revenue—

therein under a Deputation from the Supervisor of Pennsylvania in which Trusts having supported the Character of an independent and upright Officer We have every Reason to conclude that shoud he be honored by your Excellency's Appointment the Revenue Law as far as is within his Reach will be ably and faithfully executed.[1]

Fredk A Muhlenberg	Jacob Rush.
P: Muhlenberg	Jos. Hiester
Thos FitzSimons	Dan. Clymer
Tho. Scott	Peter Filbert
Thos Hartley	Gabriel Hiester
	Charles Shoemaker
	Balser Geehr

DS, DLC:GW.

1. John Witman, Jr., sought appointment as the inspector of the revenue for the second survey in Pennsylvania, which was comprised of Berks, Northampton, Luzerne, and Northumberland counties. Questions about the competency of the current inspector, James Collins, had been raised by Commissioner of the Revenue Tench Coxe in a letter to Alexander Hamilton of 15 Dec. 1792 (see Syrett, *Hamilton Papers,* 13:328–29). Although rumors of his removal evidently were circulating in December 1792, Collins remained in office for another year. Hamilton wrote GW on 23 Dec. 1793 that "Mr Collins is incapable of executing the duties of the office and that the good of the public service requires his removal" (DLC:GW). Rumors of Collins's impending dismissal surfaced again, and Witman sought the post a second time. George Clymer, supervisor of the revenue for the District of Pennsylvania, wrote Hamilton on 19 Dec. 1793 that Witman "is considered as respectable in his Character and circumstances, and is doubtless the best collector in the district . . . [and] is extremely popular among the Germans whose language he speaks" (ibid., 26:723). Frederick A. Muhlenberg wrote another letter of recommendation to GW on 20 Dec. 1793 (DLC:GW). Witman, however, failed to obtain the appointment, which went instead to John Boyd (see GW to the U.S. Senate, 29 Jan. 1794, LB, DLC:GW, and copy, DNA: RG 46, Second Congress, 1791–93, Senate Records of Legislative Proceedings, President's Messages; *Executive Journal,* 1:147–48).

To the Commissioners for the District of Columbia

Gentlemen (Private)   Philadelphia Decembr 18th 1792.
    Your letter to the Secretary of State, dated if I recollect rightly, the 5th instant,[1] intimating among other things, that you had failed in an attempt which had been made to import workmen

from Scotland, equally with that for obtaining them from Holland, fills me with *real* concern: for I am very apprehensive if your next campaign in the Federal City is not marked with vigor, it will cast such a cloud over this business, and will so arm the enemies of the measure, as to enable them to give it (if not its death blow) a wound from which it will not easily recover. No means therefore, in my opinion, should be left unassayed to facilitate the operations of next year. Every thing, in a manner depends upon the celerity with which the public buildings are then carried on. Sale of Lots—private buildings—good or evil reports—all, all will be regulated thereby; nothing therefore short of the absolute want of money ought to retard the work.

The more I consider the subject the more I am convinced of the expediency of importing a number of workmen from Europe to be employed in the Federal City. The measure has not only œconomy to recommend it, but is important by placing the quantity of labour which may be performed by such persons upon a certainty for the term for which they shall be engaged.

Upon more minute enquiry, I am informed that neither the Merchan⟨ts⟩ *here* nor in *Holland* will undertake to procure Redemptioners from Germany; and that the most eligable & certain mode of obtaining from thence such Mechanic⟨s⟩ & labourers as may be thought advisable to procure from that quarter, will be to engage some person, a German, to go from hence into Germany where he is acquainted, to procure the requisite number of men and bring them to the Shipping port, which is generally Amsterdam or Rotterdam, and that any Merchant here (who is engaged in Shipping trading to Holland) will engage to have a Vessel ready to take them on board at a time which shall be fixed, and bring them to any Port of the United States that may be specified, and receive the amount of their passage on delivery of them. The person who may be employed to go over to Germany will expect, it is said, an advance of one guinea per head for the number wanted, to enable him to pay the expences of such as may not be able to bear their own from the place where he procures them to the Shipping Port, & this advance is accounted for and taken into consideration at the time of paying for their passage when they arrive here. The customary passage it seems, is eleven guineas per head—and the compensation of the person employed to procure them is either one guinea a head for as

many as he may deliver, part of which is paid by those who employ him to go over, & part by the Merchant who furnishes the
Vessel to bring them, as he receives a benefit by the freight—
or the person employed keeps an account of his necessary expences while on this business, which is paid by his employers,
and a consideration for his services is made him according to a
previous agreement.

The term of time for which these people are bound to serve,
depends much, it is added, upon their age or ability as labourers,
or their skill as Mechanics—the former generally serve three or
four years, and the latter (if good workmen at their trades) two.
But in this case, that it would be bes⟨t⟩ for the person employed
to get them to have them indented at the time of engaging them,
specifying the number of years they are to serve to commence at
the time of their landing in the U.S.—and that he ought to be
furnished with the necessary forms of Indentures and particular
instructions on this head before he goes over—and if Mechanics of a particular description are most essential it would be well,
in order to secure their services beyond the term for which they
might be engaged for their passage, to stipulate at the time of
engaging them, that they should serve one, two or three years
over and above that time @ £ [   ] per year. And as it may happen, that some good Mechanics may be willing to come over who
are able to pay their own passage, might it not be well to empower
the person sent to engage them @ [   ] per year for (say) four
years? In all cases to provide, that if those who engage as Mechanics should be found incompetent to the business for which
they engage, from a want of skill or knowledge in it, and shall appear to have used imposition in engaging themselves as such,
they shall be obliged to serve the time of common labourers.

Should you be of opinion that it would be expedient to import
a number of workmen, and the mode here pointed out meet your
ideas, no time should be lost in carrying it into effect; and if you
have not contemplated a proper character for this business &
will inform me thereof I will endeavour to obtain one in this City
to go over to Germany, and a Merchant also to furnish the Vessel at the time & place which shall be agreed on between them.

It is not, however, my wish that the idea of importing workmen
should be confined solely to Germany—I think it ought to be
extended to other places, particularly Scotland from whe⟨nce⟩

many good & useful Mechanics may undoubtedly to be had. I have been more particular in respect to Germany because they may probably be obtained from thence on better terms than from other quarters and they are known to be a steady laborious people. It will be necessary, if you should determine upon an importation from Germany, to state the Number of Mechanics you would wish in each trade, to be brought from thence, as well as the number of labourers.

Mr George Walker who is in th⟨is⟩ City, informs me, that he shall Sail for Scotland about the first of January, & says, if he could render service in this business he would willingly do it. To get workmen is part of the business which carries him over but how far after the part he has acted with respect to yourselves you may chuse to confide in him, is fitter for you than it is for me to decide—especially as I know no more of his private character & circumstances than I do of the terms on which he would undertake to render the Service.

A thought has also occurred to me, and though crude & almost in embrio, I will nevertheless mention it. It is, if the character of Mr Hallet (from the knowledge you have acquired of it) is such as to have impr⟨es⟩sed you with confidence in his abilities & activity, whether in the unsettled state of things in France he might not be employed *this* winter in ingaging from that Country & bringing over in the Spring such workmen, and on such terms as might be agreed upon.[2]

Boston too has been mentioned as a place from whence many, & good workmen might be had but the reasons which have been assigned for the failure here are not within my recollection if I ever heard them.

Upon the whole, it will readily be perceived in what a serious light I consider delay, in the progress of the public buildings; & how anxious I am to have them pushed forward—In a word the next is the year that will give the tone to the City—if marked with energy, Individuals will be inspirited—the Sales will be enhanced—confidence diffused—& emulation created—without it, I should not be surprized to find the lots unsaleable, & every thing at a stand. With great & sincere regard & esteem I am Gentn Your Obedt Servt

Go: Washington

ALS (letterpress copy), DLC:GW; LB, DLC:GW. The illegible text in angle brackets is provided from the letter-book copy.

1. For the letter from the D.C. commissioners to Jefferson of 5 Dec., see note 1 of Jefferson's letter to GW of 8 Dec. (see also *Jefferson Papers*, 24:699–700).

2. The commissioners, after rejecting French architect Stephen Hallet's plan for the Capitol, employed him in the summer of 1793 to supervise its construction (see D.C. Commissioners to GW, 23 June 1793, and GW to Jefferson, 30 June 1793). Following GW's directions to solicit immigrant workers for the various construction projects in the federal district, the commissioners drew up at their 3 Jan. 1793 meeting "Terms for Mechanics," in which they offered to advance up to 30s. to mechanics in Europe for expenses and upon their arrival to pay the cost of their passage to the United States. The commissioners also promised to pay current American wages, that is, a daily wage of 4s. 6d. to 5s. sterling for stonecutters and masons. Half of the mechanics' daily wages would be retained until the advance and passage money had been repaid (see DNA: RG 42, Records of the Commissioners for the District of Columbia, Proceedings, 1791–1802). The commissioners also wrote Philadelphia stonecutter and sculptor James Traquair (1756–1811) on 2 Jan. 1793 asking him to engage fifty stonecutters in Great Britain who were willing to work in the United States (see DNA: RG 42, Records of the Commissioners for the District of Columbia, Letters Sent, 1791–1802). "Messrs. [John] Mason & [Joseph] Fenwick," the commissioners wrote Jefferson on 5 Jan. 1793, "will have the charge of this business in France assisted by a Letter from Mr. Hallet. Mr. [Christoph Dietrich Arnold] Delius's house, in Bremen, for Germany. Mr. [James] Hoben has fallen on measures for some from Dublin as Mr. [Collen] Williamson has for some from Scotland" (ibid., 25:24).

Tobias Lear to Thomas Jefferson

United States [Philadelphia] 18th Decr 1792.

By the President's command T. Lear has the honor to request that the Secretary of State will have Commissions made out for the following persons;

Samuel Odiorne, third mate of the New-Hampshire Revenue Cutter; to be dated 18th December 1792.

Ebenezer Perkins, third mate of the Connecticut Cutter; to be dated 18th Decr 1792.

William Loring, first mate of the New York Cutter; to be dated Novemr 15th 1792.

Caleb Stacey, third mate of the New York Cutter, to be dated Novemr 6th 1792.

William Dunton, third mate of the Pennsylvania Cutter; to be dated 22d June 1792.[1]

T. Lear has the honor to transmit to the Secretary *twenty* Commissions which have been returned to the Secretary of the Treasury from Officers of the Revenue Cutters and were yesterday sent to the President by the Secretary of the Treasury. Some of these Commissions have been resigned, & others returned on account of their tenure being limited to the *end of the next Session of the* Senate: those of the latter description have been replaced by others in the proper form.[2]

T. Lear has the honor also to transmit two Commissions, from Jno. Baker, Surveyor of Bennett's Creek in No. Carolina—one from Wm Wynn Surveyor of the port of Wynton—one from the Supervisor of the Georgia District (a Duplicate)—& one from the Inspector of Survey No. 1 in North Carolina.[3]

Tobias Lear. S.P.U.S.

LB, DNA: RG 59, George Washington's Correspondence with His Secretaries of State; LB (photocopy), DLC:GW.

1. Alexander Hamilton sent the names of the above officers to Lear on this date (DLC:GW).

2. Hamilton wrote Lear on 17 Dec. 1792 to transmit "sundry Commissions which from time to time have been returned" (DLC:GW). Those commissions have not been identified.

3. The enclosed commissions, which have not been identified, were from John Baker and William Wynne, surveyors of the customs at Bennetts Creek and Winton, N.C., respectively; John Mathews, supervisor of the revenue for Georgia; and James Read, inspector of the revenue for the first survey in North Carolina. For the resignations of Baker and Wynne, see Tench Coxe to Hamilton, 10 Nov. 1792, in Syrett, *Hamilton Papers,* 13:33. For the reorganization of the District of North Carolina, see GW to the U.S. Senate and House of Representatives, 23 Jan. 1793. For the nomination of Thomas Overton to replace James Read as inspector of the revenue for the first survey in North Carolina, see GW to the U.S. Senate, 28 Jan. 1793.

From Thomas Jefferson

[Philadelphia] Dec. 18. 92.

Th: Jefferson has the honor to send the President 2 Cents made on Voigt's plan, by putting a silver plug worth ¾ of a cent into a copper worth ¼ of a cent.[1] Mr Rittenhouse is about to make a few by mixing the same plug by fusion with the same quantity of copper. he will then make of copper alone of the same size, and lastly he will make the real cent, as ordered by Congress, four times as big. specimens of these several ways of making the cent will be delivered to the Committee of Congress now having that subject before them.[2]

AL, DNA: RG 59, Miscellaneous Letters; LB, DNA: RG 59, George Washington's Correspondence with His Secretaries of State; LB (photocopy), DLC:GW.

1. For background on the federal government's efforts to produce its own coins, see Jefferson to GW, 16 Nov. 1792 (second letter), and note 1. For Henry Voigt's appointment as chief coiner of the United States, see Voigt to GW, 13 April 1792, and note 1.

2. The experiments by Voigt and Director of the U.S. Mint David Rittenhouse probably influenced Congress in its decision to amend the standards originally established on 2 April 1792 in "An Act establishing a Mint, and regulating the Coins of the United States." "An Act to amend an act intituled 'An act establishing a Mint, and regulating the coins of the United States,' so far as respects the coinage of copper," approved on 14 Jan. 1793, specified "That every cent shall contain two hundred and eight grains of copper, and every half cent shall contain one hundred and four grains of copper" (1 *Stat.* 246–51, 299).

Tobias Lear to Henry Knox

U.S. [Philadelphia] Decr 18th 1792

By the President's commd T.L. has the honor to return to the Secy of War the letters from Genl Wilkinson wh. have been submitted to the Presidt—and to say that if there be any thing in these letters wh. in the Secy's opinion should be communicated to Congress the President wishes it might be done.[1]

T.L.

S.P.U.S.

ADfS, DLC:GW; LB, DLC:GW.

1. Knox presented the Senate on 19 Dec. an extract of a letter that he had received from James Wilkinson, "dated at fort Hamilton, the 6th of November last, with an enclosure from Major [John] Adair," commandant of the Kentucky mounted infantry (*ASP, Indian Affairs,* 1:335). Adair's letter to Wilkinson, which was written at Fort St. Clair on 6 Nov. 1792, recounted an Indian attack on his troops within sight of the fort. "Some of my men," Adair reported, "were hand in hand with them before we retreated, which, however, we did, about eighty yards, to a kind of stockade intended for stables; we then made a stand. . . . We made a manly push, and the enemy retreated, taking all our horses except five or six," which was the only great advantage gained by the Indians from this battle (ibid.). Wilkinson wrote in his letter that "the immedi-

ate consequence" of this encounter will be "an entire stop to the transport of forage to the advanced post, as our pack-horses are either destroyed or disabled, and the riflemen dismounted; in this situation I am perplexed by difficulties, as, from my ignorance of the designs of Government, and for the want of explicit orders, I am at a loss whether to direct the purchase of more pack-horses, or to encourage the riflemen to remount themselves; on these points I shall duly deliberate, and will make such decision as my judgment may direct, relying confidently on the liberality of Government for an excuse, should I err; and, in the meantime, I shall urge forward the transport of forage from fort Washington to this post, by every means left in my power" (ibid.).

Knox also submitted to the Senate on 19 Dec. a copy of a letter to him dated 17 Nov. 1792 at Lexington, Ky., from John Belli, deputy quartermaster general, who reported that he had drawn $8,090.66⅔ without orders from Knox but "by General James Wilkinson's advice." I "was necessitated so to do," Belli wrote, "or, to see the General's arrangements entirely defeated. I hope the quartermaster general will in future supply me with sums equal to the demands in this quarter: for, sir, I have already spent a great many uneasy hours for want of funds; indeed, I shall now be obliged to curtail General Wilkinson's order for pack-horses, for want of money, which this country at present does not afford" (ibid., 336).

From the Ministers and Members of the Methodist Episcopal Church in Fayette County, Pennsylvania

Pennsylvania, Fayatte County December 19. 1792
To the President and Rulers of the united states of America.

From the strongest impressions, and deepest sense of our obligations, and submission to our superior, so far as the act consistant to the law of God, and a good conscience, enacting laws to defend vertue and oppose vice.

We the Ministers and Members of the Methodist Episcopal Church residing in the western country, think it our duty to give you a true transcript of our hearts and wishs respecting the excise law, which met with such unreasonable opposition, in these parts. We are informed it has been reported to the legislators, that all the people on this side the aleghany are opposed to the excise law, which report we unanimously declare to be without foundation, and can asure you there are at least above one thousand persons in connection with us, together with a large majority of the Quakers, who not only never consented to the opposition that law met with, but earnestly wish it may be received immediately and without reluctance, and shall esteem it our duty to encourage Men to comply with it throughout our several spheres of action.[1] Signed in behalf of our community

Thornton Fleming
Valentine Cooke
William McLenahan

D, DNA: RG 59, Miscellaneous Letters.

1. For background on the opposition to the federal excise tax on whiskey by some residents of western Pennsylvania, see Alexander Hamilton to GW, 1 Sept. 1792, and notes. In response to this opposition, GW issued on 15 Sept. a proclamation calling for all citizens to comply with federal efforts to collect the excise tax. For GW's reply to Thornton Fleming (1764–1846), Valentine Cook (1765–1820), and William McLenahan, see his letter to the Ministers and Members of the Methodist Episcopal Church in Fayette County, Pa., of 30 Jan. 1793.

From Alexander Hamilton

[Philadelphia] Decr 19th 1792

The Secretary of the Treasury, presenting his respects to the President, submits the enclosed papers concerning the execution of a Contract for building a Well on Cape Henlopen.[1] He will in the course of the week wait on the President for his orders.

LB, DLC:GW.

1. For previous correspondence regarding a contract with Abraham Hargis, keeper of the lighthouse at Cape Henlopen, Del., for the construction of a well, see Hamilton to GW, 19 June 1792, and notes 2 and 3. The enclosed papers were probably those submitted by Tench Coxe in his letter to Hamilton of 18 Dec., including the contractor's account for "sinking and completing the well . . . the Amount whereof is £116:5: Pennsylvania Currency equal to 310 Dollars," which, Coxe reported, was $31.98 more than the approved contract for £104.5.2 Pennsylvania currency ($278.02). Hargis, Coxe wrote, has "rendered an account (paper A) accompanied by such vouchers as in my Judgment would be sufficient to pass his demand through the Treasury Offices were he an accountable agent, instead of a contractor. The paper (B) annexed to the estimate and Contract contains the substance of those Vouchers, carefully extracted and so placed against the items of the Estimate as to render a comparison of them easy." Coxe concluded that the additional expense was not unreasonable (DNA: RG 58, Letters Sent by the Commissioner of the Revenue and the Revenue Office, 1792–1807; extract in Syrett, *Hamilton Papers,* 13:336).

From Henry Knox

Sir.   War-department, December 19th 1792.
    In consequence of your directions, I have the honor to submit the draft of a letter to Governor Martin.[1] I have conversed with Mr Hawkins upon the subject, who is of opinion, that scouts are all that would be requisite.[2] I have the honor to be, Sir, with profound respect, Your most obedt Servt

                                        H. Knox

LS, DLC:GW; LB, DLC:GW.
    1. Tobias Lear, at GW's request, wrote Knox on 18 Dec. to transmit a letter from North Carolina governor Alexander Martin and to request "that measures may be taken by the U.S. for the protection of the frontier of that State, and to inform the Secrty that the President wishes him to report to him upon said letter as soon as he conveniently can" (DLC:GW). Martin's letter to GW has not been found.
    2. Knox's conversation probably was with North Carolina senator Benjamin Hawkins. Lear returned Knox's draft later on this date noting that "the President approves of the Answer of the Secy to Govr Martin's letter" (DLC:GW). Knox's letter to Martin has not been identified.

Tobias Lear to Henry Sheaff

Sir,   Philadelphia 19th Decr 1792
    The President of the United States begs that the Germans of this City and State will accept his best thanks, for their polite attention in directing that the German News paper should be sent to him weekly, as a mark of their respect for & attachment to him. The expressions of personal regard with which the resolution of so respectable a body was communicated, merit & receive the President's grateful acknowledgements.[1] I am Sir, with great regard, Your most Obedt Sert

                                        Tobias Lear.
            Secretary to the president of the United States

ADfS, DNA: RG 59, Miscellaneous Letters; LB, DLC:GW.
    1. Philadelphia wine merchant Henry Sheaff wrote Lear on 18 Dec. that "The Germans of this City and State Haveing their beloved President at Heart by a General Resolution of their body Requestd Mr Swyler to Furnish the German News Paper: weekly. This must be taken as a token of Regard: altho of no use to the President—I was orderd the Messeng⟨er⟩ to Forward the Same" (DLC:GW). The newspaper was the *Philadelphische Correspondenz,* published

weekly by Melchior Steiner and Heinrich Kammerer. The person requested by Die Deutsche Gesellschaft zu Philadelphia, the German Society, to furnish GW with the newspaper may have been Jacob S. Swyler, a resident of Philadelphia who in 1795 was recommended for election to the Pennsylvania legislature (see *Pennsylvania Gazette* [Philadelphia], 7 Oct. 1795).

To Anthony Whitting

Mr Whiting   Philadelphia Decr 19th 1792

The bearer Mr James Butler is the person I mentioned to you in my last as an Overlooker of the home house concern; and enclosed is the agreement I have entered into with him for that purpose.[1]

I am in great hopes, from the character given of him to me, that he may be found serviceable, keep him however to his duty, and whenever he is found difficient in it let both him & me know it. I am Your friend &ca

Go: Washington

ALS, MHi: Palfrey Family Papers.

1. GW's previous letter to Whitting was dated 16 December. The enclosed agreement has not been found.

Letter not found: from Anthony Whitting, 19 Dec. 1792. GW wrote Whitting on 23 Dec.: "Your letter of the 19th instant, enclosing the weekly reports, has been duly received."

From Francis Deakins and Benjamin W. Jones

Sir   Montgomery County [Md.] 20 Decr 1792

We now enclose you our Valuation of Mrs Sophia Mercers part of Woodstock Manor⟨,⟩ which we should have done before this had we not waited the time you Limited for a division to take place—the Sales & Quality of Other Lands in this Neighbourhood has been duly considered in our Valuation of this tract.[1] We have the Honor to be Sir your Mt Obedt Servt

Francis Deakins
Benjn W. Jones

LS, DLC:GW, in the hand of Francis Deakins.

1. For background on GW's hiring of Deakins and Jones to assess the value of Sophia Mercer's land in Montgomery County, Md., in order to settle a long-

standing debt owed by the estate of John Mercer, the father of Sophia Mercer's husband John Francis Mercer, see John Francis Mercer and GW to Deakins and Jones, 8 Dec. 1792, and note 1. The enclosed valuation has not been identified, but an entry in GW's Ledger C on 1 April 1793 credits the account of John F. Mercer: "By a Tract of Land lying in the County of Montgomery State of Maryland, Containing 519 Acres, being part of a Tract called Woodstock Manor, conveyed to me by yourself & others @ 42/. ℔ Acre . . . £1089.18." At the request of GW and Mercer, Deakins and Jones directed Hezekiah Veatch to survey this tract. The 2 Jan. 1793 survey was recorded in the general court of Montgomery County on 18 April 1794 (ViMtV). Francis Deakins wrote GW from Montgomery County, Md., on 4 Jan. 1793 that if he could provide "Any Little Service" in the future, "your commands Shall be cheerfully obeyed" (DLC:GW).

Tobias Lear to Thomas Jefferson

[Philadelphia] Decr 20th 1792

By the President's command, T. Lear has the honor to return to the Secretary of State the letter from the Treasurer of Virginia, which has been submitted to him[1]—and to request that the Secretary would inform the President where he can obtain a copy of the New Impressions of the Federal City? The President wishes to know if it would not be adviseable, in the Secretary's Opinion, to have a number of the plans of the City sent to our Ministers abroad, in order that the object may become more particularly know[n] abroad than it is at present.[2]

AL, DLC: Jefferson Papers. Jefferson docketed the letter: "Lear Tobias recd Dec. 20. 92."

1. Virginia treasurer Jaquelin Ambler reported in the enclosed letter to Jefferson of 10 Dec. the payment that morning of $10,000 "in part of the second instalment of the Monies voted by our Assembly towards the public Buildings at the Seat of Government of the United States: the residue will be paid, as soon as the state of our Treasury will enable me" (*Jefferson Papers*, 24:715). For background on Virginia's financial contribution to the new federal capital, see Jefferson to GW, 12 Nov. 1792 (first letter), and note 2, and GW to Ambler, 13 Nov., and notes.

2. GW is referring to a map of the Federal City recently completed by Philadelphia engravers James Thackara and John Vallance. For background on attempts to produce a suitable engraving of the new capital, see D.C. Commissioners to GW, 5 Oct. 1792, n.2. Following GW's suggestion, Jefferson wrote Thomas Pinckney, the U.S. minister to Great Britain, on 30 Dec. that he would send him "two dozen plans of the city of Washington in the Federal territory, which you are desired to display, not for sale but for public inspection, wherever they may be most seen by those descriptions of people worthy and likely to

be attracted to it, dividing the plans among the cities of London and Edinburgh chiefly, but sending some also to Glasgow, Bristol Dublin &c." (ibid., 803).

From Alexander Hamilton

Treasury Departmt 21st Decr 1792

The Secretary of the Treasury has the honor respectfully to submit to the President of the United States, two Contracts between the Superintendant of the Lighthouse at New London, and Daniel Harris & Nathaniel Richards, together with a letter from the Commissioner of the Revenue; from the date of which it will be seen that these papers have been overlooked for some time, a casualty from which however the service has received no injury.[1]

The Contract with Danl Harris is for his compensation as Keeper of the Lighthouse, and that with Nathaniel Richards for supplying it with oil and other necessaries. The terms of both of the objects appear to the Secretary reasonable.[2] All which is humbly submitted

Alex. Hamilton
Secy of the Treasury.

LB, DLC:GW.

1. Tench Coxe, in his letter to Hamilton of 10 Nov. 1792, enclosed "for the purpose of submission to the President, two contracts between the Superintendent of the light House at New London and Daniel Harris and Nathl Richards" (DNA: RG 58, Letters Sent by the Commissioner of the Revenue and the Revenue Office, 1792–1807; extract in Syrett, *Hamilton Papers*, 13:33–34). Jedediah Huntington was the superintendent of lighthouses, beacons, buoys, public piers, and stakes at New London, Connecticut.

2. Copies of these contracts, both dated 1 Oct. 1792, are in DNA: RG 26, Lighthouse Deeds and Contracts. Nathaniel Richards was to supply the lighthouse for one year with "strained Spermaceti Oil, Cotton wick, Candles & Soap," at a cost of $360, and Harris, as keeper of the lighthouse, received a salary of $80. Both men were to be paid quarterly. Tobias Lear, at GW's request, returned both contracts to Hamilton on 22 Dec., with a letter noting the "President's approbation annexed thereto" (DNA: RG 26, Inventory NC-31, entry 17J, Records Relating to the DLC Exhibit, "Papers Signed by Tobias Lear, 1789–93").

Letter not found: from Anthony Whitting, 21 Dec. 1792. GW wrote Whitting on 30 Dec.: "I have duly received your letters of the 21st & 26th instt."

Letter not found: to Francis Deakins and Benjamin Jones, c.22 Dec. 1792. Tobias Lear wrote to William Deakins, Jr., on this date: "The President of the United States directs me to transmit the enclosed letter to you, and beg the favor of your forwarding it to your brother Colo. Frs Deakins and Mr Jones, by the first safe opportunity that may offer after it gets to your hands" (DLC:GW).

From the French National Convention

[Paris, 22 December 1792][1]
President of the United States of North-America,

"Amidst the storms which buffet our infant liberty, it is a comfort to the French Republic, to have communication with a Republic founded as her own. Our brothers of the United States will no doubt have heard with gladness, the new revolution, which overthrew that last obstacle to our liberty. This revolution was necessary. Royalty was still existing, and in every constitution where it exists there is no true liberty. Kings and equality are incompatible with each other; it is their business to conspire against equality, and against the sovereignty of nations.[2]

"The United States of America will hardly credit it, but the national Convention have acquired proof of it:[3] the support which the ancient French Court had afforded them to recover their Independence, was only the fruit of base speculation; their glory offended its ambitious views, and the Ambassadors bore the criminal orders of stopping the career of their prosperity.

["]Nay, it is only between free nations that sincere and fraternal treaties can be formed. The liberty which the French Republic wishes to restore to the nations that shall call for her assistance, will not be polluted with similar stains; it shall be pure like herself.

"The immense distance which parts us prevents your taking in this glorious regeneration of Europe, that concern which your principles and past combats reserved to you. Single and alone against the coalition of Kings, we have shewn ourselves worthy of being called your brothers; and the ignominious retreat of their combined armies, Gennappe, Spires, Savoy, Flanders—all these successes ought to call to your remembrance Saratoga, Trenton, and York-Town.[4]

["]When will the final term of our struggles come? We do not yet know; but free americans, rely on our courage and perseverance; not a frenchman shall remain, or they shall all be free. Liberty shall become extinct in Europe, or our principles shall triumph every where over the league of despots. They have raised storms against us even in your own hemisphere; they have there excited our Islands to rebellion, but our principles and our arms will finally give them again calm and prosperity. The United States have contributed towards it, by the ample relief they have afforded our Colonies at a moment when France was too remote to give them support. Thanks to you generous americans! it is a debt which the gratitude of the French Republic discharges with heartfelt satisfaction.[5]

"The time is doubtless not far distant when the Colonies, far from being a subject of eternal rivalship and war, will only be a farther tie among nations. The time is not far distant when sound policy shall lay down the basis of commerce, not on exclusive interests, but on the conjoint interests of all, and on the nature of things. It depends on the Congress of the United States[6] to accelerate the happy moment, and the French Republic will eagerly give her concurrence to all the efforts they shall make for rivetting the political and commercial ties of two nations, who can no longer have but one common sentiment, since their principles and interests are the same."

The President of the National Convention

[Marguerite-Elie] Guadet

Translation, DNA: RG 59, Miscellaneous Letters. The translation is filed under the date of 1 Jan. 1794. The original French document used for the translation has not been determined. The address was printed in the *Gazette Nationale ou Le Moniteur Universal* (Paris) on 23 Dec. 1792.

1. The date is taken from the address in the *Gazette Nationale* and also from an English version in the *National Gazette* (Philadelphia) on 2 Mar. 1793.

2. For background on the abolition of the monarchy and the establishment of the National Convention in late September, see Gouverneur Morris to GW, 23 Oct. 1792, and source note.

3. The phrase beginning with "but" and ending with "it" does not appear in the French newspaper version.

4. The French army, after its victory of 6 Nov. over the allied armies of Austria and Prussia at Jemappes on the Belgian frontier, captured Brussels and subsequently most of Belgium. Earlier French military successes to the south included the capture of the German town of Spyer (Spires) and the province of Savoy, part of the kingdom of Piedmont-Sardinia, in late September 1792.

5. For background on the rebellion in the French colony of Saint Do-

mingue and U.S. aid to the French colonists and troops on the island, see Alexander Hamilton to GW, 19 Nov., and notes 1, 4, and 5, and Vicomte de Rochambeau to GW, 26 Nov., and note 1. For the rebellion in Martinique, see Fulwar Skipwith to GW, 25 Nov., and note 2.

6. This phrase in the French newspaper version reads: "courage des Etats-Unis."

From Alexander Hamilton

[Philadelphia] December 22d 1792.

The Secretary of the Treasury presents his respects to the President. The name of the person who was employed in superintending the erecting of the Lighthouse by mister Newton is *Lemuel Cornick*.[1] The compensation to the Keeper of the Delaware Lighthouse is 266 Dollars and ⅔ of a Dollar.[2]

LB, DLC:GW.

1. Thomas Newton, Jr., was responsible for arranging the contract for building the lighthouse at Cape Henry, Virginia. On this date GW appointed Lemuel Cornick, who had been overseeing construction of this lighthouse, as its new keeper (see Tobias Lear to Hamilton, 13 Oct. 1792, and note 1).

2. The keeper of the Cape Henlopen, Del., lighthouse was Abraham Hargis. For previous discussion of his salary, see Hamilton to GW, 18 June 1790, and note 1.

From Henry Knox

Sir   War department December 22d 1792

I have the honor to submit to you a letter from the Governor of Georgia dated the 5 instant with the deposition of Owen Bowen relatively to the murder of eight white persons.[1] I have the honor to be with the highest respect Your most obed. servant

H. Knox

LS, DLC:GW; LB, DLC:GW.

1. On 24 Dec. 1792 Bartholomew Dandridge, at GW's direction, wrote John Stagg, Jr., chief clerk of the War Department, that "the President thinks the letter &c. from the Govr of Georgia had better be laid before Congress" (DLC: GW). Knox submitted Gov. Edward Telfair's letter to him of 5 Dec. 1792 and its enclosure to the Senate on 24 Dec. (*Annals of Congress*, 2d Cong., 622–23). In the enclosed deposition, dated 3 Dec. at Richmond County, Ga., Owen T. Bowen reported that in late November the Cherokees murdered eight white residents of Franklin County, Ga., leaving their bodies "scalped, and cruelly

mangled." Telfair wrote in his letter: "It will now become indispensable that measures be taken to prevent farther outrage. Three companies of horse have already been ordered to range in that quarter where the murders have been committed, and it may be necessary that additional reinforcements be called in, to give protection and confidence to the settlers" (*ASP, Indian Affairs,* 1:336–37).

To Robert Lewis

Dear Sir,   Philadelphia, Decr 23d 1792

I wish you would, as soon as the enclosed letter gets to your hand⟨s⟩, call upon Major Harrison and endeavor to purchase from him the land therein mentioned, & for the reason therein assigned.[1]

If you can get it for a sum not exceeding forty shillings (virga curry) per Acre (wch is *a great deal more* than it is worth) close the bargain with him at once, provided, as is mentioned in the letter, the title is good, and it is not under the incumbrance of a lease— for in either of these cases I would not be concerned with the land unless I could obtain it on very low terms.

You might, after a short introduction of the subject to Major Harrison, shew him the enclosed letter—by way of bringing matters to a speedy explanation; but if you find his ideas of the value exceed 40/ pr Acre know what is the lowest terms he would sell on—the quantity of land he holds—and all the circumstances attending it, and give me notice thereof as early as you can, engaging him to wait a certain time for you to make the communication of them to me, & to receive my answer. Draw from *him* his lowest terms before *you* make any disclosure of what you would give, on my behalf.

When you was at Mount Vernon you expressed a wish to be possessed of the stud horse that was there. If he is not sold (for it was so intended when I left home) I make you a present of him.[2] I am Your Affecte Uncle

Go: Washington

ALS, NNMM: William A. Smith Collection; LB, DLC:GW.

1. See the enclosure for the other letter that GW wrote Lewis on 23 December. Robert Lewis wrote his uncle from "The Exchange Fauquier County," Va., on 4 Jan. 1793, that GW's "letter of the 23d ultimo with one inclosed of the same date, came duly to hand this day." In his letter to Lewis of 6 Jan. 1793,

GW enclosed copies of both 23 Dec. letters "on the *possibility* that the originals may have miscarried." Correspondence regarding Lewis's ultimately unsuccessful efforts to obtain William B. Harrison's land adjoining GW's Dogue Run farm, on which the gristmill stood, continued until August 1793 (see GW to Lewis, 7 Mar., 29 April, 26 July 1793, Lewis to GW, 9 Jan., 26 Mar., 17 July, 12 Aug. 1793). For GW's later negotiations to rent Harrison's land, see GW to Harrison, 4 Nov. 1798, and note 1. William B. Harrison (d. 1835) had served in Henry "Light-Horse Harry" Lee's battalion of light dragoons during the Revolutionary War.

2. GW wrote his estate manager Anthony Whitting on 6 Jan. 1793 that he had promised his nephew "the stud horse," and Whitting replied from Mount Vernon on 9 Jan. that the previous day Lewis had sent for "the Horse Sampson." See also GW to Whitting, 16 Dec. 1792, and note 14.

Enclosure
To Robert Lewis

Dear Sir,   Philadelphia Decr 23d: 1792

I have been informed within these few days that Major Harrison of Loudoun County who owns a piece of land adjoining my tract in Fairfax, is disposed to sell it, and to convert the money to more useful purposes.

I am led from the rascally set of Tenants who occupy that land —& by no other consideration whatsoever to become the purchaser of it, that I may be relieved by that means from the villainies which the livers thereon are frequently committing on my property—in the practice of which, their art & cunning is too great for detection. I have said my only motive to this purchase is to get rid of this pest of society and in saying so I have declared the honest truth; for the land would not answer for a farm being without timber, and too poor for cultivation—nor would it be profitable in Tenements because men who intended a livelihood by honest industry would give little or no Rent for it. & my inducement to buy is to get rid of those of a ⟨contrary⟩ description.

Major Harrison must be sensible that no one can be better acquainted with the land than I am—It would be unnecessary therefore (if he has any inclination to sell it) to ask a price which it will not bear—but if he is disposed to take a reasonable price and will act the par⟨t⟩ of a frank & candid man in fixing it I would not have you higgle (which I dislike) in making a bargain—I will ⟨pay⟩ ready money if we can agree—but it must be on two conditions—first—that the title is good—and secondly that it is not unde⟨r⟩ the incumbrance (any part of it) of a lease for that would defeat the sole end I should propose by the purchase—namely to purge the neighbourhood of these impure charac⟨ters.⟩

Under this view of my ideas, the knowledge you have of my sentimen⟨ts⟩ respecting the land any bargain you shall make in my behalf with Major Harrison shall be binding with me. Your Aunt unites with me in best regards for yourself and Mrs Lewis,[1] and I am Your Affecte Uncle

Go: Washington

ALS (letterpress copy), ViMtV; LB, DLC:GW. The text in angle brackets is provided from the letter-book copy.

1. Lewis was married to Judith Carter Browne.

To Anthony Whitting

Mr Whiting,   Philadelphia Decr 23d 1792.
Your letter of the 19th instant, enclosing the weekly reports, has been duly received.[1]

By Mr James Butler who left this City on friday last, I wrote you a few lines enclosing the agreement I had entered into with him.[2] I request that the Smiths Book may be put into his hands, and a regular account taken every night of what they have done in the day; and that he will see they do as much as they ought.[3] Let an Account be raised in that Book or some other, for each Plantation, and every thing done for it as regularly charged to it, as if it had been done for one of the neighbours who was to pay therefor. A practice of this sort answers too purposes—first, to see that the Smiths do their duty; and secondly, as a check upon the Plantations; who ought to account for what is received from thence, as well as for every thing else, that is furnished them in the course of the year, as soon as it shall have expired. It is my desire also that Mr Butler will pay some attention to the conduct of the Gardener & the hands who are at work with him; so far as to see that they are not idle; for, though I will not charge them with idleness, I cannot forbear saying, and I wish you to tell the Gardener so (provided you shall think there is cause for it) that the matters entrusted to him appear to me to progress amazingly slow. I had no conception that there were grubs[4] enough in the Vineyard enclosure to have employed them as many days as are reported; & sure I am that levelling the Bank ought to have taken a very little time. If it is found that the hands with the Gardener are not usefully (I mean industriously) employed, I shall withdraw them; as I did not give them to him for *parade,* to be *idle,* or to keep him in *idleness.*[5]

Mr Butler says he has been much accustomed to Hedging. I have told him how extremely anxious I am on this head; and I request you will aid him all in your power to rear them speedily. He is very fond of the French furze—and has no doubt of succeeding with the thorn—if, therefore, the berries of these are still on the trees, let them be gathered; & with every thing else that can be thought of, tried without more loss of time than is required for the proper season.

Anthony's Toe should be examined and if it requires it something should be done to it, otherwise, as usual, it will serve him as a pretence to be in the house half the Winter.[6] I have no objection to Sinah's remaining as part of the Mansion House gang; but I have strong ones for the reasons mentioned in a late letter, to her being employed in, or about the Dairy.[7] The reason which you assign however for retaining her there, has no weight with me; for it is not my intention, hence forward, that *any* of the House gang shall be employed in Fencing at the Plantations— there is no more propriety in employing them in the Post and Rail fences at Dogue run or the Ferry, than there would be in any other Sort of Fencing: Let every Plantation do their own work— they are sufficiently strong for it—and have no right to look for more aid than is to be derived from the Ditchers in that article. It would seem to me as if the progress in getting & securing the Corn at the River Plantation was extremely slow. One would not judge from this circumstance that the Crop of this Grain would prove so very short.

If you could, by means of Mr [William] Hartshorn, or any of the Merchants in Alexandria who have dealings in Loudoun, procure the deficient quantity of BuckWheat at 3/ or even 3/6 delivered at Mount Vernon, I would have you do it. Otherwise you must apply what you have to the best purposes your own judgment shall direct, for I could send none from hence at the highest of those prices.

It certainly wd be to my advantage to buy Majr Harrisons Land adjoining mine if it could be had on reasonable terms; but for *no other reason* than that which you have mentioned; but from the appearance of the new buildings which I saw on the land when I was last at home, I suspect that reason will not apply—that is— from this circumstance I apprehend he has given lease on the land, in wch case I should not be relieved from my present inconvenience by the purchase; as the riddance of bad neighbours would be the only object I could have in view. If you can, by indirect enquiries (so conducted as not to alarm the Pools) ascertain this fact & let me know the result, it would enable me to judge better of this matter.[8]

The Peach stones which were sent to you are from Georgia— desire the Gardener to pay proper attention to them.

I do not regard the temporary fall in the prices of Wheat & flour; as there is no radical cause for it—but, on the other hand the calls which occasioned the rise are still existing the prices, I will engage, will be up again; and more than probable be higher than ever before March. All the flour therefore that you can get safely stored (before the Navigation is closed) in Alexandria, will be ready for the first exports in the Spring.

It is observed, by the weekly reports, that the Sowers make only Six shirts a week, and the last week Caroline (without being sick) made only five;[9] Mrs Washington says their usual task was to make nine with Shoulder straps, & good sewing: tell them therefore from me, that what *has* been done, *shall* be done by fair or foul means; & they had better make choice of the first, for their own reputation, & for the sake of peace & quietness. otherwise they will be sent to the several Plantations, & be placed as common laborers under the Overseers thereat⟨.⟩[10] Their work ought to be well examined, or it will be most shamefully executed, whether little or much of it be done—And it is said, the same attention ought to be given to Peter (& I suppose to Sarah likewise) or the Stockings will be knit too small for those for whom they are intended; such being the idleness, & deceit of those people.[11] I am your friend and well wisher

Go: Washington

ALS, DLC:GW.

1. Whitting's letter and the enclosed reports have not been found.

2. See GW to Whitting, 19 December. GW's agreement with Butler, the new overseer at the Mansion House farm, has not been found.

3. The smith's book has not been found. Nat (Natt), married to the dower

slave Lucy at the Dogue Run farm, and George, married to the dower slave Lydia at the River farm, were the two smiths identified in Washington's Slave List of June 1799 and in his earlier list of 1786 (Slave List, 18 Feb. 1786, in *Diaries,* 4:278).

4. Grubs were roots left in the ground after clearing.

5. For GW's instructions concerning the designation of slaves to work with gardener John Christian Ehlers and for some of the projects assigned to him and his workers, see GW to Whitting, 14 October.

6. Anthony appears on the 1786 slave list as a laborer at the Mansion House farm (ibid.), but he is not on the list of June 1799. Whitting recorded Anthony as "Lame with a sore Toe" on the farm report of 30 Dec. 1792–5 Jan. 1793 (DLC:GW).

7. For GW's desire to reassign Sinah and his low opinion of the quality of her work, see GW to Whitting, 28 Oct., and note 3, and 9 December.

8. For GW's efforts to acquire William B. Harrison's land adjoining the Dogue Run farm, see GW to Robert Lewis, 23 Dec., and note 1, and its enclosed letter from GW to Lewis, 23 December. The Pools were a numerous family, some of whom lived near the Dogue Run farm on the road from GW's mill to Robert Boggess's house on the Cameron-Colchester stage road (see *Fairfax Index,* cards no. 30 and 54 for 22 Sept. 1789 and 16 Oct. 1797). For a short time during the 1750s, William Pool acted as GW's miller (see William Pool to GW, 9 July 1758, and notes).

9. Dower slave Caroline is identified as a housemaid in the 1786 slave list and again in Washington's Slave List of June 1799 where she is listed as married to Peter Hardman (Slave List, 18 Feb. 1786, in *Diaries,* 4:277).

10. The foregoing sentence was written on the left margin of the manuscript and noted for insertion at this place in the text.

11. For GW's earlier complaint about the work habits of the knitters, see his letter to Whitting of 18 Nov. 1792.

From "A Genuine Federalist"

Sir   Ohio River decr 25th 1792

How you will Brook this I know not and most probably will never know, be that as it May I hope you will attend to the following hints, so far as the[y] merit attention the[y] are Communicated by one who has neither a disposition to flatter nor to give offence and who is actuated by no other Motives than a desire to promote the publick interest and avert the evils with which we are threatned. Our Situation on the frontiers is Rather Irksome at present more especially when our Complaints against an Injust and unequal tax are endeavoured to be Construed into an Insurection[1] when our Militia after being harrased with long and fataguing duty on the frontiers, and by the express order of the

war department as well as the Executive of the States of virginia
and pennsylvania to have thier Accounts mangled and tortured
at the Sovereign pleasure of Mr Knox, is not a very agreeable Circumstance, that a part of the acounts Should be Settled and paid
whilest others for Simular Services are Rejected can only be ascribed to the Same Cause that adopted and Rendered the funding System Mysterious[2] but it is not so much my design to Criti-
cize on the proceedings of the goverment as to point out the
danger to which both the goverment and us are exposed, nor
would I have mentioned the Circumstances alluded to above,
but to Shew that it will have a tendency to Irritate the minds of
the people here and alienate theire affections from the goverment. you know our Situation well, and the disposition of the
British Can not be a secret to you, upon the appearance of
Coercive Measures by our goverment to enforce the Excise the
Bretish will offer us protection, you may think of this as you
please; but the Subject is freely Spoken of at this time among
the people and I am not Certain whether there are not Bretish
emissarys at this moment in the Country to Sound the minds of
the people on that Subject in all the Conversations I have had
thereon, this appears to be the general Opinion, that if the British will give us a free trade on the Messepipie [(]unless the Same
Can be obtained through the means of our own goverment)
every man without exception that I have heard give an Opinion
declares in favour of becoming a British Subject, at all events you
know that if we ask the British to extend their goverment to us
they will Recaive us thankfully.[3] to prevent this is the object of
the present address. and I declare most Solemnly that I have no
design either to do wrong or to hurt your feelings, but from the
purest motives to express my Ideas of this business, in order then
to quiet the minds of the people, direct that immediate payment
be maid for thire Services, its not improbable that Militia Services may be again necessary, Recommend to the Legislatuer a
repeal of the Excise law at least so far as either an immediate Repeal or as Soon as an Equal System Can be substituted in its place
but let a certain day be fixed beyound which the operation of that
Law Shall not pass. if a direct tax is thought impracticable recommend a Stamp duty this may be so Regulated that it will apply
equally, paid with Conveniency and be as productive as the Excise. the people are not so much governed by prejudice as the in-

genious Secretary seems to Imagine the word Stamp duty will be as agreeable to the freemen of america as that of Excise—obtain possession of detroit and Niagara,[4] this may be done two ways, first by a non Importation act, or secondly by raising an army Competent to the Service the first is no doubt the eligible at the same time a small force of five or six thousand active woods men may be Necessary to Cover the frontier untill the non Importation act has its desired effect. I believe the publick service would not be Injured if the present Commander in Chief of the troops Could be provided for in some other way and Genls Hand or Irvine appointed to the Command, you may probably think this Improper to be Communcated, but it Can be kept a Secret. I assure you on my part I will not mention it to any person but your self and Im sure you will not divulge it. if vouleentiers should be Required from the frontiers of pennsylvania and virginia nixt Campaign Genls Jams wood notwithstanding he lives at Richmond has the Confidence of the people here.[5] I Subscribe My Self as in fact I am a

Genuine federalist

P.S. It may be objected that a non-importation act would injure the Revinue to this I answer that the effect would be only temporary and scarcely be felt, because, every Merchant whose Circumstances would admit would import from Holland and other Countries, besides the small embarrassment the act would create would try the abilities of the Secretary and ascertain beyond a doubt whether he possess talents adeqate to the object of his appointment The army in general stands in need of a purgation, the greater part of the Officers are ill chosen and the men are worse; but I suppose the pay would not procure better, it's said Billey Faulknier is to have a Majority, if so, you will not have an officer in the army under that rank fit for the service.[6]

AL, DLC:GW. The letter is docketed as being received on 1⟨4⟩ Feb. 1793. The postscript is in the writing of a different, unidentified person. That person also may be the one who corrected erroneous spellings at five places in the main body of the letter. A note written in pencil by historian Jared Sparks appears at the end of the letter: "Evidently written by a man of some standing, & copied by an illiterate person. J.S."

1. See GW's proclamation of 15 Sept., which was issued in response to the violent opposition, especially in the western counties of Pennsylvania, to the federal excise tax on whiskey.

2. For recent delays in paying U.S. troops, see Knox to GW, 15 Sept, and

note 2. For the Washington administration's deployment and payment of militia forces, see Tobias Lear to Knox, 21 Nov., n.3. For Knox's thoughts on the use of state militias, see his "Statement Relative to the Frontiers Northwest of the Ohio," 26 Dec. 1791, in *ASP, Indian Affairs*, 197–202.

The writer blames Alexander Hamilton's financial policies, particularly "An Act making provision for the (payment of the) Debt of the United States" (see 1 *Stat.* 138–44), for the injustices produced by the federal government.

3. The Senate on 24 Jan. 1792 approved the appointment of William Carmichael and William Short as joint commissioners plenipotentiary to negotiate with Spain for the U.S. right of free navigation on the Mississippi River (see GW to the U.S. Senate, 11 Jan. 1792; *Executive Journal*, 99). Their efforts, however, failed, and it was not until the Treaty of San Lorenzo el Real of 27 Oct. 1795 that Spain agreed to grant the United States the right of navigation on the Mississippi (see Miller, *Treaties*, 318–45).

4. The British still occupied forts Detroit and Niagara in violation of the Peace Treaty of 1783 and did not withdraw their troops from those and other northern forts along the American-Canadian border until after John Jay negotiated the 1794 Treaty of Amity, Commerce, and Navigation with Great Britain (see ibid., 245–74).

5. The writer obviously opposed Anthony Wayne's recent appointment as commander in chief of the U.S. Army and preferred the leadership of Revolutionary War officers Edward Hand, James Irvine, and James Wood. For GW's opinion on the leadership of Wayne, Hand, and Irvine, see his Memorandum on General Officers, 9 Mar. 1792.

6. For the reasons some residents of western Pennsylvania might oppose Capt. William Faulkner's promotion to major, see Hamilton to GW, 1 Sept., and notes 2 and 6.

Henry Knox to Tobias Lear

½ after ten oClock Xmas Evg
My dear Sir   [Philadelphia, 25 December 1792]
Be pleased to submit some letters, or rather copies of Letters received this Evg from Genl Wilkinson. I beleive these are his *highly confidential* dispatches mentioned to Genl Wayne.[1] In addition there are some returns of stores which I do not send. The Wabash Indians will Arrive tomorrow.[2] Yours sincerely

H. Knox

ALS, DLC:GW; LB, DLC:GW. The ALS is docketed: "From The Secy of War 26 Decr 1792," and it is filed in DLC:GW under that date. The letter-book copy is dated "26th Decr 1792."

1. The letters from James Wilkinson have not been identified. Knox is referring to his own letter to Anthony Wayne of 22 Dec., in which he acknowl-

edged receiving Wilkinson's letters of 6 Nov. (see Lear to Knox, 18 Dec., n.1).
"But," Knox wrote, "I have not received any of a later date, when his highly
confidential letters arrive mentioned in his of the 14 Ultimo, copies shall be
transmitted to you" (Knopf, *Wayne*, 153). For Wilkinson's "confidential letters,"
see Knox to GW, 26 Dec., n.1.

2. For background on the visit to Philadelphia by a delegation of Wabash
and Illinois Indians, who arrived on 26 Dec. 1792, see GW to Knox, 3 Sept.
(first letter), and note 3, and Wilkinson to GW, 1 Nov., n.1.

To Thomas Newton, Jr.

Sir,   Philada December 25th 1792.

I am sorry it is not in my power to give you such precise information relative to the subject of your Letter to me of the 9th instant as may be satisfactory to yourself, or serviceable to the object mentioned in it.[1]

I do not recollect ever to have seen the Will of the Revd Mr
Green, so that I can say nothing from that; but I remember it was
impressed on my mind that the woman Sarah, of whom you
Speak, was to have had her freedom—but whether it was to have
taken place on the death of Mr Green, or on the death of his
wife, or from what other period, I am not able to say. I recollect,
however, that she lived with Mrs Green while she was a widow,
& after her marriage to Doctr Savage, but whether as a slave, or
upon other conditions is more than I know. The Revd Mister
[Bryan] Fairfax & myself were appointed Trustees on behalf of
Mrs Savage for certain purposes, but they had no relation to this
woman. If a reference to Mr Green's Will be necessary on this
subject, I presume it may be found among the Records of Fairfax County.[2] I am, Sir, &ca

                                        Go: Washington

LB, DLC:GW.
1. Newton's letter to GW of 9 Dec. has not been found.
2. For background on GW's involvement in the settlement of the estate of
the Rev. Charles Green and his widow, Margaret, who subsequently married
Dr. William Savage, see Henry Lee and Daniel Payne to GW, 24 April 1767, and
note 1, Thomas Montgomerie to GW, 24 Oct. 1788, and source note, and John
Dixon to GW, 5 Mar. 1789, n.1. For Charles Green's will, see Fairfax County
Will Book B-1 (1752–67), 398–99, in ViFaCt. The settlement of the Thomas
Colvill estate was also troublesome for GW. George Brooke, clerk of the district court at Dumfries, Va., issued a summons on 20 Oct. 1792 to James Keith
"to testify and the truth to say on behalf of George Washington Esq. in a cer-

tain matter of controversy . . . between the said George Washington and Adam Stewart and others" (MiU-C: Haskell Collection).

From Henry Knox

Sir   [Philadelphia] 5 oClock 26 Decr 1792

I have the honor to submit two letters from Brigr Genl Wilkinson with their enclosures. These were received by express, who left Fort Washington the 1st of Decr.[1] I have the honor to be respectfully Your obedient Servant

H. Knox

ALS, DLC:GW; LB, DLC:GW.

1. The letters from James Wilkinson have not been identified, but they are probably those mentioned by Knox in his letter to Gen. Anthony Wayne of 28 December. "I have received," Knox wrote, "from Brigadier General Wilkinson by express letters dated the 9th and 18 Ultimo enclosing copies to you of the 13th. November" (Knopf, *Wayne*, 154). The enclosed copies were a series of letters, which Knox had war clerk Benjamin Bankson copy, reporting problems with the shipment of payroll money and various supplies for the army (see Wilkinson to John Belli, 9, 10 Nov., Belli to Wilkinson, 9 Nov., Mahlon Ford to Wilkinson, 12 Nov., Caleb Swan to Wilkinson, 28 Oct., 10 Nov., and Wilkinson to Swan, 9 Nov. 1792, in PHi: Wayne Papers). Those letters originally were enclosed in Wilkinson's letter to Wayne of 13 Nov. from Fort Washington (PHi: Wayne Papers), and they were probably the "confidential" letters mentioned in Knox's letter to Tobias Lear of 25 Dec. 1792.

Knox in his letter of 28 Dec. informed Wayne: "It is highly proper that you should cause inquiry to be made into the nature and degree of the Confusion of Stores and Clothing complained of by Brigadier General Wilkinson." After reviewing some recent shipments, Knox observed: "There were no precautions neglected to prevent mistakes and if any have arisen they cannot with justice be charged to any persons who had the direction of the business in Philadelphia." Knox then turned his attention to another grievance: "The complaints relatively to the pay department in the district of Brigadier General Wilkinson requires an instant remedy—It certainly would have been a good opportunity by Major [Michael] Rudulph's detachment to have forwarded the money for the troops below, and you must have had some powerful reason for withholding it. . . . The Secretary of the Treasury is highly desirous the troops should be paid up and punctually every month. . . . I hope you may have received the letter of Brigadier Wilkinson of the 13th and its five enclosures, as it is of considerable importance—But if any accident should have happened to it copies shall be forwarded to you as soon as can be made" (ibid., 154–57).

Letter not found: from Anthony Whitting, 26 Dec. 1792. GW wrote Whitting on 30 Dec.: "I have duly received your letters of the 21st & 26th instt."

From Thomas Barclay

Sir   Cadiz [Spain] 27th Decr 1792

I received on the 24th of this Month, through Mr Pinckney, your Excellencys Commands of the 11th of June, to which all deference and attention possible will be shewn.[1] Mr Jefferson will naturally inform you of what I have written to him by this opportunity,[2] and therefore I shall take up no more of your time than to assure you of the respect wherewith I am, Sir, Your Most Obedient Most humble serv:

Thos Barclay

ALS, DNA: RG 59, Despatches from Consular Offices, Cadiz; ADf, DNA: RG 59, Despatches from Consular Offices, Cadiz.

1. GW's letter to Barclay of 11 June was enclosed in Thomas Jefferson's first letter to Thomas Pinckney of the same date (see *Jefferson Papers*, 24:59). GW had directed Barclay, the U.S. consul to Morocco, to carry out the duties assigned to Adm. John Paul Jones in case of Jones's death or incapacity. Since Jones died in Paris on 18 July 1792, Barclay now assumed those duties, which were to proceed to Algiers to establish peace with that nation, ransom the U.S. citizens held captive there, and act as the U.S. consul to Algiers. Barclay, however, died on 19 Jan. 1793. For background on the Algiers mission, see GW to Thomas Jefferson, 10 Mar., and note 3, Conversation with a Committee of the U.S. Senate, 12 Mar., Jefferson to GW, 1 April, and note 1, Jefferson's Memorandum on a Treaty with Algiers, 10 April, and source note, and GW to the U.S. Senate, 8 May (third letter) 1792, and note 2. For Jones's instructions, see Jefferson's letter to Jones of 1 June 1792, ibid., 3–10.

2. Barclay enclosed his letter to GW in a letter to Jefferson of 27 Dec., which Jefferson docketed as being received on 25 Feb. 1793 (ibid., 791).

Thomas Jefferson's Conversation with Washington

[Philadelphia, 27 December 1792]

Thursday Dec. 27. 92. I waited on the President on some current business. after this was over, he observed to me he thought it was time to endeavor to effect a stricter connection with France & that G. Morris should be written to on this subject. he went into the circumstances of dissatisfaction between Spain, Gr. Brit. & us, & observed there was no nation on whom we could rely at all times but France, and that if we did not prepare in time some support in the event of rupture with Spain & England we might be charged with a criminal negligence. (I was much pleased with the tone of these observations. it was the very doctrine which had been my polar star, and I did not need the successes of the Republican arms in France lately announced to us, to bring me to these sentiments. for it is to be noted that on Saturday last (the 22d) I received mister Short's letters of Oct. 9. & 12. with the Leyden gazettes to Oct. 13. giving us the first news of the retreat of the D. of Brunswic, and the capture of Spires & Worms by Custine, and that of Nice by Anselme.) [1] I therefore expressed to the President my cordial approbation of these ideas: told him I had meant on that day (as an opportunity of writing by the British packet would occur immediately) to take his orders for removing the suspension of paiments to France which had been imposed by my last letter to G. Morris, but was meant as I supposed only for the interval between the abolition of the late constitution by the dethronement of the king and the meeting of some other body invested by the will of the nation with powers to transact their affairs. that I considered the national convention then assembled as such a body, and that therefore we ought to go on with the paiments to them or to any government they should establish.[2] that however I had learned last night that some clause in the bill for providing reimbursement of the loan made by the bank to the U.S. had given rise to a question before the house of representatives yesterday which might affect these paiments; a clause in that bill proposing that the money formerly borrowed in Amsterdam to pay the French debt & appropriated by law (1790. Aug. 4. c.34.s.2.) to that purpose, lying dead as was suggested, should be taken to pay the bank, and the Presidt be authorized to borrow 2. millions of Dol. more out of which it should be replaced, and if this should be done the removal of our suspension of paiment as I had been about to propose, would be premature. he expressed his disapprobation of the clause abovementioned, thought it highly improper in the legislature to change an appropriation once made, and added that no one could tell in what that would end. I concurred, but observed that on a division of the house the ayes for striking out the clause were 27. the noes 26. whereon the Speaker gave his vote against striking out, which dividing the house, the clause for the disappropriation remained of course. I mentd suspicions that the whole of this was a trick to serve the bank under a great existing embarrasment. that the debt to the bank was to be repaid by instalments, that the 1st instalment was of 200,000 D. only, or rather 160,000 D. (because 40,000 of the 200,000 would be

the U. States' own dividend of the instalment) yet here were
2,000,000 to be paid them at once, & to be taken from a purpose
of gratitude & honor to which it had been appropriated.[3]

AD, DLC: Jefferson Papers.

1. For William Short's letters to Jefferson of 9 and 12 Oct., written from The
Hague and enclosing recent issues of the *Gazette de Leide,* see *Jefferson Papers,*
24:455–58, 474–76. After initial victories at Longwy on 23 Aug. and Verdun
on 2 Sept., the allied armies of Prussia and Austria, under the command of the
Duke of Brunswick, suffered a major defeat at the Battle of Valmy on 20 Sept.
1792. The subsequent retreat of the allied armies enabled French troops under Adam-Philippe, comte de Custine (1740–1793), to occupy the German
cities of Speyer (Spires), Worms, Mainz, and Frankfort on the Main on 29 Sept.,
4, 21, and 23 Oct., respectively, and French forces commanded by Jacques-
Bernard-Modeste d'Anselme (1740–1812) in late September to capture Nice,
a city in the kingdom of Piedmont-Sardinia.

2. See Jefferson's first letter to Gouverneur Morris, the U.S. minister to
France, of 7 Nov., in which Jefferson, acknowledging the news that the French
constitution had been suspended, wrote: "During the time of this supension,
and while no legitimate government exists, we apprehend that we cannot
continue the payments of our debt to France, because there is no person authorised to recieve it, and to give us an unobjectionable acquittal. You are
therefore desired to consider the paiment as suspended until further orders"
(*Jefferson Papers,* 24:592–94). For background on recent events in France, including the abolition of the monarchy and the election of the National Convention in late September, see Morris to GW, 23 Oct., and source note.

On 30 Dec., Jefferson added the following paragraph beneath the text of his
notes on his conversation with GW: "I took the occasion furnished by Pinckney's letter of Sep. 19. asking instructions how to conduct himself (as to the
French revolution,) to lay down the Catholic principle of republi[c]anism, to
wit, that every people may establish what form of government they please, and
change it as they please. the will of the nation being the only thing essential. I
was induced to do this in order to extract the President's opinion on the question which divided Hamilton & myself in the conversation of Nov. [   ] 92
and the previous one of the first week of Nov. on the suspension of paimts to
France and if favorable to mine to place the principle of record in the letter
books of my office. I therefore wrote the letter of Dec. 30. to Pinckney & sent
it to the President, & he returned me his approbation in writing in his note of
the same date. which see." For GW's approval of Jefferson's letter to Thomas
Pinckney, the U.S. minister to Great Britain, of 30 Dec., and for Jefferson's inclusion of the "Catholic principle" of republicanism in his letter to Pinckney,
see GW to Jefferson, 30 Dec., and note 1.

3. In compliance with section 11 of "An Act to incorporate the subscribers
to the Bank of the United States," 25 Feb. 1791, the federal government purchased $2 million of shares in the Bank of the United States with money from
loans previously obtained to pay the public debt. The bank, in turn, advanced
the government that sum to be used to reduce the public debt. The loan was
"reimbursable in ten years, by equal annual instalments; or at any time sooner,

or in any greater proportions, that the government may think fit" (1 *Stat.* 196). See also "An Act making provision for the (payment of the) Debt of the United States," 4 Aug. 1790, and "An Act making Provision for the Reduction of the Public Debt," 12 Aug. 1790, (ibid., 138–44, 186–87). In compliance with those two acts, the United States had negotiated loans with bankers in Antwerp and Amsterdam (see William Short to Alexander Hamilton, 8 Nov. 1791, n.4, in *Hamilton Papers*, 9:481–82; Ratification of the Holland Loan, 1 Sept. 1791, and Ratification Statement, 5 Nov. 1792).

On 24 Dec. 1792 the House of Representatives began debate on a bill that would authorize the president to borrow an additional $2 million to reimburse the Bank of the United States for its loan. Debate resumed on 26 Dec. and ended later that day with a vote on a motion to reduce the amount of any new loan to $200,000. The motion was defeated by the vote cast by the Speaker of the House, Jonathan Trumbull. On 27 Feb. 1793 the House resumed its debate on the bill and approved a motion to strike out the entire section authorizing a new loan (see *Annals of Congress*, 2d Cong., 753–62, 897–98). The issue was settled with "An Act providing for the payment of the First Instalment due on a Loan made of the Bank of the United States" of 2 Mar. 1793, which authorized the president to make the first payment of $200,000 to the Bank of the United States from funds already borrowed for reducing the debt (1 *Stat.* 338).

From the Massachusetts Masons

An Address of the Grand Lodge of Free and Accepted Masons for the Commonwealth of Massachusetts, To their Honored and Illustrious Brother, GEORGE WASHINGTON.

Boston December 27 A.D. 1792

Whilst the Historian is describing the career of your glory, and the inhabitants of an extensive Empire are made happy in your unexampled exertions: Whilst some celebrate the Hero so distinguished in liberating United America; and others the Patriot, who presides over her Councils; a Band of Brothers having always joined the acclamations of their Countrymen, now testify their respect for those milder virtues which have ever graced the Man.

Taught by the precepts of our Society, that all its Members *stand upon a level,* we venture to assume this station, and to approach you with that Freedom which diminishes our Diffidence without lessening our Respect.

Desirous to enlarge the boundaries of Social happiness, and to vindicate the Ceremonies of their Institution, this Grand Lodge have published a "Book of Constitutions," (& a copy for your acceptance accompanies this;) which by discovering the principles that actuate, will speak the Eulogy of the Society;[1] though they fervently wish the conduct of its Members, may prove its higher commendation.

Convinced of his attachment to its cause, & readiness to encourage its benevolent designs; they have taken the liberty to dedicate this work to one, the qualities of whose heart, and the actions of whose life have contributed to improve personal virtue, and extend throughout the World, the most endearing Cordialities: & they humbly hope he will pardon this Freedom, and accept the tribute of their esteem and homage.[2]

May the Supreme Architect of the Universe protect and bless you, give you length of days, & increase of Felicity in this World and then receive you to the harmonious and exalted Society in Heaven.[3]

John Cutler   Grand Master.
Josiah Bartlett.   Mungo Mackay   Grand Wardens.

DS, DLC:GW; LB, DLC:GW.

1. A copy of *The Constitutions of the Ancient and Honourable Fraternity of Free and Accepted Masons* (Worcester, Mass., 1792) was in GW's library at the time of his death (see Griffin, *Boston Athenæum Washington Collection*, 54).

2. At some undetermined date early in 1793, GW wrote a letter thanking the Massachusetts Masons for their testimonial and for the enclosed book (LB, DLC:GW).

3. This testimonial appeared in the 20 Feb. 1793 issue of the *Gazette of the United States* (Philadelphia).

David Rittenhouse to Tobias Lear

Sir   [Philadelphia] Thursday Decemr 27th 1792

We have begun to Assay some of the European Coins, and shall proceed tomorrow, at the Mint, if it will be convenient for the President to attend about 12 oClock.[1] Should any accident happen before that time to occasion delay, I will give you notice. I am, Sir, your most obedient humble Servant

Davd Rittenhouse

ALS, DNA: RG 59, Miscellaneous Letters.

1. For the resolution directing GW to have the gold and silver coins of France, England, Spain, and Portugal assayed, see the U.S. House of Representatives to GW, 29 Nov., and note 1. Director of the Mint David Rittenhouse submitted the assay report to Thomas Jefferson on 7 Jan. 1793, and Jefferson,

under whose jurisdiction the Mint lay, sent it to the House the next day (see Jefferson to GW, 8 Jan. 1793, and note 1).

From the United States House of Representatives

United States [Philadelphia]
Sir,   27th of Decr 1792.

In obedience to the order of the House of Representatives, I have the honor to enclose you their Resolution of this date.[1] With the most perfect respect, I am sir, Your mot Obedt & very hble Servant.

Jonathan Trumbull, speaker
of the Ho: of Representatives.

LB, DLC:GW. This letter appears under the heading: "December the 27th. The following Letter, with the Resolution enclosed was this day recd by the President."

1. The letter-book copy of the enclosed resolution, signed by John Beckley, clerk of the House of Representatives, reads: "Resolved, that the President of the United States be requested to cause this House to be furnished with a particular Account of the several sums borrowed under his authority, by the United States; the terms on which each Loan has been obtained; the applications to which any of the monies have been made, agreeable to appropriations; and the balances, if any, which remain unapplied: In this Statement it is requested, that it may be specified, at what times interest commenced on the several sums obtained, and at what times it was stopped, by the several payments made" (DLC:GW).

In response to that resolution, Tobias Lear wrote Alexander Hamilton on 28 Dec. "that the President requests the Secretary to have a statement prepared, agreeably to the Resolution of the House of Representatives, of which a copy is enclosed, to be laid before the House as soon as it conveniently can be done" (DLC:GW). Hamilton submitted his report, dated 3 Jan. 1793, to the House on 4 Jan. (see Syrett, *Hamilton Papers*, 13:451–62).

From Henry B. Baker

Honord Sir,   Philada Decr 28th 1792

You will observe by the enclosd Papers the unhappy Situation that I now labour under, and a recommendation from Colo. Henry Hollingsworth Major Edward Oldham Major Thomas M. Forman & other reputable Characters of Cecil County—I hope your honour will pardon the liberty I take, being urgd by the greatest necessity & a confidance of recieving a Small pecuniary assistance from your generous hand that was always ready to render relieve to a distressd Soldier[1]—My inability Please your honor denies me the opportunity of doing any thing in an active way towards the support of my distressd family to whom I must return nearly disconsalate—Should it not be in my Power to Procure an under Clerks place in some of the Public Offices in Town—I flater myself if your honor would be so kind as to oblige me with a line or two to Genl Knox and Colo. Hamilton, I should succeed in the application this circumstance Honord Sir, (as it is my last effort to support my dear Wife & suffering little Ones) would be recorded by kind Providance, a⟨s⟩ a fresh instance of your unlimited humanity for unhappy mortals who sufferd in the service of thier Country. In Duty bound Honord Sir, With Humble Submission I shall ever remain your most Obedt most Humb. Servt

Henry b. Baker

P.S. I hope your honor will oblige me with an answer by the Bearer Mr Sanders.[2] H.b.B.

ALS, DNA: RG 59, Miscellaneous Letters. The letter is docketed: "Mr J. H. Baker 29 Decr 1792."

Henry Baker, who had served as a lieutenant in the Maryland line during the Revolutionary War, was listed under Back Creek Hundred in Cecil County in the 1790 census for Maryland as having in his household two white males under the age of 16 and two white females (see *Heads of Families* [Maryland], 40).

1. The enclosed papers and the recommendation have not been identified. Henry Hollingsworth (1737–1803), Edward Oldham (c.1756–1798), and Thomas Marsh Forman (1758–1845), all prominent residents of Cecil County and Revolutionary War veterans, served as representatives in the lower house of the Maryland assembly in 1792. Forman, an aide-de-camp to Lord Stirling in 1779, later commanded a militia brigade during the War of 1812.

2. Neither a letter from GW to Knox or Hamilton mentioning Baker nor a reply from GW to Baker has been found.

Tobias Lear to Daniel Bowen

[Philadelphia] Decr 28th [1]792

Mr Lear presents his Compliments to Mr Bowen[1] & will thank him to send by the Bearer the six framed pictures which Mr B. bid off yesterday for the President[2]—Whenever Mr Bowen has leisure to draw off the Acct of the Prints &c. bo[ugh]t by him for the President Mr Lear will immediately pay it—and it would be pleasing to the President if he could know what would be a compensation to Mr Bowen for the trouble he has had & the politeness with which he has executed this business.

AL, NN: Washington Collection; AL (photocopy), DLC:GW, ser. 9.

1. Daniel Bowen (1760–1856) was a wax modeler and one of America's first museum proprietors. He displayed not only his own wax sculptures but also the works of various American artists in his several museums: New York City in 1789 and 1794, Philadelphia in 1790 and 1792–94, Boston in 1791 and 1795–1825. GW visited Bowen's first museum, at 74 Water Street in New York City, in September 1789 (see *Pennsylvania Packet* [Philadelphia], 24 Sept. 1789), where he saw a life-size figure of himself sculpted out of wax: "The President of the United States sitting under a Canopy, in his Military Dress.—Over the Head of his Excellency a Fame is suspended (also in Wax) crowning him with a Wreath of Laurels" (*New-York Journal, and Weekly Register,* 17 Sept. 1789).

2. Bowen, whose museum currently was in Philadelphia at 9 North Eighth Street, the "former Mrs Pine's" (see *Gazette of the United States* [Philadelphia], 29 Dec. 1792), probably purchased the six pictures for GW at the "PUBLIC SALE of Prints, Plate, Plated Ware, &c. . . . On Wednesday the 26th Inst. . . . at the House late Mrs. PINE's in Eighth street." The auction included "*A Capital Collection of* Mezzotinto and Copperplate PRINTS and ETCHINGS, Engraved by the first Artists, from Paintings of the most celebrated Painters, Ancient and Modern; being, perhaps, the most extensive and valuable Collection of PRINTS ever Imported into America" (see *Dunlap's American Daily Advertiser* [Philadelphia], 21 Dec. 1792). For the numerous prints and paintings at Mount Vernon at the time of GW's death, see Prussing, *Estate of George Washington,* 410–48.

From Gouverneur Morris

My dear Sir   Paris 28 Decr 1792.

I did myself the Honor to write to you on the twenty third of October. Since that Date, the exterior Affairs of this Country have put on a more steady Appearance. My Letter of the twenty first Instant to Mr Jefferson will communicate my View of Things, to which I could add but little at this Day.[1] I have not mention'd to him the Appointment of Mr Genest as Minister to the United States.[2] In fact, this Appointment has never been announced to me. Perhaps the Ministry think it is a Trait of Republicanism to omit those forms which were antiently used to express Good Will—In the Letter which is address'd to you is a Strain of Adulation which your good Sense will easily expound. Let it be compard with Mr Lebrun's Letter to me of the 30th of August.[3] Fact is, that they begin to open their Eyes to their true Situation; and besides, they wish to bring forward, into Act, our Guarantee of their Islands, if the War with Britain should actually take Place. Apropos of that War, I am told that the british Ultimatum is as follows. France shall deliver the royal Family to such reigning Branch of the Bourbons as the King may chuse, and shall recall her Troops from the Countries they now occupy. In this Event, Britain will send hither a Minister, and acknowlege the Republic, and mediate a Peace with the Emperor and King of Prussia.[4] I have several Reasons to beleive that this Information is not far from the Truth, and that if the Ministers felt themselves at Liberty to act they would agree to the Terms. These Terms are it is said consequential to the Sentiments delivered by Opposition in the british Parliament; which is as you will see become quite insignificant, but it was thought best to place them in a necessity of supporting the Measures of Administration. I considered these Terms (or Something very like them) in a different Point of View. If the french retire (and consequently eat up again their high tond Declarations in favor of the People and Denunciations against Kings) they will, at the next Attempt, find as many Enemies as there are Men in the neighbouring Countries, & of Course the *Mediator* will prescribe such Terms as she may think proper. Secondly as it is (almost) evident that the Republic must be torne to Pieces by contending Factions, even without any foreign Interference, her Population Wealth and Resources—*above all her Marine* must dwindle away; and as much of her Intelligence and Industry, with the greater Part of her Money Capital, must in this Hypothesis seek the Protection of Law and Government on the other Side of the Channel, her Rival will encrease both in positive and relative Power. Thirdly, an exild Monarch on the other Side of the Pyrenees (for it is at Madrid that he would probably take Refuge) would enable Britain at any Moment to distract the french Affairs, and involve the Republic in a War with Spain. Lastly, it seems an almost necessary Conclusion, that if France (in some Years of convulsive Misery) should escape Dismemberment, she would sink under severe & single Despotism, and when reliev'd therefrom (by the King or his Descendants or Relatives) she would be in a State of Wretchedness for at least one Generation. I understand that the french (in the Consciousness that their Principles have ruin'd their Colonies) are willing to pay them as the Price of Peace, but on the other Hand Mr [William] Pitt has (I am told) refus'd the Offers which the Colonists have made to him, partly because he does not wish to excite Alarm, and partly because the only useful Part of the Colonies (their Commerce) will he conceives naturally fall to Britain in Proportion to the interior Ruin which has already made great Ravages in this Country.

If the Terms offered by Britain, whatever they may be, are not accepted, I think a Declaration will *not* suddenly follow, but only an Encrease of Preparatives; because Time must be given for the Cooperators (Spain and Holland) who are both of them slow. Besides it will be necessary that a Body of prussian Troops should be collected, thro Westphalia, in the Neighbourhood of Flanders, to be join'd by Dutch Hanoverian and (perhaps) british Troops. The more the french Advance, the more they expose themselves to this Danger; and you may rely that if a large Body of Troops be thrown into Flanders, that Country will join them *eagerly* to expel or destroy the French. I think it possible that, in Case the War should break out, there may be a Treaty of Partition in which the Elector palatine may have Alsace and Lorraine in Lieu of Bavaria, and that the low Countries may be given by the Emperor (in Exchange for Bavaria) to the Duke and Duchess of York.[5] This would suit every Body but France, and She will not in such Case be consulted.

I have not yet seen Mr Genest, but Mr Paine is to introduce him to me;[6] in the mean Time I have enquir'd a little what kind of Person it is: and I find that he is a Man of good Parts, and very good Education, Brother to the Queen's first Woman; from whence his fortune originates.[7] He was thro the Queen's Influence, appointed as Chargé d'affaires at Petersburgh, and (when there) in Consequence of Dispatches from Mr de Montmorin,[8] written in the Sense of the Revolution and which he interpreted too litterally, he made some Representations in a much higher Tone than was wish'd or expected. It was not convenient either to approve or disapprove of his Conduct, under the then Circumstances, and his Dispatches lay unnoticed. This to a young Man of ardent Temper, and who feeling Genius and Talents may perhaps have rated himself a little too high, was mortifying in the extreme. He felt himself insulted, and wrote in a Style of petulance to his Chief, beleiving always that, if the royal Party prevail'd, his Sister would easily make fair Weather for him at Court: which I doubt not. At the Overturn of the Monarchy, those Letters we⟨re⟩ so many Credentials in his Favor to the new Government, & their Dearth of Men has opened his Way to whatever he might wish. He chose America, *as being the best Harbor during the Storm,* and if my Informant be right, *he will not put to Sea again untill it is fair Weather,* let what will happen.

In Addition to what I have said, respecting the King, to Mr Jefferson, it is well to mention to you that the Majority have it in Contemplation not only to refer the Judgement to the Electors of France (that is to the People) but also to send him and his Family to America which Payne is to move for. He mention'd this to me in Confidence but I have since heard it from another Quarter—Adieu my dear Sir I wish you many and happy Years.

Gouvr Morris

ALS, DLC:GW; LB, DLC: Gouverneur Morris Papers. For GW's receipt of this letter on 3 May 1793, see Morris to GW, 6 Jan. 1793, source note.

1. For Morris's letter to Jefferson of 21 Dec. 1792, which Jefferson docketed as received on 22 April 1793, see *Jefferson Papers*, 24:762–74.

2. French diplomat Edmond-Charles Genet (1763–1834) became head of the translation department in the Ministry of Foreign Affairs in 1781. He went to St. Petersburg, Russia, in 1787 as the secretary to the French legation, eventually becoming the chargé d'affaires there in October 1789. Expelled from Russia in the summer of 1792 for his revolutionary sentiments, Genet received an appointment as minister plenipotentiary to the United States on 19 Nov. 1792. Genet was greeted with much enthusiasm by republican sympathizers after his arrival in the United States the following April, but his insistence on France's right to outfit privateers and to sell their spoils in American ports, his involvement in American politics, and his schemes against the Spanish authorities in the territories of Louisiana and Florida resulted in the Washington administration's demand for his recall in August 1793 (see Notes on Cabinet Meetings, 1–23 Aug. 1793, DLC:GW). Fearing for his life if he returned to France, Genet remained in the United States and settled in New York State where he married Cornelia Tappan Clinton, a daughter of New York governor George Clinton.

3. The letter of "Adulation" to GW may be that of 22 Dec. from the French National Convention. For the letter to Morris of 30 Aug. from the French foreign minister Lebrun, see Morris, *Diary of the French Revolution*, 2:523–24.

4. Louis XVI was guillotined on 21 Jan. 1793 and his wife Marie-Antoinette died in the same manner on 16 Oct. 1793. Starting early in 1793, the combined effects of France's military aggression and revolutionary rhetoric, in ad-

dition to the execution of Louis XVI, prompted Great Britain, the Netherlands, Spain, and several other European nations to join the Austro-Prussian coalition against France.

5. Karl Theodor was the elector of Bavaria and of the Palatinate, both German states within the Holy Roman Empire, of which Francis II was currently emperor. Frederick Augustus (1763–1827), the duke of York and the second son of George III, was married to Frederica Charlotte Ulrica Catherina (1767–1820), the eldest daughter of Frederick William II, the king of Prussia.

6. English political writer Thomas Paine, famous for his encouragement of the American Revolutionary War, was an active supporter of the French Revolution. Granted French citizenship in August 1792, he was elected to the National Convention the following month (see the National Assembly of France to GW, 26 Aug. 1792). At the start of the trial of Louis XVI, Paine urged the government to banish the king to the United States rather than execute him. Paine's participation in the French Revolution decreased as more radical leaders gained ascendency during the Terror, and he was expelled from the Convention in 1793. He was arrested on 28 Dec. 1793 and imprisoned for the next ten months, during which he wrote part of *The Age of Reason*.

7. Genet's eldest sister, Jeanne-Louise-Henriette Campan (1752–1822), was first lady-in-waiting to Marie-Antoinette. Her account of life at the royal court, *Mémoires sur la vie privée de Marie-Antoinette, reine de France et de Navarre*, was published in Paris in 1822.

8. Armand-Marc, comte de Montmorin de Saint-Hérem (1745–1792), served as the French foreign minister from February 1787 to November 1791.

From James Smith

Sir,   Barrow [England] Dec. 28th 1792

As your Servant has not recd any answer as yet to his last, datd Hull June 22th 1792.[1] He take the liberty of sending a second, hoping it will arrive safe and find you in an agreeable state of health, and the enjoyment of much happiness. Sir, the purport of my last, was as follows—That having read Gordon's History of the United States,[2] and perceiving therein the glorious conquest which you were instrumental (under a kind providence) of obtaining over the arms of Despotism & oppression, and hearing of the wholesome laws that now obtain among you, together with the fertility of the soil of many parts of the united states—It likewise informed you, that I was the Son ⟨*mutilated*⟩ a Farmer in the west of yorkshire, a young man, unmarried, have been a short time at an Academy near Halifax, am now entering upon the work of the ministry, in the independant connection, & have a strong desire to come over to America, in order to see your person, and afterwards fix in some part of the united states—And lastly it requested your patronage & assistance in procuring me agreeable connections (upon the conditions of my being an honest man and peaceable Citizen) in order to encourage my coming over to America—Sir, I still continue to have thoughts of coming over to the united states, this next Summer, but having no connection with any persons there at present, I send these lines in order to commence an acquaintance with you—and to request the following favours, first, that you will acquaint me, whether there are any vacant independant congregations in Maryland, pensilvania, Virginia, or the North & South Carolinias—Second, that you will recommend me (upon the above conditions) to Dr Whitherspoon,[3] or some steady independant Ministers, as a person desirous of becoming an inhabitant of the united states, and to join in concert with them, in holding forth the glories of Emmanuel to poor Sinners—Third, that you will give me your advice upon the subject, and inform me whether I can meet with encouragement, or not, And lastly that you will answer this letter as soon as possible, after it comes ⟨*mutilated*⟩ sir, I shall think myself happy in receiving a few l⟨*mutilated*⟩ou whether you approve of my request or not—Bu⟨*mutilated*⟩ short account of the Commercial & Civil states of br⟨*mutilated*⟩ hope may not be unacceptable—Sir, trade of all ⟨*mutilated*⟩ is very brisk, foreign demands are more than can b⟨*mutilated*⟩ However I cannot assert any thing pleasing with ⟨*mutilated*⟩ to her civil state—The F. king and goverment are ⟨*mutilated*⟩ one way and many of the people another—and ⟨*mutilated*⟩ roits are expected breacking out at Hull and man⟨y⟩ other principles Towns—Mr paines rights of man have been tryed, in Court and condemned as libellous—The Effigy of Mr paine was hurried upon a sledge at Lincoln, afterwards hanged, Gibbeted, and then burnt about two weeks since It is to be feared there are going to be troublesome times in England.[4] Sir, I am your humble and Obedt Sert

James Smith

N.B. please you may direct for me—at Mr Murrays Linen Draper Barrow, near Barton Lincolnshire.

ALS, DLC:GW. The letter is docketed: "The Revd Jas Smith 20 Decr 1793." Both sides of the lower half of the second page of the manuscript are torn.

1. There is no evidence that GW replied to the letter of 22 June or this letter.

2. See William Gordon's *History of the Rise, Progress, and Establishment, of the Independence of the United States of America: Including an Account of the Late War; and of the Thirteen Colonies, from Their Origin to That Period* (London, 1788).

3. John Witherspoon (1723–1794), a Presbyterian minister and a native of Scotland, was president of the College of New Jersey at Princeton from 1768 until his death. A signer of the Declaration of Independence, he was a New Jersey delegate to the Continental Congress from 1776 to 1782, serving on the Board of War and the committee on secret correspondence for much of that time. GW's nephew George Lewis, a son of Betty Washington Lewis, had obtained a degree from the College of New Jersey in 1775. His brother Charles Lewis (1760–1775) and Martha Washington's grandson, George Washington Parke Custis, also attended this college, but neither graduated from it.

4. Revolutionary pamphleteer Thomas Paine had returned in 1787 to his native England, where he published part 2 of *Rights of Man* in February 1792. Paine's call for the abolition of the British monarchy, the creation of a republican form of government, and social reform in Great Britain found favor with radical reform groups but not with the British government. Fearing arrest, Paine fled to France later that year. The British government charged him with treason and tried him in absentia in December 1792. For the radical reform movement in Great Britain, see Edward Newenham to GW, 29 Sept., n.6.

From Alexander Hamilton

[Philadelphia] December 29th 1792.
The Secretary of the Treasury has the honor to enclose for the consideration of the President, the translation of a letter of the 27th of December, which he has received from mister de la Forest.[1] He will wait upon the President on Monday for his orders concerning the subject of it.[2]

LB, DLC:GW.

1. Neither the original receiver's copy nor Hamilton's translation of the letter from Antoine-René-Charles Mathurin de La Forest, the French consul general, has been identified.

2. GW submitted Hamilton's translation of La Forest's letter to Thomas Jefferson for consideration. According to Jefferson's letter to GW of 1 Jan. 1793, La Forest had requested that the salaries of the French consuls residing in the United States be paid through advances on the payments that the United States made on its Revolutionary War debt to France. Jefferson approved La Forest's request, and GW notified Hamilton of this in a letter written on 1 January. For the eventual resolution of this issue in favor of La Forest's request, see GW to Hamilton, 1 Jan. 1793, and notes 1 and 2.

Tobias Lear to Henry Knox

U.S. [Philadelphia] Decr 29th 1792.

By the President's command T. Lear has the honor to return to the Secy of War the Speechs of Hendricks wh. have been submittd[1]—likewise a letter from Mr Hoge to the Secy of War & the Secy's answer, wh. expresses in its conclusion the President's idea on the subject.[2]

T.L.

S.P.U.S.

ADfS, DLC:GW; LB, DLC:GW.

1. Knox, in his letter to Lear of 28 Dec., enclosed "speeches from Hendricks, to which I confess I beleive but very little regard ought to be paid" (DLC:GW). For background on Stockbridge chief Hendrick Aupaumut's unsuccessful peace mission to the Indians in the Northwest Territory, see Knox to GW, 16 Aug., n.4. For Knox's earlier report on the failure of Aupaumut's mission, and of the American peace effort in general, see Knox to GW, 6 Dec. 1792. The enclosed speeches have not been identified.

2. Neither of the enclosed letters to and from Knox has been identified. Knox's correspondent may have been John Hoge (1760–1824), who currently was a senator in the Pennsylvania general assembly representing the western counties of Washington and Fayette (1790–94). John Hoge, a veteran of the Revolutionary War, and his younger brother William Hoge (1762–1814) moved to western Pennsylvania in 1782, and together they founded the town of Washington. John Hoge was elected a member of the American Philosophical Society on 21 Jan. 1791, the same day as Alexander Hamilton and Edmund Randolph. He was elected to Congress in 1804 to fill a vacancy caused by the resignation of his brother and served until 1805. William Hoge was a member of the state house of representatives 1796–97 and served in Congress 1801–4 and 1807–9.

The subject of the letters may have been similar to that of Knox's earlier correspondence with Pennsylvania governor Thomas Mifflin concerning federal protection from Indian attacks for the state's western counties (see Knox to GW, 8 Sept. [second letter], n.6).

From the Provisional Executive Council of France

[Paris, 30 December 1792]

In the name of the French Republic

In virtue of the law of the 15th of Aug. last which attributes to the Provisory Executive council all the functions of the Executive power & of the decree of the National convention of the 20.[1] of Sep. following which maintains the public authorities which were in activity at this last epoch.

We the citizens forming the Provisory Executive council of the Republic to the US. of N. America.

Very dear, great friends & allies. The desire which the citizen Ternant has witnessed to us of returning into the military line, & of continuing to serve the Republic, has determine⟨d⟩ us to recall him, & to enjoin on him to take leave of you. We are persuaded that he will give to the Republic a new proof of his zeal in fulfilling his last functions of Minister Plenipotentiary near you by assurances the most expressive of sentiments of the most constant friendship & sincerest fraternity which it bears to the US. as of it's prayers for their prosperity & for the most perfect union between the two people.[2]

Written at Paris the 30th of Dec. 1792. the 1st year of the French republi⟨c⟩.

The citizens forming the Provisory Executive council of the republic

   signed Le Brun. Claviere. Garat. Roland. Pache. Monge.

      By the Provisory Executive council

         signed Grouvelle.[3]

Translation, in Thomas Jefferson's writing, DNA: RG 59, Communications from the Heads of Foreign States, Ceremonial Letters; D, in French, DNA: RG 59, Communications from the Heads of Foreign States, Ceremonial Letters. The original French document appears in CD-ROM: GW.

1. This date in the original French document is 21 Sept., which is the date that the newly established National Convention abolished the French monarchy by a unanimous vote.

2. In addition to this letter of recall, the Provisional Executive Council of France also approved a letter of credence on 30 Dec. 1792 for Edmond-Charles Genet, who had been designated to replace Jean-Baptiste Ternant as the French minister to the United States. The original French document and Jefferson's translation of it are in DNA: RG 59, Communications from the Heads of Foreign States, Ceremonial Letters (for the translation, see also *Jefferson Papers,* 26:48–49; the original French document appears in CD-ROM: GW). Genet and Ternant presented their respective letters to GW on 18 May 1793 (see *JPP,* 143).

3. The members of the Provisional Executive Council were Dominique-Joseph Garat (1749–1833), minister of justice; Gaspard-Louis Monge (1746–1818), minister of the navy and colonies; Pierre-Henri-Hélène-Marie Lebrun, minister of foreign affairs; Jean-Marie Roland de La Platière (1734–1793),

minister of the interior; Jean-Nicolas Pache (1746–1823), minister of war; Etienne Clavière (1735–1793), minister of public contributions and revenues; and Philippe-Antoine Grouvelle (1758–1806), secretary.

To Thomas Jefferson

[Philadelphia] Sunday Morning 30th Decr 1792
The Letter to Mr Pinckney meets my ideas—but after mentioning Sweden as the Country *most* likely to obtain Copper from, I think it would be better not to confine him to the purchase there.[1]

G. W——n

ALS, DLC: Jefferson Papers. Jefferson docketed this letter: "recd Dec. 30. 92."
1. On 29 Dec., Jefferson had sent to GW for his review a letter to Thomas Pinckney, U.S. minister to Great Britain, under the cover of a brief note of that date (DNA: RG 59, Miscellaneous Letters). Jefferson's letter to Pinckney concerns a variety of subjects including the appointment of Thomas Barclay as consul to Algiers, a request for Pinckney to procure copper from Sweden for the U.S. Mint, a directive for Pinckney to urge British officials to send instructions to their minister in the United States, George Hammond, and a notice that Jefferson soon would send the latest engravings of the plan for the federal district for distribution in Great Britain.

In regard to the American policy toward the newest French government, Jefferson wrote: "We certainly cannot deny to other nations that principle whereon our own government is founded, that every nation has a right to govern itself internally under what forms it pleases, and to change these forms at it's own will: and externally to transact business with other nations thro' whatever organ it chuses, whether that be a king, convention, assembly, committee, president, or whatever it be. The only thing essential is the will of the nation. Taking this as your polar star, you can hardly err" (*Jefferson Papers*, 24:802–4). For background on Jefferson's inclusion of the foregoing passage in this letter, see Jefferson's Conversation with GW, 27 Dec., and note 2.

A postscript was added to the letter to reflect GW's suggested alteration, and Jefferson changed the letter's original date from 29 to 30 Dec. before sending it (see ibid.).

To Anthony Whitting

Mr Whiting,   Philadelphia Decr 30th 1792
I have duly received your letters of the 21st & 26th instt, and am a little surprized to find by the last that Mr James Butler had

not reached Mount Vernon before the date of it—He left this City on the 21st and according to the usual course, & time required for the Stages to run, he ought to have been in Alexandria on Monday last, the 24th of this month.[1]

Notwithstanding the reduced number of hands at Mansion house, if Mr Butler answers the description which is given of him, he may be useful to me on many accounts; & may ease you a good deal of the particular attention which, otherwise, you would find it necessary to give to the various concerns about it. Amongst which, none I think call louder for it than the Smiths; who, from a variety of instances wch fell within my own observation whilst I was at home, I take to be two very idle fellows. A daily account (which ought regularly to be) taken of their work, would, alone, go a great way towards checking their idleness; but besides this, being always about the House (except at Haymaking & Harvest) & not far from them, he might have a pretty constant eye both to them, and to the people who are at work with the Gardener; some of whom I know to be as lazy and as deceitful as any in the world (Sam particularly)—My horses too (in the management of which he professes to have skill) might derive much benefit from a careful attention to them; not only to those which work, but to the young ones, and to the breeding mares: for I have long suspected that Peter, under pretence of riding about the Plantations to look after the Mares, Mules, &ca is in pursuit of other objects; either of traffic or amusement, more advancive of his own pleasures than my benefit.[2] It is not, otherwise to be conceived, that with the number of mares I have, five & twenty of which were bought for the express purpose of breeding, though now considerably reduced from that purpose, alone; should produce not more than Six or eight Colts a year. This I say will hardly be believed by any person who has ever been in a similar practice. The evil stands much in need of a remedy, & I request, if Mr Butler should ever reach you, that he may be told it is my desire he would endeavour to apply one. I moreover conceive (being an experimental farmer) that he will be better able to carry your directions into effect, (especially in Hay-making, Hedging and the like, in his own way) than one of the common Overseers of the Country: and in addition to these, as he writes a tolerable good hand & has a tolerable knowledge of Accts, you might derive aid from him in that way; when I was able to look after my own business it was a custom to keep as regular accounts with each of my Plantations as if the Articles delivered from the Store, from the Smiths Shop, done by the Carpenters, &ca, &ca, had gone to, or been done for, Mr Peak or any other from whom the value was to be received.[3] This under your general Superintendence (without aid) I know would not be in your power to render without neglecting other parts of your duty of more consequence; and therefore I never required it in the extent above mentioned; nor expected it. But if Butler comes to you, and merits the character given of him, an essay towards it may be made—My great fear respecting him, is, that he will be found difficient in point of activity. But as I have, in a former letter desired that admonition, or something else, may be administered to the first, and to every neglect, it is needless to repeat it in this place.[4] He is to have his Victuals cooked for him; and as he is a man who (from the accounts given of him) has seen better days than his present appearance indicates, I should suppose, if you find his deportment & behaviour decent & proper, there can be no objection to his eating with you: but in this, do what is most agreeable to your own inclination, as it is not my intention to impose any one upon you, in this way contrary thereto.

All such work as you have enumerated, I think is the duty of every Overseer to render; and if he is a man of an industrious turn he will do it, whether he is compelled by articles, or not; On the other hand, if he is of an indolent cast—(such as Jones was—)[5] all the Articles in the world would not enforce the measure longer than he, himself, was under the observation of an Overlooker, and probably, to avoid working himself, (the Negros knowing it to be his duty to do so by agreement) he would suffer them to be idle, to bribe them against a discovery of his own idleness. For these reasons I have always had doubts (where there is a large gang of hands to Overlook) of the propriety of attempting to *compell* by Articles an overseer to do more *work* than his own inclination would naturally prompt him to do, voluntarily. Indeed where there are a number of hands, his time, probably, wd be better employed in seeing them well engaged than in working himself, especially if all are not within his full view at the time.

I have not a proper recollection of the ground between the

Spring house and the Oozey ground about the place where the hound kennel stood, or, you still mistake my design; & I am led to the latter opinion, by your having begun to drain by, or from the Spring house. My intention was to have begun the drain from the *lowest* Spring at the foot of the Bank most westerly; that is— nearest the Wharf, & to have carried the water along that, *on its level* to the front of the Mansion house, as hath been described in former letters; and to let the higher ones into that drain, as may be seen by the rough sketch enclosed. I always expected, & you will find it so mentioned in one of my letters, that the Water so united, would be to be conveyed across the sunken spot (East of, &) by the Spring before you could get it to the avenue in front of the house; but I had no idea of there being other hollows west of the spring house as difficult as you represent them to be; for as to cutting through banks which are liable to Cave in, I had no idea. After this explanation of my meaning if the difficulties which you represent should still oppose themselves, I wd have the work suspended until I come home; which I presume to hope, will be in the Spring.[6]

Ascertain as near as you can how much red led (ground in Oil) it will take to complete the painting the roofs of the Old Spinning house—Salt House, Smoke house, Wash house & Coach house (adjoining) together with the four Garden houses (if not already done)—also white led to finish what was begun, and not compleated; and Oil for the whole; informing me thereof; that I may be enabled to decide whether I shall send them or not.[7] Let me know also whether the Roof of the Piaza leaks since the New shingling has been put on. You speak of the quantity of Lime which it has taken to repair the Overseers house in the Neck[8]— It is occasioned in a great measure by the profuse use of it by [Tom] davis, & the *unnecessary* strength which he gives to the mortar; in which he ought to be corrected. Of Stone lime, & the lime made from Oyster shells, the quantity differs, but the proportions of each are well ascertained for different kinds of work; for here again, Morter is made stronger, or weaker, according to the Nature of it. Rules for all these might easily be obtained, and observed. Another bad practice which he is in ought to be corrected, and that is, laying his Mortar too thick in the joints. This hurts the look of a building—rather diminishes, than adds to the strength of it—and consumes much lime.

If, as you suppose is the case, the Miller spends more time than he ought to do in his dwelling house, it is justice due to me, to inform *him* of it; and to add, that if the practice is continued your duty will require that I should be informed of it. The slow progress made by him in Manufacturing my wheat in such an open & mild fall and Winter as we have had, is, if there was Water, the strongest evidence that can be given of his indolence, and the bad use that he has made of so favorable a Season.

This mild and open weather has been a great relief to the Corn & fodder—advantage I hope has been taken of it to Husband both. But the last Report speaks of an amazing consumption (in a short time) of soft Corn at the River Plantation. I wish to hear that all your Overseers are fixed, & well in their Giers.[9]

I did not expect that the Plow which went from this place would be employed otherwise than in breaking up ground in the fall of the year;[10] I am affraid this work is backward, if but *now* you are beginning to plow for the 1st time the old Clover lot at the Mansion house; When the Brick yard & Lucern lots are also to plow, & when the former of them ought to be sown in the early part of the Spring; as well for the advantage of the Clover, as for that of the Oats with which it is Sown.

Speaking of Sowing Clover, let me request that such a machine as is described in Mr Bordleys pamphlet, be prepared, and the clover Seed sown therewith.[11] My Clover Seed has never been regularly, or well sown, notwithstanding it has been lavished upon the ground; some parts of which having none, and other parts Surcharged. Less, if distributed over the ground, will do; in some of my letters I have given you the quantities bestowed on an Acre in the vicinity of this City where it is as thick as the best Farmer would requir⟨e⟩ it to be.[12]

Has Doll at the Ferry mixed her work with that of the outhands? If not what does she employ herself in? I have no report on this head—If she knits or Sows, her work ought to be noticed in that line, & care taken that she renders a sufficiency of it.[13] Let the stud horse be delivered to Mr Robt Lewis's Order, as Mr Hartshorn did not comply with his agreement.[14] I am Your friend and Well wisher

Go: Washington

ALS, DLC:GW.

1. Whiting's letters have not been found. For GW's employment of James

Butler to oversee the workers at the Mansion House farm, see GW to Whitting, 16, 19 Dec. 1792.

2. For previous mention of the smiths Nat and George, see GW to Whitting, 23 December. For Sam's relegation to the gardener John Christian Ehlers's workforce, see GW to Whitting, 4 November. Peter may be the same slave mentioned in GW's letter to Whitting of 4 November.

3. GW's neighbor William Peake (died c.1794) and his father, Humphrey Peake (1733–1785), had been visitors to Mount Vernon and fox-hunting companions of GW in earlier years. The Peake homestead, Willow Spring, was near GW's Clifton's Neck land in Fairfax Parish.

4. For GW's previous "admonition," see GW to Whitting, 23 December.

5. For GW's dismissal of Henry Jones as overseer of the Dogue Run farm, see GW to Whitting, 9 December.

6. GW gave Whitting instructions for uniting the various springs on the river side of the mansion in his letters of 18 Nov. and 16 December. The enclosed sketch has not been found.

7. For GW's earlier instructions to paint these buildings, see his letter to Whitting of 14 October.

8. For GW's purchase of 10,000 shingles for the piazza roof, see Tobias Lear to Lovell and Urquhart, 16 Dec., n.1. For GW's instructions to repair the house used by William Garner, the overseer of the River farm (located on Clifton's Neck), see his letter to Whitting of 11 November.

9. For GW's previous criticism of miller Joseph Davenport, see GW to Whitting, 9, 16 Dec. 1792. The previous farm report has not been found. "In their Giers" (gears) means ready for work.

10. For the Dutch plow that GW had sent from Philadelphia the previous spring, see GW to Whitting, 9 Dec., and note 6.

11. For John Beale Bordley's pamphlet, see GW to Edmund Randolph, 3 Sept., and note 1.

12. GW had written Whitting on 4 Nov. regarding the amount of clover seed used in the Philadelphia area.

13. For GW's directions regarding Doll's work assignment, see the postscript added to his letter to Whitting of 4 November.

14. For GW's gift of the horse Sampson to his nephew Robert Lewis, see GW to Whitting, 16 Dec., and note 14.

To Thomas Jefferson

Dear Sir,   [Philadelphia] Monday 31st [December 1792] [1]
If you have not closed your letter to Mr Pinckney I wish you would desire him to be very attentive to the embarkation of Troops for America—especially Quebec—& to give the earliest advice of the measure—& of the numbers [2]—Yours &ca

G. W——n

ALS, DLC: Jefferson Papers. Jefferson docketed the letter: "recd Dec. 31. 1792."

1. GW erroneously dated this letter "31st Jan."

2. For Jefferson's letter to Thomas Pinckney of 30 Dec., see GW to Jefferson, 30 Dec., n.1. Jefferson included GW's request for intelligence about British troop movements in a coded letter to Pinckney of 1 Jan. 1793 (see *Jefferson Papers*, 25:6).

To Thomas Jefferson

Private

Dear Sir [Philadelphia] Decr 31st 1792

I do not recollect perfectly what your sentiments were respecting the application of Mr De la Forest—and being to give an answer to the Secretary of the Treasury on this occasion I should be glad to receive them previously thereto.[1]

The difficulty of the case you well know arises from the unauthorised request, and the hazard of advancing monies without it. I am Yours sincerely

Go: Washington

ALS, DLC: Jefferson Papers; ADf, DNA: RG 59, Miscellaneous Letters; LB, DNA: RG 59, George Washington's Correspondence with His Secretaries of State; LB (photocopy), DLC: GW. Jefferson docketed the ALS: "recd Dec. 31. 92."

1. French diplomat Antoine-René-Charles-Mathurin de La Forest had requested that the United States apply part of its Revolutionary War debt payments to the salaries of the French consuls in the United States. For background on La Forest's request and for the eventual resolution of this issue in favor of the French consuls, see Hamilton to GW, 29 Dec., and notes, and GW to Hamilton, 1 Jan. 1793, and notes. For Jefferson's approval of La Forest's suggestion, see his letter to GW of 1 Jan. 1793.

Timothy Pickering to Tobias Lear

Dear Sir General Post Office [Philadelphia] Decr 31. 1792.

Can you inform me of any of the facts or representations communicated to the president relative to news-papers, which led him to notice them in his speech, at the opening of the present session of Congress? It seemed generally to be understood to imply that obstructions to their transmission had arisen from the post office law. Were not the obstructions to the papers which should have passed *from Richmond to Staunton* a principal subject of complaint?[1]

The Committee of the House on that part of the President's speech have desired me to furnish them with such observations as occurred to me generally relative to the post office law, & the parts in which it admitted of amendment. The article of newspapers is peculiarly interesting.[2] As I am this evening or to-morrow morning to report to the Committee, an answer this forenoon will greatly oblige.[3] Dear Sir Your most obedt servt

Timothy Pickering

ALS, DLC:GW.

1. For mention of this issue, see GW's Address to the U.S. Senate and House of Representatives, 6 November. For regulations regarding the mailing of newspapers, see sections 21 and 22 of "An Act to establish the Post-Office and Post Roads within the United States," 20 Feb. 1792, in 1 *Stat.* 238.

2. The House appointed a committee on 14 Nov. to consider "that part of the PRESIDENT's Speech which relates to the transmission of newspapers" and to report what, if any, amendments to the act passed in February might be necessary (*Annals of Congress,* 2d Cong., 685).

3. Lear replied to Pickering later on this date: "I have the honor to inform you, that it was represented to the President, in such a way as to place the fact beyond a doubt in his mind, that in consequence of the rate of postage imposed on the transmission of News-papers by the Post-Office law, many persons in Virginia, who had heretofore taken News-papers from this City, had declined receiving them any longer—and that many others declared that they only continued to take them under a full persuasion that the rate of Postage woud be reduced during the present Session of Congress—and that if such reduction should not take place they would desire the printers to stop their papers.

"In addition to these strong marks of disapprobation of the rate of postage on news-papers given by individuals, he was informed that the public mind, so far as it had been expressed, in that quarter, on the subject, appeared very anxious that an alteration should take place in that part of the Post-Office law which relates to the transmission of News-Papers" (DNA: RG 59, Miscellaneous Letters).

Letter not found: to Henry Knox, 1792. ALS, sold by Goodspeed's, no. 129, item 2073, 1919. GW marked this letter "Private," and according to the catalog entry, this letter is "on matters concerning the army organization."

Letter not found: from Alexander Campbell, 1 Jan. 1793. Tobias Lear wrote Henry Knox on 30 Jan. that he had "the honor to transmit . . . a letter from Arthur Campbell to the President, which was brought here this morning." The entry for 30 Jan. 1793 in GW's executive journal recorded the receipt of a letter "from Arthur Campbell, dated Washington Jany. 1st. 1793" (*JPP*, 39).

To Alexander Hamilton

Dear Sir   Philadelphia Jany 1st 1793

After reading the enclosed letter return it to me.[1] My sentiments on the *general* principle your are acquainted with—With the one handed, under this cover, do as shall seem best to you in the case before us, & let me know the result; or, if you chuse it, I am ready to confer further with you on the subject.[2] I am always Your Sincere frd & sr.

Go: Washington

ALS, DLC: Hamilton Papers.

1. The enclosure was apparently Thomas Jefferson's letter to GW of this date.

2. On 29 Dec. 1792 Hamilton had sent GW a translation of a letter of 27 Dec. from the French consul general in Philadelphia, Antoine-René-Charles Mathurin de La Forest, to the secretary of the treasury concerning the payment of French consular salaries through advances on the American debt to France. On 31 Dec. 1792 GW forwarded to Jefferson the translation of La Forest's letter and asked for his opinion of it. Hamilton replied to GW later on Jan. 1: "Mr Hamilton wishing the President a happy New-Year, & presenting him his affectionate respects, returns the inclosed. He will wait on the President tomorrow on the subject, for a few minutes" (DLC:GW). No decision having been reached by 10 Jan., Jefferson on that date laid before GW a letter that the French minister to the United States, Jean-Baptiste, chevalier de Ternant, had written him on the subject two days earlier; GW immediately forwarded Ternant's letter to Hamilton and asked that he take it into consideration (see *JPP*, 7; *Jefferson Papers*, 25:39). On 11 Jan. "The Secretary of the Treasury waited upon the President . . . and observed—That the advance required by the French Consuls could be made without any inconvenience to the Treasury of the U.S. but as the U.S. had already paid to France the amot. of what was due to her *at present*—and as the unsettled State of things in France made it uncertain whether, when they shall have formed a permanent government, they will agree to allow of the advance thus made—the Secretary thought it was a matter which required weighty consideration and gave it as his opinion, that the President had better take the sentiments of the heads of the Departments on the subject. Which meeting the President's ideas, the Gentlemen were requested to attend the President tomorrow morning at nine O'clock" (*JPP*, 9). On the following day, Saturday, 12 Jan., the cabinet met and "thought proper to comply with" La Forest's request (ibid., 11). For Jefferson's letter to Ternant of that date, notifying him that the United States had assented to La Forest's proposal, see Tobias Lear to Jefferson, 14 Jan. 1793, n.1.

From Thomas Jefferson

Sir   Philadelphia Jan. 1. 1793.

I have duly considered the translation of the letter of Dec. 27. from M. de la Forest stating that the French Consuls here have a right to recieve their salaries at Paris, that under the present circumstances they cannot dispose of their bills, and desiring that our government will take them as a remittance in part of the monies we have to pay to France. no doubt he proposes to let us have them on such terms as may ensure us against loss either from the course of exchange of cash for cash at Philadelphia, Amsterdam & Paris, or from the difference between cash and assignats at Paris, in which latter form they will probably be paid. I do not observe any objection from the treasury that this channel of remittance would be out of their ordinary line and inadmissible on that account. taking it therefore on the ground merely of an advance unauthorised by the French government, I think the bills may be taken. we have every reason to believe the money is due to them, and none to doubt it will be paid, every creditor being authorised to draw on his debtor. they will be paid indeed in assignats, at the nominal value only, but it is previously understood that these will procure cash on the spot of the real value we shall have paid for them. the risk, if any, is certainly very small, and such as it would be expedient in us to encounter in order to oblige these gentlemen. I think it of real value to produce favorable dispositions in the agents of foreign nations here. cordiality among nations depends very much on the representations of their agents mutually, and cordiality once established, is of immense value, even counted in money, from the favors it produces in commerce, and the good understanding it preserves in matters merely political. I have the honor to be with sentiments of the most perfect respect & attachment, Sir, Your most obedient & most humble servt

Th: Jefferson

ALS, DNA: RG 59, Miscellaneous Letters; ALS (letterpress copy), DLC: Jefferson Papers; LB, DNA: RG 59, George Washington's Correspondence with His Secretaries of State; LB (photocopy), DLC: GW.

For the background to this letter and the administration's decision regarding the payment of French consular salaries through advances on the American debt owed to France, see GW to Alexander Hamilton, 1 Jan., n.2.

Tobias Lear to George Meade

Dear Sir,   [Philadelphia] January 1st 1793.

The President wishes to get from Ireland about 30 lb. or 40 lb. of the seed of the *French* Furze, which he is told may be had in Cork. The person who procures it must be careful not to get the seed of the Irish Furze which is vastly inferior to the French.

Your politness in offering to have the above mentiond seed imported for the President will apologize for the trouble of this— The price of the seed the President understands is about 1/ sterling per pound & he had directed me to send the money therefor which you will find enclosed (one ten dollar bill).[1] With great respect & esteem I am Dear Sir, Your most Obet st

T. Lear

ADfS, DNA: RG 59, Miscellaneous Letters; LB, DLC:GW.

George Meade (1741–1808), a prominent Catholic merchant of Philadelphia, served as a member of the city's common council from 1789 to 1791 and as chairman of the local prison board in 1792. Meade was among the founders of the Society of the Friendly Sons of St. Patrick in the early 1770s and the Hibernian Society in 1792. Long prosperous in the shipping trade, Meade invested heavily in undeveloped land during the 1790s. The failure of these investments during the mid-1790s brought him to the brink of insolvency. Despite his best efforts to recover his losses, Meade fell into bankruptcy in 1801.

1. For Anthony Whitting's purchase of French furze for hedging at Mount Vernon, see GW to Whitting, 18 Nov. 1792. For the Mansion House farm overseer James Butler's advocacy of the merits of French furze, see GW to Whitting, 23 Dec. 1792, and 20 Jan. 1793.

Letter not found: from Anthony Whitting, 2 Jan. 1793. GW wrote Whitting on 6 Jan.: "Your letter of the 2d instant with its enclosures came to hand yesterday."

From James Pilling

Sir   Liverpool [England] 3 Jany 1793

The Wisdom & Equity of the Laws; the genuine Freedom, both Civil & Religious, that prevail in North America, are Objects of no small Importance to the thinking mind. Upon these endearing "Rights of Man," I have formed a Determination (if God permit) to settle in that happy Land, and there spend my remaining Days.

Permit me, Sir, to ask, what Place you would recommend, for a Person, or Persons, of small Fortune, say from One to three Thousd Pounds Sterg to fix in. Kentuckey has lately been a good deal spoke of here, and I have had Proposals to purchase 20,000 Acres, or more, which have passed through several Hands, in that Country. As this State is now joined to the United States, I wish to ask you, Sir, if there be any Lands in it unpatenteed? and if so—What Price ℔ Acre? In what Latitude & Longitude? Upon what Rivers? What is the Quality of the Soil? What are the Productions, Animal, Vegetable & Mineral? By Mineral I principally mean Iron, Copper, Lead, Tin, Coals, Stone for Building, Lime Stone and Clay for Earthen Ware, and Bricks.

Sir, Your Attention to the Above, and any other Information, which Your Wisdom may see good to point out will be a Condescension consistent with that high Opinion, which Mankind have justly formed of you and your Answer will be received with much Gratitude,[1] by. sir. Your most obedt & very hble servt

James Pilling

P.S. I should like a Plan of such Lands as are to be sold. this I wish, not only for myself, but also for a number of respectable Friends, who wish to settle in America.

ALS, DLC:GW. Tobias Lear, who mistakenly docketed this letter as having been written on "2d Jany 1793," noted on the cover that it was received on 22 Feb. 1793. The addressed cover indicates that this letter was sent "℔ Falmouth."

1. No response from GW to Pilling has been found.

William White to Tobias Lear

Sir,   [Philadelphia] Jany 3. 1793.

In Regard to the benevolent Design of the President, communicated to me by you the other Day, I have to inform you, that were I to attempt to furnish a List of the proper Objects, it would necessarily be a more contracted Application of the Bounty, than is intended: For altho, like other Citizens, I have Applications from Persons of different Communions, yet an annual Duty lying on me of paying special Attention to the poor of the Churches under my perochial Care, occasions my having a Knowlege of a much greater Number of one Denomination, than of all the others.[1]

In consideration of this & of what I have occasionally learned of the Duties of the Overseers of the poor, I beg leave to suggest for your Consideration, whether it might not be best to deposit the Money with the Treasurer of that Body, giving Notice of it to the Board?[2] The Mode of doing this I can communicate to you.

Every one of these Overseers has a certain District; the poor of which are committed to his Charge. The most of them have a weekly Allowance: But I am told, that besides these, the Overseers have always a Knowlege of Families, who are driven by present Distress to solicit Charity; but would be above becoming constant Dependents on it.

Any further Information you may desire I shall have an Opp[ortunit]y of giving you in Person; I am, in the mean Time, Your very humble Servt

Wm White

ALS, MHi: Miscellaneous Bound Collection.

1. William White was the bishop of the diocese of Pennsylvania for the Protestant Episcopal Church of America (see John Churchman to GW, 5 Sept. 1792, n.5). No written communication from Lear to White has been identified.

2. A corporate body of twelve civil appointees, formally designated as the "Guardians of the Poor in the City of Philadelphia" under Pennsylvania's poor-relief legislation of 27 Mar. 1789, supervised the collection and disbursement of taxes designated for relief of the poor and directed the city's almshouse and house of employment (see William Clinton Heffner, *History of Poor Relief Legislation in Pennsylvania, 1682–1913* [(Cleona, Pa.), c.1913], 95–118).

Although the size of GW's contribution to the poor of Philadelphia in January 1793 has not been determined, on 28 Jan. 1794 GW put $250 "into the hands of Dr White to be distributed among the poor of Philada" (Presidential Household Accounts).

Alexander Hamilton to Tobias Lear

[Philadelphia] 4 Jan. 1793. Presents his compliments and writes that "The Statements went in yesterday, and are copying for the President."[1]

LB, DLC:GW.

1. Hamilton is referring to the four statements that comprised his "Report on Foreign Loans" of 3 Jan. to the U.S. House of Representatives. For the text of Hamilton's report, see Syrett, *Hamilton Papers,* 13:451–62. On 5 Jan., Hamilton sent "to the President of the United States copies of certain statements No. 1. 2. 3 & 4, which have been rendered to the House of Representatives pursuant to a resolution of the House of the 27th of Decembr last" (DLC:

GW). For background on GW's request that Hamilton prepare this report for the House of Representatives, see the U.S. House of Representatives to GW, 27 Dec. 1792, and note 1.

From Alexander Hamilton

Treasury Departmt January 4th 1793.

The Secretary of the Treasury has the honor to submit to the President of the United States two Communications, one of the 13th & the other of the 21st of December last, suggesting certain alterations in the arrangement heretofore made, within the Revenue, District of North Carolina.[1] These communications are accompanied with some supplementary documents, explanatory of them. The arrangement suggested in the last appears to me the most adviseable which present circumstances will permit—with this exception only, that the salaries proposed for the Inspectors of Surveys No. 2 and 5. be inverted; allowing to the former 100 Dollars, and to the latter 120 Dollars. The consideration that the Inspector of No. 2. is also a Collector of the Customs, dictates this suggestion.[2]

Alexander Hamilton
Secretary of the Treasury.

LB, DLC:GW.

1. The enclosed letters from Tench Coxe to Hamilton of 13 and 21 Dec. 1792 contain suggestions for the rearrangement of the revenue surveys and changes in the compensations for revenue officers in North Carolina (see both letters in DNA: RG 58, Letters Sent by the Commissioner of the Revenue and the Revenue Office, 1792–1807; extracts in Syrett, *Hamilton Papers*, 13:317–19, 346). In the 13 Dec. letter, Coxe also offered the names of three possible candidates, all veterans of the Revolutionary War, for inspector of North Carolina's first survey: Robert Rowan (c.1738–1798), a Fayetteville merchant; Thomas Callender (Calender; d. 1828), the current surveyor and inspector of the port of Wilmington; and Thomas Overton, the North Carolina assemblyman for Moore County. For previous correspondence concerning Overton's suitability for this position, see Benjamin Hawkins to Tobias Lear, 26 Nov. 1792, and note 2. For GW's appointment of Overton to the vacancy, see GW to the U.S. Senate, 28 Jan. 1793.

2. Although no written response to this letter from GW has been found, Hamilton and GW apparently discussed the issue. On 12 Jan., Coxe wrote Hamilton: "Agreeably to your Note of the 10th instant, I have the honor to inclose to you a draught of an Act of the President of the United States, calculated to establish certain alterations of the Revenue Arrangement in the Dis-

trict of North Carolina, conforming with what I presume, from your said note to be the pleasure of the President" (DNA: RG 58, Letters Sent by the Commissioner of the Revenue and the Revenue Office, 1792–1807; extracted ibid., 478). Neither Hamilton's letter to Coxe of 10 Jan. nor Coxe's draft has been identified. On 22 Jan. 1793 GW issued an executive order altering the arrangement of the revenue service in North Carolina. This order, which presumably was based on Coxe's draft, made the change in salaries that Hamilton suggested in his letter to GW of 4 January.

The rearrangement of the revenue surveys necessitated the reassignment of inspector Thomas Benbury from the third survey to the second survey. Lincoln County resident Daniel McKissack (c.1755–1818), a Revolutionary War veteran, was appointed to fill a vacancy in the fifth survey (see GW to the U.S. Senate, 28 Jan. 1793).

Henry Knox to Tobias Lear

Dear Sir.   [Philadelphia] January 4th 1793

Please to submit the enclosed letter of General Wayne[1]—Two month's pay will go as soon as the Bank can prepare the notes. The further pay must depend upon the settlement of accounts, or the payments will get into great disorder—As general Wayne has again sent for the cornplanter, the question is shall Col. Procter go upon that business? Please to return the papers after the President shall have done with them.[2] I am, Dear Sir, sincerely yours

H. Knox

LS, DLC:GW; LB, DLC:GW.

1. Anthony Wayne's letter to Knox of 28 Dec., which enclosed "the Cornplanter and New Arrow's Speech of the 8. Decem" and Wayne's "second message of the 25th Ultimo to the Cornplanter and New Arrow," has not been identified (see Knox to Wayne, 5 Jan. 1793, in Knopf, *Wayne*, 164). In response to instructions from GW, Knox submitted Cornplanter and New Arrow's speech to Wayne of 8 Dec. 1792 to the U.S. House of Representatives on 5 Jan. and to the Senate on 7 Jan., with his cover letter of 5 Jan. 1793 (see *Annals of Congress*, 2d Cong., 791; ASP, *Indian Affairs*, 1:337). In their speech the two Seneca chiefs reported on their recent meeting at Au Glaize with the hostile Indians of the Northwest Territory: "After we arrived at their towns, and had acquainted them that it was the wish of General Washington to be at peace with the whole of the Indians, even those from the rising to the setting of the sun: after they had considered, they all, as one, agreed to make a peace; but as General Washington did not let us know the terms on which he would make peace, it was referred to a council the ensuing spring, where they wish he should be present. . . . The Shawanese say, that if they make peace, it will be on these terms: The Americans to allow them all the lands they held in Sir William

Johnston's time; or, at least, that the river Ohio shall be the line, and they be paid for the lands improved on the south side of said river Ohio. These, they say, are the terms, and the only ones, on which they will make peace" (ibid.). The "Notes from Genl. Wayne's letter," recorded in GW's executive journal on 5 Jan. 1793, read: "Opinion of Cornplanter's Nephew, who was at the Council at Au Glaize—that the hostile Indians will not consent to a peace so long as a white man remains on the NW side of the Ohio—that they do not mean a cessation of hostilities 'till after the treaty in the spring. A humiliating situation to remain with his hands tied while the enemy are at liberty to act on the Offensive, which they have done with effect. He has not more Officers than to afforud one relief for the Redoubts & guards necessary for the protection and internal police of the Camp. . . . Pay of the Troops. Five months due—men in want of clothing, which they could procure if they had their pay" (*JPP,* 3).

2. Lear replied to Knox later this date: "By the President's command T. Lear has the honor to return to the Secy of War General Wayne's letter & it's enclosures which have been submitted to the President—and to inform the Secretary that the President thinks it would be best to dispatch a special Messenger to bring Cornplanter &c. to this place, as it is highly important to know with as much accuracy as possible the views of the hostile Indians. The President thinks it would be proper to lay a Copy of the Speech of Corn planter and the New Arrow before Congress—and to introduce it by observing that as that business is now before them it is thought proper to communicate to them every thing that can throw light on the subject" (DLC:GW).

On 5 Jan., Knox wrote Wayne: "The Messenger for Red Jacket left this place on the 13 Ult. It is much to be desired to receive further information on this interesting subject—The President is so anxious thereon that he has directed me to send in addition to your speech a special messenger for the Cornplanter; accordingly Col. [Thomas] Procter will depart on the 6. instant for that purpose via Pittsburgh. I sincerely hope he will come as I believe much dependence may be placed upon the importance of the truth of his information. . . . Whatever the terms may be which shall be proposed at the Au Glaize the next spring—the Government seems constrained to adopt the measure of the Conference—We shall always possess the power of rejecting all unreasonable propositions But the sentiments of the great mass of the Citizens of the United States are adverse in the extreme to an Indian War and although these sentiments would not be considered as a sufficient cause for the Government to conclude an infamous peace, yet they are of such a nature as to render it adviseable to embrace every expedient which may honorably terminate the conflict. The President of the United States is so conscious of fair and humane motives to the Indians that his hopes of pacification are founded upon the opportunity of exhibiting those motives to the Indians and impressing them with the truth thereof If the War continues the extirpation and destruction of the Indian tribes are inevitable—This is desired to be avoided, as the honor and future reputation of the Country is more intimately blended therewith than is generally supposed. . . . I believe the Citizens of no Country could more explicitly but peaceably express decided disapprobation of this War than the mass of Citizens from Maryland Eastward—Part of the Southern Citizens seem to think less of the principle of the War than the manner of carrying it on. . . .

If after trying every measure peace cannot be obtained but at the price of a sacrifice of national character, it is presumed the Citizens at large will unite as one Man in prosecuting the War with the highest degree of Vigor until it shall be advantageously terminated in all respects. . . . The situation of the Accounts with you has alone caused the pay of the troops to be with held a moment— In all probability Mr. [Daniel] Britt who is acting Pay Master under your immediate orders has a large sum of the pay of the old first regiment in his possession and it appears that no money was forwarded with Major [Michael] Rudulph so that he must also in all probability have in his possession (or the Quarter Master General) a considerable portion of the pay belonging to the troops below you. . . . I have applied for two months more pay than I before mentioned to you making in all *four* months pay,—If the Secretary of the Treasury advances this it will leave only one month of the last year as an arrear" (Knopf, *Wayne*, 164–67).

From Robert Lewis

The Exchange Fauquier County [Va.]
Hond Uncle,   January 4th 1793.

Your letter of the 23d ultimo with one inclosed of the same date, came duly to hand this day. The contents I have noted well, and shall sett off the day after tomorrow for the purpose of carrying into effect your instructions with respect to the purchasing of Major Harrisons tract of Land in Fairfax County adjoining your Mill tract. Should we bargain (as I expect we shall) no time shall be lost ere I inform you of it, and the particulars of our agreement.

I know nothing of your land individually, but was I to judge of its quality from the lands in that vincinity (which I am tolerably well acquainted with) I should not suppose that Major Harrison would have the conscience to ask more than 20/ or twenty six Shillings per acre at most. If he does, there must be improvments to enhance its value. I shall endeavor to get it upon the lowest terms I can without higgling.[1]

The Horse which you have been so good as to give me, (I am convinced), will be very valuable in this part of the Country, and, I trust, no small addition to my little income.[2] I have therefore to thank you for your kindness, and to assure you that I am gratefull. Mrs Lewis joins me in love to you and my Aunt. I remain your Affectionate Nephew

Robt Lewis

ALS, ViMtV.

1. On 9 Jan., Lewis wrote GW again from "The Exchange" in Fauquier County, Va.: "Since writing to you the 4th inst. I have been to See Major [William B.] Harrison of Loudon respecting the business you desired. He seems not at all anxious to sell his land at this time, as the purpose, for which the money arising from the sale of his land was intended, is now entirely done-away. Major Harrison appears to be an honest, candid kind of a man, and, I believe, wishes to do justice to you and himself too either by selling his land, or removing the tenants. The latter will certainly be done the next fall, as it is now too late; for the law requires six months notice for the tenants, before they can be displaced. The title I do not like, and he is unwilling to give a general warrantee. He thinks you know more of this matter than he does himself, as you were a purchaser of half the same tract of land many years ago, he therefore, suspends doing any thing farther in this business until the Spring of the year, when Congress it is probable may adjourn and you come to Virginia. Forty shillings is the least he will take per acre. I am obliged to write in great haste as a waggon going to Falmouth is now waiting, and very anxious for me to conclude" (ViMtV).

For Lewis's continuing, although ultimately unsuccessful, efforts to purchase Harrison's tract adjoining GW's Dogue Run farm, on which GW's gristmill stood, see GW to Lewis, 7 Mar., 29 April, 26 July, Lewis to GW, 26 Mar., 17 July, 12 Aug. 1793. For GW's later attempt to rent Harrison's land, see GW to Harrison, 4 Nov. 1798, and note 1.

2. During an earlier visit to Mount Vernon, Lewis had "expressed a wish to be possessed of the stud horse that was there," and GW in his letter to Lewis of 23 Dec. offered to make him "a present" of Sampson, if the horse had not been sold as originally intended. One week later, on 30 Dec., GW wrote his farm manager Anthony Whitting directing that the horse "be delivered to Mr Robt Lewis's Order." Whitting informed GW on 9 Jan. that he had sent the horse to Lewis on that date.

From the Commissioners for the District of Columbia

Sir   Washington 5th January 1793

We enclose you a list of the Squares actually devided, of those certified ready for division, and a Copy of Majr Ellicott's Return of those marked out but not yet certified for Division, as well as a Copy of Majr Ellicott's Letter to us—From the Two last you will perceive that there is at least an Uncertainty whether we shall much longer have Majr Ellicott's services, he has however shewn such a Temper in our Verbal intercourse, that we have no Apprehension of his purposely leaving the work, in a State to create Embarrasment[1]—We enclose you also his return and our Certificate of the Survey of Columbia[2] and wished to have forwarded with them distinct Accounts of the Expences incurred for that Service and the Survey of the City, in expectation that Congress will defray at least the first, and indeed it seems to us that the latter is a just Claim the one is occasioned by the execution of the immediate command of the Law, the other as a direct and necessary consequence, and a Return of this Money again to the Loans would considerably assist our Funds, but there will be no way to collect these Charges with Truth, but by going over the Vouchers for last year, our Business was mixed and the same Individuals in some Instances acted generally—We will however endeavour to have these accounts prepared against next meeting[3]—A Claim is Set up by the proprietors to be paid for the Quantity of Land in the Squares intersected by the two cross Streets and a deverging Street, we have proposed a Reference, for we are much disenclined to make a noise of our differences possibly the Demand may be relinqused[4]—You have in your memory no Doubt, the general Idea of the Expences at the time of your Addition of the Plan for a President's House with the Increase then directed and highly Ornamented as Mr Hoben has since collected, though from what grounds we do not know in proportion to the Cost of the Royal Exchange in Dublin this cost near 77900 Sterling on a view of our means, and we enclose a State for next year, we submit whehether it will not be best to take the Plan on its original Scale, adding something to the Elivation, as was agreed to be proper—There will be also the greater probability or rather Certainty of effecting the necessary work in Time[5]—Mr Blodget has been with us several days, a Recolection of some Business which makes his presence in Philadelphia almost indespensible immediately has occasioned his going off suddenly, however not before we had agreed for his Assistance at 600£ a year payable in Lots at a full price, and having matured Ideas on the most interesting points, we flatter ourselves that he will be able to assist our Funds, and Strengthen the Interest of the City in Philadelphia[6]—Mr Jefferson has obliged us by a communication of his Ideas on the Introduction of Mechanicks from Europe, as well as gaining some from Connecticut, our letter to him will be particular on these subjects, refering to that and what we shall write to Mr Blodget will, if you should wish to gain more particular Information give that Satisfaction[7]—In the progress of this letter we received Majr Ellicotts Farther letter to us enclosed, which gives his Idea of the Time still necessary for Surveying[8]—Mr Harbaugh has executed his work much to our Satisfaction, as well as the very general approbation of the Public, and Williamson for his Time has the Stone cutting in a pleasing way.[9] We are Sir &c.

Th Johnson
Dd Stuart
Danl Carroll

P.S. The Plan and certificates ar[e] too bulky for enclosure, they are intrusted with Mr Joseph Wailes of Massachussets who goes in this Stage and promises to deliver them.[10]

LB, DNA: RG 42, Records of the Commissioners for the District of Columbia, Letters Sent, 1791–1802.

1. These lists have not been identified, but one of them may have been Andrew Ellicott's "Squares Ascertained" of 5 Jan. (see DNA: Records of the Commissioners for the District of Columbia, Letters Received, 1792–1867). In the enclosed copy of Ellicott's letter to the commissioners written at the "City of Washington" on 4 Jan. 1793, Ellicott wrote: "In the execution of the Plan of the City of Washington, I have met with innumerable difficulties on account of its extreme complexity; and from its extent, the labour becomes augmented. . . . Those causes, and not want of exertions, may possibly have produced an apparent delay, in the execution of the Plan. . . . If it should be your pleasure, you may rest assured that it will be mine, to quit the further execution of the Plan of the City of Washington by the first day of May next" (DNA: RG 42, Records of the Commissioners for the District of Columbia, Letters Received, 1791–1802). The commissioners did not wait until 1 May for Ellicott's resignation but discharged him in mid-March (see D.C. Commissioners to GW, 11–12 Mar. 1793). Ellicott's dismissal was only temporary, for on 10 April he wrote his wife, Sarah (Sally) Brown Ellicott, from Georgetown: "My victory was complete; and all my men reinstated in the City, after a suspension of one month. . . . The defeat of the commissioners has given great pleasure to the inhabitants of this place" (Mathews, *Andrew Ellicott,* 99–100). For GW's intervention in the dispute and his recommendation that the commissioners reach an accommodation with Ellicott, see GW to D.C. Commissioners, 3 April 1793.

2. The return from Andrew Ellicott was his letter to the commissioners of 1 Jan., written at the "City of Washington," in which he wrote: "It is with singular satisfaction that I announce to you the completion of the survey of the four lines, comprehending the Territory of Columbia—These lines are opened, and cleared forty feet wide; that is twenty feet on each side of the lines limiting the Territory: And in order to perpetuate the work, I have set up squared mile stones marked progressively with the number of miles from the beginning on Jones's Point, to the west corner, thence from the west corner, to the

north corner, thence from the north corner, to the east corner, and from thence to the place of beginning on Jones's Point: except in a few cases, where the miles terminated on declivities, or in waters: in such cases the stones are placed on the first firm ground, and their true distances in miles, and poles marked on them. On the sides facing the Territory is inscribed, 'Jurisdiction of the United States:' On the opposite sides of those placed in the State of Virginia, is inscribed, 'Virginia.' And of those in the State of Maryland, is inscribed, 'Maryland:' On the fourth side, or face, is inscribed the Year, and present position of the magnetic-needle at that place. With this you will receive a Map of the four lines, with an half mile on each side; to which is added, a survey of all the waters in the Territory." This letter was accompanied by "a Map of the Territory of Columbia" with Ellicott's certificate of 1 Jan. describing his survey of the federal district "annexed." Ellicott's letter and certificate are in DNA: RG 42, Records of the Commissioners for the District of Columbia, Letters Received, 1791–1802, but his survey has not been identified.

The details of Ellicott's certificate were incorporated in the commissioners' certificate of 1 Jan., a copy of which reads: "We Thomas Johnson, David Stuart and Daniel Carroll, Commissioners appointed by the President of the United States, in virtue of the Act of Congress, for establishing the temporary and prermanent seat of the government of the United States; by virtue of the same Act, and of the Act amendatory therto; and agreeably to the directions of the President of the United States, expressed in his two proclamations, the first bearing date at Philadelphia on the twenty-fourth day of January 1791, the other bearing date at George-Town on the thirtieth day of March 1791, have caused the four lines of the district of territory, ten miles square, accepted for the permanet seat of government of the United States by the above mentioned Acts of Congress, to be surveyed, defined and limited, by Andrew Ellicott, in the manner following; that is to say: Beginning at a Stone fixed on Jones's Point, being the upper cape of Hunting Creek, in the commonwealth of Virginia, and at an angle, in the out-set, of 45 degrees west of the north, and runing in a direct line ten miles, for the first line: then begining again, at the said Stone on Jones's Point, and running another direct line at a right angle with the first a cross the Potomak, ten miles for the second line: then, from the terminations of the said first and second lines, running two other direct lines of ten miles each, the one crossing the Eastern Branch, and the other the Potomak; and meeting each other in a Point. These lines we have caused to be opened and cleared forty feet wide, that is, twenty feet on each side; and to perpetuate the location of the said district, we have caused squared mile-stones to be set up in each line, and marked with the number of miles, progressively from the begining on Jones's point, to the west corner thence from the west corner, to the north corner; thence from north corner, to the East corner; and thence to the beginning on Jones's Point except in a few cases, where the miles terminated on declivities or in Waters; in such cases the stones are placed on the nearest firm ground, and their true distances in miles and Poles, marked on them. On the sides of the Stones facing the territory, are inscribed the words [']Jurisdiction of the United States' on the opposite sides of those placed in the commonwealth of 'Virginia' and of those in the State of Maryland, is inscribed

'Maryland' and on the third and fourth sides, or faces, are inscribed the year wherein the Stones was set up and the present variation of the Magnetic needle at that place: As, by the certificate of the said Andrew Ellicott and the map of the said four lines of the district of territory, now called 'The Territory of Columbia,' hereto annexed, fully appears" (DNA: RG 42, Records of the Commissioners for the District of Columbia, Letters Received, 1791–1802).

3. At their meeting of 12 Feb. in Georgetown, the commissioners wrote Thomas Jefferson "respecting the expences of the Surveyors Department, with an account inclosed of the amount of expences incurred in running the permanent Lines, 2986 Dollars & 25 Cents" (DNA: RG 42, Records of the Commissioners for the District of Columbia, Proceedings, 1791–1802). For this letter, see *Jefferson Papers,* 25:170–71. The enclosed account, also dated 12 Feb., covers the surveying expenses from 1 Mar. 1791 to 8 Jan. 1793 and is in DLC: Jefferson Papers. On 19 Feb., GW received from Jefferson the commissioners' 12 Feb. letter to Jefferson and its enclosed list of expenses, and he returned both to Jefferson the following day (*JPP,* 59–60).

4. The commissioners "Wrote a letter to the Proprietors" on 4 Jan., but it has not been identified (see DNA: RG 59, Records of the Commissioners for the District of Columbia, Proceedings, 1791–1802).

5. In July 1792 the commissioners and GW selected architect James Hoban's design for the President's House and hired him to supervise its construction (see GW to the Commissioners for the District of Columbia, 8 June 1792, n.3). The enclosed statement has not been identified.

6. On 5 Jan. 1793 the commissioners appointed Samuel Blodget, Jr., "Supervisor of the Buildings and in general of the Affairs committed to our care" and gave him the authority to sell lots in the federal district on their behalf (see D.C. Commissioners to Blodget, 5 Jan. 1793, in DNA: RG 42, Records of the Commissioners for the District of Columbia, Letters Sent, 1791–1802). For Blodget's promotional activities in Philadelphia, see his letters of 26 Jan. and 1 Feb. to the commissioners in DNA: RG 42, Records of the Commissioners for the District of Columbia, Letters Received, 1791–1802.

7. For Jefferson's ideas on this subject, see his letters to the commissioners of 17 and 23 Dec. 1792 in *Jefferson Papers,* 24:749, 776. The commissioners wrote Jefferson on this same date respecting the hiring of foreign mechanics and Blodget's instructions (ibid., 25:24–25). In their letter the commissioners enclosed the "Terms for Mechanics" that they had adopted at their meeting in Georgetown on 3 Jan. (see DNA: RG 42, Records of the Commissioners for the District of Columbia, Proceedings, 1791–1802). Jefferson presented this letter to GW on 10 Jan. "for his perusal" (*JPP,* 6). For GW's thoughts on the hiring of foreign workers and for a description of the terms offered to such workers by the commissioners, see GW to D.C. Commissioners, 18 Dec. 1792, and note 2.

8. Ellicott's letter to the commissioners of 5 Jan., written in the "City of Washington," reads: "As it may perhaps be satisfactory to you, to have some information respecting the time it will yet require, to compleat the laying out of the City of Washington: I have taken that subject into consideration, and carefully examined the work done, with that which is yet to execute, and am of the opin-

ion, that it may be finished the ensuing summer, provided the work is carried on regularly, without attempting it in detatched pieces—In giving this opinion, I limit the artists to the present set of Instruments, which I have furnished at may own expense; but if another Transit-Instrument could be obtained, the work might be executed [in] less time" (DNA: RG 42, Records of the Commissioners for the District of Columbia, Letters Received, 1791–1802).

9. For the commissioners' employment of Leonard Harbaugh to erect a bridge over Rock Creek, see Benjamin Stoddert to GW, 24 Oct. 1792, n.3. For the commissioners' agreement with Collen Williamson to "superintend the stone cutting," see David Stuart to GW, 10 Dec. 1792, n.4.

10. Joseph Wales (1757–1828) of Lancaster, Mass., a veteran of the Revolutionary War and a member of the Society of Cincinnati, may have been the person entrusted to deliver these papers. GW received this letter and its enclosures on 10 Jan., and that same day he had his secretary Tobias Lear forward them to Jefferson for his consideration (*JPP*, 7).

To Samuel Powel and the Members of the Pennsylvania Senate

[Philadelphia] January 5th 1793

The President of the United States requests the pleasure of the company of the Speaker and members of the Senate of the State of Pennsylvania to dine with him on Saturday the 12th of January, at 4 O'clock.[1]

D, in Tobias Lear's writing, ViMtV.

1. Powel wrote the last names of the following Pennsylvania senators at the bottom of the manuscript page: Robert Brown, Lindsay Coats, James Dunlop, John Edie, John Hanna, Gabriel Heister, John Hoge, Thomas Jenks, Thomas Kennedy, William Montgomery, Anthony Morris, Michael Schmyser, Alexander Scott, John Sellers, John Smilie, Abraham Smith, and Richard Thomas. Current senators whose names Powel did not note were John Gloninger and Richard Peters. At "One O'Clock" on this date, Powel replied to GW: "Your Letter, addressed to the Speaker and Senate of the State of Pennsylvania, being sent to my House, did not come to my Hands 'till after the Adjourment of the Senate. I will not fail to communicate the Contents to them on Monday Afternoon, the Time to which the Senate is adjourned" (DLC:GW).

From Harriot Washington

Fredericksburg [Va.] January 5 [1793]

I hope my dear Uncle will excuse my troubleing him again, Aunt Lewis has desired me to ask you for a little money there is a few thing's I want, that I would be much obleiged to you for, she say's if you will send me some she will keep it, & I shall not get any thing but what I really want,[1] I hear the Birth night is to be kept,[2] and as every one is a going here and as I should like to go I will thank my dear Uncle if he, will be so good as to send me enough money, to get me a ⟨s⟩lite Lutestring or something, of that kind, as there is some very pretty one's here,[3] Aunt Lewis will get it for me and I will take great care of it I had a violent pain and inflamation in my jaw last week I was obleiged to have my tooth drawn, and the Doctor charged two dollar for it, Colonel Ball was here yesterday he said he had heard, from the major lately, & that he was no better.[4] If you please to give my love to Aunt Washington. I am my dear Uncle Your affectionate Neice

Harriot Washington

P.S. Aunt Lewis desirers me to give her love to you and say's she would have wrote to you but she had not time.

H.W.

ALS, CSmH: Kane Collection.

1. GW had sent Harriot Washington, who had been living at Mount Vernon since the mid-1780s under the care of George Augustine Washington's wife, Frances Bassett Washington, to the home of Betty Washington Lewis in Fredericksburg, Va., in early October 1792 because there was no one left at Mount Vernon to look after her. At that time GW had promised his sister that he would continue to provide for Harriot as he had done for the past seven years (see Harriot Washington to GW, 2 April 1790, source note, and GW to Betty Washington Lewis, 7 Oct. 1792). On 29 Jan. 1793 Betty Lewis wrote GW that she had received his letter of 14 Jan. containing "the Money for Harriot."

2. The 28 Feb. 1793 issue of the *Virginia Herald, and Fredericksburg Advertiser* reported that "an elegant BALL at the Market-House" was held in Fredericksburg on 22 Feb. to commemorate GW's birthday.

3. Lutestring, or lustring, is a glossy silk fabric used for women's dresses and ribbons.

4. George Augustine Washington, suffering from tuberculosis, had left Mount Vernon with his family in October to spend the winter at Eltham, the estate of his father-in-law, Burwell Bassett, in New Kent County, Va., where he died on 5 Feb. 1793. Col. Burgess Ball of Loudoun County, Va., was married to G. A. Washington's sister Frances.

Letter not found: to Thomas Green, c.6 Jan. 1793. On 6 Jan., GW wrote Anthony Whitting: "You will See by the enclosed to Thomas Green (which Seal before you send it to him) on what footing I have placed his continuance, or discharge."

From Henry Lee

Richmond January 6th 93

Permit me my dear president to offer my congratulations on the late unanimous renewal of affection & confidence on the part of your fellow-citizens, & to pray that the auspicious event may be attended with the happiest effects to you and to them.[1]

Col. Basset died on the fourth instant in consequence of a fall from his horse—Your amiable nephew at Eltham continues to linger without the smallest chance of recovery, and Mrs Washington enjoys a tolerable state of health in the midst of calamity[2] —this information I have from Doctor Mcclurg who attended Colo. Basset during his illness.[3]

I beg leave to present my respects to Mrs Washington & to assure you of the entire respect & attachment with which I have the honor to be Your most ob: sert

Henry Lee

ALS, DLC:GW.

1. On 5 Dec. 1792 the electoral college cast 132 votes to elect GW unanimously to a second term as president.

2. On 3 Sept. 1792 GW had written Edmund Randolph that Burwell Bassett, who was then at Mount Vernon, "was siezed hand & foot, with the Gout on the Road, & has not been out of his bed since; nor in a condition to communicate what he knows if he was disposed to do it." GW's description of Bassett's condition suggests that he suffered not from gout but from some type of stroke and that perhaps a similar episode precipitated his fatal fall in January. At the time of her father's death, Frances Bassett Washington and her husband, George Augustine Washington, were at Bassett's home in New Kent County, Virginia.

3. Dr. James McClurg (c.1746–1823), one of Virginia's most prominent physicians, studied medicine in Edinburgh, London, and Paris before returning to Williamsburg in 1773 to set up his medical practice. During the Revolutionary War he served as physician and director general of the Virginia military hospital from 1777 to 1780, and during the closing years of the war he was surgeon for the state navy. From 1779 to 1783 McClurg was a professor of anatomy and medicine at the College of William and Mary. After his professorship was discontinued in 1783, he moved to Richmond. In 1787 McClurg was appointed a member of the Virginia delegation to the Philadelphia Constitutional Convention. McClurg served as mayor of Richmond in the late 1790s and early 1800s, and he became the first president of the Medical Society of Virginia in 1820.

Letter not found: to Betty Washington Lewis, 6 Jan. 1793. On 29 Jan., Betty Lewis wrote GW: "Your letters of Januy the 6the and 14the of this Month came duly to hand."

To Robert Lewis

Dear Sir, Philadelphia Jan⟨y⟩ 6th 1793

Enclosed are copies of letters written to you agreeably to their dates. They are sent on the *possibility* that the originals may have miscarried, although the *probability*, I hope is much against it.[1]

In a late letter to Mr Whiting, at Mount Vernon, I have directed him not to sell the Stud horse, but to deliver him to your order. The sooner you send for him the better.[2]

Your Aunt unites with me in best wishes for yourself and Mrs Lewis, and with sincere regard, I am—Your Affectionate Uncle,

Go: Washington

ALS, ViMtV.

1. GW enclosed copies of his two letters to Lewis of 23 Dec. 1792 concerning the proposed purchase of a tract of land adjoining the Dogue Run farm that was owned by William B. Harrison. The enclosed copies have not been found.

2. GW had written his farm manager at Mount Vernon, Anthony Whitting, on 30 Dec. 1792 that he wished his stud horse Sampson to be "delivered to Mr Robt Lewis's Order." On 6 Jan. 1793 GW informed Whitting again that he had promised to give the horse to his nephew. Whitting informed GW on 9 Jan. that he had sent Sampson to Lewis on that day. GW had paid David Lacy £40 "for a large bay Stud Horse called Sampson" on 17 April 1790 (Ledger B, 312).

From Gouverneur Morris

My dear Sir Paris 6 January 1793

Since I had the Pleasure of writing to you on the twenty eighth of last Month I have seen Mr Genest and he has din'd with me. He has I think more of Genius than of Ability and you will see in him at the first Blush the Manner and Look of an Upstart. My friend the Marechal de Segur had told me that Mr Genest was a Clerk at £50 pr An: in his Office while Secretary at War. I turn'd the Conversation therefore on the Marechal and Mr Genest told me that he knew him very well having been in the *Ministry* with him. After Dinner he enter'd into Dispute on Commerce with a Merchant who came in and as the Question turn'd chiefly on Facts the Merchant was rather an overmatch for the Minister. I think that in the Business he is charg'd with he will talk so much as to furnish sufficient Matter for putting him on one Side of his Object should that be convenient. If he writes he will I beleive do better.[1]

I have endeavor'd to shew him that this is the worst possible Season to put to Sea for America. If he delays there is some Room to suppose that Events may happen to prevent the Mission perhaps a british Ship may intercept that which takes him out— And I incline to think that untill Matters are more steady here you would be as well content with some Delay as with remarkable Dispatch.[2] I am always yours

Gouvr Morris

ALS, DLC:GW; LB, in Morris's writing, DLC: Gouverneur Morris Papers. The ALS was docketed "From Gouvr Morris Esqr 28th Decr 1792. 6th & 10⟨th⟩ Jany 1793," with an additional notation indicating the receipt on 3 May 1793 of this packet of letters from Morris.

1. For background on Edmond-Charles Genet's career, which included service as a translator in the department of foreign affairs from 1781 to 1787, see Morris to GW, 28 Dec. 1792, and note 2. Philippe-Henri, marquis de Ségur, was the minister of war from 1780 to 1787. For the official announcement of Genet's appointment as minister plenipotentiary to the United States, see the Provisional Executive Council of France to GW, 30 Dec. 1792, n.2. According to Morris's diary, Genet dined with him on 3 Jan. (see Morris, *Diary and Letters of Gouverneur Morris*, 2:24).

2. Genet left Paris for the port city of Rochefort on 21 Jan., but inopportune weather delayed his sailing until 20 February. He arrived at Charleston, S.C., on 8 April 1793, on board the 44-gun French warship *Embuscade*.

To Anthony Whitting

Mr Whiting,   Philadelphia Jany 6th 1793

Your letter of the 2d instant with its enclosures came to hand yesterday[1]—and I am glad to find by it that Mr James Butler had arrived safe for I began to apprehend that he might have fallen sick on the Road, as he had not reached Mount Vernon at the date of your former letter of the 26th Ulto.[2]

If this person performs all the duties I have Suggested to you as proper for him to be employed in, with intelligence & zeal, I shall excuse him readily from Manual labour. And as you will Soon discover of what turn of mind he is—whether inclined to industry, or to indulgence, Whether his knowledge of Farming is real or pretended only (from the clearness & precision with which he may discourse with you on topics relating to it), Whether his dispositions are good or bad; and whether he has a head capable of arrangements or not—I should be glad to be informed, when you shall have formed a judgment of them yourself. His character as handed to me, stands exceedingly fair on the Score of Sobriety & honesty, by those with whom he has lived in this Country; and the enclosed certificate (which deposit along with his agreement) testifies to his conduct in Ireland. Mr Keating is a Clergyman of respectable character—& Major Butler (who appears on the Back of the certificate) is one of the Senators in Congress.[3] My apprehensions of James Butlers fitness, proceed from a doubt that he may want activity; & my only reason for so doubting, is founded on his clumsy appearance, and age: and again, that he will be at a loss in the management of Negros—as their idleness & deceit, if he is not Sufficiently cautioned against them, will most assuredly impose upon him. I have told him that he must Stir early & late, as I expect my people will work from day-breaking until it is dusk in the evening; and, that the only way to keep them at work without Severity, or wrangling, is always to be with them.

You will See by the enclosed to Thomas Green (which Seal before you send it to him) on what footing I have placed his continuance, or discharge; and I do hereby authorize you to Act accordingly.[4] I need not observe to you, however, that it is necessary before the latter takes place to consider how the business can be carried on without him, or some other White-man; and where, & on what terms, such an one can be had; for I am Sure, none of my Negro Carpenters are adequate to the framing, & executing such a Barn as I am about to build at D: Run.[5]

Speaking of this Barn, Let me know when it is probable it will be set about—Whether the Scantling (Oak excepted) and Plank, is actually engaged—And when to be expected? Never having been fully possessed of the poor Major's view (if he ever contemplated his disorder as fatal) in this building, I am absolutely at a loss what to say to you respecting the materials for it.[6] My *own judgment* is decidedly against expending his money for this purpose, in the hopeless state of recovery in which he is represented by his Physicians, and all who have seen him to be. On the other hand, *as he seems* so sollicitous to have it carried on, he must either think differently of his disorder from others, or his object is unknown to me. Under this view of the Subject my advice to you is, to purchase such parts of the Scantling only as are most essential & which will be first wanting by the workmen in carrying on the building, & this, without cutting it to waste; but by no means to hurry the work until matters are brought more to a crisis & certainty. I could not, before he left Mount Vernon, tell him that his case was (by every one) thought desperate; but advised him (except what could be done by his own people) to let the matter rest till the Spring—and then he should have the aid of all my people—As well Carpenters as Bricklayers, to hasten it on.

If there was an absolute necessity for refraining from Fishing with my own People, or Postponing my Hedging operations another year, I should not hesitate a moment in giving up the first; for I would make every thing yield to the latter; but I do not see the thing in this light. I expect the Hedging and every thing belonging thereto (except ditching where necessary) whether done this year, next year, or at any time thereafter, will be performed at each Plantation by the hands belonging to it. And that the proper time for this work is now, and in all weather, when the earth can be moved, between this and the budding of Spring. In a ride I took yesterday, I saw thousands of the cuttings of Willow setting out; and upon enquiry was told it was the best season to do it: if it suits one sort of cuttings, more than probable it will suit another; I therefore request this work may not be delayed a moment. It is not like fencing, grubbing, &ca that may be executed at all Seasons of the year. For this reason I should have derived more Satisfaction from reading the reports, to have found that the hands of the Ferry &ca, & the hands of Muddy hole had been employed in preparing the ground along their cross fences for the reception of Cuttings, and Seeds (if you have any to put in) than in grubbing places which could be done as well hereafter for the Crops which are to follow, or even to have omitted them if they could not as now. If under these ideas you can carry on Fishing (with my own people) and Hedging both, it will be most agreeable to me; but if one only can be done, I had rather Rent the Landing for what it will fetch, & stick to Hedging. In the first case—that is doing both—It is very probable Mr James Butler will be a proper person to Superintend the Fishery, as I presume *all* his hands must go to that business; with aid from other quarters.[7]

I should be glad to know how far you have advanced in your clearing at the Mansion house? The point between the Road leading to the Wharf, & Hell-hole, ought to be well grubbed, cleaned, smoothed, & well sprinkled with Timothy—I mean all that part which lyes with out the fence of the old clover lot, quite up to the Vineyard Inclosure: the same also on the other side of the Road, between that and the cross fence by the Vault & old hound kennel.[8]

If the Wool is all spun up, in what manner do you mean to employ the Spinners? They must not be idle; nor ought the Sewers to have been so when they were out of thread: If they can find no other work, let them join the out door hands. Myrtilla & Delia had better, I conceive, do this altogether, as their will be enough without them for all the purposes of Spinning & Sewing.[9]

More than an hundred bushels of Buck wheat will, I should Suppose, be nearly or quite adequate to all your wants. If it is sown in good season, and the ground is well prepared, three pecks to the Acre will be enough, of Seed that is fresh & good.

If you think the Wheat in No. 2, at Muddy hole, will not be too much injured by turning the young Mules on it, I do not object to the measure; and with respect to the young Jack, it is my earnest wish that he may be fed high—Winter & Summer—to see to what size he can be made to grow.

As I have promised the stud horse to Mr Robt Lewis, I would not have him disposed of otherwise. I shall write to him by this opportunity to send for the horse.[10]

I Suppose Mr Hooe receives my flour upon the same terms he Stores other goods; No other I have a right to expect; but I conceive that he ought to insure it against embezzlement—or waste, occasioned by improper usage in tossing it about. However, if you Store up on the Same terms others do, I can expect no more.[11]

When you are well informed of the conditions on which Majr Harrison lets his Land to Pool &ca I shall be better able to decide upon the propriety of becoming the purchaser of it. My opinion of its being under lease was occasioned by the New building I discovered on it, but this was no more than conjectural evidence of the fact.[12] I remain Your friend & Welwisher

Go: Washington

ALS, NN: Washington Collection.

1. Whiting's letter to GW of 2 Jan. and its enclosures have not been found.

2. Whiting's letter to GW of 26 Dec. 1792 has not been found. Butler, whom GW had hired in December 1792 as an overseer on his Mansion House farm,

had left Philadelphia for Mount Vernon on 21 Dec. (see GW to Whitting, 16, 19, 23 Dec. 1792).

3. The enclosed certificate has not been identified. GW's agreement with Butler, which has not been found, had been enclosed in GW's letter to Whitting of 19 Dec. 1792. The "Clergyman of respectable character" is probably Thomas Keating (c.1743–1793), who had been assistant pastor of St. Mary's Roman Catholic Church in Philadelphia from May 1789 until later that year when he was sent to Charleston, S.C., where he established St. Mary's Church, the first Catholic church in that state. It is uncertain when Keating left South Carolina, but he was in Philadelphia at the time of his death on 23 Mar. 1793. Pierce Butler was one of the senators from South Carolina.

4. GW's letter to Green has not been found. Although GW had long been disgusted by Green's drunkenness, laziness, and general incompetence, his desire to assist Green's wife Sarah, the daughter of his former body servant Thomas Bishop, prevented him from dismissing Green. In the late summer of 1794, however, Green left GW's employ "of his own accord" (see GW to William Pearce, 21 Sept. 1794, ALS, ViMtV; ALS [letterpress copy], DLC:GW).

5. On 28 Oct. 1792 GW had informed Whitting of his resolution to build a barn at the Dogue Run farm. See GW's Plan for a Barn, which he enclosed in his letter to Whitting of 28 Oct., and his letters to Whitting of 4 Nov. and 2 Dec. 1792.

6. GW seems to have changed the subject of this paragraph abruptly from the proposed barn at the Dogue Run farm to the construction underway on his property at Clifton's Neck. On 25 Oct. 1786 GW had written to his nephew George Augustine Washington that "it is my present intention to give you at my death, my *landed* property in the neck, containing by estimation between two & three thousand acres. . . . And under this expectation & prospect . . . when it perfectly suits your inclination & convenience, be preparing for, and building thereon by degrees." G. A. Washington had left Mount Vernon in late October to spend the winter in New Kent County, Virginia. For earlier correspondence concerning the wisdom of continuing construction on the major's house, see GW to Whitting, 9 Dec. 1792. After his nephew's death from tuberculosis in February 1793, GW instructed Whitting to stop work on the house (see GW to Whitting, 24 Feb. and 3 Mar. 1793).

7. For GW's earlier instructions regarding the fishery and hedging, see his letters to Whitting of 14 Nov. and 2 Dec. 1792, respectively.

8. The burial vault was southeast of the Mansion House. For the location of the old kennel, which had recently burned down, see GW to Whitting, 9 Dec. 1792, n.12.

9. Myrtilla (Matilda; d. 1832), a spinner at the Mansion House farm, had belonged to GW since at least 1774. After GW's death in 1799, she apparently remained at Mount Vernon with her husband, Boatswain (see Memorandum List of Tithables, c.July 1774; Slave List, 18 Feb. 1786, in *Diaries*, 4:277–78; Washington's Slave List, June 1799; Hirschfeld, *Washington and Slavery*, 215). Delia may be the 35-year-old spinner whom GW leased from Mrs. Penelope Manley French in 1799 (see Washington's Slave List, June 1799).

10. For the background to GW's gift of a stud horse to his nephew Robert

Lewis, see Lewis to GW, 4 Jan., n.2, and GW to Lewis, 6 Jan. 1793, and note 2. Whitting informed GW on 9 Jan. that he had sent "the Horse Sampson" to Lewis on that date.

11. GW stored some of his flour at the Alexandria warehouse of Robert Townsend Hooe, which was located on Hooe's Wharf on the Potomac River at the southwestern corner of Duke Street. For Whitting's shipment of 100 barrels of flour to Alexandria at this time, see Whitting to GW, 9 Jan. 1793. By 28 April, GW could report that he had "141 barls of Superfine, & 149 barls of common flour" stored at Hooe's warehouse (see GW to John Fitzgerald, 28 April 1793). For GW's negotiations with Hooe for an acceptable purchase price for his flour, see GW to Hooe, 17, 29 May, Hooe to GW, 23 May, and GW to Whitting, 29 May 1793.

12. GW previously had raised this issue in his letter to Whitting of 23 Dec. 1792. For the background to GW's attempt to purchase a tract of land adjoining his Dogue Run farm from William B. Harrison, see GW to Robert Lewis, 23 Dec., and the enclosed letter from GW to Lewis of the same date, and Lewis to GW, 4 Jan. 1793, and note 1. GW's opinion of the Pool family was that "a more worthless set are no where to be found" (see GW to William Pearce, 14 Dec. 1794, ALS, ViMtV; AL [letterpress copy; incomplete], DLC:GW). For further information on the Pool family, see GW to Whitting, 23 Dec. 1792, n.8.

From David Stuart

Dear Sir,   Ge: town 7th Jany 93

Agreeable to your request in your late letter to me, I now send you a list of all the sales both public & private, which have been made in the city of Washington.[1] The persons whose names are opposite to the red crosses, bid at our desire: these lots of course remain with us—The square bought by Mr Blodget, was in the same situation, 'till his last visit here, when he agreed to take it on himself, and gave us reasons to expect he would set about improving it immediately—It is yet doubtfull, whether he may not allso take those opposite to N:B: in red[2]—It was my wish to have sent you the list at the first of our meeting; but our Clerks have been so much engaged, that I have not been able to get it made out sooner. I am with the greatest respect Your affecte Servt

         Dd Stuart.

ALS, DLC:GW. GW received this letter on 10 Jan. (see *JPP,* 7).

1. Stuart apparently was responding to a request that GW had made in his letter to Stuart of 30 November. Although the enclosed list has not been identified, GW already had received a considerable amount of information about the sale of lots in the Federal City. For the sale of October 1791, see Stuart to

GW, 19 Oct., nn.1–2, and D.C. Commissioners to GW, 21 Oct. 1791. For a summary of the sale of October 1792, see D.C. Commissioners to GW, 13 Oct. 1792, n.1. For "private bargains" agreed to since the public sale in October 1792, see Stuart to GW, 10 Dec. 1792, and note 3.

2. For Samuel Blodget, Jr.'s purchase of square 688 near the proposed site of the U.S. Capitol, see D.C. Commissioners to GW, 13 Oct. 1792, and note 2. Nathan Bond was one of several Boston speculators who had purchased lots near the site designated for the President's House (see Stuart to GW, 10 Dec. 1792, and note 3).

From Thomas Jefferson

[Philadelphia] Jan. 8. 93.

Th: Jefferson has the honor to inclose to the President 3. copies of the papers on the subject of the coins. he does not see however that it is necessary to send one to the Senate; unless usage has rendered it so.[1]

he has retained the Directors *original* statement, thinking it ought to be of record in his office, as it may be the foundation of a law.[2]

AL, DNA: RG 59, Miscellaneous Letters; LB, DNA: RG 59, George Washington's Correspondence with His Secretaries of State; LB (photocopy), DLC:GW.

1. Jefferson enclosed a copy of the letter of 7 Jan. sent him by Director of the Mint David Rittenhouse, a copy of Rittenhouse's 7 Jan. report on the recent assay of foreign gold and silver coins, and a draft cover letter for GW to send to the U.S. House of Representatives, which reads: "According to the request expressed in your Resolution of the 29. of November, I have caused Assays and other proper experiments to be made at the mint of the united States, of the gold and silver Coins of France, England, Spain, and Portugal, and now lay before you the result" (DNA: RG 59, Miscellaneous Letters). For the House's resolution, see the U.S. House of Representatives to GW, 29 Nov. 1792, and note 1.

Jefferson also enclosed an introduction to the assay report and Rittenhouse's 7 Jan. letter, which reads: "The Secretary of State, to whom was referred, by the President of the United States, the Resolution of the House of Representatives of the 29th of Novr 1792 on the subject of Experiments on the Coins of France, England, Spain, and Portugal, Reports, That assays and experiments have been accordingly made at the Mint, by the Director, and under his Care and inspection, of sundry gold and silver Coins of France, England, Spain, and Portugal, and a statement of the quantity of fine metal and alloy in each of them, and the specific gravities of those of Gold given in by the Director, a copy of which, and of the letter covering it, are contained in the papers marked A and B" (DNA: RG 59, Miscellaneous Letters). Paper A was a copy of Rittenhouse's letter to Jefferson of 7 Jan., which reads: "I have herewith enclosed the result of our Assays &c. of the Coins of France, England, Spain, and Portugal. In the course of the Experiments a very small source of Error was detected, too late for the present occasion, but which will be carefully guarded against in future" (DNA: RG 59, Miscellaneous Letters). Paper B was a copy of the assay of gold and silver coins conducted at the U.S. Mint on 7 Jan. 1793 by David Ott under Rittenhouse's supervision (DNA: RG 59, Miscellaneous Letters; see also *Jefferson Papers*, 25:32–33). Jefferson, not GW, sent his introductory paragraph and documents A and B to the House of Representatives later on 8 Jan. 1793 under a brief cover letter of that date. He apparently did not send a copy to the Senate (see *Jefferson Papers*, 25:37–39; *Annals of Congress*, 2d Cong., 801). For GW's possible presence during at least part of the assay process, see Rittenhouse to Tobias Lear, 27 Dec. 1792.

2. GW approved on 9 Feb. 1793 "An Act regulating foreign Coins, and for other purposes" (1 *Stat.* 300–301).

From William Moultrie

Sir,   Charleston [S.C.] 8th January 1793

Agreeably to a resolve of the Legislature of this State, I have the honor herewith to transmit to you, a copy of an Oath made by Benjamin Cleveland respecting the murder of some Cherokee Indians.[1] I have the honor to be, with great respect, Your most Obt hume Servt

Willm Moultrie

ALS, owned (1992) by Mr. Gary Hendershott, Little Rock, Arkansas.

1. Benjamin Cleveland (1738–1806) had risen to the rank of colonel in the North Carolina militia during the Revolutionary War and had played a prominent role in the American victory at Kings Mountain in October 1780. Cleveland later moved to South Carolina, where he was a justice of the peace for Pendleton County for many years. Cleveland's deposition of 1 Dec. 1792, given in Pendleton County, reported that "on the 26th day of October last the Leach, old Will & his Son the Duke of Simbs with three other Cheroke fellows," came to his house on the Tugaloo River, "under the protection of a Flag." Leach told him "that they were delegated with powers from the well disposed Towns of their Nation to come to him . . . with a peace talk." The Indians also provided Cleveland with "some very interesting & important intelligence concerning the measures which had been & were about to be adopted by the disaffected part of their Nation." They left his house later that day and crossed the Tugaloo River into Georgia. There "in the night of the 28th, or the morning of the 29th of October last, before, or about day break on the said Morning," a group of armed men fired on them, killing Leach and Old Will. Cleveland wrote that "this cruel act was done in Franklin County in the State of Georgia by a party of men said to be about thirty in number, said to be all Georgians and said to live at or near the Mulberry Grove on broad River. . . . soon after the said Indi-

ans were killed under the protection of a flag as aforesaid, a party embodied, said to consist of eighty or ninety men marched into a peaceable Town of the Cherokees, about 40 Miles distant from our frontier Settlements in a hostile manner, killed one or more Indians (the rest fled to the mountains) burned their houses destroyed the Corn, & carried off what plunder they found there, which would anywise answer their avaricious purposes, That he believes this Bandity were raised in the same Settlement, and had with them all, or most of the party who were engaged in the murder of the Flag as aforesaid and that he hath since heard, that a much stronger party from the same County in Georgia, is gone, or about to go to destroy another peaceable Town of the Cherokees—where they expect to get more plunder than they did in the last Town they destroyed" (filed under the date of 8 Jan. 1793 in DNA: RG 59, Miscellaneous Letters).

On 2 Feb., Tobias Lear transmitted to Henry Knox by GW's command "a lettr from Govr Moultrie, enclosing a deposition relative to the murder of certain Cherokee Inds by a party of Geo[r]gians in Oct. last" (DLC:GW).

Pass for Jean-Pierre Blanchard

[Philadelphia, 9 January 1793]

TO ALL TO WHOM THESE PRESENTS SHALL COME.

The bearer hereof, Mr. Blanchard a citizen of France, proposing to ascend in a balloon from the city of Philadelphia, at 10 o'clock, A.M. this day, to pass in such direction and to descend in such place as circumstances may render most convenient—THESE are therefore to recommend to all citizens of the United States, and others, that in his passage, descent, return or journeying elsewhere, they oppose no hindrance or molestation to the said Mr. Blanchard; And, that on the contrary, they receive and aid him with that humanity and good will, which may render honor to their country, and justice to an individual so distinguished by his efforts to establish and advance an art, in order to make it useful to mankind in general.[1]

Given under my hand and seal at the city of Philadelphia, this ninth day of January, one thousand seven hundred and ninety three, and of the independence of America the seventeenth.

GEORGE WASHINGTON.

Printed transcript, DLC: Institute of Aerospace Sciences Papers.

1. Jean-Pierre Blanchard (1753–1809), who had arrived at Philadelphia on the *Ceres* on 9 Dec., was the first person to make balloon flights in England, Germany, and Poland, and in 1785 he and John Jeffries were the first to cross the English Channel by air.

Blanchard's balloon flight at Philadelphia on 9 Jan. was described in the 16 Jan. issue of the *Pennsylvania Gazette* (Philadelphia): "Mr. Blanchard, the bold ÆRONAUT, agreeably to his advertisement, at five minutes past ten o'clock, on Wednesday morning, the 9th instant, rose with a BALOON from the Prison Court in this city, in presence of an immense concourse of spectators there assembled on the occasion. The process of inflating the Baloon commenced about 9 o'clock.—Several canon were fired from the dawn of day, until the moment of elevation—a band of music played during the time of inflating, and when it began to rise, the majestic sight was truly awful and interesting— the slow movement of the band added solemnity to the scene. Indeed the attention of the multitude was so absorbed, that it was a considerable time e'er silence was broke by the acclamations which succeeded.

"As soon as the clock had struck 10, every thing being punctually ready, Mr. Blanchard took a respectful leave of all the spectators, and received from the hands of the President a paper, at the same time the President spoke a few words to him, who immediately leaped into his boat, which was painted blue and spangled; the baloon was of a yellowish coloured silk, highly varnished, over which there was a strong net work—Mr. BLANCHARD was dressed in a plain blue suit, a cocked hat and white feathers. As soon as he was in the boat, he threw out some ballast, and the baloon began to ascend slowly and perpendicularly whilst Mr. BLANCHARD waved the colours of the United States and also those of the French Republic, and flourished his hat to the thousands of citizens from every part of the country who stood gratified and astonished at his intrepidity. After a few minutes, the wind blowing from the northward and westward, the baloon rose to an immense heighth, and then shaped its course towards the southward and eastward. Several gentlemen rode down the Point road, but soon lost sight of it, for it moved at the rate of 20 miles an hour.

"About half after 6 o'clock the same evening, Mr. BLANCHARD returned to this city, and immediately went to pay his respects to the President of the United States.—He informed that his æriel voyage lasted forty-six minutes, in which time he ran over a space of more than 15 miles, and then descended a little to the eastward of Woodbury, in the state of New-Jersey—where he took a carriage and returned to Cooper's ferry—and was at the President's, as we have already mentioned, at half past 6 o'clock that evening." Thus ended Blanchard's forty-fifth aerial flight and his first on the North American continent.

Blanchard had tried to defray the cost of this flight through the sale of subscription tickets for five dollars apiece. Unfortunately, on 9 Jan. the "neighbouring lots and buildings to the jail were crouded with *gratis* spectators, while but few, we were sorry to see, within the walls [of the prison], contributed toward defraying the charges of this costly experiment. . . . A number of Gentlemen, we understand who enjoyed the sight of this magnificent experiment from without the Prison court, understanding, from positive authority, that M. Blanchard's subscriptions would fall several hundred pounds short of his expences, opened a subscription, which contains already a number of respectable names" (*General Advertiser* [Philadelphia], 3, 10 Jan. 1793). On 25 Jan. the *General Advertiser* printed a letter Blanchard had written to its editor, Benjamin Franklin Bache, on 24 Jan. in which he reported that although "Some gentlemen understanding that my loss, by the last experiment, is upwards of 400 guineas, were kind enough to open subscriptions, to cover the expence . . . their success has not answered to their wishes, by a great deal." Even so, "as many avow it as their intention to reserve their subscription for a second experiment I have thought it encumbent on me to endeavour to afford the opportunity." On 17 June 1793 Blanchard "entertained the citizens" of Philadelphia with a demonstration "of the Parachute, which succeeded, to the admiration of all the spectators. The weather being wet, prevented the ascension of the balloon to the height intended, but every particular of the experiment was effected, and the balloon and parachute fell in Arch street, near the Delaware, the animals [used in the experiment] coming down safe" (*Pennsylvania Gazette,* 19 June 1793).

From the Commissioners for the District of Columbia

Sir   Washington 9th Jany—1793
     After closing our Letter of the 5th we wrote Majr Ellicott—a copy is sent,[1] to which we soon received the inclosed answer[2]— We feel a strong disinclination to go into discussions before the public and believe we shall not be led or drove[3] into it. We are Sir with the greatest respect & esteem Your Obt hble Servts
                                                                    Th. Johnson
                                                                    Dd Stuart.
                                                                    Danl Carroll

LS, DLC:GW; LB, DNA: RG 42, Records of the Commissioners for the District of Columbia, Letters Sent, 1791–1802.

     1. The D.C. commissioners' letter to Andrew Ellicott of 8 Jan. reads: "We have before us your two letters of the 4th and 5 Inst.—It can answer no good purpose to go minutely into the subject of the first, and therefore we decline it, but in general without pretending to a scientific acquaintance with your professional Art we cannot sacrifice so much of our sincerity as to say otherwise than that our expectations have been much disappointed as to the Time, the work of surveying has been on hand, and have often mentioned to you our wish of strengthing you with every assistance in our power to expidite it—If your not being able to effectuate the wishes of the public and ours should perfect your resolution to leave us by the first of may, we wish to be on a certainty some time before, for it will be most manly, & agree best with our real inclination to part on good Terms & with as little injury to the business as possible.
     "Your Letter of the 5th mentions your opinion that the work may be finished next Summer—whether you continue through or not, we wish every measure to be pursued to shorten the Time as much as may be consistent with accuracy for you must have often observed our difficulties & chagrin at being obliged

to act on the existing State of the work & which has obliged us to trouble you often with particular Requests" (DLC:GW).

2. Andrew Ellicott's reply to the D.C. commissioners, written at Georgetown on 8 Jan., reads: "I wish you to direct Mr Gantt to furnish me with copies of my letters of the 4th and 5th of this month as they will be necessary in replying particularly to yours of this date—That you should pass a general censure on work which you say you do not understand and great part of which I am sure you never saw, is to me a most extraordinary circumstance—You will please to recollect that the sale of lots last year was not as extensive as it might have been by two thirds, owing to the property being uncertain & the necessary public notice not being given to enable you to divide without the concurrence of the proprietors—All Hamburgh was ready for division by the first day of June last and yet not one sale could be made on that part of the City—*this I trust was no neglect of mine*[.] General censures are in my opinion the most unge⟨ner⟩ous mode of commencing an attack, I shall therefore make it a point to vindicate myself as publicly as possible—I claim no merit from doing my duty but would just direct your attention to the plan of the City of Washington—In bringing that forward to serve the cause in which we have been mutually engaged I have lost one of my oldest and most valuable friends and in the execution received your disapprobation—You may rest assured that my exertions will be directed to forwarding the execution of the plan of the City untill the first day of May next when I shall quit the service" (DLC:GW).

3. In the letter-book copy this word is "drawn."

From Anthony Whitting

Honrd Sir   Mount Vernon Jany 9th 1793
    Your Letter of the 30th of Decemr I had the Honor to receive, in my last I mentioned Mr Butlers being at Mount Vernon[1] he seems a well inform'd man & may be a Good Judge of farming but I find he like all others first from Europe thinks Great improvements may be made in agriculture he has been with the hands while Grubbing on the side of hell hole Swamp & he Got a Spade & tried the Soil of the Swamp & told me at Dinner there was some fine manure there he seemd to think it a Great acquisition and I believe would wish to see it all hauld out on the Land I had the same ideas when I came first to this Country.
    I have perticularly examined the Ground from the Wharf to the Visto since the receipt of your Excellencys Letter which Containd a Sketch of what was intended, & still think the Collection of water from the different Springs to front of mansion house will be very difficult,[2] there are many hollows to pass three of Which I think at least five feet lower than the banks on each side

of them. if the water Should be carried across them in a trunk it would then deprive me of the water running down them which is the most considerable & should the drain be cut deep enough to collect that water (which certainly ought to be Collected) it must in many places as above be at least five feet deep and not less then three or four in every part whether you Sir supposed this to be the Case I dont know. I still think it is not impossible but are of the same way of thinking I was, that it will take an immensity of Labor I have examined the Paint & Oyl the latter of Which is now nearly exhausted I found in the Store 3 Small kegs of red paint very dry & hard which I believe had been there some years we Soften'd it by boiling it in the Oyl and have used the Greatest part of it the roofs of the houses take a Great deal of paint The Salt house & 3 Garden houses out of 4 are finishd & the Smoke house allmost done[3] we Shall want a bll of Oyl & a keg of red paint & it must not be a small one to finishd the Other houses & five or six kegs of White to go over what has been only primed & it would look well if the Cornice of Smoke & Salt houses was painted over now the roof is new painted Indeed there is a Great deal of painting wanting the pillars of the Piazza are very naked, & many other places are wanting paint So that if your Excellency Chuses to have them done there is no danger of sending too much White Lead—4 or 5 of the small kegs which white paint is Generally put in will do What has been began & not finishd abt the [slave] Qu[arte]rs Green house[4] &c. perhaps Salt & Smoke house. The Piazza roof has not leakd since it was Covered.

The Old Clover Lot at Mansion has been Several weeks plough'd. The brick yard inclosure[5] I think will be the better for lying 'till spring as it now is as buck Wheat leaves the Land very light & I much question but it will be more mellow in Spring then if it had been turnd up to have been beat with the rains & run to Gether by frosts The Lucerne Lot I think I will plough (if the weather continues fine) to morrow as from its being Stony & Gravelly the above case will not happen. The Lots abt mansion house I will sow with Clover myself and am persuaded I can sow it as regular as any machine ever made use of One may notwithstanding be made for the use of Others places as no dependence can be placed in the Overseers Sowing regular.

Doll at Ferry has been Sick some time past has lately been Swingling flax[6] but as I took her of the report nothing has been said of her work or Sickness I have this morning had her brought in a Cart to mansion house & intend her to be learn'd to knit[7] there wants more knitters the plaid Stockings Given to the people wont last them more then two or three weeks & I could wish them to have all knit Stockings.

Mr Robt Lewis Sent yesterday for the Horse Sampson I have this morning sent him[8] he requested his boy to have him Shod if he had no Shoes on, the Smiths being only just finishing there kiln I had to send for some Coal & had him Shod this morning.

Yesterday Visited Mount Vernon Lord Galloway Son of the Earl of Galloway in Scotland he has been it seems thro Nova Scotia & the thirteen States is at present at Alexandria Mr Willm Wilson came with him to Mount Vern. he is Going to the Northwd & will I expect call on your Excellencys in passing[9] he was highly delighted with the Situation of Mount Vernon but much surprized at the number of Acres in Cultivation he ask'd me what number of ploughs we work'd I told him about thirty he said it far exceeded any number he ever knew off.

I have sent a 100 blls of flour to Alexa. this week but we have a Great deal of trouble of Getting it from the mill I am forced to send the Waggon & Carts to haul it to the Oyster Shell Landing & then each bring a Load to the Old fish house below Bishop's the tides have been very low but the Weather fine for Getting it away I have allways met the Boat in Town 'till this day When it is Gone alone with 50 blls I wrote to Smith to inspect it as it comes out of the boat[10] we had part of our Load on Monday[11] not inspected I Got him to inspect it as we unloaded it & it passed with Credit I hope it will do the same to Day. flour is worth abt 1/6 ⅌ bll more then last week three Brigs have past this morning up, so that I hope it will not be worse in price.

The Clover seed & every thing mentioned in the Bills of Lading & invoices have come safe to hand.[12]

The fences at River plantn are a Serious matter and I hardly know where timber is to be found for the repairs of them By some means however they must be made Good for I cannot bear to see such fences, there hands (men) must be now Constantly employd in this business & women likewise as soon as rails can be Got in putting them up Mr Stewart[13] & myself have been all thro the woods he seems to think the timber not so very Scarce but he has lived in a part Where it is Generally so which makes him think more favorable of them woods I have signified to him a desire of having the fences all put in repair for such is there present situation that no hog can hardly be kept in any field— the post & rail fences around the Clover Lot will let a hog thro half Grown, Your Excellencys was mentioning that Gang might come over to mansion house Grubbing but I had rather see there fences put in Good order if you Sir have no Objections they have a Good winters work there to compleat this & I most heartily wish it may be done. I am Honrd Sir Your Obdt Servt

A. Whitting

ALS, DLC:GW.

1. Whitting's most recent letter to GW, which was written on 2 Jan., has not been found. For the hiring of James Butler as overseer of the Mansion House farm, see GW to Whitting, 6 Jan. 1793, and note 2.

2. For background on GW's attempt to unite the various springs on the river side of the mansion at Mount Vernon, see GW to Whitting, 28 Oct., 18 Nov., 2, 16, 30 Dec. 1792. GW had enclosed the sketch, which has not been found, in his letter to Whitting of 30 Dec. 1792.

3. The salt house and smokehouse were located on the north and south lanes, respectively, west of the mansion house. The four garden houses were at each end of the upper and lower gardens. The two nearest the mansion were necessaries, and the other two served as storehouses for tools.

4. The new slave quarters and the adjoining greenhouse were northwest of the mansion next to the upper garden.

5. Brickyards and kilns had been built at several locations at Mount Vernon over the years, usually near current construction sites. In 1792 a brickyard was located near the new slave quarters and the greenhouse.

6. Swingling was the process of beating flax in order to remove the coarse or woody particles in it.

7. For GW's earlier instructions that Doll be taught to knit, see GW to Whitting, 4 Nov. 1792.

8. For background on GW's gift of a stud horse to his nephew Robert Lewis, see Lewis to GW, 4 Jan., n.2, and GW to Lewis, 6 Jan. 1793.

9. John Stewart (1736–1806), the seventh earl of Galloway (Scottish), served as a member of the House of Commons from 1761 until 1773 and subsequently as a representative peer for Scotland in the House of Lords until 1790. The person who accompanied Alexandria merchant William Wilson to Mount Vernon was probably the earl's eldest son, George Stewart (1768–1734), currently a commander in the Royal Navy who was styled Lord Garlies from 1773 to 1806 when he succeeded his father as the eighth earl of Galloway. No evidence has been found that he visited GW in Philadelphia in 1793.

10. For background on the shipment of flour to Alexandria, see GW to Whitting, 6 Jan. 1793, and note 11. Alexandria merchant Alexander Smith, whose store specialized in groceries and bolting cloth, currently served as flour inspector there (see Miller, *Artisans and Merchants of Alexandria*, 2:129–30).

11. Whitting is referring to Monday, 7 Jan. 1793.

12. For the purchase and shipment of this clover seed and for GW's planting instructions, see GW to Whitting, 9 Dec. 1792, and note 5. The bills of lading and invoices may be those enclosed in GW's letter to Whitting of 16 Dec. 1792.

13. William Stuart was GW's new overseer at the River farm. He apparently held this position until GW's death. By 1802 he had become manager of the Custis White House plantation in New Kent County, Va., a property controlled by Dr. David Stuart by virtue of his marriage in 1783 to Eleanor Calvert Custis, the widow of Martha Washington's son, John Parke Custis.

From Uriah Forrest

Sir   Georgetown 10th January 1793.

Having at heart the growth & prosperity of the federal City I have for many months made it a point to promote all in my power whatever appeared to be the views of those directing its improvement even in instances where my judgement could not be convinced the measures were quite proper[.] Because from the altercation which took place betwixt the commissioners and major L'enfant and in which I with other proprietors interfer'd perhaps improperly but certainly too intemperately I was led to reflect perhaps more than I had otherwise done & from that reflexion & from observation I am convinced the City has infinately more to dread from the discord and want of Union in its friends than from all the power of its Enemies[.][1] Thus impressed you will not wonder at my endeavouring to heal the breach between the Commissioners and mr Ellicot on the first intimation I had of it[.][2] I suggested to one of the commissioners it was better to overlook any waste of time or trifling expence of money which I understood was objected to the Surveyor than to suffer him to be discontented much less that it should be generally known there existed new differences between those directing & executing the business of the City and to Mr Ellicot I urged every thing in my power[.] But on Tuesday I heard with great concern it had been ineffectual for on the morning of that day it was pretty generally spoken that He intended to attack their conduct in the public prints and had given them notice to provide a successor.[3]

He had left Town before I received this information and I therefore sent out to the City to try and dissuade him from it[.] I inclose herein copy of his answer[.][4] I understand several letters have passed between the commissioners & him[.] I have not seen any of them nor have I been particularly informed the contents more than that in general they contained much acrimony.

I consider the Event and particularly the Time of it as very unfortunate and have thus early troubled you respecting it in the hope that some expedient may be fallen on to effect an accommodation or if that cannot be brought abou⟨t⟩ to guard as much as possible against any ill effects from i⟨t⟩.

I confidently trust You will accept of the Motives which have induced me to trouble you on the occasion as a sufficient apology for the freedom I have taken and pray you to beleiv⟨e⟩ that of the whole number of those who respect & esteem you there is not one more sincere than Sir Your most Obedient very humble Sert

Uriah Forrest

ALS, DNA: RG 59, Miscellaneous Letters.

1. For background on events leading to the dismissal in February 1792 of architect and engineer Pierre L'Enfant as surveyor general and supervisor of the construction of the new capital, see L'Enfant to GW, 21 Nov. 1791, editorial note; see also GW to L'Enfant, 28 Feb. 1792. For support of L'Enfant by Forrest and other D.C. proprietors, see D.C. Commissioners to GW, 21 Dec. 1791, n.5.

2. For earlier mention of the commissioners' dissatisfaction with the work of surveyor Andrew Ellicott and for Ellicott's show of "Temper" in "Verbal intercourse" with the commissioners, see, respectively, David Stuart to GW, 10 Dec. 1792, and D.C. Commissioners to GW, 5 Jan. 1793, and note 1.

3. For Ellicott's letter of resignation, see D.C. Commissioners to GW, 5 Jan. 1793, n.1.

4. The enclosed undated copy of Ellicott's letter to Forrest reads: "According with You in opinion that an immediate Attack on the conduct of the Commissioners, may be attended with some disadvantag⟨e⟩ to the City, and conceiving that delaying it till may, the time I shall certainly leave the city, Cannot effect my reputation, I have determined to postpone till that period, A newspaper investigation, but as to Your request & Recomendation that I should rescind my resolution of quitting all concern with them, & with the city, while under their Government, it is quite out of the Question—This resolution I have not taken up from any sudden impulse, but from a conviction of some months Standing, that delays will attend the execution of the plan of the City, and blame must be the portion of those to whom the work is intrusted, when directed by men unacqua[i]nted with its principals, and the nature of such busin[e]ss—My early opinion in favor of the permanent residence, being fixed at this place, must be known too well to admit of a doubt, this opinion has produced an attachment, which added to a desire of Compleating the permanent lines, and fixing some principal points in the City, on which its bueaty Materially depends, are of the reasons, why I continued in the Employ, after receiving directions from one of the Commissioners, to quit the work which I had just begun on the Eastern

Branch and lay out the Canal, Intended to Join the Tiber & St James Creek, It was by obeying this order, that the sale of lots on that Valuable river was prevented, and for which I have been so undeservedly Censured.

"An Attempt to execute so complex a plan, in small detached pieces, which has hitherto been the System, directed by the Commissioners, will not only be attended with delay, but—produce innumerable inaccuracies, The Commissioners, although, from their appointment intended to overlook (or at least if possible to comprehend in some measure, the nature of) the different branches of business, carrying on in the City, could never Yet be prevailed upon, by any arguments of mine, to go over one work; and rather than take the trouble, of examining the permanent lines, they reported without seeing them—Those who are concearned in preserving the bueaty of the plan, will do well in using their endeavors, to obtain some good Mathematitian, well acquainted with the use of Instruments to complete it: Otherwise some person, or other, unacquainted with the bussiness, and too mean to act with independance, will probably be appointed to finish a work begun and forwarded by Major L'Enfant & myself" (DNA: RG 59, Miscellaneous Letters).

On 15 Jan., Tobias Lear wrote Thomas Jefferson: "As the Secretary of State may be about to write to the Commissioners respecting the addition of the City to be marked in the survey of the federal territory, the President sends him the enclosed w[hic]h he has just received from Mr Forrest, that he may see more particularly the situation ⟨of⟩ matters between Mr Ellicott & the Commissioners" (DLC: Jefferson Papers).

Tobias Lear to Thomas Jefferson

[Philadelphia] Thursday January 10th 1793
The President orders T. Lear to return to the Secretary of State the letter from Mr Pinckney—the one from Mr Johnson and that from Mr Livingston, which have been submitted to the President's perusal;[1] and to observe that the President thinks it is to be regretted[2] that Mr Pinckney does not say anything in his letters relative to certain matters which he was instructed to be particularly attentive to.[3]

AL, DLC: Jefferson Papers; ADf, DNA: RG 59, Miscellaneous Letters (mistakenly filed under 16 Jan. 1793); LB, DNA: RG 59, George Washington's Correspondence with His Secretaries of State; LB (photocopy), DLC: GW. Jefferson docketed the AL as received on 10 Jan. 1793.

1. The enclosed letters included Thomas Pinckney to Jefferson, 5 Oct. 1792, Joshua Johnson to Jefferson, 9 Oct. 1792, and Henry Walter Livingston to Jefferson, 5 Oct. 1792. Jefferson received these letters on 9 Jan. and presented them for GW's review later that same day (see Summary Journal of Public and Private Letters in DLC: Jefferson Papers; *JPP*, 5). Pinckney's letter concerns his

recent interview with Lord Grenville, British foreign secretary, on the subject of British impressment of American seamen. Pinckney did not receive a satisfactory answer to American complaints, but he did obtain Grenville's promise that "he would consider the business more fully and the result shoud be the subject of a future conference to take place at an early period" (*Jefferson Papers*, 24:441–43). Joshua Johnson, the U.S. consul for London, was displeased with the financial terms of his appointment and indicated in his letter to Jefferson his desire to resign, agreeing only to stay in the post "until the President shall be pleased to appoint some other person to take my place" (ibid., 453–55). The letter from Henry Walter Livingston, secretary to Gouverneur Morris at Paris, has not been identified, but GW's executive journal contains a summary of its contents: "gives a statement (by Mr. Morris' order) of the propositions which took place between Genl. Demouriez & the King of Prussia—wh. statement is essentially different from what has been received through other channels." This summary, as well as GW's notes on Pinckney and Johnson's letters, is in *JPP*, 5.

2. In the draft this phrase reads: "is much to be regretted."

3. Lear may be referring to the instructions in Jefferson's letter to Pinckney of 14 June, which Jefferson repeated in his letter to Pinckney of 30 Dec. 1792, to find skilled artisans willing to come to the United States in order to work at the newly established U.S. Mint (*Jefferson Papers*, 24:74–76, 802–4). Lear, however, may be alluding to Jefferson's latest letter to Pinckney, written at Philadelphia on 1 Jan. 1793, in which Jefferson wrote, in code: "I have it in charge from the President of the United States, to desire you to be very attentive to the embarkation of troops from the British dominions in Europe, to those in America, and particularly to Quebec—and to give us the earliest advice of their numbers, destination, object and other material circumstances" (*Jefferson Papers*, 25:6). For GW's directive to Jefferson, see his first letter to him of 31 Dec. 1792. GW may have hoped that Pinckney would include information on British troop movements in his letter, even before receiving specific instructions to do so.

From Robert R. Livingston

Sir   New York 10th Jany 1793

I do myself the honor to transmit you a copy of the first part of the proceedings of the society for the promotion of agriculture arts & manufactures in this State.[1] Tho this first essay may contain little information that will appear new to you yet I am persuaded that you will not see with indifference any attempt for the improvement of agriculture since its interests are closely connected with the prosperity of the country & distinguished by your patronage & attention.[2] I have the honor to be Sir with the highest respect & essteem Your Most Obt Hum: Servt

                                            Robt R. Livingston

ALS, PHi: Gratz Collection; ALS (photocopy), DLC:GW, ser. 9.

1. A copy of part 1 of the *Transactions of the Society, Instituted in the State of New-York, for the Promotion of Agriculture, Arts, and Manufactures* (New York, 1792) was in GW's library at Mount Vernon at the time of his death (see Griffin, *Boston Athenæum Washington Collection,* 149).

2. On 10 Feb. 1793 GW wrote Livingston from Philadelphia: "It was not 'till the 8th instt that I had the pleasure to receive your letter of the 10th Ulto, with a copy of the first part of the proceedings of the Society for the promotion of Agriculture, arts & Manufactures in the State of New York, which accompanied it.

"While I beg you to accept my best thanks for your politeness in sending me this book, I, with pleasure, bestow the tribute of praise that is due to the patiriotic characters who have instituted & supported So useful a society.

"Convinced as I am that the prosperity of our Country is closely connected with our improvement in the useful arts, I sincerely rejoice to find another establishment, calculated to promote its best interests, added to those truly valuable ones which before existed. I pray you to make a tender of my best respects to Mrs [Mary Stevens] Levingston—and to your good Mother [Margaret Beekman Livingston] & family at the mannor when you See them—in which Mrs Washington cordially unite" (ALS, NHi; Df, in Tobias Lear's hand, DNA: RG 59, Miscellaneous Letters; LB, DLC:GW).

From Gouverneur Morris

(private)

My dear Sir   Paris 10 January 1793

As I have good Reason to beleive that this Letter will go safely, I shall mention some Things which may serve as a Clue to lead thro Misteries—Those who plannd the Revolution which took Place on the tenth of August sought a Person to head the Attack, and they found a Mr Westermann whose Morals were far from Exemplary. He has no Pretensions to Science or to Depth of Thought, but he is fertile in Ressources and endued with the most daring Intrepidity. Like Cæsar he beleives in his Fortune—When the Business drew towards a Point, the Conspirators trembled; but Westermann declard they should go on. They obey'd because they had trusted him too far. On that important Day his personal Conduct decided (in a great Measure) the Success. Rewards were due, and military Rank with Opportunities to enrich himself were granted.

You know Something of Dumouriez. The Council distrusted him. Westermann was commission'd to destroy him, should he falter. This Commission was shew'd to the General. It became the Band of Union between him and Westermann—Dumouriez open'd Treaty with the King of Prussia.[1] The principal Emigrants, confident of Force and breathing Vengeance shut the royal Ear. Thionville was defended because a Member of the constituent Assembly saw in Lafayette's Fate his own.[2] Metz was not deliver'd up because Nobody ask'd for the Keys, and because the same Apprehensions were felt which influenced in Thionville. The King of Prussia waited for these Evidences of Loyalty untill his Provisions were consum'd. He then found it necessary to bargain for a Retreat. It was worth to Westermann about ten thousand Pounds. The Council, being convinc'd that he had betray'd their bloody Secret, have excited a Prosecution against him for old Affairs of no higher Rank than petit Larceny—He has desir'd a Trial by Court Martial.

You will judge whether cordial Union can subsist between the Council[3] and their Generals—Verniaux[,] Guadet &ca are now I am told the Intimates of Dumouriez, & that the present Administration is to be overturn'd, begining with Pache the Minister of War—You will have seen a Denunciation against these Members of Assembly for a Letter they wrote to Thierry the King's Valet de Chambre. This Affair needs Explanation, but it can be of no present Use.[4]

The King's Fate is to be decided next Monday the fourteenth. That unhappy Man conversing with one of his Counsel on his own Fate, calmly summed up the Motives of every Kind and concluded that a Majority of the Convention would vote for referring his Case to the People and that in Consequence he should be massacred—I think he must die or reign.[5] yours always and truly

Gouvr Morris

ALS, DLC:GW; LB, DLC: Gouverneur Morris Papers.

1. For background on revolutionary events in France, including the storming on 10 Aug. 1792 of the Tuileries, where Louis XVI and his family were living, the arrest of the king, the establishment of a republican government, and France's war with Austria and Prussia, see Gouverneur Morris to GW, 23 Oct. 1792, and source note. François-Joseph Westermann (1751–1794), a native of Alsace, served several years in the French army before receiving an appointment to a magisterial position in Strasbourg in 1788. His radical revolutionary inclinations eventually led him to Paris, where he played a leading role in the storming of the Tuileries. As a member of General Dumouriez's staff, he as-

sisted in the negotiations that led to the withdrawal from France of the Prussian army following its defeat at Valmy on 20 Sept. 1792 by the French forces under Dumouriez's command. Westermann participated in Dumouriez's conquest of Belgium in the fall of 1792 and invasion of the Netherlands in February 1793. Following General Dumouriez's defection to the Austrians in the spring of 1793, Westermann was investigated by a commission of the National Convention, and although he admitted an Austrian attempt to bribe him, he was found innocent of any impropriety and returned to active military service. Early in 1794 previous charges of treason were revived by the French government, and Westermann was guillotined on 5 April 1794.

2. After the king's arrest in August 1792 and the suspension of the monarchy, Lafayette's opposition to the creation of a new government led to his removal from military command and his indictment by the government. On 19 Aug. he fled France, but he was arrested by Prussian forces while crossing France's border. Transferred to Austrian custody in May 1793, Lafayette was imprisoned at Olmütz until his release in September 1797. Thionville, a port on the Moselle River, is in northeast France, near the Luxembourg border and seventeen miles north of Metz. It was under siege from 24 Aug. to 14 Sept. 1792, when the arrival of additional French troops forced the Prussians to abandon the siege.

3. For a list of members of the French Provisional Executive Council as of 30 Dec. 1792, see the French Provisional Executive Council to GW, 30 Dec. 1792, n.3.

4. Royal valet Marc-Antonine Thierry de Ville-d'Avray (1732–1792) had been a vehicle for clandestine correspondence between Louis XVI and Girondin leaders Pierre-Victurnien Vergniaud (1753–1793) and Guadet before the storming of the Tuileries. Vergniaud, a member of the former Legislative Assembly, now served in the newly elected National Convention. He presided over the king's trial by that body and voted for the king's execution. Vergniaud himself was guillotined on 31 Oct. 1793.

5. After a trial before the National Convention, Louis XVI was found guilty of conspiracy and criminal activities against the general security of the state. Contrary to the king's expectation, the National Convention voted against allowing the people to decide his fate, and the king was executed on 21 Jan. 1793.

From Edward Weyman, Jr.

Charleston South Carolina January 10 1793
The Humble Petition of Edward Weyman Sheweth!
That by the death of Edward Weyman, his father, the place of Surveyor of the Port of Charleston is become vacant,[1] and the Collector of the said Port having honoured your Petitioner with the said appointment until a permanent one is made, therefore prays that you will be pleased to confirm him in the same—Your

Petitioner is induced to this from his knowledge of the business of the Office, and his father not leaving his private affairs in so elegible a situation as he could expect, and the whole dependence of an aged Mother resting solely on the success of this application[2]—And your Petitioner as in duty bound will ever pray.

Ed. Weyman

ALS, DLC:GW.

1. Edward Weyman, Sr. (1730–1793), a glass grinder and upholsterer who had been born in Pennsylvania, married Rebecca Breintnall in 1751 and moved to South Carolina by the mid-1750s. A member of the Sons of Liberty in the 1760s and of several secret correspondence committees in the early 1770s, Weyman was elected to the first and second South Carolina provincial congresses in 1775 and 1776 and state general assemblies in 1776, 1779–80, and 1782. While serving as a lieutenant in the Charleston artillery battalion in 1780, Weyman was captured by the British and exiled to St. Augustine. Exchanged in the summer of 1781, he subsequently joined Francis Marion's brigade as an artillery captain. Following the Revolutionary War, Weyman was searcher for the port of Charleston c.1783–88. GW appointed him surveyor of Charleston on 3 Aug. 1789 and port inspector on 6 Mar. 1792.

2. Isaac Holmes was the collector of the customs for the port of Charleston. South Carolina senator Pierce Butler wrote GW on 6 Feb. about Weyman's interest in this position. For the nomination of Edward Weyman, Jr. (1768–1813), as surveyor and inspector of the port of Charleston, see GW to the U.S. Senate, 18 Feb. 1793. The Senate confirmed Weyman's appointment on the following day (*Executive Journal*, 1:129).

From Cincinnatus

SIR, [11 January 1793]

YOU have not often been troubled with anonymous addresses, it may therefore be thought proper, that some apology be made you for the obtrusion of this; but the novelty of the measure must be justified by the necessity of the case, and by that claim which your injured companions in arms have to your patronage and protection,—derived from those professions and promises made to them by you when their commander in chief. They then respected you as they ought, as soldiers they gloried in you, as friends they loved you; they once thought their affections for you reciprocal, and would even now reluctantly give up that belief.

My address to you will be in plain republican language. I do not pretend to understand those prudent forms of decorum, those gentle rules of discretion, which courtly softness may prescribe.

No man knows as well as you the services, sacrifices and sufferings of the late army; your tribute of acknowledgements is on record,—it does justice to your head and heart; but Sir, by what fatality has it happened, that your countenance, which once delighted and animated them, is now withdrawn from their support?—There was a time, when the army never would have believed, that you could be at the head of government for four years, without making one effort,—without expressing a single wish for a retribution of their services. Can it be possible, Sir, that you have abandoned the known rules of right, to adopt the quibbling distinctions of the Treasury? The army have now come forward, *quasi unâ voce,* and have thrown themselves on the justice, the humanity and gratitude of Congress—to ask that as a gratuity which they ought to receive as a right.—Such men, struggling with adversity, must always be an interesting scene to them;—at sight of so much virtue in distress your natural benevolence will take the alarm and anticipate their acts of humanity.

The individuals of the late army thought themselves interested, and were therefore active, in the change that effected the present government. The languor and inability of the old one deprived them of their stipulated wages; but the change has been the reverse of their expectations; for they are not only not benefited, but really injured by it, inasmuch as they not only do not receive any of their own dues, but are compelled to contribute to pay those very dues to others, without any sort of equivalent or compensation paid to them. If they were justifiable in overturning the old government, because it could not do them justice, how much less reason have they to support the present one which does them injustice.

The present government has been liberal to the late army in nothing but neglect and contempt. It may be worth while to pause a little and reflect on the probable effects of a continuance of these measures.—If nothing shall now be granted them, they will feel cut off from all hopes of redress,—and in that you lop off their attachment to government—methinks I see you startled at the idea of so extensive an amputation.

Sir, the *salus reipublicæ* might again require a practice of those lessons, the army learnt in their youth before they are too old:— now is the time to purchase the exclusive right to their tactical knowledge—it may be had at the low price of paying them their honest demands;—it will infuse a portion of new health into the government and enable it to bear its infirmities.

A single ray of well directed sympathy from you will dissipate a cloud which is overshadowing your own honourable fame.

I have addressed myself to the individual members of Congress, through the same channel, on this subject, with such arguments as, to my understanding, are unanswerable.

CINCINNATUS

Printed copy, *General Advertiser* (Philadelphia), 11 Jan. 1793; printed copy, *National Gazette* (Philadelphia), 23 Jan. 1793.

This letter is one of four first printed in the *General Advertiser* under the pseudonym of Cincinnatus. The others are "To the Individual Members of Congress," 8, 14 Jan., and "To the Victorious & Patriotic Officers of the French army," 21 January. They also appear, respectively, in the issues of the *National Gazette* for 19, 23, and 26 January. The author of these letters has not been identified. The recurrent themes in these four letters are the author's opposition to the system adopted by the Washington administration to fund the public debt and his call for some type of compensation for the original recipients of government securities, which included many veterans of the Continental army. In many cases the original owners had been induced by economic circumstances to sell their certificates at depreciated prices to speculators who now reaped large profits under Alexander Hamilton's financial system.

On 14 Jan. a "memorial of the officers of the late Delaware line of the Continental Army, in behalf themselves and the soldiers of the said line, was presented to the House [of Representatives] and read, praying that the depreciation which accrued on the certificates of debts granted them for military services rendered during the late war, may be made good to them, or such other relief afforded them as the present circumstances of the United States will admit. *Ordered*, That the said memorial be referred to the Committee of the Whole House to whom are referred the memorials of the late officers and soldiers of the lines of New Hampshire, Massachusetts, New York, Pennsylvania, and Maryland." That same day "the House resolved itself into a Committee of the Whole . . . and took into consideration the memorials." Discussion on the issue continued into the next day's session, and on 16 Jan. the members approved a resolution that these memorials "ought not to be granted" (*Annals of Congress*, 2d Cong., 811–27).

From Benjamin Hawkins

Senate Chamber 11th of Jany 1793

I send you herewith the papers mentioned this morning.[1] Mr [Robert] Morris acknowledging himself in the Senate, a party concerned, (and as such, would not vote) moved to postpone the consideration of the last memorial, assigning as the reason, "that the Indians in question, would soon be in this city, that the company meant to apply to them, on the subject, and *had reason to believe,* that they would not hesitate to acknowledge the validity of their claim."[2] I have the honor to be, with the Sincerest attachment sir, your obedient servant

Benjamin Hawkins

ALS, DNA: RG 59, Miscellaneous Letters.

1. An entry in GW's executive journal indicates the receipt of this letter on this date and describes its enclosures as "a pet[it]ion from persons calling themselves the Illonois & Wabash Land Companies which had been presented to the Senate during their last session—with the report of a Committee of the Senate upon said petition, and the observations of the agents of said Companies upon the Report" (*JPP,* 9–10). The petition of 12 Dec. 1791 from the Illinois and Wabash Land Company, signed by stockholders James Wilson, a prominent Philadelphia lawyer and president of the company, William Smith, an Episcopal clergyman and former provost of the College of Philadelphia, and Jonathan Shee, the treasurer of the city of Philadelphia, reads: "That, during the years 1773 and 1775, your memorialists purchased from different Indian Tribes, aborigines and possessors of the Country, lying on part of the waters of the rivers Ilinois and Ouabache, two parcels of land, as described in the deeds now in their possession, and which, when required, are ready to be produced.

"That the consideration, as specified in the aforementioned deeds, was at least as valuable as any that was given on similar occasions—That the negociation was of the most publick notoriety—That the meaning and intention of the parties were interpreted and explained by persons duly qualified, of whom his Britannick Majesty's interpreter was one; all deposing, that they were present, either at the delivery of the bargained property to the Indians, or at the execution of the deed, as will be found authenticated by *Hugh Lord* Esquire, captain in the eighteenth british regiment and then commanding in that Territory. The registry of Kaskaskais will also shew the record of the whole transaction.

"That further formalities (if, from the British government, more were necessary to be obtained) were prevented by the almost immediate rupture with Great Britain.

"That the property of the Lands in question was at the time of purchase in the natives.

"That however clear the claim of the *Company* to the whole of their purchase may be; they hesitate not to express their willingness and desire that a reasonable *compromise* upon the subject may take place between the United States and them.

"They therefore *pray,* That your honorable house may appoint a committee to *hear* and *report* upon, the justice of their case, and such proposals as they shall lay before it. This *prayer* they with confidence, hope will be complied with; both from your known love of justice and the evident advantage that must result to the community, if by a compromise with the company, the necessity of a second purchase from the natives wou'd be precluded. Of this but little doubt can be entertained since the Indians never have denied, and are still ready, as the Company are credibly informed, to acknowledge the honesty of the purchase made from them by your memorialists" (DNA: RG 59, Miscellaneous Letters).

The report of the U.S. Senate committee, apparently made sometime between December 1791 and April 1792, reads: "That the Claims of the petitioners are founded on two deeds mentioned in the said petition, one of which to William Murray and others who are called the Ilionois Company is dated July 5th 1773—and the other to Lord Dunmore and others who are stiled the Wabash Company bears date October 18th 1775.

"That the said petitioners have proposed to surrender and convey to the United States all the Lands described or meant to be described in the abovementioned Deeds from the Indians on the Proviso that the United States reconvey to the Company one fourth part of the said Lands.

"That in the opinion of the Committee Deeds obtained by private persons from the Indians without any antecedent authority or subsequent confirmation from the Government could not vest in the Grantees mentioned in such Deeds a Title to the Lands therein described.

"That the said Petitioners do not suggest any such antecedent authority or subsequent confirmation in the present case—and therefore in the opinion of the Committee the said petitioners have not a legal Title to the said Lands.

"That the proceeds of the sales of Lands in the western Territory belonging to the United States are appropriated towards discharging the Debts for the payment whereof the United States are holden.

"The petitioners alledge that the considerations specified in the said Deeds were paid to the Indians and were at least as valuable as any that were given on similar occasions, and that the Indians named in the said Deeds were owners of the Land—On these points the Committee give no opinion—but for the reasons above expressed they think it would not be expedient for the government of the United States to accede to the abovementioned proposition of the Petitioners" (DNA: RG 59, Miscellaneous Letters).

The memorial from the Illinois and Wabash Company of 11 April 1792, signed by the same men as the earlier petition, reads: "That they have seen the Report, which your Committee have made upon the former Memorial on behalf of the said Company.

"That the said Committee have assumed as law, and as the basis of their Report, a Principle, which, in the humble Opinion of your Memorialists, is not founded on the Law of the Land.

"Wherefore your Memorialists pray that they may be heard, personally or by Counsel, before you, in opposition to the principle of the said Report" (DNA: RG 59, Miscellaneous Letters).

This appeal for congressional recognition of the company's pre–Revolutionary War purchases of four tracts of land, containing an estimated 60 million acres in the Northwest Territory, was denied. For a brief history of the Illinois and Wabash Land Company and its unsuccessful attempts to validate its claims, see Alvord, *Illinois Country*, 301–2, 340, 381–87. See also *Account of the Proceedings of the Illinois and Ouabache Land Companies* (Philadelphia, 1803); *ASP, Public Lands*, 1:27, 72–75, 160–61, 189, 2:108–20, 253.

2. For the current visit to Philadelphia by representatives from the Illinois and Wabash Indians, see James Wilkinson to GW, 1 Nov. 1792, n.1. At GW's command Tobias Lear wrote Henry Knox later on this date "to transmit to the Secretary a letter & its enclosures which the President has recd from Mr Hawkins.

"The President requests that the Secretary will take the subject of this letter & papers into consideration—and see the President upon them tomorrow morning at *nine* O'clock—and that the Secretary will then bring with him the Book—or documents of Instructions which have been given to the Commissioners who have been appointed to treat with the Indians—The President expects at that time the heads of the other Departments to be with him also.

"The President Observes that it will not be necessary to have any of the Instructions &c. copied for the purpose of bringing here" (DLC:GW).

On 12 Jan. 1793, according to GW's executive journal, the "Heads of the Departments and the Attorney General of the United States, waited on the President this morning at nine o'clock, according to appointment.... The Secretary of War was this day directed by the President to make inquiry of the Interpreters, whether any persons & who had held any conversation with the Indians since they have been in the City on the subject of Land—and to order the Interpreters, in the most pointed manner, not to communicate to the Indians a single sentence from any person relative to purchasing their Lands" (*JPP*, 11).

Tobias Lear to Thomas Jefferson

[Philadelphia] Friday January 11th 1793

T. Lear is ordered by the President of the U.S. to transmit to the Secretary of State a letter and its enclosures, together with a draft of the survey of the federal district, which he has received from the Commissione[r]s.[1]

The President requests that the Secretary will take this matter into consideration and report to the President his opinion whether it should be laid before Congress or not.[2]

Tobias Lear.
Secretary to the President of the United States.

ALS, DLC: Jefferson Papers; ALS (letterpress copy), DNA: RG 59, Miscellaneous Letters; LB, RG 59, George Washington's Correspondence with His Secretaries of State; LB (photocopy), DLC:GW. Jefferson mistakenly docketed the ALS as received "Jan. 8. 93."

1. For these documents, see D.C. Commissioners to GW, 5 Jan. 1793, and notes 1, 2, 7, and 8.

2. For Jefferson's reply, in which he recommended sending the commissioners' "report with a plat of the boundary" to Congress, see his letter to GW of 18 February.

Henry Knox to Tobias Lear

My dear Sir.   [Philadelphia] Jany 11. 1793.

Will you please to submit to the President of the United States the enclosed letters from major general Wayne, and to inform him that as the paymaster has arrived at head quarters, pay, to complete the army for the last year, will be prepared, and forwarded instantly.[1] I am, dear Sir, Yours sincerely—

                                                           H. Knox

LS, DLC:GW; LB, DLC:GW.

1. An entry in GW's executive journal for 11 Jan. 1793 indicates GW's receipt of two letters that Anthony Wayne had written to Knox earlier this month. One was "a private Letter, dated Legionville, Jany. 1st. 1793 on the subject of the *Address,* from the Officers" (*JPP,* 9). This letter has not been found, but its substance appears in Wayne's letter to Knox of 12 Dec. 1792, in which Wayne enclosed "a copy of an address of the Officers of the Legion of the United States, at this place upon a subject that has patriotism experience & humanity for it's basis: i e the inadequacy of the ration allowed the soldiery—which is by no means sufficient for their comfort or support, unaided by either root or vegetable, & from which the situation & nature of the service, can not possibly be procured;—nor is it to be expected that the meat or bread kind (after being drove & carried so great a distance thro' a Wilderness) can be equal in quality to what cou'd be obtained in a highly cultivated country." After observing that the American ration was "far short" of that allowed British troops, Wayne wrote: "From a full conviction in my own mind that this is a business which merits the serious and early attention of Congress—I have to request, that you will be so good as to submit that *address* to the President of the U S, who I am persuaded will recommend to the immediate consideration of the Federal Legislature, such addition to the ration as he may deem proper and adequate for the comfort & support of the soldiery" (Knopf, *Wayne,* 150–51). Knox replied to Wayne in a private letter of 22 Dec. that "the memorial of the officers, is considered by the President and your other friends, as an extremely improper measure, and tending to produce insubordination and every military evil consequent thereon. . . . You will understand, that it is the manner, more than the matter, which is considered as exceptionable. Although it is difficult to conceive, why the ration should be less sufficient now, than for fifteen years past—few or no complaints having been made against its sufficiency, it being nearly the same as that of the late war—The subject will however be duly considered" (ibid., 152).

The second enclosed letter, according to GW's executive journal, was "an Official one, date Legionville Jany. 5th. 1793," which "mentions the arrival of the Paymaster [Caleb Swan] at Pittsburg" (*JPP,* 9). This letter, which is in Knopf, *Wayne,* 162–64, under the date of 4 Jan. 1793, begins: "I have the honor to acknowledge the receipt of yours of the 22nd. Ultimo, & sincerely regret that the *Address* of the Officers upon the subject of rations has been consider'd 'as prejudicial to order & discipline' but as I have already explain'd that business in my private letter of the 1st. Instant, I hold it unnecessary to enlarge upon a subject that has been totally misconstrued both as to design & tendency, nor will it effect either order or discipline both of which have been introduced, into the Legion with a rapidity & promptitude, not often experienced equalled or excelled in any period of the late War, nor will it be relaxed as long as I have the honor to continue in Command." Wayne also reported "that from Appearances the Indians are watching an Oppertunity to make an other stroke at the Convoy's," that he has "Order'd the Dragoons about thirty in Number to descend the Ohio tomorrow from Fort Washington," and that he has "found it Necessary" to make several "promotions in the Cavalry until the pleasure of the Pre[siden]t is known there being a real want of Officers."

Lear replied to Knox later this date: "By the President's command T. Lear has the honor to return to the Secretary of War the Letters from Maj. Genl Wayne which have been submitted to the President" (DLC:GW).

From Thomas Jefferson

[Philadelphia] Sunday Jan. 13. 93.

Th: Jefferson has the honor to send to the President a sketch which he has submitted to a gentleman or two in the legislature on the subject of Indian purchases.[1]

he sends him also two letters recd last night from mister Gouverneur Morris. the correspondence referred to in one of them, is in French, and being improper to go into the hands of a clerk, Th: J. is translating it himself for the use of the President. it is lengthy, and will require a good part of to-day to do it.[2]

AL, DNA: RG 59, Miscellaneous Letters; AL (letterpress copy), DLC: Jefferson Papers; LB, DNA: RG 59, George Washington's Correspondence with His Secretaries of State; LB (photocopy), DLC:GW.

1. Jefferson's enclosure reads: "Be it enacted &c. that no person shall be capable of acquiring any title, in law or equity, to any lands beyond the Indian boundaries & within those of the U.S. by purchase, gift, or otherwise, from the Indians holding or claiming the same: and that it shall be a misdemeanor in any person, punishable by fine & imprisonment at the discretion of a jury, to obtain, accept, or directly or indirectly to treat for, any title to such lands from

the said Indians or any other for them. But where any such Indians shall of their own accord desire to sell any part of their lands, and it shall be deemed the interest of the U.S. that a purchase shall be made, the same shall be done by treaty or convention, to be entered into by the President of the U.S. & ratified by two thirds of the Senate according to the constitution: to enure to the use of the states respectively, where the said lands lie within the limits of any state, they paying the price, and to the use of the U.S. where such lands lie within any territory ceded to them by particular states" (DNA: RG 59, Miscellaneous Letters). James Madison was probably one of those congressmen who received a copy of this enclosure since he introduced a modified version of Jefferson's memorandum as an amendment to a bill on Indian trade currently under consideration (see *Annals of Congress,* 2d Cong., 827; *Madison Papers,* 14:441–42). Congress incorporated Jefferson's idea to impose criminal penalties on those who attempted to purchase Indian lands without proper authorization, but with modifications to his wording, in "An Act to regulate Trade and Intercourse with the Indian Tribes," approved on 1 Mar. 1793 (1 *Stat.* 329–32).

2. The two letters Jefferson had received recently from Gouverneur Morris were dated 19 and 27 Sept. 1792 (*Jefferson Papers,* 24:404–5, 419–22). The letter of 19 Sept. contained copies, in French, of Morris's letters to the French minister of foreign affairs, Pierre-Henri-Hélène-Marie Lebrun, of 20 Aug., 1 Sept., and 17 Sept. 1792 and of Lebrun's letters to Morris of 30 Aug., 8 and 16 Sept. 1792, all of which Jefferson translated for GW and delivered to him later on this date (see *JPP,* 18). Morris, in his letter to Lebrun of 20 Aug., complained that the seal on a recently received letter "has been opened by authority of the government" and asked Lebrun "to prevent such violations." Lebrun responded to Morris's complaint on 8 Sept., assuring him that he had "communicated" Morris's displeasure to the mayor of Paris and that "there was not the smallest intention to fail in respect to your person or to the character with which you are invested." On 30 Aug., Lebrun wrote Morris that, the suspension of the king notwithstanding, the United States was obligated to provide the previously agreed upon $800,000 debt payment to the relief of the French colony of Saint Domingue. Morris replied on 1 Sept. that, as he had observed previously, he had "*never been authorised to meddle*" in the arrangements made for the repayment of the American debt to France. He did, however, review the United States's current financial agreements with France and concluded that "the result is, that in every state of the case, the reimbursements, hitherto due, are all paid." In addition, because of the tone of Lebrun's letter of 30 Aug., Morris requested his passport to leave France. Lebrun wrote Morris on 16 Sept. asking him to remain in Paris and to wait for "new instructions from your constituents; in short continue to treat, without interruption or delay, the affairs which interest the two people." On the following day Morris agreed in writing to do so, but he renewed his request for a passport. For a summary of the contents of these enclosures, see ibid., 12–16. Letterpress copies of Jefferson's translations of the Morris-Lebrun correspondence are in DLC: Jefferson Papers. Also enclosed were brief extracts (in French) from the *Journal des débats et des décrets* (Paris) for 15 Sept. 1792, in which Claude-Louis Masuyer (1759–1794), a representative for Saône-Loire in the Legislative As-

sembly and subsequent National Convention, called for the restoration of law and order in Paris, and for 16 Sept. 1792, in which Jean-Marie Roland de La Platière (1734–1793), minister of the interior, denied any responsibility for the recent spate of unauthorized arrests in Paris (DNA: RG 59, Despatches from U.S. Ministers to France). For background on recent political events in France, see Morris to GW, 23 Oct. 1792, and source note.

The letter from Morris to Jefferson of 27 Sept. contained two enclosures: an extract of a letter from William Short to Morris of 7 Sept. 1792, in which Short asked Morris to join with him and Thomas Pinckney in requesting the Austrian government to release Lafayette "in the name of the U.S. as a citizen thereof," and an extract of Morris's answer to Short of 12 Sept. 1792, stating Morris's opposition to this proposal (both are in DNA: RG 59, Despatches from U.S. Ministers to France). See also Morris's letter to GW of 23 Oct. 1792, and note 1, for Morris's mention of these letters to GW.

On 15 Jan. 1793 Tobias Lear wrote Jefferson: "If the Secretary of State has not already sent to the Secretary of the Treasury the letters from Mr G. Morris, relative to the French debt, the President will thank the Secretary to send them to him (the President) as he expects to see the Secretary of the Treasury this morning and will give them to him" (DLC: Jefferson Papers). Morris's letter of 19 Sept. and its enclosures were returned to GW on this date and "put into the hands" of Alexander Hamilton. GW and Hamilton then discussed the contents of these documents and several other letters relative to the repayment of the American debt to France and the conduct of William Short, the U.S. minister to The Hague who also oversaw the financing and repayment of the American debt (see ibid., 18–21).

To Anthony Whitting

Mr Whiting,   Philadelphia Jany 13[–14]th 1793

Your letter of the 9th instant with the several reports therein, came duly to hand;[1] & to such parts as require it, I shall reply.

I never had it in contemplation to with-draw the hands from the River, or any other Plantation to aid at the Mansion house, if their work should be required at home: therefore I find no difficulty in releasing the River force from this Service, if there is *really* work enough to employ them at home; which is indeed very probable, as they have spent all the fall—& half the Winter in getting in their Corn: a thing hardly ever heard of before in the worst of weather, much less in such as we have had; & which perhaps never was seen before. If there was any way of making such a rascal as Garner pay for such conduct, no punishment would be too great for him.[2] I suppose he never turned out of mornings until the Sun had warmed the Earth; and if *he* did not, the *Negros* would not: and if you do watch the motions of these people (now & then) in the Mornings—it will, more than probably be the case with the rest who are on standing wages; & who feel no interest in the Crop, whether it be great or small: For in this case, principle, & a regard for reputation, are the only motives to stimulate industry. and, unfortunately, too few of that class of (common) Overseers, are over burthened with either of these.

I am perfectly sensible of the scarcity of Timber at the River Plantn; and the distance it is to draw at some others; and this, principally (but aided by many others) is the reason why for many years back, I have been labouring but in vain to substitute live, instead of dead fences; and which I will no longer, under any pretences whatsoever, delay doing. My frequent and long absences from home prevented my attending to the business personally; and no recommendation, nor indeed orders, could draw the attention of those to whom I entrusted my affairs—in the manner it ought—for the seasons were either suffered to pass away before the measure was thought of by them, or, the work executed in such a manner as to produce no good effect. Now, as I mean to make hedging a *business,* and a *primary one,* and when I add that, I cannot be more disappointed, or disobliged by any thing, than in neglecting the Season, and the means to accomplish the measure; I shall hope to be relieved in a few years from the great consumption of timber which such a quantity of Fencing as I have, will occasion; and the consequent transportation of the Rails to such a variety of cross fences as there are but which—in the first instances at least—might be made of any sort, or kind of hedge that would turn horses, Cattle & Sheep; Hogs not being admitted.

It would be folly to place cuttings of either Willow or Lombardy Poplar in grounds they will not grow; and you & the Gardener— on the spot—must be the best judge of these—substitute therefore what you may think best in their places. I look upon either, & both of these trees to be excellent for rearing a hedge quick; but conceive they ought to be fronted, or backed, with some other plant that is more stubborn, & durable too, if they can be had; in order to make a lasting, & formidable hedge.

You propose a change in the course of the Fence from the back of the young clover-lot to the river; but I do not understand on what line, or how you propose to run it. My idea, was not to alter the fence of the Brick yard lot, unless to draw it as much up the hill (just above [Thomas] Green's house) as it could be done to be out of the view of the House; & then, from the No. East Corner thereof, to run such a fence as you seem to have in contemplation (below the Summit of the hill also, so as to be hid from view) until it reached the hollow by Boatswains house thence to the outer fence in the nearest direction—I meant moreover, to have run another fence from the No. West Corner of the New Clover lot, by the road at the turn & gully, until it shd strike the outer fence near the gate by Richds house,[3] which would have thrown all the intermediate ground into one Inclosure to be divided hereafter at pleasure, into Smaller lots, if necessary—This would leave all the Hill sides—the broken grounds—& Swamps below—which contain most grass—for a common pasture: and the way to get in to it might be by a continuation of the lane by the New quarter, & back of the Smiths shop to the head of the hollow by the Wild Cherry tree;[4] and wch would be the road also to the old fish house landing, without passing through Gates or Bars or lot itself. The reason why I had not mentioned this matter to you before, was, that I conceived work enough had been cut out already, without enumerating more; but as you seem to look forward, on acct of hedging &ca I mention these ideas without being tenacious of them. My object in clearing the grounds *out side* of the pasture, along the Road from the Gum Spring,[5] was, that you might see the Mansion house as soon as you should enter the little old field beyond it.

I have no objection to your pursuing your own judgment as to the time fittest for plowing the Brick yard Inclosure provided the grain & grass-seeds are sown therein as early as possible. I wish both were *now* in the ground; & hope every exertion possible has been made this mild & open weather to forward your plowing generally for it is highly probable that February & March may be unfit for this business; in which case, & not embracing the fine weather you have had, the business, & your crops consequently, will be exceedingly backward.

Although you may sow the grass-seeds at the Mansion house yourself it is my wish nevertheless that a Machine (described by Mr Bordley) may be made to sow it at the other places; for in unskilful hands the seed is wasted, and the ground not productive, on account of the irregularity in the sowing it.[6] It is my wish that the Buckwheat, sowed for manure, could be got into the ground as early as possible after the frosts are over, that, when the first growth therefrom has ripened seed enough to stock the ground a second time, it may be again plowed in, which will afford a second dressing before it is seeded with grain.

Mr Butler's ideas may require correction, & to be assimilated a little more to the nature of our climate & Soil; but I by no means disapprove of the idea of trying the efficacy of the mud which may be extracted from Hell hole, if he can contrive to get it up. I do not mean on a large scale. This would be expensive, but if ⟨one⟩ attempt was made on a few square rods of the poorest ground in the adjacent lot, with different quantities on each, the experiment might, & unquestionably would, ascertain a fact which may be of great importance to know—and as experiments of this sort can be made at a small expence it is wonderful & inexcusable they are not oftener attempted. And though it may be imprudent to risk a whole field of Turnips, for the purpose of folding upon (until the land can be brought into better order) yet it would certainly be right to practice this upon a small scale at first; and advance by degrees, and according to the utility & the advantages which are found to flow from it. Mr Young (of Suffolk in England) who, unquestionably, understands the *principles* of farming as well as any man in England, and who has had as much practical knowledge, has given it as his *decided* opinion that the Stock of every farm ought to be supported by the fallows.[7] By fallows (for he reprobates the idea of naked Fallows) he means Turnips, Cabbage, Beans Clover and such like as are best adapted to the Soil. & which are part of his rotation Crops. His great Desiderata is, that large Crops cannot be raised without large Stocks of Cattle & Sheep—Nor large Stocks of these without the Fallows abovementioned; which are the *best* if not the *only* proper preparation for Crops of grain. To get fully into a practice of this sort, in this Country, must be more than the work of a year, two, or three, but if it is never begun it can never be executed—Turnips (where the land is fit for it) folded on, & Clover, seems to be his plan.

As there appears to be more difficulty in carrying the Water to the Visto in front of the Mansion house than I had conceived the work may be suspended until my arrival. But what is the reason that Davenport will not make the experiment I directed with 100 bushls of Wheat? If it is delayed, the object I had in view cannot be answered by it—which was, to ascertain whether it would be best, & most for my interest to sell my Wheat in the grain, or after it was manufactured. He certainly must be a very indolent man![8] There is no doubt in my mind, but that both Wheat & flour will be as high before the middle of March as it has been yet, or more so; a continuation of the cause (and in a degree better known than it was) of the rise in the prices of these articles will not loose its effect—but as the sales of mine will depend in some measure upon the Cash in Alexandria, it is my desire that you will keep me pretty regularly informed of the Alexandria prices, that I may govern myself accordingly.

I will, by the first Vessel to Alexandria send Oil & paint agreeably to your Memorandum.[9] The Pillars of the Piaza & other parts of the Mansion house must be examined & repaired before they are painted—after which I will have both sides of it & ends painted & sanded. as well as the Pillers—I requested the Major to have a sufficient quantity of white, & fine sand brought from below for this purpose (if what I had was insufficient) but whether it ever was done or not I am unable to say.[10] for in too many cases it has happened that, the directions given in letters (when not immediately executed) are laid by & never thought of more, unless I have renewed them. When you receive the paints I shall send from hence, the Cornice of the Salt & Smoke houses may be painted white in the manner you have suggested.

By the last weeks report you have been grubbing in the old meadow at D. Run. Which meadow is it that you call the old? If it be that by the Overseers house, I hope all that was left unfinished at the former clearing of it will be now compleated, except such trees as ought to be left for Shade & ornament near the house; & all the trash entirely removed from it. By the same weeks report, from Muddy hole, a blank for the qty of Buckwheat is left. It is better not to touch a subject than to leave it unfinished.[11]

Let Mr Crow know, that I view with a very evil eye the frequent reports made by him of Sheep dying.[12] When they are destroyed by Dogs it is more to be regretted than avoided perhaps—but frequent *natural deaths* is a very strong evidence to my mind of the want of care—or something worse—as the sheep are culled every year & the old ones drawn out. I wish you well—and am Your friend &ca

Go: Washington

N.B. The enclosed seeds are from the Maliga Grape desire the Gardener to Plant, and give proper attention to them.[13]

P.S.—Jany 14th 1793. I beg that the Mill may not be idle for want of Wheat—The Sooner indeed the residue of the Crop can be delivered there the better, and less waste will be sustained. Let me know how many Stacks remain to be got out at the River Plantatn—What you suppose they will yield—and how much Wheat you conceive is in the Barn at the Ferry & French's.[14]

ALS, DLC:GW.

1. The enclosed reports probably included the farm reports for 30 Dec. 1792–5 Jan. 1793 (DLC:GW).

2. William Garner had been dismissed recently from his position as overseer at the River farm (see GW to Whitting, 9 Dec. 1792).

3. For Richard's house, see GW to Whitting, 4 Nov. 1792, n.6.

4. GW is referring to the north lane, which was located northwest of the mansion house. The blacksmith shop was located on the eastern side and the new slave quarters on the western side of this lane.

5. The Gum Spring was on the south branch of Little Hunting Creek, where the road from Mount Vernon joined the main road from Alexandria to Pohick Church.

6. John Beale Bordley described in detail a box for sowing clover seed in his pamphlet *Sketches on Rotation of Crops* (Philadelphia, 1792). For GW's receipt of this pamphlet the previous fall, see GW to Edmund Randolph, 3 Sept. 1792. GW also owned the 1797 edition of this pamphlet at the time of his death (see Griffin, *Boston Athenæum Washington Collection*, 27–28). GW previously had instructed Whitting to build such a box in a letter to him of 30 Dec. 1792.

7. Correspondence between GW and the English agriculturalist Arthur Young had commenced in 1786 (see Young to GW, 7 Jan. 1786, and GW to Young, 6 Aug. 1786). For works on agriculture by Arthur Young that were in GW's library at the time of his death, see Griffin, *Boston Athenæum Washington Collection*, 95, 230–32, 273, 548.

8. For GW's instructions to his miller, Joseph Davenport, see GW to Whitting, 16 Dec. 1792.

9. For Whitting's estimate of the amount of oil and paint needed for various buildings at Mount Vernon, see his letter to GW of 9 Jan. 1793.

10. Sand was applied to the freshly painted surface of the beveled wood siding of the mansion house and the outbuildings on the north and south lanes to give these structures the appearance of stone. For GW's earlier concern about having enough sand for painting, see George Augustine Washington to GW, 15–16 April 1792.

11. GW is referring to the farm reports for 30 Dec. 1792–5 Jan. 1793 (DLC:GW).

12. Hyland Crow was hired in 1790 as overseer of Ferry and French's farm (see Ledger B, 351). Whiting's farm reports for 30 Dec. 1792–5 Jan. 1793 show the death of two sheep on that farm (DLC:GW).

13. GW's note is written in the left margin of the first manuscript page of this letter. In his letter of 20 Jan. to Whiting, GW wrote: "Enclosed you have some Seeds of the (bleu) Maliga grape. . . . Those sent last were of the White kind— in other respects the same." Málaga, a province in southern Spain, was known for fortified wines made from the several varieties of grapes grown there.

14. The postscript is not filed with this letter, but separately in DLC:GW, ser. 8, Miscellaneous Papers, Subseries A: Correspondence and Miscellaneous Notes.

From Thomas Bee

Dear Sir   Charleston [S.C.] 14 January 1793.

The Office of Surveyor of the Customs for this Port being vacant by the death of Mr Weyman[1]—I have presumed once more to trouble your Excellency & to Sollicit you, in favor of my Brother Joseph Bee, who has by the Events of the War lost the greatest part, if not the whole of a very handsome property, and has now a Wife and three Children to support—he was one of those who was captured at the fall of Charleston in 1780, & from his known Opposition to the British, sent among others to St Augustine, after his Exchange, he joined the Southern Army as a Volunteer in Col. [William] Washingtons Cavalry, where he continued in *constant* service, until the Evacuation of this Town.[2]

Mr Izard & major Butler will be able to give any further information that may be deemed requisite,[3] with sentiments of the greatest Esteem & respect I remain your Excellencys most Obt & very hume Servant

Tho. Bee

ALS, DLC:GW.

1. For an earlier report of Edward Weyman, Sr.'s death, see Edward Weyman, Jr., to GW, 10 Jan. 1793.

2. Joseph Bee (1746–1815), who had supplied provisions to the Continental army during the Revolutionary War, was arrested by the British after the surrender of Charleston in 1780 and was exiled to St. Augustine. Exchanged in the summer of 1781, Bee served in the South Carolina senate in 1782. At the end of the war in 1783, Bee owned 1,200 acres in St. Paul Parish, 400 acres in St. Bartholomew Parish, and forty-three slaves.

3. U.S. Senator Pierce Butler of South Carolina wrote GW on 6 Feb. about Joseph Bee's interest in this position. No letter of recommendation from South Carolina's other senator, Ralph Izard, has been found. GW nominated Edward Weyman, Jr., not Bee, as the surveyor and inspector of the port at Charleston on 18 Feb. 1793.

Tobias Lear to Thomas Jefferson

United States [Philadelphia], January 14th 1793
By the President's command T. Lear has the honor to return to the Secretary of State the letter to the Minister of France, relative to the supply of money to pay certain Bills drawn by the administration of St Domingo, which has been submitted to the President;[1] and to inform the Secretary, that the President, presuming that the contents of said letter is[2] conformable to the arrangements made on that subject, approves of the same.

Tobias Lear.
Secretary to the p[r]esident of the United States

ALS, DLC: Jefferson Papers; ALS (letterpress copy), DNA: RG 59, Miscellaneous Letters; LB, DNA: RG 59, George Washington's Correspondence with His Secretaries of State; LB (photocopy), DLC:GW. Jefferson docketed the ALS as "recd Jan. 14. 93."

1. Jefferson, in his letter to Jean-Baptiste Ternant of 14 Jan. 1793, wrote: "I have laid before the President of the United States your Letter of the 7th. instant, desiring a supply in money, on account of our debt to France, for the purpose of paying certain Bills drawn by the Administration of St. Domingo, and for procuring necessaries for that Colony, which supply you wish should, with those preceding, make up the amount of four millions of Livres. . . . But having, in a former letter expressed to you our desire that an authentic and direct sanction may be obtained from the Government of France for what we have done, and what we may hereafter be desired to do, I proceed to inform you that motives of friendship prevailing over those of rigorous caution, the President of the United States, has acceded to your present desire." Money also will be provided, Jefferson wrote, as "expressed in your other letter of the 8th. relating to the Consuls of France.

"I have, however, Sir, to ask the favor of you to take arrangements with the Administration of St. Domingo, so as that future supplies from us, should they be necessary, may be negotiated here, before they are counted on and drawn for there. Bills on the French Agents here to be paid by us, amount to Bills on us; and it is absolutely necessary that we be not subject to calls, which have not been before calculated and provided for" (see *Jefferson Papers,* 25:51–52). For background on Ternant's request that part of the American debt be applied to the expenses for France's colony of Saint Domingue, see Alexander Hamilton to GW, 19 Nov. 1792, and note 1. For background on the request from French diplomat Antoine-René-Charles-Mathurin de La Forest that the United States assign a portion of its debt payments to the salaries of the French consuls in the United States, see GW to Hamilton, 1 Jan. 1793, and note 2. See also *JPP,* 16–18.

2. In the letter-book copy this verb is correctly conjugated as "are."

Letter not found: to Betty Washington Lewis, 14 Jan. 1793. On 29 Jan., Betty Lewis wrote GW: "Your letters of Januy the 6the and 14the of this Month came duly to hand."

Timothy Pickering to Tobias Lear

Dear Sir,   Philaa Jany 14. 1793.

The inclosed letter from Samuel Freeman Esqr. of Portland I should have presented long ago: but laying it by in my desk *very safely,* it has been overlooked.[1] Perhaps it may now be of no consequence. Possibly you may know Mr Freeman. He has written to *me* in consequence of an acquaintance formed by his being the postmaster at Portland. I take him to be of a very respectable character there; and that his information may be relied on for its truth and impartiality. If the point to which it refers be not decided, be so good as to present it to the President. I am with great regard Your most h'ble servt

                                   T. Pickering

ALS, DLC:GW.

1. Samuel Freeman (1743–1831) of Portland, District of Maine, was a delegate to the Massachusetts provincial congress in 1775 and to the Massachusetts house of representatives in 1776 and 1778. He served as a clerk of the court for forty-five years, beginning in 1775, and as the register for the probate court until 1804 when he became a probate judge. From 1776 until 1805 Freeman was postmaster of Portland. His many publications include *The Columbian Primer, or The School Mistresses Guide to Children, in Their First Steps to Learning* (Boston, 1790), *The Town Officer* (Portland, 1791), *The Probate Auxiliary* (Portland, 1793), *A Valuable Assistant to Everyman, or, The American Clerk's Magazine* (Boston, 1794), *The Massachusetts Justice* (Boston, 1795), and *Extracts from the Journals Kept by the Rev. Thomas Smith* (Portland, 1821).

The enclosed letter from Freeman to Pickering has not been identified, but it may have been a recommendation for an acquaintance's appointment to the post of U.S. marshal for the District of Maine, a position that soon would become vacant due to the election of its current occupant, Henry Dearborn (1751–1829), to the U.S. House of Representatives (see David Servall to Tobias Lear, 20 Feb. 1793).

From Jonathan Rhea

Sir   Monmouth County New Jersey January the 14th 1793

If my zeal and I hope faithfull services during the late Revolution,[1] my exertions in detecting the treachery of Depeyster, and what I then and still do believe to have been an intended assassination,[2] entitules me to the liberty of recommending, or the soliciting a favor, if it can be granted with propriety, I shall beg leave to ask the appointment of my brother James Rhea to the commission of an Ensign in the now standing army, I wish not to deceive nor to recommend improperly, my brothers character during the late war, was that of a good soldier, he was young but in the Militia of this county, he was a volunteer in the late unfortunate action under General St Clair with the Indians, and from the information of some of my old brother officers he there behaved well.[3] I have the honor to be with the most affecte regard & respect Your Obdt Servt

Jonathan Rhea

ALS, DLC:GW.

1. Jonathan Rhea (1754–1815), who had been appointed an ensign in the 2d New Jersey Regiment in January 1777, was promoted to second lieutenant in 1778 and lieutenant in 1781, and he was brevetted to the rank of captain in 1783. A prominent lawyer in Trenton, N.J., after the war, Rhea served as the clerk of the New Jersey Supreme Court from 1793 to 1807, as the quartermaster general for the state from 1807 to 1813, and as a presidential elector in 1793.

2. Pierre De Peyster was a resident of Newark, N.J., at the beginning of the Revolutionary War. Although he had signed an oath of allegiance to the American cause, De Peyster offered his services as a spy to the British following the Battle of Trenton in December 1776. In May 1782 an incriminating letter was intercepted from De Peyster to Sir Guy Carleton, the British commander in chief at New York City. The Americans arrested De Peyster and condemned him to death, but he escaped from captivity in September 1782. The following December he sailed to England, where he eventually became a merchant in Yorkshire.

3. Jonathan Rhea's brother James Rhea was a lieutenant in the levies of 1791, serving under Gen. Arthur St. Clair at the army's defeat by hostile Indians on 4 Nov. 1791 while encamped at the present-day site of Fort Recovery, Ohio (see William Darke to GW, 9–10 Nov. 1791, and source note; "Denny Journal"; Guthman, *March to Massacre*). He did not receive a military appointment from GW but did achieve the desired appointment as an ensign in the U.S. Army in January 1799, during the presidency of John Adams. By 1807 Rhea had risen to the rank of captain, and by May 1810 he was command-

ing the troops at Fort Wayne, in present-day Indiana. Found derelict in his duties in 1812 because of continual drunkenness, Rhea was forced to resign from the army.

From Alexander Hamilton

Treasury Departmt January 15th 179[3].[1]

The Secretary of the Treasury has the honor to submit to the President of the United States the enclosed Letter from the Commissioner of the Revenue respecting the Lighthouse on Tybee Island.[2] The arrangement which he proposes appears to the Secretary an adviseable one. If it shall be approved by the President, measures will be immediately taken for carrying it into execution.[3]

A. Hamilton

LB, DLC:GW.

1. The manuscript is mistakenly dated "1792."

2. Tench Coxe's letter to Hamilton of 4 Jan. 1793, communicating a "plan of repairs of the light House on Tybee Island at the Mouth of the Savannah River," suggests replacing the wooden "lantern by one made of Iron," erecting a "balcony or gallery without and around the lantern for the purpose of keeping the glass in as clean and transparent a condition as possible," and reducing "the unprecedented height of this light House" by 23 feet (DNA: RG 58, Letters Sent by the Commissioner of the Revenue and the Revenue Office, 1792–1807). The Tybee lighthouse had been severely damaged by fire the previous November (see *National Gazette* [Philadelphia], 5 Dec. 1792).

3. On 16 Jan., Tobias Lear wrote Hamilton: "By the President's command T. Lear has the honor to return to the Secretary of the Treasury the letter from the Commissioner of the Revenue respecting the Light House on Tybee Island; and to inform the Secretary that the President approves of the arrangements therein suggested by the Commissioner for the rebuilding or repairing said Light House" (DNA: RG 26, Inventory NC-31, entry 17J, Records Relating to the DLC Exhibit, "Papers Signed by Tobias Lear, 1789–93").

From Thomas Jefferson

Sir   Philadelphia Jan. 15. 1793.

On further consideration I have thought it may be as well to omit the proposition for making any *addition* however small to the foreign fund, till the next session of Congress, by which time it will be more evident whether it is necessary or not.[1] I have the honor to be with the greatest respect Sir Your most obedt & most humble servt

Th: Jefferson

ALS (letterpress), DLC: Jefferson Papers.

1. Congress voted to extend the 1 July 1790 act appropriating $40,000 for the expenses of the diplomatic establishment of the United States in "An Act to continue in force for a limited time, and to amend the act intituled 'An act providing the means of intercourse between the United States and foreign nations,'" which GW signed on 9 Feb. 1793 (see 1 *Stat.* 128–29, 299–300).

Index